Ius Gentium: Comparative Perspectives on Law and Justice

Volume 104

Ius Gentium is a book series which discusses the central questions of law and justice from a comparative perspective. The books in this series collect the contrasting and overlapping perspectives of lawyers, judges, philosophers and scholars of law from the world's many different jurisdictions for the purposes of comparison, harmonisation, and the progressive development of law and legal institutions. Each volume makes a new comparative study of an important area of law. This book series continues the work of the well-known journal of the same name and provides the basis for a better understanding of all areas of legal science.

The *Ius Gentium* series provides a valuable resource for lawyers, judges, legislators, scholars, and both graduate students and researchers in globalisation, comparative law, legal theory and legal practice. The series has a special focus on the development of international legal standards and transnational legal cooperation.

Michele Graziadei · Lihong Zhang
Editors

The Making of the Civil Codes

A Twenty-First Century Perspective

 Springer

Editors
Michele Graziadei
Law Department
University of Torino
Torino, Italy

Lihong Zhang
East China University of Political Science
and Law
Shanghai, China

ISSN 1534-6781   ISSN 2214-9902 (electronic)
Ius Gentium: Comparative Perspectives on Law and Justice
ISBN 978-981-19-4992-0   ISBN 978-981-19-4993-7 (eBook)
https://doi.org/10.1007/978-981-19-4993-7

Preface

Over the past twenty years, many countries around the world have promulgated new civil codes or have revised their civil codes. After prolonged work, the People's Republic of China enacted its first civil code in 2021. It appears that codification, far from losing momentum, is alive and well in our epoch, although the mythology surrounding the first civil codes is by now a thing of the past.

This is a propitious moment to bring to the attention of readers a wide-ranging examination of the state of the art concerning civil codifications around the world. Although this book does not cover every significant experience, the essays collected in it offer our readers a substantial set of contributions on civil codifications, for a total of 16 jurisdictions. An introduction and three thematic essays complete the overall picture. Remy Cabrillac's essay provides a general reflection on civil codifications; Sabrina Lanni's contribution discusses how some recent civil codes cover environmental issues, and a final essay by the late Rodolfo Sacco addresses the relationship between the civil codes and their interpreters. Our views on the subject are presented in the introduction to the volume.

The first idea to produce a volume like this took shape during a conference organized by the editors on the making of the civil codes, which was held at the University of Torino in 2016. The papers collected in this volume do not issue out of that conference but have been produced independently for this publication, with the exception of the contribution by the late Rodolfo Sacco, which is the speech he delivered at the closing session of that conference. Rodolfo Sacco passed away in March 2022, as we were working to complete the typescript for publication. Many of his ideas were a source of inspiration for the editors of this book.

We are immensely grateful to the distinguished colleagues who have joined for this collaborative project. They have patiently waited for the production of this book during the pandemic, while the final conference around this project that we intended to announce as a surprise for them could not be organized. Their commitment to the production of the book has been a formidable encouragement all along the way.

While the work on the book progressed, we contracted many debts with those who helped us to prepare the typescript for publication. We therefore wish to express our gratitude to Michael Gardiner, legal officer at the Newfoundland and Labrador

Court of Appeal, who edited several of the contributions to this book, and to Davide Caudana, Marco Giraudo, and Elisa Verra, who provided editorial assistance by checking consistency with the house style. We are also grateful to Ms. Lydia Wang, editor for the Social Sciences, Springer Asia, for her unfailing support and to Ms. Shalini Shelvam and Ms. Karthika Purushotha, who oversaw the preparation of the typescript for publication. The financial support provided by the Law Department of the University of Torino through its excellence programme (2018–2022) funded by the Italian Ministry of Education, University and Research, and by the Collegio Carlo Alberto, Torino, is gratefully acknowledged.

Torino, Italy   Michele Graziadei
Shanghai, China   Lihong Zhang
April 2022

Contents

Editors and Contributors

About the Editors

Michele Graziadei is Professor of Comparative Private Law, University of Torino; President of the Società Italiana per la ricerca nel diritto comparato—SIRD; Past president of the European Association of Law Faculties; Member of the executive board of the International Association of Legal Science; Titular member of the International Academy of Comparative Law; corresponding member of the Accademia delle Scienze (Torino), Collegio Carlo Alberto Fellow. He is the author of over 100 publications in several languages. His recent publications include *Comparative Law, Transplants and Receptions* in M. Reimann, R. Zimmermann (eds.), *The Oxford Handbook of Comparative Law* (2nd edn OUP, 2019); M Graziadei, LD Smith (eds.), *Comparative Property Law: Global Perspectives* (Elgar, 2018).

Lihong Zhang is Professor of Law at East China University of Political Science and Law (Shanghai, ECUPL), a holder of Ph.D. degree in law of University of Rome "La Sapienza", Vice Secretary-General of China's National Society of Civil Law, Standing Director of China's National Society of European Law, Director of China's National Society of Comparative Law, Director of the Roman Law and European Law Research Center of ECUPL. He been a visiting professor at the University of Paris "Panthéon Assas", University of Turin, National University of Singapore, Münster University, Catholic University of Leuven, Jagiellonian University, University of San Francisco and University of Macerata and he has been delivering the academic speeches at many world-renowned universities, such as Harvard University, University of California at Berkeley, Georgetown University, Hitotsubashi University and the National University of Seoul.

Contributors

Arroyo Amayuelas Esther University of Barcelona, Barcelona, Spain

Arslan Gizem Department of Civil Law, Kadir Has University, Istanbul, Turkey

Baysal Başak Department of Civil Law, Kadir Has University, Istanbul, Turkey

Cabrillac Rémy Faculté de droit et science politique, Montpellier, France

Cannarsa Michel Lyon catholic University, Lyon, France

Graziadei Michele Law Department, University of Torino, Collegio Carlo Alberto, Torino, Italy

Heirbaut Dirk Ghent University, Ghent, Belgium

Kemelmajer de Carlucci Aida Rosa National Academy of Law and Science of Buenos Aires, Buenos Aires, Argentina

Kim Sang Yong Faculty of Law, Yonsei University, Seoul, South Korea

Kozuka Souichirou Faculty of Law, Gakushuin University, Tokyo, Japan

Lanni Sabrina University of Milan, Milan, Italy

Liu Qiao City University of Hong Kong, Hong Kong, China

Morin Michel Université de Montréal, Montreal, QC, Canada

Paulus Christoph G. Humboldt-Universität zu Berlin, Berlin, Germany

Pavlov Andrej A. Law Faculty, St. Petersburg State University, St. Petersburg, Russia

Pichonnaz Pascal Department of Law, University of Fribourg, Fribourg, Switzerland

Poveda Velasco Ignacio Maria University of Sao Paulo, Sao Paulo, Brazil

Rasskazova Natalia J. Law Faculty, St. Petersburg State University, St. Petersburg, Russia

Rudokvas Anton D. Law Faculty, St. Petersburg State University, St. Petersburg, Russia

Sacco Rodolfo Emeritus of the University of Torino, Torino, Italy

Tomasevicius Filho Eduardo University of Sao Paulo, Sao Paulo, Brazil

van Dongen Emanuel G. D. Molengraaff Institute for Private Law, Utrecht University, Utrecht, The Netherlands

Vékás Lajos Eötvös Loránd University Budapest, Budapest, Hungary

Wang Liming Renmin University of China, Beijing, China

Zhang Lihong East China University of Political Science and Law, Shanghai, China

Abbreviations

ABGB	Allgemeines bürgerliches Gesetzbuch
ADC	Anuario de derecho civil
Am J Comp L	American Journal of Comparative Law
AÜHFD	Ankara Üniversitesi Hukuk Fakültesi Dergisi
BCEHC	Boletín del Centro de Estudios Hipotecarios de Cataluña
BGB	Bürgerliches Gesetzbuch
BOA	Boletín Oficial de Aragón (Official Journal of Aragón)
BON	Boletín Oficial de Navarra (Official Journal of Navarre)
Br J Can Stud	British Journal of Canadian Studies
BW	Burgerlijk Wetboek
C d D	Cahiers de Droit
c.c.	Codice civile
C.C.Q.	Civil code of Quebec
Can Bar Rev	Canadian Bar Review
CC	Civil Code
CCC	Chinese Civil Code; Argentinian Civil and Commercial Code
CC Cat./CCC	Catalan Civil Code
CCJC	Cuadernos Civitas de jurisprudencia civil
CCRO	Civil Code Revision Office
CISG	United Nations Convention on the International Sale of Goods
CN	Constitución de la Nación Argentina
Colum J Asian L	Columbia Journal of Asian Law
D. lgs	Decreto legislativo delegato
Dalhousie LJ	Dalhousie Law Journal
DCC	Dutch Civil Code
DCFR	Draft Common Frame of Reference
DOGC	Diario Oficial de la Generalitat de Cataluña
DP	Draft Proposals (of Japan's Civil Code (Law of Obligations) Reform Commission of Japan)
EC	Constitución española
ECC	European Economic Community

ECHR	European Convention on Human Rights
ECtHR	European Court of Human Rights
ERPL	European Review of Private Law
EU	European Union
Eur JL Reform	European Journal of Law Reform
ff.	Following
FTA	Free Trade Agreement
GRUR	Gewerblicher Rechtsschutz und Urheberrecht
Harvard Law Rev	Harvard Law Review
Hong Kong LJ	Hong Kong Law Journal
IJLI	International Journal of Legal Information
InDret	InDret. Revista para el análisis del derecho
IR	Interim Report (Chukan Shi'an) Concerning the Amendments to the Civil Code (Law of obligations) of Japan
ISTAT	Istituto Nazionale di Statistica
İÜMHE	İstanbul Üniversitesi Mukayeseli Hukuk Enstitüsü
J Civ L Stud	Journal of Civil Law Studies
JCL	Journal of Comparative Law
JO	Journal Officiel
JT	Journal des Tribunaux
KCC	Korean Civil Code
l.	Legge ordinaria
LC	Legislative Council (Houesei Shingikai) of Japan
Louisiana Law Rev	Louisiana Law Review
Loy L Rev	Loyola Law Review
Manitoba Law J	Manitoba Law Journal
McGill Law J	McGill Law Journal
Melb U L Rev	Melbourne University Law Review
Minroku	Daishin'in Minji Hanketsuroku (Records of the Great Court of Judicature Civil Cases) of Japan
Minshû	Saikô Saibansho Minji Hanreishû (Collection of the Supreme Court Civil Cases) of Japan (Between 1922 and 1946)
MoJ	Ministry of Justice
MÜHF	Marmara Üniversitesi Hukuk Fakültesi
NBW	Nieuw Burgerlijk Wetboek
NPC	National People's Congress
OECD	Organization for Economic Co-Operation and Development
OHADA	Organisation pour l'harmonisation en Afrique du droit des affaires
OR	Outline of Reform (Yoko An) Concerning the Amendments to the Civil Code (Law of obligations) of Japan
Osgoode HLJ	Osgoode Hall Law Journal
PECL	Principles of European Contract Law
PRC	People's Republic of China

RabelsZ	Rabels Zeitschrift für ausländisches und internationales Privatrecht
RC	Civil Code (Law of Obligations) Reform Commission (Minpô (Saiken Hô) Kaisei I'inkai) of Japan
RCDP	Revista Catalana de Dret Privat
RDC	Revista de Derecho Civil
RDS	Revue de droit suisse = ZSR
RDUS	Revue de Droit de l'Université de Sherbrooke
RGD	Revue générale de droit
RIDC	Revue internationale de droit comparé
RJB	Revue de la Société des juristes bernois
RM Themis	Rechtsgeleerd Magazijn Themis
RSFSR	Russian Soviet Federative Socialist Republic
SPC	Supreme People's Court
SPR	Schweizerisches Privatrecht
Stanf LR	Stanford Law Review
STS	Sentencia del Tribunal Supremo
Texas Int'l LJ	Texas International Law Journal
TS	Tribunal Supremo
U Tokyo JLP	University of Tokyo Journal of Law and Politics
UC Davis L Rev	University of California, Davies Law Review
Unif L Rev	Uniform Law Review
Univ Toronto Law J	University of Toronto Law Journal
UPICC	Unidroit Principles of International Commercial Contracts
USP Law School J	University of Sao Paulo Law Journal
USSR/SSSR	Union of Soviet Socialist Republics
WG	Working Group
WiRO	Wirtschaft und Recht in Osteuropa
WPNR	Weekblad voor Privaatrecht Notariaat en Registratie
WTO	World Trade Organization
ZEuP	Zeitschrift für europäisches Privatrecht
ZGB	Zivilgesetzbuch
ZJapanR	Zeitschrift für Japanisches Recht
ZPO	Zivilprozessordnung
ZSR	Zeitschrift für Schweizerisches Recht = RDS

On Civil Codes: A Twenty-First Century Perspective

Michele Graziadei and Lihong Zhang

Abstract Civil codes are an effort to provide stability and coherence to several areas of the law. Despite the growing complexity of contemporary societies, codification as a legislative technique has not been abandoned. Codification is, however, just one option on the table. This introductory chapter explores why this option has been so successful, though the mythologies surrounding the first civil codifications are by now behind us, and much has changed both in society and in legal theory since the time those first codes were put into force.

1 The Force of an Idea

Codification, once more, really? Why should a new book be devoted to a topic that has already been widely covered by so many important contributions? This introductory chapter provides some reflections that may help answer this question and put this book into perspective.

The theme underlying this collection of essays is that civil codes—both old and new—represent an attempt to provide stability and coherence to several areas of the law, offering a comprehensive approach to the regulation of a whole set of civil relations by setting coordinated rules applicable to them.[1] Although codification

---

[1] For a general view of civil codification see: Parise and Van Vliet (2018), Wang (2014a, b), Rivera (2013), Vargas (2011), Cabrillac (2002), Cappellini and Sordi (2002), and Sacco (1993).

M. Graziadei (✉)
Law Department, University of Torino, Collegio Carlo Alberto, Torino, Italy
e-mail: michele.graziadei@unito.it

L. Zhang
East China University of Political Science and Law, Shanghai, China
e-mail: lihongzhang111@qq.com

typically serves these purposes, it is also true that legal change will still occur over time, even though a civil code has been enacted. The challenging task of balancing conflicting legal principles and demands is not over once a code is enacted. The search for stability, coherence, and adaptability continues in various ways after a code civil enters into force, for example when innovations are introduced into the law without amending the code. Eventually, the code as it was enacted turns out to be just a milestone along the road to new legal developments.

The question for us is, therefore, how stability and change are managed in the presence of ongoing legal development under the civil code of a country. The problem was already familiar to the drafters of the French civil code. A few famous lines from the preparatory works of the French civil code by the eminent Jean-Étienne-Marie Portalis show clear awareness of this:

> A code, however complete it may seem, is no sooner finished than thousands of unexpected questions present themselves to the magistrate. For these laws, once drafted, remain as written. Men, on the other hand, never rest. They are always moving; and this movement, which never ceases and whose effects are variously modified by circumstances, continually produces some new fact, some new outcome.
>
> Many things are therefore necessarily left to the authority of custom, to the discussion of learned men, to the arbitration of judges.[2]

The papers collected in this volume provide an interesting and up-to-date set of new responses on this point. These various responses have matured in countries that have experienced different socioeconomic and political trajectories, such as Argentina, Brazil, China, Japan, Russia, South Korea and Switzerland, or that by now are members of the European Union, such as Belgium, France, Germany, Italy, Hungary, The Netherlands, and Spain. Codification may be achieved under different political regimes.

At the end of a long intellectual journey, we will not try to sum up the findings by each contributing author who was so kind to join in the effort. We prefer to let them speak with their own voices. Rather, our task is to present in a concise way our thoughts on these issues in a modest attempt to cast some light on them.

It should be clear from the outset that this volume does not cover those projects that in recent decades explored the possibility of a uniform civil codification for Europe. Instructive as they are, both for their ambitions and their limits, that part of the story relating to the codification of civil law is mostly left out of this book. The conditions for civil codification in a multinational, culturally diverse space like the one constituted by the European Union present issues that are different from those prevailing at the national level, where the value and costs of reducing legislative particularism in civil and commercial matters are usually debated against a different background.

Nevertheless, many of those projects have been a source of inspiration for national reformers of the law. Reform efforts both inside and outside Europe have considered them, along with other nonbinding legal texts, such as the Principles of European Contract Law and the Unidroit Principles on International Commercial contracts.

---

[2] Portalis (1801).

All these international legal materials illustrate how some of the tasks of codification are accomplished by other means in a transnational setting.[3]

Having made this choice, namely, not to discuss codification at the EU level, the codification landscape in European countries is still evolving under the pressure of EU legislation and the case law of the European Court of justice. Provisions incorporated into the civil codes of the European countries that derive from EU must therefore be interpreted and applied in conformity with it. National civil codifications in Europe thus are integrated at the EU level to an unprecedented level because EU law by now covers a whole range of disparate matters, from package travels to product liability, to transactions on digital platforms, etc... It has often been remarked that EU legislation presents a challenge to the national civil codes because of its pointillistic and ad hoc character.[4] The other face of the same coin is the concrete risk that EU law is interpreted in light of national legal concepts and categories, rather than as a law that has its own ends, as it should be, although in the elaboration and interpretation of EU law comparative law has a definite role to play.[5]

The European Convention of Human Rights and the jurisprudence of the Strasbourg Court tasked with its application are also taken into account when considering the limits to purely national approaches to codification in Europe. Their influence on national law is particularly visible in areas such as family law.

National codifications in Europe are therefore now under the shared roof of supranational norms. The European situation has no exact parallel in other contexts, given the level of integration experienced by the countries belonging to the EU, and yet national experiences across the world often speak of cosmopolitan attitudes and of the impact of international trends on codification processes. One could quickly come to the conclusion that this is the visible effect of accentuated globalizing trends. Although these trends are present on the contemporary scene, the history of codification shows that borrowing, adaptation, and contamination, along with a measure of original creation, were there from its very beginning. The first civil codes were drafted on the basis of a variety of materials mostly drawn from the Roman law sources, which did not have a national character; they also reinstated several (non national) customary rules and in doing so took advantage of the available legal literature. Subsequent civil codifications have benefitted from a close examination of previous codes, whether enacted at home or abroad[6]; more recent codifications have drawn from international conventions and soft law texts as well.[7]

Our epoch is defined by an increased recourse to legislation to govern disparate fields of the law, including those areas of the law that have been codified. This is due to the growing complexity of contemporary societies, to the major role of the contemporary State in the regulation of the economy, and in arbitrating or recognizing the claims of the various constituencies and organised interests. Nonetheless, the civil

---

[3] For an excellent discussion Jansen (2010).

[4] See, e.g., Roth (2002).

[5] See, e.g., Lenaerts (2003, 2017); Graziadei (2020).

[6] Mirow (2001).

[7] See, e.g., Guo et al. (2021) and Pietrunko and Richter (2020).

codes have maintained their importance among the source of law in a high number of jurisdictions all around the world.[8] The most populous country in the world—the PRC—is, for the moment, the latest country to join the club of countries that opted for codification, with its civil code of 2020. This achievement confirms once more that codification is one of the most powerful techniques in the hands of a legislator.

On what grounds is this power based?

One would look in vain for a single, compelling answer on the point. Legislators have often refrained from taking upon themselves the task of setting out the law applicable to the whole range of civil and commercial relationships. Codification of the law is, after all, just one option on the table, and a relatively recent option when considering the history of law through the ages from a global perspective.[9]

Furthermore, the common law world still offers the view of large tracts of the law relating to civil and commercial relationships that are not enacted in the form of a code. They are mostly left to the care of judges and commentators, with the occasional intervention of the legislator. This happens despite the great amount of attention given in common law jurisdictions to the possibilities offered by codification, its merits and defects.[10] In continental Europe, the laws of the Nordic countries (Finland, Denmark, Iceland, Sweden, Norway) developed without following the path of the neighbouring countries. They all avoid comprehensive civil codifications, taking a rather sceptical view of their utility.[11]

Law reformers have often launched codification as a reaction to the unbearable disorder of the law, its lack of intelligibility, or its inaccessible nature. Similar motives already feature at the entry door of one of the world's most famous legal compilations, namely, the Digest of Justinian:

> ….we have found the whole extent of our laws which has come down from the foundation of the city of Rome and the days of Romulus to be so confused that it extends to an inordinate length and is beyond the comprehension of any human nature.[12]

Unsurprisingly, the urge is then to remedy similar defects and to provide a single statement of the law, which should be free from discrepancies, repetitions, and contradictions. This is not the occasion to consider whether Justinian's Digest lived up to the challenge,[13] but to note that similar statements are often found in the preparatory works of compilations and codes of all ages, including the Chinese civil code of 2020 as a resounding call for action.

---

[8] For the thesis that we live in an age of decodification see Irti (1999). This stimulating diagnosis has sparked an international debate. The evidence collected since the first publication of Irti's book shows that codification is far from dead. As Cabrillac's contribution to the present volume makes clear, codification is still enjoying an excellent state of health, although the ethos of codification has changed since the epoch of the first civil codes. See as well on these points Vargas (2011); Sacco (1983).

[9] Pirie (2021).

[10] See, e.g., Giliker (2021) and Weiss (2000).

[11] See, e.g., Juutilainen (2013).

[12] D. 1.17.1.1 (trans. ed. by Watson).

[13] More on this in Mantovani (2016)

Since the Enlightment, the idea of an accessible, orderly set of laws gained ground in Europe.[14] Eventually, by the beginning of the nineteenth century, the impulse to provide a single set of laws to govern civil relations for the whole the polity carried the day with the French (1804) and the Austrian (1811) codifications. Order and intelligibility are usually one of the principal justifications given for the codification effort, but the desire to pursue similar goals is not enough to have a codification, however. Justinian's Digest does not qualify as a codification, although the Emperor intended to bring (more) order to the law. To pick a twentieth century example, the drafters of the English Law of Property Act 1925 worked to remedy the messy state of English property law, to make it more certain and intelligible. The resulting text is not a codification either. It is too rich in detail, and it still requires sound knowledge of the previous practice of the law to master it.

To move beyond similar commonplace observations, one rapidly comes to the conclusion that a comprehensive, systematic statement of the law, such as that which is found in a civil code, is available only if the way toward that ultimate goal has been carefully prepared. All the powers of a legislator cannot deliver on this, unless a systematic treatment of the law is made available to it, typically because scholarly works have laid the foundations for satisfying this need. The point has been aptly made by James Gordley: "...continental scholars were systematic before they had codes. It was their very success in systematizing the law that made the codes possible".[15]

The second element of continuity between the old and the new law entrusted to the civil codes is the assumption that authoritative texts are the source of the law. For centuries, jurists educated at the universities have been trained to find the law in the text of Justinian's compilation (and in the *Corpus juris canonici*, as far as canon law was concerned). The importance of customary law in medieval and modern Europe was immense, but the tendency to put customary law in writing reveals how even custom in the end falled prey to the mindset of lawyers educated at the universities and their ability to work with texts. Obviously, the raise of printing was a formidable push in the same direction.

Contemporary observers may quickly label this posture as the quintessential, foundational mythology of the civil law tradition.[16] Mythology it is, because during the entire epoch of the ius commune the law did not cease to change and evolve in different directions, to experience a variety of cultural influences, and to adapt to the new material conditions of life in society.[17] However, much is lost if the crucial point is missed: it was a mythology *with a purpose*—hence it is appropriate to approach

---

[14] See Coing (1997) and van der Bergh (2007).

[15] Gordley (1998, 735).

[16] See, e.g., Legrand (1995).

[17] On this last point, see, e.g., with respect to the relation between Roman law, commerce and industrialisation in nineteenth century Germany: Whitman (1990, 221 ff).

the phenomenon as a form of ideology.[18] By following this path, jurists trained at the universities established for themselves the same type of technical legitimation that is claimed through expertise in the form of high learning (*scientia*)—they indeed represented themselves as the lights of the *scientia iuris*—*Rechtswissenschaft, science du droit*, an objective form of knowledge of the law.[19] The anchoring of jurists to the ontological plane, namely, the self-representation of *scientia iuris* as knowledge built on a compact nucleus of nonnegotiable values, waranted by certain texts, historically lent credibility to the legal profession and conveniently protected it from political criticism to a large extent, and above all enable them to work even when centralised state structures were yet to emerge.[20] To put it in a line, the jurists knew how to 'naturalise' their notion of the law. Public law, however, was never wholly tied to the same premises; it emerged later as a system of law, and to this day it is only partially codified.

With the advent of the modern codification movement, the text was still, once more, at the centre of the scene, commanding, if possible, even closer attention, but it was no more ruling as an old monument of the antiquity in the name of legal science. The source of its legitimation had changed, becoming an act of positive legislation.

Here we have a turning point. In Europe, the first civil codifications represented both the culmination of the scholarly dominance of legal development and a break with the previous tradition.[21] The pithy propositions that make up a code are quite different from those collected in Justinian's compilation. The former are on their face much less open to discussion and argumentation than the latter, being cast as a set of rules.[22] For the first time in the entire history of the civil law, the legislature stepped in to claim competence to govern the entire subject matter of civil relationships, marriage and successions included, for the whole polity. By doing so, the code implicitly—perhaps beyond the intention of its makers—emphasized the national, rather than the universal dimensions of the law, as an expression of political will.[23]

---

[18] For this framing: Orestano (1982) and Kroppenberg and Linder (2014) are less explicit, but their argument points in the same direction. A similar analysis can be developed as well by reflecting on judicial style in civilian and common law jurisdictions: see Lasser (2004).

[19] On this strategy: Wieacker (1996), and for a critique of its standard presentation Tuori (2020). For a more complex reconstruction, which integrates the various components of the medieval legal order: Grossi (2010) and the authors cited in the previous note.

[20] See, the literature cited in fn. 19 and Luongo (2018).

[21] This aspect is emphasized by Paolo Grossi, who holds the French civil code to be the apogee of unprecedented 'absolutistic' tendencies, which turned legislation into the pre-eminent source of the law: Grossi (2010). On patterns of continuity of the law after the entry into force of a new codification see, e.g., with respect to the German civil code: Zimmerman (2001).

[22] See Gordley (1998).

[23] Some codes proclaimed faith in nationalism as well. For example, the Italian Civil Code of 1942, art. 12 (preliminary title), provides: "In applying the law one cannot attribute to it any other meaning than that made evident by the proper meaning of the words according to their connection, and by the intention of the legislator. If a dispute cannot be decided with a specific provision, it refers to the provisions governing similar cases or similar matters; if the case still remains doubtful, it is decided according to the general principles of the legal system ('ordinamento giuridico') of the State.". The

The references to reason and equity in the preparatory works of the French civil code, as well as the homage paid by § 7 of the Austrian Civil Code of 1811 to the principles of natural law, still reflected those old universalistic tendencies. However, the choice to enact the code in the vernacular language, rather than in Latin, conveyed a new message: that there was a strong link between the law and the territorial power that enacted it. In the nineteenth century, the civil code is the expression of a wider effort of the State to set a modernising, rational plan for society, in which the raising bourgeoisie has a major role to play.[24]

Nevertheless, continuity with a number of solutions going back to the old law and its doctrines was warranted, when compatible with the new political and economic order, even when the code intended to provide a fresh start, as the French civil code did, by proclaiming the abrogation of all the previous sources of law.[25]

The power of the code was thus related to its rational plan or to its systematic character, to the accessibility of it, thanks to the resulting simplification of the sources of the law, and to the possibility of reading the law in the modern language as part of a message that rendered the code the law of the nation. The force of the idea is clearly intelligible at this point: it is the force of formalism writ large. A civil code is not meant to last just a few years; it is a declaration of the law that is cast in a form that should be durable because it is of a high level of generality. The idea that the code is also a complete statement of the law—albeit a fiction—is a fiction that falls in line with assumptions backing the authority of the code.

Before proceeding to the discussion of these ideas, one further point must be highlighted. Even in nineteenth-century Europe, codifications were adopted in very different contexts and pursued different philosophies. For example, at first, in many European countries, codification implied the reception of a foreign code rather than the elaboration of an original text. In the same period, outside Europe, in Asia, the elaboration of a code implied, first of all, the creation of a whole new terminology to translate alien legal concepts and the rapid acculturation to the intellectual background of Western law, as happened in Japan, during the Meiji period.[26] Under colonial or semicolonial conditions, the code did not apply to the entire population of a country either (and even in Europe the application of the code could be contested in some contexts, e.g. in some parts of the countryside).[27]

The ideal of a continuity between the letter of the code and the works of its interpreters in all these contexts was a mere hypothesis, not necessarily warranted by

---

latter part of the norm was a tribute to the autarchic ideology of the fascist regime, and should now be reformed.

[24] Canale (2009).

[25] Article 7 of the French Civil Code provides: "From the day on which these laws are enforceable, the Roman laws, ordinances, general or local customs, statutes, regulations, cease to have the force of general or particular law composing this code."

[26] Kitamura (1993). On the recent modernisation of the language of the Japanese civil code see the contributions by Kozuka (in this volume) and Ortolani (2018).

[27] Bell (2014).

the facts.[28] The translation of foreign legal literature into the local languages—where and when it occurs—is a poor surrogate for the initial lack of original works produced by the local jurists. In these contexts, the civil code hardly carries with it the same symbolism that it gained elsewhere and the law may show hybridity, adaptations, and contaminations.[29]

2   The Code Is Dead, Long Live the Code

In the previous section, we sketched a genealogy of civil codes. A reflection on the present relevance of civil codifications invites the following question as well: when do codes die?

There are famous pictures representing the birth of codes and scholarly articles dedicated to failed codification projects, but the final chapters in the lives of civil codes are seldom discussed, although the death of codification in general has been predicted with a certain emphasis.

It is tempting to say that a first factor determining the death of a code is simply its old age. With the passage of time civil codes become decrepit too. The incremental change that is initially deemed compatible with them, in the end, disfigures them. Although old codes are "in force", their vigor is much diminished, the letter is still there, but the spirit is often gone. A system that was once codified then turns out to be uncodified: codification silently unravels over time, and the code is virtually dead, as it no longer speaks to reality.

Prior to several both recent and less recent reforms, the oldest code of Europe, the French civil code, risked this fate.[30] France has always been presented as a leading civil jurisdiction, putting great faith in codification as a legislative technique. However, by the close of the last century, the French civil code was rapidly losing ground to the law formed outside it and to the weight of its own judicial application on a massive scale. New theories and rules sanctioned by judicial practice and by academic writings found no direct support in the code and yet submerged it. Under these conditions, the code had lost its *raison d'être*. This danger was just as apparent in Belgium, and Belgium quickly proceeded to reform its civil code as well. For the same reasons, the German civil code has undergone a vast reform of the law of obligations in 2002. This was the occasion to incorporate into the code new statutory provisions to bring the code in line with doctrinal and judicial developments, as well as to integrate consumer contract law of European origin into the BGB and

---

[28] Those of study the history of the French civil codification in nineteenth century Europe know, for instance, that its interpretation in the German lands beyond the Rhine was guided by conceptual approaches different from those prevailing in the same epoch France. Looking beyond Europe, both the case of Japan and China are telling. On the legacy of Legalism and Confucianism in the Chinese experience with codification see the chapter by Zhang in this book.

[29] Timoteo (2021).

[30] See, e.g., Mazeaud (2004).

to undertake reforms going beyond consumer law. The German legislature accommodated tendencies emerging at the European and international levels concerning general contract law as well. After this reform, new provisions were introduced in the code in recent years, such as those dealing with medical treatment contracts and those concerning the implementation of European directives on consumer rights, mortgage credit, and package travel. The most recent additions to the code in the field of contracts concern architect and engineering contracts (§§ 650p ff.). The reform process is evident in other parts of the code as well; for example, the law on foundations was amended in 2021.

A closer look at the life of civil codes to detect factors at the origins of their obsolescence highlights at least three elements affecting the vitality of a codification in the absence of reactions to outdateness, usually in the form of recodification.

The first is a change in the values that dominate certain aspects of social life. The protection of fundamental human rights, in particular, of personality rights, in recent codifications is a case in point. The dedication of a specific book of the new Chinese civil code to the protection of personality rights provides a good example of this dynamic.[31]

Family law is a typical instance in this respect. Family law experienced change on a large scale between the second half of the twentieth century and the first decades of the twentieth century in many countries. In this period, family law inherited from the past, based on the inequality of the spouses, was repealed to lay down completely new foundations for it in a wide number of jurisdictions. A legal revolution has taken place, and it is still ongoing, concerning, e.g., the role of gender in its relation with family law. Until this wave of reforms, the codes that enacted the old law were mere relics from the past in the eyes of the new generations who rejected them. To provide another example of legal change related to the onset of new values with respect to the area of patrimonial relationships, the birth of consumer law in the twentieth century is connected to a new assessment of private autonomy and its role in market relationships; the ideology of contract prevailing in the nineteenth century, extolling the sanctity of contracts, was eventually abandoned.

The second factor of change is the emergence of new material conditions of life in society. This may bring with it new law to remedy a legal regime that turns out to be dysfunctional. Pressure on civil codes are abundant.

The average life span in European societies has increased dramatically in the last century. This poses entirely new problems for the law of succession. When the first civil codes were enacted, the rules on forced heirship usually benefitted minors or a young people. Today, it is not unusual for a daughter or a son aged 65 (or more) to succeed to parents aged 85 (or more). Traditional forced heirship rules working under these conditions take on an altogether different socioeconomic meaning. Hence, the need to amend the laws governing succession upon death.

Consider as well the advent of modern traffic in the twentieth century: compulsory automobile insurance soon became a necessity. Similarly, the large-scale development of industrial activities is at the origins of the provisions of the civil codes on

---

[31] See Prof. Wang's chapter in this book.

emissions among neighbouring properties. One could go on in the same vein to illustrate, for example, how the introduction of electricity as a new source of energy posed several legal puzzles to codifiers. Presently, the rise of artificial intelligence and automated contracting through platforms is leading to the creation of new rules that will have to be accommodated into civil codes sooner or later, while self-driving cars are on the legislative agendas of many countries. Assisted reproduction techniques, and other disruptive technologies in the field of life sciences, also impact traditional civil law rules in a number of ways.

Third, a code may suffer desuetude because it provides rules that are ill designed, as happens when the code fails to intercept the needs of those who should use it.

Consider the evolution of the rules on the taking of security over movables. They provide a nice example of the evolution of legal practice outside the framework provided by the Code. In Germany, the codal rule that requires the handing over of goods to a creditor to give security for credit (BGB § 1205) was quickly sidestepped by legal practice, with the support of decisions rendered by the Supreme Court just a few years after the German civil code was enacted.[32]

With the benefit of hindsight, one can conclude that BGB § 1205 is a dysfunctional provision because it effectively prevents the debtor from creating a security right over goods (usually raw materials) that the same debtor must transform in the production process. The law of security thus rapidly began developing along lines different from those provided for by the Code. In an area of the law that is dominated by formalism, such as property law, private autonomy played around the code with relative ease.

When the code begins showing obsolescence, the typical reaction is to reform it.

The number of new provisions that are incorporated into old civil codes shows that obsolesce is no fatal illness, if cured. Like an old palace, a code can be renovated. This is usually the preferred course of action.

The growth of an entire new set of rules can also be accommodated into a new, separate code, with a rationality of its own. The enactment of a consumer code in several countries (e.g., France, Italy, Spain) is a clear example of this dynamic.

The substitution of an old code with an entirely new code is the fruit of more ambitious plans. Among other countries, Italy, Québec, and the Netherlands made this choice in the twentieth century. Once more, the response to obsolesce of an old codification is a fresh effort directed at codification. In both cases, the new codifications could draw inspiration from an increased plurality of sources, exploiting the most recent advances of legal science at the time. The nineteenth-century visions of private law underlying the German and French civil codes have been left behind by these codifications. A new complete codification is thus perhaps the best evidence of the growth of a new legal consciousness; but a new legal consciousness does not necessarily lead to abandoning codification as a technique to set out the law.

---

[32] The first of these decisions is RZ 8 November 2004, RGZ, 146. The Court thus confirmed a line of decisions preceding the entry into force of the BGB. Kötz (1987) shows that the possibility to 'take the civil codes less seriously' is far from rare in several contexts.

3 The Letter and the Meaning of a Code

Civil codes are texts sanctioned by state authority. Thus far, we have implicitly assumed that these texts have the ability to constrain their interpreters. We have also assumed that this quality is not everlasting, nor to be taken for granted as an empirical fact. However, what about the general, philosophical question raised by similar remarks: do texts, even if sanctioned by authority, constrain interpreters? Alternatively, to put the same question in slightly more provocative terms: are sceptics justified to think that jurists all too often must be pulling rabbits out of empty hats when interpreting the civil codes?

As far as the law is concerned, general questions such as these are better answered after inspecting the historical record.

The history of the civil law tradition in Europe would be inexplicable if the legal professions had not managed to gain strong legitimation as a social force managing legal change over time. This legitimation was gained thanks to the capacity of jurists to distance their theoretical and practical activity directed at preventing or solving disputes from the sheer exercise of unbridled political power. In the civil law world, the texts they worked with became one of the strongholds of the notion of legality which embodies such ideal. This foundation expressed (and is) a *commitment* to be bound by the relevant texts, whether they are sanctioned by tradition alone, or by a democratic legislature, under a constitution.[33] Still, in either case, those texts do not speak without an interpreter. Agreement by jurists on a certain opinion establishes its authority. Judicial pronouncements weight in the same matter because they are deliberated by (independent) decision makers after hearing the reasons advanced by both parties in a dispute. The attribution of meaning to the provisions of a code (more generally: to legislative enactments) is a social act that is governed by conventions in all codified systems. The local legal culture may be more or less inclined to allow an open discussion of them. The code itself may speak or remain silent about them.[34] In any case, over time, methods of interpretation change, and the culture of the interpreter of the code changes as well. Nonetheless, those conventions are far from imaginary. As John Merryman noted: "...to understand a contemporary civil law system you have to know where it comes from and what its image of itself is... In most of the civil law world legal professionals believe in that image. Even those who do not believe in it often feel compelled to act as though they do".[35] With this remark, a profound truth is unveiled. There is an element of subjectivity and creativity in every act of interpretation, although one may wish to deny it, or may even be bound by convention to deny it. These remarks do not dispense lawyers from looking for a theory of interpretation of law under the code, but rather help to build a better

---

[33] For brilliant analysis of the notion of 'commitment' and its role in furthering comparative projects Valcke (2018).

[34] Guzmán Brito (2011).

[35] Merryman (1987). On judicial styles as the manifestation of such assumptions see the important contribution by Lasser (2004). Sacco's pioneering, profound work on legal formants and cryptotypes is very much relevant here. See on this his chapter in this book.

comparative understanding of it by leading to an ethnography of it. In 1948, Roscoe Pound concluded that legal systems need to be studied functionally as instruments of social control and that legal precepts and the interpretation and application thereof need to be developed "with respect to the social ends to be served".[36] This is still broadly true today, and lawyers have lost their legitimation time and again when they have lost sight of this need.

A further point to keep in mind is that texts are not all the same. The authority of the text varies with its quality. Codifications can be judged on the basis of formal criteria, although different drafting styles legitimately reflect different professional ideals and assumptions about the law. Text with a high degree of generality—such as those providing the rules on extra contractual liability contained in many civil codes— allow for massive integration of meaning and for a good amount of discretion in determining the outcome of a litigation. References to 'good faith', 'reasonableness', 'public policy', 'good morals', and the like perform similar functions. Even in the presence of such formulas, the fundamental principle of justice that extols equality requires that similar cases be decided in a similar way. This principle puts a heavy argumentative burden on those who support the application of a different rule with respect to similar facts because an exception to the rule must be justified.

In several contemporary legal systems, this justification is sometimes upheld by constitutional arguments. The open-ended nature of many constitutional provisions is an invitation to develop cogent arguments for or against a certain solution. Since many contemporary constitutions are rich repositories of values, they do provide a way to approach the interpretation of the code that is liable to influence its application, although this is by no means a universal rule.[37] On the other hand, if the constitution is understood mostly as a political document, the code may help to entrench values that would otherwise fail to obtain recognition at the political level. The recent Chinese codification of personality rights in its civil code looks like an attempt to move in this direction and is telling about the rich debates behind the making of the Chinese civil code.[38]

4 The Reasons for a Lasting Legacy

Codification is by now a quintessential component of many legal systems. Its legacy is profound, although the views about codification and its contexts have changed over time.

In this introduction, we have argued that civil codifications should be read against the background of a legal tradition. Civil codifications provide the texture of the general law applicable among subjects in civil matters. For centuries, jurists trained

---

[36] Pound (1948).

[37] See, e.g., Sajo and Uitz (2005), Barkhuysen and Lindenbergh (2006), and Oliver and Fedtke (2007).

[38] Seppänen (2016, spec. p. 110 ff).

at the universities in the West have found this frame of reference in a text (and then, perhaps even more often, to be honest, in the interpretations developed over that text). The contemporary function of the code is still to lay down that general texture of the law, to offer an authoritative representation of it.

Traditions can grow spontaneously and exhibit original traits; they can be imitated or invented. They be betrayed, if necessary. The story of codification across the world draws upon all these possibilities. In any case, civil codes as propositional enactments of the law call for interpretations. They are not self-sufficient, even when they proclaim they are.

Just as constitutions do not live without constitutionalism, civil codes are put into practice by lawyers who understand their language, their doctrines, their policy choices, and who are trained for this. The sheer manifestation of political will is not enough to create these skills and capacities (although it can destroy them). More is needed to create them, and this is why lawyers receive specific training in the law. Any attempt to limit their call by ignoring the complexity of their standing (e.g., by turning them into burocrats, or mere servants of power, public or private) risks backfiring in terms of the credibility of their work.

A high level of coherence between the text of the code and these components of the law that make its interpretation is not to be taken for granted, however. The text as written is a fact, its meaning, as it results from the work of its interpreters, evolves over time. Adherence to new values, new theoretical views and new societal demands typically creates distance between the text and its interpreters. A wide gulf between them emerges when the foundations of the code are alien to the local professional culture and to society at large.

The perception of fault lines in the tradition leading to the codes has become sharper over time. The illusion that a text in the form of a civil code will defeat the complexity of the law once and for all has finally vanished. Codifications will challenge their interpreters. They will have to confront the problem of how to balance or coordinate conflicting legal principles, deal with issues that the code failed to address, or did not cover brilliantly. However, the seductive ambiguity of codification remains, and this new awareness only makes it more intriguing in the end.

References

Arnaud A-J (1969) Les origines doctrinales du Code civil français. LGDJ, Paris

Atias C (2009) L'influence des doctrines dans l'élaboration du Code civil. Histoire de la justice 1:107–120

Barkhuysen T, Lindenbergh SD (eds) (2006) Constitutionalisation of private law. Martinus Nijhoff Publishers, Leiden, Boston

Bell GF (2014) Codification and decodification: the state of the civil and commercial codes in Indonesia. In: Wang WY (ed) Codification in East Asia: selected papers from the 2nd IACL thematic conference. Springer, Cham, 39–50

Cabrillac R (2002) Les codifications. Presses Universitaires de France, Paris

Canale D (2009) The many faces of the codification of law in modern continental Europe. In: Grossi P, Hofmann H (eds), A history of the philosophy of law in the civil law world, 1600–1900. Springer, Dordrecht, 135–183

Cappellini P, Sordi B (2002) Codici: Una riflessione a fine di millennio. Giuffrè, Milano

Coing H (1977) An intellectual history of European codification in the eighteenth and nineteenth centuries. In: Stoljar S (ed), Problems of codification, 16

de Lasser M, S.-O.-l'E, (2004) Judicial deliberations: a comparative analysis of transparency and legitimacy. Oxford University Press, Oxford

Giliker P (2021) Codification, consolidation, restatement? How best to systemise the modern law of tort. International & Comparative Law Quarterly 70(2):271–305

Gordley J (1998) Codification and legal scholarship. UC Davis L Rev 31:735

Graziadei M (2020) The European court of justice at work: comparative law on stage and behind the scenes. Journal of Civil Law Studies 13:1

Grossi P (2010) A history of European law. Wiley, Blackwell, London

Guo P, Zhang S, Li L (2021) CISG and Chinese contract law reform in the new CCC: impacts, interactions and implications. Journal of Contract Law 37(3):192–215

Guzmán Brito A (2011) Codificación del derecho civil e interpretación de las leyes. Las normas sobre interpretación de las leyes en los principales códigos civiles europeo-occidentales y americanos emitidos hasta fines del siglo XIX. Iustel, Madrid

Irti N (1999) L'età della decodificazione. 4th ed. Giuffrè, Milano

Jansen N (2010) The making of legal authority. Non-legislative codifications in historical and comparative perspective. Oxford University Press, Oxford

Juutilainen T (2013) Finnish private law: Statutory system without a civil code. In: Rivera JC (ed) The scope and structure of civil codes. Springer, Dordrecht, pp 155–180

Kitamura I (1993) Problems of the translation of law in Japan. Victoria University of Wellington Law Review 23:143

Kötz H (1987) Taking civil codes less seriously. Modern Law Review 50(1):1–15

Kroppenberg I, Linder N (2014) Coding the nation. Codification history from a (post-) global perspective. In: Duve T (ed) Entanglements in legal history: conceptual approaches. Max Planck Institute for European Legal History, Frankfurt am Main, 67–99

Legrand P (1995) Antiqui juris civilis fabulas. University of Toronto Law Journal 45:311–362

Lenaerts K (2003) Interlocking legal orders in the European Union and comparative law. International and Comparative Law Quarterly 52(4):873–906

Lenaerts K (2017) The European court of justice and the comparative law method. European Review of Private Law 25(2):297–311

Luongo D (2018) La metodologia del commento nei trattati sull'interpretatio iuris di età umanistica. AION (filol.) Annali dell'Università degli Studi di Napoli "L'Orientale", 40(1):197–239

Mazeaud P (2004) Le Code civil et la conscience collective française. Pouvoirs 3:152–159

Mantovani D (2016) More than codes. In: du Plessis PJ, Ando C, Tuori K (eds) The Oxford handbook of Roman Law and society. Oxford University Press, Oxford, p 23

Merryman J (1987) Letter to the editor American Journal of Comparative Law. 35:438–441

Oliver D, Fedtke J (eds) (2007) Human Rights and the private sphere. A Comparative Study, Routledge, New York

Oppetit B (1998) Essai sur la codification. Presses Universitaires de France, Paris

Orestano R (1982) Ideologia, parola da non far più paura: Per una 'radiografia' della scientia iuris. Foro italiano, 105, V, c. 157–176

Ortolani A (2018) The many languages of Japanese legal language. Handbook of Communication in the Legal Sphere. de Gruyter, Berlin, pp 450–477

Mirow MC (2001) Borrowing private law in Latin America: Andrés Bello's use of the Code Napoléon in drafting the Chilean civil code. In: Louisiana Law Review 61(2), 291–329

Parise A, van Vliet L (eds) (2018) Re- De- Co-dification?New Insights on the Codification of Private Law. Eleven International Publishers, The Hague

Pietrunko S, Richter G (2020) DCFR as a basis for a modern codification-the revised Moldovan civil code. Osteuropa Recht 65(2):173–206

Pihlajamäki H (2015) Private law codification, modernization and nationalism: A view from critical legal history. Critical Analysis of Law, 2(1)

Pirie F (2021) The rule of law: a 4,000-thousand year quest to order the world, London, Profile Books

Portalis EM (ed. or. 1801) Preliminary Address on the First Draft of the Civil Code Presented in the year IX by Messrs. Portalis, Tronchet, Bigot-Préameneu and Maleville, members of the government-appointed commission. available in English translation at: https://www.justice.gc.ca/eng/rp-pr/csj-sjc/ilp-pji/code/index.html#Endnote1 (last consulted on 2 January 2022)

Pound R (1948) Comparative law and history as bases for Chinese Law. Harvard Law Review 61:749–762

Rivera JC (ed) (2013) The scope and structure of civil codes. Springer, Cham

Roth WH (2002) Transposing "pointillist" EC guidelines into systematic national codes—Problems and consequences. European Review of Private Law 10(6):771 776

Sacco R (1983) Codificare: modo superato di legiferare? Rivista di diritto civile I:117–135

Sacco R (1993) I codici civili dell'ultimo cinquantennio. Rivista di diritto civile I:311–316

Sajo A, Uitz R (eds) (2005) The constitution in private relation: expanding constitutionalism. Eleven International Publishers, Utrecht

Soleil S (2005) Le Code civil de 1804 a-t-il été conçu comme un modèle juridique pour les nations? in Forum historiae iuris. http://www.forhistiurde/zitat/0503soleil.htm

Seppänen S (2016) Ideological conflict and the rule of law in contemporary China. Cambridge University Press, Cambridge

Timoteo M (2021) Lungo sguardo verso Oriente: il nuovo codice civile cinese, Rivista trimestrale di diritto e procedura civile, 1157–1174

Tuori K (2020) Empire of law: Nazi Germany, exile scholars and the battle for the future of Europe. Cambridge University Press, Cambridge

Valcke C (2018) Comparing law: comparative law as reconstruction of collective commitments. Cambridge University Press, Cambridge

van den Berg PAJ (2007) The politics of European codification: a history of the unification of law in France, Prussia, the Austrian Monarchy and the Netherlands. Europe Law Publishing, Groningen

Vargas C (2011) Codification as a socio-historical phenomenon. 2nd reprint ed. with an Annex & Postscript. Szent István Társulat, Budapest

Weiss GA (2000) The enchantment of codification in the common-law world. Yale Journal of International Law 25(2):435–532

Wang WY (2014a) Codification in East Asia: selected papers from the 2nd IACL thematic conference, Springer, Cham, Heidelberg, New York, Dordrecht, London

Wang WY (ed) (2014b) Codification in international perspective: selected papers from the 2nd IACL Thematic Conference (Vol. 1). Springer Science & Business Media

Whitman JQ (1990) The legacy of Roman law in the German romantic era: historical vision and legal change. Princeton University Press, Princeton

Wieacker F (1996) A history of private law in Europe: with particular reference to Germany. Weir trans. Oxford University Press, Oxford

Zimmermann R (1995) Codification: history and present significance of an idea. European Review of Private Law 3:95–120

Zimmerman R (2001) Roman law, contemporary law, European law: the civilian tradition today. Oxford University Press, Oxford

Michele Graziadei is Professor of Comparative Private Law, University of Torino; President of the Società Italiana per la ricerca nel diritto comparato - SIRD; Past president of the European Association of Law Faculties; Member of the executive board of the International Association of Legal Science; Titular member of the International Academy of Comparative Law; corresponding member of the Accademia delle Scienze (Torino), Collegio Carlo Alberto Fellow. He is the author of over 100 publications in several languages. His recent publications include *Comparative Law, Transplants and Receptions* in M. Reimann, R. Zimmermann (eds), *The Oxford Handbook of Comparative Law* (2nd edn OUP, 2019); M Graziadei, LD Smith (eds), *Comparative Property Law: Global Perspectives* (Elgar, 2018).

Lihong Zhang is Professor of Law at East China University of Political Science and Law (Shanghai, ECUPL), a holder of Ph.D. degree in law of University of Rome "La Sapienza", Vice Secretary-General of China's National Society of Civil Law, Standing Director of China's National Society of European Law, Director of China's National Society of Comparative Law, Director of the Roman Law and European Law Research Center of ECUPL. He been a visiting professor at the University of Paris "Panthéon Assas", University of Turin, National University of Singapore, Münster University, Catholic University of Leuven, Jagiellonian University, University of San Francisco and University of Macerata. He has given lectures at many world-renowned universities, such as Harvard University, University of California at Berkeley, Georgetown University, Hitotsubashi University, and the National University of Seoul.

The Codifications at the Beginning of the Twenty-First Century

Rémy Cabrillac

Abstract Codification has an insolent vitality at the start of the twenty-first century. Codification is indeed one of the most important global legal phenomena of the 20th and early twenty-first centuries. The strength of codification is undoubtedly to have known how to evolve without denying its past. In contemporary times, codification has two different forms: codification-modification and codification-compilation. However, codification has ceased to be the exclusive domain of the state, opening up to private codification and supranational codification.

1 Codification: An Outdated Form of Legislation?

Is codification an outdated form of legislation?[1] This question could flourish in the middle of the twentieth century as a reaction of doubt and even anxiety that gripped those faced with the perpetuation of a continuing crisis in the sources of law. The acceleration of legal time, echo of the acceleration of history and of an acceleration of the social and technical evolutions that the law would try to follow, did not fail to worry.[2] In response to this challenge, the French public authorities have multiplied, in a disorderly manner, the rules that entangled and telescoped, transforming the French-style garden into an inextricable *maquis*, leading to great legal uncertainty,

---

[1] «La codification, forme dépassée de législation?», XI congrès international de droit comparé, Caracas, 1982, in particular, Sacco (1983).

[2] Savatier (1948).

R. Cabrillac (✉)
Faculté de droit et science politique, Montpellier, France
e-mail: remy.cabrillac@umontpellier.fr

© The Author(s), under exclusive license to Springer Nature Singapore Pte Ltd. 2023
M. Graziadei and L. Zhang (eds.), *The Making of the Civil Codes*,
Ius Gentium: Comparative Perspectives on Law and Justice 104,
https://doi.org/10.1007/978-981-19-4993-7_2

which was periodically denounced not only by the political[3] or judicial authorities[4] but also by the general public.[5]

The decodification process,[6] through the multiplication of special rules governing a subject outside the structure of a code,[7] hit hard the traditional codes adopted in the nineteenth century during the golden age of codification. "The vow of eternity", which would inhabit any code, according to the beautiful formula of Chancellor d'Aguesseau,[8] proves to be illusory. Dean Cornu astutely observed with respect to such eternity that "Who believes he writes on stone will never have written except on sand, waking up disillusioned with lapidary dreams".[9] Is codification still possible and desirable if it risks being so quickly obsolete?

At the turn of the millennium, other questions were added to these initial doubts, born of the globalization of the law.[10] Such globalization has led to fierce competition between legal systems. Is the civil law tradition of codification the most rational and efficient form of organizing legal rules? The debate has raged on following the publication of the World Bank's Doing Business reports, in particular the 2004 Understanding Regulation report, which presented the Common Law as the most economically efficient legal system.[11]

In addition, globalization has weakened traditional politico-geographic divisions. Can state-level codification continue while international standards play an increasingly important role in national legal orders and while the framework of the nation state, inherited from the Renaissance, seems obsolete or at least singularly limited during a time of globalization and regional supra-state grouping?

The best answer to these doubts can only be pragmatic; it lies in the insolent health of codification at the start of the twenty-first century. Codification is indeed one of the most important global legal phenomena of the 20th and early twenty-first centuries.

Many countries undertook progressive recodifications, notably of their civil code, during the twentieth century, starting with certain areas particularly sensitive to social developments, such as the law of persons or family law, and then extending this recodification to other matters, such as contract law. A particularly revealing example is that of Germany, which reformed its law of persons and family law in the second half of the twentieth century[12] before renovating the part of the BGB relating to the

---

[3] Balladur (1997, p. 193): « Proliferation of ever more complex texts, in ever more numerous matters, instability of rules that we want to adapt to all situations, to all changes, degradation of the purity, of the quality of the legislation, obscurity and sometimes contradiction between the aims pursued».

[4] Cf. Conseil d'Etat, Rapport 2006, *Sécurité juridique et complexité du droit.*

[5] Eliakin (2013).

[6] Irti (1978); Thunis and Mensbrugghe (1998).

[7] Cabrillac (2002, p. 114).

[8] *Préambule de l'ordonnance sur les donations de 1731.*

[9] Cornu (1996, p. 370).

[10] Delmas-Marty (1998).

[11] Association Capitant (2006).

[12] Franck (2000, p. 819).

law of obligations.[13] Japan has also just recently conducted a partial amendment of its civil code.

Other countries have opted for global recodification. Some countries have done so for purely technical reasons. For example, the Netherlands replaced its obsolete civil code from 1838 with a new civil code, the NBW, which essentially came into effect on January 1, 1992.[14] Political considerations have sometimes arisen mixed with these technical considerations. As an illustration, we can cite the example of Quebec. Quebec replaced the Civil Code of Lower Canada (1866), which was dominated by liberalist ideology and the influence of Catholicism, with the Civil Code of Quebec, which entered into force on January 1, 1994.[15] In the same spirit, in 2002, Brazil replaced the Civil Code of 1916, which was based on a very conservative ideology, with a resolutely progressive civil code.[16] Argentina adopted a new civil code with resolutely modern civil law, which entered into force on August 1, 2015.[17]

Finally, a global recodification is sometimes justified by essentially political considerations: this is how the Russian Federation adopted a new civil code, which entered into force in 1996, replacing the civil code adopted within the framework of the USSR in 1922.[18] The same phenomenon occurred in the countries of central and eastern Europe, as shown, among others, by the new Civil Code of Romania adopted in 2011.[19] In China, a civil code was adopted after a long process[20] on 28 May 2020, and it came into force on the 1st of January 2021.[21]

Many works of recodification in progress across the five continents, such as that in Iraq[22] or those in the countries of Central Europe (to cite but a limited number of examples), testify to the contemporary vitality of codification.

Better still, countries that traditionally did not seem interested in codification have decided to adopt a civil code. For example, the Hungarian Civil Code of 1960[23] constitutes the first civil code in this country with old roots of customary law. The fall of communism did not stop this movement, a new civil code having been adopted in 2014. Even common law countries remained have paid some tributes to codification.[24]

---

[13] Witz (2002).

[14] Cf. Van Dunne (2004, p. 337).

[15] Cabrillac (1993).

[16] de Siebeneichler de Andrade (2016/2021, p. 57).

[17] Cabrillac (2015).

[18] Translated in English (*Civil Code of the Russian federation*, Oxford University Press, 2003) or French (*Code civil de la Fédération de Russie*, Juriscope, 2005).

[19] *Le Code civil roumain, vu de l'intérieur, vu de l'extérieur*, PU Bucarest, 2014.

[20] Shi (2006).

[21] Cabrillac (2020). See as well *RIDC*. 2019/3, and in particular Shi, «La rédaction du Code civil chinois entre compilation et innovation», p. 946.

[22] Sharpe (2008, p. 2448).

[23] Zajtay (1970, p. 477).

[24] Halpérin (2009, p. 177).

The balance sheet of this brief panorama is eloquent: contrary to popular belief, the continental law to which codification is consubstantial constitutes a legal system contemporarily expanding throughout the world. This finding is hardly surprising. The criticisms levelled against the lack of economic efficiency of codification are based on questionable methods of evaluation and are far from unanimous among economists. The continental European model and, in particular, the French codes[25] seem as, if not more, effective than a body of case law providing a specific response to each fact-specific case submitted to a particular judge.

The strength of codification is undoubtedly to have known how to evolve without denying its past; actually, the emergence of new forms of codification has not damaged the sustainability of traditional forms.

2   The Sustainability of Traditional Forms of Codification

To remedy the crisis in the sources of law, the French legislator has attempted to take multiple avenues alleged to simplify the law: impact studies, evaluation of legislation, experimental legislation, etc. It is clear that the results did not match expectations. The main remedy for this crisis of law still lies in codification, which in contemporary times took two different forms (2.1) codification-modification and (2.2) codification-compilation.[26]

2.1   The Codification-Modification Approach

The codification-modification approach is that which performs a substantive modification of the existing codified law, following the example of the Civil Code of 1804, which profoundly modified the French law of the time. French law has essentially undergone three codification-modifications that have marked the last decades. The first two operated an overall recodification of a subject whose regulations had aged to the point of becoming unsuitable for contemporary society. A new Code of Civil Procedure replaced the 1806 version in 1975. A new Penal Code, adopted in 1992 and entered into force in 1994, replaced the old Penal Code of 1810.

Several attempts to recode the whole of the French Civil Code failed, particularly those attempts in 1904 and 1945. The renewal of the French Civil Code came from reforms in the law of persons and family law undertaken in 1960 under the direction of Dean Carbonnier. The scope of these reforms had an impact well beyond their respective fields of law. These reforms ensured a "quiet revolution"[27] of French civil law. These reforms have initiated a new style of legislation dominated by several

---

[25] Cabrillac (2011).

[26] Cabrillac, op. cit., p. 189.

[27] Cornu (2013).

characteristic features: disengagement from the law in favor of other rules of social organization, willingness to propose several different legislative models, and the attribution of a moderating power to judges through guiding conceptual frameworks. These ideas inspired the reforms of civil law undertaken thereafter, such as the ordinance of March 23, 2006 amending the law of sureties or the order of February 10, 2016 reforming the law of contracts and the regime of obligations. The passing of an ordinance (under art. 38 of the Constitution), is a pseudoprimary legislative procedure allowing the executive branch of the French Government to pass legislation coming immediately into effect on a temporary basis until such legislation eventually receives the authorization of the French Parliament or lapses.

In the classic subjects of civil procedure, criminal law, civil law hitherto governed by Napoleonic codes, of which they have endeavored to respect the spirit and the letter, different codification-modifications have been undertaken. This fidelity to historic legislation has made it possible to avoid contemporary legislative flaws in these matters and curbed normative disorder. Indeed, these codification-modifications tried to respect the same concern for the elegance of form and basic coherence, which characterized the old codes.

This elegance is first reflected in the search for a legislative style that recalls that of the codes of the nineteenth century and contrasts singularly with the clumsy and tangled formulas of the contemporary legislator.

To limit itself to the single example of the French Civil Code, the recodification undertaken wanted to dip its pen in the ink of Portalis to prolong this marvelous style, in the perfect balance between technical and contemporary language, and between abstract and concrete language, which has largely contributed to its success and longevity. Thus, to extend the spirit of the famous articles of the Napoleonic Code of 1804, contemporary coders have chiseled out both organized and expressive formulations just as esthetic as those from 1804, for example, article 310 of the French Civil Code, which states: "All children whose parentage is legally established have the same rights and the same duties in their relations with their father and mother".

Elegance is also reflected in the respect for a harmonious structure that symbolizes the classicism of the French spirit in the artistic field. The general plan, the secondary headings, the continuous numbering, the fundamental place recognized in the basic subdivision that constitutes the article, everything in these codification-modifications indicates a concern for a beautiful and well-ordered law.

Thus, while making important modifications to the plan of the Code of Civil Procedure of 1806, successor legislators nevertheless retained a rational presentation illustrating the course of the civil trial, characterized by a logical continuity going from the general to the specific.

We can observe in the same spirit that civil recodification is scrupulously inscribed in the general structure of the Civil Code of 1804, trying to spare it as much as possible, sometimes at the cost of daring acrobatics.[28]

These codification-modifications also respect the substantive consistency of the codified material, which constitutes the essence of any codification. For example, the

---

[28] Cornu (1964, p. 157).

1975 French Code of Civil Procedure has been lauded both by doctrinal scholars and by practitioners because it retains a certain unity of inspiration in the rules of civil procedure.[29] Likewise, the civil recodification that has occurred piece by piece since 1960 created inevitable risks of discrepancy between texts with different vintages, but despite this, the unity of the modern French Civil Code cannot be seriously questioned. The French Civil Code is inhabited with the same breadth, with the same soul, transcending the diversity of the texts that compose it.[30]

The coherence of these recodifications undoubtedly largely results from the unity of inspiration that has inhabited each recodification. In fidelity to the classic model of code, these contemporary codification-modifications were in fact almost always entrusted to a single man, a single legislative draftsman.

Thus, the French Code of Civil Procedure was essentially designed by Dean Cornu. The "guiding principles of the trial", which constitute the first 24 articles of the code, and the frontispiece, which symbolizes his conception of the trial, bear his mark so much that the Keeper of the Seals of the time, Jean Foyer, noted: "we could call it, in all justice, the Cornu Code".[31]

The French Penal Code gives concrete expression to the ideology of human rights, which permeates its very structure and many of its particular provisions, at the instigation of Mr. Robert Badinter, who largely contributed to the political compromises essential for its adoption.[32]

As for the reforms of the French Civil Code, it goes without saying that they were essentially drafted or at the very least inspired by Dean Carbonnier, who initiated an original legislative style, incontestably creating a path toward a new model of codification. These codification modifications, although they may have put an end to the existing normative disorder, were not adapted to new issues in the fields of labor law and consumer protection law resulting from highly technical and rapidly changing regulations.

Another type of codification was then favored by the public authorities, referred to as codification-compilation.

2.2 Codification-Compilation

Codification-compilation constitutes the gathering of scattered laws and regulations into a single corpus, without the substance of the law thus collected being modified.

To remedy the anarchic proliferation linked to the crisis of the law, the French government decided, the day after the Second World War ended, to create, by a decree of May 10, 1948, a commission in charge of studying the codification and the simplification of both legislative and regulatory texts. The objective of the public authorities

---

[29] Cadiet and Canivet (2006).

[30] Cabrillac (2001, p. 730).

[31] Foyer, p. 323.

[32] Badinter (1988).

was to bring order to the existing legislative thicket as quickly as possible. They decided to proceed with the codification of the existing legislative and regulatory texts by decree, without modification other than pure form and without intervention of the Parliament. The term "administrative codification" is sometimes used to refer to this type of codification. This Commission did considerable work until 1988, developing numerous codes in various fields.

The government intended to relaunch this form of codification by a decree on September 12, 1989 to establish a Superior Codification Commission which, according to the text of the decree, "takes over from the previous one" and is "charged with working to simplify and clarify the law". This Commission has thus attached itself to an ambitious program of compiling the rules governing many matters that have recently appeared in the French legal order. The Superior Codification Commission has adopted numerous codes since it took office, the most emblematic examples of which include the Intellectual Property Code (1992), the Consumer Code (1993), the Monetary and Financial Code (2000), the Heritage Code (2004), and the Transport Code (2010). The only Napoleonic code to have been the subject of a codification-compilation is the Commercial Code in 2000.

More than 70 codes and statistics now show that approximately half of French law is now codified.[33] The public authorities intend to maintain this effort to adopt new codes and follow up on existing codes, as evidenced by one circular of May 27, 2013. This codification-compilation is based on a fundamental principle, symbolically recalled by a law of April 12, 2000 relating to the rights of citizens in their relations with the administration,[34] that of the stability, consistency, or constancy of law. The laws are codified without modification other than to the pure form of the written law. This principle of the constancy of law is essentially justified by time constraints. Only a codification with respecting the constancy of law "allows codes to be drawn up without slowing them down or losing them in the examination and debate of any substantive reform" (Circular of May 30, 1996, art. 2.1.1). Indeed, because of the principle of the constancy of law, codification-compilation occurs without it being necessary for the adoption of a code to get bogged down in the long and complex legislative process. Many codes have been adopted by ordinance.

This principle of constancy of law codification/codification-compilation has been subjected to several criticisms.

It was first criticized for constituting a historical betrayal of the very concept of a code. A large segment of civil law doctrine, marked by the shadow of Napoleonic codifications, considers that compiling is not codifying. The argument no doubt seems excessive. The concept of a code has taken various forms throughout history. The Roman codifications and most of the codifications until the XVIIth century were more or less only codification-compilations. The advent of the concept of

---

[33] *Rapport de la Commission supérieure de codification*, 2012, p. 9 (www.legifrance.gouv.fr).

[34] Loi n° 2000–321 du 12 avril 2000, art. 3, al. 2: «This codification must be doing so without changing the law…».

codification-modifications, which knew its paroxysm with the Napoleonic codes, only dates from the XVIIIth century.[35]

The constancy of law approach of codification-compilation was then criticized for allowing substantive changes beyond its purported limitation to simple changes in form. Among other examples, the inclusion of a particular text in a new legal context (e.g., that of a broader code in contrast to an act of narrower scope) can, through interpretation based on the placement of such text, have significant consequences on the substance of the law. To counter this argument, consider that, since Justinian, history shows that a compilation inevitably leads to modifications of the law without altering the quality of the codification-compilation thus adopted.[36] However, making changes without prior consultation with the scientific community or even more importantly with Parliament is hardly satisfactory in a democratic society.

Another argument was put forward that codifying without modifying the law is devoid of purpose since it does not allow the law to be adapted to changes in society. The defenders of the codification-compilation approach in keeping with constancy of law principles replied that a codification-compilation could provide an essential starting point for a later modification, providing a check-up of the state of the law to allow future legislators to better subsequently deal with the weaknesses of such laws (Circular of May 30, 1996, art. 2.1.1).

Consequently, the assessment of these codification-compilations seems to us to be generally positive, all the more so since they are contained on and available through a very efficient tool, the Legifrance website. On this site, the texts of the various codes, updated daily, can be consulted in their current version and more often than not even in previous or future versions. Whatever the faults or weaknesses of the codification-compilation approach, one must acknowledge that it improves the accessibility of the law to the general public, a rule of law imperative to which the Constitutional Council is very attached.[37]

The main limit of codification-compilation lies in its inability to bring together legal standards other than legislative or regulatory standards that proliferate today. International or European standards, decisions of domestic courts, decisions of the Court of Justice of the European Union or the European Court of Human Rights, nonstate rules or spontaneous rights remain beyond the reach of a codification-compilation. This limitation is all the more unfortunate since it contrasts with the ambition of completeness of the contemporary codifier who wishes to codify the whole of existing law.

In this context, new forms of codification have developed.

---

[35] Cabrillac, op. cit., p. 37.

[36] Gaudemet (2000, p. 249).

[37] Cf. Zadrany (2011) and the decisions cited therein.

3   The Emergence of New Forms of Codification

Codification has ceased to be the exclusive domain of the state, opening up to (3.1) private codification and (3.2) supranational codification.

3.1   Private Codification

The aura of the Napoleonic codifications masked the survival of private codifications throughout the XIXth and XXth centuries, of which the success of the private editions of the codes, published by Dalloz or Lexisnexis, constitute topical illustrations. A real resurgence of private codifications was witnessed from the end of the XXth century forward. As seen in any codification cycle, private codification is the first response to a crisis in the sources of law resulting from the disorderly proliferation of laws and regulations generating legal uncertainty. Jurists confronted with this crisis are the first to suffer from it and therefore to try to remedy it by codifying it long before the public authorities eventually take over the work.[38] Private codification efforts are not a modern phenomenon but exist wherever laws exist at a certain intersection of complexity and disorder, for example, Hermogenian and Gregorian codifications in the Roman Empire, the Gratian Decree in medieval canon law, private compilations of customs such as that of Philippe de Beaumanoir in Middle Ages, and the Brisson Code in the Renaissance.

The resurgence of private codification at the end of the twentieth century and the beginning of the twenty-first century takes the form of private codes of scholarly origin intended to remedy a legal insecurity born from the imperfection of existing legal texts or even their absence. They constitute a "legal offer", to use the beautiful expression of Jean Carbonnier and Pierre Catala,[39] a spontaneous offer of a code in this case, which does not correspond to an order from the public authorities. Two illustrations seem emblematic of this phenomenon.

The first developed in the European framework.[40]

A first working group, chaired by a Danish professor, Ole Lando, in the 1980s brought together academics from the different member countries of the European Union to develop a text to serve as a draft for a future code of European contract law. Thus, the *Principles of European Contract Law* (PECL) was born, the first version of which dates from 1995 and has since continued to be enriched and updated. This project was included in a more ambitious initiative, the development of a European civil code, bringing together all private law. This project was initiated in 1998 by the German professor Christian von Bar. A second working group was convened on the initiative of Professor Giuseppe Gandolfi, the Academy of European Privatists, founded in 1992 brought together academics from different member countries of the

---

[38] Cabrillac, op. cit., p. 68.

[39] Carbonnier, Catala, de Saint-Affrique and Morin (2003).

[40] Cabrillac (2016).

European Union on the same principle to draw up a European Code of Contracts, the draft text of which was disseminated in 1983.

The second illustration concerns the law of French obligations. Despite the important creative role of case law, the texts of the French Civil Code relating to the law of obligations, which date mostly from 1804, have aged and no longer provide the necessary legal certainty. On the strength of this observation, a project to renovate the French law of obligations under the French Civil Code was launched by Pierre Catala and handed over to the public authorities in 2005. A second project was prepared within the framework of the Academy of Moral and Political Sciences under the direction of Professor François Terré and disseminated in 2009.

This resurgence of private codification is to be welcomed. It constitutes a stimulating challenge for the doctrine whose role was in decline but now rediscovers the essence of its mission, "criticism, ideation, reflection, invention, innovative imagination".[41] The development of private codifications of scholarly origin constitutes a formidable catalyst for the debate of ideas in the contemporary legal world. It also has the merit of placing academics in the heart of the city whose rules they are trying to develop.

Two questions do not fail to arise, even if they seem far from critical.

The first relates to the legitimacy of the individual initiator of the codification and incidentally of the working group with which they have chosen to surround themselves. It is easy to denounce the lack of legitimacy of those whose authority is self-proclaimed.[42] We can, however, trust the legal community not to allow a project to be carried out by a leader with little scientific credibility. The example of French projects reforming the law of obligations is revealing, and the scientific authority of Pierre Catala or François Terré is indisputable. Therefore, the challenge to their legitimacy can only be marginal and relate, for example, to the composition of the working group (roles given to practitioners, political orientation of its members… etc.).

The second question relates to the dissemination of these codifications. Are they not doomed to remain dead letters, without benefiting from the binding force of official codifications? The answer to this question is certainly negative. It should first be noted that these private codifications play important roles in legal and judicial practice. For example, users of the law, particularly in international commercial contracts, do not fail to refer to the Lando Principles.[43] The courts also give them a nonnegligible status. One author noted that the Lando Principles have led to some notable developments in French case law.[44] As we have observed, "scholarly codification therefore continues its long ascent toward the status of rule of positive law".[45]

In addition, the history of the cycles of codification shows, once again, that the public authorities frequently distribute the private codifications and are inspired by

---

[41] Bredin (1981, p. 112).

[42] Cf., for example, for the draft of European civil Code: Lequette (2002).

[43] Deumier (2008, D. 494).

[44] Fages (2003, D. 2386).

[45] P. Deumier (2008, 66).

them. Such is the case of the Justinian codification, with the Hermogenian and Theodosian codifications, of the official writing of customs by the ordinance of Montils-les Tours with the use of private customaries, of the Corpus Juris canonici with the Gratian Decree, and of royal ordinances with the Code of Barnabé Brisson.[46]

The same phenomenon is, for example, occurring with the two illustrations of private codifications of scholarly origin previously mentioned. European institutions have encouraged the adoption of a draft common frame of reference and a proposal for the regulation of a common European commercial law that is very much inspired by the Lando Principles (No. 2). Similarly, the ordinance of February 10, 2016, reforming the French law of contracts and the law of obligations was largely inspired by the Catala and Terré projects.

These private codifications of scholarly origin sometimes combine with the development of supra-state codifications.

3.2 Supranational Codification

Codification has always flourished in the framework of a state, and this relationship between nation and code has reached its climax since the XVIth century with the advent of the modern state. However, over the past forty years, supra-state codifications have been developed. International structures grouping several states from the same geographical area have established and have developed harmonized or even uniform laws with respect to certain subjects in the form of a code.

The already mentioned draft of the European Code of Contracts is a revealing example. We can also mention that of "OHADA", the treaty creating the Organization for the Harmonization in Africa of Business Law (in French, OHADA, Organization pour l'harmonisation en Afrique du droit des affaires). This treaty signed in Port Louis on October 17, 1993[47] between sixteen African countries and open for accession by any member state of the African Union, has for its main objective: "…the harmonization of commercial law in the member states through the development and adoption of common rules which are simple, modern, and adapted to the situation of their respective economies…" (art. 1 of the Treaty). Today, it brings together seventeen African countries. Within the framework of OHADA, uniform acts are adopted. These acts are real codifications of specific subjects that are directly applicable in all Member States and have the full binding force of law (art. 10 of the Treaty). Several uniform acts are currently in force covering a variety of fields of law, for example, commercial law, arbitration law, the law governing class actions, and the law of securities. A uniform act relating to contract law is also being drafted. We can equally evoke the movement of codification of contract law in additional regions of the world.

---

[46] Cabrillac, op. cit., p. 79.

[47] One Treaty was adopted in Quebec, October 17, 2008 to renforce the organization.

In Central America, a draft code of international contracts has just been prepared by French academics and practitioners[48] under the patronage of the Association Capitant pour le System d'Intégration Centro-Américain (SICA), an international organization whose goal is to progressively develop uniform standards under the umbrella of a Central American Court of Justice uniting six countries. Similar projects are being developed in South America, Asia and a number of Arabic countries.

A trend that deserves to be welcomed is that these supra-state codifications, without constituting private codifications since they most often arise from an official order and are not thus a spontaneous offer of code, give a large weight to doctrine. They most often involve lawyers from different countries, or even from different continents, and prove to be a formidable in vivo laboratory of comparative law.

From an economic/commercial point of view, when it comes to a code, such as a code governing the law of contracts, the impact on trade in an area, however difficult to assess precisely, seems only to be positive.

However, this movement of supra-state codifications conceals in itself the risk of excessive standardization, not within each regional group often sharing similar rules but rather at the global level. Montesquieu previously denounced the dangers of such standardization: "there are certain ideas of uniformity which sometimes seize the great minds (because they touched Charlemagne) but which infallibly strike the small ones".[49]

To use the example of the various regional movements for the codification of contract law, there is an undeniable tropism toward a single model, that of the *Unidroit Principles of International Commercial Contracts*. It does not seem correct to us that contract law be the same in Buenos Aires, Tokyo, and Yaoundé, in defiance of the national legal traditions thus condemned to disappear. Acculturation can only flourish if the grafted law is in sync with the society in which it will apply. Resistance movements have sometimes appeared in the face of a standardized code, disconnected from existing more local legal traditions. Thus, a first draft of a uniform act relating to contracts within the framework of OHADA, drawn up very directly inspired by the Unidroit Principles, was considered to be too far removed from the law currently applicable in the member states. A second draft more consistent with the diversity of legal traditions of the member states is presently being developed.

Codification, both in its traditional and novel forms, can be an effective remedy to the contemporary crisis of the sources of law, but it still has to be used with sagacity. The future of codification thus depends on its ability not to fall into the flaws that characterize the law. As Bruno Oppetit observed, "if codification can restore its traditional virtues to the law, it will be subject to a bright future, otherwise it will suffer from the same discredit".[50]

---

[48] Rémy Cabrillac, Mario Celaya, Denis Mazeaud, Yves Picod.

[49] *De l'esprit des lois*, Book XXIX, Chapter IXI.

[50] Oppetit (1998, p. 66).

References

Badinter R (1988) Présentation du projet de Code pénal. Dalloz, Paris

Balladur E (1997) Caractères de la France. Plon, Paris

Bredin J-D (1981) Remarques sur la doctrine. In: Mélanges P. Hébraud. PU Toulouse, Tolouse

Cabrillac R (1993) Le nouveau Code civil du Québec. Dalloz, Paris, 267

Cabrillac R (2001) Le Code civil à la fin du XX ème siècle. In: Etudes offertes à Pierre Catala. Litec, Paris

Cabrillac R (2002) Les codifications. PUF, Paris

Cabrillac R (ed) (2011) Quel avenir pour le modèle juridique français dans le monde ? Dalloz, Paris

Cabrillac R (2015) Le nouveau Code civil et commercial de la Nation argentine: l'éclatante réussite d'un audacieux pari. Dalloz, 2397

Cabrillac R (2016) Droit européen comparé des contrats, 2nd edn. Lextenso, Paris

Cabrillac R (2019) Introduction au droit, 12th edn. Dalloz, Paris

Cabrillac R. (2020) Le Code civil chinois. Dalloz, 1375

Cadiet L, Canivet G (2006) De la commémoration d'un code à l'autre: 200 ans de procédure civile en France. Lexisnexis, Paris

Capitant A (2006) Les droits de tradition civiliste en question. A propos des rapports Doing business, Paris

Carbonnier J, Catala P, de Saint-Affrique J, Morin G (2003) Des libéralités, une offre de loi. Defrénois, Paris

Cornu G (1964) La lettre du code à l'épreuve du temps. In: Mélanges René Savatier. Dalloz, Paris, p 157.

Cornu G (1996) Codification contemporaine : valeurs et langage. In: L'art du droit en quête de sagesse. PUF, Paris, p 370.

Cornu G (2013) Introduction, les personnes, les biens, 11th edn. LGDJ, Paris

de Siebeneichler de Andrade F (2016/2021) O modelo do Codigo brasilero de 2002 sob a perspectiva das funçoes atuais da codificão. Roma e America, Diritto comune, p 57

Delmas-Marty M (1998) Trois défis pour un droit mondial. Seuil, Paris

Deumier P (2008) L'utilisation par la pratique des codifications d'origine doctrinale. Dalloz, 494

Eliakin P (2013) Enquête sur ces normes qui nous tyrannisent. Robert Laffont, Paris

Fages B (2003) Quelques évolutions du droit français des contrats à la lumière des Principes de la commission Lando. Dalloz, 2386

Foyer J (1998) Le nouveau Code de procédure civile. In: Le nouveau code de procédure civile vingt ans après. La Documentation Française, Paris

Franck R (2000) Le centenaire du BGB : le droit de la famille face aux exigences du raisonnement politique, de la Constitution et de la cohérence du système juridique . Revue internationale de droit comparé, p 819

Gaudemet J (2000) La codification et l'évolution du droit . In; Id. Sociologie historique du droit. PUF, Paris

Halpérin J-L (2009) Profils de mondialisation du droit. Dalloz, Paris

Irti N (1978) L'età della decodificazione. Giuffrè, Milan

Lequette Y (2002) Quelques remarques à propos du projet de Code civil européen. Dalloz, 2202

Oppetit B (1998) Essai sur la codification. PUF, Paris

Rapport de la Commission supérieure de codification (2012) www.legifrance.gouv.fr

Sacco R (1983) La codification, forme dépassée de législation? In: Rapports Italiens au XI° Congrès International de Droit Comparé – Caracas 1982. Giuffrè, Milan, p 65

Savatier R (1948) Les métamorphoses économiques et sociales du droit civil d'aujourd'hui. LGDJ, Paris

Siebeneichler de Andrade F (1997) Da codificaçao, Cronica de un concepto. ed. Do avogado, Brasil

Sharpe J (2008) L'état du droit en Irak. Dalloz, 2448

Shi J (2006) La codification du droit civil chinois au regard de l'expérience française. Bibl. Droit privé, t. 475, LGDJ, Paris, préf. M. Delmas-Marty

Shi J (2019) La rédaction du Code civil chinois entre compilation et innovation. Revue internationale de droit comparé, p 945

Terré F (1980) La crise de la loi. Archives de philosophie de droit, p 17

Thunis X, Mensbrugghe F (1998) Codification et décodification: le droit comparé à contribution. Cahiers de la Faculté de droit de Namur, n° 7

Van Dunne M (2004) Lawyer's paradise or paradise lost: the Dutch civil code of 1992 as an exponent of the 19th century legislative tradition. In: Le code Napoléon, un ancêtre vénéré, Mélanges offerts à Jacques Vanderlinden. Bruylant, Bruxelles, p 337

Witz C (2002) La nouvelle jeunesse du BGB insufflée par le droit des obligations. Dalloz, 3156

Zadrany A (2011) Codification et Etat de droit, thèse, Paris II

Zajtay I (1970) L'importance de l'évolution de l'ancien droit hongrois au point de vue de la théorie des sources. Revue internationale de droit comparé, p 477

Rémy Cabrillac is Professor of Civil Law and director of the private law department at the University of Montpellier. The author of a dozen monographs in civil law, his book "Les codifications", was translated into several languages (Russian, Spanish, Romanian and is currently being translated into Chinese). He has written more than one hundred fifty publications in French and foreign journals, as well as collaborations in collective works, published both in France and abroad. Prof. Cabrillac has been the director of 40 doctoral theses. He has been appointed as an expert to carry out advisory activities in the field of civil law or codification by different governments and administrations (New Caledonia, China, Cameroon, Chile... etc.). He is a member of several international associations, such as the *Société de législation comparé* and the Henri Capitant Association, and is a member of the editorial board of a dozen legal journals worldwide.

Civil Law in Spain is Plural, as Are Its National Civil Codes

Esther Arroyo Amayuelas

Abstract The codification of Spanish civil law did not achieve the desired uniformity in all of Spain. Indeed, the Spanish Civil Code mainly reflected the law of Castille and respected territorial laws in force in other parts of the country. Later, within the framework of the plurality of civil legislation that was recognized in the Spanish Constitution, Catalonia (and other territories) gradually developed their competence in civil matters. On occasions, this has made it possible to overcome the passivity of the state legislator in regard to dealing with the lack of modern reforms in the CC. A civil code imposes rationality and legal security and provides the opportunity to craft law tailored to the particular needs and interests of the society for which the civil code is intended. Beyond juridical incentives, there are also political motivations behind codification. Beyond serving as a symbol of the Catalan nation and strengthening its own personality, today the reasons for a Civil Code for Catalonia are better understood when considering the importance of civil law in regulating relations between citizens in a rapidly changing modern age.

1 Introduction

The codification movement in Europe found its highest expression in the nineteenth century. Codification is a process that culminates in the establishment of a national legal tradition that promotes its own law to the detriment of the European *ius commune*. In a civil code, rules are systematized and logically ordered by subjects. A civil code is subdivided under increasingly specific divisions. "Books" are often the broadest division found in a civil code. For instance, there may be one book for a broad subject such as family law. Books are then further divided into titles (e.g., marriage), then into chapters (e.g., solemnization of marriage) and finally to numbered articles, which would be specific provisions of law. In addition to specific rules, civil codes contain general principles that allow it to be adapted to a

E. Arroyo Amayuelas (✉)
University of Barcelona, Barcelona, Spain
e-mail: earroyo@ub.edu

© The Author(s), under exclusive license to Springer Nature Singapore Pte Ltd. 2023
M. Graziadei and L. Zhang (eds.), *The Making of the Civil Codes*,
Ius Gentium: Comparative Perspectives on Law and Justice 104,
https://doi.org/10.1007/978-981-19-4993-7_3

variety of specific cases that may not be explicitly accounted for in the articles of the civil code (e.g., diligence of the good father of a family/reasonable person standard; abuse of rights; good faith; good morals and public order). There are therefore not as many laws as there are cases to be solved. A civil code always follows a rational system. Provisions on marriage will often be followed by provisions on separation and divorce. However, a civil code does not necessarily also impose a uniform regime across an entire nation. The general trend of uniformity was adopted in France, Italy and Germany, but in Spain, the situation was different because different regional civil laws subsisted despite the existence of a national civil code. Historical Spanish codification did not keep pace with the European codification movement. One of the first codes, the French Napoleonic code, dates from 1804. In contrast, only a collection of laws called the *Novísima Recopilación* was produced in Spain in 1805.

The Spanish Civil Code of 1889 remains largely unchanged in many key respects. If it has resisted the passage of time, it is partly thanks to piecemeal codal reforms and creative works of jurisprudence by the Spanish judiciary. However, despite these efforts, the CC no longer provides answers to a modern society's problems on a multitude of subjects. Today, there are a series of events paying homage to the CC on its 130th anniversary, which, surely, more than celebrating its existence, highlight the reasons that require a recodification to be undertaken.[1] In contrast, the territorial laws that the CC has been allowed to exist are now better adapted to modern society and its issues. In the pages that follow, reference will be made to the evolution of the civil law in Catalonia, where some time ago, the legislator initiated a codification process that remains unfinished to date. This unfinished codification process is justified by the convenience of progressively and constantly promoting the updating and modernisation of Catalan civil law institutions.

2 The Coexistence of Civil Codes in Spain

Spanish civil codification covers almost a century of frustrated attempts to achieve a single civil code for the entire Spanish nation.[2] The Civil Code of 1889 repealed the law previously in force in Castille (art. 1976 II CC) and was declared to be subsidiary to the law in force in each territory (old art. 12.2 CC; current art. 13.2 CC), except for some provisions that are compulsory throughout the whole Kingdom (e.g., effects of the laws and the general provisions for their application, as well as provisions regarding the solemnization of marriage).

---

[1] See Order JUS/74/2019, of 28 January, creating the Working Commission for the Commemoration of the 130th Anniversary of the Enactment of the Civil Code (BOE of 1.02.2020). For the time being, see Código Civil: 130 Aniversario (2020). A parallel could be drawn with the book Le Code civil (1804–2004) Livre du Bicentenaire (2004), although this celebration was also aimed at exalting the national code at a time when the possibility of a European one was on the horizon.

[2] For the defense of Catalan civil law against the introduction of a Spanish Civil Code, see Harty (2002).

One of these territories that had its own civil law, different from the law in force in the territories of the Castilian Crown, was Catalonia. In 1960, Catalan civil law was organised and systematized in a Compilation of the Special Civil Law of Catalonia. It was not a code but rather a collection of particular legal institutions, proper and exclusive to Catalan civil law; in other words, it did not regulate all situations of daily life and only contained isolated legal institutions that could continue to exist because of their peculiarity in relation to the CC. The Compilation of Special Civil Law of Catalonia was a restricted endeavour that necessarily had to avoid contradicting or becoming redundant with respect to the CC. That is why the Compilation was presented as a "special" law, as opposed to the "general" law of the Civil Code.[3]

After the adoption of the Spanish Constitution, at the end of the last third of the twentieth century, the context was favorable to the promotion of the codification of Catalan civil law because of the constitutional recognition of legislative pluralism in civil matters.[4] The result is a civil code that is designed to be malleable in the hands of the legislature in that it is progressively elaborated and easy to update in terms of numbering, modern in terms of content, and still unfinished.[5] Rather than just referring to a code, therefore, we should speak of codification as a process. Other autonomous communities, such as Aragon and Navarre, have recently followed a similar process of modernisation and updating of their own law, although in their case the name "code" has been omitted or is accompanied by the adjective "foral".[6]

3   Resilience v. Obsolescence of Codes

In the nineteenth century, codification revolved around the axis of unity: a single law for all citizens, without distinction of class or concessions to particularism. However, society is unequal, and this inequality is acknowledged in many civil law jurisdictions. This fact is often reflected in consumer protection laws or the law of leases, where the law seeks to correct for an existing inequality of power between parties. Moreover, the Spanish Constitution has now taken over matters that were formerly covered by the CC (e.g., family, property, marriage, personality rights, associations, and foundations). This means that the CC is not the only instrument that provides the governing principles for social organization, nor is it the only one that can be used to interpret the basic categories of the system. In part, this is also a consequence of

---

[3] For historic Catalan legal tradition, see Badosa Coll (2003) and Oleart (2014). On the Spanish codification process, see also, Arroyo Amayuelas (2006, pp. 3–7).

[4] See below Sect. 4.

[5] Martín-Casals (2004) and Arroyo Amayuelas (2014).

[6] Legislative Decree 1/2011, of 22 March, of the Government of Aragon, which approves, under the title of "Code of Foral Law of Aragon", the Revised Text of the Aragonese Civil Laws (BOA of 29.03.2011); Foral Law 21/2019, of 4 April, on the modification and updating of the Compilation of the Civil Law of Navarre or Fuero Nuevo (BON of 16.04.2019). For the terms "common" and "foral" law, see Jacobson (2002, pp. 320–322). On the development of civil laws, their limits and potentials, in the different Spanish Autonomies, see Bayod López (2019).

the impact of European private law, which is continuously influencing national legal orders. The question therefore arises as to whether codification is an anachronistic project, in view of the constant production of special laws outside the code and the fact that attempts to recodify civil law in Spain have had little or no success.[7]

3.1 The Recodification Trend

There have been major reforms in the civil codes of many countries, and fundamental parts of the economic life of the twenty-first century have been modernised. This has led to talk of recodification, if sometimes only partial or limited to patrimonial law. It is precisely the ability of the codes to be updated that has contributed to maintaining their validity. In North America, Quebec promulgated its new civil code in early 1992 to simplify and modernise the law, which also brought in new institutions such as *trust* in that civil law jurisdiction.[8] In Europe, Germany recodified its civil law in 2002, and the conflict between the orientation of national contract law and that of European Union contract law (in particular consumer law) made it desirable to incorporate the latter into the BGB to promote coherence and improve understanding. That adaptation made it possible to define the BGB as a site on which a building is permanently under construction, thus ruling out the possibility of condemning it to be a mere museum.[9] The French legislator preferred an autonomous codification of consumer law and proceeded to a comprehensive reform of the law of obligations and contracts (undertaken in 2016),[10] soon to be followed by another reform in the field of civil liability.[11] Further amendments are also under way in other countries, such as Belgium,[12] Hungary, and Romania.[13] Following the European model, the drafting of a Chinese Civil Code aims to consolidate existing legislation, with the same objective of consolidating the sources of law into a rationally organized system to adapt them to contemporary society.[14]

3.2 The Obsolescence of the CC

In Spain, a large part of civil law no longer corresponds to the outdated rationale of the original Spanish Civil Code. It is true that its preliminary title and, above all, family

---

[7] Different points of view in Roca Trias (2015).

[8] See Beaulne (2015) and Cantin Cumyn (2002).

[9] See Zimmermann (2005, pp. 226–228).

[10] On the French reform, see Cartwright, Whittaker (2017).

[11] Borghetti and Whittaker (2019).

[12] Geens (2016), Wéry and Dirix (2015), and Stijns (2016).

[13] Menyhárd and Veress (2017). See generally, Rivera (2013).

[14] Shi (2019), Wang (2020). Previously, Zhang (2009).

law have undergone major reforms (the latter being a constitutional imperative), but others, equally necessary, have been made outside the CC. Among the most significant is the regulation of consumer contracts, which are partially regulated in a recast text that is not even complete. The CC is also residual in other contexts. For example, the codified regulation of leases, which still enshrines the principle of *emptio tollit locatum* ("sale breaks hire") (art. 1571 CC), has long been overtaken by sectoral legislation on housing leases (art. 14 LAU).[15] On the other hand, the codified regulation of the services contract, initially designed for the subordinate work of domestic servants (see the grotesque second part of art. 1584 CC)[16] has not been applied for many years. The provisions of the CC that still refer to the liability for latent defects in the purchase and sale of livestock (art. 1491 ff CC) or to the right of the owner of a swarm of bees to pursue it over another's property (art. 612 CC) have lost their usefulness. There is no doubt either that the rules on legal persons are insufficient or that the periods of extinctive and acquisitive prescription are poorly adapted to current needs. There is no trace of personality rights in the Code either and the rules on contract formation or precontractural liability are missing. However, it is fair to acknowledge that marriage in *articulo mortis* (imminent danger of death) (art. 52 CC) or wills in the event of an epidemic (art. 701 CC) have regained their relevance in times of COVID-19.

At the same time, judges through jurisprudence are increasingly involved in the creation of law. This is why, for example, the *rebus sic stantibus* clause has been accepted in Spanish civil law.[17] It is also thanks to case law that it is possible to distinguish between obligations of means and of results, although it would seem that this is a universal legal transplant.[18] Judges have breathed life into the codified institutions to such an extent that they are incomprehensible to legal operators who are not familiar with case law. Three examples, in contractual matters, illustrate this very well: the interpretation of an abstract and polysemic term such as the cause of

---

[15] About this maxim, see Du Plessis (2012). In Spain, the principle was very nuanced in the Urban Lease Act of 1994 (LAU), but was fully recovered in a main amendment of this Act, by Act 4/2013, of 4 June [see Arrieta Sevilla (2019)]. It was fortunately abandoned again in a new amendment of the Act, by Royal Decree-Law 7/2019, of 1 March, on urgent measures concerning housing and rent, which incorporates the original LAU rule, according to which sale breaks hire only if it occurs after the 5th year of the contract; if the lease had been previously registered in the property register, subsequent sale never breaks.

[16] Art. 1584 Spanish CC: "A domestic servant destined to the personal service of his master, or his family, for a specific time, may resign and be dismissed prior to expiration of the term; but if the master were to dismiss the servant without just cause, he shall compensate him by paying him the salary due and fifteen more days' salary. The master shall be believed, unless evidence to the contrary is provided: 1. As concerns the amount of the salary of the domestic servant; 2. As relates to the payment of salaries accrued in the current year".

[17] As result of the Spanish financial crisis of 2008, see STS of 30.06.2014 (ECLI:ES:TS:2014:2823) and 15.10.2014 (ES:TS:2014:5090). However, see now STS of 15.01.2019 (ECLI:ES:TS:2019:57). For Spanish case law see http://www.poderjudicial.es/search/indexAN.jsp

[18] For the distinction, originally, in the French doctrine, see Demogue (1925, T. V, n. 1237, pp. 536–544). On the reception in Europe of this duality, Ranieri (2010, pp. 31–32).

the contract or the obligation (arts. 1261.3, 1274 CC); the setting of the conditions for termination of the contract, e.g., essential nonperformance (art. 1124 CC), or the conditions for the exercise of the action for hidden defects (art. 1484 CC), which has been distinguished from the *aliud pro alio* doctrine. The Law of Succession is a second field in which the importance of case law renders the CC a significantly incomplete legal reference.[19]

3.3 The Failed Attempts at Comprehensive Reform

In the area of obligations, contracts, and civil liability, the CC has remained almost completely unchanged for 130 years since its promulgation. There has been no lack of attempts at modernisation, but all have been in vain due to the lack of political momentum. Preliminary projects to reform the Civil Code have come from governmental institutions as well as private academic initiatives. To date, none have been successful.

Specifically, we note the complete failure of a proposal made by Sect. 2 (on commercial matters) of the General Codification Commission in 2013, which aimed to regulate a general and special part of the law of obligations and contracts in a new commercial code. This plan was prompted by the understanding that contracts not involving business were considered to be residual and that consumer contracts (where one party is always a business) belong to the commercial rather than the civil sphere.[20] The most recent proposal for a reform of the CC (which no longer maintains the distinction between civil and commercial contracts) is that promoted, on private initiative, by the Spanish Association of Civil Law Professors, led by Prof. Rodrigo Bercovitz.[21] This initiative also incorporates part of the results of the more modest (failed) preliminary draft of the (partial) reform of the Civil Code drawn up in 2009 by Sect. 1 (on Civil matters) of the General Codification Commission.[22] It is not an excessively disruptive proposal, but the influence of soft law and other European codifications is clear. The convergence of solutions with the recent reform

---

[19] Parra Lucán (2019a, b). The Spanish Minister of Justice of the previous government announced specific reforms on forced share (currently 2/3 of the inheritance) and liability for the estate debts (currently *ultra vires*, as a rule), which, by the way, should already have been made public. See the Order of 4 February 2019 on the website of the General Codification Commission https://www.mjusticia.gob.es/cs/Satellite/Portal/es/actividad-legislativa/comision-general-codificacion/propuestas#id_1288783424421.

[20] For criticism, Parra Lucán (2014). See the new Proposal for a Preliminary Draft Law on the Commercial Code, presented after the opinion of the Council of State in March 2018, available at: https://www.mjusticia.gob.es/cs/Satellite/Portal/es/actividad-legislativa/comision-general-codificacion/propuestas.

[21] See Spanish Association of Civil Law Professors, *Proposal for a Civil Code,* Madrid, Tecnos, 2018. Text and updates, on the Association's website at: http://www.derechocivil.net/publicaciones/propuesta-codigo-civil. See Parra Lucán (2019b).

[22] The proposal was only intended to reform the law of obligations and contracts. See Fenoy Picón (2013). There was previously in Spain a Proposal for the reform of the contract of sale.

of the French law of obligation is particularly noteworthy, and it is to be welcomed that one of them is the removal of the cause of the contract.[23]

In line with these recent failures at reform, the fate of the (rather few) papers that Sect. 1 (on Civil matters) of the General Codification Commission made public on its website between 2011 and 2012 (others are not dated) is not clear. The most recent reform of the Civil Code is again partial and aims at abolishing the legal regime of incapacity in the case of deficiencies that prevent a person from governing himself. This is being done in accordance with the principles of the New York Convention on the Rights of Persons with Disabilities of 13 December 2006.[24]

4 The Emergence of a Civil Code in Catalonia

In 1918, the Assembly of the *Mancomunitat* (a political institution formed by the association of the four Catalan provinces)[25] proposed codifying Catalan civil law, but the dictatorship of Primo de Rivera put an end to these efforts by dissolving the institution (Decree 12 March 1925). The idea resurfaced in the Second Spanish Republic (1931), with the proclamation of political autonomy for Catalonia, but was unfortunately interrupted by the Spanish Civil War (1936–1939). With the dictatorship of Francisco Franco (1939–1975), it is known that only one Compilation (1960) could be approved.

The path toward a Catalonian civil code began slowly, with the recovery of national autonomy following the approval of the Spanish Constitution in 1978 and the assumption of powers in civil matters in the Statute of Autonomy of Catalonia. The Parliament of Catalonia has been enacting specific acts on civil matters, which are of application in its territory (art. 111–5 CC Cat). However, the Catalan legislator cannot legislate on matters that the Constitution attributes solely to the State (art. 149.1.8 EC).[26] This reservation of State powers means that the Catalan Civil Code is necessarily incomplete. Furthermore, the legislative power in civil matters ought to extend to the *preservation, modification* and *development* of civil law. According

---

[23] For a comparison between the French reform and the Spanish Association of Civil Law Professors' Proposal, see Arroyo Amayuelas (2017).

[24] See BOE of 3.06.2021.

[25] Mancomunitat de Catalunya (1919, pp. 8–9, 61–66). See broadly, Balcells et al. (1996, pp. 479–488) and Balcells (2010).

[26] Art. 149.1.8ᵃ of the Spanish Constitution: "[T]he State holds exclusive jurisdiction over the following matters: civil legislation, without prejudice to the preservation, modification and development by the Autonomous Communities of their civil laws, *fueros* or special rights, whenever these exist; in any event the enactments relative to the application and effectiveness of legal provisions, legal-civil relations arising from the forms of marriage, the keeping of records and drawing up of public instruments, bases of contractual obligations, rules for resolving conflicts of law and determination of the sources of law in conformity, in this last case, with the rules of the *fueros* or with those of special laws".

to some, this shows how incomplete regional powers are; in fact, it is quite the opposite because these three concepts describe all the possible modalities of exercising competence.

An organization has been created to lead the Catalan codification following the example set by the most civil jurisdictions. The Observatory of Private Law of Catalonia was created to analyze the feasibility of a future Catalonia Code. Together with it, the Catalan General Codification Commission was established to study and organize the underlying rules of the Catalonian legal system that could eventually become the new CC Cat.[27]

4.1 Codification: An Unfinished Process

In the exercise of its power, the Catalan legislator has updated civil law in Catalonia, first by carrying out reforms in the Compilation of the Special Civil Law of Catalonia, subsequently by enacting a series of special acts, and finally by codifying specific areas of civil law. This codification took place in two phases. First, the law of succession was codified in 1991. Second, family law was codified in 1998. Each codification led to its own separate code. From 2002 onward, sectoral codification was abandoned in favor of a more comprehensive codification of civil matters in a single body of law. The updated inheritance and family codes became two books of this new civil code, and other special laws that already existed were incorporated into the other books of the CC Cat. Book VI is the last one that has been enacted; it is presently incomplete, but the Catalonian legislature is continuing its work to finish it. For the time being, it incorporates the already existing legislation on rustic lease contracts and the contract for the conveyance of land in exchange for future construction and offers completely new regulations on sale and mandate contracts.

4.2 The Political Reasons for Codification

There are always political reasons behind the idea of codifying the law, and in Catalonia, these have been promoted for a long time. The drafting of a separate civil code is an attempt to break the inertia of presenting Catalan civil law as a subordinate appendix to what judges and lawyers have traditionally perceived as common or general law. In short, better law, because it is more complete (the CC).[28] For this reason, art. 111–5 CC Cat now makes it clear that, in Catalonia, the only common law is Catalan law.

---

[27] Decree 395/2011, of 27 September, *of the Catalan Codification Commission and the Catalan Private Law Observatory* (DOGC of 29.09.2011).

[28] Arroyo Amayuelas (1998).

Another advantage of codification is technical because it simplifies and improves access to the law by providing an internal order and unity that allows the public as well as the judiciary to benefit from a better understanding of the law. In fact, although disguised as a technical advantage, there is also a political motivation to this. It is clear that a singular CC for Catalonia, acting as a symbol of a comprehensive and unified body of law, is more culturally significant than disparate statutes and regulations. As a result, a civil code can develop a special significance as an element of national identity and an instrument of social cohesion for the jurisdiction in which it applies.

4.3 The Code and the Catalan Legal Tradition

In Catalonia, codification is not simply a way of presenting the law but a reform process that, in addition to the consolidation, harmonisation and ssytematization of special acts, aims to update and modernise civil law. This requires the law to be adapted to society and demands a change of existing laws in both content and language. An overall positive assessment of the reforms it incorporates deserves to be highlighted, although the Civil Code of Catalonia (CC Cat) is not modernized in all the matters it covers (e.g., it still maintains the need for the institution of the heir in the will; or the principle *nemo pro parte testatus pro parte intestato decedere potest*). Modern legislators must overcome the approach that has traditionally driven legislative action in Catalonia. This traditional approach has required reforms based on maintaining a balance between the desire for renewal and the preservation of the historical spirit of Catalan law. In theory, this means that while the legislature seeks to implement modern reforms, any new laws must find their legitimacy by demonstrating how they are derived from the historical Catalan legal tradition. This approach is in reality often a formality as opposed to a substantive governing principle and is not always faithfully reflected in articles of law. This demonstrates the difference between the historical imperatives burdening a compilation in contrast to the modern flexibility of codification. Even if abrupt changes are not advisable, and the Catalan legal tradition remains necessary for the interpretation of current law (art. 111–2 CC Cat), the time has long since come for profound modernisation and renovation. This means that history can no longer serve as a basis to legitimise and/or justify the present legal system and its laws as it did when the 1960 Compilation was written.

4.4 Systemic Risks

The idea of systemic risks is intended to refer to the suspicion of unconstitutionality that always surrounds Catalonian legislation and the high probability that acts enacted by the Catalan Parliament will end up being challenged before the Constitutional Court. In fact, Act 29/2002, which approved the structure of the Civil Code of Catalonia and its Book I, was challenged by the President of the Spanish Government. Among the arguments of the State lawyer, many of them political rather than legal, was that the Spanish Constitution prohibited Catalonia from having a civil code. However, the case was eventually withdrawn in 2004. Another case was filed against art. 129 of the Autonomous Statute of Catalonia. This article recognizes the competence of the *Generalitat* (Catalan Executive) in civil matters. The ruling of the Constitutional Court 31/2010 of 28 June[29] stated that the article could only be constitutional if it was interpreted in accordance with the theses of the "connected or related institutions", as defined in other previous rulings of the same court.[30] In essence, this means that the Autonomous Communities cannot legislate on any matter of civil law even if not expressly reserved to the State and may only legislate in accordance with the principles inspired by their existing laws and in conformity with the compiled civil law existing prior to the Spanish Constitution. Put another way, autonomous communities can only legislate with respect to institutions that show a connection with those previously established or within the margins of their general principles of law. Previous Catalonian acts or parts thereof had been considered unconstitutional for this very reason. In some cases, such acts were slated to be included in the modern code.[31]

On this ground but also because there was a suspicion of infringement of State competence on the fundamental guidelines of contractual obligations ("*bases de las obligaciones contractuales*"),[32] a new action of unconstitutionality was brought against Book VI of the CC Cat. Surprisingly, this time, the ruling of the Constitutional Court 132/2019 of 13 November declared Book VI of the CC Cat to be constitutional (except for one provision).[33] The Court concluded that the doctrine of the "connected institutions" should not only refer to institutions covered by the Compilation but could also take into account any connection with new institutions stemming from other subsequently enacted legislation, i.e., once the competence to legislate had already been assumed. This decision recognizes the validity of Book VI of the CC Cat, but it cannot be ignored that the judgment had four individual votes, and six out of twelve sitting judges were against the majority decision.[34] Be that as it may, it is interesting to note that the Court rightly considers consumer sales to be a civil matter, which, as has already been pointed out, is a contentious area of law being debated between civil and commercial legal scholars. Moreover, the Court held that codified

---

[29] BOE of 16.07.2010.

[30] Ruling of the Constitutional Court 88/93 of 12 March (BOE of 15.4.1993) and 156/93 of 26 May (BOE of 28.05.1993).

[31] See ruling of the Constitutional Court 95/2017, of 6 July on the so-called "Catalan Intermediate Tenures". For criticism, see Vaquer Aloy (2009). In 2019, two new rulings were issued that affected other Catalan Acts: ruling of the Constitutional Court 7/2019, of 17 January, concerning the Act on digital wills, which modified Books II and IV of the Civil Code of Catalonia; and ruling of the Constitutional Court 13/2019, concerning the Act on urgent measures in the field of housing.

[32] See art. 149.1.8 Spanish Constitution in fn 25.

[33] BOE of 19.12.2019.

[34] Nor is Spanish legal doctrine very much in line with the reasoning of that judgment. See Bercovitz Rodriguez-Cano (2020); García Rubio (2019). However, see Assúa González (2020).

consumer sale law is constitutional, although the Catalan competence on consumer protection in other areas was disputed in preceding rulings.[35] The judgment also sets out that *bases de las obligaciones contractuales* is what is essential and must function as a general criterion for all contracts in Spain to guarantee legal unity in favor of economic activity. This does not mean that the Catalan regulation cannot be different from that contained in State law; it only means that Catalonian legislation should not violate the essential principles contained in the CC. This would include principles such as the primacy of autonomy of will, the absence of formalism in contracts, the role of contracts in the transfer of property, or good faith.

5 Structure and Contents of the CC of Catalonia

According to the plan outlined in Title I of Act 29/2002, the *First Act of the Civil Code of Catalonia,*[36] the CC Cat will consist of six books: Book I, containing general provisions governing the sources of the law and the rules for its application (including prescription and caducity (*decadenza*)); Book II, on natural persons and family law; Book III, on legal entities, including associations and foundations; Book IV, on the law of succession; Book V, on the law of property; and Book VI, on the law of contracts, including consumer contracts. The CC Cat is structured around six books, which is two more than the CC. The CC Cat incorporates more modern rules in several areas when compared with the Spanish one. A number of these modern novelties are highlighted below.

5.1 Prescription and Caducity

The effects of time on claims and rights have been developed *ex novo* in Title II of Book I of the CC Cat. Its provisions on prescription and caducity (*decadenza*) are much more complete than those in the CC and more appropriate to modern times, with periods of prescription of 10, 3, and 1 year(s). The general limitation period is 10 years, as opposed to the 30 years previously established in art. 344 of the Compilation (art. 121–20 CC Cat) and the 15 years of the original art. 1964 of the CC (since 2015, lowered to only 5).[37]

---

[35] See ruling of the Constitutional Court 54/2018 of 24 May 2018 and 13/2019 of 31 January 2019.

[36] See Art. 6 Act 29/2002, of 30 December, *First Act of the CC Cat* (DOGC of 13.01.2003).

[37] See art. 1964.2 Spanish CC, as amended by Act 42/2015, of 5 October 2015 (BOE of 6.10.2015).

5.2   Person and Family Law

Book II systematically regulates for the first time the law of natural persons, which is now more in line with the European and International frameworks than the CC. It is not by chance, therefore, that the provision on the moment in which the person acquires legal capacity, at birth (art. 211–1.1 CC Cat; cf. art. 7 Convention on the Rights of the Child), has obliged the Spanish legislator to repeal the rule in the CC that still made such acquisition dependent on the course of the 24 h after the umbilical cord was cut, which, furthermore, required that the person born had a human figure (former art. 30 CC). It is significant that the new Spanish rule—which is in line with the Catalan rule—was imposed after the promulgation of the abovementioned Book II of the CC Cat and not after the signing and ratification of the Convention on the Rights of the Child, which happened many years before. Book II CC Cat also establishes a modern rule on "commorient death" (when two individuals die in such a way that it is impossible to determine who died first). Art. 211–2.2 CC Cat establishes that people who die as a result of the same accident just 72 h apart are understood to have died at the same time. This cannot be true in reality because, clearly, one dies before the other, and it is too great a fiction to think otherwise.

Other provisions deal with minors' and adults' legal capacity and decision making in the medical field. It should be remarked that the pioneer rule on living wills is, as in many other previous cases, a clear example of legal transplantation within the State.[38] Concerning adults' protection, Title II of Book II incorporates a wide variety of protection instruments. The most interesting instruments are those that provide models of assistance to vulnerable people without the need for prior incapacitation, such as the German *Betreeung*, on the one hand (which in Catalan is called "*assistència*", arts. 226–1 to 226–7 CC Cat), and the enduring powers of attorney, on the other ("*poders en previsió de pèrdua de capacitat*", art. 222.2 CC Cat). Over time, there have been new amendments (e.g., amendments that prevent people with intellectual disabilities from automatically losing the right to vote, art. 211–3.4 CC Cat).[39]

The very same Book II CC Cat stands out for its incorporation of a broad conception of the legal idea of the family. Unlike the current national framework in Spain, Book II includes innovative provisions regulating (unmarried) partnerships[40] and

---

[38] See on that, Navarro-Michel (2005) and Ferrer i Riba (2011).

[39] See Final Provision of L. 3/2017, of 15 February, *of Book six of the Civil Code of Catalonia, regarding obligations and contracts, and the modification of Books one, two, three, four and five* (DOGC of 22.02.2017).

[40] See Tarabal Bosch (2016). Other Autonomous Communities have regulated this matter to some extent. However, see the Constitutional ruling 93/2013, of 23 April, against Act 6/2000, of 3 July, on unmarried couples in Navarre (BOE of 23.5.2013). This ruling established that comprehensive legislation, applicable even against people's will, could infringe on their freedom as individuals (art. 10 of the Spanish Constitution). Therefore, partners must be left free to choose the rules they deem appropriate or voluntarily submit to the legal ones. For an overview, see Egusquiza Balmaseda (2009). The Constitutional ruling 81/2013, of 11 April, as regards the Act 11/2001, of 19 December, on de facto unions of the Autonomous Community of Madrid, focused on the lack

prenuptial agreements in anticipation of a break-up (a novelty inspired by US soft law, arts. 231–20, 234–5 CC Cat).[41] Book II CC Cat includes the possibility of giving parents shared custody of their children in cases of marital crisis, and with reference to step-parents recognizes certain decision-making powers and custody rights (art. 236–14, 236–15 CC Cat). The regime of separation of property between spouses is maintained as a legal regime, although this is not the predominant trend in Europe. Economic compensation for the spouse who has worked for the household or for the other spouse with insufficient remuneration has undergone significant adjustments. The amount of economic compensation recoverable in the two aforementioned scenarios is a maximum of a quarter of the difference between the original assets and the increase in the assets of the spouse who benefited from the unpaid or underpaid contributions of their spouse (art. 232–5 CC Cat).[42] In matters of parentage by means of assisted reproductive technologies, the consent of the (married or unmarried) partner (man or woman) of the woman who is undergoing such assisted reproduction suffices to establish the consenting partners rights as a parent (arts. 235–3, 235–8.1, 235–13.1 CC Cat). State law, on the contrary, does not provide for the consent of a woman who is not married to the recipient woman, apart from other differences.[43]

5.3 Law of Succession

Book IV CC Cat introduced substantial reforms in the current law of succession. However, it still maintains classic, obsolete principles, such as the incompatibility between intestate and testate succession.[44] In this new Book IV, testamentary freedom is extended with new causes of unworthiness and with the adoption of precautions that seek to prevent the coercion of elderly testators (art. 412–5.2 CC Cat). A forced share or reserved portion is still a fixed amount of one quarter of the inheritance, regardless of who and how many people are entitled to it, but reforms have been introduced that create uncertainty. One of these is the new cause of disinheritance due to the manifest absence of family relationship to the deceased, provided that this situation is exclusively attributable to the beneficiary (art. 451–17.2 e CC Cat), which is an open clause that favors judicial discretion and, consequently, legal uncertainty.[45]

---

of legislative powers on civil matters. On the diversity of models prevailing in this area of the law and its constitutionality, see Martín Casals (2013), Lamarca Marquès (2014), and Navarro-Michel (2014).

[41] See Anderson (2012, p. 28).

[42] Farnós Amorós (2016).

[43] See an overview of Book II CC Cat in Lamarca (2016) and Ferrer Riba (2010).

[44] For an overall perspective on the new Book IV CC Cat, see Arroyo Amayuelas – Anderson (2011).

[45] Arroyo Amayuelas - Farnós Amorós (2016) and for further case-law evolution, see Arroyo Amayuelas (2019). On forced share in the whole of Spain, see Cámara Lapuente (2020) and specifically on Catalan law, see Anderson (2014).

Book IV CC Cat improves the likelihood of successfully transferring a family business by means of an inheritance agreement (prohibited in the CC) but still requires the grantors to have familial or kinship ties (art. 431–2 CC Cat). On the other hand, the heir's liability for the deceased's debts is only *intra vires* if he takes inventory in the time and manner legally provided for (arts. 461–14, 461–17, 461–20 CC Cat). Regarding intestate succession, the position of the surviving spouse is improved. The spouse inherits in the absence of children, but in advance of the grandchildren, if all the children who are in common with the deceased repudiate the inheritance (art. 442–2.2 CC Cat). If there are children, the surviving spouse only has the right to the usufruct of the entire inheritance; the novelties are that this usufruct now extends to the forced share (art. 442–4.1 CC Cat), is for life and is not extinguished by the widower's new marriage or partnership (art. 442–4.3 CC Cat). In addition, it can be commuted to a quarter of the inheritance and the usufruct of the family home (art. 442–4 CC Cat).[46] Book IV is governed by the principle of full equality in succession between married and unmarried couples.

Over time, there have also been new amendments to govern and recognize the validity of digital wills (e.g., arts. 411–10, 421–2, 421–4 CC Cat).[47]

5.4 Contract Law

Book VI CC Cat on the law of obligations and contracts is the most innovative because for the first time, it includes a complete regulation of the contracts of sale, mandate, and lease (rustic and urban, but the latter is still being drafted).[48] The gradual Europeanisation of the law in this area has greatly facilitated legislative activity in Catalonia and the updating of this part of Catalan civil law. The most obvious example is that provided by the regulation of sale.[49] At first, the legislator only wanted to repeal the traditional Catalan provisions still in force, according to which a sale of immovable property may be rescinded by the seller when the price paid by the buyer is less than 50% of the value of the property. The rules on *rescisión por lesión ultra dimidium* originally dated from 1960 and had their roots in the *ius commune* and customary law. This originally simple idea later culminated in a more ambitious proposal, namely, the *ex novo* regulation of the sale contract. The Common European Sales Law (CESL) rules on unfair exploitation helped to reformulate the

---

[46] For an overview of the legal regulation of intestate succession in Catalonia, see Tarabal Bosch (2014).

[47] Act 10/2017, of 27 June, *of the digital will and modification of the second and fourth books of the Civil Code of Catalonia* (DOGC of 29.06.2017). Constitutional Court ruling 7/2019, of 17 January declares the unconstitutionality of certain of its provisions dealing with the creation of an electronic registry of digital wills.

[48] See, however, Act 11/2020, of 18 September, *of urgent measures on price control in urban leases* (DOGC 21.09.2020).

[49] Miquel-Sala (2019, pp. 370 ff.); Arroyo Amayuelas (2016, pp. 333–339).

rules for *ultra dimidium* rescission in a new article, but ultimately, the latter has not been repealed, and unnecessarily, both institutions now coexist in the CC Cat.[50]

Catalonia has a Consumer Code, but it does not embrace consumer contracts. Therefore, consumer law also has a place in Book VI, especially in a contract of sale.

6 The Relevance of the Code as a Common of General Law for Catalonia

The Catalan legislator aims to emphasize the expansive relevance of the principles governing civil law institutions to express the civil code's role as the law to be generally applied in Catalonia. To this end, art. 111–4 CC Cat establishes that the provisions of the CC Cat constitute common law in Catalonia.[51] Therefore, Catalan Law is to be preferentially applied (art. 111–5 CCC), except for certain subjects regulated by the State that are of a general direct application (i.e., the matters listed in art. 149.1.8ª Spanish Constitution). Expressed in other words, where the *Generalitat* holds exclusive jurisdiction, Catalan civil law applies to its territory preferentially to any other. Therefore, in Catalonia, the first and main source of civil law is Catalan civil legislation. The CC Cat is the "general and common law" that will fill the gaps whenever a special statute needs to be completed. The CC Cat is as "common or general" in Catalonia as the CC is in the rest of Spain. This does not mean that the State's civil law contained in the CC (the traditionally named "common law") has ceased to be applicable as subsidiary legislation in Catalonia. CC Cat, art. 111–5 confirms this point. Art. 149.3 of the Spanish Constitution and art. 4.3 CC impose the general subsidiarity of the CC and, more generally, of all Spanish civil legislation. The difference is now that the Catalan codified civil law intervenes in this hierarchy above the CC (art. 111–4 CCC). Plus, in cases where Catalan legislation is insufficient and the State's law is to complete it, the latter will only be applied if it does not conflict with the Catalan civil provisions or with the principles that sustain them (art. 111–5 II CC Cat).

7 Conclusion

The civil code is an appropriate legislative technique from a formal point of view because it imposes rationality and legal security and from a social point of view because a codification process addresses the particular needs and interests of the society for which the civil code is intended. In Catalonia, the purpose of codification

---

[50] For criticism, Martín-Casals (2018, pp. 280–287) and Arroyo Amayuelas (2016, pp. 338–339). On unfair exploitation, see Barceló Compte (2019) and Gómez Calle (2019).

[51] For the same principle in the Preliminary Provision of Quebec Civil Code, see Bisson (1999). In Catalonia, see Badosa Coll (2007).

is not to restore the lost hegemony of a civil code, as has happened in other countries that have entered the process of recoding, but to achieve it for the first time. A civil code confers a prestige that compilations lack. Moreover, a compilation only aims to consolidate the past and is an attack on the evolution of law. This is something that civil codes try to overcome. The Catalan legislator has often demonstrated that they are capable of reacting faster to social change than their Spanish counterpart. The latter has indeed failed to introduce those reforms that are necessary to update the CC and thus to bring it into the modern age.

References

Anderson M (2012) Marital agreements: Spanish case-law v. the 2010 Catalan reform. Confronting the Frontiers of Family and Succession Law: Liber Amicorum Walter Pintens. 1:23–40

Anderson M (2014) An outline of the catalan forced share system. IJLI 42(1):35–46

Anderson M, Arroyo Amayuelas E (eds) (2011) The law of succession: testamentary freedom. European perspectives. Europa Law Publishing, Groningen

Arrieta Sevilla LJ (2019) La recuperación de la regla venta quita renta en los arrendamientos de vivienda. ADC 1:53–100

Arroyo Amayuelas E (1998) Vigència i aplicació del dret a Catalunya segons la jurisprudència del Tribunal Suprem: 1875–1888. BCEHC 79:360–386

Arroyo Amayuelas E (2006) The Plurality of Civil Codes in Spain. Spanish Decodification versus Catalan Codification. Aracne, Roma

Arroyo Amayuelas E (2014) Die Entwicklung des Zivilrechts in Katalonien und das neue katalanische Zivilgesetzbuch. ZEuP 3:584–607

Arroyo Amayuelas E (2016) Some thoughts on the proposal of the common European sales from a Catalan perspective. Osservatorio del diritto civile e commerciale 1:329–340

Arroyo Amayuelas E (2017) A Spanish perspective on the general theory of contract. In: Cartwright J, Whittaker S (eds), The code Napoléon rewritten. French contract law after the 2016 reforms, pp 361–385

Arroyo Amayuelas E (2019) Libertà di testare, solidarietà familiare e diseredazione. Verso un sistema di clausole generali di privazione della legittima?. In: Tescaro M - Scola S (eds) Casi controversi in materia di diritto delle successioni, pp 641–656

Arroyo Amayuelas E, Anderson M (2011) Catalan law between modernisation and tradition: a general overview of the 2008 reform of the law of succession. In: Anderson M, Arroyo Amayuelas E (eds) The law of succession. Testamentary freedom. European Perspectives, pp 41–72

Arroyo Amayuelas E, Farnós Amorós E (2016) Kindship Bonds and emotional ties: lack of a family relationship as ground of disinheritance. ERPL 2:203–222

Assúa González CI (2020) Conexión y bases de las obligaciones contractualesa propósito de la STC 132/2019. Derecho Privado y Constitución 37:235–272

Badosa Coll F (2003) Quae ad ius Cathalanicum pertinet. The Civil Law of Catalonia, ius commune and legal tradition. In: MacQueen H L, Vaquer A, Espiau S (eds) Regional Private Laws and codification in Europe, pp 136–163

Badosa Coll F (2007) El caràcter de dret comú del Codi civil de Catalunya. RCDP 8:19–46

Balcells A (2010) El projecte d'autonomia de la Mancomunitat de Catalunya del 1919 i el seu context històric. Parlament de Catalunya, Barcelona

Balcells A, Pujol E, Sabater J (1996) La Mancomunitat de Catalunya i l'autonomia. Proa, Barcelona

Barceló Compte R (2019) Ventaja injusta y protección de la parte débil del contrato. Marcial Pons, Barcelona

Bayod López C (ed.) (2019) La Constitución española y los derechos civiles españoles cuarenta años después. Su evolución a través de las sentencias del Tribunal Constitucional. Tirant lo Blanch, Valencia

Beaulne J (2015) Droit des fiducies, 3rd ed. Wilson & Lafleur, Montréal

Bercovitz Rodriguez-Cano R (2020) Comentario a la STC 13 de noviembre de 2019. CCJC 113:277–314

Bisson AF (1999) La disposition preliminaire du Code civil de Québec. McGill LJ 44:539–565

Borghetti JS, Whittaker S (eds) (2019) French Civil Liability in Comparative Perspective. Hart, Oxford

Cámara Lapuente S (2020) Forced Heirship in Spain. In: Reid K G C, De Waal M J, Zimmermann R (eds) Comparative Succession Law. III: Mandatory Family Protection, pp 139–174

Cantin Cumyn M (2002) La fiducie, un nouveau sujet de droit?. In: Beaulne J (ed.) Mélanges Ernest Caparros. Wilson & Lafleur, Montréal, pp 129–143

Cartwright J, Whittaker S (eds) (2017) The Code Napoléon rewritten. French Contract Law after the 2016 Reforms. Hart, Oxford

Código Civil: 130 Aniversario (2020). Wolters Kluwers, Madrid

Demogue R (1925) Traité des obligations en général. V. Rousseau, Paris

Du Plessis Paul J (2012) Historical evolution of the maximum 'sale breaks hire'. In: Van der Merwe C, Verbeke AL (eds), Time-Limited Interests in Land, pp 19–32

Egusquiza Balmaseda MA (2019) Las parejas de hecho y el Tribunal Constitucional. In: Bayod López (ed), La Constitución española y los derechos civiles españoles cuarenta años después. Su evolución a través de las sentencias del Tribunal Constitucional, pp 81–106

Farnós Amorós E (2016) Monetary compensation and 'selfless dedication' to the family". In Lauroba Lacasa, E, Ginebra Molins, E. (dirs.), Matrimonial property regimes in Spain, pp 215–234

Fenoy Picón N (2013) The Spanish obligation and contract law and the proposal for its modernization. In: Schulze R, Zoll F (eds) The Law of Obligations in Europe, pp 397–430

Ferrer i Riba J (2011) Protection against incapacity and private autonomy in Spanish Law. In: Löhning M et alii (Hrsg) Vorsorgevollmacht und Erwachsenenschutz, pp 245–261

Ferrer Riba J (2010) El Derecho de la persona y de la familia en el nuevo libro segundo del Código civil de Cataluña. InDret 3:1–3

García Rubio MP (2019) Incertidumbre y alguna cosa más en la interpretación constitucional del poder normativo sobre la materia civil. RDC 4:1–43

Geens K (2016) The jump to the right of tomorrow. Recodification of the basic legislation (https://bit.ly/droitdemain)

Gómez Calle E (2019) Desequilibrio contractual y tutela del contratante débil. Aranzadi, Cizur menor

Harty S (2002) Lawyers. Codification and the origins of Catalan nationalism. Law and History Review 2:349–384

Jacobson S (2002) Law and nationalism in nineteenth-century Europe: the case of Catalonia in comparative perspective. Law and History Review 2:307–347

Lamarca Marquès A (2014) The unconstitutionality of cohabitation regulation—Two decisions of the Spanish constitutional court. In: Witzleb, Norman et al. (Hrsg.), Festschrift für Dieter Martiny zum 70. Geburstag, pp 1141–1161

Lamarca Marquès A (2016) The changing concept of 'family' and challenges for family law in Spain and Catalonia. In: Scherpe J (ed) European Family Law, II, pp 289–308

Lauroba Lacasa E, Ginebra Molins E (eds) (2016) Matrimonial property regimes in Spain. Société de Legislation Comparé, Paris, Paris

Le Code civil (1804–2004) Livre du Bicentenaire (2004). Dalloz, Paris

Löhning M et alii (eds) (2011)Vorsorgevollmacht und Erwachsenenschutz. Gieseking, Bielefeld

MacQueen HL, Vaquer A, Espiau S (eds) Regional Private Laws and codification in Europe. Cambridge University Press, Cambridge

Mancomunitat de Catalunya (1919) El dret català i la codificació. Barcelona

Martín Casals M (2013) El derecho a la convivencia "anómica" en pareja: ¿un nuevo derecho fundamental? InDret 3:1–43

Martín-Casals M (2018) Avantatge injust i lesió en més de la mitat: una duplicitat necessària i convenient?. In: Serrano de Nicolás Á (ed) Estudios sobre el Libro Sexto del Código Civil de Cataluña, pp 251–292

Martín-Casals M (2004) Die Kodifizierung des katalanischen Zivilrechts im europäischen Rahmen. ZEuP 3:677–684

Menyhárd A, Veress E (eds) (2017) New civil codes in Hungary and Romania. Springer, New York

Miquel-Sala R (2019) Das Sechste Buch des katalanischen Zivilgesetzbuches: neues Kaufrecht unter europäischem Einfluss. ZEuP 2:358–384

Navarro-Michel M (2014) Same sex couples in Spain and Catalonia. IJLI 42(1):47–54

Navarro-Michel M (2005) Advance directives: The Spanish Perspective. Med Law Rev 13:137–169

Oleart O (2014) From Legal Compilations to legal codes: A Catalan legal history approach (18th–20th Centuries). IJLI 42(1):1–21

Parra Lucán MA (2019a) La actualización del Derecho de Sucesiones en la Jurisprudencia de la Sala 1.ª TS. La Ley. Derecho De Familia 22:10–25

Parra Lucán MA (2019b) La necesidad de un nuevo Código civil para la sociedad del siglo XXI. Diario La Ley n° 9515, of 11 November 2019

Parra Lucán MA (2014) La doble codificación en España y la frustración del proceso de unificación del Derecho privado. Eur Dirit Priv 3:897–925

Ranieri F (2010) Dienstleistungsverträge: Rechtsgeschichte und die Italienische Erfahrung. In: Zimmermann R (Hrsg), Service Contracts, pp 2–41

Reid KGC, De Waal MJ, Zimmermann R (eds) (2020) Comparative Succession Law. III: Mandatory Family Protection. OUP, Oxford

Rivera JC (ed) (2013) The scope and structure of civil codes. Springer, New York

Roca Trias E (ed) (2015) Codificaciones del Derecho privado en el s. XXI. Civitas, Madrid

Scherpe J (ed) (2016) European family law, II. Cheltenham, Elgar

Schulze R, Zoll F (eds) The law of obligations in Europe. Sellier, Munich

Serrano de Nicolás A (ed) Estudios sobre el Libro Sexto del Código Civil de Cataluña. Marcial Pons, Barcelona

Shi J (2019) The drafting of the Chinese civil code: between compilation and innovation. RIDC 4:945–965

Spanish Association of Civil Law Professors, (eds) (2018) Proposal for a civil code. Tecnos, Madrid

Stijns S (2016) Faut-il réformer le Code civil? - Réponses et méthodologie pour le droit des obligations contractuelles et extracontractuelles:les obligations contractuelles. JT 19 (6647): 305–311

Tarabal Bosch J (2016) Stable Cohabitation in the Catalan Civil Code. In Lauroba Lacasa, E, Ginebra Molins, E. (dirs.), Matrimonial Property Regimes in Spain, pp. 271–288

Tarabal Bosch J (2014) The law of successions I: intestacy under Catalan Law. IJLI 42(1):28–34

Tescaro M, Scola S (eds) (2019) Casi controversi in materia di diritto delle successioni, II. ESI, Napoli

Van der Merwe C, Verbeke AL (eds) (2012) Time-limited interests in land. Cambridge University Press, Cambridge

Van Erp S, Vaquer A (coords) Introduction to Spanish Patrimonial Law. Comares, Granada

Vaquer Aloy A (2019) La conexión suficiente y las bases de las obligaciones contractuales. In: Bayod López (ed), La Constitución española y los derechos civiles españoles cuarenta años después. Su evolución a través de las sentencias del Tribunal Constitucional, pp 47–80

Vaquer A (2006) Introduction. In: Van Erp S - Vaquer A (coords) Introduction to Spanish Patrimonial Law, pp 1–17

Verbeke AL, Scherpe JM, Declerck, C (eds) (2012) Confronting the frontiers of family and succession law: Liber amicorum Walter Pintens. Vol. 1, Intersentia, Antwerp

Wang Z (2020) On the Constitutionality of Compiling a Civil Code of China. Springer, New York

Wéry P, Dirix E (2015) Pour une modernisation du Code Civil, JT 29(6615): 625–626

Witzleb N et al. (ed) (2014) Festschrift für Dieter Martiny zum 70. Geburstag. Mohr Siebeck, Tübingen

Zhang L (2009) The Latest Developments in the Codification of Chinese Civil Law. Tulane Law Review 83:999–1038

Zimmermann R (2005) The new German law of obligations. Oxford University Press, Oxford

Zimmermann R (ed) (2010) Service Contracts. Mohr Siebeck, Tübingen

Esther Arroyo Amayuelas is Full Professor of Civil Law at the University of Barcelona. Since 2015, she has held the EU Private Law Jean Monnet Chair at the same university. As a member of the Group *Acquis*, she took part in the development of European Private Law through the Network of Excellence created by the Sixth Framework Programme for Research of the European Union (2005–2009). Fellow of the German DAAD (2003) and of the Alexander von Humboldt Foundation (2006–2007). Since 2010, during the winter semester, she teaches at University of Münster in the Language and Law Program for foreign jurists (Lehrauftrag: FFA—Program).

The Making of the Turkish Civil Code

Başak Baysal◉ and Gizem Arslan◉

Abstract The adoption of the Turkish Civil Code based on the Swiss Civil Law on October 4, 1926, was probably the most important movement of the legal revolution that followed the Turkish Revolution. In other words, it was one of the most significant steps taken toward the modernization of Turkish society. The new Turkish State departed from its religious foundation and instead was built on secularism. These laws laid the blueprints for a new society by reconstituting the basis of private law through the introduction of new regulations in the laws of persons, inheritance, property, and family. Two major difficulties were encountered during the process of adopting this Civil Code. The first major difficulty was inherent in translation, initially arising from their translation and further complicated by the Turkish language reform in the 1930s. The second major difficulty was the resistance that the new Civil Code received as a result of its radical changes in the regulation of family law. However, we argue that Turkish society, which has a culture of its own, has over time adapted itself to these new laws. Therefore, a significant conclusion that can be drawn from the modernization process in Turkey is that civil law rules can be successfully adopted by a country even when they come from different cultures and societies.

1 Introduction

Important laws were enacted and entered into force in Turkish private law in the 2000s for a variety of reasons related to political, social, and economic developments that occurred in the country. An interesting outcome of introducing such laws is a perceived increase in the importance of the methods used in law-making. The procedures and techniques used during the making of the law are key to ensuring their legal legitimacy. Acceptance of the laws by society is the result of social debate and

B. Baysal (✉) · G. Arslan
Department of Civil Law, Kadir Has University, Istanbul, Turkey
e-mail: basak.baysal@khas.edu.tr

G. Arslan
e-mail: gizem.arslan@khas.edu.tr

© The Author(s), under exclusive license to Springer Nature Singapore Pte Ltd. 2023
M. Graziadei and L. Zhang (eds.), *The Making of the Civil Codes*,
Ius Gentium: Comparative Perspectives on Law and Justice 104,
https://doi.org/10.1007/978-981-19-4993-7_4

negotiation; therefore, it is of central importance that an enactment relies on healthy social debates. The procedures and principles adhered to during the process are closely associated with the validity of the rule of law and democratic state principles in a modern state.[1] Another important aspect of law-making is the ability of the law-making procedures and principles to permit the law-maker to respond to the needs of society.

In the case of a major change in a social order or legal system, in lieu of large social debates, some laws and regulations may be adapted from other countries, and society may be expected to simply accept them. Regulations that have to be adopted by Turkey during the process of its integration into the European Union are an example of such a major change.[2]

In some cases, the desired changes were implemented for revolutionary purposes. Indeed, the law-making process was historically different in Turkey. The founders of the new Republic of Turkey ensured the integration of the state into the modern world through such drastic changes after the collapse of the Ottoman Empire. For the law to transform society, adaptation of laws that were essentially incompatible with the existing social culture became a necessity.[3]

The Turkish Civil Code and the Code of Obligations, two significant laws that would change the trajectory of Turkish private law, were adopted in 1926. These laws were initially made based on a translation of the Swiss Civil Code and the Swiss Code of Obligations. The reason for this adaptation movement is essentially based on the idea of the Turkish revolution and the modernization pursued by the new Turkish state. This paper examines the relationship between the Turkish Revolution and the process of adopting Western laws with a focus on how such laws were both adapted to Turkish society and shaped Turkish society.

2   An Overview of the Concept of Modernization in Turkey

Codification means, narrowly speaking, combining the rules of law that are disorderly or unwritten in a state to create a comprehensive and complete legal system. A law-making movement can occur for economic, social, or political purposes depending on the legal policy of a state.[4]

In the last years of the Ottoman Empire, movements of law adaptation and lawmaking took place. These movements emerged during "Tanzimat" (1839–1876), the period of modernization and reform, driven by both economic and political considerations. In particular, economic relations with Europe required the Ottoman Empire to change its religion-based rules. During this period, some codes, such as the Commercial Code, were modeled on foreign laws. However, the conservative

---

[1] Altan (2015), p. 11–13; Baysal (2016), p. 20 ff.

[2] Bakırcı (2015), p. 27.

[3] Atamer (2008), p. 724 ff.

[4] Örsten Esirgen (2011), p. 33.

structure of the Ottoman Empire did not allow for such a direct adoption in the field of civil law. Despite this conservative structure, there were attempts and endeavors to make a civil code during this period. In fact, "the Mecelle" (Ottoman Civil Code) emerged from these efforts.[5]

However, the Mecelle, the first civil code in the history of Islamic and Turkish law, was criticized for not having regulated the law of persons and family law.[6] Although various efforts were made to overcome these deficiencies by the commissions established in the following periods, a comprehensive civil code did not materialize.[7]

The Republic of Turkey was founded in 1923 after the collapse of the Ottoman Empire. It was hardly possible for the new state to be governed by the Ottoman legal system because the latter was based on Islam, whereas the new state was built on secularism. Therefore, new laws had to be adopted in almost every field. The most important of these laws was the civil code, which is closely concerned with all aspects of society.[8]

When viewed from this perspective, the adaptation that occurred in Turkish society following the Turkish Revolution is parallel with the law adaptation process in the 20th century. The driving force of both movements is modernization and westernization. Note that what is meant by modernization in the Republic of Turkey is not the same as the one in the previous period under the Ottoman Empire. After the Turkish Revolution, in contrast to legal reforms during the Ottoman Empire, secularization became an indispensable element of modernization.[9] The laws adopted from Europe before the Turkish Revolution were based on the separation of the legal system of the state from those governing private law, such as family law and the law of persons. The laws adopted after the revolution were based on the unification of the legal system via a secular system.[10] Since a national legal unity was essential in the newly established Republic, society had to be regulated singly and uniformly. A secular civil code was the heart of this modernization due mainly to its impact on the lives of the Turkish people.[11] For this reason, the adoption of the Turkish Civil Code, which affected the fundamental dynamics of society such as production, property, and familial relations,

---

[5] Kılıçoğlu (2016), p. 1718.

[6] Atamer (2008), p. 725 ff.

[7] Örsten Esirgen (2011), p. 45.

[8] Kılıçoğlu (2016), p. 1720.

[9] Zwahlen (1976), p. 249.

[10] Kubalı (1973), p. 44; Zwahle (1973), p. 146.

[11] Hasan Ali Yücel, well-known writer and minister of education, spoke explicitly about the relationship between the reception of the Civil Code and the modernization process in Turkey: "The reception of Western law is the acceptance of civilization. In particular, the adoption of family law is a future of civilized life": Öztan (1996), p. 85.

is considered the foremost step of modernization.[12] For this reason, the Civil Code overshadows the 1921 and 1924 Constitutions as a legal revolution.[13]

During Tanzimat, the period of modernization and reform between 1839 and 1876, civil law was the area least affected by modernization.[14] The Mecelle (Ottoman Code of Civil Law) was based on Islamic Law and was the primary source of law regulating obligations. Other fields of private law, especially family law, were not regulated under any secular state law and were instead under laws derived from Islamic law.[15] However, the Turkish Revolution required entirely abandoning Islam-oriented legal principles, thereby basing the Civil Code on secularism. As a result of rapidly shifting from laws derived primarily from Islamic law to wholly secular laws, the preparatory work of the first commission was by many not well received. The practices during the Tanzimat period aimed at finding a compromise between Shari'a and Western principles.[16] However, this was in contradiction with the idea of a modern secular Turkey.[17] It was thought that such a compromise could increase the influence of Islam on society and pave the way for transforming Turkey back into a religious state.[18]

As a result of such fears of a resurgent religious state, the idea of accepting a secular system for all legal institutions prevailed over the idea of revising the existing Islamic Law. The economic development model was ensured by effectively protecting property through a general theory of obligations and commercial law and the current modern property regime. The legal basis of the socioeconomic structure, which was ensured via the revolution, relied on a process of adopting laws largely derived from those found in foreign jurisdiction. Therefore, the translation, adoption, and adaptation of European laws was chosen over pursuing a longer *de novo* law-making process.[19]

However, Turkish law adaptation is different from other legal systems that adopted laws from other countries. In particular, the existence of law adaptation activity in

---

[12] Papachristos (1975), p. 24; In the Turkish preamble, it was stated that Mecelle and the legal rules based on religious principles would not be compatible with the new regime because religious dogmas constitute a huge obstacle to modernization, and the Turkish society had to adapt themselves to the age: Üskül Engin (2014), p. 36.

[13] Serozan (1999), p. 748–750; The 1921 and 1924 Constitutions are important developments in the Turkish history. The principle of national sovereignty appeared in 1921 Constitution for the very first time after the parliament was formed in 1920. The 1924 Constitution, accepted after the proclamation of the Republic in 1923, altered the state's regime and included an emphasis on laicism: See: Tanör (2020), p. 255 & 294.

[14] Kubalı (1973), p. 49.

[15] Elbir (1953–1955), p. 286.

[16] Elbir (1953–1955), p. 286; Tandoğan (1965–1966), p. 422.

[17] Zwahlen (1973), p. 146. For more detail: Velidedeoğlu (1944), p. 338 ff.

[18] Postacıoğlu (1956), p. 63 Tandoğan (1965–1966), p. 423; Zwahlen (1973), p. 145/146.

[19] Papachristos (1975), p. 24; Two commissions were established shortly before the foundation of the Republic, one in 1923 and the other one year later to make a new civil code. The drafts prepared by these commissions were not found suitable from the perspective of the new Republic and consequently a more radical solution was sought and found in the adoption of the 1926 Civil Code: Üskül Engin (2014), p. 32.

postcolonial African countries stemmed from the long-term and historical colonization of these countries. In contrast, Turkey has never been a colony of the Western States.[20] Having not had Western principles forced upon it Turkey does not bare the same reticence to drawing on Western legal principles and when convenient adopting legislation similar to Western jurisdictions. As a result, the adoption of such laws into Turkish law has been relatively successful in shaping social relations.[21]

3 Other Laws Affected by the Legal Adaptation Movement

The Swiss Civil Code is not the first example of a law adopted after 1920.[22] The Italian Zanardelli Penal Code of 1889, adopted in Turkish Law in 1926, is the last and most significant adoption of law that occurred in the classical period. The relevant Italian Penal Code was replaced by the "Rocca Law" during the Mussolini period. The new Italian law was under positivist influence and ensures significant penalties for crimes against the state. After they were adopted in Italy, these crimes were added to the Turkish Penal Code. This Code remained in force in Turkish Law until 2005, after which the national Penal Code repealed and replaced it.

The provisions in the third, fourth, and fifth sections of the Turkish Commercial Code were also based on the model of the Swiss Commercial Code. During that process, Italian, German, and French laws were analyzed as well. The old Commercial Code was an independent law that was prepared by Ernest E. Hirsh, who studied the development of similar laws in Western Europe.[23] The new Turkish Commercial Code is also an independent law prepared by a commission comprised essentially of professors of law and entered into force in 2012, similar to the Turkish Code of Obligations.[24]

In addition, in 1927, the old Civil Procedure Code was prepared based on the Code of Canton of Neuchatel (Switzerland), and French and German laws were also taken into account. It entered into force after various fundamental changes were made and remained in force until 2011, when the new Law of Civil Procedure entered into force.

---

[20] When a legal system or a law is transferred to another country, it often represents a divergence from the values of the country is accepting the law. This is the matter that the colonized countries faced. Turkey, however, went through this adaptation process willingly. Therefore, in Turkey this adaptation movement was considered a "reception": Üskül Engin (2014), p. 32.

[21] Scholler (1996), p. 8.

[22] Mumcu (1996), p. 17 ff.

[23] Karayalçın (1957), p. 34 ff.

[24] OG 14.2.2011, Nr. 27846.

4 Why the Swiss Civil Code was Chosen

Regarding the decision to adopt a civil code, the legendary justification for the Civil Code dated 1926 was expressed by *Mahmut Esat Bozkurt* as follows: "The Turkish people should not adapt the modern civilization to themselves, but themselves to the requirements of the modern civilization, and at any cost."

It proved to be a very important decision for the Turkish government to choose to adapt Turkish law based on the Swiss Civil Code among the German, French, and Swiss options.[25] In the beginning, it might not be clear why the Swiss Civil Code was preferred.[26] The selection of Cantonal laws, in particular, might not seem suitable for a country with a unitary state structure. However, the Minister of Justice of the Atatürk cabinet, *Mahmut Esat Bozkurt,* had other critical concerns that led him to his decision to advocate for the Swiss Civil Code.[27] First, the Swiss Civil Code was the most recent civil code of that time. Second, it ensured gender equality to a larger extent than other laws.[28] While the German Civil Code was also among the most recent laws at the time, it was casuistic and not easily comprehensible and applicable in a different legal culture.

The Swiss Civil Code included general regulations and provided judges with broader discretion, which played a vital role in the decision to adapt the Swiss Civil Code[29]. The Turkish Civil Code allowed for the creation of case law.[30] The Turkish Civil Code gave judges the freedom to act as a "lawmaker" (*modo legislatoris*). The judge can act as a legislator under Article 1(2) of the Turkish Civil Code when there is a gap in existing legislation.[31] This flexibility was one of the main grounds

---

[25] Özcan (2002), p. 147 ff; Bozkurt (1944), p. 11–12.

[26] For a different perspective and background of the reception of the choice to rely on the Swiss Civil Code see: Atamer (2008), p. 731 ff: "The young Turkish republic, which on the one hand tried to transform herself into a European country, on the other hand was very careful to underline its independence. In this concept reception of the Swiss Civil Code offered a perfect solution from this point of view".

[27] Lipstein (1956), p. 10–23; Tercier (1997), p. 6.

[28] Tandoğan (1965–1966), p. 424.

[29] Akipek (1973), p. 59.

[30] Elbir (1953–1955), p. 284; Zwahlen (1973), p. 148; Tandoğan (1965–1966), p. 424.

[31] Cf. AE von O (1977), p. 681.

for the adoption of the Swiss Civil Code.[32] Turkish judges enjoy using this exceptional power, which allows for applying the law easily from a foreign.[33] Therefore, Turkish judges could apply their theoretical background and adapt a civil code from a completely different culture into their national legal system where legislators failed to provide them with legislation governing a particular subject. After the foundation of the Turkish Republic accepting general rules and entitling judges with the possibility of becoming a lawmaker was a very efficient decision during the adoption of the civil code. In Turkey, the public confidence in judges made the process of adapting the new laws to Turkish society easier and made it more likely for such laws to be embraced by Turkish society.[34]

Lastly, at the time, there were many French-speaking academics and a number of Swiss-educated officials in higher positions of authority in Turkey tilting the scale toward the Swiss Civil Code.[35]

5 The Effects of the Law Adaptation Movement on Modernization

In this section, we seek to analyze some key aspects to understand how law adaptation has affected the modernization of Turkish society. What novelty has the Swiss Civil Code brought about? How and why did modern Turkish law differ from its historical law? What are some of the difficulties experienced while adopting and implementing this more modern law, and how were they overcome?

The steps taken toward modernization in the early years of the Republic were revolutionary and uncompromising. Since modernization essentially meant westernization, social transformation and the development of a new culture were inevitable. Hence, the Civil Code was not a law that aimed at reflecting the traditions of society. Instead, the Civil Code was expected to change these traditions.[36]

Given the key role of family in the structure of society, the most significant change was introduced in family law following the adoption of the Swiss Civil

---

[32] *Eugen Huber* who is the creator of the Swiss Civil Code was inspired by the works of François Gény, Méthode d'interprétation et sources en droit privé positif (1919). A judge's entitlement of acting as a legislator is based on the Gény's idea that a Code itself is not self-sufficient; François Gény, Méthode d'interprétation et sources en droit privé positif (1919), Von Overbeck, Louisiana L. Rev., 37, (1977–1977) (n.2) 685; Richard Groshut, The Free Scientific Search of François Gény, The American Journal of Jurisprudence 17 (1972), 16; Meunier (2014), (n.8), p. 356; Kadner Graziano (2013) (n.30), p. 698 fn.38; See also Duncan Kennedy/Marie Claire Belleau, François Gény aux Etats-Unis, in François Gény, Mythe et Réalités 1899–1999 Centenaire de Méthode d'Interprétation et Sources en Droit Privé Positif, Essai Critique, eds. Claude Thomasset, Jacques Vanderlinden & Philippe Jestaz, (2000).

[33] Akipek (1973), p. 59.

[34] Elbir (1953–1955), p. 282–303; Baysal (2016), p. 37.

[35] Ataay (1978), p. 71; Atamer (2008), p. 731.

[36] Üskül Engin (2014), p. 33.

Code.[37] Among the key novelties were official marriages, monogamy, relative equality between spouses, the right to request a divorce being granted to both parties, legal regulations concerning illegitimate children, and paternity regulations. These changes were accompanied by a host of other important developments, such as the right of inheritance of women and girls, the land registry and the principle of publicity, the protection of personal rights, and the family name, which have been adopted by way of the new Turkish Civil Code.

The most distinctive difference between historical and modern laws is in relation to marital property. The Turkish Civil Code stipulates three different property regimes. Spouses may freely choose one of the three regimes during the marriage, yet the separation of estates is the default legal regime.[38] That the legal regime is separation of estates contributed to inequality and disadvantaged women, in particular, women with no income given that it was uncommon for women to participate in the labor force at the time. The Turkish Civil Code (1926) was amended by the new Civil Code in 2002. Since 2002, the regime of participation in acquired property has been the default legal matrimonial regime.

The Turkish Civil Code differs from the Swiss Civil Code with respect to separation and divorce. According to Turkish divorce law and legislation, a spouse cannot file for divorce as a result of their spouse committing adultery if he/she had forgiven his/her spouse's unfaithfulness. The forgiving party loses the right to file for divorce. The new Civil Code includes the same provision. On the other hand, divorce via abandonment is permitted. The absence of the spouse, abandonment, need not exceed two months. This difference originates from the Turkish social structure. In the Turkish family structure, the absence of the spouse is considered a strong indicator of the breakup of the spouses.[39]

Some changes arise from the close familial relationships in Turkish society. For example, first the Supreme Court and then the new Turkish Civil Code recognized the right of the parents as well as the grandparents to have a relationship with the child.[40] These differences provide Turkish civil law with an independent character. The interpretation and application of the Turkish Civil Code along with the broad discretion of the judge created deviations from the original Swiss laws. However, the exercise of discretion has limits that Turkish judges must respect.[41] Hence, Turkish civil law follows that of Switzerland in general.

Differences arose during the modernization in property law concerning different registration requirement periods. Continuous possession of land for a period of 20 years that is uncontested by any lawsuit allows the possessor of the title to acquire ownership via an extraordinary statute of limitations.

---

[37] Zwahlen (1973), p. 148–151; Lipsteinp (1956), p. 17–23.

[38] Krüger (1976), p. 287 ff. (300); Außerdem Velidedeoğlu (1959), p. 146.

[39] Zwahlen (1973), p. 175 ff.

[40] YİBK (Supreme Court Decision of Joint Chambers) November 18, 1959, M. no. 12/D. no. 29, OG 10482.

[41] Zwahlen (1976), p. 254.

6 Problems Faced During the Adaptation Process

The Swiss Civil Code was not translated *verbatim*; there were some minor divergences from the original law, and Cantonal Law was ruled out.[42] Some other significant differences in adaptation stem from the characteristics of Turkish society; however, these differences do not originate from Islamic Law. Instead, the objective was better adaptation of the civil code to the Turkish social structure.[43] However, the aim of this study is not to focus on all these differences but to emphasize the most significant ones.

It is common to experience some challenges during law adaptation processes. To begin with, translating a civil code written in a foreign language for a different culture and society is a challenging task. Problems arising from the adoption of these laws at the time are likely strong indicators for determining how successful the adaptation and modernization of such laws would be in the future. Initially, it took a long time to overcome translation problems and conflicts with existing doctrine and judgments. The Swiss Civil Code was translated from French, and its German copy was ignored, which resulted in concerns that many translations were wrong.[44] Nearly all of these problems were resolved by way of reference to Turkish doctrine and judicial decisions.[45] Turkish doctrinal scholars sought to correct the mixed and ambiguous terms via theological interpretation by paying special attention to the German language. Consequently, in preparing the New Civil Code adopted in 2002, the German law was also analyzed to prevent translation or interpretation problems that could have arisen.

Another complication resulting from the original translation of the Swiss Civil Code was that the Turkish translation of the laws included many Arabic and Persian words used at the time of adoption but removed from the Turkish language by the language reform during the 1930s. As a result, many such words became obsolete, and most Turkish society no longer understood the Turkish legal language, including the Civil Code. One reason for having chosen the Swiss Civil Code was comprehensibility, yet this advantage was lost in the years following its translation.[46] This was resolved by simplifying the legal language in the New Civil Code of 2002.

There is no doubt that there is a strong interaction between the structure of the family and the structure of society. While the family structure directly affects the structure of society, revolutionary changes in society also shape the family structure.[47] Compared to the other fields of private law, family law is the most affected by traditions, religion and general moral principles.[48] Family relationships, which have been shaped by traditions for decades, centuries, or millennia, cannot be entirely

---

[42] Tercier (1997), p. 7.

[43] Velidedeoğlu (1959), p. 141 f.

[44] Zwahlen (1973), p. 157.

[45] Tercier (1997), p. 7.

[46] Zwahlen (1973), p. 156.

[47] Üskül Engin (2014), p. 36.

[48] Gören-Ataysoy (1976), p. 263 ff.

transformed all at once simply by passing laws.[49] As a result, apart from the translation issues, the greatest challenge during the making of the Turkish Civil Code based on the Swiss Code was faced in the reform of family law. One such challenge is in the area of religious marriages. While Turkish Law forbids unmarried persons to marry in a religious ceremony, such marriages are particularly common in certain locations and may be considered an official marriage in the eyes of the local people.[50] The legal minimum age for marriage can be considered another controversial topic. The first law stipulated that the minimum age of marriage was 17. However, it was later reduced to 15 for women (and 14 by court order) since girls are traditionally married at an earlier age than 17 in certain locations. The New Civil Code alters the age of marriage to 17 for both sexes (16 by court order). These developments indicate that distinctions, which might have been historically necessary, are no longer relevant in the present.

Another problem at the time of the adaptation of laws arose from insufficient time and infrastructure regarding personal records and other technical aspects of implementing the laws in practice. The principle of publicity had been adopted, but challenges arose with respect to property law due to a lack of infrastructure to effectively facilitate public access to records. However, these problems were quickly addressed by modernizing the population registry and land registry systems.

7 Post-adaptation Period

The main difference between secular civil law and Islamic law is that the new law manages to progress with modern developments in social life. Many changes were made in 75 years between the adoption of the Turkish Civil Code and the New Turkish Civil Code, which entered into force in 2002. Some of these changes were made by the legislator, and some were made through constitutional court decisions.

The Turkish Civil Code of 1926 reflected the patriarchal understanding that was typical at the time. Over time, however, this civil code significantly changed the legal status of women and children who had no rights under Islamic Law and gave them an individual identity.[51] The status of the woman and the child born out of wedlock are relevant examples. While such issues in Turkish National Law are not parallel to the Swiss Law, they were resolved via reform laws and constitutional judicial decisions. While women's participation in the labor force depended on the consent of their husbands per the former Civil Code, the Constitutional Court has removed this requirement.[52] The Constitutional Court also annulled the provision

---

[49] Elbir (1953–1955), p. 286.

[50] Zwahlen (1973), p. 175.

[51] Serozan (1999), p. 752.

[52] Anayasa Mahkemesi (Constitutional Court) November 29, 1990, D. no. 30/31, OG 21272.

that constituted inequality for the inheritance right of a child born out of wedlock.[53] In 1990, legislators made a corrective decision to equalize the status of a child born in a marital union with a child born outside a marital union.[54]

After the adoption of the Civil Code of 1926, amendments to Turkish private law continued to be made, for instance, by Law 3444,[55] until 2002. As a result of this law, significant developments took place in the areas of personal protection, gender-related changes, and facilitation of divorce in addition to consensual divorce. Such changes, together with the changing society, created the need for a new law. Therefore, the New Civil Code that was prepared considering the changes in the Swiss Civil Code was adopted in 2002.

The Swiss Civil Code has influenced the New Civil Code, implying that Turkey has not departed from adopting laws from Western countries. The New Turkish Civil Code (2002) still has the same objective as the original Civil Code of 1926 to modernize the Turkish legal and social order. This ideal started with the Turkish Revolution and continues with the modernization of Turkish society.

In this framework, we conclude that the Western rules have been successful in Turkey. While some challenges were faced, they were resolved in time. We believe that the law adaptation process has had an excellent influence on the success of the Turkish Revolution. In line with this argument, Elbir introduced the Switzerland-Turkey sample as a successful example of model harmonization with European Law and noted that harmonization concerns could be addressed through this model in the 1950s.[56] The adaptation process demonstrated that it is possible to apply the same civil law rules to different cultures and societies. Harmonizing rules is certainly a challenging task, yet it can be successful. Furthermore, this tradition encourages law-makers and doctrinal scholars to overcome the harmonization problems in the process of Turkey's accession to the EU.

8   Conclusion

Law is an effective instrument to transform social structures despite the challenges that might be experienced in the process. The law adaptation movement that occurred after the Turkish revolution is an excellent example demonstrating how law can be used to transform a society. The Turkish Civil Code, adopted by translating the Swiss Civil Code in 1926, is based on the principle of secularism, reflects the world view of the new state and is the touchstone for the modernization of Turkish society. The main goal of the adoption of the civil code was to abandon Islam-oriented laws and ensure westernization through changes to the family structure.

---

[53] AYM (Constitutional Court) September 11, 1987, D. no.1/18. YİBK (Supreme Court Decision of Joint Chambers) February 2, 1997, M. no. 1996/1, D. no. 1997/1; Kılıçoğlu (2016), p. 1718.

[54] Law no. 3678, November 14, 1990.

[55] OG 12.05.1988, Nr. 19812

[56] Elbir (1953–1955), p. 297/298.

It is common to face resistance when a law is introduced to alter the structure of a conservative institution, such as the family. Traditions and social norms cannot be immediately eliminated merely by the passing of laws. However, after the adoption of the Civil Code, the adaptation of Turkish society to the law was and is remarkable. Notwithstanding the challenges encountered during the adaptation process, due mainly to the particular characteristics and traditions of Turkish society, we conclude that the overarching goal of the adoption of a civil code and Turkish society's adaptation to it has to a large extent been achieved.

References

Akipek JG (1973) Türk Medeni Kanunu V. I Ankara

Altan A (2015) Kanun Yapma Tekniği Açılış Konuşması. In: TBB Ankara, pp 11–20

Ataay A (1978) Neden İsviçre Medeni Kanunu. In: Medeni Kanun 50. Yıl Sempozyumu 1. Tebliğler. İÜMHE İstanbul, pp 59–72

Atamer YM (2008) Rezeption und Weiterentwicklung des Schweizerischen Zivilgesetzbuches in der Türkei. RabelsZ 72:723–754

Bakırcı F (2015) Yasa Yapma Sürecinin Hızlandırılması ve Sakıncaları. In: TBB Ankara, pp 21–62

Baysal B (2016) Lawmaking in Turkish Private Law. In: Basedow J, Fleischer H, Zimmermann R (eds) Legislators, Judges, and Professors. Mohr Siebeck, Tübingen, pp 20–32

Bozkurt ME (1944) Türk Medeni Kanunu Nasıl Hazırlandı? In: Medeni Kanunun XV. Yıldönümü İçin, Hrsg. İstanbul Üniversitesi Hukuk Fakültesi, İstanbul, pp 11–12

Elbir HK (1953–1955) L'expérience turque et le problème de l'unification du droit privé. Unification du droit, pp 282–303

Gören-Ataysoy Z (1976) Die Fortbildung rezipierten Rechts. ZSR 263

Kadner GT (2013) Is it Legitimate and Beneficial for Judges to Compare? European Review of Private Law 3, p 698 ff

Karayalçın Y (1957) Ticaret Hukuku Dersleri I, 2. Aufl., Ankara

Kılıçoğlu A (2016) Medeni Kanunumuzu Nasıl Değiştirdik. MÜHF Hukuk Araştırmaları Dergisi 22(3):1717–1757

Krüger H (1976) Fragen des Familienrechts: osmanisch-islamische Tradition versus Zivilgesetzbuch. ZSR, p 287 ff

Kubalı HN (1956) Les facteurs déterminant de la réception en Turquie et leur portée respective. Annales de la Faculté de Droit d'Istanbul 6:44–52

Lipstein K (1956) The Reception of Western Law in Turkey. Annales de la Faculté de Droit d'Istanbul 6:10–23

Meunier G (2014) Les travaux préparatoires from a French Perspective: Looking for the Spirit of the Law. RabelsZ 78:346–360

Mumcu A (1996) Siebzig Jahre westliches Recht in der Türkischen Republik: Eine rechtshistorische und aktuelle Bilanz in Westliches Recht in der Republik Türkei 70 Jahre nach der Gründung, Scholler, Heinrichs/Tellenbach, Silvia (Hrsg.) Baden-Baden

Örsten Esirgen S (2011) Osmanlı Devleti'nde Medeni Kanun Tartışmaları: Mecelle mi, Fransız Medeni Kanunu mu? Ankara Üniversitesi Osmanlı Tarihi Araştırma ve Uygulama Merkezi Dergisi (OTAM) 29:31–48

von Overbeck AE (1977) Some Observations on the Role of the Judge under the Swiss Civil Code. Louisiana Law Rev 37:681–700

Özcan MT (2002) Modernisation and Civil Law: The Adoption of the Turkish Civil Code and its Political Aspects. Annales de la Faculté de Droit d'Istanbul 51:166–176

Öztan B (1996) Türkisches Familienrecht nach 70 Jahren ZGB. In: Westliches Recht in der Republik Türkei 70 Jahre nach der Gründung, Scholler, Heinrichs/Tellenbach, Silvia (Hrsg.), Baden-Baden, p. 85 ff

Papachristos AC (1975) La réception des droits privés étrangers comme phénomène de sociologie juridique. Paris, 1975

Postacıoğlu İ (1956) Quelques observations sur la technique de réception des Codes étrangers à la lumière de l'expérience turque. Annales de la Faculté de Droit d'Istanbul, pp.63-74

Scholler H (1996) Vorwort. in: Westliches Recht in der Republik Türkei 70 Jahre nach der Gründung, Scholler, Heinrichs/Tellenbach, Silvia (Hrsg.), Baden-Baden, p. 1 ff

Serozan R (1999) Cumhuriyet ve Medeni Kanun. In: Cumhuriyetin 75. Yılı Armağanı, Hrsg. İstanbul Üniversitesi, İstanbul, pp 748–750

Tandoğan H (1965–1966) L'influence des codes occidentaux sur le droit privé turc, en particulier la reception du code civil suisse en Turquie. AÜHFD 1965–1966, pp 417–436

Tanör B (2020) Osmanlı-Türk Anayasal Gelişmeleri. YKY İstanbul

Teroier P (1997) La réception du droit civil suisse en Turquie. ZSR 1997, p 1 ff

Üskül Engin ZÖ (2014) Medeni Kanun ve Toplumsal Dönüşüm. In: 1. Türk Hukuk Tarihi Kongresi Bildirileri. Onikilevha İstanbul, pp 31–42

Velidedeoğlu HV (1944) İsviçre Medeni Kanunu Karşısında Türk Medeni Kanunu. Medeni Kanunun 15'inci Yıldönümü İçin Ed. İstanbul Üniversitesi Hukuk Fakültesi, pp 348–364

Velidedeoğlu HV (1959) Türk Medeni Hukuku Umumi Esaslar. 6. Ed., İstanbul

Zwahlen M (1973) Les écarts législatifs entre le droit civil turc et le droit civil suisse. ZSR, pp 141–186

Zwahlen M (1976) L'application en Turquie du Code civil reçu de la Suisse. ZSR, pp 249–264

Başak Baysal is Professor of Law and Dean of Faculty of Law at Kadir Has University that she joined in 2019. Previously, she was an Associate Professor, Faculty of Law, Istanbul University. She is member of the executive board of the International Association of Legal Science. She received her PhD in Civil Law from Istanbul University. Her research interests include contracts and torts, and her recent publications include "Influence du droit européen en Turquie et en Suisse, Journée Turco Suisse", VSIR 75, (with Werro/Heckendorn-Urscheler), Schultess, 2015 and "Tort Law", On Iki Levha Publishing, Istanbul, 2019.

Gizem Arslan is Assistant Professor of Law at Kadir Has University Faculty of Law, Department of Civil Law; previously Assistant Professor of Law, Vocational School of Justice at Bandirma Onyedi Eylül University. She was also a Lecturer (part-time) at Nisantasi University in 2019. She received her PhD in Civil Law from Istanbul University. Her doctoral thesis focuses on liability for abnormally dangerous activities in US law. As part of her doctoral work, she was a visiting scholar at St. Mary's University (Texas) in 2014. She was a member of the Istanbul Bar Association in 2004-2018. Her most recent publication is Phantom Risks and the Problem of Causation (2018) in the Journal of Social Sciences, Istanbul Commerce University.

The Perpetual French Codification

Michel Cannarsa

Abstract The bicentenary of the French *Code civil* at the beginning of the twenty-first century has fulfilled its symbolic function. In the wake of the bicentenary, the French legal community rose up to the challenge of perpetuating the *Code's* legacy. Major reforms have taken place, or are about to take place, in the field of private law: contract law, law of secured transactions, law of extracontractual liability, law of specific contracts… All these reforms aim to, among other things, restore the *Code civil* as the core of private law. This chapter provides a view on the recent codification process in France, highlighting its methods, actors and purposes through the most recent examples of reforms in private law. It also questions the capacity of the code to preserve its *rayonnement* on the entire system of private law and considers the various challenges posed by the pace of social, economic and technological evolution.

1 Introduction

What do we have in mind when we talk about codification? The meaning of codification seems simple at first sight but can obviously refer to various realities, depending on place and time factors, among others. The definition of codification could therefore be a good starting point when aiming to provide a portrait of codification in France in the twenty-first century. Of course, the aim is not simply to reiterate what has been said previously in much deeper, better and systematic ways[1] but to pay due tribute to a polysemic concept and to establish a more consistent approach toward the most recent examples of codification. For several centuries, the meaning of the term codification was very different from what it came to represent in nineteenth-century Western

---

[1] Codification is the subject of an extensive literature. See among many others: Beignier (1996); Cabrillac (2008); Catala (2004); Gazzaniga (1996); Halpérin (2003); Malapert (1861); Martin (2003); Oppetit (1998); Terré (1993); Zenati-Castaing (1998) (2011).

M. Cannarsa (✉)
Lyon catholic University, Place des Archives, 10, 69002 Lyon, France
e-mail: mcannarsa@univ-catholyon.fr

M. Graziadei and L. Zhang (eds.), *The Making of the Civil Codes*,
Ius Gentium: Comparative Perspectives on Law and Justice 104,
https://doi.org/10.1007/978-981-19-4993-7_5

Europe. By the second half of the twentieth century, it had also come to mean something quite distinct and may well be subjected to shifts in meaning in decades to come. Historically, codification represents a compilation of a vast number of disseminated statutes characterised by a relative consistency and systematicity. Codification has served as a political symbol of unification, prestige and power. It is an ongoing clean-up of old codes (recodification): a seemingly permanent process of "under construction". At the same time, however, the concept of codification is sufficiently universal and homogeneous to describe common realities, challenges and legislative policies, no matter the jurisdiction concerned. Most jurisdictions, especially within the civil law legal system, therefore face the same problems and share the same objectives when they tackle the issue of codification.

What is of interest at this stage in the evolution of legal orders, especially as far as the French legal order is concerned, is to ask different questions (and provide tentative answers) to grasp the reality of codification in previous years, in the current period and in the foreseeable future. The questions addressed in the following pages are aimed at shaping reflections on codification, with a view to drawing out the substance of the debate. In addition, recent, ongoing and forthcoming legislative reforms in the field of private law can shed helpful light on these reflections. They therefore serve to illustrate the different issues and questions raised throughout the chapter.

2   The Meaning of Codification (What Is Codification?)

The meaning of codification in France is not significantly different from that of other civil law jurisdictions. However, the well-known history of codification in France, magisterially embedded in the Napoleonic Codes of the early nineteenth century, leads to a consideration that codification in France indeed has different meanings. The codes and especially the *Code civil* are not only practical, didactical, legal and political realities but also a symbolic and almost mythological expression of French law. This symbolic narrative around the *Code civil* still resonates, despite it being only partially true even at the time when the *Code* was enacted. The "codification-compilation" dimension of the *Code* was indeed far from marginal, considering the historical existing legal substrate.[2] However, the Napoleonic codification was also a major shift compared to previous legislative and codification techniques.

The disparity between the narrative and reality seemed to widen throughout the 200 years of the codes' existence. In contrast to this narrative, quite early on and with increasing intensity, both the French courts and legal scholarship (though the *École de l'exégèse* expressed the very opposite approach) began shaping positive law

---

[2] Martin (2003) stresses the mythological dimension of the *Code civil*, considered as a rupture with the previous legal system, whereas it is a stage in a long maturation process (e.g., p. 214); Gazzaniga (1996) shows how customary law, royal ordinances, especially under the ministries of Colbert and D'Aguesseau but also in the philosophical thought of Voltaire, Diderot and Montesquieu, among others, provided the "raw material" and the method for the Napoleonic codifiers.

in different areas of private law through creative interpretation and adjustment—the older the *Code civil* became, the more courts had to create law. This was formally done on the basis of the *Code civil*. In practice, however, case law often went well beyond what the drafters of the code and the legislator set out in the relevant texts.

French private law has therefore been shaped in the past 200 years by a combination of case law, legislative reforms, and doctrinal ssytematization, leaving not just the *Code civil* but also the *Code de commerce*, merely a residual status in some areas of law. While this erosion process took place, a different codification movement developed, especially after the Second World War[3] and with growing intensity in the past 20–30 years.[4] It is obvious that what codification meant in the nineteenth century is quite different from what it means in the twentieth and twenty-first centuries. However, as we shall discuss below, the last five years in France have seen a renewed belief in and commitment toward systematicity and codification. The symbolic dimension, 200 years after the Napoleonic codes were enacted, is not absent, but in the first decades of the twenty-first century, there has indeed been a genuine effort by the legislator and legal scholarship to restore the lustre of the *Code civil*. This effort has been quite in contrast with the legislative activity of the last 20–30 years, where legislative inflation and codification-compilation have been at play.

Currently, the official database of French law (*Légifrance*) lists 75 different codes. It is therefore obvious that few of these codes represent anything more than a compilation of statutes and regulations. Focusing on codes having a particularly direct relationship with private law and commercial law, apart from the *Code civil* and Code of commerce, the insurance code, the consumer code, the construction and housing code, the financial and monetary code and the intellectual property code do indeed contain rules that will have an impact on the law of contracts, property law, the law of persons, tort law and law of secured transactions, just to name a few. However, apart from these, the majority of codes in the abovementioned *Légifrance* list deal with public law, administrative law and State-related activities, i.e., subjects that reflect, among others, the State's intervention in the economy. This is why the recent reforms of the law of contracts,[5] the law of secured transactions, bankruptcy law, the forthcoming reform of the law of torts, international private law[6] and specific contracts,[7] bring the codification or recodification process back to its symbolic core.

---

[3] A decree of 10th May 1948 (n° 48–800) established a public body in charge of codification and simplification of legislative and regulatory texts: *Commission supérieure chargée d'étudier la codification et la simplification des textes législatifs et réglementaires.*

[4] A new public body replaced the above mentioned *Commission supérieure chargée d'étudier la codification*: the *Commission supérieure de la codification* (Superior Commission for Codification), established by decree n° 89–647 of 12 September 1989.

[5] Amendment of the Civil Code by Ordinance n° 2016–131 of 10th February 2016 relating to the law of contract, the general regime of obligations and proof of obligations, entered into force on 1st October 2016, and was ratified by Act No. 2018–287 of 20th April 2018.

[6] Pailler (2021).

[7] Stoffel-Munck (2020).

3   The Objectives of Codification (Why Do We Codify?)

Any codification process has several objectives. A contradiction between these various objectives is not rare. There is indeed a need to balance conflicting interests (most of the time at least) with the perspective of reaching the proper solutions that will keep the members of a given society together. The objectives of a codification process will also vary in accordance with historical, (geo) political, economic and social circumstances.[8] The Napoleonic codification in France was certainly as much a political as a legal achievement. The five Napoleonic codes are still called the "*cinq grands Codes napoléoniens*"[9] and have the abovementioned almost mythological dimension and role. Napoléon has been one of the great legislators to whom History pays a legitimate tribute. As François Terré stated, "great legislators in history, [...], have also been great codifiers".[10] The codifications of the nineteenth century probably had higher philosophical and political objectives. To unify the State and the Nation around a code but also put an end to social unrest[11] were among the principal aims of the Napoleonic codification. In addition, for a long time, there existed the necessity to conciliate the evolving nature of law with the search for stability at certain points in history.[12] Regarding the philosophical impetus, the *Lumières* period, jusnaturalism and jusrationalism but also mathematical rationalism, paved the way for various codifications in Europe and eventually for legal positivism.[13] As Carbonnier perfectly stated, "codification is more than a multiplier of statutes: there is in it a spirit of a system, [...] an intention of political renewal, as well as the hope to suspend the course of history."[14]

From a technical point of view, codification is also a remedy against dispersed legislation and is therefore the expression of a rationalization effort.[15] This indeed appears to be the prevalent dimension of codification.[16] Due to the current inflation of legislative texts, this technical objective (which also has a political dimension, considering the need and obligation to make the law accessible) seems to have gotten the upper hand over the more philosophical, theoretical and political objectives[17] and led to a reflux of the idea of codification in the second half of the twentieth century, especially as far as economic life is concerned.[18] This phenomenon puts the holistic dimension of the system at risk and produces many different subsystems,

---

[8] Terré (1993), p. 33.

[9] See ministerial circular of 30th May 1996 on codification of legislative and regulatory statutes, Official Journal n° 129 of 5th June 1996.

[10] Terré (1993), p. 33.

[11] Oppetit (1998), p. 11.

[12] Terré (1993), p. 32.

[13] Ibid., p. 35.

[14] Our translation, quoted in Oppetit (1998), p. 9.

[15] Ibid., p. 12; see also p. 55, quoting Vanderlinden (1967).

[16] Ibid., p. 58.

[17] Ibid., p. 12.

[18] Ibid.

thus undermining the idea of a common law (*droit commun*). It is due in part to the antagonism between sectorial interests and their temptation to emancipate themselves from the general legal order (and from the law itself), which seems to characterise contemporary societies and markets.[19]

Governmental authorities have also been concerned with the necessity to pursue the principle "ignorance of law is no excuse" ("*nul n'est censé ignorer la loi*"), which requires the enabling of citizens to better understand their rights and obligations. For example, a 1996 ministerial circular reiterated these objectives, pertaining to the general issue of accessibility and intelligibility of the law.[20] Hence, codification is seen as the best way to collect the various legislative and regulatory rules applying to a given area of social and/or economic life, with the objective of organizing said rules in the most systematic and consistent manner. Simplification and correction of certain codified provisions will generally complement this "compilation-codification" process with a view to making the law more accessible to both citizens and economic operators and rendering it simpler and clearer. Beyond these practical effects also lies one of the conditions of adherence to the rules and to the social pact. The current French draft for the reform of extracontractual liability is an illustration of the attempt to reinforce accessibility and legal certainty in a legal area where most positive law is based on case law.[21]

The attractiveness of the legal order is also a key concern for governments and legislators. Attractivity supposedly measures itself in economic but also in political and cultural terms. By assessing legal systems in terms of economic efficiency and by downgrading civil law systems, the World Bank's "Doing Business" reports were perceived as a provocation, if not a declaration of legal war, by a significant part of French legal academia and beyond.[22] The 2016 reform of the law of contracts offers a good example of a response aiming to counteract the lost attractivity of French law. Indeed, the report to the French President accompanying the 2016 ordinance reforming the law of contract leaves no doubt in this regard.[23] This is how, for

---

[19] Ibid., p. 13.

[20] See fn 9. It was followed by a similar circular dated 27th March 2013. Between the two circulars, around twenty codes have been adopted and nine codes have been "recodified", including the *Code du commerce* and the *Code du travail*. In the 2013 circular, the then Prime Minister stated that approximately 60% of laws had been codified alongside 30% of regulatory texts. It is worth remembering that the objective of clarity and intelligibility has constitutional value: see *Conseil constitutionnel*, decision of 16th December 1999, n° 99–421 DC, Official Journal, of 22nd December 1999 and *Conseil constitutionnel*, decision of 26th June 2003, n° 2003–473 DC, Official Journal, of 3rd July 2003.

[21] See report n° 663 of 22nd July 2020 by senators Jacques Bigot and André Reichardt on extracontractual liability and the draft bill n° 678, presented before the Senate on 29th July, 2020.

[22] Association Henri Capitant (2006), Les droits de tradition civiliste en question—A propos des Rapports Doing Business de la Banque Mondiale (Vol. 1 and 2). Société de Législation Comparée, Paris.

[23] *Rapport au Président de la République relatif à l'ordonnance n° 2016–131 du 10 février 2016 portant réforme du droit des contrats, du régime général et de la preuve des obligations*, Official Journal n° 0035 of 11 February 2016: https://www.legifrance.gouv.fr/jorf/id/JORFTEXT0000320 04539: "[...] the international stakes of such a reform of French law are economic: the "Doing

example, the historical notion of *cause* was removed from the new version of the *Code civil*, the legislator considering that said notion was insufficiently defined and therefore a source of legal uncertainty.[24] For the same reason, the scope of application of the newly introduced control of unfair contractual terms in the *Code civil* has been limited to preformulated standard contracts.[25] Even if the protection of weak contractual parties and contractual fairness were also invoked by the legislator in the aforementioned reform, (economic) attractivity was most certainly prevalent. The same rationale applies to the very recent reform of the law of secured transactions[26] and of bankruptcy law,[27] as indicated in the reports accompanying the ordinances.[28] In both reforms, the objective of reinforcing the efficiency and attractivity of French law in terms of international investments is clearly stated. More precisely, the reform of the law of secured transactions aims to not only increase both the efficiency and legal certainty of proprietary securities but also to simplify and modernise rules on the contracts of guarantee and on the assignment of claims, not just in the *Code civil* but also in the *Code de commerce* and the monetary and financial code. All these aspects of this reform share increased attractiveness of French law as their objective.[29]

The influence of international law also assigns further objectives to codification. The obligation to place legal orders in conformity with international law, especially EU law, as well as to conform with the decisions of superior courts (the European Court of Human Rights and the Court of Justice of the European Union) is a major drive for change (and apparently, increasingly, a source of national debate). During the process of reform of the law of contract, the various European projects of harmonization of private law, as well as comparative studies, have played quite a significant role in inspiring the drafters of the reforming ordinance.[30] The transposition of EU

Business" reports published by the World Bank, which regularly put forward common law legal systems, have contributed to the development of the image of a complex, unpredictable and unattractive French law. In this context, a more readable and predictable law of contract, with a focus on simple drafting and a clearer and a more didactic presentation, is likely to attract foreign investors and operators wishing to connect their contracts to French law".

[24] Ibid. The aforementioned notion has been replaced by "*contrepartie*", in article 1169 of the *Code civil*: "[a]n onerous contract is a nullity where at the moment of its formation, what is agreed in return for the benefit of the person undertaking an obligation is illusory or derisory." For a critical perspective on the removal of the "*cause*", see Chénedé (2016), pp. 85–87; Wicker (2020).

[25] Ibid.

[26] Ordinance n° 2021–1192 of 15th September 2021 *portant réforme du droit des sûretés*.

[27] Ordinance n° 2021–1193 of 15th September 2021 *portant modification du livre VI du code de commerce*.

[28] *Rapport au Président de la République relatif à l'ordonnance n° 2021–1192 du 15 septembre 2021 portant réforme du droit des sûretés*, Official Journal n° 0216 of 16 September 2021, and *Rapport au Président de la République relatif à l'ordonnance n° 2021–1193 du 15 septembre 2021 portant modification du livre VI du code de commerce*, Official Journal n° 0216 of 16 September 2021.

[29] See the report on ordinance n° 2021–1192.

[30] See *Rapport au Président de la République relatif à l'ordonnance n° 2016–131 du 10 février 2016 portant réforme du droit des contrats, du régime général et de la preuve des obligations,*

directives impacting private law can quite often be a challenge when the national legislator wishes to preserve the coherence of the national legal framework as much as possible. For example, the French consumer code underwent a recodification in 2016,[31] less than 20 years after it entered into application[32] to make its structure more accessible, to harmonise its content and to preserve its accessibility.[33] Being mostly the law of the single market, EU law can reinforce the impression that the efficiency of the legal order is increasingly the driver of codification and/or recodification, leaving national legislators with a residual scope of intervention.

In other areas of private law, namely, the law of persons and family law, the objectives of codification and recodification are naturally different from those in the areas of contract and specific contracts, extracontractual liability, commercial law, etc. The protection of the individual, freedom of choice, equality between men and women, equality between children, nondiscrimination on sexual grounds, etc., are increasingly predominant in the numerous reforms of the *Code civil* in the past 50 years. Moreover, as we will discuss later, the national legislator generally has more leverage in these areas. Indeed, in principle, these societal reforms do not have significant economic impacts. The aforementioned reforms are therefore somewhat easier to adopt and have contributed to maintaining the *Code civil* up-to-date in these areas. In addition, because these legal areas are generally outside the scope of EU competences, national legal sovereignty can express itself with far fewer constraints.

4   The Drafters of Codification (Who Is the Codifier?)

Sooner or later, the codifier is of course the legislator. The codifying process, however, generally involves many different stakeholders, and parliament does not necessarily play a major role, nor is it involved at all stages of the process. As previously mentioned, a *Commission supérieure chargée d'étudier la codification et la simplification des textes législatifs et réglementaires* (Higher Commission responsible for studying the codification and simplification of legislative and regulatory texts) was established in 1948 and then replaced in 1989 by the *Commission supérieure de la codification* (Higher Commission on Codification).[34] This administrative body is under the Prime Minister and is in charge of planning codification priorities. It establishes codification methodology in an annual report and coordinates the various

---

mentioning the Unidroit principles, the PECL, the Gandolfi code, the DCFR and the comparative studies by the *Société de législation comparée* and the *Association Henri Capitant*.

[31] Ordinance n° 2016–301 of 14th March 2016 *relative à la partie législative du code de la consommation*.

[32] Act n° 93–949 of 26th July 1993 *relative au code de la consommation (partie Législative)*.

[33] *Rapport au Président de la République relatif à l'ordonnance n° 2016–301 du 14 mars 2016 relative à la partie législative du code de la consommation*, Official Journal n° 0064 of 16 March 2016.

[34] https://www.gouvernement.fr/commission-superieure-de-codification.

ministries' services in charge of drafting new codes. It also has a consultative function when existing codes are under a modification process. The existence of the aforementioned commission and the number of existing codes confirms that codifying remains a priority of French governments and that they have been relatively successful in achieving this result. This approach has a bureaucratic dimension, which is sometimes criticized.[35] For example, the reform of the law of contract was mainly written by the so-called *Bureau du droit des obligations* of the Ministry of Justice, whose composition and functioning were not particularly transparent at the time of drafting. In addition, the Ministry of Justice is sometimes challenged in its initiative and drafting competences by other ministries, particularly the Ministry of Finance and Economy.

Various would-be codifiers generally compete to have their say in the drafting of a code or in updating old codes that will eventually be reissued, thus demonstrating competition among different law providers. In fact, most codifications are the assemblage of many different contributions. Legal scholarship has played a central role in past codifications, both upstream by providing a systematic and didactic formalisation of positive law and downstream by drafting codes' proposals. In the aftermath of the Second World War, several highly regarded legal academics authored major reforms of the *Code civil*. Jean Carbonnier had a long and substantial influence on various reforms dealing with family law and the law of persons.[36] The recent reform of the law of contract saw the involvement of a number of academics who, at the beginning of the 2000s, took part in research groups under the lead of Pierre Catala and François Terré. These two groups released reform proposals of the law of obligations that paved the way for the 2016 reform of contract law. The more recent reforms of the law of secured transactions and the proposed reforms of the law of specific contracts (and property law) are considered closely connected to draft reforms prepared by different academic groups within the *Association Henri Capitant*.[37] The involvement of academics is sometimes at the express request of the Ministry of Justice.[38]

On another note, the past two decades have seen successive governments taking increased control over the recodification process. The French Constitution allows the government to adopt ordinances in matters of legislative competence.[39] The advantage of this legislative procedure is of course that it is faster than the parliamentary one, the latter requiring a series of debates and votes by the two chambers of the parliament. The ordinance procedure, once the enabling law (*loi d'habilitation*) has been adopted, gives the government ample freedom to draft the new rules. Once the

---

[35] Terré (1993), p. 44.

[36] See, e.g., Rude-Antoine (2007).

[37] Revet (2020). For example, Michel Grimaldi (for the law of secured transactions) and Jérôme Huet (for the law of specific contracts) have chaired groups within the association that drafted the aforementioned proposals.

[38] Stoffel-Munck (2020), indicating that he has been appointed as the chairman of the commission in charge to draft the reform of the law of specific contracts.

[39] Article 38 of the Constitution.

ordinance is adopted, it can enter into force almost immediately, without even waiting for the ratification act (*loi de ratification*). The government has made extensive use of the ordinance procedure in recent years. This is how the reforms of consumer law, the law of contract and the law of secured transactions were adopted. This faster procedure is an increasingly useful tool to meet the implementation deadlines of the numerous EU directives into national law. However, for such important aspects of private law, such as the law of contract, the law of extracontractual liability, the law of specific contracts, etc., parliament has encountered increasing difficulties in accepting being deprived of its role as the main lawmaker. The reform of the law of contract is a good example of this phenomenon; the Senate "took back control" of its law-making power at the ratification stage, with significant amendments and extensive debates over the proposed legislation. Moreover, considering the political reactions of the past years, the government committed itself to preserving parliament's initiative for the next round of reforms, in particular the one pertaining to extracontractual liability.

In an increasing number of areas, legislative competence is no longer an exclusively national competence. The competence of the EU, especially within the framework of the completion and functioning of the single market, is extensive. The fact that the single market is also becoming a digital single market has had a multiplier effect on the EU's aforementioned sphere of competence. The law of persons, family law and property law are outside of the direct competence of the EU,[40] which does not imply, however, that national legislators are completely free to exercise their national prerogatives. Indeed, if a domestic regulation constitutes a (disproportionate) barrier to one of the freedoms of the single market, then it might have to be put in conformity. However, beyond these rather preserved legal areas, as everyone knows, consumer law, contract law, extracontractual liability, company law, commercial law, insurance law, competition law, etc., have been, and continue to be, hugely influenced and impacted by rules of EU origin. This means that the drafter of significant parts of private law (and their correspondent articles in various codes) is the EU legislator (usually the Council of the EU and the EU Parliament, on the basis of the ordinary legislative procedure). This chapter is of course not the proper place to discuss the EU legislative process, the influence of Member States within it, or its democratic functioning. Let us simply stress the fact that the transposition of EU directives (or, increasingly, the direct application of EU treaties, the EU Charter of Fundamental Rights and EU regulations) makes the task of keeping the various elements of a

---

[40] The same legal areas are, however, closely connected with the rights and freedoms of the European Convention on Human Rights and are therefore quite often subject to decisions of the European Court of Human Rights. This sometimes leads to legislative reforms in order to put national law in conformity with its decisions. For example, in a case about the difference between "legitimate" children and children of adulterous unions, leading to a difference in treatment of an adulterine child in the division of the estate (resulting from the old version of articles 759 and 760 of the *Code civil*), the European Court of Human Rights ruled in the *Mazurek* decision of 1st February 2000 that French law was in breach of article 1 of Protocol No.1 and article 14 of the convention. The concerned articles of the *Code civil* were consequently modified in the aftermath of the decision.

national legal system together even harder and is probably inherent to the fact that national and EU legal orders are intertwined.

The number of would-be codifiers also creates an emulative context and therefore competition among them. As courts are, to a certain extent, "daily codifiers", codification is also the opportunity for the legislator (but also for academia) to restore everyone's status and place as lawmakers in the legal system. There are several examples in French private law where most applicable positive legal rules are based on the decisions of the *Cour de cassation*. The law of extracontractual liability is probably the most obvious one. The situation could hardly be different considering the 200 or more years of existence of the *Code civil*. This phenomenon is an invitation to reflect on the possibly limited relevance and effects of codification, as there appears to be an inevitable "programmed obsolescence" of codes. This "programmed obsolescence" is reinforced by the speed of socioeconomic transformation in recent years, especially considering the various paradigmatic shifts that technologies have produced.

5   The Content of Codification (What Do We Codify?).

As previously mentioned, France is particularly keen on codifying as much as possible. There are currently 75 codes (even if some of them are redundant) in the official electronic database *Légifrance*,[41] including 30 abrogated codes. A total of 26 of the codes in force are relatively recent, as they entered into force in the twenty-first century. Most of these codes do not deal directly with private law. However, approximately a dozen of them can fairly be considered to remain, with varying degrees of distance, within the gravitational force of the *Code civil*. As a result, through efforts to maintain the *Code civil* as the shining star of private law, its *droit commun* (common law) progressively grows in intensity. The reform agenda of the past 20 years (dealing with the law of contract, law of secured transactions, law of prescription, consumer law, etc.) has in large part been focused on the preservation of the integrity of the *Code civil* and of its "magnetic force".[42]

Leaving aside the many codes without a significant impact on private law, the codification and revision/recodification agenda is determined according to multiple factors. The previously mentioned *Commission supérieure de la codification* is in charge, with the supervision of the Prime Minister, to define the agenda. The excessive dissemination of sources of law, as well as the risk for the system's coherence, the lack of intelligibility and accessibility and the other objectives detailed in the previous paragraphs, provide the criteria for identifying the content of codification. Depending on the importance given to one particular objective as opposed to another, the legislator will focus on certain areas with priority.

---

[41] https://www.legifrance.gouv.fr/liste/code?etatTexte=VIGUEUR&page=1#code.
[42] Revet (2020).

Substantial family law and law persons, as previously mentioned, are in the (almost) free hands of the national legislator, even though these areas increasingly come under the influence of (supranational) fundamental rights.[43] Moreover, updating these parts of private law, which reflect society's evolution, its morals, and its political orientation, cannot be left to case law without significant difficulties. Hence, the number of reforms in these areas is rather high. Starting in the 1960s, a non-exhaustive list gathers together laws on matrimonial regimes,[44] parental authority,[45] divorce,[46] bioethics,[47] succession rights,[48] family name,[49] filiation[50] and same-sex marriage.[51] Needless to say, all these reforms have extensively modified the first book (of persons) of the *Code civil*.

5.1 Law of Contract

In contrast, until recently, the law of contract and of extracontractual liability have proved to be somewhat immune from textual reforms, whereas their substance has been heavily modified and extended by courts over the 200 years following the adoption of the *Code civil*. After the 2016 reform of the law of contract, the third book (*Des différentes manières dont on acquiert la propriété*—"Different Ways to Acquire Property") of the *Code* has been largely reshaped in its structure and content, especially Title III (*Des sources des obligations* -"Sources of Obligations"). While most of the reform has been dedicated to the integration into the *Code civil* of existing solutions based on case law[52] and to their didactic presentation, contractual fairness objectives have pushed some rules beyond their pre-existing scope of application.[53] True innovations were also introduced, some of which are mentioned in

---

[43] Cayrol (2020), speaks of *"fondamentalisation"* of civil law.

[44] Law n° 65–570 of 13th July 1965 *portant réforme des régimes matrimoniaux*.

[45] Law n° 70–459 of 4th June 1970 *relative à l'autorité parentale*.

[46] Law n° 75–617 of 11th July 1975 *portant réforme du divorce*, revised by Law n° 2004–439 of 26 May 2004 *relative au divorce*, revised by Law n° 2016–1547 of 18 November 2016 *de modernisation de la justice du XXIe siècle*.

[47] Law n° 94–653 of 29th July 1994 *relative au respect du corps humain*, revised recently by Law n° 2021–1017 of 2 August 2021 *relative à la bioéthique*.

[48] Law n° 2001–1135 of 3rd December 2001 *relative aux droits du conjoint survivant et des enfants adultérins et modernisant diverses dispositions de droit successoral*.

[49] Law n° 2002–304 of 4th March 2002 *relative au nom de famille*.

[50] Ordinance n° 2005–759 of 4th July 2005 *portant réforme de la filiation*.

[51] Law n° 2013–404 of 17th May 2013 *ouvrant le mariage aux couples de personnes de même sexe*.

[52] For example, the duty to inform within the contract formation phase has been codified in art. 1112–1 of the *Code civil*, reflecting the case law of the *Cour de cassation* and extending the duty of good faith to the precontractual stage.

[53] See Chénedé (2016), pp. 28–30. See also, e.g., art. 1171 *Code civil*: "In standard contracts, any non-negotiable term, preformulated by one of the parties, which creates a significant imbalance in the rights and obligations of the parties to the contract is deemed not written. [...]."

the following examples. Article 1100–1 formally recognizes, for the first time, the category of unilateral juridical acts and therefore of unilateral legal commitments and submits them to the same rules as contracts.[54] The distinction between bespoke contracts and standard contracts is also formally stated in article 1110, which allows the application of specific protective provisions to the latter category.[55] Reception theory in the formation of contracts is also introduced[56] with the various preparatory contracts, as well as the consequences in case of breach, now regulated into the *Code*.[57] The sanction of economic duress, expressing the spirit of commutative justice, now completes the previous traditional definition of the term.[58] Hardship was eventually introduced as well by the 2016 reform and is one of its biggest innovations, going as far as to allow courts, on the request of a party, to revise the contract or put an end to it.[59] Assignments of contracts are also now possible on the basis of article 1216 and constitute a stand-alone category, different from the mere accumulation of assignment of claims.[60] The concept of contract suspension is also newly introduced in article 1220.

5.2   Law of Secured Transactions

Regarding the very recent reform of the law of secured transactions introduced by ordinance n° 2021–1192 of 15th September 2021, this latest amendment completes previous reforms in the field laid out in ordinance n° 2006–346 of 23rd March 2006, which focused mainly on contractual guarantees, and in law n° 2007–211 of 19 February 2007, which introduced the long-awaited *fiducie*—(trust) into French law.[61] The 2021 reform impacts approximately 220 articles of the *Code civil* and mainly deals with proprietary securities and contracts of guarantee, with a view to modernising them.

---

[54] "Juridical acts are manifestations of will intended to produce legal effects. They may be based on agreement or unilateral. As far as is appropriate, they are subject, both as to their validity and as to their effects, to the rules governing contracts."

[55] Article 1171 on non-negotiable terms and article 1190, which imports the *contra-proferentem* interpretation rule in standard contracts from the consumer code into the *Code civil*: "[in] case of ambiguity, a bespoke contract is interpreted against the creditor and in favor of the debtor, and a standard-form contract is interpreted against the person who put it forward."

[56] Article 1121: "[a] contract is concluded as soon as the acceptance reaches the offeror. It is deemed to be concluded at the place where the acceptance has arrived."

[57] See article 1123 on pre-emption agreements and 1124 on unilateral promises (note: bilateral promises are left out).

[58] See article 1143: "[t]here is also duress where one contracting party exploits the other's state of dependence toward him and obtains an undertaking to which the latter would not have agreed in the absence of such constraint, and gains from it a manifestly excessive advantage."

[59] Article 1195 *Code civil*.

[60] Chénedé (2016), pp. 169 ff.

[61] Barrière (2013).

Proprietary securities were not in the scope of the 2006 reform, making their modernisation a strategic objective of the actual reform. The 2021 reform therefore deals mainly with the aforementioned legal proprietary securities and removes obsolete chattel privileges while reinforcing the pledge of claims and property as security.[62] The reform also provides, in article 2323 of the *Code*, for a theory of proprietary securities, which thus far was omitted.[63] Indeed, it encompasses not only traditional securities, based on a preferential right but also proprietary-based securities granting an exclusive right to the creditor.[64] Article 2325 clarifies that a proprietary security for a third party has a proprietary nature and not a personal one.[65]

More generally speaking, proprietary securities are at the core of the September 2021 reform through the improvement of the security function of *fiducie*[66] and the recognition of the security function of assignment of claims[67] on one side and assignment of a sum of money on the other.[68]

Apart from the proprietary securities, the new version of article 2288 of the *Code civil* provides a new definition of the contract of guarantee. It is, however, new only on a formal level, as the substance of the notion remains unchanged.[69] A number of innovations are proposed in the introduction of the "subcontract" of guarantee at article 2291–1,[70] and of a new article 2297 concerning the most awaited reform of the written mention requirement on the contract of guarantee.[71] From the perspective of codification, it is worth mentioning that this requirement was previously addressed in the consumer code.[72] With the objective of reinforcing the status of the *Code civil* as

---

[62] Simler, Delebecque (2021), p. 5.

[63] Pellier (2021a, b), p. 30.

[64] Ibid.

[65] Ibid., p. 31.

[66] *Fiducie* as a security is modernised through a reduction of its formalism (the requirement of an estimate of the value of the property transmitted is no longer necessary and the fiduciaire/trustee may now sell the property given in *fiducie* at a price different from that set by the expert if a sale at that price is not possible, even though the requirement of an expert's report is maintained in order to ensure the protection of the settlor). It is also improved through the possibility to secure a future claim, as it is the case for the other *in rem* securities.

[67] See new articles 2373 ff of the *Code civil*. Article 2373 states that: "[o]wnership of a claim may be assigned as security for an obligation by virtue of a contract concluded under articles 1321 to 1326."

[68] Pellier (2021a, b) La propriété, p. 53. Article 2374 now states that: "[t]he ownership of a sum of money, either in euros or in another currency, may be assigned as security for one or more present or future claims."

[69] Simler (2021), p. 9.

[70] "A subcontract of guaranty is a contract by which a person undertakes to pay the guarantor what the debtor may owe him under the contract of guaranty."

[71] "Subject to nullity of his commitment, the natural person guarantor shall himself indicate that he undertakes as guarantor to pay to the creditor what he is owed by the debtor in the event of the latter's default, up to an amount in principal and accessories expressed in words and figures. In the event of a difference, the guarantee is valid for the amount written out in full." Simler (2021), p. 11.

[72] Articles L. 314–15 and L. 341–5-1 consumer code. The said articles are therefore abrogated.

the common private law, the written requirement is now stated in the *Code*.[73] Pursuant to the new article 2297, every natural person stipulating a contract of guarantee has to formally, through a written mention on the contract, approve the guarantee,[74] even if, and that is one of the major changes, the formalism applicable to the mention is relaxed.[75] Last, the new article 2298 of the *Code civil* is considered, as far as contracts of guarantees are concerned, as the most important part of the reform. It allows the guarantor to oppose the creditor any exception that the debtor was entitled to, thus restoring the accessory dimension to the guarantee after a period of uncertainty in case law.[76]

5.3   Extra-Contractual Liability

While the original basis of extracontractual liability is individual fault and negligence, the theory of risk gained momentum at the end of the nineteenth century and inspired new regimes of liability for damages caused by things in custody. These new regimes were developed by courts on the thin basis of the five original articles of the *Code civil*. Almost one hundred years later, at the end of the twentieth century, courts added a general regime of liability for damages caused by others (based on the social risks created by specific activities requiring certain additional categories of persons to be catered for) to the special regimes of vicarious liability. The current rules of civil liability in France therefore depart significantly from their original setting in the 1804 version. The radical evolution of French extracontractual civil liability on the basis of court action made the French civil liability system one of the most victim-oriented. As far as personal injuries are concerned, their compensation is at the center of the civil liability system. Compensation has indeed been the main objective of French courts through a continuous extension of the scope of liability and by limiting as much as possible the role of fault as a condition to trigger liability and compensation.

To bring more legal certainty to the entire system of civil liability, codify existing rules based on case law and introduce modern solutions, the French Ministry of Justice released a draft reform bill on 13 March 2017,[77] which was inspired in part by previous academic projects.[78] To preserve the parliament's competences and

---

[73] It is worth mentioning that the same "centralization" effort has been made about the pledge, as the reform cancels many articles that were previously within the code of commerce and in different specific statutes, in order to gather most of the legal provisions dedicated to the pledge into the *Code civil*: see Séjean-Chazal (2021), pp. 40 ff.

[74] There is an extension of the scope of the mandatory written mention, whereas the consumer code applied only to specific categories of contracts or persons (specific loans and to business creditors).

[75] Simler (2021), p 13.

[76] Simler (2021), p 15.

[77] The Draft Reform Bill has been translated into English by S. Whittaker, in consultation with J.-S. Borghetti. The translation is available at: http://www.textes.justice.gouv.fr/art_pix/reform_bill_on_civil_liability_march_2017.pdf.

[78] Catala (2007); Terré (2011).

sensibility after the government-driven reform of the law of contract, a new draft bill was issued by the Senate in July 2020.[79] The draft mainly adopts solutions based on case law and is mostly a "*codification à droit constant*", i.e., a codification of existing rules. In certain areas, the new bill seeks to clarify the specific case law. Regarding the structure of the proposed legislation, a new general article (1243) establishes the principle of liability for damages caused by others while limiting this liability to the cases listed in the following articles. The aim of the limitative list is to exclude new causes of action that courts could "create". The proposed article 1244 also states that there can be no liability for damages caused by others, unless it is proven that the act causing harm is of such a nature as to trigger the liability of the person committing the act. This is consistent with the previous state of case law regarding employers' liability for the damages caused by their employees, but it revisits in a stricter sense the *Levert* decision of 10 May 2001 relating to parents' liability for damages caused by their children.[80]

The draft new article 1248 aims at clarifying preexisting case law in the field of employer liability for harm caused by employees, especially regarding the causes of exoneration of employer liability.[81] The aforementioned provision confirms the employer's strict liability for harm caused by the employee while providing a definition of the notion of "principal" (employer),[82] which until now resulted from individual courts decisions. Regarding parental liability for damages caused by their children, the reform states that parents will be responsible in thus far as they exercise parental authority (article 1245 of the draft reform bill includes all cases of responsibility for damages caused by the minor).[83] As such, it is important to emphasize

---

[79] *Proposition de loi portant réforme de la responsabilité civile*, n° 678 of 29th July 2020. Due to the current political setting, the conclusion of this legislative process is highly unlikely any time soon.

[80] Indeed, in this decision, the *Cour de cassation* held that a simple causal harmful act of the child was sufficient to trigger his/her parents' liability: decision of 10th May 2001, *Bulletin des arrêts des chambres civiles* 2001, II n° 96, p. 64.

[81] "An employer is liable strictly for harm caused by his employee. An employer is a person who has the power to give orders or instructions to his employee in relation to the performance of his functions.

In the case of transfer of the relationship of employment, this liability is borne by the beneficiary of the transfer.

An employer or a beneficiary of such a transfer is not liable if he proves that the employee acted outside the functions for which he was employed, without authorisation and for purposes alien to his attributions. Nor is he liable if he establishes collusion between his employee and the victim.

An employee is not subject to any personal liability except in the case of intentional fault, or where without authorisation he acted for purposes alien to his attributions."

[82] It is stated that the principal is the one who has the power to give the agent orders or instructions in connection with the performance of his duties (draft art. 1248).

[83] "The following are liable strictly for the action of a minor:

– his parents, to the extent to which they exercise parental authority;
– his tutor or tutors, to the extent to which they are charged with care of the minor's person;
– the person charged by judicial or administrative decision with organizing and controlling the minor's way of life on a permanent basis. In these circumstances, the parents' and tutor's liability of such a minor cannot be engaged."

the removal of the previous condition of (legal) cohabitation with the minor. The removal of this condition certainly goes in favor of the victim who has a guarantee of compensation. Thus, and even in the event of parental separation, both parents will be jointly liable - the justification being that separation has in principle no effect on the joint exercise of parental authority.

In addition, the draft reform bill covers cases in which the minor is entrusted to another person by a judicial or administrative decision in addition to the legal situation of the tutor. In these cases, the liability of the parents cannot be engaged. All cases of liability for damages caused by the minor are strict liabilities, according to which an exemption will be possible only in case of a fault of the victim or in case of *force majeure*. In addition, the fault of victims not considered legally responsible (which can be understood as minors of a very young age or persons suffering from a temporary, or long-term, mental disorder at the time of the act) does not constitute a cause of exemption except when it assumes the characters of *force majeure*. In this sense, the preliminary draft is partly based on a well-established case law.[84] Concerning liability for damages caused by adults in custody, the proposed new articles 1246 and 1247 of the draft reform bill cover these two cases of liability distinguishing between permanent and intermittent custody, with different conditions and a different legal regime for these two situations.[85] In the case of a natural or legal person entrusted by an administrative or a judicial decision to organize and control the activity of other persons, the option is strict liability. Only the proof of a foreign cause (that is, fault of the victim, *force majeure* or action by a third person) can exonerate the liable person. Regarding persons who organize the activity of others on the basis of a contract, liability is based on fault, as it is possible to escape from liability by proving the absence of fault.

French extracontractual liability is in a situation of high complexity due to the significant extension of its original setting through the courts. It is also definitely oriented toward an objective of (almost) systematic compensation of victims of personal injuries. The downside of the actual situation is a lack of clarity and legal certainty, which certainly deserves to be fixed. The draft reform bill of civil liability would complete the 2016 reform of the law of contracts. However, one could also wonder whether the simple codification of existing case law would be sufficient to make French law of extracontractual civil liability able to face the challenges of new industrial and social risks, especially in the area of new technologies.

---

[84] Court of cassation, Plenary Assembly, 9th May 1984, *Bulletin des arrêts des chambres civiles* 1984, A.P. n° 2 and 3.

[85] "A person charged by judicial or administrative decision with organizing and controlling an adult's way of life on a permanent basis is liable strictly for the action of such an adult placed under their supervision" (draft article 1246); "Other persons who take on by contract, and by way of their business or profession, a task of supervision of another person or the organization and control of the activity of another person, are liable for the damages caused by the adult or child supervised unless they show that they did not commit any fault in their task." (Draft article 1247).

6   The Methods of Codification (How and How Much Do We Codify?)

It is a common understanding that codification refers to a rationalization and system-atization process (generally reflected in the code's substantive provisions but also in its structure) and that it should focus on broad principles[86] and rules[87] while preserving the flexibility of the legal order. Codification thus creates a system.[88] As Lawson stated, "there are often occasions when it is advantageous to sum up and simplify the law on a particular topic. [...] If the law on a topic is not capable of being set out as a series of general principles, there is no great point in trying to codify it. [...] If a code becomes old, like the French civil code, then, even if it is amended from time to time, it may ultimately produce a type of law which is not very different from a common law system",[89] and "all codes have aimed at some measure of abridgement, that is to say, the laying down of principles and rules of some breadth, and have omitted as far as possible the application of those rules or principles, leaving it to the interpretation of the commentators and courts."[90]

As Bruno Oppetit observes, a "doctrine of codification should be established, by defining its objectives and methods."[91] From that perspective, and due to the important number of codes in France, codification is at the same time a consistent and systematic organization of legal rules (e.g., the *Code civil*, *Code de commerce*, *Code pénal*, etc.), as well as a codification-compilation of otherwise dispersed provi-sions. As previously mentioned, the French *Commission supérieure de la codifica-tion* is responsible for drafting and implementing the codification agenda. Within this framework, the main method in the past 30 years has been the "*codification à droit constant*" (codification of established law), which nonetheless has allowed the clarifi-cation, modification and occasional renewal of existing rules (the reform of the law of contract being a good example from this perspective). The *Commission supérieure de la codification* has its own "doctrine" of codification and defines the drafting style ("légistique" and "codistique").[92] It stresses, for example, the importance of introductory parts ("titres liminaires" or "subdivisions chapeaux") of annexes (e.g., including sources of European and international law that the French legislator cannot codify in the core provisions of a specific code as it does not have the competence to repeal European and international legal rules). Moreover, an official *Guide de légistique*, drafted by the *Conseil d'État*, is regularly published and provides rules,

---

[86] Lawson (1960), p. 4, speaks of "super-eminent principles".

[87] Oppetit (1998), p. 37.

[88] Ibid., p. 23: "la codification vise à la mise en système des normes juridiques".

[89] Lawson (1960), pp. 5–6.

[90] Ibid., pp. 2–3, adding: "They have at the same time tried to state the rule or principle in such form that there should be little doubt of their interpretation."

[91] Oppetit (1998), p. 21: "il conviendrait d'esquisser une véritable doctrine de la codification, définissant ses objectifs et ses méthodes."

[92] See, e.g., Commission supérieure de codification, Annual Report 2019, p. 5.

principles and methods to be followed in drafting legislative texts.[93] All this can easily give the impression of a technocratic/bureaucratic approach, which has been duly criticized.[94]

According to Bruno Oppetit, the reluctance to codify in modern times can be attributed to the fact that legal norms are becoming more and more specific and less and less general and abstract[95] in large part because of a growing technocratic influence in governments and parliaments.[96] The EU origin of a significant number of legal norms tends to augment the phenomenon, as will the regulation of technologies, especially AI. From the perspective of codification, there seems to be a possible conflict between, on the one hand, relying on general and abstract rules, principles (e.g., good faith) and prescriptions, and drafting very technical and extensive regulations, on the other. Computerisation of legal norms and ever bigger and more efficient databases is possibly a way forward. It would also be a useful tool to identify inconsistencies between norms and codes on a continuous basis and therefore preserve the coherence of the legal order. It could, however, have a lasting impact on the style of legislative drafting. On the subject of electronic databases, the aforementioned *Légifrance* official database is certainly a very effective tool in terms of the accessibility of legal norms. One could even think of the progressive emergence of a legal "metaverse".

7   The Time and Place of Codification (When and Where to Codify?)

7.1   Time for Codification

Quoting Portalis, "the codes that govern peoples are created over time; however, in reality, we do not create them".[97] This expresses the idea of a continuous sedimentation process. According to François Terré, the frequency of codification is irregular and depends on the circumstances.[98] As stressed previously, some parts of the *Code civil* went unmodified for more than 200 years. However, the necessity to adapt the legal framework to the evolution of the ecosystem seems to have increased the pace of reforms dramatically, which is hardly compatible with the time needed for a proper codification or recodification.[99] The frantic pace of production of legal norms

---

[93] See the 3rd edition, published in 2017, especially pp. 109–115 regarding codification. The guide is available at: https://www.legifrance.gouv.fr/contenu/Media/Files/autour-de-la-loi/guide-de-legistique/guide-de-legistique-edition-2017-format-pdf.pdf.

[94] Terré (1993), p. 44.

[95] Oppetit (1998), pp. 33–34.

[96] Ibid., p. 25.

[97] Preliminary address on the first draft of the Civil Code, 21st January 1801.

[98] Terré (1993), p. 33.

[99] Oppetit (1998), p. 32.

at national and European levels leads to partial, sectorial and successive reforms[100] and makes it even harder to identify an opportune time for codification. Successful codification requires a certain harmony between the present, the past and the future, which is hard to attain.[101]

The past 30 years have been a period of intense codification and recodification. The 200th anniversary of the *Code civil* certainly played a symbolic part in the impetus behind legal reform in recent years. The German recodification and European harmonization projects have played their parts as well, provoking a notable "national awakening". One could, however, have the feeling that codes (and legal norms, generally speaking) are currently set for "premature obsolescence" and that codification can no longer represent what it has done for the last two centuries. Hence, the possible advent of permanent or perpetual codification.

7.2 Place for Codification

The question as to where legal norms should be codified can have a number of different meanings. First, as there is not one single code for private law, it is not always obvious where a specific norm should end up. There are indeed cases of concurring provisions in different codes, putting at risk the central position of the *Code civil* as the common law of the private law system. One example among others is the question of the exploitation of one contractual party dependence, which is a newly introduced provision in the *Code civil* (article 1143)[102] and a provision in the *Code de commerce* (article 420–2 & 2).[103] The duty to inform is another example considering that it is present not only in the *Code civil* (article 1112–1) but also, among others, in the consumer code (L. 111–1) and in specific contexts such as the insurance contract (article L132-5–2 imposing specific information duties for providers of life insurance contracts and capitalisation insurance contracts). Deciding where to codify a specific norm therefore has consequences not only in terms of the respective scope of application of different codes but also in terms of legal certainty and legal consistency.

A second question refers to the material dimension of codification: a code used to be a big red book (most of the time). The *Code civil* is published as a commented volume consisting of more than 3000 pages, with a new (relatively)[104] updated edition published every year. One could argue, however, that the "hardware" approach will

---

[100] Ibid.

[101] Terré (1993), p. 42.

[102] See fn 58.

[103] "The abuse by an undertaking or a group of undertakings of the state of economic dependence of a customer or supplier is also prohibited, if it is likely to affect the functioning or structure of competition. Such abuses may consist in particular of refusals to sell, tied sales, discriminatory practices as referred to in articles L. 442–1 to L. 442–3 or range agreements."

[104] For example, the 2022 edition of the *Code civil* by one of the main publishers was unable to include the new provisions deriving from the August 2021 Bioethics Law.

become obsolete, considering the growing interest in big databases into which AI-fuelled search tools might significantly transform the code into an "object". The codes may well become increasingly intangible, and their virtual version would most likely be better adapted to an ever-changing legal landscape. Smart programmes could also help in identifying inconsistencies and redundancies and correct them, possibly automatically. The concept of a code for a given legal and socioeconomic area corresponds, among others, to the idea that a single book (e.g., the *Code civil* or the *Code de commerce*) makes it easier to access the information contained in it. A "smart" legal design and efficient electronic versions and search tools would probably change the landscape and make the law more accessible and intelligible. The future location of codes will therefore be increasingly the world of electronic databases, and this may well have an impact on codification techniques and legal drafting.

A third question is about the right level of codification: subnational, national or international. Except for local exceptions (as in Alsace-Moselle or in some of the Overseas Territories), the national level in France is the only admissible level of codification, especially as far as private law is concerned. The national framework appears inherent to codification.[105] However, European legal integration can hardly be ignored, not only due to existing European pieces of legislation with a more or less direct impact on private law (e.g., 85/374/EEC directive on product liability, the unfair contract terms directive 93/13/EEC, the consumer rights directive 2011/83/EU, the consumer sales and guarantees directive 1999/44/EC, repealed and replaced by 2019/771/EU directive on certain aspects concerning contracts for the sale of goods, 2019/770/EU directive on certain aspects concerning contracts for the supply of digital content and digital services) but also considering the unfruitful attempts in the last 25 years to harmonise more significant parts of private law. The full harmonization approach, which represents the most recent trend in the EU legislative agenda, tends to accentuate the impact of EU legislation on national codes. In addition, EU legislative projects in the field of new technologies and AI (e.g., consumer protection in the digital age, platform regulation, liability of AI, etc.) is also likely to have a lasting and structural effect, possibly putting the future of national codes in jeopardy.

8 Conclusion

Contemporary reality is complex, making its legal regulation complex and, at the same time, ever more necessary. One could wonder whether codes, considering their long maturation process, are the right answer to complex questions and situations, even in the traditional area of private law. Codes certainly play a major (democratic) role in keeping the law accessible and comprehensible in a society characterized by ever-growing complexity. On a formal level, however, legal design in the twenty-first

---

[105] Oppetit (1998), p. 62.

century should be different from what it was 200 years ago and even before. The use of technological tools could certainly be increased to achieve a variety of results, such as the consistency of the entire legal framework and making the law simpler, clearer and more accessible to "ordinary" citizens.

The bicentenary of the French *Code civil* has played its symbolic function, and the French legal community rose up to the challenge of perpetuating the *Code*'s legacy. The significant efforts by legal scholars to offer modernised private law rules to the legislator deserve to be highlighted. These efforts enable the preservation of the consistency of the entire system of private law, with the *Code civil* remaining its center of gravity. However, it remains to be seen whether the various reforms of recent years will have a lasting effect. Indeed, several phenomena put the integrity of national legal orders at risk. A first phenomenon is the increasing international origin of legal norms, especially within the European legal order. While European legal integration has several positive sides, it tends also to jeopardise the traditional architecture of national private law. When European legislative action is combined with increasing technical regulation (as is the case with machinery, AI and other new technologies), the aforementioned effect on national private law is increased. This second phenomenon is just at its beginning and is certainly set to last. A third phenomenon, connected to the previous one, corresponds to the increasing attempts to emancipate technology from traditional legal systems and to create what we could call alternative legal "metaverses" (e.g., alternatives to traditional legal tools based on blockchain technologies). Parallel "techno-legal" orders may develop, undermining the capacity of traditional legal sources to shape social and economic relations.

Only time will tell whether the recent and upcoming didactic and modernising reforms will make the *Code civil* fit for the entire twenty-first century, or if the current period will be seen retrospectively as its swan song. Beyond the monument of the *Code civil*, what is at stake is a common law (*droit commun*), regardless of the legal order concerned. This objective has merited the broad commitment of the French legal community of the past years and certainly deserves the continuing and renewed commitment of future generations of lawyers, whatever the social, economic and technological landscapes will be.

References

Barbier H (2016) Les grands mouvements du droit commun des contrats après l'ordonnance du 10 février 2016. Revue trimestrielle de droit civil 247

Barbier H (2020) De l'articulation de l'article 1171 du code civil avec l'article L.442–1 du code de commerce. Revue trimestrielle de droit civil 375

Barrière F (2013) La fiducie. Répertoire de droit civil

Beignier B (1996) La codification. Dalloz, Paris

Cabrillac R (2008) La recodification en France. Editions universitaires d'Avignon, Avignon

Catala P (2004) Les techniques de codification: l'expérience française. Revue juridique de l'Océan Indien 77–84

Catala P (ed) (2007) Proposals for reform of the law of obligations and the law of prescription (trans: Cartwright J, Whittaker S) http://www.justice.gouv.fr/art_pix/rapportcatatla0905-anglais.pdf

Cayrol N (2020) Le droit civil aujourd'hui. Revue trimestrielle de droit civil 502

Chénédé F (2016) Le nouveau droit des obligations et des contrats. Dalloz, Paris

Fages B (2021) Droit des obligations. LGDJ, Paris

Gazzaniga J-L (1996) Le code avant le code. In: Beignier B (ed) La codification. Dalloz, Paris, pp 21–32

Halpérin J-L (2003) L'histoire de la fabrication du code : le Code Napoléon. Pouvoirs 107:1121

Lawson FH (1960) A Common Lawyer Looks at Codification. Inter-American Law Review II:1–6

Malapert (1861) Remarques historiques sur la codification. Revue critique de législation et de jurisprudence XIX:3–15

Martin X (2003) Mythologie du Code Napoléon. Aux soubassements de la France moderne. Dominique Martin Morin, Poitiers

Mignot M (2021) Le nantissement de créance. La Semaine Juridique 43–44:46–52

Oppetit B (1998) Essai sur la codification. Presses universitaires de France, Paris

Pailler L (2021) La codification du droit international privé français à l'heure européenne. La Semaine Juridique, Édition Notariale 25:1233–1235

Pellier J-D (2020) L'extension de la protection contre les clauses abusives. Revue des Contrats 4:75

Pellier J-D (2021a) Les dispositions générales relatives aux sûretés réelles. La Semaine Juridique 43–44:30–33

Pellier J-D (2021b) La propriété retenue ou cédée à titre de garantie. La Semaine Juridique 43–44:53–59

Revet T (2020) Droit Commun. Revue des Contrats 3:1

Rouvière F (2020) Qu'est-ce que le droit civil aujourd'hui ? Revue trimestrielle de droit civil 538

Rude-Antoine E (2007) Jean Carbonnier et la famille. Transformations sociales et droit civil. L'année Sociologique 57:527–543

Séjean-Chazal C (2021) Le gage du Code civil retrouve ses lettres de noblesse. La Semaine Juridique 43–44:40–45

Simler Ph (2021) Réforme du cautionnement. La Semaine Juridique 43–44:9–29

Simler Ph, Delebecque Ph (2021) La réforme des sûretés, enfin … La Semaine Juridique 43–44:3

Stoffel-Munck Ph (2020) La préparation d'une réforme des contrats spéciaux. Revue des Contrats 4:1

Terré F (1993) La codification. ERPL 1:31–46

Terré F (ed) (2011) Pour une réforme du droit de la responsabilité civile. LGDJ, Paris

Vanderlinden J (1967), Le concept de code en Europe occidentale du XIIIe au XIXe siècle: essai de définition. Éditions de l'Institut de sociologie, Bruxelles

Wicker G (2020) De la survie de la cause. Ébauche d'une théorie des motifs. Recueil Dalloz 1906

Zenati-Castaing F (1998) Les notions de code et de codification (contribution à la définition du droit écrit). In: Antonmattei P-H, Garello J, Atias C, Frison-Roche M-A (eds) Mélanges Christian Mouly. Litec, Paris, pp 217–253

Zenati-Castaing F (2011) L'avenir de la Codification. RIDC 2:355–384

Michel Cannarsa is Professor of Private Law and Dean of the Faculty of Law at Lyon Catholic University (UCLy). His areas of research are law and technology, international and European law, commercial law, comparative law, consumer law, law of obligations, and legal translation. His recent works have focused on the interaction between law and technology, contract, and products liability law, including, The Cambridge Handbook of Artificial Intelligence—Global Perspectives on Law and Ethics (Cambridge University Press, 2022, with L. DiMatteo and C. Poncibò), The Cambridge Handbook of Lawyering in the Digital Age (Cambridge University Press, 2021, with L. DiMatteo, M. Durovic, F. De Elizalde, A. Janssen and P. Ortolani), The Cambridge Handbook of Smart Contracts, Blockchain Technology and Digital Platforms (Cambridge University

Press, 2019), "Interpretation of Contracts and Smart Contracts: Smart Interpretation or Interpretation of Smart Contracts?", [2018] 26 European Review Private Law (2018), Issue 6, pp. 773–785, "Remedies and Damages," in « Chinese Contract Law, Civil and Common Law Perspectives », (L. DiMatteo and C. Lei, Cambridge University Press, 2017, pp. 377–403). He is a fellow of the European Law Institute, a member of UCLy Research Unit's Scientific Committee as well as of UCLy Vulnerability Research Group's Scientific Committee.

The Making, Meaning and Application of Civil Codes in the Netherlands

Emanuel G. D. van Dongen

Abstract The early Dutch codifications must be considered as a means to achieve unification. At the beginning of the unitary State, the latter claimed a monopoly on law making, and its laws became the only formal source of law. The next codification, the Dutch Civil Code of 1838, which was the product of the beliefs of the bourgeoisie class, led to a formalistic attitude of the courts and legal doctrine. Only in the early twentieth century did the primacy of law formation slowly shift from the legislature to the courts. Then, it became clear that the Dutch civil law codification was not unique and complete. However, law making by judges led to a lack of uniformity and legal certainty. A drafting process that started in 1947 led to a new Civil Code in 1992, which codified previous case law and solved the remaining lacunae and technical ambiguities. This code did not, however, have a constitutional, unifying role, nor did it lead to a fundamental change in practice. Due to its corrective mechanisms, such as open norms, future developments can be more easily dealt with, and courts are given free leeway in law making. Although this Civil Code is still the cornerstone of private law, actual law making, at least in tort law, is largely performed by the courts. The Code lacks the element of exclusiveness or completeness. In the long run, it is a question whether a national codification is the best way forward.

1 Introduction

The introduction of codifications is regarded as a major turning point in law: the period of *ius commune* ended, and various all-encompassing codifications came into existence.[1] Codifications were introduced in the Netherlands and abroad in various areas of law, including private law. They were promulgated by the government, which exercised authority over its subjects, and with exclusive force issued by that

---

[1] Zimmermann (2000, p. 1) and Milo et al. (2014, pp. 5–6).

E. G. D. van Dongen (✉)
Molengraaff Institute for Private Law, Utrecht University, Utrecht, The Netherlands
e-mail: E.G.D.vanDongen@uu.nl

© The Author(s), under exclusive license to Springer Nature Singapore Pte Ltd. 2023   89
M. Graziadei and L. Zhang (eds.), *The Making of the Civil Codes*,
Ius Gentium: Comparative Perspectives on Law and Justice 104,
https://doi.org/10.1007/978-981-19-4993-7_6

government.[2] The Dutch Civil Code (*Burgerlijk Wetboek*), like other codifications such as the French *Code Civil*, in addition to being a (more or less) exclusive source of law, is also a source of knowledge of the law and a systematic arrangement of the law. In specific cases, courts must decide not on the basis of judicial precedents but by applying and interpreting the Civil Code. However, the role of the judge as '*la bouche de la loi*', as formulated by Montesquieu in his *De l'Esprit des lois* (1748; if ever understood in that way), changed in the Netherlands following the establishment of this system. Although Dutch codifications still hold a central place in the Dutch legal system, for hundreds of years, judges have also begun making law.

To understand the making and meaning of codifications of private law in the Netherlands, this contribution will start with a discussion of Dutch codifications in the nineteenth century, including the role of legal sources and the three legal actors ('legal formants'[3]): the courts, the legislature and legal doctrine. Subsequently, the changing role of the courts, of case law and the codifications up to 1992 will be discussed, including legal formalism (*legisme*), the changed perception of the task of the courts in relation to 'law finding', legal reasoning, and the impact of European private law and fundamental rights. A key focus in this contribution will be the relationship between the legislature and the judiciary: the maker and the user of the Civil Code. The judiciary can regard its decisions as a form of dispute resolution but also as the creation of a legal norm, taking into consideration the implications of legal judgments for the (development of the) law. However, this is only possible when legal decisions are considered a source of law, so this issue will also be discussed. In discussions on the relationship between the legislature and the judiciary, the question of judicial activism is often raised, although this is not something that is easy to define. Multiple definitions can be found in the literature.[4] Activism is often contrasted with judicial restraint. Nevertheless, the term activism is sometimes used as a mask for a substantive position—the favored position being sound and the alternative position being 'activist'.[5] Therefore, because this term is so unclear and vague, it will be avoided where possible. The Urgenda case will be discussed further in the article, a case that has received much attention in the Netherlands and abroad. Finally, a conclusion will be provided on the (future) role of the Civil Code and the role of the judiciary in the Netherlands.

2 Dutch Nineteenth Century Codifications: The Dawning of a New Era

The story of Dutch codification projects begins immediately after the establishment of the Batavian Republic (in 1795). A codification movement emerged, and a committee

---

[2] Lokin and Zwalve (2014, p. 20).

[3] Sacco (1991, pp. 1–34).

[4] Waele (2009, pp. 45ff).

[5] Easterbrook (2002, p. 1401).

was installed in 1798 to put an end to the legal diversity left over from the *Ancien Régime*, known as the Committee of Twelve. Codification was considered a means to achieve unification, and the movement was not only a response to local diversity but also an expression of faith in the ordering power of rational thinking—the guiding principle of the Enlightenment.[6] The introduction of Codes in 1798 was the final act to complete the unitary State. The State thus claimed its monopoly on lawmaking, and its laws became the only formal source of law.[7] The political situation soon changed, however, when in 1806 a new kingdom was created by the Treaty of Paris. Louis Napoleon, the brother of the French emperor, became the King of Holland. On 1 May 1809, the Code Napoléon for the Kingdom of Holland (*Wetboek Napoleon ingerigt voor het Koningrijk Holland*) came into force. This Code was formally declared to be exclusive and brought about legal unity, not only as a practical instrument but also as a constitutional tool that was intended to forge the political identity of the new 'nation'.[8] This codification was based on the French *Code Civil* but adapted specifically to the Dutch situation by a committee of legal practitioners. The introduction of this Code led to a fundamental change in the practice of law: judges and lawyers now had to base their decisions on a provision in this Code, and it abolished all former law that was rooted in the Roman law tradition. Mandatory interpretation by law led to the disciplining of judges who were previously independent. At the same time, the doctrine was also dethroned from its position as the oracle of justice.[9] A transition to an exclusive, national codification occurred: the dawning of a new era.[10] However, this code had little practical significance, and legal doctrine hardly welcomed it either, which can be explained by the conservative attitude of legal scholars and practitioners. The new code was not in line with the spirit of the times; it was too different, too new, and worst of all not truly 'Roman'.[11]

Soon, however, on 1 March 1811, the French codes, including the Code Napoléon, came into force as a result of the annexation of the Netherlands by France. The exclusivity of the codifications, an important political and procedural function, also served to subject judges to the primacy of the law and to achieve legal unity and legal certainty. (Dutch) legal doctrine first only explained and, later, annotated the Code.[12] Following the defeat of Napoleon and the restoration of the Kingdom of the Netherlands of 1815, French codes continued to apply until the national Dutch codes had been constructed. Following the independence of Belgium in 1830, another codification in civil law was introduced in the Netherlands in 1838. The French Civil Code served as an important source for this new code, and thus continuity was assured. The new code was legally comprehensive and exclusive. Furthermore, it fit well within

---

[6] Grosheide (2010, p. 22).

[7] Jansen (2014, p. 21).

[8] Van den Berg (2014, pp. 48, 51, 69).

[9] Lokin (2010, pp. iv–v).

[10] Van Dievoet (1943, p. 3).

[11] Grosheide (2010, pp. 29–30).

[12] Brandsma (2010, p. 41).

the political-constitutional perspective of national unity and within philosophical and legal philosophical tendencies such as rationalization and universalisation.[13]

3   The Role of the Judiciary in the Nineteenth Century

Although the Dutch Constitution might currently resemble a judicially enforced constitution, it was originally a politically enforced constitution. The constitution originally features reluctance about any role for judges with respect to the enforcement of constitutional values.[14] The notion of division of powers was laid down in Article 115 of the Dutch Constitution of 1848, which states that laws are inviolable, i.e., the so-called prohibition to review the constitutionality of legislation (statute law). Previously, in the period between 1815 and 1848, formal laws were tested materially, which might lead to a denial of the binding force of legal provisions. The prohibition of constitutional review, introduced by the Constitution of 1848, thus represented a break with existing practice.[15] The display of judicial restraint shown by the prohibition of courts to review the constitutionality of legislation expresses a tradition of scepticism about the role of the courts in a democracy, originating from the post-French Revolution idea that 'a proper government demands a clear and rigid separation of powers'.[16] The French notion of separation of powers brought with it a modest role for the courts. British ideas on parliamentary sovereignty also influenced the notion of the prohibition of judicial constitutional review in the constitutional reforms of 1848.[17]

Codes such as the French *Code Civil* and the Dutch Civil Code of 1838 are products of the ethical and economic beliefs of the bourgeoisie class, which in the course of the nineteenth century gained sufficient power to occupy key positions in the State apparatus. They are also tailored, or at least applicable, to the economic reality of that time, which makes the focus on codification understandable.[18] The efforts of Dutch lawyers up to 1870/1880 were mainly focused on becoming accustomed to the legal provisions and their connections. The formalistic attitude of the courts and legal doctrine form the practical side of the liberal, bourgeois State governed by law. It was only a decade after the birth of the Dutch Civil Code in 1838 that formalism became dominant in legal doctrine.[19] Formalism adopted a political-constitutional point of view, based on the idea of the *trias politica*, that the primacy of the creation of law should lie as far as possible with the legislature, not with the courts.[20] The

---

[13] Milo (2010, p. 11).

[14] Uzman (2018, pp. 257, 259).

[15] Bos (2010).

[16] Claes and Van der Schyff (2008, p. 128).

[17] See Uzman (2018, pp. 261–262).

[18] Kop (1982, p. 6).

[19] Ibid., p. 31.

[20] Van den Bergh and Jansen (2011, p. 132).

courts had to apply the law, clarify it using interpretation methods, and, where the law was silent, administer justice.[21] To the formalists, judicial decisions were not considered a source of law; that was something reserved for legislation. The all-encompassing position of formalism only emerged in the Netherlands in the second half of the nineteenth century. Interpretations by the courts did occur, of course, but added no new elements to the existing law. Nor did *communis opinio* of legal doctrine or prevailing lines of thought in case law constitute positive law. The fact that the task of legal doctrine was regarded as being clarification of the law must be placed in a time and a jurisdiction in which private law codifications, in a period of relative social stability, were seen as the main means of regulation in the government-free sphere.[22]

As already stated, around 1870, legal doctrine obtained a better grip on the codification. A new response to the dominant position of formalism took place around 1880. This movement of free interpretation of the law (*vrije rechtsvinding*) then became the mainstream, although it had already existed before.[23] At the same time, a desire for radical legal reform emerged, spurred on by developments in modern transport, the so-called 'social issue' and the many technical errors in the Civil Code. In these times of social unrest when the legislature did not take action, a model in which only the legislature makes the law no longer appeared to be an adequate regulatory model for solving social conflicts.[24] Consequently, the interpretation of the law by the courts took on the character of law making.

4 The Changing Role of the Judiciary in the Early Twentieth Century

Around the turn of the century, a movement emerged in legal doctrine, which showed more interest in developments in the judiciary. In the period after the Dutch Civil Code of 1838, the primacy as to the role of law formation slowly shifted from the legislature to the courts. Over time, partly due to thorough study and partly as a result of social developments, new flaws came to light. The legislature failed to act, and as the consequences for the judicial community became more serious, the courts were asked to try to develop a fairer legal system. This call was answered by the Dutch Supreme Court in 1919. However, to interpret this case in the correct context, we should start with another case that occurred before in 1910.

In the 1910 *Zutphen neighbor* case, a person living above a storage house that had a water leak refused to shut down the main water supply. As a result, the owner of the property inside the storage house suffered damage from the water. In this case, mere negligence was regarded as insufficient grounds to establish unlawfulness and

---

[21] Cf. Art. 13 of the General Provisions Act of 1829. See Jansen (2015, p. 67).

[22] Kop (1982, p. 34).

[23] Jansen (2015, pp. 119, 133).

[24] Kop (1982, pp. 6-7).

liability.[25] Although the result in this case was unjust, the president of the Supreme Court, Justice Aernout Ph.Th. Eyssell (1837–1921), in his contribution in *Themis* in 1911, argued that by accepting that mere carelessness would lead to unlawfulness, freedom of competition in general would be negatively affected.[26] It could be argued that this alarming and prominent case in 1910 was not formalistic but actually displayed 'activism'. The Supreme Court, under the presidency of Eyssell, ruled in an activist way on the grounds of pronounced purposes of legal policy. There was much agreement among colleagues that at times of extraordinary criticism, the Supreme Court had to take on a political role in the fight against emerging socialism and the ongoing attacks on bourgeois society.[27] The strict approach taken by the Supreme Court led to criticisms, which were in line with the plea of Utrecht professor Molengraaff (1858–1931) to fight unfair competition (thus calling for a less narrow view of Art. 1401 of the Dutch Civil Code) in his article in the *Rechtsgeleerd Magazijn* of 1887.

Before the legislature could take action, the Supreme Court had already changed its position as to the interpretation of unlawfulness pursuant to Article 1401 of the 1838 Dutch Civil Code. In the famous *Lindenbaum/Cohen* landmark case in 1919, the Dutch Supreme Court, dealing with unfair competition, ruled that—next to acts that violated a written rule or a subjective right—acts contrary to unwritten rules of conduct can be regarded as unlawful.[28] The decision was made under the presidency of a new president, W.H. de Savornin Lohman (1864–1932). In this case, no legal provision existed that prohibited provoking a breach of duty of confidentiality. Although it could be thought that this was a loophole in the law, this is incorrect since there was still a solution present—namely, denial of the claim. Nevertheless, it could be said that the need for a particular result sometimes creates a loophole,[29] as in this case. The decision by the Supreme Court in the *Lindenbaum/Cohen* case in 1919 was made at the time of a legal proposal in a similar vein to change the legal provision on unlawful acts and thus crossed this legislative process with the formal legislature. This decision was therefore debatable at that time from the point of view of the power relationship between the legislature and the judiciary in a democratic constitutional state.[30]

This decision is often considered a novelty: a break with formalism and a breakthrough toward a freer interpretation of law or of 'law finding'—in contrast to the famous 1910 case of the *Zutphen neighbor*. However, to say that the (general) approach taken by Dutch law was formalistic is incorrect or in any case incomplete. Already by the end of the nineteenth century, jurists were searching for ways to create more freedom for the courts to enable them to take more account of societal

---

[25] Supreme Court (*Hoge Raad*, HR) 19 June 1910, *W.* 1910, 9038.

[26] Van Maanen (1999, p. 39).

[27] Van den Bergh and Jansen (2011, p. 140).

[28] HR 31 January 1919, *NJ* 1919, 61.

[29] Van der Linden (2013, p. 98).

[30] Rijpkema (2007, pp. 53–57).

developments. Decisions by lower courts allowed compensation for the infringement of patents.[31] Strict formalism was not practiced throughout the whole nineteenth century. Regarding the requirement of 'unlawfulness' (in Art. 1401 DCC
(1838)), the majority of writers of legal doctrine pleaded for a broad interpretation
of 'unlawfulness', and until 1883, broad liability would apply in decisions of the
Dutch Supreme Court.[32] This only changed under the presidency of Justice Eyssell,
especially in 1905, when the Supreme Court decided to put a stop to the way lower
courts were fighting unfair competition. This came from the belief that rapid industrialisation was best served by a restriction on appeals to unfair competition, which
also involved a strict interpretation of unlawfulness.[33]

The *Lindenbaum/Cohen* case shows that the Dutch codification was only partially
a description of the law and that this was not unique and complete.[34] Furthermore,
when interpreting the reason for change concerning the role of the courts, the view
of one of the justices in the *Lindenbaum/Cohen* case, Rhijnvis Feith (1868–1953), is
relevant. He believed that judges must play a role in the development and creation of
the law. Simultaneously, another justice, Bernard C.J. Loder (1849–1935; one of the
justices ruling in the famous 1910 case) opposed free interpretation of the law.[35] Free
interpretation of the law, however, was not what happened in *Lindenbaum/Cohen* but
what was argued by, among others, Isaac H. Hijmans (1869–1937), professor at the
University of Amsterdam. In his *Het recht der werkelijkheid* (1910), he advocated
judicial activism, in which law finding took 'reality' as a starting point and that the
law should not be seen as directive when establishing the law. The 'law of reality',
as Hijmans called it, was, however, not at the forefront of legal doctrine in private
law during the first half of the twentieth century.[36] Nevertheless, the 1919 judgment
marked a new era. The ease with which the courts were able to remedy a number
of flaws in legislation was very encouraging. Confidence in the actions of the courts
grew, even to the extent that for a long time calls for law review were few and far
between.[37]

---

[31] Van den Bergh and Jansen (2011, p. 140).

[32] Van Maanen (1999).

[33] HR 6 January 1905, *W.* 8163; see also Van Maanen (1999).

[34] Kop (1982, p. 53).

[35] Florijn (1994, p. 69).

[36] Van Boom (2013, p. 44).

[37] Florijn (1994, p. 89). Furthermore, in the first decades of the twentieth century, it became accepted
that settled case law is not only a source of knowledge of the law, but can also be a source of law.
See Jansen (2015, p. 258).

5   Reform of the Code: The New (Un)Completed Civil Code of 1992

The Dutch Civil Code of 1838 had many lacunae, many unclear wordings and inner contradictions, which led to calls for these deficiencies to be remedied. Due to lacunae and technical ambiguities, the law was formed by the judiciary, which led to a lack of uniformity and legal uncertainty.[38] The increase in judicial decisions that had to be consulted before one could establish one's rights and obligations was another reason for the recodification of the Civil Code.[39] For a long time, political necessity for recodification was lacking, and there was little interest in it besides from private law practitioners. This only changed after World War II, when the political elite became more receptive toward innovation.[40]

Already in 1938, the Leiden professor Eduard Meijers (1880–1954)—a jurist closer to legal formalism than to free interpretation of law—pleaded for a complete recodification of the Civil Code.[41] Paul Scholten (1875–1946), professor at the University of Amsterdam, pleaded the contrary, however; namely, that recodification was impossible and gaps had to be filled in by the judiciary.[42] Both professors had a lasting influence on legal science. It was Scholten's *General Method of Private Law* (1931), in particular the chapter on the methods of private law, with which he gained great fame. Scholten opposed legal formalism and the purely legal-dogmatic method. His view of law finding was a synthesis between the application of law (legal formalism) and law finding.[43] In doing so, he anticipated subsequent Dutch case law and legislation. In 1947, Meijers was assigned the task of drafting a new civil code, probably due to the personal interest and influence of the Minister of Justice, Johannes H. van Maarseveen (1894–1951). To create the new civil code, the old 1838 Civil Code was explicitly taken as a starting point. When Meijers died in 1954, the project had almost been completed.[44] He was succeeded by J. Drion, professor at the University of Leiden, J. Eggens, Advocate-General at the Supreme Court, and F.J. de Jong, Justice at the Supreme Court. Following the death of Meijers, the progress of the project slowed down.[45]

It was not until the year of the European unification in 1992 that the Netherlands acquired a national codification, i.e., a truly Dutch-made codification, albeit with a high degree of academic learnedness.[46] After a book on Family Law and the Law of Persons (book 1—already in force in 1970) and on Legal Persons (book 2—already

---

[38] Engelhard and Giesen (2012, pp. 148–149).

[39] Smits (2014, p. 247).

[40] Lokin and Zwalve (2014, p. 377).

[41] Jansen (2015, pp. 226 ff).

[42] Engelhard and Giesen (2012, p. 149).

[43] Langemeijer (1950, pp. 135–136).

[44] Hondius (2002, p. 21).

[45] See also Florijn (1994, esp. Ch. 4).

[46] Lokin (1994, pp. 111–142).

in force in 1976), books followed Patrimonial Law (book 3), Inheritance Law (added in 2003), Property Law (book 5), Law of Obligations (book 6), Specific Contracts (book 7), Transport (book 8) and International Private Law (added in 2012).

6 The Codification of 1992: Still the Central Focus of Attention

In the decades preceding the introduction of the new Civil Code, courts were already applying anticipatory interpretations in their decisions,[47] understanding the ruling law in light of the future Code of 1992. This method of interpretation places judicial activism in a different light. Law making by the courts is not the product of pure activism but because legitimation is possible, if not from a codification then from another objective angle, such as forthcoming legislation. In this sense, judicial activism should be understood in light of (a technique of) legal argumentation because a certain solution is desired (by society) using a different argument than had been used until that time.

The Civil Code of 1992 includes its own correction mechanisms, such as reasonableness and fairness, unjust enrichment, and open norms allowing for the incorporation of future developments.[48] In the twentieth century, the legislature had already begun to lose control of law making, a development that continues to this day. Although the Civil Code is still a cornerstone of the law, actual law making, at least in the area of tort law, is largely performed by the courts. In general, there is a division of tasks: the legislature makes suggestions for continuity through abstract and general formulations, and the courts adjust the law according to changes in society. In this way, the law is flexible, albeit not very sustainable (the paradox of codification).[49] Case law is accepted as a source of law, alongside codes and legislation. In the literature, the meaning of codification has changed visibly and may be understood as 'mere' legislation, without the element of exclusivity or completeness.[50]

The coherence of civil law that was present in 1992 has already crumbled as a result of the application of legal rules of European (Union) origin.[51] This has affected the established national private law structure, changing the framework for legal relationships between private parties through legislation as well as legal adjudication.[52] Based on Article 19(1) of the Treaty on the European Union, Member States shall provide remedies sufficient to ensure effective legal protection in the areas covered by Union law. It is therefore necessary to study the interconnections with the Civil Code to determine which remedies can be invoked in the event of a violation of Union law

---

[47] Hartkamp (1992, p. 7).

[48] Hartlief (2018, p. 1776).

[49] Van den Berg (2012, pp. 199–201).

[50] Vranken (2004, p. 2).

[51] Hartlief (2018, p. 1777).

[52] Mak (2016, p. 270).

in relation to private parties.[53] Dutch courts are obliged to interpret national law in conformity with EU directives. This is particularly important in private law because a directive has no direct effect between private individuals.[54] International legal standards arising from dialog between supranational judges and national Supreme Court judges are becoming increasingly important.[55] Furthermore, private regulations and private law also exist outside the Civil Code.[56]

In the Netherlands, fundamental human rights can be found in the Dutch Constitution and in international human rights treaties. The European Convention on Human Rights (ECHR) of 1950, in particular, is becoming increasingly important. At first, when the ECHR entered into force in the Netherlands in 1954, Dutch courts were extremely hesitant to apply the ECHR let alone use it to override parliamentary legislation.[57] Until the 1980s, there was hardly one case in which the Supreme Court found a violation of a Convention right, confirming its hesitant approach.[58] This changed in the 1980s,[59] which became a high point in the Dutch Supreme Court's decisions concerning fundamental rights review, considering the ECHR as an enforceable Bill of Rights. The rise in the impact of the human rights treaties was triggered by the fact that the European Court of Human Rights considered the ECHR to be a living instrument and was reading positive obligations into some of its provisions for the States that were party to the convention. In addition, the Netherlands became party to the International Covenant on Civil and Political Rights in 1979, which added some extra protection in addition to the ECHR.[60] After the 1980s, a slow retreat set in. From the 1990s onward, the Supreme Court did not see itself empowered to set aside national legislative provisions based on inconsistency with the ECHR, and a prevailing interpretation by the European Court was deemed necessary.[61]

Currently, Dutch courts tend to consider fundamental rights in private law disputes (i.e., in horizontal relationships) to a varying extent, depending on the field of law: its relevance is more acknowledged for tort law than for contract law, particularly for property law.[62] Fundamental human rights generally have only a subtle impact on private law relationships. Courts, when solving disputes, mostly apply fundamental rights as one of the factors to be taken into account. Fundamental rights are also used as a source of inspiration when tracing general law principles or when interpreting and applying open private law norms.[63] In the case of a violation of a fundamental rights provision, an injured party may file a claim based on a wrongful act, Article 6:162

---

[53] Ibid., p. 271.

[54] See Hartkamp (2019), no. 181 ff.

[55] Loth (2014).

[56] Smits (2015, pp. 536–538) and Giesen (2020, p. 15).

[57] Uzman (2018, p. 265).

[58] See for a notable exception, HR 23 April 1974, *NJ* 1973/272.

[59] Uzman et al. (2011, pp. 656–657).

[60] Gerards and Fleuren (2014, p. 225).

[61] Uzman et al. (2011, p. 658).

[62] Cherednychenko (2016, pp. 453–471).

[63] Ibid., p. 468.

Dutch Civil Code (DCC), which can serve as a gateway. In tort law, fundamental rights can also influence the rules for loss compensation, in particular immaterial losses. In the past, fundamental human rights did not convince the Dutch Supreme Court to award emotional distress damage compensation.[64] The issue of whether the mere infringement of a fundamental right constitutes a ground to award immaterial damage compensation is a topic of debate. Recently, the Dutch Supreme Court gave a clear, negative answer to this question in the *Heavy detention regime* case.[65] In this case, a person was sentenced to life imprisonment but had been wrongfully detained for 350 days in the highest security prison in the Netherlands instead of being detained under a less severe detention regime.

7 The Legislature and the Courts: 'Two Partners in the Business of Law'[66]

In 1959, in the famous *Quint/Te Poel* case, the Supreme Court had already created law by ruling that in cases not specifically laid down in statutory law, a solution that fits within the system of statutory law and is consistent with the cases laid down in the law must be found.[67] Accordingly, legal obligations do not have to be directly rooted in a legal provision. Subsequently, the Supreme Court supplemented and refined this rule further. The Supreme Court is cautious where the system of the law does not provide sufficient guidance; it has to choose between different solutions, and it is impossible to properly assess the consequences of its autonomous choice.[68] Initially, the courts' task was modest: fill in the gaps, i.e., lend a hand where the legislature has missed something. Gradually, this task extended to include not only what was not forgotten by the legislature but also what it found too difficult.[69] A greater appeal to the judicial role of the courts followed as a result of the increasing legalization of society and the periodic inability of politicians to agree on statutory regulation on important issues such as abortion, the right to strike, and euthanasia. These social issues are therefore submitted to the courts, as well as issues of international law, such as EU law and the ECHR.[70]

Lawmaking has become inherent in the judicial process. If needed, courts go further than strictly applying statutory provisions, for example, by deviating from the literal wording of the statutes to resolve cases and by creating new rules. Currently,

---

[64] This restrictive approach led to criticism in legal literature. Finally, a reform led to the acceptance of emotional distress damage which entered into force on 1 January 2019. See *Staatsblad (Stb)* 2018, 132.

[65] HR 15 March 2019, ECLI:NL:HR:2019:376.

[66] Taken from Vranken (2005), no. 9.

[67] HR 30 January 1959, ECLI:NL:HR:1959:AI1600.

[68] De Graaff (2019, pp. 9, 11).

[69] Boogaard and Uzman (2016).

[70] Kop (2011).

it is widely accepted that the legislature cannot deal entirely with all lawmaking and that lawmaking activities by the courts are indispensable. Creation of law has thus become a joint venture of the courts and the legislature, leading to a shared responsibility.[71] While the task of developing legal rules was originally a byproduct of the work of the Dutch Supreme Court, currently, it is considered one of its core tasks.[72] Questions are raised, from a constitutional law perspective, about the legal basis of the lawmaking task of the courts,[73] attracting both support and criticism. In his important work, Gerard J. Wiarda, president of the Supreme Court, ascertained a shift from the notion of a judge since 1838 as *bouche de la loi* (Montesquieu) to a judge as arbiter, deciding on fairness.[74] The shift from more heteronomous to more autonomous forms of law finding is the result of doctrine, case law and legislation, and the influence of European law.[75] The legislature's contribution to this shift can be found in the use of the role that vague norms (open concepts) in legislation and the role these vague norms started to play (see also below).[76] The *Lindenbaum/Cohen* and *Quint/te Poel* cases, discussed above, show fairness as a complementary source of unwritten law. It is interesting that Justice F.J. de Jong (1901–1974), a representative of Meijers' line of thought, drafted the *Quint/te Poel* decision and later became a member of the triumvirate that, after the death of Meijers, was charged with drafting a new Civil Code.[77]

The 'new' Civil Code of 1992 facilitated the courts becoming increasingly less restricted in relation to the law, allowing them to set aside statutory provisions under certain circumstances.[78] The task of the (supreme) court to develop and create law is desirable to keep the law up-to-date, enabling it to respond to current events in society and to be flexible and avoid injustice. Even after the introduction of the new Civil Code in 1992, activities on this front did not stop. In 2008, Abas wrote that since the introduction of the new Civil Code, the Supreme Court had brought about more substantive changes than the 1992 Code had brought in comparison to the old Civil Code of 1838.[79] In the new Civil Code, case law from the preceding period is codified, including the idea that the courts must perform a specific interpretation of open norms. In fact, by doing so, the legislature provided the courts with leeway, or even delegated them power, for law making, thus preventing a relapse to legal formalism.[80]

Due to the (continuing) silence of the (democratically legitimate) legislature (in the field of private law), it has been argued that the constitutional legitimation for courts

---

[71] Feteris (2016, pp. 17–18) and Giesen (2020, pp. 7, 10).

[72] See Feteris (2014, pp. 71 ff).

[73] Kortmann (2005, pp. 250–252).

[74] Wiarda (1999, p. 15).

[75] Van Gerven and Lierman (2010, pp. 226–227).

[76] Bruning (2016, pp. 76–77).

[77] Klomp and Steenhoff (1998, p. 14), Zwalve (2007, p. 208, note 3), and Bruning (2016, p. 85).

[78] Kop (2011).

[79] Abas (2008, pp. 193–198).

[80] Giesen (2020, pp. 15, 24, 82).

to operate is growing.[81] However, this sometimes goes even further—for example, in cases where courts argue that the legislature did not choose the best solution and thus they argue it away.[82] Although the Netherlands does not have a formal system of precedents, in practice, precedent decisions made by the same or higher courts are very important. According to Article 12 of the General Provisions Act of 1829, judges are forbidden to render verdicts in the form of a general decree, disposition or regulation. However, at present, this rule seems to have had its day.[83] Furthermore, although the Supreme Court starts from an individual dispute, it currently looks to some extent 'beyond the individual dispute'.[84] As a result of the Act on Requests for a Preliminary Ruling to the Dutch Supreme Court in civil law matters, which came into force in 2012, it can now perform its judicial task sooner and more frequently, which may lead to a (slightly) altered understanding of its task.[85] Apart from this change and the possibility created by Protocol 16 to the ECHR, continuing on the path of Article 80a of the Dutch Judiciary Act, increasing contacts between the Supreme Court and lower courts will lead to more lawmaking by the Supreme Court in the future.[86]

8 Enforcement of Constitutional Values: The Urgenda Case

The current shift in ideas on climate policy and climate change, both social and political, recently stepped into the limelight in the Urgenda case.[87] The Dutch perceptiveness of the idea of public interest litigation as a way to enforce constitutional values will be touched upon here. A court that openly intervenes in the political process is at odds with the Dutch tradition of a politically enforced constitution, according to which it is the task of Parliament to implement constitutional values. The Urgenda case, although procedurally a matter of private law, is similar to the earlier 'activist' or politically controversial Reformed Political Party (*Staatkundig Gereformeerde Partij*) case in 2010,[88] which was essentially a public/constitutional law issue of general government policy.

Urgenda requested that the Dutch State take measures to reduce CO2 emissions in the Netherlands by 40% before the end of 2020, or at least by a minimum of 25%, compared to the level of emissions in 1990. The targets of the Dutch State are lower, which would imply insufficient action to prevent climate change. Urgenda brought

---

[81] Uzman (2013, p. 161) and Giesen (2020, p. 25).

[82] See, e.g., HR 27 May 2005, *NJ* 2005/485.

[83] Jansen (2008, pp. 2, 29).

[84] Giesen (2020, p. 101).

[85] Ibid., p. 43.

[86] Feteris (2016, pp. 19–22).

[87] HR 20 December 2019, ECLI:NL:HR:2019:2006. The following text is based on Van Dongen and Keirse (2020), no. 45 ff., where this case is dealt with more elaborately.

[88] HR 9 April 2010, ECLI:NL:HR:2010:BK4549; Uzman (2018, pp. 267–268).

a collective action (cf. Art. 3:305a DCC) against the Dutch State, arguing that the Dutch State is knowingly exposing its citizens to danger and is thus committing an unlawful act (Art. 6:162 DCC). Urgenda asked the court to oblige the State to reduce emissions by at least 25%. The Court of Appeal upheld the decision of the court of first instance, although it changed the grounds for liability by applying Articles 2 and 8 ECHR as the basis for its judgment. The Supreme Court, upon appeal in cassation, based its judgment on the UN Climate Convention (1992) and on the State's legal obligation to protect the lives and well-being of citizens in the Netherlands. The Netherlands is included among the Annex I countries that must take the lead in combatting climate change and be committed to reducing greenhouse gas emissions. These legal obligations are anchored in Articles 2 and 8 ECHR. According to the Supreme Court, the State has not explained why a lower reduction can be considered justified and still lead, over time, to the reduction targets accepted by the State.

The perspective taken by the state is a constitutional perspective, stating that decisions on the reduction of gases must be made by politicians. According to the Supreme Court, however, the State has a constitutional duty to apply the rulings of the European Court of Justice. The courts must provide legal protection as an (essential) element of democracy and must protect the limits of the law. The Supreme Court therefore ruled that the Court of Appeal thus agreed with the ruling of the Court of Appeal, namely, that the State is obliged to take measures to actualise a 25% reduction by the end of 2020, due to the risk of climate change that could seriously affect the residents of the Netherlands in their right to life and well-being.

This decision demonstrates the continuing constitutionalisation of civil law.[89] Furthermore, as already stated, it serves as an example of public interest litigation based on Article 3:305a DCC. Although the Urgenda decision can be questioned from the *trias politica* perspective, one could also argue, with Van Gestel and Loth, that public interest litigation may well be seen as an expression of democratic legitimation, as long as the State and the courts sufficiently respect the policy freedom of the State and objectify and justify their normative actions.[90] In fact, this is the core element in the discussion on lawmaking and judicial activism. I agree with Van Gestel and Loth that there is no infringement of the policy freedom of the State in this case. The courts did not make up this minimum percentage—for years, the government had agreed on it as the minimum requirement to stop irreversible climate change, and it had signed climate agreements in Paris.[91] With regard to lawmaking, the fact that this decision essentially concerns public law issues of general government policy makes a difference for the context and nature of lawmaking. This is not to say that judicial lawmaking is no longer legitimate. From an institutional perspective, it does make a difference whether the Supreme Court engages in far-reaching law making in an area where the political bodies are silent and the law making is limited to the mutual relationship of mutual groups or persons in society or legal judgments such

---

[89] Giesen (2020, p. 111).

[90] Van Gestel and Loth (2019, p. 647).

[91] Ibid., p. 655.

as the Urgenda case, which deal with highly politicized issues and raise questions about the allocation of values in the public interest.

9   The Future of the Dutch Civil Code

The Dutch Civil Code is a collection of recent legislation as well as remnants of past legislation, of Dutch as well as European origin, of case law and of doctrinal thought. Introduced in 1992, it is a relatively recent civil code. Nevertheless, it seems that the notion of presenting law in an all-embracing and systematic way is as prominent as it was two centuries ago. Shortly before the introduction of the new Code, the European Parliament in 1989 had even called for the elaboration of a European civil code,[92] an indication that this trend toward codification was even present at the European level.

One reason for the (re)codification of 1992 was to make the whole private law system more consistent and to reduce the huge amount of case law that had to be consulted to establish the specific rights and obligations of subjects.[93] The new Code did not have a constitutional, unifying role—as it did at the time when nation states began to emerge—nor did it lead to fundamental changes in legal practice. It was rooted in past legal tradition, thereby assuring continuity. At the time of its promulgation, the Code encompassed all norms in a systematic and clear way, although some parts (whole books, as well as lesser reforms) were added later and some parts are still to be included. Formally, it replaced all previous statutory laws, customs and authorities, although the strength and continuity of legal tradition remains evident in case law. This strength was facilitated by anticipatory interpretations by the judiciary in rulings given in the decades preceding the new Civil Code.

In the literature, the meaning of codification has shifted visibly and can be read as 'mere' legislation, without the element of exclusivity or completeness.[94] The Civil Code is not a universally binding code but elaborates generally accepted legal principles and standards in a way that reflects the socioeconomic needs of the time.[95] Some have argued that the current situation no longer fits the exclusiveness of codifications. The Civil Code nevertheless remains the center of gravity of private law in the Netherlands (thereby suggesting continuity), although the main emphasis in relation to lawmaking, for example in the area of tort law, has shifted to the judiciary, which adjusts the law to the changing society.[96] Perhaps as a result of such developments and the division of tasks between the legislature and the judiciary, it will be possible for the new Code to pass the test of time.

That said, the question of whether a national codification is the best way to go forward in the long run still applies. The old argument that it is better to ensure one

---

[92] Official Journal of the European Communities 1989, No. C 158/400.

[93] Smits (2014, pp. 245, 247).

[94] Vranken (2004, p. 2).

[95] Cf. Hirsch Ballin (2018).

[96] See also Van den Berg (2012, p. 200).

law for one market and/or community is no longer a relevant motive for a national codification,[97] considering the international character of the market, nor is the argument of creating constitutional unity. It has been suggested that in a post-Westphalian world, new forms of legitimacy need to be found outside the familiar forms developed for nation states, i.e., law developed by national parliaments.[98] A Code could be considered from the perspective of accessibility and predictability of the law as a means to manage information. It is indeed questionable whether a codification is the best way forward to achieve the goals of accessibility and predictability. These goals might be better reached, as Smits argues, by moving toward ways of digital legal information management, including the essential electronic means to achieve this.[99]

Acknowledgements The author would like to thank Dr J.M. Milo and Professor J. Uzman for their critical remarks on a draft version of this article.

References

Abas P (2008) De Hoge Raad Als Wetgever. Trema 5:193–198

Boogaard G, Uzman J (2016) Tussen Montesquieu en Judge Dredd. Over rechter, politiek en rechtsvorming. In: De Graaff R et al. (eds) Rechtsvorming door de Hoge Raad. Ars Aequi Libri, Nijmegen, pp 63–74

Bos E (2010) Toetsing van wetten tot 1848. Nederlands Juristenblad 85(11):666–671

Brandsma F (2010) Balsem uit nieuwe en wijze Wetten. Tweehonderd jaar Wetboek Napoleon ingerigt voor het Koningrijk Holland. In: Lokin JHA, Milo JM, and Van Rhee CH (eds) Tweehonderd jaren codificatie van het privaatrecht in Nederland. Chimaira BV, Groningen, pp 33–44

Bruning M (2016) Over redelijke wetstoepassing en hanteerbaarheid van het Nederlands privaatrecht'. In: De Graaff R et al. (eds) Rechtsvorming door de Hoge Raad. Ars Aequi Libri, Nijmegen, pp 75–107

Cherednychenko OO (2016) The impact of fundamental rights on Dutch private law: revolution or evolution? In: Trstenjak V, Weingerl P (eds) The influence of human rights and basic rights in private law. Springer, Cham, pp 453–471

Claes M, Van der Schyff G (2008) Towards judicial constitutional review in the Netherlands. In: Van der Schyff G (ed) Constitutionalism in the Netherlands and South Africa. Wolf Legal Publishers, Nijmegen, A Comparative Study, pp 123–142

De Graaff R (2019) Zestig jaar Quint/te Poel: Ruimte voor rechterlijke rechtsvorming in het verbintenissenrecht. Nederlands Tijdschrift voor Burgerlijk Recht, pp 4–11

De Waele HCFJA (2009) Rechterlijk activisme en het Europees Hof van Justitie. Boom Juridisch, The Hague

Easterbrook FH (2002) Do liberals and conservatives differ in judicial activism. University of Colorado Law Review 73(4):1401–1416

---

[97] See Smits (2012, pp. 296–310).

[98] Smits (2011, pp. 119 ff).

[99] Smits (2014).

Engelhard E, Giesen I (2012) The impact of institutions and professions in the Netherlands. In: Mitchell P (ed) The impact of institutions and professions on legal development. Cambridge University Press, Cambridge, pp 142–168

Feteris MWC (2014) Beroep in cassatie in belastingzaken. Kluwer, Deventer

Feteris M (2016) Voorwoord. In: De Graaff R et al. (eds) Rechtsvorming door de Hoge Raad. Ars Aequi Libri, Nijmegen, pp 17–25

Florijn EOHP (1994) Ontstaan en ontwikkeling van het nieuwe Burgerlijk Wetboek. Datawyse/Universitaire Pers Maastricht, Maastricht

Gerards JH and Fleuren JWA (2014) The Netherlands. In: Gerards JH and Fleuren JWA (eds) The implementation of the European Convention on Human Rights and of the judgments of the ECtHR in National Case Law. Intersentia, Antwerp, pp 217–260

Giesen I (2020) Rechtsvorming in het privaatrecht. Kluwer, Deventer

Grosheide FW (2010) Het Wetboek Napoleon en de Geest der Eeuw. In: Lokin JHA, Milo JM, and Van Rhee CH (eds) Tweehonderd jaren codificatie van het privaatrecht in Nederland. Chimaira BV, Groningen, pp 21–31

Hartkamp AS (1992) Wetsuitleg en rechtstoepassing na de invoering van het nieuwe burgerlijk wetboek. Kluwer, Deventer

Hartkamp AS (2019) Mr. C. Assers Handleiding tot de beoefening van het Nederlands Burgerlijk Recht. 3. Vermogensrecht algemeen. Deel I. Europees recht en Nederlands vermogensrecht. 4th edn. Kluwer, Deventer

Hartlief T (2018) Waarin een klein land groot. Nederlands Juristenblad 25:1776–1778

Hirsch Ballin E (2018) De betekenis van het Nieuw BW in de Nederlandse rechtsstaat. Nederlands Juristenblad 25:1779–1782

Hondius EH (2002) The genesis of the principles of European Contract Law and of modern Dutch Private Law. In: Busch D et al. (eds) The principles of European Contract Law and Dutch Law. Ars Aequi Libri, Nijmegen, pp 13–27

Jansen CJH (2008) Over de plaats en functie van de Wet, houdende Algemeene Bepalingen der Wetgeving van het Koningrijk (1829). Ars Aequi, pp 22–29

Jansen CJH (2014) The study of Roman Law in the Netherlands in the early 19th century. In: Milo JM, Lokin JHA and Smits JM (eds) Tradition, codification and unification. Comparative-historical essays on developments in Civil Law, Intersentia, Cambridge, pp 17–27

Jansen CJH (2015) De wetenschappelijke beoefening van het burgerlijke recht in de lange 19e eeuw. Kluwer, Nijmegen

Klomp RJQ and Steenhoff GJW (1998) G.J. Wiarda. Schets van leven en werk. Wiarda Instituut, Utrecht

Kop PC (1982) Legisme en privaatrechtswetenschap. Legisme in de Nederlandse Privaatrechtswetenschap in de negentiende eeuw. Kluwer, Deventer

Kop P (2011) Rechtsvorming door de Hoge Raad? Nederlands Juristenblad 16:1040–1044

Kortmann CAJM (2005) De rechtsvormende taak van de Hoge Raad. Trema, pp 250–252

Langemeijer GE (1950) Meijers en de Rechtsdogmatiek. Rechtsgeleerd Magazijn Themis, pp 132–148

Loth MA (2014) De Hoge Raad in dialoog. Tilburg University, Tilburg

Lokin JHA (1994) Waarin ook een klein volk groot kan zijn. In: Lokin JHA (ed) Tekst en uitleg. Opstellen over codificatie en interpretatie naar aanleiding van het nieuwe Burgerlijk Wetboek, Vof Chimaira, Groningen, pp 111–142

Lokin JHA (2010) Voorwoord. In: Lokin JHA, Milo JM, Van Rhee CH (eds) Tweehonderd jaren codificatie van het privaatrecht in Nederland. Chimaira BV, Groningenp, pp iii–vi

Lokin JHA, Zwalve WJ (2014) Hoofdstukken uit de Europese Codificatiegeschiedenis, 4th edn. Boom Juridische uitgevers, The Hague

Mak C (2016) De Hoge Raad als Europese civiele rechter. In: De Graaff R et al. (eds) Rechtsvorming door de Hoge Raad. Ars Aequi Libri, Nijmegen, pp 269–280

Milo JM (2010) Tweehonderd jaren privaatrechtelijke codificatie: Het Wetboek Napoleon ingerigt voor het Koningrijk Holland. Perspectieven voor verleden en heden. In: Lokin JHA, Milo JM,

Van Rhee CH (eds) Tweehonderd jaren codificatie van het privaatrecht in Nederland. Chimaira BV, Groningen, pp 1–19

Milo JM, Lokin JHA and Smits JM (2014) Tradition, codification and unification—an introduction. In: Milo JM, Lokin JHA and Smits JM (eds) Tradition, codification and unification. Comparative-historical essays on developments in Civil Law. Intersentia, Cambridge, pp 1–11

Rijpkema P (2007) Lindenbaum-Cohen: Einzelfallgerechtigkeit of beleid? In: Janse R, Taekema S, Hol T (eds) Rechtsfilosofische annotaties. Ars Aequi Libri, Nijmegen, pp 53–57

Sacco R (1991) Legal formants: a dynamic approach to comparative law. Am J Comp L 39(1):1–34

Smits JM (2011) Kodifikation ohne Demokratie? Zur Legitimität eines Europäischen (Optionalen) Zvilgesetzbuches. In: Joerges Chr, Pinkel T (eds), Europäisches Verfassungsdenken ohne Privatrecht—Europäisches Privatrecht ohne Demokratie? ZERP-Diskussionspapier 1/2011, pp 119–132

Smits JM (2012) What do nationalists maximise? a public choice perspective on the (Non)Europeanization of private law. European Review of Contract Law 8:296–310

Smits J (2014) On the vocation of our age against codification: on civil codes in the information society. In: Milo JM, Lokin JHA, Smits JM (eds) Tradition, codification and unification. Comparative-historical essays on developments in Civil Law, Intersentia, Cambridge, pp 245–255

Smits JM (2015) Het privaatrecht van de toekomst. Tijdschrift Voor Privaatrecht 52(2):517–547

Uzman J, Barkhuysen T, Van Emmerik M (2011) The Dutch Supreme Court: a reluctant positive legislator? In: Brewer Carias A (ed) Constitutional courts as positive legislators. Cambridge University Press, Cambridge, pp 645–688

Uzman J (2013) Constitutionele remedies bij schending van grondrechten: over effectieve rechtsbescherming, rechterlijk abstineren en de dialoog tussen rechter en wetgever. Kluwer, Deventer

Uzman J (2018) Changing tides: The Rise (and Fall?) Of Judicial Constitutional Review in the Netherlands. In: Ferrari G F et al (eds) The Dutch Constitution beyond 200 Years: tradition and innovation in a multilevel legal order. Eleven International Publishing, The Hague, pp 257–271

Van den Berg PAK (2012) De paradox van de codificatie: Over de gevolgen van codificatie in Europa voor de rechtsvinding. RM Themis 4:199–201

Van den Berg P (2014) Constitutive rhetoric: The case of the "European Civil Code". In: Milo JM, Lokin JHA and Smits JM (eds) Tradition, codification and unification. Comparative-historical essays on developments in Civil Law. Intersentia, Cambridge, pp 45–70

Van den Bergh GCJJ, Jansen CJH (2011) Geleerd recht. Een geschiedenis van de Europese rechtswetenschap in vogelvlucht. Kluwer, Deventer

Van Boom WH (2013) Empirisch privaatrecht. Enige beschouwingen over de rol van empirisch onderzoek in de hedendaagse privaatrechtswetenschap. Tijdschrift voor Privaatrecht 50/1, pp 7–84

Van Dievoet E (1943) Het burgerlijk recht in België en in Nederland van 1800 tot 1940. De rechtsbronnen. De Sikkel, Antwerp/Martinus Nijhoff, The Hague

Van Dongen EGD, Keirse ALM (2020) The Netherlands. In: Karner E, Steininger BC (eds) European Tort Law Yearbook 10 (2019). De Gruyter, Berlin/Boston, pp 409–437

Van der Linden T (2013) Het legaliteitsbeginsel in de privaatrechtelijke rechtsvinding. BW-Krant Jaarboek 28:87–107

Van Gerven W and Lierman S (2010) Algemeen deel. Veertig jaar later. Kluwer, Mechelen

Van Gestel R and Loth M (2019) Voorbij de trias politica. Over de constitutionele betekenis van 'public interest litigation. Ars Aequi, pp 647–655

Van Maanen GE (1999) De Zutphense juffrouw en de ontrouw bediende van Lindenbaum, 2nd ed. Ars Aequi Libri, Nijmegen

Vranken JBM (2004) Verantwoording. In: Vranken JBM Giesen I (eds) Codificatie en dynamiek. Instrumenten ter begeleiding van de omgang met codificaties. The Hague, pp 1–6

Vranken JBM (2005) Mr. C. Asser's Handleiding tot de beoefening van het Nederlands Burgerlijk Recht. Algemeen Deel***. Kluwer, Deventer

Wiarda GJ (1999) Drie typen van rechtsvinding. 4th edn., revised by T. Koopmans. W.E.J. Tjeenk Willink, Deventer

Zimmermann R (2000) Roman Law, Contemporary Law, European Law. The Civilian Tradition Today. Oxford University Press, Oxford

Zwalve WJ (2007) review of 'D.M.A. Gerdes, Derdenverrijking, Deventer 2005 (Kluwer), 290 pagina's + XII.' WPNR 6701:208–212

Emanuel G.D. van Dongen is Associate Professor of Private Law at the Molengraaff Institute for Private Law, Utrecht University. As a researcher, he is affiliated with the Utrecht Center for Accountability and Liability Law, the Montaigne Centre for Rule of Law and Administration of Justice and the Empirical Research into Institutions for Conflict Resolution, Utrecht University. He has been a visiting professor at the universities of Roma Tre, LUISS, and the University of Torino. He is holder of the rotating TPR Private Law Chair 2021–2022 at the University of Ghent.

The Italian Civil Code at Eighty: Facing Old Age

Michele Graziadei

Abstract Italy's civil code is eighty years old. In this chapter, I will consider the evolution of the law in Italy since the entry into force of the Italian civil code in 1942. Although the formal structures of the code have largely remained the same over the years, the case for a new codification is becoming compelling. In the eighty years since the enactment of the code, the country has witnessed the fall of fascism, the establishment of the Republic and the return to democracy, a rapid modernisation, and the consequent change of social values. Several areas of the law have therefore experienced profound transformations. European Union law and the jurisprudence of the European Court of Human Rights have also deeply influenced Italian law. The Republican Constitution has been a key factor in consolidating the evolution of the law. At present, there is little chance that Italy will soon introduce a new civil codification, but the Italian civil code of 1942 is now facing old age; the efforts to keep it up to date on the basis of a piecemeal approach to reform should probably give way to more ambitious plans for a new civil codification.

1   The Making of the Italian Civil Code of 1942.

The present civil code of Italy originated in turbulent times because it was enacted in the last year of Mussolini's fascist government, in the midst of the Second World War.[1] Up to the entry into force of the new text in 1942, the Kingdom of Italy had a civil code (1865) which was greatly indebted to the French civil code. It also had a commercial code (1882) that was an original product of Italy's scholarship on

---

[1] There are no critical editions of the preparatory works of the code. Ranieri (2012) and Caprioli (2008) provide a brief, informative summary of the drafting process and of the key features of the Italian civil code. Recent studies dedicated to the making of the code include: Rondinone (2003, 2020) and Sandonà (2020). On the contemporary legal culture: Cavina (2014), Grossi (2010), and Irti (1990). For a general assessment: Sacco (2013).

M. Graziadei (✉)
Law Department, University of Torino, Torino, Italy
e-mail: michele.graziadei@unito.it

© The Author(s), under exclusive license to Springer Nature Singapore Pte Ltd. 2023   109
M. Graziadei and L. Zhang (eds.), *The Making of the Civil Codes*,
Ius Gentium: Comparative Perspectives on Law and Justice 104,
https://doi.org/10.1007/978-981-19-4993-7_7

commercial law.[2] The original version of the civil code of 1942 had several provisions making reference to the odious racial laws enacted under the fascist regime in 1938.[3] Following the tenets of fascist ideology, the civil code proclaimed its adhesion to corporativism, and cultivated a nationalistic outlook of the law.[4] Nonetheless, the civil code reflected as well the formalistic positions of large sectors of Italian legal culture under the dictatorship, which is exemplified by statements such as the following:

> The systematic method handed down to us by our glorious legal school" [is based on princi-ples which, due to]: "their solidity and vitality, resist any new codification, adapt wonderfully to the new social needs and form as well […] the basis of […] the new social legislation.[5]

Hence, although the code favored the intervention of the State in the economy and in private relationships (e.g., by expanding the sphere of voluntary and contentious jurisdictions in family matters),[6] in the years following the end of fascism, many scholars (including some of those directly involved in the making of it, such as Filippo Vassalli) highlighted that much of its contents were not derived from fascist doctrines, or developed as corollaries of them.[7] By and large, the civil code consol-idated doctrines and rules rooted in the legal theory and judicial practice evolving under the previous civil code and the legislation enacted during or after the First World War.[8]

The drafters of the civil code of 1942 did not introduce into Italian law a general part of the code following the model of the *Allgemeiner Teil* of the German civil code, although German scholarship had left a deep mark on the Italian academic world by the 1920s.[9] The civil code was thus divided into six books, prefaced by a set of norms on laws in general, which contained norms on the sources of law, on the interpretation of laws, and on private international law (*disposizioni sulla legge in generale*). Book I of the code was dedicated to persons and family; book II to succession upon death; book III to property and real rights; book IV to the law of obligations; book V ('on labor') covered both labor relations and the regulation of firms, partnerships, and companies; book VI on the protection of rights covered the law of evidence, public records, and security rights as well as miscellaneous rules

---

[2] The historiography on the nineteenth century codes is presented and discussed by Ferrante (2012).

[3] On the racial laws in general: Livingston (2014) and Gentile (2013). On the racial laws, the civil code, and Italian legal scholarship see, e.g., Navone, (2019), with further references; Treggiari (2013, 2008), Somma (2005), and Teti (1998).

[4] Stolzi (2015) covers the recent historiography on fascism and the law in Italy.

[5] Azzariti et al. (1943, p. V); for a critical discussion: Somma (2005, p. 35 ff.) and Treggiari (2008), highlights that this was by no means the only orientation prevailing among scholars, and that fascism could count on willing supporters, who were clearly ready to support antiformalism.

[6] Padoa Schioppa (2017).

[7] On this debate: Rescigno (2013).

[8] For the documentation of this opinion and its critique: Somma (2005, p. 35 ff.) and Cappellini (1999). Vassalli's views on this are presented in an essay published after the end of the Second World War: Vassalli (1947). On the legacy of the legislation enacted to cope with the consequences of the first world war: Moscati (2016).

[9] Cian (2013).

on the enforcement of rights (such as the rules on limitation periods). The new civil code unified civil and commercial law pursuant to the design first advocated fifty years earlier by Cesare Vivante, a leading commercial law professor (although in his later life Vivante had changed his opinions on the point).

As far as patrimonial law is concerned, the civil code was drafted in continuity with the fundamental features of French civil codification, although the rhetoric of the regime tended to emphasize the purely national character of it. Political hostility toward France undermined the French-Italian project for a joint code of the law of obligations, which floundered in 1937 and was officially abandoned in 1939.[10] Resistance to that project was also motivated by the changing landscape of Italian private law, which was no longer in line with the liberal ideas underlying the French-Italian project. Those ideas had been defended by prestigious names such as Vittorio Scialoja and Mariano d'Amelio, who later were to play an early but limited role in the elaboration of the codification project supported by fascism.[11]

Beyond the rhetoric highlighting the national character of the code, its key features, as far as the law of obligations is concerned, are nonetheless still in line with those of the French civil code. Contract is the central pillar of the law of obligations (art. 1321 ff.); *inter vivos* legal acts of a patrimonial nature are regulated by reference to the rules governing contracts, insofar as they are applicable to them (art. 1324 c.c.). The requirement of *causa* to have a valid contract is maintained (arts. 1325, 1343–1345 c.c.). With respect to the transfer of property, the Italian civil code adopts consensualism (art. 1376 c.c.). The law of extracontractual liability is open ended, rather than based on a list of protected rights, such as that set out in § 823 BGB (art. 2043 c.c.). Nonetheless, the drafters of the code also appreciated the findings of German legal thought. For example, the code introduces a first set of general rules on the law of agency (*rappresentanza*) (1387 ff. c.c.) which were until then lacking. Furthermore, the language of the code pays close attention to the conceptual innovations produced by German legal science. Since the code was completed in a relatively short time and in haste, at least as the final phase of the codification process was concerned, the defective coordination of certain parts of it is apparent, and its terminology suffers from the same problem.[12]

The code intends to deal with problems that showed the shortcomings of classical liberal contract law. For example, it provides for an obligation to negotiate contracts in good faith (art. 1337–1338 c.c.). For the first time in Europe, it regulated standard form contracts and unfair contractual terms (arts. 1341–1343 c.c.). The civil code established the duty of monopolists to contract with any interested party (art. 2597 c.c.). In the case of supervening unforeseen circumstances, rendering contractual performance more onerous than it could reasonably have been anticipated, contracts may be terminated unless the parties agree on a voluntary adaptation of the contract to the new circumstances (arts. 1467–1469). The intention to overcome the legacy of classical liberalism is present in other areas of the law as well, such as the law of

---

[10] Alpa and Chiodi (2007).

[11] Chiodi (2020, p. 216 ff).

[12] Vassalli (1947).

property, which highlights a productivist design unknown to the previous civil code. This took shape during the 1930s, when the economy fell under the control of the State, as a consequence of the great depression of 1929.[13]

2 The Transition to Democracy in the Aftermath of the Second World War and the Renovation of Italian Legal Culture

When fascism fell in 1943, the immediate decision of the interim government was to delete from the Italian civil code those repugnant provisions that could not remain in force after the fall of the regime, being the direct expression of it, such as the norms proclaiming adhesion to racism, to corporativism, and to the fascist ideology.[14] Due to the way the code had been drafted, those norms could be removed from it without altering the legal structure within which they were nested. To give an example, art. 1175 of the code originally provided that "The debtor and the creditor must act fairly, in accordance with the rules of corporativist solidarity". It was sufficient to abrogate the last words: "in accordance with the rules of corporativist solidarity" to preserve the remaining part of rule. Once these amendments were passed, it soon became clear that the civil code was bound to remain in force, despite its tainted origins. In the following years, there were only modest gestures hinting at the possibility of introducing a new civil code.[15]

After the constitutional referendum held in 1946, Italy became a Republic. The republican constitution entered into force in 1948. The content and language of the 1948 constitution was new, reflecting the ideals of a democratic, pluralistic, social state. The constitution rejected a purely statist conception of the legal order and recognized the autonomy of the various social formations,[16] thus overcoming the old organicist conception that focused on the family as foundation of the state. The Constitutional Court, which held its first hearing in 1956, showed that constitutional law could have a vital role in the evolution of Italian private law by giving voice to the pluralistic dimensions of the constitution.[17]

The post war period was characterised by the flourishing of new intellectual energies leading to a process of profound renovation and change of the Italian legal culture. This process was set in motion by the return of the country to democratic politics and to a pluralistic social life, while the economy experienced a boom, and

---

[13] Jannarelli (2007).

[14] Royal d.l. 20 January 1944, n. 25; D. lgs. lt. 14 September 1944, n. 287.

[15] Somma (2005, 40–41).

[16] Grossi (2020) and Rescigno et al. (2017).

[17] On the history of the Constitutional Court: Barsotti et al. (2015); for a rich, enlightening examination of the progressive role played by the constitution and by constitutional law as a means to rethink private law: Pennasilico (2011); the works of Pietro Perlingieri represent the high point of this trend: see Perlingieri (2006).

profound social transformations were seconded by the growth of the welfare state. The vanishing of the cult of the State, which had reached its peak during fascism, left place for the expression of pluralism in the various ambits of social life, with growing intensity by the end of the 1960s, in parallel with the diminishing role of legal formalism and conceptualism.[18]

Among those who greatly contributed to the development of new trends in the field of private law, the names of Guido Alpa, Francesco Galgano, Antonio Gambaro, Gino Gorla, Luigi Mengoni, Pietro Perlingieri, Pietro Rescigno, Stefano Rodotà, Rodolfo Sacco, Vincenzo Scalisi, Pietro Trimarchi stand out. Contemporary Italian civil law is therefore the expression of several revolutions. This shows how even an apparently stable codification is bound to be challenged by profound social transformations and by the evolution of the law, driven by fresh intellectual forces and new social conditions.

The methodology of Italian jurists has indeed profoundly changed since the 1950s. The change is manifest if we consider the increasing weight given to argumentations based on constitutional values, with special reference to the centrality of the human person and human dignity,[19] the increasing attention given to judicial decisions as a factor in the evolution of the law and the balancing of various considerations that takes place through them, the visible role of comparative law as a method of interpretation and—last but not least—the influence of nonnational legal sources on Italian law and legal scholarship.[20] Nonetheless, sociolegal approaches in Italy still have limited traction in many legal debates (although they have a clear impact on certain sectors of the law, such as family law and labor law). In these debates, legal formalism—every now and then—is vigorously defended,[21] even if this is by now understood as a rearguard move.[22]

As a formal recognition of the growing impact of EU law and international law on the Italian legal system, art. 117 of the constitution has been amended to reflect this evolution. Meanwhile, the role of the state in the economy has been redefined with the rise of the regulatory state in the 1980s,[23] and the integration of the Italian economy in the European single market and in the global economy.

In the following pages, I will examine what trends have shaped the evolution of family and succession laws, the law of property, and the law of obligations since the entry into force of the Italian civil code in 1942. I will not discuss how labor law or commercial and business law have changed because they are outside my field of expertise, although they have been reformed in depth as well.

---

[18] Grossi (2021) and Sacco (2005). Breccia (1999) highlights lements of continuity and discontinuity in private law in the post World War II period.

[19] See, e.g., Rodotà (2018).

[20] Alpa et al. (1999) and Marini (2016).

[21] See, e.g., Irti (2016).

[22] Vettori (2020).

[23] Sordi (2020).

3 The Law of Persons and Family Law

As mentioned above, the increasing pluralism of Italian social life since the 1960s influenced the development of the law. The law of persons and family law are two areas of the law in which the Italian civil code as originally conceived has been completely overtaken by subsequent developments.

Freedom of association, that in Italy enjoys constitutional protection (arts. 3, 18 Const.), is a fundamental component of life in a democratic society. The first book of the Italian civil code of 1942 regulates associations with legal personality and foundations (arts. 41–42). Both are subject to the supervision of the public authorities, while unincorporated associations, which the civil code barely mentions, are free from it. All these entities could not receive donations or acquire land or immovables without governmental approval under the original provisions of the civil code. These restrictions were abolished in the late 1990s (l. 127/1997). A thriving third sector has thus developed in Italy in the last fifty years. The relative diffidence with which the State originally approached nonprofit entities has been completely reversed since the 1980s. To cater to the needs of NGOs, Italy has now adopted a code for the third sector (Codice del Terzo Settore—d. lgs. n. 117/2017), which applies to a whole range of nonprofit entities, as well as new legislation relating to social enterprises (d. lgs. 112/2017). The norms of the civil code on associations and foundations have been left untouched, however. Currently, the only new norm inserted in the text of the code is art. 42-bis, which provides new rules for the transformation of associations into foundations, their mergers or demergers.

The sketchy provisions of the civil code relating to personal identity (art. 6–10 c.c.) are now massively integrated by judicial decisions relating to the civil protection of personality rights (name, reputation, personal identity, image, right of publicity, etc.).[24] Data Protection legislation (i.e. the GDPR) is increasingly important in this respect as well. Legislation has also regulated organ donations by a living donor (see, e.g., l. 458/1967; l. 483/1999) or from a dead person (l. 91/1999). Consent for medical treatment and living wills are regulated by recent legislation (l. 217/2017). Medically assisted procreation was first regulated in 2004 (l. n. 40/2004), and the Constitutional Court then overturned the ban on using donor sperm and eggs in fertility treatments, which was part of a divisive set of restrictions on assisted reproduction contained in the legislation passed by Parliament (judgment n. 162/2014).

The original version of the civil code allowed a couple who no longer intended to live together to obtain a decree of judicial separation, but marriage was indissoluble. Divorce was introduced in Italy in 1970 (l. n.898/1970, n. 898), despite the opposition of the Christian Democrats. In 1974, a political movement promoted an unsuccessful referendum to repeal the new law. Voters supported divorce, delivering a landmark victory for those who demanded change in the area of family law. In the following years, Parliament passed a fundamental reform of family law (l. n. 151/1975). The reform abolished the civil code rules on marital power and the role

---

[24] These developments have been accompanied by a rich scholarly discussion: Alpa and Resta (2019).

of the husband as head of the family, which were the direct expression of a patriarchal conception of the family, thus advancing the equality of the spouses. With the reform, parental responsibility was equally shared by the members of the couple. Community property became the default regime for marital property. In case of separation or divorce the parents are to have joint custody of the children (l. 54/2006). More recent reforms have regulated divorce and separation proceedings, establishing that if a couple has no children under the age of majority and no property to divide a simple joint declaration before the civil registrar will separate or divorce the couple (l. d. n. 132/2014, l. n. 162/2014). Six months of consensual separation are now sufficient as a prerquite for a divorce. In case of nonconsensual separation, divorce may be pronounced one year after a couple begins living separately (l n. 55/2015). Previously, three years of separation were a prerequisite to obtaining a divorce. The Constitutional Court has intervened to make sure that the rules for the attribution of the family name to children no longer favor the attribution of the father's family name to a newborn.[25] Adoption was reformed in 1983 to allow for the adoption of children lacking proper parental care (l. n. 184/1983). Further reforms of adoption laws were enacted in the following years (e.g., l. n. 173/2015) and more are currently being considered by the legislature. Meanwhile, with the entry into force in Italy of the New York Convention on the Rights of the Child, the best interest of the child has become the lodestar of judicial decisions concerning the well-being of children. Children born out of wedlock now enjoy exactly the same rights as children born to a married couple. The law no longer draws the distinction between legitimate and illegitimate children (d. lst. n. 145/2013; l. 219/2012).

Italian family law was changed once more in 2016 to introduce civil unions for same-sex partners and specific rights for partners, regardless of their sexuality, if they "live as a couple in a stable relationship" (l. n. 76/2016, on *unioni di fatto or convivenze*). To date, however, Italy has not introduced marriage for same-sex couples. The matter has been widely debated, but the opposition to it, by the Catholic Church and political parties close to it has been decisive, although contested by many. An amendment to the Italian legislation on private international law provides for the recognition of same-sex marriage celebrated abroad as a civil union (art. 32-bis, l. 218/1995). Prenuptial agreements are currently considered invalid, although a recent bill to reform the civil code advances a proposal to reverse the rule (see below para. 7).

Concerning natural persons, law no. 164/1982 provided a first set of rules on the rectification of sex for transexual people. According to art. 1 of this law, a birth certificate can now be amended to alter the sex originally entered on it: 'subsequent to a modification occurring in [a person's] sexual characteristics' (art. 1). In 2015, the Court of Cassation ruled that the public interest in the definition of gender cannot lead to sacrifice a person's psychological and physical integrity. The ruling excludes the necessity of surgical treatment of a person's sexual organs to proceed to the rectification of their sex on their birth certificate. In the same year, the Constitutional Court also reiterated the central role of the judge in assessing the appropriateness of

---

[25] Constitutional Court, Judgment 131/2022.

surgery; therefore surgery should not be considered a prerequisite for the rectification of sex on identity documents (judgment n. 221/2015).

The civil code was amended in 2004 to provide a tailored measure of protection for people with diminished autonomy (l. n. 6/2004, on *amministrazione di sostegno*). More reforms in this area of the law are forthcoming, and they will probably lead to the abolition of tutela for adults, which is now considered an anachronistic regime.

4   The Law of Succession

The law of succession has been affected by few changes since the entry into force of the Italian civil code. This does not mean that the original provisions of the civil code are still functional; on the contrary, they are by now rather dysfunctional. The introduction of divorce in Italy was not followed by a reform of a spouse's forced share (legitimate portion) on inheritance. Therefore, since the codal provisions on a spouse's forced share are still those that were introduced when marriage was indissoluble, here we have a first set of problematic rules. The significance of forced share rules has also changed as a consequence of the greater average length of life in Italy, which is the second highest in the world (after Japan). The lack of substantial reforms of the law since its entry into force in 1942 is criticized because it is all too common to have adults who have already received all they need to have success in their life from their parents as beneficiaries of forced shares. The National Council of Notaries announced a reform project to address some of these problems in 2019. This initiative should also introduce into Italian law a new formality, the certificate of succession (cp. article 67 of Regulation (EU) No. 650/2012). It is not yet clear whether this project will be successful, however. The projects favor individual autonomy as a way to allow for a more satisfactory and equitable planning of succession upon death. Although no overall reform has thus far modernised the law of succession, some of the glaring problems linked to the original text of the civil code have been approached. The transfer of donated assets is now regulated in a slightly more functional way, because the possibility to clawback donations violating the reserved share of the forced heirs has been limited (l. n. 80/2005; d.l n. 35/2005). Furthermore, a specific type of agreement (patto di famiglia) has been introduced (l. 55/2006) to facilitate the intergenerational transfer of family businesses (arts. 768-bis to art. 768-octies c.c.).

5   The Law of Property

The law of property has been amended repeatedly since the enactment of the civil code. The rules on condominiums (arts. 117 ff.) have been reformed in 2012 (law n. 220/2012). The new provisions clarify their scope of application and provide for a more precise indication of the common parts of the building; they regulate the intended use of the common parts as well as the conditions that justify the detachment of individual owners' units from the central heating system. The new rules facilitate innovations to improve the use of buildings, such as the removal of architectural barriers, the installation of video surveillance systems, and the recourse to systems for the production of wind or solar energy. Improved, more stringent rules governing the power and duties of condominium administrators are also a feature of the reform. A complex set of rules enacted between 1969 and 2005 now governs the sale of parking lots, given their chronic shortage. The rules on acquisitive prescription have been improved by allowing for the registration of the transcript of a mediation procedure concerning the acquisition of title over an immovable by acquisitive prescription in the land register (l. n. 98/2013). A reform of the law relating to rural properties facilitated the acquisition of property by acquisitive prescription (l. n. 346/1976). In 2005, the Italian Parliament introduced the possibility of designating immovable properties to a specific purpose or destination for the life of a specific living person or 90 years (l. n. 273/2005, introducing art. 2645ter c.c.). This rule was initially introduced to protect the right of persons with disability to live in their home, although the new provision inserted in the code can also have wider applications. Since the entry into force in Italy of the Hague Convention of 1985 on the law applicable to trusts and their recognition, Italians can set up trusts governed by foreign laws over assets located in Italy. This possibility is not merely theoretical : there are over a hundred cases by the Court of Cassation dealing with such trusts created in Italy. Actually, the above mentioned l. 273/2005 was a first attempt to introduce in Italy a legal device that could replicate some of the effects of a trust recognized under the Hague Trust Convention of 1985. Timesharing of property ownership was first regulated in Italy by d. lgs. n. 427/1998 following directive 94/47/CE. The consumer code of 2005 replaced the 1998 decree so that *multiproprietà* is now regulated by arts 69 ff. of that code, with further amendments also introduced in that code (d. lgs. n. 79/2011, n. 79). The law on common lands approved by Parliament in 2017 reverses the previous tendency to favor individual property ownership over commons (l. n. 168/2017, *Norme in materia di domini collettivi*). This law recognizes these particular proprietary regimes as the primary legal order of the original local communities. They are endowed with the capacity for autonomy and the continued management of properties historically governed under a model of intergenerational co-ownership. The relevant community exercises, in collective or individual form, rights of enjoyment (l. n. 168/2017, art. 1). Under this law, the Republic has the task of protecting and enhancing the assets that are enjoyed collectively as fundamental elements for the life and development of local communities. They perform—as ecological components of the system—an important function of conservation and safeguarding of the natural and cultural heritage and are a source of renewable resources to be used for the benefit of territorial communities. Wildlife (belonging to certain protected species), which was previously *res nullius,* was declared to be the property of the State in 1977, protected in the interest of the national community (l. n. 968/1977).

Cultural property has been regulated by a separate code since 2004 (d. lgs. n. 42/2004, *Codice dei beni culturali e del paesaggio*), while actions to recover cultural property are now governed by the Unidroit Convention on stolen or illegally exported cultural objects (Rome, 1995) (ratified in Italy by l. n. 213/1999).

The civil code does not recognize nonpossessory security interests over movables, except in the form of retention of title clauses or statutory privileges. This cautious approach to secured transactions has been eroded by a whole range of provisions. Some of them originate from EU legislation, while others were introduced by national reforms. Directive 2002/47/EC on financial collateral arrangements introduced forms of nonpossessory securities with respect to cash or financial instruments. The directive was implemented in Italy in 2004 (d. lgs. n. 170/04). At the national level, new legislation introduced nonpossessory security interests over specific products, such as certain hard cheeses or ham, and more recently wines and spirits. The intent to overcome the approach based on the original vision of the civil code is clear. With the enacting of d.l. n. 59/2016, and l. n. 119/2016, A new set of rules on nonpossessory pledges entered into force in 2016 (d.l. n. 59/2016 and l. n. 119/2016). Entrepreneurs can now register a nonpossessory pledge to secure present or future credit granted to them or to third parties, with the provision of the maximum amount guaranteed, relating to the operation of the business. A nonpossessory pledge may be established on movable property, whether present or future, including intangible property, intended for the operation of the undertaking and on claims arising out of or in connection with that operation (with the exception of registered movable property, which is subject to a different regime). Unless otherwise provided for in the contract, the debtor or the third party granting the pledge is authorized to transform or dispose the objects of the pledge. The Ministry of Finance opened the relevant register in 2021 (d. m. n. 114/2021 on registro dei pegni). With respect to hypothecs, a new law regulating the "prestito vitalizio ipotecario" introduced a home equity release product that allows elderly homeowners to access (part of) the equity in their home without having to disrupt their living arrangements (l. n. 44/2015).

6   The Law of Obligations

At first glance, the law of obligations enacted by the Italian civil code in 1942 seems to be a rather stable component of the civil code. This impression, however, fades away after a more accurate assessment of the present state of the law is carried out.

A major factor in the changing of the law, as enacted by the code, has been the evolution of EU law. With increasing frequency since the 1980s, the EU enacted legislation with an impact on the law of obligations. The directive on unfair contractual terms (Directive 93/13/EEC) and the directive on the liability for defective products (Directive 85/374/EEC) are two early instances of such legislation. The civil code provides that unfair terms in a standard contract are not binding unless specifically approved in writing (art. 1341 cc.). This technique does not provide adequate protection to the weaker party, as one more signature on the contractual document is enough to make unfair terms binding. The EU directive made those terms ineffective, notwithstanding any consent specifically given to them, thus leaving the parties free to concentrate on the negotiation of the essential element of the price of the goods or services bargained for. The rules implementing Directive 93/13/EEC of 5 April 1993 on unfair terms in consumer contracts were at first incorporated into the civil code. They are now contained in arts. 33 ff. of the consumer code of 2005. This code also regulates the liability of producers for defective products originating from Directive 85/374/EEC (Consumer Code, art. 114 ff).

The wide list of subsequent EU instruments relating to the law applicable to contracts can now be found in any book on European contract law and will not be repeated here.[26] It is sufficient to recall that the civil code is supplemented by the various provisions of the consumer code of 2005 implementing a whole range of   directives. The consumer code introduces rules governing consumer contracts, where various forms of contractual asymmetry operate to the disadvantage of consumers. Further rules on certain specific contracts (e.g., consumer credit) are contained in other sectorial consolidations such as the legislation on banking law (d. lgs. n. 385/1993). By and large, all these texts follow the same logic, namely, to protect the party affected by informational asymmetries or whose market power is limited. Other acts intend to remedy the same type of asymmetry with respect to franchisees (l. n. 129/2004) or subcontractors (l. n. 192/1998), sanctioning the abuse of dependency in these economic relationships according to a policy developped by the national legislature.

Since the 1980s, a great number of public utilities in Italy have been privatized. Contracts for services with consumers for gas, electricity, etc., are regulated by independent agencies that are also responsible for the activation of consumers' dispute resolution bodies. The enforcement of the rules on unfair contractual practices introduced by EU legislation is the task of an independent public body (*Autorità garante della concorrenza e del mercato*). Recently, Italy introduced legislation to facilitate collective actions by consumers (see arts. 840-bis to 840-sexiesdecies c.p.c.). Such actions may be brought against companies or bodies managing public services or public utilities with respect to acts and conducts carried out in the performance of their respective activities.

Business practices evolve and the civil code has also been amended to make room for new legal techniques or for the adaptation of old legal techniques to new business needs. The civil code's rules on the assignment of claims (art. 1260 c.c.) have thus been supplemented by legislation on factoring operations involving the sale of claims by way of assignment to a funder (l. n. 52/1991 n. 52). Regulations concerning financial leasing were introduced in 2017 (l. n. 124/2017, art. 136). Under the new legislation, a finance lease is a contract whereby the bank or financial intermediary undertakes to purchase or construct an asset according to the instructions of the user, who assumes all the risks, including the risk of loss. The asset in question is made available to the user for a period of time for a given consideration. At the expiry of the contract, the user has the right to acquire the ownership of the asset at a predetermined price or, in the event of failure to exercise this right, the obligation to return it.

---

[26] See, e.g., Schulze and Zoll (2021).

The law of extracontractual liability has been changed by both EU and national initiatives. The most salient EU innovation, after the introduction of a specific regime to govern the liability for defective products mentioned above, is perhaps the harmonisation of the law relating to environmental liability (Directive 2004/35/EC, as amended). The implementation of Italian legislation is contained in the environmental code (d. lgs. n. 152/2006), as supplemented by the civil code. More recently, the EU General Data Protection Regulation, art. 82 provides for the compensation of material and immaterial damages resulting from data protection breaches, thus replacing previous national legislation in the same matter.

At the national level, the law relating to medical liability was completely reformed in 2017 (l. 24/2017). The reform instituted a regime that is more protective of individual physicians, whose liability is governed by the provision of the civil code on extracontractual liability (2043 c.c.), while hospitals are held liable according to the rules on contractual liability of the civil code (art. 1218 c.c.). Compulsory insurance is now mandatory for all medical personnel, and a compensation fund is made available for the victims of medical accidents who are not covered by such insurance.

On paper, the rules of the civil code on extracontractual liability are essentially still the same rules that were first enacted in 1942 (arts. 2043–2059). Nonetheless, the law changed as a consequence of subsequent developments.[27] Since the 1970s, both the Constitutional Court and the Court of Cassation have rendered judgments that have profoundly changed the landscape of law. They have been encouraged to do so by doctrinal contributions exploring the role of the law of extracontractual liability in a modern society. The first of these developments is the practical abolition of the rule that excluded the compensation of nonmaterial damages, except in the cases expressly provided for by the law (art. 2059 c.c.). Nonmaterial damages are now routinely awarded in all cases, despite the letter of the code. Arts. 138–139 of the private insurances code (d. lgs. n. 209/2005) provides rules for the compensation of certain bodily injuries that have no patrimonial consequences. These articles are among the few legislative texts that expressly acknowledge the new approach to the compensation of nonmaterial damages now prevailing in the courts. A second development that should be mentioned here concerns the wider scope of protected interests under the general provision on extracontractual liability (art. 2043 c.c.). The law as elaborated by scholarly writings and judicial decisions now provides for the compensation of a much larger number of unjust infringements of rights and interests than the ones at first allowed for under the same text of the civil code. This reflects the more complex nature of life in society today and the richer set of values and expectations that deserve protection under such conditions. Several of these values are at the core of constitutional provisions, such as the right to health (art. 32 Const.). Both the Constitutional Court and the Court of Cassation have repeatedly rendered judgments that highlight how constitutional values influence the determination of the range of protected interests by the provisions of the civil code on extracontractual liability. Therefore, although the civil code has not changed, the law has changed.

---

[27] For a full discussion: Bussani (2020).

7   By Way of Conclusion: Texts, Interpreters, Codifiers

The Italian experience with codification shows that, far from being a perennial monument of lasting legal principles, the civil code is bound to become obsolete in due time, even if it manages to survive a radical regime change, such as the fall of fascism, as the Italian civil code of 1942 did.

The code makers can successfully manage to insert in the civil code new rules that emerged prior to the enactment of the code to consolidate and systematize them. They can draft the civil code to support those doctrines that represent the state of the art when the code is prepared. However, they can hardly anticipate what the (not so near) future will bring. The fate of the Italian civil code squarely confirms this. Legislators can neither foresee how fundamental values or social life shall change, nor anticipate how the material conditions of life in society shall be transformed by new scientific and technical inventions.

If further evidence is needed to show how the flux of change over time is bound to affect the vitality of a codification, let us consider the present relevance of the general introductory section of the Italian civil code containing dispositions on the law in general (*disposizioni sulla legge in generale*). These norms now look like a relic from the past. Art. 1 of this part of the civil code (on the sources of law) is simply misleading, being completely outdated: it does not even mention the Constitution among the sources of Italian law. Art 12 of the *disposizioni* on the methods of interpretation of the law in general still endorses the narrow, nationalistic ideas of the drafters of the code.[28] This provision is by now dead letter, as our judiciary is fully aware of the necessity to interpret the law in accordance with the Constitution, the relevant international sources, and EU law. Referring to foreign laws as a means of comparison is also practiced in high-profile civil cases. Furthermore, the Italian rules on private international law, which were once in this part of the civil code, are mostlyreplaced by the l. n. 218/1995, reforming private international law, and by the relevant EU regulations on private international law.

The long list of amendments and supplementary legislation that was passed over the years to correct or supplement the original text of the civil code speaks volumes about the limits of the vision that supports the making of a code. This aspect of the Italian experience teaches a lesson of more general value about codification as a long-term project for a country. Nobel prize winner Selma Lagerlöf once said: "Culture is what remains when one has forgotten everything we had learned". One is tempted to remark that, with respect to the civil codes, the opposite is true: the specific cultural elements that go into the making of the civil code may quickly lose their importance. What remains are the rules that survive them and the form in which they are cast.

On the other hand, civil codes are compatible with legal change. They can be amended and thus receive a new lease of life by way of periodic reforms. It is also true that the law often changes, although the text of the code is not altered. For example, in Italy, most developments concerning the law of extracontractual liability

---

[28] Gorla (1969).

occurred without changing the text of the code. Doctrinal and judicial developments in this area of the law reflected the growth of society's pluralism and the need to protect a wider range of material and nonmaterial interests, values, and expectations. Between the text as a historical fact and the rules of law that are applied as an outcome of the process of interpretation, there is the context in which interpreters operate. Their culture and their sensibilities are liable to change over time to respond to new intellectual and societal challenges as they did in Italy. A civil code is a system that is designed to capture the general texture of the law applicable to civil relations. That texture is inevitably bound to evolve as society evolves, even when the text remains the same over time. No civil code can manage to halt such evolution; it will take place even if the code does not second it. One of the key figures among the drafters of the civil code of 1942, Prof. Filippo Vassalli, openly acknowledged this. Looking back upon his experience as a codifier in the early 1950s, in a famous essay titled *Estrastatualità del diritto civile,*[29] on the relationship between the power of the state and the principles and rules of law governing civil relationships, Vassalli made the point that the attempt to assert the dominion of the State over civil law is a late manifestation of the sovereignty of the State and is bound to recede with it. Vassalli's analysis was based on the rise of humanitarian law, the tendency of trade to overcome barriers among states, and the decline of state sovereignty in the new international order established in the aftermath of World War II. Seventy years after this far-sighted analysis, Italian civil law is no longer composed of rules enacted exclusively at the national level; this is a part of a more general global trend. The European Convention on Human Rights and the jurisprudence of the Strasbourg Court set limits on what national legislatures and courts can do. National codifications in Europe must allow for the development of the European single market as emerging from EU law. The formation of private law beyond the State is an immanent feature of the present age.[30] Nevertheless, the flux of national legislation in the field of civil law is not receding. Part of this recent legislation in Italy is now entrusted to specific codes, such as the consumer code, the private insurances code, the code of industrial property, of cultural property, for the third sector, etc. The search for principles and order is indeed a permanent necessity, even when more legislation is forthcoming.

The trajectory of EU law and of much contemporary legislation shows that to respond to the challenge of complexity under these conditions, jurists have no choice but to cultivate fruitful dialogs with the several areas of knowledge that are the core of the contemporary developments in all contexts of life. These are technical and scientific disciplines but also social disciplines such as economics, sociology, and anthropology, beyond the classical reference to philosophy, including political philosophy. If unable or unwilling to draw on the accumulation of knowledge generated by different research traditions, the task to govern the complex worlds of environmental protection, health, banking and finance, information technology, etc., will slip from the hands of lawyers; will increasingly elude those who are not equipped for the

---

[29] Vassalli (1951). On Vassalli's thought, see the important essay by: Grossi (1997).

[30] Barsotti and Graziadei (2021) and Jansen and Michaels (2008).

task.[31] Lawyers will then be rule takers, rather than rule makers, unable to answer the call to meet their manifold social responsibilities with credibility.

The trends described in this chapter make the case for a new codification for Italy. The Italian civil code of 1942 has now passed the age of its maturity, and it is beginning to look decrepit. If the chance of having a European civil code is indefinitely postponed, as it seems to be, the time has come to think about what a new Italian civil code will look like. The reform projects presented by past governments have a rather limited scope.[32] They do not truly lay down the foundations for a new civil codification. The academic debate over the reform of the civil code in Italy has just begun, and it is yet to be seen whether it will produce viable outcomes.[33] My prediction is that if a new Italian Civil Code shall arrive, it shall not arrive too soon. For the moment, the search for principle in legislation that is symbolised by the civil code must therefore continue by other means, with full awareness of the new contexts in which civil codes are located and of the growing complexity of the tasks and roles fulfilled by lawyers in modern societies.

References

Alpa et al (1999) Le fonti non scritte e l'interpretazione. Trattato di diritto civile diretto da Rodolfo Sacco, Utet, Torino

Alpa G, Chiodi G (eds) (2007) Il progetto italo francese delle obbligazioni. Giuffrè, Milano

Alpa G (2018) Diritto civile italiano: Due secoli di storia. Il Mulino, Bologna

Alpa G, Resta G (2019) Le persone fisiche e i diritti della personalità. In: Trattato di diritto civile diretto da Rodolfo Sacco, Utet, Torino

Alpa G (2020) Tecniche di codificazione e creatività del giudice. Note sul disegno di legge per la riforma del codice civile. Questione giustizia, 63–66

Azzariti FS, Martinez G, Azzariti G (1943) Diritto civile italiano. disposizioni sulla legge in generale e libro I del codice - parte generale - persone - matrimonio e filiazione - altri istituti del diritto delle persone, 2nd ed. Cedam, Padova

Barsotti V, Graziadei M (eds) (2021) Il diritto oltre lo stato: Atti del 6. Convegno nazionale SIRD, Firenze, 25–27 ottobre 2018. Giappichelli, Torino

Barsotti V, Carozza PG, Cartabia M, Simoncini A (2015) Italian constitutional justice in global context. Oxford University Press, Oxford

Breccia U (1999) Continuità e discontinuità negli studi di diritto privato - Testimonianze e divagazioni sugli anni anteriori e successivi al secondo conflitto mondiale. Quaderni Fiorentini per la Storia del Pensiero Giuridico Moderno 28:293–509

Bussani M (2020) L'illecito civile. In: Trattato di diritto civile del consiglio nazionale del notariato diretto da Perlingieri. E.S.I., Napoli

Cappellini P, Sordi B (eds.) (2002) Codici. Una riflessione di fine millennio. Giuffrè, Milano

---

[31] Gambaro (2002).

[32] See Atto Senato n. 1151, XVIII Legislatura, Delega al Governo per la revisione del codice civile. Dossier—n. 131; Dossier del Servizio Studi sull'A.S. n. 1151 available at: https://www.senato.it/leg/18/BGT/Schede/Ddliter/dossier/51488_dossier.htm. On it, Alpa (2020).

[33] Cuffaro and Gentili (2021), Alpa (2020), and Sirena (2020).

Cappellini P (1999) Il fascismo invisibile: Una ipotesi di esperimento storiografico sui rapporti tra codificazione civile e regime. Quaderni fiorentini per la storia del pensiero giuridico moderno, 175–292

Caprioli S (2008) Codice civile: Struttura e vicende. Giuffrè, Milano

Cavina M (2014) Giuristi al bivio: le facoltà di Giurisprudenza tra regime fascista ed età repubblicana. CLUEB, Bologna

Chiodi G (2020) Costruire una nuova legalità: il diritto delle obbligazioni nel dibattito degli anni Trenta. In: Birocchi I, Chiodi G, Grondona M (eds) La costruzione della legalità fascista negli anni Trenta. RomaTrePress, Roma, 201–260

Cian G (2013) L'evoluzione del sistema privatistico italiano e l'influsso tedesco: spunti per una riflessione generale. In: Perlingieri P, Tartaglia Polcini A (eds) Novecento giuridico: i civilisti. E.S.I, Napoli, 19–31

Cuffaro V, Gentili A (eds) (2021) Materiali per una revisione del codice civile, vol 1. Giuffrè, Milano

Ferrante R (2012) Il problema della codificazione. Istituto della Enciclopedia Italiana, Roma

Gambaro A (2002) Codici e diritto giurisprudenziale. In: Cappellini P, Sordi B (eds) Codici. Una riflessione di fine millennio. Giuffrè, Milano

Gentile S (2013) La legalità del male. L'offensiva mussoliniana contro gli ebrei nella prospettiva storico-giuridica (1938–1945). Torino, Giappichelli

Gorla G (1969) I precedenti storici dell'art. 12 disposizioni preliminari del codice civile del 1942 (un problema di dritto costituzionale?). Il Foro italiano 5:112–132

Grossi P (2021) Il diritto civile in Italia fra moderno e posmoderno: dal monismo legalistico al pluralismo giuridico. Giuffrè, Milano

Grossi P (2020) Oltre la legalità. Laterza, Bari-Roma

Grossi P (2010) Scienza giuridica italiana: un profilo storico. Giuffrè Milano

Grossi P (1997) Il disagio di un 'legislatore' (Filippo Vassalli e le aporie dell'assolutismo giuridico). Quaderni Fiorentini per la storia del pensiero giuridico moderno 26:377–405

Irti (1990) La cultura del diritto civile. Utet, Torino

Irti (2016) Nόμος e lex. (Stato di diritto come Stato della legge). Rivista di diritto civile, 589–598

ISTAT (2021) Matrimoni e unioni civili in forte calo, in lieve diminuzione anche i divorzi. https://www.istat.it/it/files/2021/02/Report-matrimoni-unioni-civili-separazioni-div orzi_anno-2019.pdf

Jannarelli A (2007) Il dibattito sulla proprietà privata negli anni Trenta del Novecento, Agricoltura Istituzioni Mercati, 1000–1032

Jansen N, Michaels R (eds) (2008) Beyond the state: rethinking private law. Tübingen, Mohr Siebeck

Livingston MA (2014) The Fascists and the Jews of Italy. Mussolini's Race Laws, 1938–1943. Cambridge University Press, Cambridge–New York

Marini G (2016) L'Italian style fra centro e periferia ovvero Gramsci, Gorla e la posta in gioco nel diritto privato. Rivista Italiana per Le Scienze Giuridiche, Nuova Serie 6:95–157

Navone G (2019) Il divieto di matrimonio razzialmente misto nella legislazione fascista. Europa e diritto privato, 121–140

Moscati L (2016) La legislazione di guerra e il contributo della civilistica romana, Rivista italiana per le scienze giuridiche, pp 349–367

Padoa Schioppa A (2017) A history of law in Europe. Cambridge University Press, Cambridge

Pennasilico M (2011) Legalità costituzionale e diritto civile. Rassegna di diritto civile, 840–876

Perlingieri P (2006) il diritto civile nella legalità costituzionale, 3nd ed. Editoriale Scientifica Italiana, Napoli

Ranieri F (2012) Codice civile. In: Max Planck encyclopedia of European Private Law-Max-EuP 2012. https://max-eup2012.mpipriv.de/index.php/Codice_Civile

Rescigno P, Resta G, Zoppini A (2017) Diritto privato. Una conversazione. Il Mulino, Bologna

Rescigno P (2013) Codici: Storia e geografia di un'idea. Laterza, Roma-Bari

Rodotà S (2018) Vivere la democrazia. Laterza, Roma-Bari

Rondinone N (2020) Impresa e commercialità attraverso il «lato oscuro» dell'unificazione dei codici. Giappichelli, Torino

Rondinone N (2003) Storia inedita della codificazione civile. Giuffrè, Milano

Sacco R (2013) A civil code originated during the war (The Italian Codice Civile). In: Rivera JC (ed) The scope and structure of civil codes. Springer, Dordrecht, pp 249–265

Sacco R (2005) Prospettive della scienza civilistica italiana all'inizio del nuovo secolo. Rivista di diritto civile, 417–441

Sacco R (1983) Codificare: modo superato di legiferare? Rivista di diritto civile, 117–135

Sandonà A (2020) Della tutela dei diritti. Storia del VI libro del codice civile italiano. Giappichelli, Torino

Schulze R, Zoll F (2021) European contract law. Nomos Verlag, Baden-Baden

Sirena P (2020) (ed) Dal «Fitness Check» alla riforma del Codice Civile. Jovene, Napoli

Somma A (2019) Verso la grande trasformazione. Il primo conflitto mondiale e la disciplina dell'ordine economico nell'esperienza italiana. www.historiaetius.eu-15/2019-paper2

Somma A (2005) I giuristi e l'Asse culturale Roma-Berlino: Economia e politica nel diritto fascista e nazionalsocialista. Klostermann, Frankfurt am Main

Sordi B (2020) Diritto pubblico e diritto privato: una genealogia storica. Il Mulino, Bologna

Stolzi I (2015) Fascismo e cultura giuridica: persistenze ed evoluzioni della storiografia. Rivista di storia del diritto italiano, 57:257–285

Teti R (1998) Documenti di archivio sul libro I del codice civile. Rivista di diritto civile 3(1):355–388

Treggiari F (2013) Legislazione razziale e codice civile: un'indagine stratigrafica. In: Speciale R (ed) Le leggi antiebraiche nell'ordinamento italiano: Razza diritto esperienze. Patron, Bologna, pp 105–122

Treggiari F (2008) Questione di stato. Codice civile e discriminazione razziale in una pagina di Francesco Santoro-Passarelli. In: Treggiari F, Diurni G, Mari G, Per saturam. Studi per Severino Caprioli, I. Fondazione Centro Italiano di Studi per l'Alto Medioevo, Spoleto, 821–868

Vassalli F (1947 repr 1960). Motivi e caratteri della codificazione civile. Rivista italiana per le scienze giuridiche, 76–107 (reprinted in Studi giuridici, III, 2, Giuffrè, Milano)

Vassalli F (1951) Estrastatualità del diritto civile. In: Studi in onore di Antonio Cicu, Giuffrè, Milano, 481–490

Vettori G (2020) Effettività tra legge e diritto. Giuffrè, Milano

Michele Graziadei is Professor of Comparative Private Law, University of Torino; President of the Società Italiana per la ricerca nel diritto comparato—SIRD; Past president of the European Association of Law Faculties; Member of the executive board of the International Association of Legal Science; Titular member of the International Academy of Comparative Law; corresponding member of the Accademia delle Scienze (Torino), Collegio Carlo Alberto Fellow. He is the author of over 100 publications in several languages. His recent publications include *Comparative Law, Transplants and Receptions* in M. Reimann, R. Zimmermann (eds), *The Oxford Handbook of Comparative Law* (2nd edn OUP, 2019); M Graziadei, LD Smith (eds), *Comparative Property Law: Global Perspectives* (Elgar, 2018).

Blitzkrieg Codification: The 2020 Belgian Civil Code

Dirk Heirbaut ⓘ

Abstract In the early nineteenth century, Belgium received all of Napoleon's codes. Despite a call for national codifications in the 1831 Constitution of independent Belgium, Napoleon's 1804 Civil Code survived until the twenty-first century. However, in 2016, the Minister of Justice Koen Geens communicated a large-scale recodification program, including a new Civil Code. The code was planned to consist of nine books in an order determined by pragmatic—not doctrinal—considerations without a common method for editing the parts of the code. By 1 November 2020, Book 8 had already entered into force, and Parliament had already approved Book 3, with Books 4 and 5 and a part of Book 2 already being submitted to it. Among the factors explaining this success are the pragmatism and flexibility of the drafting process, the lack of truly revolutionary reforms and the enthusiasm for a new code that Minister Geens generated among law professors and politicians. Thus far, the drafters of the code have not yet dealt with some controversial issues of family law, so that some of the hardest work is still ahead of them. However, there is no doubt that almost two hundred years after independence, Belgium has finally emancipated its private law from France.

1 Introduction

At the time of writing, the Covid-19 pandemic struck Belgium very hard, and the country's inefficiency also manifested in many other ways. For example, after the elections of 26 May 2019, it took until 30 September 2020 to form a new full-fledged federal government. However, this state, which failed the Covid-19 exam and had only a lame-duck federal government, managed to work on a new civil code.

D. Heirbaut (✉)
Ghent University, Ghent, Belgium
e-mail: Dirk.Heirbaut@ugent.be

M. Graziadei and L. Zhang (eds.), *The Making of the Civil Codes*,
Ius Gentium: Comparative Perspectives on Law and Justice 104,
https://doi.org/10.1007/978-981-19-4993-7_8

Undeterred by the pandemic, a first book entered into force on 1 November 2020,[1] and even during the worst moments of the pandemic, Parliament received drafts of other parts.[2]

When compared to the realizations of neighboring countries, this is an impressive feat. Even though the Netherlands has achieved more than other Western European countries with its 1992 Civil Code, a Dutch scholar does not hesitate to call the pace of reforms in Belgium "breathtaking".[3] This becomes even more amazing from a Belgian point of view. When asked, many Belgians will claim that their country's legal and judicial system is actually a great example of the country's inefficiency. Although a legal historian would probably not be willing to go that far, they should admit that until recently, Belgium's record as a codifying state was not very good. In this context, the new Civil Code means a revolutionary break with the past, which begs for an explanation. Moreover, the new Civil Code is only one, albeit major, part of a larger program of reform and recodification that already boasts many successes. Last but not least, the whole undertaking officially started at the end of 2016, meaning that the results arrived very fast. While examples abound of states that have worked even faster, these cases were either due to a complete change of society that necessitated an overhaul of the existing law (e.g., Central Europe after the fall of the Berlin wall) or due to a nondemocratic government that could push through reforms without opposition (e.g., Napoleonic France). In Belgium, no revolution has shaken the country, and its democratic institutions fully participate in the codification effort. Thus, a mystery confronts us: how did Belgium suddenly become an overachiever of codification?

The following pages will try to clarify this mystery. A first part of the text will present a very brief overview of previous failures to enact a new Civil Code for Belgium (2), followed by the 2016 recodification program and its motives (3). For our story, even more important is the actual implementation, particularly the ways of realizing the new Civil Code. After giving a brief overview of the Code's structure (4), the methods for drafting the code are addressed (5). A provisional list of the current results (6) will lead to some explanations both for the achievements reached thus far (7) as well as their continuation in the near future (8). Finally, even if successfully completed, the infant Code will soon be exposed to a particular challenge that, if left unaddressed, will endanger its success in the long term (9).

---

[1] Text up to date until 1 November 2020. I want to thank Florenz Volkaert, Filip Batselé and Stephen Hewer for correcting my text. Needless to say, any remaining errors are entirely my own. All websites referred to were last consulted on 10 August 2020, unless stated otherwise. Art. 75 al. 1 of the Loi du 13 avril 2019 portant création d'un Code civil et y insérant un livre 8 "La preuve", Moniteur belge 14 May 2019.

[2] Proposition de loi portant le livre 2, titre 3, "Les relations patrimoniales des couples" et le livre 4 "Les successions, donations et testaments du Code civil", Chambre des Représentants de Belgique, Documents parlementaires, 20 May 2020, 1272/1.

[3] Wissink (2017, 1147).

2   The History of Private Law Codification in Belgium

A legal historian has an easy task writing the history of Belgian private law insofar as this history has to be relevant for current law. Before 1795, hundreds of customary legal systems dominated the legal landscape of the Southern Low Countries, today's Belgium. The French Revolution unified the country's law by abolishing the old law and replacing it with French Law. Napoleon continued the Revolution's work by promulgating his Civil Code (1804), Code of Civil Procedure (1806), Commercial Code (1807), Code of Criminal Procedure (1808) and Criminal Code (1810). As the Belgian territories were just a part of France at that time, they also received these Napoleonic Codes. In 1815, after Napoleon's final defeat at Waterloo, today's Belgium and the Netherlands formed one state, the United Kingdom of the Netherlands. This United Kingdom wrote its own codes as symbols of its independence, and it planned to have them enter into force in 1831. By then, however, the Belgians had already seceded from the United Kingdom of the Netherlands. Belgium disregarded the new codes, as it intended to repeat history and write its own texts. The 1831 Constitution called for Belgian codes to be promulgated as soon as possible, but thereafter, no one really heeded the codification article. In fact, of Napoleon's five great codes, two (the Civil Code and the Code of Criminal Procedure) survived until the twenty-first century. The 1867 Criminal Code and the 1967 Judicial Code replaced the Napoleonic texts but lacked innovation and remained staunchly within the French orbit. The only original creation of independent Belgium was its Commercial Code. As Belgium's Parliament wanted to stimulate the country's economy, it replaced the old code piecemeal during the second half of the nineteenth century without following the French example, as France's industrialization lagged behind compared to Belgium. Thus, Belgium deviated from the French pattern only when necessary for the former's economic success. In short, the dream of national Belgian codifications never became reality. Parliament finally recognized this state of affairs in 1970 by removing the codification article from the Constitution altogether.[4]

The failure to codify has been most glaring for private law. Belgium's founding generation never enacted more than a new statute on real securities to replace the most defective part of Napoleon's Civil Code. However, Belgium could have gifted itself with a great new civil code in the 1880s. In 1879–1885, François Laurent, author of a leading treatise on the Napoleonic Code and the country's greatest law scholar at that time, wrote a draft new civil code for Belgium.[5] Unfortunately, Laurent's shortcomings doomed the text as much as his erudition guaranteed its quality. Laurent was an anticatholic zealot who saw his draft code as a weapon against the Catholic Church. This could have worked for the anticlerical liberal government, which had invited Laurent to write his text, but by the time he had finished the job, the Catholic party had come to power and would not relinquish its monopoly over government until the dawn of the First World War. Moreover, even for most hardliners in the Liberal Party, Laurent had gone too far in his text by revolutionizing family law,

---

[4] Heirbaut (2017a).

[5] On the Laurent draft Code, see Bruyère (2019).

for example, by awarding equality to married women.[6] After their 1884 electoral victory, the Catholics appointed a commission to write another draft Civil Code, the goal of which was more to bury Laurent's draft rather than obtaining actual results.[7] Although a few calls for a new Civil Code surfaced every now and then, those fell on deaf ears, politicians did not show much enthusiasm.[8] By early 2016, law scholars had resigned themselves to this state of affairs. An article by Peeraer and Samoy described the then consensus: a new code being impossible, the best to strive for would be mini-codes.[9] These texts, following the 2004 Code of Private International Law, would reform a part of private law, but without any overarching scheme or philosophy.

Nevertheless, a truly major codification still remained possible in Belgium. At the bicentennial of the French Commercial Code in 2007, Belgium's Commercial Code had become a shade of its former self. Statutes on Bankruptcy and Arrangements with Creditors (1997), the Code of Companies (1999) and other texts such as the Code of Private International Law (2004) robbed it of most of its content. As such, these newcomers led to a decodification of commercial law, a group of minor texts taking the place of the great code.[10] In 2007, a new venture started with work on a Code of Economic Law, which integrates major economic regulations and consumer protection. Parliament enacted this Code in 2013–2015. This new major code was the work of the Ministry of Economic Affairs. Strangely, the Ministry of Justice was not involved at all.[11] The Ministry of Economic Affairs had not wanted the Ministry of Justice's cooperation because it feared the latter's involvement would have derailed the project. The early 2016 consensus has to be understood in that context. Even if a major codification in Belgium was still possible, it was not feasible to realize it under the guidance of the Ministry of Justice, mostly due to the latter's disinterest. With the Civil Code falling under the Ministry's competence, this effectively sealed the fate of a possible new Civil Code.

3   The 2016 Recodification Program

At the end of 2016, the consensus on the impossibility of a new Civil Code suddenly fell apart. On 6 December 2016, Koen Geens, the then minister of justice, communicated his recodification program under the title: 'The leap toward the law of tomorrow'.[12] Only words such as 'revolutionary' and 'breath-taking' can do justice to its ambitions. The minister wanted:

---

[6] For an elaborate analysis of Laurent's draft on women's rights, see Bruyère (2019, 301–387).

[7] Cf. Stevens (2006).

[8] Heirbaut (2005, 27–28).

[9] Peeraer and Samoy (2016, 601–618).

[10] Heirbaut (2005, 46–47).

[11] Byttebier and Wera (2013).

[12] Geens (2016).

- a new Criminal Code.
- a New Code of Criminal Procedure.
- a Code of Enforcement of Sentences.
- a new Civil Code.
- a revision of the Code of Economic Law and the dismantling of the Commercial Code.
- a revision of the Code of Companies.

Before checking whether the results after 2016 correspond in any way with these grand ambitions, it is necessary to look at the motives behind the codification program, distinguishing the minister's personal motives from the more general motives of recodification. As it is clear that without Minister Geens, there would have been no recodification program, a brief overview of his personal history is in order.[13] Koen Geens entered politics as what in Dutch is called a 'white rabbit' (*wit konijn*). The term describes an outsider who has not run for public office but is suddenly called upon by a political party to take an important position if the party for whatever reason cannot find or agree upon an insider. In 2013, the Flemish Christian-Democrat Minister of Finance in the federal government had to resign, and Koen Geens, who had not presented himself at the ballot box previously, became Minister of Finance. White rabbits may disappear as soon as they appear, but Geens managed to do well both in office as well as in running for office. His popularity in the 2014 elections led him toward the post he had really coveted, namely, Minister of Justice. He proved himself to be a man with a mission, namely, to ensure that Belgians would become proud of their legal and judicial system by putting the citizens' interests, and not those of the legal professions, first.[14] He presented his plans by using the analogy of the triple jump: first the hop, then the step and finally the jump.[15] The hop addressed immediate concerns of the Ministry of Justice, for example, making sure that it would pay its bills on time, a sad but recurring problem. The second jump, the 'step', meant the realizations of quick wins to achieve a more efficient justice system. The jump finally had two parts: establishing the court of the future and recodification. To understand the importance of the latter, one has to look at the minister's personal history. Koen Geens is both a successful practicing lawyer, co-founder of one of Belgium's most prestigious law firms and a professor of company law at Leuven University. He also fulfilled several tasks for and in government. He served a few years as chief of staff for the head of the Flemish Regional Government and authored the 1999 Code of Companies together with his French-speaking colleague Anne Benoît-Moury. Although Parliament approved of their text, Geens was dissatisfied with the result. The politicians had only allowed Geens and Benôit-Moury to write *à droit constant*

---

[13] For the biographical information, see Over Koen Geens (www.koengeens.be/minister/over).

[14] See, e.g., the following press release, Het nieuwe goederenrecht helpt burenconflicten oplossen én voorkomen, 2020 (https://www.koengeens.be/news/2020/01/30/het-nieuwe-goederenrecht-helpt-burenconflicten-oplossen-en-voorkomen).

[15] Geens (2016, 1).

(with unchanged law),[16] meaning that the new Code could have a new text and structure but could not be changed in substance from the pre-existing law. From 2007 on,
Geens started to criticize the code he had written himself because he had not been
allowed to make any fundamental changes.[17] The story should have ended there,
but the events of 2013–2014 gave Geens the leverage to start turning his ideas into
reality. Looking back, the true surprise is not so much that he wanted to change the
Code of Companies but that he also wanted to recodify so many other branches of
the law. At the same time, no one can deny that a minister who has actually drafted
a code is the right person to direct a major recodification project.

Apart from Geens' personal motives, there are many other good reasons for recod-
ifying Belgian Law. Inevitably, social evolution outpaces a code, and an update of
the law becomes necessary. Good judges can fill the gap somewhat by establishing
new rules, but judges are limited in that they can only deal with those problems that
appear before the courts. Moreover, many judges are reluctant to introduce reforms,
as that clashes with the older idea that the judge should apply, but not make the law.
Equally, case law by its very nature is chaotic: a judge can rule on a single issue, but
they cannot turn a plethora of leading cases into a coherent whole. If judges agree
on the need to solve a certain problem, they may not always agree on the specific
solution, and the Court of Cassation, which hears appeals in last resort against decisions of lower courts and tribunals on points of law, cannot ensure that all cases are
solved in a uniform way. The same holds for specialized legislation by Parliament:
Parliament may not be interested, and when it votes an Act, the latter may leave a
lot unresolved or lead to more chaos. Consequently, citizens have long had problems
understanding and applying the law, and even law professors can no longer claim to
know the law. In addition, older national codes, such as the Napoleonic Civil Code,
were originally conceived as autonomous texts without having to take into account
constitutional, international, European and regional law. Their inflexible structure
does not allow them to handle such interference without losing their coherence.[18]

All these motives appear in the Geens recodification program, which offers more
details. For example, updating the law means taking technological evolution, such as
digitisation, into account.[19] The program also allows for more autonomy and flexibility for the parties without being at the detriment of a weaker party.[20] Case law and
special legislation are brought back into the fold by integrating them into the new
Code, which allows for the multilayered nature of private law, a 'lasagne' of regional,
national, European and international elements.[21] The Minister and the drafters of the
Civil Code have another, private-law specific motivation: restoring to the Civil Code
its central legal position.[22] This clearly applies in the Code's relation to case law

---

[16] On this French concept, see Suel (1995).

[17] Geens (2007a, 2007b).

[18] Geens (2016, 3–5).

[19] See, e.g., Geens (2016, 32).

[20] See, e.g., Geens (2016, 37–38).

[21] Geens (2016, 28).

[22] Dirix and Wéry (2015–2016).

and special legislation. The impression is even that some specialists of private law still yearn for the days when the Civil Code was the 'undisputed king' and would not mind seeing the Civil Code regain its preeminent positioning compared to the country's other codes. For the economic codes (Code of Economic Law and Code of Companies and Associations), a major motive is to attract foreign investors to Belgium by enacting a clear and concise law.[23] To a lesser extent, this motive also applies to the property law and law of obligations of the Civil Code.[24]

Some motivations are also remarkably absent. Nationalism has been an important motive for codification in most other countries, but in the Geens recodification program, it is absent. No one sees recodification as a way to emphasize Belgium's identity or claims that Belgium can serve as a model for other countries. It seems then that the general lack of Belgian nationalism also affects the country's jurists. Last but not least, for the Civil Code, there is a motive that should be overriding, but that is in fact completely ignored. Recent research by Johan Vandevoorde has shown that the decision in 1830 to prevent the codes of the United Kingdom of the Netherlands from entering into force was invalid, both according to the law of the new state of Belgium and according to the law of the United Kingdom of the Netherlands, so that the newly independent Belgium 'illegally' continued to use the French codes.[25] This did not apply to the Code of Criminal Procedure, and for the other codes, this problem no longer exists, as later legislation, e.g., the reforms of the Commercial Code mentioned above, (unknowingly) amended it. However, for the Civil Code, the problem remains: from 1830 until the present day, the law in force has been the 'wrong' law. No one cared then, no one cared in 1904 when a Dutch lawyer pointed this out and no one cares today, even though Vandevoorde has made a convincing argument based on well-documented research. However, there is no denying that in this context, a new civil code is necessary to finally settle the problem of the validity of the French civil code in Belgium.

Before starting the analysis of the new Civil Code, it may be worthwhile to indicate that the codification program has gone beyond hopes and ambitions to actual realizations. By the summer of 2020, the Belgian Parliament had approved a new Code of Companies and Associations, the major reform of the Code of Economic Law intended by the minister went through successfully, and the old Code of Commercial Law was abolished.[26] A draft new Criminal Code[27] and a draft new Code of Criminal Procedure circulate in parliament[28] and a draft Code of Enforcement of Penalties is

---

[23] See Houben and Meeusen (2020).

[24] Cf. Stijns (2018, 410).

[25] For a summary, see Vandevoorde (2018).

[26] For a survey of these reforms, see Heirbaut (2021a).

[27] In two versions: Proposition de loi instaurant un nouveau Code pénal, Chambre des Représentants de Belgique, Documents parlementaires, 24 September 2019, 417/1 and 12 February, 1011/1.

[28] Proposition de loi contenant le Code de procédure pénale, Chambre des Représentants de Belgique, Documents parlementaires, 11 May 2020, 1239/1.

ready.[29] Belgium also has a new Code of Maritime Law since 2019, but this Code is the result of an older project, unrelated to the work of the Ministry of Justice.[30] Even if one takes into account that the recodification of private law had already started more than a year before the official announcement of 6 December 2016,[31] the period for achieving the impressive results just mentioned remains remarkably short. This speed invites the comparison advanced in the title with the Second World War term 'Blitzkrieg'. As the parts below will show, there are more similarities that meet the eye too.

4   The Structure of the New Civil Code

To evaluate the work on the new Civil Code thus far, one should know that its drafting method differs from that of the recodification program applied to the other codes. Instead of having one body that is responsible for the complete text, the code's books have been parcelled out to several drafting entities. There is no overall commission or individual steering of the whole process. True, there are two coordinators, but they have not been involved, thus far, in the books on family law (including patrimonial family law).[32] Apart from that, there was also Minister Geens himself, but in September 2020 he decided not to continue as a minister in the federal government.[33] A member of his staff originally served as a liaison between most drafters,[34] but later quit, so continuity was largely lacking. Moreover, not just is there no common editorial board writing the Code, a common method is equally absent. To understand the rest of this text, the reader should first become acquainted with the structure of the new Belgian Civil Code:

The Code contains nine Books[35]:

Book 1: General Provisions.
Book 2: Persons, Family and Property Relations of Couples.
Book 3: Goods.
Book 4: Successions, Gifts and Wills.
Book 5: Obligations.

---

[29] Cf. Note de politique générale. Justice, Chambre des Représentants de Belgique, Documents parlementaires, 24 October 2018, 11–12.

[30] Loi du 8 mai 2019 introduisant le Code belge de la Navigation, Moniteur belge, 1 August 2019.

[31] Officially, minister Geens only appointed the drafting commissions of the new Civil Code on 30 September 2017 (Arrêté ministériel du 30 septembre 2017 portant creation des Commissions de réforme du droit civil, Moniteur belge, 9 October 2017), but the decree doing so also states that the minister had already charged the experts with drafting a text by a simple letter in the summer of 2015.

[32] Geens (2016, 27 note 1, 43, 49, 52, 58).

[33] See below.

[34] Geens (2016, 31, 37, 43,49, 52, 58).

[35] Art. 2 Loi portant création d'un Code civil.

Book 6:   Specific Contracts.
Book 7:   Security Rights.
Book 8:   Proof.
Book 9:   Prescription.

Readers should immediately dispel any notions that this structure has been based on great theories about the structure of private law. It is also useless to look at the influence of an Institutional, a Pandectist or any other theory-based structure for that matter. Topics that other codes already dealt with were excluded, and pragmatism seems to have been the main impetus for the structure and organization of the Code. For example, specific contracts receive their own book because the decision was taken from the start to discuss these only at a later stage.[36] In doing so, Belgium shows it has learned from the Dutch experience. There, the new (Dutch) Civil Code officially entered into force in 1992. However, for many specific contracts, the text was not yet ready, and the new law only appeared later. Even today, for a very few specific contracts, the text of the old code in the so-called Book 7a is still the law of the Netherlands, keeping the numbering of the old code.[37] Whereas the Dutch arrived at this by chance, Belgium has designed from the start that, for some time, the articles on specific contracts will survive with their numbering from the old Code.[38] In contrast, the new books have their own numbering, which is not continuous but starts from one for each book. Generally, the work on the different books is parallel, not sequential. This means that the goal is not to finish the whole text in one effort or to finish the books in their particular order but only to finish each individual book as soon as possible, with the exception of Book 6 (Particular contracts), which has to wait for Book 5 (General law of obligation, general law of contracts and tort law). This approach may even occur within a book. Thus, the drafts on the property relations of married couples[39] and tort law[40] proceed at a different pace from the rest of Books 2 and 5 to which they belong.

To the ordered mind of many jurists, this may seem like a recipe for madness, but there is a logic behind it. First, the Dutch experience taught that making a major code in one go is not truly feasible. The Dutch finished Book 1 in 1970, Book 2 in 1976, and most of the others in 1992 but still had to wait until 2003 and 2012 for Books 4 and 10. This does preclude that the aforementioned Book 9 may never arrive.[41] Second, Belgium had good experiences with constructing a modular code with its new commercial law in the second half of the nineteenth century[42] and its more recent

---

[36] Geens (2016, 29).

[37] For the c.70 old articles that still remain, see https://wetten.overheid.nl/BWBR0006000/2019-01-01.

[38] Geens (2016, 29).

[39] Proposition de loi portant livre 2, titre 3 et le livre 4 du Code civil, 17.

[40] Proposition de loi portant insertion du livre 5 "Les obligations" dans le nouveau Code civil, Chambre des Représentants de Belgique, Documents parlementaires, 16 July 2019, 6.

[41] On the history of the Dutch Civil Code, see Florijn (1996) and Veen (2001).

[42] Heirbaut (2005, 35–41).

Code of Economic Law.[43] The main advantage of and the argument for this chaotic method remains that it offers more guarantees of success. The comparison with the Blitzkrieg is useful here. Instead of all the troops going to the frontline as one block, so that any obstacle will halt the whole group's progress, the individual sections rush forward as soon as they can. If some of them encounter an obstacle, the others can still press on. For now, this approach has already led to promulgated laws for Book 3 (January 2020)[44] and Book 8 (April 2019).[45] Parliament has already received the drafts of Book 4 and Book 5 (minus tort law) and a part of Book 2.[46] Drafts of Book 1[47] and the tort law of Book 5 are ready.[48] Books 7 and 9 are mainly meant to 'recycle' recent legislation[49] in a codification *à droit constant*[50] and book 6 will come later anyway. For now, drafting Book 2 looks like the major remaining problem. Thus far, the Belgian approach to private law codification may lack elegance but makes up for that by swiftly achieving results. Essential is the willingness to change the original plan if the circumstances demand so. For example, the original idea was to have the new Code appear on the scene with Book 5, the law of obligations.[51] In the eyes of many Belgian jurists, the law of obligations is still the apex of private law, so it was evident to start with it. However, since the obligations drafts have encountered the most resistance,[52] that option was out. Minister Geens then had the meagre Book 8 kick off the new Code. While this led to the complaint that 'the wagon had become the locomotive',[53] the train at least was on track and continued running.

This approach also has disadvantages. For a long time, Belgian jurists will have to cope with two codes (old and new). Drafters of a book or a part thereof will not always know the rest of the new law. Book 1 presented specific problems. When the drafters of Books 3 and 5 wrote their text, the work on Book 1 had not even started. This would not have been an inconvenience had all books been autonomous in and of themselves, which is not the case. Therefore, the drafters of other books had to tackle certain topics that should have belonged to Book 1. One way of solving that problem is by moving such a topic to Book 1 later on,[54] another just to leave

[43] Byttebier and Wera (2013, 206–207).

[44] Loi du 13 avril 2019 portant création d'un Code civil.

[45] Loi du 4 février 2020 portant le livre 3 « Les biens» du Code civil, Moniteur belge, 17 March 2020.

[46] Proposition de loi portant livre 5 nouveau Code civil; Proposition de loi portant livre 2, titre 3 et le livre 4 du Code civil.

[47] However, this draft is not yet public.

[48] See Bocken et al. (2019). There is a more recent version, which has not yet been made public.

[49] See, for example, Dirix and Sagaert (2014).

[50] Cf. Geens (2016, 29).

[51] Art. 2 Avant-projet de loi du 30 mars 2018 portant creation d'un Code civil et y insérant un livre 5 «Les obligations» (text consulted on: https://www.law.kuleuven.be/verbintenissenrecht/voo rontwerp-van-wet-verbintenissenrecht.pdf).

[52] See in particular Storme (2018).

[53] George (2019).

[54] Chances are great that this may happen with abuse of rights, now art. 5.7 Proposition de loi livre 5, as this concept is relevant for every part of private law, not just the law of obligations.

it in the book where it happened to end up. The result of the latter approach is that Book 1 has now been downgraded. The originally recodification program called it a General Part,[55] the 2019 Act promulgating Book 8 then already reduced it to General Dispositions.[56] Another problem concerns the numbering within the books. Given that Books 2, 5 and 6 will not be produced in one gulp, it makes sense not to have a numbering by book but by title within a book. This approach was chosen for Book 2 and should make it easier to 'plug in' new titles. However, the drafters of other books did not opt for this, and now a fixed number of articles has to be reserved for parts that arrive later,[57] irrespective of how long these parts will actually be.

5   The Methods of Editing the Code

As the previous paragraph already indicated, there is no common method for editing the different parts of the Belgian Civil Code. The approach is to take what works and to discard what does not. This becomes clear when one looks at the drafters. For the criminal law drafts, the Minister's cabinet and officials of his Ministry played an important role, but for economic and private law, external experts have been domi-nant because the Ministry of Justice lacks in-house expertise. For these experts, a bewildering variety of names and combinations exist, such as expert, editor, coordi-nator, and member of a workgroup. Persons can be active for more than one text and in more than one capacity. Their number can also vary from one to fourteen. The groups of experts may have existed previously, and Minister Geens co-opted them into his work or they may have come into existence because of the work on their part of the Code.[58] All of the external experts worked for free.[59] The expert is usually a law professor, though in many cases in combination with legal practice, mainly at the bar.[60] The latter has led to the criticism that the drafters may have served the interests of law firms, though that concerned mostly the work on the Code of Companies and Associations, not the Civil Code.[61]

The workflow also varied. A common process for arriving at a reform may be described as follows. First, experts, together with the Minister's cabinet and the administrative staff of the Ministry of Justice, write down the principles underpin-ning the reform. These are then discussed within the government and the competent commissions of Parliament. Afterwards, experts, cabinets and administrations write

---

[55] Geens (2016, 30).

[56] Art. 2 Loi portant création d'un Code civil.

[57] For example, in Book 5 articles 5.141–5.211 have been reserved for tort law.

[58] See Heirbaut (2018, 407–408).

[59] Cf. U onderschat het primaat van de politiek (interview with Minister of Justice, Koen Geens), De Standaard, 20 March 2019.

[60] See for example, for the drafter of the new tort law, Heirbaut and Jousten (2021).

[61] Maak de onzichtbare macht zichtbaar, De Standaard, 23 March 2019; Beroep? Topadvocaat en ghostwriter van de Wetstraat, De Standaard, 16 March 2019.

a draft. This draft is then scrutinized by a group composed of representatives of all of the government's ministers, which may lead to amendments. In a next stage the ministers themselves discuss the new version. If approved, the draft goes to the Legislative Section of the Council of State, Belgium's supreme administrative court. Its remarks on the draft's quality mostly lead to a new round of discussions and amendments by the ministers' representatives and, if all goes well, to a final approval by the ministers. Thereafter, the text, which has been revised several times, arrives in Parliament. Broad consultation with all stakeholders in the previous stages should ensure that by this point a consensus has been reached.[62] In fact, for the drafts of Books 3, 5 and 8, there had even been a consultation of the public at large, which had the chance to make comments.[63] This public element has been called a success, but that depends on what one considers success. The number of persons and institutions reacting was rather low, and most reactions came from the legal and financial world.[64]

As the modus operandi above shows, Minister Geens wanted to ensure that the drafts had a good chance of receiving parliamentary approval. In some cases, he even joined and took over initiatives of members of parliament. This happened for the 2017 and 2018 Acts on successions and the property relations of married couples.[65] The minister also inserted codification articles into these acts, allowing the government to integrate these parts of the law into the new Civil Code without having to pass through Parliament because this would amount only to a *codification à droit constant*.[66] When presented with the draft Royal Decree implementing these codification articles, the Legislative Section of the Council of State nevertheless objected because, in its opinion, the draft did change the content of the law, which was not allowed. The minister gave in and submitted the draft to Parliament.[67] As this example proves, speed may be an overriding concern, but it still has to take a backseat to democratic control by Parliament. In that, Belgium is very unlike France, where for example, the 2016 new contract law used the shortcut of an ordinance by the government.[68] The cooperation between Parliament and the Minister is not one-sided. For example, both before and after the 2019 elections, members of parliament submitted the ministerial drafts as member's bills[69] because that was deemed more opportune, as no one knew whether Minister Geens would retain his position after the formation of a new

---

[62] Geens (2016, 5).

[63] Dirix and Wéry (2017).

[64] Cf. Keereman (2018a, 8).

[65] Heirbaut (2018, 409).

[66] Art. 72 Loi du 31 juillet 2017 modifiant le Code civil en ce qui concerne les successions et les libéralités, Moniteur belge, 1 September 2017; art. 75 Loi du 22 juillet 2018 modifiant le Code civil et diverses autres dispositions en matière de droit des régimes matrimoniaux, Moniteur belge, 27 July 2018.

[67] Proposition de loi portant le livre 2, titre 3 et le livre 4 "Les successions du Code civil, 4–6.

[68] Ordonnance n° 2016–131 du 10 février 2016 portant réforme du droit des contrats, du régime général et de la preuve des obligations (https://www.legifrance.gouv.fr/eli/ordonnance/2016/2/10/JUSC1522466R/jo/texte).

[69] Example Servais Verherstraeten for Proposition de loi portant livre 5 nouveau Code civil.

government. As he decided not to join the new government formed on 30 September 2020, this was indeed a wise approach.

6 Why Does It Work This Time?

Given that Belgium failed to enact its own civil code in the past, why is this time different? A first explanation lies exactly in the difference between the past and the present. When the country became independent in 1830, the nationalism of the day may have called for new codes, but very soon a more pragmatic attitude took over. By keeping the French codes, Belgium did not have to invest in the development of its own law.[70] In fact, it is doubtful whether in 1830, Belgium had the in-house legal expertise to write codes that would have deviated from the French model. The country not only lacked scholars but also case law, which could have paved the way for a new code. Even François Laurent, a Belgian patriot, still saw his draft Civil Code for Belgium as a Franco-Belgian text, and in his 33-volume treatise on the Napoleonic Code, he incorporated French case law, as there simply was not enough Belgian material. In the twentieth century, this changed. Already in the 1930s, Henri De Page had enough Belgian cases to fill the next great treatise on private law in Belgium. Whereas De Page still had to refer to French doctrine,[71] Belgium also caught up for that after the Second World War.[72] By now, Belgium has indeed acquired enough expertise both in the law schools and in the court rooms to produce its own codes. It is interesting to make a comparison with Luxemburg. Given that both Belgium and France are currently reforming their private law, two choices confront Luxemburg: either to keep on following the French lead or go its own way like the Belgians. For now, it seems that a pragmatic attitude prevails. Luxembourgish law does not (yet) have the expertise to stand on its own, and it is better to keep on profiting from France's efforts.[73]

The previous paragraph only explains why the time is now ripe in Belgium for a new code but not why the current project is successful. The crucial element is that, for the first time in history, Belgium has a real plan for a new Code, the 2016 recodification program. In the past, ministers of justice, insofar as they were interested in a new Code, got sidetracked by the politics of the day or gave up as soon as they encountered resistance. Minister Geens's attitude, hopefully continued by his successors, can be summed up as follows: there will be incidents anyway, but the great work must go on.[74] In this, it helps that for private law Geens called upon external

---

[70] There was a whole industry in nineteenth century Belgium producing pirated editions of French law books (Verbeke 1994, 115–135).

[71] Heirbaut (2017b, 293–294).

[72] Heirbaut (2017a, 14–15, 17–18).

[73] Ancel and Prüm (2020, 26).

[74] Geens K, Nieuwjaarstoespraak Orde van Vlaamse balies, 27 januari 2015 (https://www.koengeens.be/news/2015/01/27/nieuwjaarstoespraak-orde-van-vlaamse-balies); "Koen Geens: "Als ik de

experts.[75] Even if his own cabinet and the Ministry's officials had to cope with crises, the experts continued to work. This explains why neither the terrorist attacks in Brussels in March 2016 nor the coronavirus pandemic stopped the recodification project.

Like any good plan, the recodification program set its priorities. Once again, the recodification program looks like a blueprint for a Blitzkrieg offensive. If you know that your tanks, in this case codification drafts, will encounter an obstacle, simply drive around it and leave its elimination for another day. This attitude is most of all visible in Book 2. Many problems, such as same sex marriages, have been settled for some time and will not create any ripples.[76] More difficult to handle are transgender and nonbinary people, adoption and filiation. In all of these fields, Minister Geens has kept reforms outside the codification program so that, should the Constitutional Court declare a part of a reform statute unconstitutional, such will not hinder the codification process.[77] The Constitutional Court had indeed stricken down parts of 2017 statutes on transgender people and adoption,[78] which proves the wisdom of this approach. For filiation law, the situation is murky. The Constitutional Court has produced an important body of case law, but some of its decisions have been controversial. Therefore, a 2018 statute has changed filiation law but only for uncontroversial issues. For the remainder, a ministerial commission on the law of filiation still needs to find its own consensus, which then has to survive the scrutiny of Parliament and the Constitutional Court.[79] Under these circumstances, it is indeed better to leave transgender people, adoption and filiation out of the codification's scope.

Like a Blitzkrieg offensive, the codification program accepts that no battle plan survives contact with the enemy and that flexibility, not a rigid adherence to the plan, wins the day. This may mean that the sequence of events needs to be changed, as has already been indicated for the central role originally planned for Book 5, now taken over by Book 8. It also meant that in the case of fierce resistance, the Minister did not insist and saved his energy for another day in the hope that sooner or later the wanted reforms would become possible anyway. Once again, Book 2 offers the best example. The 2016 codification program left no doubt about the personal feelings of Minister Geens, a Christian Democrat, concerning couples. First, he wanted to restrict the blessing of the law to affective relations. For married couples, he proposed to better protect the weaker party in separations of property by new mandatory rules. For unmarried couples in an established relationship, he also foresaw a minimum

---

verkiezingen moet winnen door mensen bang te maken, dan verlies ik ze liever" (interview with Koen Geens), Het Laatste Nieuws, 30 maart 2019).

[75] Cf. U onderschat het primaat van de politiek (interview with minister of justice, Koen Geens, De Standaard, 20 March 2019).

[76] Loi du 13 février 2003 ouvrant le mariage à des personnes de même sexe, Moniteur belge, 28 February 2003.

[77] Cf. Geens (2016, 29).

[78] Cannoot (2020).

[79] Verschelden (2019, 61–62, 69).

set of mandatory rules, once again to protect the weaker partner.[80] However, Geens could not convince the liberal parties in the governing coalition to agree to all this and had to give up his plans.[81] Paradoxically, his willingness to accept his defeat ensured the overall success of the codification. By losing the battle, he could continue to try and win the war.[82] In other words, tactical defeat may turn out to be strategic victory.

The acceptance of the various drafts is helped by the fact that they does not rock the boat too much. Innovations can be divided into two groups. The first consists of merely legislative innovations, i.e., the new rule has already been embraced for some time by case law, the codification only cementing existing jurisprudence by giving it an official, parliamentary stamp of approval. The best example of this is the tort law project. Whereas in the old Code a mere six articles sufficed to set out tort law, the new Code will expand this to seventy-one articles. However, an overwhelming majority of them mainly attempt to enshrine established precedents into legislation.[83] Therefore, objections are unlikely. A second group of innovations may cause more problems: novelties defended by scholars.[84] On these truly new articles, not everyone may agree. The drafters have foreseen resistance, and a major strategy for countering criticism is calling in comparative law. It is impossible to discern much of a pattern in the references to foreign codes and European or international texts, such as the Draft Common Frame of Reference, as the drafting body for each part of the code just quotes whatever pleases it. Thus, the drafters of Book 3 like the Civil Code of Québec the most, whereas the drafters of Book 5 ignore it almost completely. The only common element is that all drafters call in comparative law to support their own views and ultimately their choices. Quotes of foreign codes or European and international texts are mostly instrumental. They did not inspire the drafters' decisions but were used to justify them ex post facto.[85] This implies that the reference to foreign law, the external element, takes on more importance when the drafter fears that they will encounter more internal opposition. The 2016 codification program illustrates this, when it mentions the fiduciary contract, some kind of 'trust light'.[86] Given the traditional abhorrence of the trust in Belgium, opposition seemed inevitable. Therefore, Minister Geens listed many other Continental countries, which already had a similar instrument.[87] In the end, this failed. Parliament did not accept the fiduciary contract, as it feared that this would open the doors for tax evasion.[88] That the comparative argument is only an instrument becomes clear when one looks at the

---

[80] Geens (2016, 38–42).

[81] Keereman (2018b, 8).

[82] See for more on this, Heirbaut (2021a).

[83] Bocken et al. (2019, 30).

[84] See, e.g., Bocken et al. (2019, 33–35).

[85] See Heirbaut (2021b).

[86] Keereman (2018a, 9).

[87] Geens (2016, 47).

[88] Proposition de loi portant insertion du livre 3 "Les biens" dans le nouveau Code civil. Amendements, Chambre des Représentants de Belgique, Documents parlementaires, 10 December 2019, 173/2, 15.

use of legal history in the commentaries to the drafts. When the drafters do not like current Belgian law, they call in comparative law. However, when the comparative data show that a change of Belgian law is overdue and nevertheless the drafters prefer the Belgian tradition as an exception to the rule, then suddenly the history of Belgian private law justifies their choice. Remarkably, this 'Belgian' tradition does not go beyond Napoleon and is French in origin. An example is the *causa*, the requirement of a cause to contract. Even France has given in and has finally gotten rid of it, but the drafters of Book 5 still stick to the *causa* because to them 'tradition' has made it sacrosanct.[89]

In legal literature, the drafts have not sparked much criticism, apart from Book 5. The latter has drawn some fire, both for its general part and the section on tort law. However, the various attacks are of a rather divergent nature. One critic does not at all like that the drafts describe the normal person as 'the prudent and reasonable debtor' and prefers to stick to the old formula of the 'good family father',[90] thereby ignoring that most Belgian society has already said farewell to this idea a long time ago. The only fundamental criticism, thus far, came from Matthias Storme, one of Belgium's brightest law scholars, who attacked the dogmatic underpinnings of some choices by the drafters and even questioned the need for a new Code.[91] Two of the drafters countered his criticism, but reading their text the substantive arguments seems to matter less than their main justification: modernization is necessary and should not be hindered by doctrinal discussions.[92] In other words, it is better to have a new Code as soon as possible than to strive for an ideal Code that will never become reality. It seems that most law scholars share this pragmatic attitude. Moreover, as leading specialists have written the drafts, it has become hard to criticize their texts. Even for the Legislative Section of the Council of State, it has been hard to point out defects in the substance of the drafts. In addition, both the Legislative Section and other outsiders had to deal with so many drafts, not just of the recodification program but also Minister Geens's many other reforms, that it has become impossible to give all of them the critical attention they need.[93] To return to the Blitzkrieg analogy, so many tanks are rushing forward, that trying to stop one of them, just means that all the others can and will continue.

The 'love affair' between law professors and the code also reflects the changed nature of codification since the time of Napoleon. For Napoleon, the code expressed the legislator's will. Judges were only to apply it, and professors had to stick to paraphrasing the code. Events thereafter have shown that in reality the judges developed the law as it pleased them.[94] Codification has now become a way for the law scholar

---

[89] See for the drafters' view, Stijns (2020, 225–238).

[90] Letter of lawyer J. Boury, Réforme du Code civil: le droit en perte de valeurs, to newspaper Le Soir, 18 April 2019.

[91] Storme (2018, 17).

[92] Dirix and Wéry (2018, 16–17).

[93] Cf. Raad van State: 'Toezicht op wetten schiet tekort', De Standaard, 19 March 2019.

[94] See Gläser (1996).

to take back control from the judges. After all, even if the drafts mostly follow established case law, the drafting professors decide whether or not the draft will do so. Thereby, they (and not the judges) have become the final authorities on the law. The promulgation of the Code does not have to end this. After all, who is in the best position to interpret the Code: Parliament, which has voted on the draft, or the professors who wrote it? In short, the Code is the instrument of the law professor in trying to get the upper hand over the practitioners. Hence, the only numerous protests came from an open letter against the draft tort law signed by several practicing lawyers in French-speaking Belgium.[95] Even if it should score a minor victory, the practitioners' protest does not seem to be a major obstacle because changes in substantive private law do not seem to lead to a popular debate.[96] In contrast, for procedure and the court system, the situation is completely different. The Judicial Code and the Code of Criminal Procedure have a direct impact on the power of legal professions, and any proposal of change in these fields of law leads to much more virulent reactions.[97] Last but not least, practitioners have not been absent in the drafting process. Many professors have a double hat, teaching at university and working as practitioners at the same time.[98] During the drafting, practitioners were consulted, which ensured that the drafters could change their texts to meet the practitioners' approval.[99] Moreover, those practitioners who had not yet been consulted individually could have used the consultation of the public at large to make their remarks.

7 Landmines on the Road to Completion?

Thus far, only two Books have passed through Parliament, which still leaves seven to go. Much remains to be done, and in September 2020, the captain left the ship. Koen Geens, who had started the recodification program, decided not to continue as Minister in a new government. Is the future of recodification in Belgium thus in danger? Will Geens' tanks—after a first successful offensive—run into unexpected landmines, leaving them stranded?

Fortunately, there is no doubt that the reforms of the Civil and other codes will go ahead. In its coalition agreement of 30 September 2020, the new government expressly commits itself to continuing the recodification program.[100] Moreover, the new Minister of Justice, Vincent Van Quickenborne, had already pleaded for

---

[95] Lutte (2019) with approximately 150 cosigning practicing lawyers.

[96] In this case, there was a reply (Dubuisson and Bocken [2019]), but it did not generate a protracted discussion.

[97] See Heirbaut (2021a).

[98] See, e.g., Dubuisson and Bocken (2019, 731).

[99] Cf. Geens (2016, 5).

[100] Magnette P, De Croo A, Verslag van de formateurs, 2020 (consulted on: https://www.standaard.be/cnt/dmf20200930_94514804, 1 October 2020), 62.

a 'masterplan' to reform the Civil Code in 2004.[101] There are also elements guaranteeing the continuation of the recodification effort regardless of the personal wishes of a future Minister of Justice. First, by now so many members of parliament and law professors have become involved that the new code is no longer a dream of just one person.[102] Another element is that Books 3 and 8 have become the Sagrada Familia of Belgian law. Like the first parts of Gaudi's unachieved cathedral in Barcelona, on which work started in 1882, Books 3 and 8 will stand as calls to finish the job (and a lot faster than in Barcelona). Minister Geens himself has strengthened this by a textbook example of framing. When Book 8 enters into force on 1 November 2020, two civil codes will coexist in Belgium. It would make sense to reserve the name 'Civil Code' for the 1804 Civil Code and to describe its successor as the 'New Civil Code' because it is the new kid on the block after all. However, the 2018 Act introducing a Civil Code and inserting Book 8 into that Code states that from 1 November 2020 on the 1804 Code will be called 'Old Civil Code' and that the newcomer will just be the 'Civil Code'.[103] This imposes a new frame, the new Code will be seen as 'the' code and the 1804 Code as an anomaly. Thus, the names for the two codes are not neutral but gently nudge jurists toward the new Code.

Anticipation will also play a role. In fact, this will help to save Book 5, despite all criticism. The draft of the new tort law has not yet been submitted to Parliament because the commission took its time and the upshot of this is a very elaborate text. A jurist who has the draft and its commentary can dispense with reading all of the literature on tort law. As the current Code contains only six articles on tort law and the draft one structures and amends current case law, judges will inevitably look to this handy text and apply it before it has even been voted by Parliament. For the rest of the law of obligations in Book 5, some scholars have already indicated some occasions where judges have applied the draft in anticipation of it becoming law.[104] Even though their claims may be exaggerated,[105] there is no doubt that anticipation contributes to path dependence. It makes it easier to continue on the planned path to approve the draft. The Geens-armada will continue to conquer.

8 Future Challenges

The biggest but most common mistake of codifiers is thinking that their job is done when the new law has been promulgated. In reality, the job just begins at that point, and in some cases, strengths may become weaknesses. No one will deny that it is

---

[101] Heirbaut (2005, 27–28, note 85).

[102] For the names of the law professors involved, see Geens (2016).

[103] Final paragraph of art. 2 Loi portant création d'un Code civil.

[104] Stijns (2018, 415–428), Wéry (2018), and Dirix and Wéry (2020).

[105] The scholars indicating influences of the draft are actually some of its authors and not neutral outsiders. More doubts about a possible influence of the draft in a specific judgment in Peeraer (2020, 47).

good that the current codification project proceeds at a rapid pace, but a slower rate of advancement also has its advantages. It allows practitioners more time to prepare the shift to the new law.[106] Thus far, generous transition periods of more than a year, much longer than the ordinary ten days after the publication of a new law, seem to have enabled a smooth transition.[107] More problematic is the tactic of setting aside problematic issues, as sooner or later they have to be approached. The conundrum may be the law of filiation. In 1987, Belgium finally enacted new legislation to conform to the European Court on Human of Right's ruling in the 1979 Marckx case, which had deemed Belgian law in this area discriminatory.[108] The years after 1987 have become a 'calvary' for the legislator. Neither the 1987 Act nor any of its successors have received the full approval of the Constitutional Court, which has always found something to criticize in new filiation law.[109] In fact, one may wonder whether it is even possible to write a subtitle on filiation for Book 2, Title 2, that can ever pass the Constitutional Court's strict scrutiny. In addition to topics that are covered by the current Code, much legislation outside the Code exists. In some cases, the new Code will integrate them[110]; in other cases, the drafters do not want to do so, as this costs valuable time and/or may lead to a debate derailing their draft. Thus, in tort law, almost all of the special regulations will continue to exist after parliament's approval of the current draft.[111] This means that the Code will fail partially to achieve one of its goals: to reunite private law legislation in one text and thereby make it more accessible. Once again, this needs to be remedied sooner or later.

As usual, social evolution will eventually outpace the code, making updates necessary. If these are as haphazard as the previous amendments to the current Code, it will not take long before the new Code becomes a monstrosity. If Napoleon's Code has by now become a dilapidated building instead of a venerable institution, the Code of Minister Geens amounts to the construction of a new house. The problem is that, for now, the house owner has not yet foreseen that he will have to invest in the upkeep of his new dwelling. Consequently, it will not take long before it risks becoming as ramshackle as its predecessor. Another recent Belgian code shows how to avoid this. The Ministry of Employment and Labor has been the driving force behind the 2010 Social Criminal Code. An advisory council guards the future coherence of the Code by advising its application and implementation and the integration of existing and new legislation into the Code.[112] It could be a good idea to establish such an advisory council for the new Civil Code as well. This council could also be useful to address

---

[106] Cf. Wissink (2017, 1148).

[107] For example, about one and a half yearss for the new property law (Art. 39 Loi du 4 février 2020 portant le livre 3).

[108] Paula Marckx, the single mother who started this case, passed away in the summer of 2020 at the age of 94, after a life with many careers as a model, journalist, helicopter pilot and airport CEO (De vrouw die ouderschap loskoppelde van het huwelijk, De Standaard, 30 June 2020).

[109] See Gallus (2016) and Verschelden (2005).

[110] Example product liability (Bocken et al. 2019, 17–22).

[111] Bocken et al. (2019, 36).

[112] Art. 96–98, Code social pénal, Moniteur belge, 1 July 2010.

construction errors. No code has ever been free of errors in its design,[113] but given the speed of the Belgian codification process, more construction errors may pop up than is usual.

9   A Final Problem

Last but not least, the new Civil Code may not be the end. Koen Geens at one moment confessed that his ultimate dream is a unique code,[114] a Civil Code that contains what is now covered by the Civil Code, the Code of Private International Law, the Code of Economic Law and the Code of Companies. Whether such a Belgian 'supercode' may ever be possible will depend on a completely different element, which has been rather absent in this text but inevitably crops up in any discussion of Belgium: the linguistic issue. In 2018, Flanders, the Dutch-speaking part of Belgium, changed a small part of the Civil Code for which it was competent,[115] and one year later, it installed its first ever Minister of Justice.[116] These, in themselves minor, events may herald a new trend in which the competence for private law moves to the regional level. If that happens, the latest Civil Code of Belgium may also become its last…

10   Addendum

The Belgian codification Blitzkrieg has moved so rapidly that it easily left behind the manuscript of this article submitted in the fall of 2020. In 2022 Belgian parliament approved Books 1, 4 and 5 and a part of Book 2. If anything these most recent events have confirmed the analysis in this article. For example, because objections to the tort law draft could have been an obstacle for the passage of Book 5 through parliament, tort law was taken out of this book. It is now the topic of Book 6. This means that specific contracts are bumped from Book 6 to Book 7. However, security rights could not go from Book 7 to Book 8, because Book 8 on proof is already in force. Therefore security rights find their home in Book 9, displacing prescription to Book 10. Once again, this proves that pragmatism determines the structure of the Belgian Civil Code and not any great theory about private law.

---

[113] Thus, the twenty-fifth anniversary of the Dutch Civil Code led to a book on fifty of its construction errors: Van de Pol et al. (2017).

[114] Exposé d'orientation politique. Justice, Chambre des Représentants de Belgique, Documents parlementaires, 17 November 2014, 20/18, 33.

[115] Decreet van 9 November 2018 houdende bepalingen betreffende de huur van voor bewoning bestemde goederen of delen ervan, Moniteur belge, 7 December 2018.

[116] Vraagtekens bij plannen voor Vlaamse justitie, De Tijd, 9 October 2019.

References

Ancel P, Prüm A (2020) Introduction. In: Ancel P, Prüm A (eds) Réformer le droit des contrats? Analyse comparée autour du droit luxembourgeois. Larcier Brussels, pp 15–26

Bocken H, Dubuisson B, Jocqué G, Schamps G, Vansweevelt T, Delvoie J, Zammito B (2019) La réforme du droit de la responsabilité extracontractuelle. Le projet de la Commission de réforme du droit de la responsabilité. La Charte Bruges

Bruyère M (2019) Principes, esprit et controverses. L'Avant-projet de Code civil de François Laurent ou l'oeuvre séditieuse d'un libre penseur, unpublished PhD thesis Ghent University

Byttebier K, Wera T (2013) De codificatie van het Belgisch economisch recht. In: Alofs E, Casman H, Van den Bossche A (eds) Liber amicorum André Michielsens. Kluwer Mechelen, pp 193–242

Cannoot P (2020) Grondwettelijk Hof dwingt verdere hervorming geslachtsregistratie af. Tijdschrift Voor Familierecht 10:17–26

Dirix E, Sagaert V (2014) The new Belgian Act on security rights in movable property. European Property Law Journal 3:231–255

Dirix E, Wéry P (2015–2016) Tijd voor een hercodificatie van het Burgerlijk Wetboek. Rechtskundig weekblad 79:2

Dirix E, Wéry P (2017) Consultatie Nieuw Burgerlijk Wetboek. Tijdschrift Voor Belgisch Burgerlijk Recht 7:531–532

Dirix E, Wéry P (2018) Nieuw verbintenissenrecht: dogmatische discussies mogen noodzakelijke modernisering niet in de weg staan. Juristenkrant 373:16–17

Dirix E, Wéry P (2020) Le nouveau Code civil: un état de la situation. Tijdschrift Voor Belgisch Burgerlijk Recht 10:322–324

Dubuisson B, Bocken H (2019) La réforme du droit de la responsabilité: «Un droit commun applicable à tous». Réponse à Me Isabelle Lutte. Journal Des Tribunaux 138:729–731

Florijn E (1996) Ontstaan en ontwikkeling van het nieuwe Burgerlijk Wetboek. Universitaire Pers Maastricht

Gallus N (2016) Filiation. Bruylant Brussels

Geens K (2007a) 200 jaar vennootschapsrecht in perspectief: Quo vadis ius societatum? Tijdschrift Voor Privaatrecht 44:75–90

Geens K (2007b) Tweehonderd jaar vennootschapsrecht in vogelvlucht. In: Buyle J-P, Derijcke W, Embrechts J, Verougstraete I (eds) Tweehonderd jaar Wetboek van Koophandel. Larcier Brussels, pp 97–108

Geens K (2016) Le saut vers le droit de demain. Recodification de la législation de base. www.koengeens.be/fr/politique/recodification-de-la-législation-de-base/recodification

George F (2019) Le nouveau droit de la preuve. Quand le huitième wagon devient locomotive! Journal des Tribunaux 138:637–657

Gläser M (1996) Lehre und Rechtsprechung im französischen Zivilrecht des 19. Jahrhunderts. Klostermann Frankfurt

Heirbaut D (2005) Hebben/hadden onze ministers van justitie een 'civiel' beleid? Kluwer Mechelen

Heirbaut D (2017a) The Belgian legal tradition: does it exist? In: Kruithof M, De Bondt, W (eds) Introduction to Belgian law. Kluwer Mechelen, pp 1–24

Heirbaut D (2017b) Weg met De Page? Leve Laurent? Een pleidooi voor een andere kijk op de recente geschiedenis van het Belgische privaatrecht. Tijdschrift Voor Privaatrecht 54:267–321

Heirbaut D (2018) The sleeping beauty awakens: Belgium's new law of inheritance as a first step of the greatest recent recodification program in Western Europe. Zeitschrift Für Europäisches Privatrecht 26:407–408

Heirbaut D (2021a) De Blitzkrieg van Geens: en wat daarna? (forthcoming)

Heirbaut D (2021b) References to foreign law in the commentaries to the new Belgian Civil Code (forthcoming)

Heirbaut D Jousten A (2021) Der belgische Vorentwurf zum neuen Deliktsrecht (forthcoming)

Houben R, Meeusen J (2020) The competition for corporate charters: Belgium wants a (bigger) piece of the pie. ZEuP 28:11–46

Keereman A (2018a) Je schrijft niet om de vijf jaar een nieuw burgerlijk wetboek" (interview with Eric Dirix). Juristenkrant 364:8–9

Keereman A (2018b) Een consequenter en meer solidair huwelijksvermogensrecht" (interview with Alain Verbeke). Juristenkrant 371:8–9

Lutte I (2019) La réforme du droit de la responsabilité civile: un vrai débat de société. Journal des Tribunaux 138:682–683

Peeraer F, Samoy I (2016) The Belgian Civil Code: how to restore its central position in modern private law. European Review of Private Law 24:601–618

Peeraer F (2020) Ook bij koop op plan moet nietigheid (of onwerkzaamheid) niet verder gaan dan nodig. Tijdschrift Voor Bouwrecht En Onroerend Goed 18:44–49

Stevens F (2006) 'Où est donc passé la commission de révision?' La révision du Code civil en Belgique à la fin du XIXe et début du XXe siècle'. In: Macours G, Martinage R (eds) Les démarches de codification du moyen âge à nos jours. KVAB Brussels, pp 213–221

Stijns S (2018) Het aankomend verbintenissenrecht in de recente rechtspraak van het Hof van Cassatie. Tijdschrift Voor Belgisch Burgerlijk Recht 8:406–428

Stijns S (2020) La disparition de la cause du contrat. Rapport belge. In: Ancel and Prüm, Réforme, pp 225–238

Storme ME (2018) Een nieuw verbintenissenrecht: oude wijn in nieuwe zakken. Juristenkrant 372:17

Suel M (1995) Essai sur la codification à droit constant. JO Paris

Van de Pol F, Beumens T., de Kluiver C, Overheul M, Trapman L (eds) (2017) Vijftig weeffouten in het BW. Ars Aequi Nijmegen

Vandevoorde J (2018) Le Code Napoléon est-il encore en vigueur en Belgique? Journal des Tribunaux 137:279–280

Veen (2001) En voor berisping is hier ruime stof: over codificatie van het burgerlijk recht, legistische rechtsbeschouwing en herziening van het Nederlandse privaatrecht in de 19de en 20ste eeuw. Cabeljauwpers Amsterdam

Verbeke C (1994), Belgian law: an annotated bibliographic guide to reference materials. CBBB Brussels

Verschelden G (2005) Origineel ouderschap herdacht: pleidooi voor een globale hervorming van het afstammingsrecht. Die Keure Bruges

Verschelden G (2019) Partiële reparatie van het afstammings- en naamrecht. Commentaar bij de titels 3 en 4 van de wet van 21 December 2018. Tijdschrift Voor Familierecht 9:61–76

Wéry P (2018) L'avant-projet de réforme du droit des obligations et ses premiers échos en jurisprudence. Tijdschrift Voor Belgisch Burgerlijk Recht 8(2018):296

Wissink M (2017) Omzien en Vooruitzien. Tijdschrift voor privaatrecht 54:1147–1151

Dirk Heirbaut is Francqui research professor at Ghent University and member of the Royal Flemish Academy of Belgium for Science and the Arts. His research focuses on medieval and feudal customary law, the comparative history of private law codifications, private law in Belgium since the French Revolution, and the methodology of legal history.

The Making of the Argentine Civil and Commercial Code

Aida Rosa Kemelmajer de Carlucci

Abstract The purpose of this chapter is to provide a brief overview of the Civil and Commercial Code in force in the Argentine Republic since August 1, 2015, and to explain its general guidelines. It explains the way to manage decodification, the importance of the constitution and the human rights treaties in the system of private law and the special functions of general principles.

1 Purpose of This Paper

This paper provides a brief overview of how the Argentine Civil and Commercial Code (CCC) came into force in Argentina in 2015, namely how it was prepared, and explains its general features.

2 Some Relevant Facts

In February 2011, Ricardo Lorenzetti, Helena Highton and myself were appointed by the President of the Argentine Republic and accepted the challenge of preparing the draft law, which eventually formed the basis of the current CCC. Federico di Lorenzo, the efficient secretary of the commission, coordinated the work of more than one hundred Argentine jurists, comprised of 30 groups, and entrusted with proposing the rules of the different parts of the future code.

The first great difference with the repealed Civil Code (CC) dated from the nineteenth century, effective from 1871 to 2015, which necessarily included many partial amendments, was the way in which it was drafted. The original Civil Code was

A. R. Kemelmajer de Carlucci (✉)
National Academy of Law and Science of Buenos Aires, Buenos Aires, Argentina
e-mail: aidakemelmajer@carlucci.com.ar

M. Graziadei and L. Zhang (eds.), *The Making of the Civil Codes*,
Ius Gentium: Comparative Perspectives on Law and Justice 104,
https://doi.org/10.1007/978-981-19-4993-7_9

prepared by Vélez Sarsfield,[1] who worked alone in a country where the rate of illit-
eracy was 80%. At that time, there were very few specialists in civil law, and as in
France, the job of the interpreters of law and doctrinal scholars was undervalued. In
fact, when Jacques de Maleville, one of the jurists appointed by Napoleon to draft the
French Civil Code, published an article in which he analyzed the discussions in the
Conseil d'État and proposed guidelines of interpretation, Napoleon exclaimed "My
code is lost", fearing that the comments would distort the text. As a man of this time,
the emperor considered commentators to be a kind of "corrupter" of the meaning
of the law. That is the reason why, to avoid that particular descriptor, Jean Bugnet,
professor at Dijon, said: "I do not know the Civil Law; I only teach the Napoleonic
Code."

The Argentine situation in the twenty-first century is very different. Great teachers
have developed a private law that, in many aspects, is at the forefront not only of
the legislation and doctrinal scholarship of Latin American countries but also has
adopted advanced solutions even when compared with European law. The CCC in
force is not an individual work but the result of the effort of the cooperation of many
jurists.

The preparatory process was deeply democratic. While the project was being
drafted, the Argentine community became aware of what was being written. Before
the submission of the preliminary draft, countless conferences, courses, consultations, etc., were given throughout the country; furthermore, the different parts of the
draft were distributed among the other members of the subcommittees.[2] Books and
articles with comments were published nearly everywhere one would care to look.[3]
These contributions were critical. The intention was that with criticism, which was
more or less in good faith, with greater or lesser ideological bias, the text of the draft
law would be improved.

3 The Concept of Code. Managing Decodification. Some Instruments to Facilitate It

The concept of code in the nineteenth century was different from the current one. At
that time, it was stated that: "coding is, on one hand, an exhaustive work, in whole
or in part, which ensures a certain security of the legal order, in particular, because
it gives people, within a country, better *accessibility* to the Law. In addition, from

---

[1] This is recognized by Law No. 340, which approved the Civil Code "drafted by Dr. Dalmacio Vélez Sarsfield".

[2] This methodology proved useful to correct many original mistakes.

[3] For example, Rev Derecho Privado y Comunitario, 2012-I y 2012-2, Bs. As., ed. Rubinzal, 2013; Revisión de la Ley de Daños, 2012-3, Bs. As., ed. Rubinzal, 2012 y 2014-1, 2 y 3, Bs. As., ed. Rubinzal, 2014; Rev. del Colegio de Abogados de la Plata, special ed., November 2012; Rev. de Derecho mercantil, de consumo y de sociedades, año III, no. 5, October 2012; Cuaderno Legal Familiar, No 28, Bs. As., ed. Ley, May 2012; Rivera (2012), Vitolo (2012a, b), Lopez Mesa (2012), and A.v. (2012).

the point of view of Congress, it is an act of authority in search of *stability and permanence*".

Exhaustiveness was expressed in Sect. 22 of the repealed Argentine Civil Code, which stated: "What is not explicitly or implicitly stated in any section of this Code cannot have the force of law in civil law, even if such a provision had been previously in force, either by a general law, or by special law".

However, this aspect of codification was called into question by Portalis in his famous Preliminary Speech: "A code, however complete it may seem, is no sooner finished than thousands of unexpected questions present themselves to the magistrate. For these laws, once drafted, remain as written. Men, on the other hand, never rest. They are constantly moving; and this movement, which never ceases and whose effects are variously modified by circumstances, continuously produces some new fact, some new outcome. Many things are therefore necessarily left to the authority of custom, to the discussions of learned men, to the arbitration of the judge".[4]

Moreover, today, "*completeness*" is openly contradicted by the undisputed phenomenon of *decodification,* which the CCC does not (and cannot) erase. Rather, it expressly maintains the statutes contained in special laws. In other words, it respects the unstoppable phenomenon of decodification. Therefore, in the words of Natalino Irti, a "new exegesis" must "rationalize the role of microsystems and compose systemic coherence".[5]

Precisely, the CCC is intended to be the instrument of integration of all microsystems of private law. In other words, there is "dialog" among different sources. Special laws and microsystems do not exist in isolation, in the void, or without interrelationships. On the contrary, although these microsystems have specific rules, interpreters may use the CCC as an instrument for integrating different sources into the system. For example, the principles of good faith, prohibition of abuse of law, etc. (arts. 10/13 CCC), all of them apply in the context of special statutes as well, such as insurance law, navigation codes, environmental law, etc.

Quite often, interpretation is done *dialogically,*[6] it needs a "dialog of sources".

The phrase "dialog of sources" derives from International Law as explained by Erik Jayme.[7] The plurality of sources, which is typical of postmodern law, requires the coordination of laws within the legal system. This is a condition for efficiency and justice at a time marked by the tendency to legislate on the most varied, often converging, subjects, both in domestic and international law. It is a question of applying, simultaneously, both coherently and co-ordinately, several sources to eliminate the incompatible norm only when there is an insurmountable contradiction. Flexible coordination of sources restores coherence by identifying complementarities, convergences, and harmonies.

---

[4] Portalis (1978, pp. 35–37).

[5] Irti (1992, pp. 113–114 and 191).

[6] Sozzo (2012, p. 150).

[7] Jayme (1995, p. 259).

Of course, this "dialog" is not always easy; sometimes there is a real "overflow" of sources[8] by the inclusion of some branches, such as bioethics and the environment, that are interdisciplinary by themselves.

The CCC helps the new exegesis by incorporating various sections explaining the order of application of the rules (arts. 1, 2, 150, 768, 963, 964, 1709, 1834, etc.). Sections of this type are necessary in a code that, as I said, expressly recognizes the phenomenon of decodification, as the repeated referrals to special laws shows. I will now focus on some examples of express recognition of special laws.

The provisions of the preliminary title concerning:

– the existence of abuse of a dominant position in the market, which are governed by *the specific provisions referred to in special laws* (art. 11).
– the assignment of rights with respect to a human body, which have no commercial value but affective, therapeutic, scientific, humanitarian or social value, can be done by the holder of such rights provided that such values are respected as stipulated in the *special laws* (art. 17).
– the indigenous communities' rights to own the lands they occupy are exercised in accordance with the National Constitution and the *special law.*

The first book stipulates as follows:

– legal entities have a different personality from that of their members, with the exceptions that may be found in *special laws* (art. 143).
– the exercise of individual rights must be compatible with collective rights and should not affect the functioning or sustainability of ecosystems of flora, fauna, biodiversity, water, cultural values, landscape, among others, according to the criteria provided for in the *special law* (art. 240).
– The new housing protecting system also refers to "local regulations" for the determination of economic unity in rural properties (art. 256).

The Second Book makes provisions for assisted human reproduction and has left the regulation of many issues to the *special law*; thus, sections 567, 575 and 577 refer to prior, informed and free consent and other requirements established by the *special law.*

The complexity of the system should not be intimidating.

a. First, this complexity existed before the CCC. Lawyers and judges deal with it daily; it has not been invented by the CCC, which, as stated before, has favored its understanding by establishing solution-oriented provisions.
b. Moreover, numerous rules mirror the case law of the Supreme Court of Justice of the Nation. This "*living law*" incorporated into the CCC is very useful to interpret the system. For example, according to the Supreme Court, the declaration of unconstitutionality is the *last ratio* of the legal order and will only be pronounced if there is no other way to integrate the rule in order to bring it in agreement with

---

[8] Pérez Luño (2011).

the Constitution[9]: "interpretation must be based on the words of the law, but must be consistent with the content of other provisions, because the various parts of the law form a coherent unity and it is necessary make a balance with the whole", and "the unspecified legal concepts arising from principles and values are rules of integration and axiological control, so it is appropriate to disqualify decisions manifestly contrary to the legal values that constitute the legal order" among other examples.

c. Emphasis has been placed on grammar to enable a better understanding of the CCC. The Commission tried to draft the rules as clearly as possible to facilitate their understanding both by professionals and the general public. Efforts have been made to preserve, wherever possible, those words already known and used by Argentine legal scholars and Argentine courts. However, there have been many modern social, scientific, cultural, and economic changes. For these reasons, new expressions have inevitably been incorporated to reflect new phenomena and legal trends.

d. Finally, it is true that flexible notions, such as *"restricted capacity"* and *"age and degree of maturity"*, must be managed by lawyers, judges, and other legal professionals. However, these expressions were already known as part of our legal jargon (for children, law 26,061; for mental health, law 26,657, etc.).

4 The Role of the Judge: The Constitutionalization of Private Law. The Value of Principles

The judge, this person who, in the nineteenth century, was the "mouth that pronounces the words of the law", according to Montesquieu's quotation, today has an active role; the new code increases it, for various reasons, included, but not limited to, the following:

a. The Human Rights Treaties and the Constitution, expressly mentioned in sections 1 and 2 of the CCC, oblige the judge not only *to subsume* the facts into the rules but also to *weigh* principles in hard cases, when fundamental rights are in conflict, using the *proportionality principle.*

Much has been said about the constitutionalization of private law. The document attached to the Draft Law explained: "In the new Code there is *a communicability of principles between Public and Private Law* in almost all the basic points. For the first time in Argentina there is in the Code *a connection between Constitution and Private Law* consistent with the decisions of the courts and the Argentine legal scholars".

In line with this, Andrés Gil Dominguez says that the CCC implies a "nonstop passage from a 19th-century code, which responded to the scheme of a legislative rule of law, to a code of the twenty-first century, which incorporates as a general

---

[9] Constitutional Court, 288:325; 290:83; 292:190; 301:962; 324:3345, 4404; 325:645, among others.

structure of interpretation and application the paradigm of the constitutional and *conventional* rule of law".[10]

Such an assertion is correct. In Argentina, "constitutionalization" means a *"constitutional body of law"*, wherein human rights treaties have been incorporated. These treaties, such as the American Convention on Human Rights, created courts responsible for the interpretation and implementation of these treaties, such as the Inter-American Court of Human Rights. The effectiveness of the supra-legal hierarchy of laws requires that each country follow the interpretation of these courts. It has been clearly asserted that "the national interpreter and the inter-American interpreter are doomed to understand each other through the practice of a fluid judicial *dialog to prevent a loss of effectiveness*".[11]

CCC's adherence to the so-called trend favouring the "constitutionalization" Private law is evidenced from sect. 1 onward. It has well been said that this trend "deals with very important issues that compromise a certain model of society". This assertion is implicit in Alberdi's words in his famous debates[12] with Vélez Sarsfield: "The Civil Code of a country is the part of legislation that aims to develop the natural rights of its inhabitants considered as members of the family and the civil society. These rights are essential to human beings".[13]

The CCC contains fundamental principles and strives to make them a factual reality. For example, the *constitutional* protection of housing (art. 14 of the CN) is clear in the housing legal regime (arts. 244/256 CCC), which gives more security to a greater number of people than the previous law.

As stated before, in many cases, lawyers and judges must "weigh", and "reconcile", values, rights, and safeguards in conflict. Perhaps, a paradigmatic case to show the tension between principles is a plenary ruling entered by the National Court of Appeals hearing Commercial Matters, which analyses the conflict between the abstract nature of a bill of exchange and the right of access to justice of a debtor who is a consumer living outside the Court's jurisdiction. The decision held that "The abstract causal relationship[14] with the underlying transaction, as any other special provision derived from the law, cannot prevail over general constitutional laws issued by the Congress of the Nation, in compliance with the Constitution itself. Consumer rights are a kind of human rights or, more particularly, a *constitutionalized civil*

---

[10] Gil Dominguez (2015, p. 43).

[11] Pizzolo (2015, p. 623).

[12] De Domingo (2002, p. 251) and Bilbao Ubillos (1997, p. 273).

[13] The controversy was started by Alberdi (repr. 1920); Vélez replied with *El folleto del Dr. Alberdi*, in El Nacional, June 1868, p. 255–279 repr. in *Juicios críticos sobre el proyecto de código civil,*Buenos Aires, ed. imprenta José Tragant, págs. 231/256. Alberdi replied con *Efectos del sistema federal en la unidad tradicional de la legislación civil de las repúblicas de Sud América*, Obras Selectas, Buenos Aires, ed. La Facultad, 1920, t. IX, Escritos jurídicos, vol. 2, pág. 280/330.

[14] "Abstracción cambiaria" means that there is no need to show the cause or motive backing the negotiable instrument. In other words, there is no need to make reference to the underlying transaction that originated the the instrument to make it enforceable.

right".[15] For this reason, even if both of them are strong principles, the Court prioritizes the right of access to justice and, consequently, authorizes the judge, even *ex officio*, to declare his territorial incompetence in an enforcement proceeding of the debt resulting from the negotiable instrument against a human being, whose domicile is very distant from the place where a company (a bank, an insurer, etc.) have brought the lawsuit according to what is written in the document.

It is necessary to remember Cicero: "When I put up the arguments for a cause, for a defense, I do not count them, I weigh them." This is the reason why the balance is one of the oldest and most constant symbols of justice.[16]

Overall, the CCC entrusts and requires the judge to make *reasonable* decisions[17] (art. 3), "capable of ensuring rationality".[18]

b. The relevance of principles.

As Giorgio Pino says, the "discovery" of legal principles has been one of the core issues of the last fifty years; they are an almost routine instrument in legal argumentation.

Many criticisms have been made to the CCC for using principles and rules. Some authors said that the role of legal principles as a source of law has weakened; others discuss the use of the word 'principles' when CCC lists rules and vice versa. For example, sect. 31, under the heading *"General Rules"*, provides that the restriction on the exercise of legal capacity is governed by "the following general *rules*". Among others, it mentions "the presumption of capacity", which in truth is said to be a principle.

In fact, the CCC distinguishes principles and rules, but between the great diversity of theories about these concepts, it adheres to those that hold that the distinction principles/rules is not always strong. In some cases, the distinction is weak; it is a question of degrees and, consequently, that distinction is not always relevant to the resolution of the conflict. The important thing is that, in most cases, weighting will be the basic methodological criterion to solve a situation where fundamental rights are in conflict.

Such conflicts can also arise in human rights microsystems. For example, family housing in the marital crisis is usually attributed to the spouse who must take care of the children so as not to change their place of living and protect the best interest of the children. However, what to do if the parent who must leave the house is a visually handicap person, who has organized such property in such a way that they can work normally, to be able to provide assistance to the children?

---

[15] Cámara Nacional de Apelaciones en lo Comercial. Autoconvocatoria a plenario s/competencia del fuero comercial en los supuestos de ejecución de títulos cambiarios en que se invoquen involucrados derechos de consumidores, 29/6/2011, elDial.com—AA6CB4; ED 244-59; JA 2011-III-285; Doc. Jud. Año XXVIII, n° 1, 4/1/2012 pág.7, voto del Dr. Heredia.

[16] Robert (1998, p. 53).

[17] Iniguez (2012, p. 237).

[18] Prieto Sanchís (2003, pp. 131–132).

5   The Human Being, Center of the System. Dignity and Autonomy

The protection of *human beings* as the focus of the system is closely linked to the notion of *dignity,* and this is associated with the concept of *autonomy*.

Two Spanish authors say that "biological evolution left human beings on the beach of the history. Then, the great cultural evolution began, the arduous humanization of man himself and reality", but humans were left "without an instruction manual, and we struggle to establish ourselves as species *endowed with dignity;* we want to build a new essence with the biological essence received. Dignity is not in the past but is the future".[19]

This dignity was especially considered by the Supreme Court of the Nation in the leading case "Diez", 7/7/2015, when the court ruled, with undisputed endorsement for patients' rights, that such a person, who had been in a vegetative state for more than two decades, had the right to leave this world with dignity, detaching himself from the hydration provided to him only to extend an unworthy life.

Dignity walks alongside autonomy, that is, the possibility of each one deciding or choosing with respect to their own life. Carlos Nino[20] explained that "Personal autonomy is the ability of a human being to decide what we want to do with our lives, to design and implement our own vital plan, as sustained by Emmanuel Kant. However, for such autonomy to be effective, people must have real choices, and sometimes, for that option, they need the help of the State."

Therefore, the state should not hinder that autonomy or subscribe to the dogmatism of preconceptions, such as "family public order" or the "presumption of fraud".[21]

Autonomy, which is synonymous with freedom, has changed traditional notions such as *minors, capacity, disability, and representation* based upon the understanding that they are no longer adequate to describe the whole regime of acts involving the child and the person with limitations caused by mental health deficiencies.[22] Hence, the expression "age and degree of sufficient maturity" (mentioned in the International Convention on the Rights of the Child), which is in numerous provisions of the CCC (Arts. 24, 26, 66, 404, 425, 595, 596, 598, 608, 613, 617, 626, 627, 639, 679, 690, 707), and the new legal regime for persons deprived of health (art. 32 last part).

Argentine courts show great reasonableness in their rulings by applying these concepts.

For example, 3/9/2015, the Court of Minors No. 1 of Corrientes authorized a teenage girl who lives with her aunt to conduct her own administration (alternatively, with the assistance of her aunt if needed) of the allowance that her father receives from the State because even if he has a daughter, he provides no assistance to her.

---

[19] Marina and De La Válgoma (2000, p. 17ff).

[20] Nino (1989).

[21] Gaspar Lera (2016, p. 255).

[22] Ferrando G (1999, p. 59); conf. Lisella (1984) n° 16 ss. Kraut and Diana (2012).

Another case: Two teenagers who, having different parents, consent to being adopted by their mother's husband, a third person who truly fulfils the role of father of both; one adolescent agreed to a full adoption while the other wanted a simple adoption. Both wished to use the first surname of the adopter. The judgment thus responds to what the sufficiently informed adolescents expressly requested of the Court.

Finally, as Gil Dominguez says, "when Sect. 1 refers to "the cases" is protecting each person, because it is linked to pluralism and the idea that each person, as part of their life plan, has the right to be considered and to get a response according to his/her owness".[23]

6 Methods of Interpretation

The CCC is more concerned about the "aims of the law" than about the "intention of the legislator". On the other hand, the repealed Civil Code contained the famous "notes" that Vélez incorporated at the bottom of each article. There is no doubt that these notes were a valuable instrument of access to knowledge, since in the nineteenth century, there were fewer books to aid in the interpretation of the text. Today, there is an excess of literature, almost everybody reads and writes, thanks to the educational policy started, precisely, by Domingo F. Sarmiento, president by the time the Civil Code was enacted.

The "originating" intention is no longer the central element of the interpretation of the Code. sect. 2 uses "aims"; it is useless to look back, like Lot's wife, who remained immobilized. Briefly speaking, today we don't need to know the "original meaning"; this is the "nonoriginalist" interpretation, typical of constitutional law, which sneaks into private law.

The activist "nonoriginalist" approach to interpretation has been accepted by the Inter-American Court of Human Rights and the Supreme Court of Justice of the Argentine for many years now. Indeed, in 1934, in the *Avico case,* the Argentine Supreme Court said: "Constitutional rules must be interpreted in such a way as to adapt to the actualities or demands of modern life, without stubbornly searching into the intention of its authors a hundred years ago".

The acceptance of this method of interpretation is fully justified. As Valencia Zea pointed out in Colombia when explaining his project of a private code, "each generation claims its own criteria; not to impose old ideas enables its evolution and progress". "The argument of authority, or genuine meaning of the law, has only a relative value. We cannot expect our way of thinking to be the same as that our successors, nor could our ancestors link us to their ways of conceiving and resolving legal problems".[24]

---

[23] Gil Dominguez (2015, p. 43).

[24] Valencia Zea (1980, pp. 15–16).

Apparently, even the Bible itself demands this kind of interpretation; Rabbi Sergio Berman says: "The Bible should be read more like a script than as a scientific paper. The text tends to explain the meaning of *why,* more than *how the facts were.* This text is enshrined *in meaning*, not by the historical verification of the events narrated in it".[25]

7   The Method of the Civil and Commercial Code. The Unification of Civil and Commercial Contracts. Consumer Law

Like the repealed code, the CCC is divided into a preliminary title and books. Books are divided into titles, titles into chapters, and chapters into sections.

The difference is, on the one hand, that the preliminary title has been "enriched". Divided into four chapters, it implies the recognition that written law is not the only source of law. This preliminary title incorporates general principles, such as good faith and the prohibition of abuse of the law and fraud. As Diez Picazo pointed out, "Inserting a norm into the preliminary title contributes very effectively to energizing it. The preliminary title is like the *entrance door to* the entire legal system. Having a piece of machinery at the door, where everyone sees it and can think of using it, is not quite the same as having it left in a hidden corner of the building. In other words, almost all jurists know the preliminary title. Additionally, reaching the forgotten ins and outs of some sectors requires more educational training and more erudition".[26]

The CCC has six books instead of four as the former one. There is now a complete book devoted to family relationships and another to the law of succession.

The First Book deals with *persons*, then with *objects,* and finally with *legal relationships.*

The Second Book regulates *familial relationships.* In the plural, several forms of family are accepted and not just the one grounded on marriage.

The Third Book refers to the Law of Obligations. Title One regulates the General Theory of Obligations; how they arise, how they are terminated, etc. Title Two regulates the Law of Contracts. The great novelty introduced in the CCC is the distinction between two ways of entering into contracts: (i) the traditional one, offer and acceptance; (ii) the new one, contracts concluded with pre-established general clauses and in which the adhering person may or may not be a consumer. For example, a businessperson buys insurance through standard forms provided by an insurance company or by a third party, without any chance of discussing the terms and conditions of the contract: it's the so-called *"take it or leave it"* approach.

---

[25] Bergman (2009, p. 50).

[26] Diez Picazo (1982, p. 10).

These types of one-sided adhesion contracts may or may not contain unfair clauses. The CCC regulates such clauses; this regulation is very important since, in Latin America, there are smaller, weaker companies that do business with more powerful companies, some of them multinationals, which impose the conditions of contracts upon them. The CCC deals with judicial review of unfair clauses, which is possible, even if they have been approved by an administrative authority. These are rules that protect small businesses, many times forgotten by national laws.

Title Three addresses some aspects of consumer relationships. The CCC has not delineated the entirety of consumer protection laws. The code regulates only what has been referred to as the "hard core" of the system. The decision to do so was not easy. Comparative law shows several models. Clearly, some, but not all, consumer-related issues must be incorporated into the CCC because this is a fast-changing subject matter. Consequently, if we consider this characteristic, a first option is to keep both regulations separate (as in Italy, France, etc.). The other criterion accepted in Germany, Quebec and Argentina is to introduce just the fundamental concepts in the code. The Commission understood that a twenty-first century code cannot ignore the consumer, especially since Argentina's Constitution expressly mentions and protects this "vulnerable" person.

Consequently, rules connecting two basic points have been introduced:

i. rules dealing with consent, and
ii. rules solving the imbalance between consumers and providers. For example, provisions concerning abusive practices (arts. 1096/1099), special arrangements (arts. 1104/1116), and unfair terms (art. 1117/1122) are included in the code. In addition, protection was extended to other specific areas, such as banking contracts (arts. 1384/1389), private cemeteries (art. 2111), timesharing (art. 2100), to name a few. Moreover, a bridge was built between consumer law and the environmental law under sect. 1094, providing that the rules governing consumer relations must be applied and interpreted in accordance with the principle of access to *sustainable consumption.*

The Commission explained the functioning of consumer law by taking into account the special law and the CCC. General principles of consumer protection incorporated into the CCC are the "minimum protection", so (i) there are no obstacles for the special law to establish higher conditions in favor of the consumers, and (ii) at the same time, the special law may respect those minima without affecting the system.

Title Four refers to private civil and commercial contracts (sale, lease, agency, distribution, etc.)

As a great Spanish professor once said, "the commercial code was a fossil with the mummies of contracts that long ago disappeared from the business world, without ruling the new ones".[27] The unification of civil and commercial contracts was acclaimed by Argentine legal scholars for years. However, one of the first measures taken by the Commission was to enquire very well-known professors as

---

[27] Garrigues Díaz-Cañabate (1981).

to whether unification was appropriate or not. Unfortunately, the report came when the Commission had already sent the bill to the Ministry of Justice.

Either way, in this respect, the CCC follows a project drafted in 1998. The authors of that document explained:

> At that time (1804), there was a sharp division between civil law (which was considered the legal continent of the *agricultural* economy) and commercial law (to which *trade and industry* were attributed). Circumstances varied over time. Georges Ripert rightly described the phenomenon of the expansion of acts of commerce: "Actions of ordinary life are carried out today in a business-like manner. The contract is no longer an agreement concluded after a long discussion, drafting a double-copy letter. It is adhesion to pre-established clauses, printed out in a form, and at a fixed price. Rural life itself does not escape that commercialization. We learn about agricultural credit and crop warrant and paying bills by letters of credit." A person who does not acquire any property can spend his life without going to a notary, but he cannot stop going to a bank every day. In our region, Augusto Teixeira de Freitas led to unification by referring to "that dreadful duplication of civil laws" and the absence of "any reason requiring a Commercial Code". The First National Congress of Commercial Law, held in Buenos Aires in 1940, approved a motion advocating for the enactment of a single code of obligations, both civil and commercial. As of 1926, the Second National Conference of Lawyers had appointed a commission of jurists to carry out work to simplify the rules of the law of obligations. The VI National Bar Conference, held in La Plata in 1959, went further and approved the following statement: "1. The enactment of a single Code of Private Law is desirable; 2. To achieve that purpose, as an immediate step, a single Code of obligations and contracts should be enacted; 3. As a further pull, the unification of the private law of Latin American States must be reached". Acdeel E. Salas stated that "a synthesis of the so-called civil and commercial law is necessary, since both regulate the same legal substance: the relationships of individuals with each other". Bridging the gap between the two main areas of law has already occurred in Argentina. The insolvency of nontraders was soon subjected to the same procedure as that applied to traders (sect. 310, Law 19.551, now sect. 2, Law 24.522), subject to the commercial judge (Law 22.093). The use of securities has become widespread. Law 17.711 incorporated into the Civil Code a number of principles derived from the commercial system.

Equally important, the CCC opted to favour the legal solution derived from the Commercial Code in the event of divergences between the two bodies of law. As an illustration of this, in the tension between pecuniary interest (commercial) and presumption of gratuitousness (civil), the balance is inclined toward the commercial nature, as in the contract of deposit (sect. 1357) and agency (sect. 1322).

However, some negative comments have been raised against the methodology used. In fact, an author asks himself: What is left of commercial law?[28] The answer is everything, mainly because commercial matters remain in the Special Law outside the CCC.

Finally, it must be taken into account that commercial law is no longer the status of traders; the "humanization" of commercial law began a long time ago.[29]

---

[28] Vitolo (2012a, b, p. 167).

[29] Alegria (2010).

8 Another Aspect of Constitutionalization. The Issue of Effectiveness.

The constitutionalization of private law implicitly carries its effectiveness. It has been said:

> The "judicial process points to the crucial time in which the protection of rights prevails. Moreover, this is the highest and most critical instance, since judicial protection constitutes the last resort, the last protections provided by the law, which intended to operate when spontaneous observance of the provisions has been infringed and all other forms of protection have failed. Consequently, the failure of judicial protection unescapably means a deficit in the operation of the rules of substantial law.[30]

That is why this CCC contains many procedural rules aimed at giving efficient application of any judgment (e.g., section 553 and 557, measures to ensure alimony and communication rights) and, although discussed by a minority sector of Argentine legal scholars, it accepts valid instruments for the best exercise of substantial law, such as the "dynamic evidentiary burden", in the field of civil liability (sect. 1735), and in family law (sect. 710).

In brief, despite the great crisis of our judiciary, the CCC shows trust in judges. As Portalis[31] said in his memorable Preliminary Speech: "We have kept ourselves from the dangerous ambition of regulating and foreseeing everything. Positive laws will never be able to completely replace the use of natural reason in the chores of life…The task of the law is to broadly fix the highest principles; establish fertile principles and not descend into details. The judge, penetrated by the general spirit of laws, is the one tasked with its application."

Judges, of course, must understand that time is usually fundamental to the exercise of rights. They should remember the African proverb:

> Every morning, a gazelle wakes up in Africa. She knows she has to run faster than the fastest lion if she does not want to be killed. Every morning, a lion wakes up in Africa. He knows he has to beat the slowest gazelle if he does not want to starve. It does not matter if you're a lion or a gazelle: When the sun comes up, you had better start running.

9 Conservation and Innovation

Every recoding process has parts of conservation and parts of innovation or greater rupture with the past.

The CCC has conserved much, not only in the method but also in the content, except with respect to the rights of the human being, especially in the field of familial relationships.

Deep regulatory innovation lies in family law. Change should not disturb the general public because it reflects a modern reality and the constant and settled case

---

[30] Luminoso (1999, p. 27).

[31] Portalis (1978, pp. 35–37).

law of the Inter-American Court of Human Rights. In short, this is the acceptance that we must begin to revise the classic constructed paradigms on heterosexuality and male/female dualism because, as the Court says, "as part of contemporary societies there are social, cultural and institutional changes aimed at more important developments of all life choices" and "the American Convention does not find a closed concept of family, let alone the protection of traditional model exclusively"; "all forms of family have advantages and disadvantages and each family has to be analyzed in particular, not from a statistical point of view."[32]

The loss of the centrality of marriage is counterbalanced by the growth of the role that filiation plays as a founding act of the family; reality has even eroded the traditional categories of filiation, so the CCC has had to introduce a new category, namely, filiation assisted by human reproduction techniques (arts. 560/564).[33]

10 What Was Left Along the Way and What Was Changed from the Initial Draft

Some changes were not even proposed by the Commission, perhaps because of an excess of caution. For example, it would have been desirable to eliminate the classification of artificial persons into public and private, or to authorize in some cases, as in Brazil, a divorce issued by the administrative authority.

Moreover, as is well known, along the path ranging from the submission of the preliminary draft to the enactment of the CCC, some points were left out, such as the responsibility of the State (finally regulated for a limited area, by law 26,944, which may raise some constitutional doubts); the right to access drinking water (proclaimed in numerous international declarations and in the water codes of some provinces); homogeneous individual rights (whose regime is being built by the rich case law of the Supreme Court of Justice of the Nation); *postmortem* human assisted reproduction and surrogacy (thus leaving a gap that is causing legal problems to children born as a result of these techniques, solved by the judges); deterrent pecuniary sanctions to be applied to those who attack the environment; and the duty of cooperation of the Argentine authorities in favor of people residing in our country who want to adopt abroad (last paragraph of sect. 2635, a deletion that will surely be ignored by good Argentine judges, who will continue to comply with this collaboration by application of the general rules of private international law).

Nevertheless, in my opinion, the overall result is positive. Of course, as Ripert said, it is easier to replace aged material with a new machine in a factory than to replace traditional legal equipment with the new legal order. He noticed that in France, after forty years of the enactment of the law recognizing women's legal equality, the

---

[32] I have explained these changes in the introductory chapter of the book that I have codirected with Marisa Herrera and Nora Lloveras, *Tratado de Derecho de Familia según el código civil y comercial de 2014*, Santa Fe, Rubinzal, 2014, t. I, pp. 9–94.

[33] Stanzione MG (2012, p. 201).

French notaries continued to call the woman's husband to validate an act for which they need not appear. We can find no better example of conservatism.

As a Chinese proverb says, "when winds of change blow, some people build walls, some build mills." The Argentine legal scholars, Argentine courts and successive legislators after 1871 built wonderful mills. Vélez died on 30 March 1875, at the age of seventy-five; he had four years of his life to see how the new winds consolidated the course of history. One way or the other, his work transcended him and lasted for nearly a century and a half. The hundreds of Argentine jurists working at CCC are aware that today the aims must be much more modest and that is why we have not built a mill to stand tall and long in the wind but instead we have built a bridge between the historical laws and the laws that future generations will undoubtedly demand tomorrow.

References

Alberdi, JB (1920) Efectos del sistema federal en la unidad tradicional de la legislación civil de las repúblicas de Sud América, Obras Selectas, t. IX, Escritos jurídicos, vol. 2 ed. La Facultad. Buenos Aires, pp 280–330

A.v. (2012) Reformas al derecho comercial en el Proyecto de Código Civil y Comercial de la Nación. Legis, Buenos Aires

Alegria H (2010) Régimen legal de protección del consumidor y derecho comercial, LL 2010-C-821

Bergman S (2009) Celebrar la diferencia. Unidad en la diversidad, ed. B. Argentina SA. Buenos Aires, p 50

Bilbao Ubillos, JM (1997) La eficacia de los derechos fundamentales frente a particulares. Ed. Centro de estudios políticos, Madrid, p 273

Cámara Nacional de Apelaciones en lo Comercial. Autoconvocatoria a plenario s/competencia del fuero comercial en los supuestos de ejecución de títulos cambiarios en que se invoquen involucrados derechos de consumidores, 29/6/2011, elDial.com—AA6CB4; ED 244–59; JA 2011-III-285; Doc. Jud. Año XXVIII, n° 1, 4/1/2012 pág.7, voto del Dr. Heredia

De Domingo T (2002) El problema de la drittwirkung de los derechos fundamentales: una aproximación desde la filosofía del Derecho. Rev. Derechos y Libertades, Madrid, año VII, January-Dicember, p 251

Diez Picazo L (1982) Prólogo in Wieacker F El principio general de la buena fe. Civitas, Madrid, p. 10

Ferrando G (1999) Libertà, responsabilità e procreazione. Cedam, Padova, p 59

Garrigues Díaz-Cañabate J (1981) Setenta y cinco años de derecho mercantil, en Estudios de Derecho mercantil en homenaje al profesor Antonio Polo. ed. Revista de Derecho Privado, Madrid, p 264

Gaspar Lera S (2016) Los negocios de configuración del patrimonio común en la sociedad de gananciales: autonomía privada de los cónyuges y Registro de la propiedad. Rev. Crítica de Derecho inmobiliario, XCII(753)(January/February):255

Gil Dominguez A (2015) El Estado constitucional y convencional de derecho en el código civil y comercial. Ediar, Buenos Aires, p 43

Herrera M, Nora Lloveras N (2014) Tratado de derecho de familia según el código civil y comercial de 2014. t. I, Rubinzal, Santa Fe, pp 9–94

Kraut A, Diana N (2012) Un breve panorama de la legislación, la jurisprudencia y el proyecto de código civil y comercial, Una imprescindible relectura del status jurídico de las personas con discapacidad mental. Rev. de Derecho Privado y comunitario 2:141

Iniguez MD (2012) Reglas generales de las personas jurídicas y contratos asociativos. Rev. d. Privado y Comunitario 3:237

Irti N (1992) La era de la decodificación. Bosch, Barcelona

Jayme E (1995) Identité culturelle et intégration: le droit internationale privé postmoderne. Recueil des Cours de l' Académie de Droit International de la Haye, II, Nihjoff, Haye

Lisella G (1984) Interdizione "giudiziale" e tutela della persona. Gli effetti dell'incapacità legale. E.S.I., Napoli

Lopez Mesa, M (ed) (2012) Estudios sobre el proyecto de nuevos estudios civiles y comerciales código, ed. Contexto, Resistencia

Luminoso A (1999) Quale processo per la famiglia. Ricognizione dell'esistente e prospettive di riforma. In: AV, Quale processo per la famiglia e i minori. Giuffrè, Milano, p 27

Marina JA, De La Válgoma M (2000) La lucha por la dignidad. Anagrama, Barcelona

Nino C (1989) Ética y derechos humanos. Astrea, Buenos Aires

Pérez A (2011) El desbordamiento de las fuentes del derecho. La ley, Madrid

Pizzolo C (2015) Las normas interconectadas (entre la primera y la última palabra en derechos humanos), LL 2015-D-623

Portalis JEM (1978) Discurso preliminar del proyecto de código civil francés, trad. De Manuel de Rivacoba y Rivacoba, Edeval, Valparaíso, pp 35–37

Prieto Sanchís L (2003) Neoconstitucionalismo y ponderación judicial. In: Carbonell M (ed) Neoconstitucionalismo(s), Trotta—IIJ de la UNAM, Madrid, pp 131–132

Rivera, JC (dir) (2012) Comentarios al Proyecto Civil y Comercial Código de la Nación

Robert CN (1998) Naissance d'une image: la balance de l'equité. In Justice et equité, Dalloz, Paris

Sozzo G (2012) Consumo digno y verde: humanización y ambientalización del derecho del consumidor. Sobre los principios de dignidad del consumidor y de consumo sustentable. Rev. D. Privado y Comunitario, p 139

Stanzione MG (2012) Rapporti di filiazione e terzo genitore: le esperienze francese e italiana. In: Famiglia e Diritto 2:201

Started Alberdi JB (1920) Proyecto de código civil para la República Argentina, repr. in Obras Selectas, t. IX, vol. 2, Escritos jurídicos. La Facultad, Buenos Aires 2:173–254

Valencia Zea A (1980) Proyecto de Código de Derecho privado. Bogotá, pp 15–16

Vélez (1868) El folleto del Dr. Alberdi, en El Nacional, págs. 255/279, repr. In Juicios críticos sobre el proyecto de código civil, José Tragant, Buenos Aires, ed. imprenta, pp 231–256

Vitolo DR (2012a) El derecho comercial en el proyecto de código civil y comercial de la Nación. ¿Qué queda de él? Rev. de derecho privado y comunitario 3:167

Vitolo, DI (2012b) Reformas al régimen de protección de los consumidores en el proyecto de código civil y comercial de la Nación, Ed. Ad-Hoc

Aida Rosa Kemelmajer de Carlucci is Professor of civil law. She has a Phd from the University of Mendoza. She is a member of the National Academies of Law and Science of Buenos Aires and Córdoba. She is also an honorary member of the Royal Academy of Law and Legislation of Madrid, Spain. In 2016, she received the Konex Award from Brillante as the most prominent humanities personality of the last decade in Argentina, one of the highest distinctions awarded in Argentina in the social sciences.

Civil Law and Social Changes in Korea in the Past 30 Years

Sang Yong Kim

Abstract The Republic of Korea has experienced a period of rapid social change, which is generally referred to as "compressed and shortened development". Since the Seoul Olympics in 1988, social changes have progressed more rapidly. Korea has responded quite successfully to the rapid social changes in the field of civil law. However, not all aspects of Korean civil law responded as successfully as others. The development of property law in the Korean Civil Code has lagged behind the development of family law. Property Law has mainly responded to social changes through the legislation of special acts. Family Law has responded promptly and continuously through a number of amendments of the KCC while also developing by way of adoption and amendment of special family law acts. As a result of such different responses, it could be said that property law in the KCC is more akin to a top down "Law in the Book" legislative exercise, where family law is in contrast "Law in Action", resulting from the influences of the advocacy of women-led women's rights civic groups, academic works of progressive family law scholars, and judgments of unconstitutionality and constitutional nonconformity of clauses of the KCC by the Constitutional Court. Presently, in the field of property law, high increases in real estate prices, real estate speculation, irregular real estate transactions by abnormal legal methods, and the incomplete recapture of windfalls are becoming growing social problems. It is hoped that in the future, real estate transactions could be normalized by way of notarization of the contract of purchase and sale and by developing legislation that facilitates the recapturing of windfalls resulting from social development projects. Much work has been done to help Korean civil law keep pace with a rapidly changing Korean society, but much work remains to be done. In the field of family law, it should be noted that the rights and interests of children whose parents have divorced should be subject to strong legal protections. Minors should be protected against the misuse of the internet through the use of sophisticated smartphones and other electronic devices. Moreover, the growing number of immigrant foreign workers, North Korean escapees, and refugees arriving in Korea has created a strong need for the legislation of an act of equal treatment (e.g., an anti-discrimination act or equality

S. Y. Kim (✉)
Faculty of Law, Yonsei University, Seoul, South Korea
e-mail: lawkimsy@gmail.com

© The Author(s), under exclusive license to Springer Nature Singapore Pte Ltd. 2023
M. Graziadei and L. Zhang (eds.), *The Making of the Civil Codes*,
Ius Gentium: Comparative Perspectives on Law and Justice 104,
https://doi.org/10.1007/978-981-19-4993-7_10

act) to protect such individuals from discrimination. Ultimately, Korean civil law shall pursue and realize justice and love, which are the eternal and utmost important values of mankind. Justice and love are the ultimate goals of the KCC and all special civil acts. This paper proposes that Korean society should evolve beyond extreme individualistic egoism and gradually transition into communitarianism. Korean civil law shall be imbued with the characteristics of social law in parallel with the changes of Korean society toward communitarianism.

1 Introduction: Characteristics of Social Changes and Challenges During the Last 30 Years in Korea and Deficiencies in the Responses of the Civil Law in Korea

1.1 Social Changes and Challenges in Korea During the Last 30 Years

History progresses by way of challenge and response. Civil law also develops as a response to social changes and challenges. For the past 30 years, Korea has progressed rapidly, simultaneously, and over a short period of time into a high information, hyper connected, globalized, and individualized society, with lower birth rates, aging population demographics, lower rates of marriage, and increasing divorce rates, which is increasingly polarized as a result of the rise in industrialization and urbanization that began in the 1960s. Furthermore, Korea has experienced two large economic shocks due to a foreign currency deficiency (once in 1997 and again in 2008). More than 1.5 million foreign workers and many refugees have immigrated to Korea. Recently, more than 33,000 North Korean have escaped into South Korea. During the past 30 years, Koreans have enjoyed economic prosperity and abundance, but Koreans have also lived with a high level of social tension. Korea was particularly impacted by the COVID-19 pandemic beginning in late 2019 early 2020.

To such social changes and challenges, responses of civil law have been slow and insufficient. Continuous high increases in the price of land and housing have become a severe social problem.[1] Windfalls due to real estate speculations are not recaptured by way of tax (income or otherwise) and flow fully with limited tax consequences into the hands of the owners of land and housing.

---

[1] See, Jeong (2018).

1.2 Responses to Social Change by Way of a Series of Partial Amendments of the Korean Civil Code

Since the implementation of the KCC, in 1958, the property law section has been very partially amended three times (in 1984, 2011 and 2015), and the family law section has been more broadly amended three times (in 1977, 1990, and 2005), continuing with further, more minor, partial amendments from 2005 to 2020.[2] In 1984, the KCC was updated to include provisions concerning sectional superficies to provide a legal framework to support the construction of subways and the development and use of underground properties (§ 289-2 KCC). In 2011, a KCC provision on minority guardianship was updated to facilitate the appointment of a guardian (§ 928 ff. KCC) and provisions concerning the court's powers of appointment and supervision in relation to adult guardianship were amended to address the social challenges resulting from a growing elderly demographic (§§ 9 ff., §§ 936 ff. KCC). Furthermore, the age of majority was lowered to 19 years of age by amendment in 2011. Before then, it had been 20 years of age (§ 4 KCC). Finally, in 2015, tourist travel contracts were given a prescribed form (§§ 674-2 to 674-9), and strong protections for a guarantor were introduced (§§ 428-2, 428-3, 436-2 KCC). In addition to the abovementioned amendments of the KCC, the lion's share of the civil law's response to social changes and challenges has been carried out by way of legislation in the form of numerous special civil acts.

In reference to the three periods of broad amendments of the KCC section on family law, many important legal principles were introduced or amended.

The amendment of the family law section of the KCC in 1977 introduced numerous legal principles, including but not limited to, the principle of constructive majority by marriage of a minor (§ 826-2 KCC), the joint exercise of parental authority by both parents (§ 909 (2) KCC), legal reserve of inheritance (§§ 1112ff. KCC), and presumption of co-ownership where ownership in property is uncertain between husband and wife (§ 830 (2) KCC). In 1990, amendments introduced the ability to make a claim for the division of property against the other party at the time of divorce (§§ 839-2, 843 KCC), consideration of contributory portion of an inheritor in the case of inheritance (§ 1008-2 KCC), and joint burden of living expenses for communal life of husband and wife (§ 833 KCC), among other reforms. In 2005, the legal concept of the "head of the family" was removed from the KCC, while provisions were added concerning full adoption (§§ 908-2ff.), the denial of paternity by child (§ 846 KCC), and the shortening of litigation period of action of denial of paternity (§ 847 KCC). Most notably among the 2005 amendments was the deletion of the long-standing traditional prohibition of marriage between parties with the same surname (historically related to being from the same clan) and being from the same geographical region (§ 809 KCC).

The reason why family law has been more broadly amended than property law comes from a number of factors, including the strong amendment movements from

---

[2] Since the implementation of the KCC to 2020, it had been amended a total of thirty times.

women-driven women's rights civic groups pushing to shift the paradigm of the family away from traditional Confucianism-oriented family law, a growing body of modern scholars providing support for the idea of more democratic, gender-equal family law, and judgments of unconstitutionality or constitutional non-conformity by the Constitutional Court on the undemocratic and Confucianism-oriented clauses of family law in the KCC.[3]

It is not to be thought that the overall responses of the KCC in light of social changes and challenges during the past 30 years were timely or sufficient; however, as a result of the actors outlined above, progress has been made.

2   Series of Projects of Amendment of the Korean Civil Code

2.1   Two Attempted Projects of Amendment of the Korean Civil Code's Law of Property Fall Short of a Successful Complete Revision

Since 1999, the KCC has undergone major amendments of its section on property law. The first project of amendment began in 1999, with the first draft being proposed in 2004. The first draft contained sweeping reviews of whole areas of the property law section of the KCC, including lowering the age of majority from twenty years of age to nineteen,[4] changing from the permission principle to the authorization principle in relation to the establishment of a juristic person, concise regulations on floating sum mortgages, three categories of nonperformance combined into a unified principle of nonperformance of obligation, exclusion of the fault of the obligor in the case of the rescission of a contract, strict liability of a supervisor with respect to a ward in their care, etc.

However, the first amendment draft, which was submitted to the National Assembly by the Administrative Government in 2004, was never passed into law owing to the expiration of the term of the members of the National Assembly. According to the Korean Constitution, all draft acts submitted to the National Assembly for deliberation are abandoned when the term of the members of the National Assembly expires (Proviso of Article 51 of the Constitution). As a result, the first amendment draft was abandoned in 2008.

From 2009, work began on the second draft amendment of the KCC's property laws, which was not completed until 2014. At this time, it had been planned not to

---

[3] Lee (2018, pp. 531–532) and Shin (2018, pp. 412–414).

[4] The age of majority has been lowered to 19 years of age in 2013. The voting age has been lowered to 18 years of age as of 2020 by the *Public Official Election Act*. Therefore, minors could vote in national elections. In the near future it appears that the age of majority will be lowered to 18 years of age in line with the voting age.

submit one global draft amendment as in 2004 but to submit numerous partial drafts of particular sections of property law separately. Although more effective than the previous attempt, only provisions concerning adult guardianship, contracts governing tourism, and new protections of guarantors were added or amended. After such partial success, the remaining outstanding partial drafts were also automatically abandoned because of the expiration of the term of the members of the National Assembly.

Given this failure to significantly alter the law on property, the KCC could not fully and appropriately respond to Korea's emerging social changes and challenges. Therefore, in place of an amendment of the KCC, numerous special civil acts were enacted to attempt to achieve what the KCC could not. Judgments of the Constitutional Court and the Supreme Court also assisted in allowing the existing civil law to respond to such changes.

2.2 Amendment of Family Law in the Korean Civil Code a Relative Success

The KCC's provisions governing family law have been amended to respond relatively successfully to the emerging social changes and challenges in Korean society. In addition to major amendments of the KCC's family law provisions in 1977, 1990 and 2005, more minor partial amendments have been continuously carried out in 1997, 2009, 2011, 2012, 2014, 2016, 2017 and 2020, as they were needed. A particularly significant partial amendment occurred in 2011, which introduced new rules surrounding adult guardianship to address the issues concerning Korea's aging population. Adult guardianship encompasses 4 subtypes of guardianship: adult guardianship,[5] limited guardianship,[6] specific guardianship[7] and guardianship by contract. Of these four types of guardianship, three are statutory, while guardianship by contract is not. Adult guardianship is designed and regulated for the protection of property and the person of an incompetent adult. Guardians for incompetent adults are selected and appointed by the family court (§ 936 (1) KCC). In principle, the standard number of guardians is one, but where necessary, multiple guardians may be appointed (§ 930 (2) KCC). Juristic persons (e.g., a corporation) may also have a guardian appointed and fall under guardianship (§ 930 (3) KCC). A guardian as an agent of a ward can perform juristic acts on behalf of their ward (§ 938 KCC).

The reasons why family law could be successfully amended where property law failed to progress have lied, as outlined in greater detail above, in a combination

---

[5] Adult guardianship can be commenced by adjudication by the family court for a person who continuously lacks the capacity to manage affairs due to mental restraints (§ 9 (1) KCC).

[6] Limited guardianship can be commenced by adjudication by the family court for a person who demonstrates insufficient capacity to manage affairs due to mental restraints (§ 12 (1) KCC).

[7] Specific guardianship can be commenced by adjudication by the family court for a person who requires temporary guardianship or guardianship for any specific affairs due to mental restraints (§ 14–2 (1) KCC).

of initiatives by civic groups, scholars, the Constitutional Court, and the Supreme Court. In addition to these reasons, members of the National Assembly could not help consider the democratic potential of woman voters as a key target demographic to win elections. However, the projects to amend the KCC's provisions on family law have not been completely sufficient to meet the social changes and social challenges in Korean society.[8] It is noted in particular that the KCC's provisions concerning the protection of children are lacking.

An increasing divorce rate has placed the issue of the governance of the support and maintenance for the children of divorcing parents in the forefront of Korean society. To support such children, the *Act on Enforcing and Supporting Child Support Payment* was introduced in 2014. Through this act, the Child Support Agency was established in 2015. The main work of this governmental body is to inform the divorced payer of their obligation to pay child support to the recipient of child support. In 2020, the KCC was amended to introduce protections for sexually abused minors: the period of extinctive prescription of the right of sexually abused minors to claim compensation from their abuser was amended to begin only from the time the child reached the age of majority (§ 766 (3) KCC). Therefore, any sexually abused minor mayflies a claim for damages within three years from the time they reach the age of majority (presuming they or their legal representative have knowledge of both damages and the identity of their abuser) (§ 766 (1) KCC) and within 10 years from the age of majority (the standard based on the prescription period from the time at which an unlawful act was committed presuming the victim has no knowledge of their claim in damages or the identity of the abuser in the first three years but gains such knowledge before ten years pass) (§ 766 (2) KCC).

An unaddressed recommendation of certain modern scholars is that where an individual passes intestate, the share of inheritance to potential beneficiaries should be divided in proportion to the contribution of the potential beneficiary to the person or estate of the deceased prior to their passing.[9]

---

[8] Lee, op. cit., p. 532.

[9] Eom (2020, p. 9).

3 Legislative Action by Way of Special Civil Acts Outside the Korean Civil Code for a Timely Adaptive Response to Social Changes and Challenges

3.1 Legislative Responses to Growing Migration to Urban Centers, Shifting Social Structures, and Rapid Increases in the Price of Land and Housing by Reason of Growing Industrialization and Urbanization

Industrialization and urbanization have been rapidly progressing in Korea since the beginning of the 1960s. They have brought both positive and negative effects. On the positive side, large amounts of land have been developed, countless factories have been built and operated, providing employment opportunities, new cities have emerged and flourished, and high-rise housing apartments have been erected to meet the housing needs of a growing urban population. On the other hand, the price of land has skyrocketed, low-income individuals have encountered difficulties securing affordable housing lease contracts, the quality of the environment has significantly degraded, problematic levels of land speculation have been widespread, and abnormal land transactions occurring by way of irregular legal methods have created windfall profits for the few to the detriment of the many.

To tackle such social and economic side effects of industrialization and urbanization, many special civil acts have been proposed and enacted, and new legal institutions have been created. The legal notion of partitioned ownership of a building was created to facilitate the registration of the ownership of each partitioned part of an aggregate building through the *Act on the Ownership and Management of Aggregate Buildings* (1984).

Land ownership can be transferred from seller to buyer when two legal conditions are met: (1) there is a contract between the seller and the buyer, and (2) the transfer of ownership from the seller to the buyer is registered (§ 186 KCC). However, in the general practice of land transactions, many abnormal transaction methods have emerged to secure windfalls resulting from high increases in land prices. Through such abnormal transaction methods, land speculations have spread wildly. To curb and control land speculations, legal measures on irregular land transaction methods have been taken to address concerns relating to the use nominal trusts,[10] registration of sale from the first seller directly to the last buyer without registration of the

---

[10] Several types of nominal trust are used in practice. Explaining it by way of example; A is a land owner, and then in the registry B is recorded as the owner on the basis of a nominal trust contract between A and B. Furthermore, A sells his land to B, and then in the registry C is recorded as the owner on the basis of a nominal trust contract between A and C with the consent of B. Furthermore, A sells his land to B and B is recorded as the owner in the registry, but the recorded owner, B, is not real owner, because the real owner, C, has concluded a nominal trust contract with B. In this case, the seller A does not know about the nominal trust contract between B and C. By way of the nominal trust contract, the unrecorded real owner exercises the rights of ownership, not the recorded nominal owner.

intermediate buyer,[11] false descriptions of the cause of registration, etc. The contract of nominal trust and transfer of ownership on the basis of the nominal trust contract has been rendered null and void under by legislation (§ 4 *Act on the Registration of Real Estate under Actual Titleholder's Name*(1995)). Registrations from the first seller directly to the last buyer without registration of the intermediate buyer are now administratively controlled and punished (§§ 8 Nr.1, 9 Nr. 1 *Act on Special Measures for Registration of Real Estates*(1990)). In reference to the regulation of registration from the first seller directly to the last buyer without registration of the intermediate buyer, the Supreme Court ruled that under existing legislation, such action shall be administratively punished, but the transfer of land ownership shall ultimately remain effective.[12]

Another means of regulating the sale of real property is that all sale contracts for the transfer of real estate are required to be reported to a local governor or city mayor within 30 days from the date of conclusion of the contract of sale (§§ 3 ff. *Act on Report of Real Estate Transaction* etc. (2016)). The land sale report system was created in 1978 by the amendment of the *Act on National Land Use and Management*. To execute a contract for the sale of land within the boundary of a designated area, permission must be sought from the relevant governor or city mayor (§§ 10 ff. *Act on Report of Real Estate Transaction* etc. (2016)). This permission system of the contract of sale of land also began in 1978 through the amendment of the *Act on National Land Use and Management*. Moreover, the transfer of land ownership shall be registered with the corresponding local registry within 60 days from the date of full payment of the sale price of such land (§§ 2 ff. *Act on Special Measures for the Registration of Real Estate*). Since 2006, it is required to record the sale price of the land in the relevant registry (§ 1 (1) Nr. 9 *Registration of Real Estate Act, §§ 47-5, 47-6 Regulation of Registration of Real Estate*).

To recapture windfalls due to continuously increasing real estate prices, extreme legal measures were taken in 1989: the excessive profits tax on the sale of land by *the Land Excess Profits Tax Act* (1989), regulations imposed on the owners of housing sites by the *Act on Ceilings on the Ownership of Housing Sites* (1989), and development charges by the *Restitution of Development Gains Act* (1989). These three acts have been referred to as being based on the idealistic conception of public land ownership. The concept of public land ownership means that land shall not be treated as a kind of commodity but as a natural resource. Therefore, land ownership can be regulated and controlled more strictly by statutes for the purpose of public interests on land, even though land would be owned by private persons. However, the *Land Excess Profits Tax Act* was declared as not conforming with the Constitution by the Constitutional Court in 1994[13] and repealed by the National Assembly in 1998. The Act on *Ceilings on the Ownership of Housing Sites* was repealed in 1998 and

---

[11] Explaining it by way of example, A had sold his land to B. B without registration of his name resold it to C, and then transfer of ownership in the registry is carried out from A directly to C without registration of the intermediate buyer (in this case B).

[12] Judgment of the Supreme Court on Jan 26, 1993, 92 Da 39,112.

[13] Judgment of the Constitutional Court on Jul. 29, 1994, 92 Heonba 49, 52.

declared unconstitutional by the Constitutional Court later in 1999.[14] Until now, the *Restitution of Development Gains Act* remains in effect, but development charges have become lighter and lighter.[15] Starting in 2005, an aggregate real estate tax has been levied on increased real estate prices that exceed the recognized price under the *Aggregate Real Estate Tax Act* (2005). Furthermore, from 2006, a rebuilding charge shall be levied on the excessive gains of a homeowner due to their rebuilding their house under the *Restitution of the Excess Rebuilding Gains Act*.

In financial practice, real estate securities have been created in the form of floating sum mortgages or provisional registrations. For the protection of the debtor, mortgagor and guarantor, the floating sum mortgage is regulated and guided by governmental financial authorities, and security through provisional registration is regulated by the *Provisional Registration Security Act* (1983).

For the secure and stable living situation of the residential lessee, lease periods are not permitted to be shorter than two years without the consent of the lessee to a fixed term of less than two years (§ 4 *Housing Lease Protection Act* (1981). The rights of a lessee also act as a counter balance against the purchaser of a leased residential property by the new buyer from the original owner (§ 3 *Housing Lease Protection Act*); a deposit shall be repaid to the lessee preferentially when the leased housing is to be auctioned (§§ 3-2, 8 *Housing Lease Protection Act*). In addition to a residential lease, a lessee of commercial buildings is also similarly protected as in the case of residential leases according to the *Commercial Building Lease Protection Act* (2001). In contrast, the lease period of a commercial building can be prolonged by renewal of the lease contract up to 10 years (§ 10 (2) *Commercial Building Lease Protection Act*). In 2020, the rights of a residential lessee were strengthened. Residential lessees can renew their lease contract for more than two years at the time of the expiration of the original lease contract for two years. The duration of residential leases shall not be contracted for less than two years under such circumstances (§ 4(1) *Housing Lease Protection Act*). Therefore, the lessee can live at the leased house for at least 4 years. The lessor can reject the renewal of the lease contract only if the lessor or his or her lineal ascendant or his or her lineal descendant intend to live at the leased property (§ 6-3 (1) Nr 8 *Housing Lease Protection Act*). A final noteworthy protection for lessees is that rent shall not be increased by more than 5% of the original contracted rental value for the duration of the lease, and it shall not be increased within 1 year from the original lease contract or from the time of the last increase(§ 7 *Housing Lease Protection Act*).

To address growing concerns regarding environmental degradation due to industrialization and urbanization, a strict liability regime was adopted for offences deemed to be infringements on the environment (§ 31 *Framework Act on Environmental Policy* (1990)).

---

[14] Judgment of the Constitutional Court (Full Bench) on Apr. 29, 1999, 94 Heonba 56 (Hearings of another 66 cases were joined to this proceeding).

[15] See, Kim (2017, pp. 100–104).

3.2 Evolution of Consumer Protection Laws to Protect Emerging Consumer Class Transitioning to a Consumer Based Economic Model

In parallel with its industrialization and urbanization, Korea has progressed into prosperity and, at the same time, a society with greater risks for a growing consumer base owing to mass production and mass consumption. To protect consumers from unfair contracts, consumer contracts have been regulated under the *Regulation of Standardized Contracts* (1986). For example, a buyer can make use of a discretionary withdrawal of an acceptance of a contract if they do so within 7 days from the acceptance date of a contract of sale (§§ 5 ff. *Installment Transactions Act* (1991), §§ 7 ff. *Door-to-Door Sales,* etc. Act (1991)).

Since 2002, manufacturers of defective movables have been held to a standard of strict liability in reference to their products. From 2013 forward, punitive damages are awarded in Korea to an injured individual where an injury resulted from an intentional act or gross negligence on the part of the manufacturer (§ 3 (2) *Product Liability Act*). The recovery of such punitive damages is limited to at most threefold the actual provable damages of the individual claimant.

3.3 Acceptance of and Participation in the International Trend Toward Globalization

Korea should accept and participate in the worldwide trend toward globalization. In 1995, Korea joined the World Trade Organization (WTO) as an original member nation, and in 1996, Korea became a member of the Organization for Economic Co-Operation and Development (OECD).

Due to insufficient preparations by the Korean government, these steps toward globalization resulted in an economic crisis due to a deficiency of foreign currency in 1997. To overcome this economic shock and to encourage foreign investment, the limitations on the highest interest rates were eliminated by the repeal of the *Interest Limitation Act* in 1998. After recovering from this economic crisis, the *Interest Limitation Act* was newly enacted in 2007. The highest allowed interest rate under the new *Interest Limitation Act* reached 30% per year. Since its peak, the rate has been gradually lowered, and it is now 24% per year.

To let banks and firms dispose of enormous bad claims (i.e., bad bonds, bad debts), asset-backed securities (ABS) and mortgage-backed securities (MBS) were introduced through the *Asset-Backed Securitization Act* in 1998 and the *Korea Housing Finance Corporation Act* in 2003. In 2005, Korea also ratified and accepted the CISG (United Nations Convention on Contracts for the International Sale of Goods). However, there are some aspects of the KCC that are not harmonized with the provisions of the CISG: classifications of nonperformance of debt as contrasted with a unified (one type) of nonperformance, requirement of fault of the obligor for the rescission of the contract by the obligee, calculation of damages on the basic principle of proximate causal relationship instead of foreseeability in the case of nonperformance of contract and torts.[16]

Continuing its trend of embracing globalization, the Korean government has negotiated and signed many FTAs (Free Trade Agreement) with foreign countries starting in 2003. It was understood by the Korean government that in preparation for the negotiation of future FTAs, it was necessary to encourage the competitiveness of the Korean agricultural sector. Therefore, the *Agricultural Land Act* was passed in 1994, giving farmers the ability to own farmland indefinitely, farmland has also been able to be leased freely, and agricultural companies have been able to be established. Korea's first FTA was with Chile; it was signed in 2003 and came into effecting 2004.

The world economic crisis of 2008 was well overcome without additional special measures in the field of civil law. From 2012, the creation of the right to place a security on present existing movables, movables to be manufactured in the future, and on present and future claims was permitted in accordance with the *Security Act on Movables, Debt,* etc. (2010). The abovementioned security on movables and debts can be used only by juridical persons and businessmen, whose trade names are registered in accordance with the *Commercial Registration Act* (§ 2 Nr 5 *Security Act on Movables, Claims,* etc.)

3.4 Changes of Practice and Theory of Juridical Acts with Growing Importance of Artificial Intelligence, Information Technologies, and the Advent of Hyper-Connected Societies

Currently, almost all transactions concerning goods as well as financial transactions are done online. Therefore, contracts for transactions are concluded with offer and acceptance through electronic declaration of intention. Moreover, contracts are written in electronic documents, signatures are completed by electronic methods, and notarizations are also realized electronically.

The time of sending and receiving an electronic declaration of intention is simultaneous with its being sent by computer (§ 6 *Basic Act on Electronic Documents and Electronic Transactions* (2012)[17]). The legal validity of electronic documents was explicitly recognized in Sect. 4 of the *Framework Act on Electronic Documents and Electronic Transactions* as well as in the KCC.

In conjunction with the extensive use of the internet by consumers, a need was created to secure, avoid the leaking of, and prevent the misuse of consumer data and electronic transaction data. To meet this challenge, the Korean National Assembly

---

[16] See, Kim (2002).

[17] Originally in 1992, the *Basic Act on the Electronic Transactions* was legislated and in 2012, it was extensively reviewed and renamed the *Basic Act on Electronic Documents and Electronic Transactions.*

enacted the *Act on Fair Indication and Advertisement,* which came into force in 1999, *the Act on the Consumer Protection in the Electronic Commerce Transactions,* etc., which came into force in 2002, and the *Personal Information Protection Act,* which came into force in 2011.

3.5   Responses of the Civil Law to the Extensive Immigration of North Korean Escapees

A large number of North Korean escapees moving into South Korea generated many novel legal questions that required answering. Would a North Korean escapee be granted a divorce from a spouse who remained in North Korea? Were North Korean bigamous marriages valid? Could prescription/litigation periods for the recovery of an inheritance of North Korean escapees in South Korea be extended?

Under article 19-2 of the *Act on Protection and Settlement Support for North Korean Escapees* in 2007, an escapee can litigate a divorce against a spouse remaining in North Korea. Under article 6 of the *Acton Special Cases concerning Family Relationship, Inheritance,* etc. (2012) an exception is made to the prohibition on bigamy between residents of South Korea and North Korea the second marriage of an escapee in South Korea (under certain conditions) shall be valid, even though his or her first spouse continues to live in North Korea. Under article 11 of the *Act on Special Cases Concerning Family Relationship, Inheritance,* etc. (2012), for the recovery of an inheritance of North Korean escapees in South Korea, the prescription period of 3 years from knowledge of the infringement of their inheritance right or 10 years from the occurrence of the infringement of the inheritance right shall be calculated from the date of their arrival in South Korea.

4   Modification of the Korean Civil Code by Judgments of the Constitutional Court and the Supreme Court

Important Judgments of the Constitutional Court and the Supreme Court played a large supporting role for the KCC's responses to the social changes and challenges in Korea. Originally, a real estate lease's longest permitted duration was 20 years (§ 651 KCC). This clause of the KCC was declared unconstitutional in 2013, thus permitting leases to be of a longer duration.[18] A Supreme Court ruling came out in support of the upward readjustment of the retirement age of its employees to 65 years of age from 60 in the past.[19] These two points have not been written into the KCC. The other judgments of unconstitutionality and constitutional unconformity have been wholly integrated into the KCC.

---

[18] Judgment of the Constitutional Court on Dec. 26, 2013, 2011 Heonba 234.

[19] Judgment of the Supreme Court (Full Bench) on Feb. 21, 2019, 2018 Da 248,909.

The Supreme Court has also sought to push the civil law forward on social issues by clarifying the rights of certain children. In 1999, the Supreme Court ruled that a baby that is the result of an insemination of a spouse by a male who is not one of the spouses in the marriage shall be presumed to have the same standing as any other child resulting from the marriage.[20]

5   Diversification of Legal Methods to Remedy Damages

There has been a diversification of options available to potential plaintiffs to seek damages in the case of civil action in Korea. Two tracks to seek civil damages exist: first, a standard civil procedure by way of the *Civil Procedure Act* and second, voluntary civil conciliation (settlement) proceedings by way of the *Judicial Conciliation of Civil Disputes Act*. Every potential plaintiff is therefore able to take their legal actions for damages to court selectively through civil procedure or civil conciliation.

In Korea, numerous judicial frameworks to facilitate conciliation in specific fields of law have emerged through a proliferation of conciliation acts:

- Conciliation for the payment of damages for consumer disputes by the *Framework Act on Consumers*;
- Conciliation for environmental disputes by the *Framework Act on Environmental Policy*;
- Conciliation for remedies of damages through medical malpractice by the *Act on Remedies for Injuries from Medical Malpractice* and *Conciliations and Mediation of Medical Disputes*;
- Conciliation for deliberation and mediation of housing lease disputes by the *Housing Lease Protection Act*;
- Conciliation for deliberation and mediation of commercial building lease disputes by the *Commercial Building Lease Protection Act*;
- Conciliation for financial disputes by the *Act on the Establishment, etc., of Financial Services Commission*; and
- Conciliation for disputes relating to personal information by the *Personal Information Protection Act*.

In addition to these field-specific conciliation proceedings, the procedure for class actions in the case of security transactions is outlined in the *Securities-Related Class Action Act*. Legal actions taken by associations (referred to in Korea as "Verbandsklage" as a result of this legal action being based on the German collective action model) also have field-specific legislation for legal actions taken by consumer protection associations under the *Framework Act on Consumers* and legal actions by personal information protection associations according to the *Personal Information Protection Act*. To proceed by way oaf class action or a *Verbandsklage* in the situations outlined above, a class representative (a.k.a., a representative plaintiff) or plaintiff

---

[20] Judgment of the Supreme Court (Full Bench) on Oct. 23, 2019, 2016 Meu 2510.

association must apply for and receive leave (permission) from the court to proceed with the action. Through class actions, class members can be compensated for losses resulting from certain security transactions. However, through *Verbandsklage,* the only remedy available to plaintiff associations is the granting of an injunction by the court.

6   Conclusory Evaluation of the Past and Future Evolution of Korean Civil Law

Overall, the response of the KCC to social changes and challenges over the past 30 years has been relatively appropriate but not completely sufficient. In the field of property law, the majority of the legislative response to such changes and challenges were accomplished by way of new legislation apart from the KCC and the amendment of existing special civil acts in the field of property law, not by amendment of the KCC. However, in the field of family law, the KCC has proven more adept at responding to social change through prompt and continuous amendment. The reason for this appears to lie in the negative attitude of civil law professionals and the business community to the amendment of the property law section of the KCC, in contrast to the otherwise positive activities of women-driven feminist civic groups, progressive family law scholars, and the Constitutional Court pushing for the reform of the family law section of the KCC.

Despite past and present legislative efforts, issues concerning large increases in real estate prices, real estate speculation, irregular real estate transactions, and insufficient recapture of windfalls have not been completely resolved. There is some hope that in the future real-estate transactions could be normalized by way of a notarization requirement for contracts of sale and that real estate windfalls resulting from social developments are recaptured.

It is also critical that antiquated provisions of the KCC be updated. Of special importance would be the need to modernize the rule concerning special servitudes outlined in § 302 KCC.[21] However, while modernizing this provision, legislators must seek to respect and maintain its critical role in facilitating important Korean traditional land use methods even with the emergence of a more technological sophisticated society built around industry, information technology, and artificial intelligence.

Korean codifiers and the drafters of special acts have a great deal of work ahead of them. Presently, there is a growing desire to ensure that children whose parents have divorced be granted greater protections than they were historically. Legislators must seek to protect minors against growing risks related to their use of the internet

---

[21] § 302 KCC: Where the inhabitants of a certain area, as a collective body, are entitled to take grass or trees, catch wild animals, take earth or sand, rear live stock, or take other profits from the land of the area owned by another person, the provisions of this chapter shall apply mutatis mutandis subject to the custom of each locality.

through sophisticated smartphones and other electronic devices.[22] Korean society increasingly seeks greater equality for foreign workers, North Korean escapees, and refugees. There is a strong need for an act of equal treatment (e.g., an anti-discrimination act or equality act), which should be legislated as soon as possible. Furthermore, to ensure the consistent application of the law, conflicts between the KCC and special civil acts should be eliminated through a project of harmonization. These conflicts are at times glaring and ripe for correction, as illustrated by the differences between the floating suretyship of article § 428-3 in the KCC and the floating suretyship of article § 6 in the *Special Act on the Protection of Guarantors* (2008).

Recently, however, it seems that the hard work of amending the KCC and related civil acts has stalled. The government has been trying to change the highly technical legal language of the KCC that is difficult for the general public to understand into more colloquial, comprehensible, and accessible language since 2017. The bill of amendment for this updating of the language of the KCC was submitted to the National Assembly in 2019. The draft bill, however, was abandoned in 2020, owing to the expiration of the term of the members of the National Assembly.

Ultimately, Korean civil law shall pursue and realize justice and love, which are the eternal and utmost values of mankind. Justice and love are the ultimate goals of the KCC and all special civil acts.[23] It is my opinion that Korean society shall evolve into one of communitarianism from the present extreme individualistic egoism and that Korean civil law shall be embodied with characteristics of social law in parallel with the changes of Korean society into communitarianism.

References

Eom KC (2020) Differentiation of share of inheritance according to his or her contribution to parents. Korea Bar Association Newspaper, Apr. 13

Han SI, Kim SH (2018) Textbook of law of relatives and inheritance. Hwasan Media, Seoul

Jeong WH (2018) History of land speculations in Korea. Volume 3 by the Research Institute for Law, the Bible and history. PNC Media Co., Seoul

Kim H (2014) Die Nacherfüllung als Rechtsbehelf des Käufers nach CISG, deutschem und koreanischem Recht, Studien zum ausländischen und internationalen Privatrecht, Nr. 310, Mohr Siebeck, Tübingen

Kim SY (1996) Comparative security law of immovables, 2nd edn. Beobweon Publishing Co., Seoul

Kim SY (2002) Comparative contract law. Beobyeongsa Publishing Co., Seoul

Kim SY (2013) Comparative Law of Revolving Mortgages. Hwasan Media, Seoul

Kim SY (2015) Theory of natural law and legal policy. PNC Media, Seoul

---

[22] In the present day SNSs (Social Networking Services) through ICTs (Information & Communication Technology) are used for the sexual exploitation of children. To protect children from such exploitation, the *Act on the Protection of Children and Juveniles from Sexual Abuse* was enacted in 2009 and came into force in 2010. So long as technology and social circumstances continues to change there will remain a continuing need to strengthen the rights of children to claim for support, and to protect the safe and peaceful everyday living of their lives.

[23] See, Kim (2019).

Kim SY (2016a) Textbook of general part of law of obligations. 3rd ed. Hwasan Media, Seoul

Kim SY (2016b) Textbook of special part of law of obligations. 3rd ed. Hwasan Media, Seoul

Kim SY (2017) Theory of justice on land. Vol. 2 by the Research Institute for Law, the Bible and History. PNC Media Publishing Co., Seoul

Kim SY (2018a) Textbook of general part of civil law. 4th ed. Hwasan Media, Seoul

Kim SY (2018b) Textbook of property law. 4th ed. Hwasan Media, Seoul

Kim SY (2019) Justice and love as perspective direction of legal policy. Volume 5 by the Research Institute for Law, the Bible and history. PNC Media Publishing Co., Seoul

Kim SY (2021) A study on necessity of enlargement of communitarian land use: In terms of modernization of special servitude. J Nat Sci, Repub Korea, Humanit Soc Sci 60(1)

Lee SW (2018) Past developments and future tasks of family law. In: Changes of Korean private law for past 70 years and perspective in the future: memorial book for the anniversary of 30th year of the late Prof. Kim Zeounghan. Beobmoon-Sa Publishing Co., Seoul

Shin YH (2018) Trends of amendment and points of issues of civil law. In: Trends and issues of jurisprudence in Korea. The National Academy of Sciences, Republic of Korea

Yun JS (2016) Textbook of law of relatives and inheritance. Bakyoungsa Publishing Co., Seoul

Sang Yong Kim is Professor emeritus at the faculty of law of Yonsei University, President of the Korea Civil Law Association (since 2007), President of the Korean-German Law Association (since 2011), and Academic Advisor for the Korea Legislation Research Institute (1990–Present). Professor Kim is Humboldt Research Awardee (Humboldtpreisträger, 2006) and a member of the National Korean Academy of Sciences, Republic of Korea (since 2009).

Between Globalization and Localization: Japan's Struggle to Properly Update Its Civil Code

Souichirou Kozuka

Abstract The law to amend Japan's Civil Code was approved in 2017, after more than a decade of work since the Japanese Ministry of Justice announced its intention to fundamentally review the Code in 2006. The pronounced goals were to adapt the Civil Code to economic and social changes since its codification at the end of the nineteenth century and to make the Code easier for the general public to understand. However, the amendments made are mostly of a technical nature, making the reform a "triumph of legal technocrats." Most of the innovative proposals were rejected, and academics are already talking about the possibility of developing interpretations of the adopted text with reference to rejected proposals as guidance. The omission of policy issues from the Code and the large role expected of lawyers and courts in driving interpretative developments are typical of how the law has evolved in Japan. Thus, the reform of Japan's Civil Code does reflect the characteristics of Japanese law.

1 Introduction

In May 2017, amendments to the Civil Code, generally known as the "reform of the law of obligations",[1] were approved by the Diet (Japanese Congress). Except for postwar reform to the family law section, it was the first time since the Civil Code's original codification in 1896 that a large part of it was amended with regard to substantive rules. The modernisation of the Code in 2004 replaced the classic Japanese (written in *katakana*, pursuant to the style used in the nineteenth century) with modern phrases (in *hiragana*), making only minor substantive changes to the

---

[1] The literal translation of the original Japanese "saiken hô" is "the law of claims", rather than obligations. However, this chapter uses the term that many readers will be familiar with for the sake of convenience.

S. Kozuka (✉)
Faculty of Law, Gakushuin University, Tokyo, Japan
e-mail: souichirou.kozuka@gakushuin.ac.jp

© The Author(s), under exclusive license to Springer Nature Singapore Pte Ltd. 2023   181
M. Graziadei and L. Zhang (eds.), *The Making of the Civil Codes*,
Ius Gentium: Comparative Perspectives on Law and Justice 104,
https://doi.org/10.1007/978-981-19-4993-7_11

provisions. Therefore, "the first substantive reform to the Civil Code on a large scale" is an apt description for the 2017 amendments. The amendments entered into force on 1 April 2020.

The reform took place over more than a decade. The official process of deliberations at the Legislative Council (LC) commenced in response to Request No. 88 of the Minister of Justice in 2008. However, this process was preceded by apparently private examination by a group of academics that commenced in 2006 and concluded with the publication of the private Draft Proposals (DP) in 2008. Given that several Ministry of Justice (MoJ) officials participated in the group, the private process could justifiably be regarded as part of the MoJ's continued efforts toward fundamental reform of the Civil Code. The private group, known as the Japanese Civil Code (Law of Obligations) Reform Commission (RC), was formed shortly after the MoJ announced its plan to reform the Civil Code (law of obligations) in February 2006.[2] It was not until 15 years later that the amendments entered into force and thus became applicable in Japanese society.

Japan was not the only jurisdiction to reform its Civil Code. It was not a coincidence that the project originated only a few years after the 2002 modernization of the Law of Obligations (*Schuldrecht*) in Germany. Movements toward codification of the European Civil Code surged after that year, culminating in publication of the Draft Common Frame of Reference (DCFR) in 2009, and then waned before the Japanese reform process reached its conclusion. In the meantime, the French Civil Code has gone through reform, implemented by the Ordonnance of 2016. As is usual with the legislative process in Japan, thorough studies of major jurisdictions abroad were made during reform deliberations, including references to those jurisdictions' reforms as well as drafts produced in the process (such as the Drafts for reform of the French Civil Code by Prof. Catala, Prof. Terré and the French Ministry of Justice). On the other hand, there are local features unique to Japan, which has made Japan's reform of its Civil Code distinct from the reform completed by its European counterparts.

This chapter intends to examine the reform of Japan's Civil Code, focusing on its process, policies and outcomes. It follows up on a piece focusing more on the interest group analysis that the author published together with Prof. Nottage when the reform process was still underway.[3] Although the practical impacts of the reform on various transactions warrant careful examination, this chapter will not analyze the amendments made in detail.[4]

The chapter is structured as follows. First, an overview of the reform process is provided (2). Then, a concise history of the Civil Code in Japanese society during the hundred-odd years since its codification is given to understand the context of the

---

[2] The announcement on reform of the Civil Code (law of obligations) (February 2006), available at http://www.moj.go.jp/MINJI/minji99.html (in Japanese).

[3] Kozuka and Nottage (2014)

[4] For an overview of Japanese contract law based on the Civil Code postreform, see Sono et al. (2019).

reform (3). The next section describes the policies that underpinned reform deliberations (4). It is followed by an examination of which proposals made it into the final bill and which did not (5). The potential for future developments under the amended Civil Code is then briefly discussed (6). The chapter's conclusion is based on the analysis conducted in these five sections and finds the Japanese reform to have been a triumph of legal technocrats. The conclusion also identifies one important characteristic of Japanese law: it is *Juristenrecht* (lawyers' law), relying heavily on academic discourse and case law developments in adapting legal rules to real-life demands (7).

2 Overview of Japan's Civil Code Reform of 2017

2.1 The Origins of the Project

Takashi Uchida was a key figure in the initial stages of civil code reform. He had been professor of civil law at Tokyo University until 2007, when he resigned, many years in advance of his retirement age, to devote himself to the reform of the Civil Code. Uchida served as secretary general of the RC and, after resigning from Tokyo University, was nominated Senior Advisor to the MoJ and advised the Ministry on reform until 2014, when the overall shape of the reforms was largely settled.

In his earlier days, Uchida was well known as a leading academic specializing in contract law. In particular, he pointed to the difficulties that the classic contract theory faced and argued that existing contract law did not reflect real-life contractual relationships and, among other things, the local realities of Japan. He then advanced a controversial argument that practicing lawyers, in particular judges, resort to general principles such as the principle of good faith when faced by the need to adapt to the endogenous norms arising from real life in Japan and required to provide an acceptable solution.[5] It seems that Uchida's zeal for civil code reform emanated from his aspiration to introduce Japan's local elements into the civil code to make the latter more "fit" for Japanese society.

The experience of participating in the drafting of the UNIDROIT Principles on International Commercial Contracts (UPICC) may have convinced Uchida that it was the right time to put Civil Code reform on the legislative agenda.[6] In the early 2000s, many countries, mostly in transition from a former socialist regime to a market economy, were working on codification by making reference to internationally promulgated rules, including the UPICC. Producing a locally fit Code by referring to globally accepted rules with modifications made where necessary seemed to be the universal approach that Japan could follow. At a time when Japan enjoyed its status as the sole advanced economy in Asia, China's economy still lagging well

---

[5] Uchida (1993).

[6] See the detailed comparison of the DP and UPICC in Uchida (2011).

behind Japan's, it was even possible to dream of the reformed Japanese Civil Code becoming the Asian model of codification.

It was indeed timely to talk about such a dream, as Japan finally acceded to the United Nations Convention on the International Sale of Goods (CISG) in 2008. The acceptance of these universally recognized sales law rules, although rather belatedly, given its large share in international trade, had removed the impediments for Japan to take the lead in establishing a unique (possibly non-Western) model of contract law. Those academics who followed the European developments were already aware that the CISG as well as the relevant European laws affected the German law of obligations so significantly that the latter had renounced many doctrines that had been considered to form the basis of the German law. Thus, it was anticipated that Japanese contract law would also need to depart from the "old" doctrines imported from German law in past decades.

Looking back from the present, the prospects for reform held in the late 2000s were too optimistic. In particular, Uchida's argument focusing on the role of the good faith principle did not garner support when presented at the Assembly of the Japanese Academy of Private Law. Kashu, then a retired judge teaching civil law at a university, responded that Japanese judges prefer to adhere to classical contract law. According to Kashu, when a judge appears to derogate from the classic contract law framework, this is simply an unsatisfactory compromise to deal with a complicated case.[7] It was therefore questionable that practicing lawyers could share the view that the Civil Code needed reform to adapt to real life in Japan.

2.2   The Progress of Deliberations for Reform

With its difficult future yet unknown, the RC commenced an overall examination of the law of obligations. The examination was wide in scope and covered not only contract law but also the general rules of the law of obligations (*Allgemeines Schuldrecht*), including liability from default, assignment of receivables and fraudulent conveyance, as well as relevant provisions in the general rules of the Civil Code (*Allgemeiner Teil*), such as the rules on mistake, rescission and prescription. This result largely coincided with the scope of the 2010 version of the UPICC. The approach of the RC was essentially to review comparative law. Not only Western jurisdictions, such as France, Germany, England (Sale of Goods Act), the Netherlands, Quebec and the United States (Uniform Commercial Code) but also Asian jurisdictions, such as the Republic of Korea (South Korea), PR China, the Republic of China (Taiwan), Vietnam and Cambodia, were covered, reflecting the intention for Japan's reform to establish the Asian model of contract law. Global and regional uniform rules, namely, the CISG, UPICC, European Principles of Contract Law (PECL) and DCFR, were also often referenced.

---

[7] Hoshino and Iwaki (1992, pp. 73–74).

The RC concluded its work in 2008 and published its proposals for reform, DP, in five-volume books written in commentary style: black letter rules with elaborate comments and comparative law notes.[8] Later that year, the LC established a Working Group (WG) to respond to the Minister's abovementioned Request (Request No.88). After that, the WG replaced the RC as a forum for deliberations. Uchida sat on the secretariat's side as the MoJ's senior advisor, and many members of the RC participated either as members or associate members.[9] The WG held its first meeting on 24 November 2009. The emphasis on comparative law continued, especially in the early stage of the deliberations, as evidenced by references to foreign sources in the WG materials.

After having 26 meetings, the WG published an Interim Summary of Issues (*Ronten Seiri*) on 12 April 2011.[10] While seeking public comment on this document, the WG continued its deliberations and adopted the Interim Report (*Chukan Shi'an*) (IR) on 26 February 2013,[11] at its 71st meeting. Public comments were again solicited and considered by the WG, which further continued deliberations until publishing the Tentative Outline of Reform (*Yoko Kari'an*) on 26 August 2014.[12] The latter was developed into the final Outline of Reform (*Yoko An*) (OR) at the 99th meeting of the WG,[13] held on 10 February 2015. The OR was quickly drafted into a bill to amend the Civil Code, which was submitted for approval to the Diet. The Diet was occupied with another agenda and needed two more years to finally approve the Bill, although there was not much debate among representatives.

In addition to opposition to individual proposals, there was harsh criticism of the project as a whole. The leader of the movement against the RC and LC process was Masanobu Kato, a famous professor of civil law. He argued that any reform should be modest, simply restating case law and established practices. Although Kato was a member of the RC (not belonging to small groups that worked actively on the drafting of the DP), he formed another group that produced its own proposal for reform in 2009. As the MoJ's reform process progressed, Kato escalated his criticisms against the MoJ's reform, eventually claiming that the reform was manipulated by hidden interests of the MoJ and some academics.[14] It was ironic that the finally adopted Bill ended up more in line with what Kato had argued for: modestly codifying the case law and accepted rules while discarding most of the ambitious proposals originally envisioned by the DP.

---

[8] For details of the DP in English, see Kamo (2010).

[9] On the overlap between members of the RC and WG, see Kozuka and Nottage (2014, p. 238).

[10] Available at http://www.moj.go.jp/shingi1/shingi04900074.html (only in Japanese).

[11] Available at http://www.moj.go.jp/shingi1/shingi04900184.html (only in Japanese).

[12] Available at http://www.moj.go.jp/shingi1/shingi04900227.html (only in Japanese).

[13] Available at http://www.moj.go.jp/shingi1/shingi04900244.html (only in Japanese).

[14] Kato (2015).

3   Background to the Reform: The Civil Code in Society

3.1   *Codification in the Late Nineteenth Century*

Request No. 88 of the Minister of Justice demanded two issues to be considered in examining the reform of the Civil Code: (a) how to adapt the Code to changes in the economy and society since codification and (b) how to make the Code easy for the general public to understand. To understand this demand, the status of the Civil Code in Japanese society needs to be examined, going back to its original codification in the late nineteenth century.

Codification in Japan was part of modernisation efforts after opening up the country under pressure from the Western Powers. In fact, codification had the more immediate purpose of gaining full equality with those powers by amending the "unequal" treaties that the premodern Tokugawa government concluded, under which Japan's Western counterparts retained extraterritorial jurisdiction and other privileges.[15] It was a prerequisite for negotiating the amendment of the unequal treaties that Japan be equipped with a modern judicial system. By using the modern term, the Japanese government in the late nineteenth century was required to transplant the Western-style legal system to equate itself with its Western counterparts.

As a result, there was a large gap between the Civil Code and Japanese society from the beginning. The text of the Civil Code closely resembled that of Western Codes, but daily life and commercial transactions in Japan when the Code was adopted in 1896 were much different from those in Europe. Nevertheless, the Japanese codification differed from the transplant that took place due to colonization in various places outside Europe. Instead of copying the whole legal system of a European country, Japanese drafters enjoyed the freedom to hunt for several models and cherry pick from among them.[16] While the French legal system transmitted by Gustav Boissonade, who spent from 1873 to 1895 in Japan and educated young Japanese at the MoJ, had significant influence, the drafts of the German Civil Code (BGB) also had extensive impacts, not least affecting the arrangement of the Japanese Civil Code. Its model was the second draft of the BGB, pursuant to the Pandekten system but placing the Book on the law of Property (*Sachenrecht*) before the Book on the law of obligations (*Schuldrecht*). The drafters did not fail to turn their eyes to the common law, the most famous provision being that on recoverable damages (now art. 416 of the Civil Code), which was a restatement of *Hadley v Baxendale*.[17] Matsumoto argues that Japanese law is a mixed legal system in a broad sense.[18] The legal institutions and legal thought of various jurisdictions have commingled so that no single legal system can be regarded as the "mother" system.

---

[15] Nottage (2019, p. 202).

[16] Ishikawa (2013, p. 64).

[17] 9 Ex. 341; 156 Eng. Rep. 145.

[18] Although with regards to tort law, not contract law; see Matsumoto (2015).

3.2   Changes in Society and New Challenges

Shortly after codification, Japanese society started to change as a result of industrial-isation after victory in wars against China (Qing Dynasty) and the Russian Empire. This industrialisation brought about urbanisation and changed people's lives in large cities. It also affected traditional communities in rural areas through penetration of the market economy. The result was a rise in social problems in the early twen-tieth century (*Taisho* era; 1912–1926).[19] Labor conditions at modern factories have become a serious issue as an increasing number of people have started to be employed in industry. Conflicts concerning the lease of land and houses, as well as disputes over the tenancy of farms, rose in number. Furthermore, the validity of standard contracts drew the attention of lawyers after the Great Kanto Earthquake of 1923, as most insurance conditions exempted an insurer from liability to indemnify victims for property damages due to an earthquake.[20] The Civil Code, which transplanted classic contract law from Europe, was not able to address these social problems.

Japan's devastating defeat in the Second World War did not directly result in further social change, except with regard to family matters. During the first decade after the War, people struggled to reconstruct the society they used to live in before the War. Then, economic growth during the 1960s and 1970s resulted in modernisation of Japanese society, which again gave rise to various challenges to private law. The rapid increase in the number of automobiles has made traffic accidents a frequent occurrence. Mass production also causes pollution of the environment and consumer accidents. Although these were mainly issues of tort, contracts were also relevant with regard to consumer transactions.

The third challenge that Japanese society experienced emerged in the 1990s, after the end of the Cold War. That society, traditionally rather insulated due to its geographical features, faced globalization as both products and the capital market became global after the confrontation between capitalist and socialist worlds came to an end. At the same time, the opening up of the Internet accelerated the digitization of society, which further transformed Japan. The Judicial System Reform, decided in 2002, was the Japanese judiciary's response to these challenges. It may not be coincidence that the Civil Code reform was put on the agenda a few years after the implementation of the Judicial System Reform. Having radically reformed the court system and legal education, Japanese lawyers needed to consider the reform of substantive rules. The focus naturally turned to the Civil Code, which governed the legal rights and obligations of those in society.

---

[19] Vanoverbeke (2004, pp. 14–19).

[20] Kozuka (2013, pp. 212–213).

3.3   Special Statutes and Case Law as Responses

Interestingly, the Japanese Civil Code (except for the family law section, which was completely changed after the Second World War) had been exempt from fundamental amendments, even though Japanese society had experienced transformation several times. Instead, when a legal response was needed, special statutes were introduced without affecting the basic rules in the Civil Code. Thus, in the *Taisho* era, the Land Tenancy Law and House Tenancy Law (modified and integrated into the Land and House Tenancy Law in 1993), as well as the Law on Personal Guarantee, were enacted. The consumer problems recognized during postwar economic growth were addressed decades later by the Consumer Contracts Act of 2000, again in the form of a special statute. As a response to the challenges of digitisation, the Act on Electronic Signature was enacted in 2001. Finally, relating to globalization, the CISG was implemented by way of direct application, without being integrated into the Civil Code.

In some cases, especially when the gap between the Civil Code and real life is better addressed by the case-by-case approach, case law has had a role to play. Examples include the doctrine of "continuous contracts", intended to provide justifiable solutions to problems arising from long-term contracts, often observed in distributorships and supply chains.[21] This should be understood against the role of precedents in Japan, which is much different from that in traditional civil law jurisdictions. Not only academics but also the courts recognize precedents as de facto binding on later cases as the source of law (*Rechtsquelle*).[22] This view of precedents dates back to the *Taisho* era, a time of social turmoil. Faced by challenges due to industrialisation and urbanisation, Japanese legal academics turned their eyes to the gap between legal texts and social reality. The leading figure was Izutaro Suehiro, civil law professor of the then Imperial University of Tokyo who introduced legal realism after spending years in the US. Suehiro instigated the study of court cases, inspired by the precedent-driven law-making process in the US. Eventually, in response to these academic initiatives, the courts also gave weight to precedents.

3.4   Implications for Civil Code Reform

In light of the above-explained developments in the last century, two issues could have been anticipated regarding civil code reform. One was whether to integrate special statutes into the Civil Code. If the Civil Code were left intact when addressing new challenges because of the cost of and time needed to amend the Code, then reform would be an opportunity for the Code to absorb the statutes kept independent. However, if the Civil Code were to remain unaffected by policy decisions and the

---

[21] See Taylor (1993).

[22] Kozuka (2020b, pp. 67–72).

products of interest group politicking left to special statutes, the conclusion would be the opposite.

The other issue was whether to restate and codify case law in the reformed Code. In this context, it is interesting that Suehiro emphasized the need to focus on the "local color" of a legal system and tried to identify a Japanese "local color", which he claimed was absent in the legal literature of the time, in court cases.[23] Even if the text of the Code were transplanted from, and identical to, other jurisdictions in the West, Suehiro expected that its application in Japanese court cases would reveal uniquely Japanese features. One might note that Suehiro's quest for the "local color" of the Civil Code was taken up a century later by Uchida, whose focus was on local elements in contract law. If so, restating case law could contribute to codification reflecting local elements of Japan, as was originally envisaged.

4 Policies Adopted by the Reform

4.1 Observed Policies

There is no official statement explaining the policies that underpinned the reform. Therefore, an observer must identify such policies from the amendments made. This is not an easy task, not least because the amendments were made to numerous provisions covering various subjects. In fact, it would be a surprise if each and every amendment, even small ones, was derived from only a few principles. Nevertheless, a thorough examination of the amendments reveals that there are several "lines of thought" based on which many of the amendments were developed. Below, four are identified.

4.1.1 Loose Consensualism

The most striking principle underpinning Japan's Civil Code reform is loose consensualism. Consensualism here refers to the consequences of a certain action being justified by the actor's agreed undertaking. Concerning liability from default, which was one of the most hotly contested issues, fault-based liability was abandoned, and the rule loosely based on consensualism replaced it. To be more precise, the new text provides that the debtor shall compensate for damages when the debtor fails to perform its obligation or when that obligation is impossible to perform, provided, however, that the debtor is exempted from liability when the default is not attributable to the debtor in light of the contract or other cause of the obligation, as well as the general sense of trade (art. 415(1)). Here, the debtor's liability for default is essentially founded on its own undertaking to perform a certain obligation. Exemption

---

[23] Suehiro (1921), Preface.

arises from the contract (or other cause of the obligation), which might provide for conditions limiting the liability of the debtor.

However, comparing the Civil Code after reform with previous reform proposals reveals that consensualism in the adopted text has been significantly compromised. The DP proposed the rule that a debtor shall be exempt from liability for default only when the default arose from an event not undertaken by the debtor. In the IR, a rule similar to the DP proposal was included as Alternative A, alongside a proposal referring to exemption in case the default was not attributable to the debtor, which was Alternative B. The reference to "events not attributable to the debtor" reflected the rule before reform. The final text adopts Alternative B in IR, with traces of consensualism found in the mention of "contract" as a criterion of attribution. Even this criterion is further compromised by the additional reference to the "general sense of trade", which was absent in the IR. The IR simply made reference to the "meaning of the contract." In this sense, consensualism in the reformed Civil Code is (very) loose.

Loose consensualism does not only appear in the provision on default liability. With regard to the right to avoid the contract when another party fails to perform its obligation, the amended provision includes a proviso that the right of avoidance cannot be exercised if the failure to perform the obligation is insignificant in light of the contract and the general sense of trade (art. 541). While this restriction on the right of avoidance is, in fact, a restatement of established case law,[24] the standard for significance of default is found in what was undertaken in the contract. Furthermore, such consensualism is again compromised by reference to the general sense of trade.

Another important provision based on loose consensualism relates to the impossibility of performing the obligation. Discarding the doctrine under the Civil Code before the reform, the newly added provision takes the position that a contract is not initially void even when it is impossible to perform from the time when the contract was formed (see art. 412-2). Apparently, this provision reflects consensualism in the sense that a contract that the parties have consented to is to be held valid. As elsewhere, this consensualism is loose, as indicated by a definition of impossibility that refers to "the contract or other cause of obligation, as well as the general sense of trade."

A related reform has been made to remedies in case the seller delivers goods that do not conform with the requirements of the contract. The view that the seller's liability for delivering goods with latent defects is a unique type of liability distinct from general liability for default, which was seemingly adopted by case law under the Code pre-reform, is now rejected. Under the post-reform Code, the seller's liability is governed by the rules on general liability for default. The only specific rules for the former relate to the variety of remedies available to the buyer, including a request to repair the goods, deliver substitute goods, or replenish the goods (art. 562(1)), or, when the seller does not meet these requests, to reduce the amount to be paid (art. 563(1)).

---

[24] Supreme Court, 21 November 1961, *Minshû* vol. 15, issue 10, p. 2507.

4.1.2 Consistencies within the Code

The second principle is to ensure consistencies within the Civil Code. To be more specific, where similar provisions contained differing rules, efforts were made to coordinate them.

This principle is best observable in service contract provisions. Inspired by the Dutch Civil Code (art. 7:400) and the DCFR (Book 4, Part C), the DP proposed introducing a category of "service contract", which has gained importance in the modern economy.[25] The parallels with European sources are not precise, however, as the "service contract" under the DP was considered to be a concept comprising contracts of employment (*Dienstvetrag*), work (*Werkvertrag*), mandate (*Auftrag*) and deposit (*Verwahrung*) as subcategories. The idea had been discarded before the WG published the IR. However, the consistencies among the four types of contracts, originally considered subcategories of the service contracts, were strictly implemented in the final provisions.

Under the Code post-reform, two types of mandate contracts are distinguished based on renumeration arrangements. The Code pre-reform assumed that the mandatary is paid for its performance of the mandated services. The newly added provision addresses the arrangement under which the mandatary is compensated for the outcome of its service (art. 648-2), as in the case of lawyers or real estate brokers working on a contingency fee basis. The new Code then treats the former (traditional) type of mandate in an equal manner to a contract of employment. In particular, when the performance of a service is frustrated, the mandatary is entitled to partial payment regardless of whether the frustration is attributable to the mandatary (art. 648(3)). This rule is identical to that found in the equivalent provision regarding contracts of employment (art. 624-2). On the other hand, the contingency fee-based mandate is regulated in parallel with contracts of work. In the case of frustrated service, the mandatary shall be compensated to the extent that the mandator benefits from the outcome of partial performance (art. 648-2(2), applying art. 634 for the contract of work).

In a similar vein, the rules on submandate (permissible when the mandator consents to it or it is required for a compelling reason; art. 644-2(1)) are unified with the rules on the subdeposit (art. 658 (2)). Furthermore, the effects of submandate (art. 644-2(2)) and subdeposit (art. 658(3)) are coordinated with the rules on the subagent in the Book on General Rules (art. 106(2)).

4.1.3 Solving the Problems Created by the Mixture of Legal Systems

Somewhat related to the policy of internal consistency, the reform addressed some widely recognized problems arising from the fact that the Japanese legal system is a mixed legal system in the broad sense. Some of the institutions transplanted from

---

[25] Minpô (Saiken Hô) Kaisei Kentou I'inkai (2010), p. 9.

French law conflicted with the institutions modeled on German law. These problems have been solved by implementing locally developed practices and doctrines.

One example relates to the law on fraudulent conveyance. Before the reform, the Civil Code provided for a system based on the Paulian action (*action paulienne*) under French law. A creditor was entitled to rescind a fraudulent transaction through the court. However, the provisions were vaguely drafted and difficult to understand. Furthermore, although the Code provided that rescission by the Court should benefit all claimants, the Great Court of Judicature (the predecessor of the Supreme Court before the Second World War) in its early days held that a transaction, if successfully rescinded, becomes nonexistent only against the defendant (either the recipient or third party beneficiary, as the case may be), not vis-à-vis others.[26] Case law, although established as precedent, was inconsistent with bankruptcy law modeled on German insolvency law, which demanded equal treatment among general creditors.

The Civil Code post-reform carefully drafted the conditions under which a transaction could be rescinded: either when the debtor's assets are diminished in amount (or converted into a more liquid type of asset (art. 424-2)) or when payment is made to a specific creditor over competing creditors at the time the debtor is already insolvent (art. 424-3). Regarding the effects of rescinding the transaction, it is explicitly stated that the fraudulently transferred asset or its value shall be returned to the debtor so that all the creditors may benefit from it (art. 424-6). It was also made clear that the effects of the court decision rescinding the transaction are binding on the debtor and all the creditors (art. 425). Thus, the civil code after the reform essentially aligns with bankruptcy law, although the proposal in the DP (retained in the IR) to prohibit the rescinding creditor from receiving the returned asset by itself was not accepted (see art. 424-9(1)). As a result, the rescinding creditor can fully satisfy its claim by the received sum at the cost of other creditors, as is the case under the Code prior to the reform.

The creditor's right to subrogate to the debtor's claim was also a source of confusion. Again, the Civil Code appeared to be based on the French system, specifically the oblique action (*action oblique*), and the provisions were not sufficiently clear. The Code also seemed to be inconsistent with the procedure of civil execution, regulated by the Civil Execution Act drafted under the strong influence of (though not identical with) German law.

Case law was also difficult to understand, as there were cases where the court admitted a claimant to subrogate to the claim of the debtor even though the debtor was solvent. One example is a case in which the purchaser of a piece of land demanded that the uncooperative seller agree to change the registration in the land registry, which in fact remained with the previous owner (the seller to the seller). In such a case, the purchaser was entitled to subrogate to the seller's right against the previous owner to update the registration so that the registered owner could be changed first from the previous owner to the seller and then, based on the purchaser's own right, from the seller to the purchaser.

---

[26] Great Court of Judicature, 24 March 1911, *Minroku* vol. 17, p. 117.

The civil code after the reform explicitly provided for such use of subrogation for the purpose of "securing a claim to change the registration" (art. 423-7). By specifying this exceptional use, it has become easier to understand that subrogation (other than for that use) is permitted only when the debtor is insolvent, although the new regulation still lacks an explicit requirement to that extent. The procedure has been further detailed, with the number of relevant provisions expanding from one to seven. However, the proposal to prohibit the subrogating creditor from satisfying its claim by receiving payment from the subrogated claim, included in the DP and retained in the IR, has not been adopted (see art. 423-5), as in the case of the rescission of a fraudulent transaction.

Finally, the Civil Code before the reform included a few provisions on securitised claims, possibly in line with the French tradition. They have long been ignored because the doctrine of negotiable instruments (*Wertpapier*) has developed in the field of commercial law, which is dominated by the German approach. The basic difference is that the German approach distinguishes the instrument as the medium and the claim represented by it, while the French tradition focuses on the claim as embodied in the instrument. Based on the work of commercial law academics, the relevant provisions have been completely redrafted according to the German *Wertpapierrecht* (art. 520-2 to 520-20).

4.1.4   Sporadic (and Modest) Paternalism

Some provisions in the amendments Bill adopt the paternalistic approach of limiting the freedom of contract to protect the interests of the weaker party. One such provision is found in the rules on standard contracts. As mentioned above, the standard contract has been an issue since the early twentieth century. It was questioned how clauses not negotiated by the parties, often without an opportunity for one of the parties even to look at them, could be binding. The Great Court of Judicature held that the parties are presumed to have consented to be bound by a contract incorporating standard clauses.[27] Nevertheless, the court lacked a tool to regulate an unfair or unreasonable clause, except when the clause was so unfair as to be against the *ordre public* (public policy).

Under the reformed civil code, a standard contract validly binds the parties if (a) the parties agree on the adoption of standard clauses in the contract or (b) the party having prepared the standard clauses 'presents' to the other party that those clauses will be incorporated into the contract (art. 548-2(1)). For public service companies, such as railway operators, road vehicle transport operators and telecommunications service operators, their respective business regulations have added a provision that the publication of a standard clause is deemed as "presenting" the clause under the Civil Code. As an exception to this framework, a standard clause is not binding if it limits the right or expands the duty of the other party and unilaterally harms the interests of that other party in such a manner as to be against the principle of good

---

[27] Great Court of Judicature, 24 December 1915, *Minroku* vol. 21. p. 2182.

faith in light of the manner and circumstances of the transaction as well as the general sense of trade (art. 548-2(2)). The initial proposal in the IR to introduce regulation of a surprise clause, apparently inspired by the German Civil Code (sec. 305c) and the UPICC (Art. 2.1.20), was strangely merged with the regulation of an unfair clause and drafted based on the general regulation of unfair clauses in a consumer contract (art. 10, Consumer Contracts Act).

Another example of a paternalistic approach is the personal guarantee. The personal guarantee was already an issue in 2004, when the Civil Code was redrafted in modern language. The 2004 amendments introduced protection of a guarantor of a revolving guarantee as long as the guaranteed claim was a pecuniary debt. After controversies, it was decided that some, but not all, of those amendments should be expanded in scope and become applicable to any revolving guarantee by an individual guarantor. The adopted rules are that the maximum amount of debt to be guaranteed be stipulated in advance (art. 465-2(2)); that such stipulation be made in writing (art. 465-2 (3)); and that the guaranteed amount of debt be fixed when the guarantor becomes insolvent (art. 465-4). Furthermore, a personal guarantee to cover a pecuniary debt arising from business operations, including a revolving guarantee that can cover debts arising from business, must be consented to in writing and notarised (art. 465-6(1)). This requirement is not applicable when the guarantor is the manager or controlling shareholder of a company and guarantees debts arising from the company's activities (art. 465-9).

4.2   Analysis of the Four Policies

Intriguing questions here are how the four policies were developed and on whose initiative. It seems that (loose) consensualism derived from the CISG. There is no surprise that the CISG, which Japan acceded to the year before the WG held its first meeting, affected the Civil Code. As mentioned, many academic members of the WG (and RC) knew that the CISG had significant impacts on German contract law doctrine. Therefore, there is a good reason to presume that the CISG also influenced the reform of Japan's Civil Code indirectly through these impacts. While modest paternalism is not observable in the CISG, the combination of consensualism and modest paternalism is the basic policy of the UPICC. Thus, one may safely conclude that the policy framework of Japan's Civil Code reform conforms with the ideas of Uchida and the globalists who led deliberations at the RC and WG.

The focus on technical consistencies within the Code, as well as efforts to solve problems arising from the mixture of legal systems, seem to be more domestic in their origins. Indeed, treating contracts of employment and work in parallel with contracts of mandate and deposit was severely criticized by a legal historian.[28] Such persistent emphasis on the rearrangement of provisions for the sake of apparent consistency, which this author names "ahistorical radicalism", is also observed in the reform of

---

[28] Koba (2010, pp. 208, 211–212).

the transport law (included mainly in the Commercial Code) adopted in 2018.[29] This fact implies that technical consistencies were the concern of the MoJ rather than the academic members engaged in the reform. Legal technocrats were concerned about having a consistent, self-contained legal system but were not interested in exploring the historical background of such a system.

It is interesting to observe that there seems to be little difference between the policies underpinning the amendments made, the proposal (DP) by the RC, and the private proposal by the group led by Kato. Despite Kato's harsh criticisms, his group's counterproposal is no less technical in nature. The group does not have conspicuous policy positions, such as more interventionist in favor of socially disadvantaged people or more market-oriented to support the competitive market. Seemingly, there is a common understanding about the status of the Civil Code among lawyers in Japan, whether in academia or in practice: the Civil Code should be policy-neutral and unaffected by interest group politicking. Uchida even claimed that the exploratory work by the RC as an academic group had the advantage of being immune to the pressure of interest groups.[30]

The orientation toward neutrality in terms of policy is related to the fact that the proposal to integrate the Consumer Contracts Act into the Civil Code was never seriously considered. Curiously, lawyers advocating consumer interests were not in favor of this proposal. They claimed that such integration would prevent timely amendments in the future, as the Civil Code is far more difficult to amend than consumer law. Those lawyers may also share the view that the Civil Code must not be the subject of interest group politics.[31]

The general public, however, may have a different view. Laypersons are usually not interested in technical issues of law. Given the time and costs that public servants had spent, the expectation was that the product of their work, namely, the reformed Civil Code, would visibly improve society. It is in this context that the amendments paternalistically protecting the weaker party's interest deserve attention. Neither the proposal to exclude a surprise clause in a standard contract nor the proposal for strict regulation of a personal guarantee was included in the DP. Both proposals were introduced in the course of deliberations at the WG. These topics were featured in the media when the reform Bill was submitted to the Diet and then approved. MoJ's legal technocrats may have shrewdly included these items to appease both the media (representing the general public) and lawyers (as experts) concerned to ensure the policy neutrality of the Civil Code.

---

[29] Kozuka (2020a).

[30] Uchida (2011, p. 709).

[31] See Kihara (2012).

5   Achievements of the Reform

5.1   Scale Down of the Reform

To evaluate the reform, one needs to examine what has been achieved and what has not. The OR, which is the final product of the LC, includes 40 headings, most of which consist of a few paragraphs. Each paragraph essentially addresses one reform item. In addition to the topics mentioned above in examining policies underpinning the reform, the OR includes topics such as the law on mistake, prescription, assignment of receivables, set-off, formation of a contract and individual types of contracts.

Although it may appear to cover a broad range of topics, the reform, in fact, was scaled down significantly in the course of deliberations. That fact is obvious when comparing the OR with the IR and, further back, with the DP. The DP included several innovative proposals, including restructuring the Code's arrangements and codifying new concepts. It proposed, for example, that the prescription (time limitation) of claims be separated from acquisitive prescription and be moved from the Book on general rules to the Book on obligations. It also proposed codifying rules relating to change of circumstances, interpretation of contracts, settlement arrangements, liability from the negotiation process of a contract (Japanese equivalent to *culpa in contrahendo*) and continuous contracts (long term contracts). These are rules mostly developed by case law without foundation in the text of the Civil Code. The innovative proposals described in this paragraph do not feature in the Code, despite Uchida's hope to draft a Code that accounted for its uniquely Japanese context. The only new concept introduced was the assumption of debts, developed by academic doctrine under the German influence and recognized by case law since the 1920s.[32]

5.2   Simple Quantitative Analysis of the Reform

To examine the extent to which the reform has been scaled down, the author has compared the DP, IR and OR in more detail. The DP, edited in the style of black letter rules and comments, included 600 operative rules. The author counted the DP rules adopted, almost as proposed, by the IR and OR.[33] For the proposals in the IR and OR that do not correspond to any proposal in the DP, the author examined whether

---

[32] Great Court of Judicature, 25 March 1926, *Minshû* vol. 5, p. 219; Great Court of Judicature, 9 May 1921, *Minroku* vol. 27, p. 899.

[33] It is, of course, not easy to judge whether a proposal in the DP is adopted "almost as proposed" by the IR or OR given that the drafting style of the DP is different from the MoJ's style of drafting. The difficulty is increased when the approaches to the topic are not identical. Although possibly arbitrary and imprecise to some extent, the author has tried to capture the intention of the DP's proposals, referring to the comments where necessary, and examined whether that intention is achieved in the IR or OR. When a rule in DP are adopted in part and rejected in part in the IR or OR, the adopted rule is counted as 0.5.

these were substitute proposals on an issue for which the DP proposed a different rule or original proposals on an issue that the DP did not deal with (including those issues the DP discussed but did not propose any rule on).

The results are striking. Only 216 and a half of the DP rules were adopted by the IR. 97 and a half rules in the IR are substitute proposals for those in the DP. This means that half of the topics that the RC raised were dropped from the table of deliberation in the early stages of deliberations. By the author's count, the IR listed 334 rules, including 20 new proposals that were not included in the DP. However, the OR included only 248 rules, with 86 rules dropped from the table. This means that the volume of reform in the OR shrunk to approximately three quarters of that in the IR, less than half compared with the ambitious DP. Furthermore, among the 216 and a half DP rules adopted by the IR, only 138 were accepted in the OR. Thus, the "survival rate" of the 600 DP proposals was 23%, less than a quarter. It is no wonder that Omura deplored in a book reviewing the outcome of the reform that most of what had been claimed as the basic features of Japan's Civil Code reform had disappeared.[34]

A closer look reveals that the survival rate varies depending on the subject. Many DP proposals regarding the creditor's right of subrogation (oblique action) and fraudulent conveyance (Paulian action), securitised claims, and the assumption of debts survived; 8 and a half out of 20, 14 out of 21, and 7 out of 15, respectively. As already discussed, the first two address the mainly technical problem arising from the mixture of legal systems, while the third is a restatement of case law established for almost a century. It is quite obvious that DP proposals fared better when dealing with amendments of a technical nature. More controversial proposals were met with backlash, with DP-derived proposals often substituted by rules retaining existing provisions and practice.

5.3 Triumph of Legal Technocrats

In brief, the reform was a triumph of legal technocrats. It has addressed confusion arising from ambiguous provisions and old case law and clarified minor issues using case law and undisputed doctrine. Yamamoto argues that the frustration of more ambitious proposals is due to the unanimity rule of the LC and minimalism in the style of drafting.[35] It may be true that the LC's unanimity rule, complied with in practice though not stipulated anywhere, makes it difficult to achieve any controversial reform. Nevertheless, the conservative outcome is striking when compared with the reform of other laws, for example corporate law, heavily driven by policy considerations.[36] Such a conservative outcome must be considered in light of the widely held view discussed above that the Civil Code should be policy-neutral and not subject to

---

[34] Omura and Dogauchi (2017, p. 499).

[35] Yamamoto (2017, pp. 141–146).

[36] See Goto et al. (2017).

interest group politicking. When policy considerations play a limited role, advocates of a new proposal must convince others that this proposal will improve the relevant existing rule in a technical sense. This will be no mean feat.

Minimalism, as Yamamoto claims, describes the MoJ's approach of drafting only necessary rules and not codifying what can be understood from other provisions or what can be arranged by private agreement. This is not unique to the drafting of the Civil Code and is in fact always the case with law reform administered by the MoJ. It is doubtful that this approach has satisfied the second component of Request No. 88 to make the Civil Code easier for the general public to understand, as outlined above. Nevertheless, for legal technocrats, simpler text may be more convenient, as long as trained lawyers can share a common understanding of the text.

One may wonder who the "legal technocrats" that dominated the codification process are. The MoJ officials who serve as the secretariat of the LC are mostly seconded judges experienced in civil matters. There are also judges who sit as members of the WG during the LC's deliberations as representatives of the court. As a result, judges have a large influence over the enactment of basic laws, such as the Civil Code, at the MoJ.[37] It should be remembered that Kashu, as an experienced judge, rejected Uchida's theory to expect the flexible use of the good faith principle. When a judge finds the need to come to an equitable solution under the specific facts of the case, they prefer to rely on more specific provisions to develop an interpretation that will lead them to the solution, rather than turn to a general principle giving wide discretion, such as the principle of good faith. Similarly, the plan of Uchida and other academics to create an innovative Code was too ambitious for judges engaged in law-making as legal technocrats. Ultimately, the latter took control of the reform.

6 Prospects for the Future

Having seen that ambitions for fundamental reform have shrunk to a smaller scale, academics have realized the importance of their future role. Omura argues that, with the support of civil society, proposals made in the course of deliberations, even those frustrated, may inspire future case law and academic doctrine developments.[38] Although limited to the subject of service contracts, Sumida also argues that the proposals not adopted will guide interpretation of the adopted texts.[39]

If the Code is to be policy neutral and the drafting style is minimalist, the interpretation of the Code's text by lawyers will naturally play a large role. In this sense, Japanese law is a kind of *Juristenrecht* (lawyers' law). The legislative process does not conclude controversies. Rather, it forms the starting point from which lawyers compete with each other by developing their own interpretations. This development

---

[37] Kozuka and Nottage (2014).

[38] Omura and Dogauchi (2017, p. 505).

[39] Sumida (2018)

will be facilitated by the emphasis given to precedents, which is closer to the common law than traditional civil law jurisdictions.[40]

If Japanese law is understood as *Juristenrecht*, one may wonder whether the initial aspiration to produce a civil code that reflects Japan's local features was an appropriate one. The reformed Code does not codify uniquely Japanese rules or doctrines, not even those developed by Japanese courts' precedents. Arguably, the "local color" of Japan's Civil Code does not exist in such rules and doctrines. Rather, Japanese lawyers' approach to the Civil Code, demanding the policy neutrality of the Code and expecting developments of law by lawyers, is the uniquely Japanese feature. To them, law is a technical subject, and policy issues are hidden behind the scenes (or dealt with elsewhere through interest group politicking). In that sense, although contrary to Uchida's hope, the Civil Code reform ending up in the triumph of legal technocrats does in fact reflect the "local color" of Japanese law.

7 Conclusions

The fundamental reform of the Japanese Civil Code was finally concluded in 2017 and is now in force. Comparing the initial ambitions and the finally adopted text, an observer might form the view that the reform was significantly frustrated. The scale of the reform became modest, innovative proposals were not included, and even local doctrines developed by case law failed to be codified. Such an outcome might appear curious, given that the criticisms of the project, made most prominently by Kato, hardly succeeded in a political sense. A closer examination, however, reveals that the approach to reform adopted a Japanese "local color". Interest group politicking was carefully avoided in deliberations over the Civil Code to keep it policy neutral. The minimalist style of drafting that excluded ambitious (but not unanimously supported) proposals resulted in simple text, leaving ample room for academics and practicing lawyers to develop the law through interpretation of that text. Even though this has frustrated another intended goal of the reform, namely, to create a civil code that is easy to understand for the general public, the adopted text is in line with Japanese law being "lawyers' law." In these respects, the reform was indeed uniquely Japanese.

It is true that Japanese society has changed since the time the Civil Code was adopted in 1896. It is also true that the Code needs to adapt to this change. However, how such adaptation is made is affected by the *modus operandi* of local law and lawyers. This *modus operandi* is so deeply rooted in society that a piece of legislation to amend the Civil Code cannot change it.

Acknowledgements The author acknowledges funding for his research from the Japan Society for the Promotion of Science, identifier 20H00051.

---

[40] Kozuka (2020b, pp. 54–57).

References

Goto G, Matsunaka M, Kozuka S (2017) Japan's gradual reception of independent directors: an empirical and political-economic analysis. In: Baum H, Puchniak D, Nottage L (eds) Independent directors in Asia: a historical, contextual and comparative approach. Cambridge University Press, Cambridge, pp 135–175

Hoshino E, Iwaki K (1992) シンポジウム 現代契約法論 (Symposium: the modern contract law theory). Shihô 54:3–125

Ishikawa H (2013) Codification, decodification, and recodification of the Japanese civil code. Univ Tokyo J Law Politics 10:61–80

Kamo A (2010) Crystalization, unification, or differentiation? The Japanese civil code (Law of obligations) reform commission and basic reform policy (Draft proposals). Columbia J Asian Law 24:171–212

Kato M (2015) 迫りつつある債権法改正 (The reform of the law of obligations approaching). Shinzansha, Tokyo

Kihara H (2012) Japan's civil code reform and consumer protection. Ajia Hôgaku 47:72–84

Koba A (2010) 「債権法改正の基本方針」に対するロマニスト・リヴュー、速報版 (The Romanist review on the "basic policy on the law of obligations reform", an interim version). Tokyo Daigaku Houka Daigakuin Lô Revû 5:195–215

Kozuka S (2013) Japanese earthquake insurance in context. In: Hsu Y-M, Tsuji Y (eds) International business law in the 21st century: challenges and issues in East Asia. Cambridge Independent Press, Cambridge, pp 207–220

Kozuka S (2020a) Maritime law codification in Japan: elements considered and those not considered. In: Pepłowska-Dąbrowska A, Nawrot J (eds) Codification of maritime law: challenges, possibilities and experience. Informa Law, London, pp 217–231

Kozuka S (2020b) The style and role of judgments by Japanese courts: how they are written and read. Zeitschrift für Japanisches Recht 49:47–75

Kozuka S, Nottage L (2014) Policy and politics in contract law reform in Japan. In: Adams M, Heirbaut D (eds) The method and culture of comparative law, essays in honor of Mark Van Hoecke. Hart Publishing, Oxford and Portland, pp 235–253. The longer version is available at: https://papers.ssrn.com/sol3/papers.cfm?abstract_id=2360343

Matsumoto E (2015) Tort law in Japan. In: Bussani M, Sebok AJ (eds) Comparative Tort Law: global perspectives. Edward Elgar, Cheltenham and Northampton, pp 359–384

Minpô (Saiken Hô) Kaisei Kentou I'inkai (ed) (2010) 詳解債権法改正の基本方針 (The basic policy on the law of obligations reform in details), Vol V. Shoji Homu, Tokyo

Nottage L (2019) The development of comparative law in Japan. In: Reimann M, Zimmermann R (eds) The Oxford handbook of comparative law, 2nd edn. Oxford University Press. Oxford, pp 201–227

Omura A, Dogauchi H (eds) (2017) 解説民法 (債権法) 改正のポイント (Lectures on the major issues of the reform of the civil code (law of obligations)). Yuhikaku, Tokyo

Sono H, Nottage L, Pardiek A, Saigusa K (2019) Contract law in Japan. Kluwer Law International, Alphen aan den Rijn

Suehiro I (1921) 物権法 (The property law). Yuhikaku, Tokyo

Sumida M (2018) 委任 (The contract of mandate). In Shiomi Y, Chiba E, Katayama N, Yamanome A (eds) 詳解改正民法 (Revised civil code in detail). Shoji Homu, Tokyo

Taylor VL (1993) Continuing transactions and persistent myths: contacts in contemporary Japan. Melbourne Univ Law Rev 19:352–398

Uchida T (1993) 現代契約法の新たな展開と一般条項 (1) ~ (4) (The new developments of the modern contract law and the general clause, Parts 1–4), NBL 514: 6–11, NBL 515: 13–21, NBL 516: 22–32. NBL 517:32–40

Uchida T (2011) Contract law reform in Japan and the UNIDROIT principles. Uniform Law Rev 14:705–717

Vanoverbeke D (2004) Community and state in the Japanese farm village: farm tenancy conciliation (1924–1938). Leuven University Press, Leuven

Yamamoto K (2017) 民法の基礎から学ぶ民法改正 (Leaning the civil code reform from the basics of the civil code). Iwanami Shoten, Tokyo

Souichirou Kozuka (Ph.D., Tokyo) is Professor of Law at Gakushuin University, Tokyo. He specializes in commercial law, corporate law and maritime, air and space law and has taught at Chiba University (Chiba), Sophia University (Tokyo), Keio University (Tokyo) as well as at the Tokyo seminar sponsored by Ritsumeikan University & ANJeL (Australian Network for Japanese Law). His recent publications in English include "The Style and Role of Judgments by Japanese Courts: How They are Written and Read", *Zeitschrift für Japanisches Recht* No. 49 (2020), pp. 47–75, and *Implementation of the Cape Town Convention and the Domestic Laws on Secured Transactions* (2017, Springer). He is correspondent of UNIDROIT (the International Institute for the Unification of Private Law) and Associate Member of the International Academy of Comparative Law (IACL).

The Chinese Civil Code: The Problem of Systematization

Qiao Liu

Abstract This chapter assesses the systematization of the Chinese Civil Code ('CCC') by using multiple internationally accepted criteria. It concludes that while the CCC has generally adopted a logical macro structure akin to the BGB, a number of problems currently exist at a micro level, which severely diminishes the systematization of the Code. Inconsistency between different provisions, repetition, inadequate use of cross-referencing, and the overly broadness of some provisions have been identified as the major problems in this regard. The uneasy relationship between provisions governing obligations in general and provisions governing contracts only within Title 1 of Book III Contracts also poses a potential challenge. By identifying and analyzing these problems, the present chapter hopes to contribute to their future solution by way of legislative amendments and judicial interpretations.

1 Introduction

The promulgation of the Chinese Civil Code ('CCC') is a landmark in the legal history of the People's Republic of China ('PRC'). As the first piece of PRC legislation with 'Code' in its title, the CCC has been hailed by President Xi Jinping as 'a major achievement in developing socialist rule of law in the new era' and a milestone that 'systematically integrates the civil legal norms developed by long-term practices during more than 70 years [construction] of the New China'.[1] While it is undeniable that the CCC, along with the 'positive energy' it generates, has much to commend it, any future reflection and improvement upon the CCC depends on an objective and unprejudiced assessment of its pros and cons. Such an assessment is necessarily

---

[1] See Xi Jinping (delivered 15 June 2020), Fully Understand the Significance of the Enactment of the Civil Code, Better Protect the Rights and Interests of the People Lawfully. Additionally, see, Xinhua (2020, p. 19).

Q. Liu (✉)
City University of Hong Kong, Hong Kong, China
e-mail: qliu5@cityu.edu.hk

© The Author(s), under exclusive license to Springer Nature Singapore Pte Ltd. 2023　　　203
M. Graziadei and L. Zhang (eds.), *The Making of the Civil Codes*,
Ius Gentium: Comparative Perspectives on Law and Justice 104,
https://doi.org/10.1007/978-981-19-4993-7_12

technical in nature and forward-looking, unconcerned with resurrecting any debate during the drafting and deliberation of the CCC. Its sole purpose is to promote better understanding and actions with respect to the practical use of the code.

The CCC may be assessed by comparison to a number of different benchmarks. Therefore, a comparison may be conducted between the CCC and (1) previous 'Laws' (in the Chinese context, such 'Laws' refer specifically to legislation promulgated by the National People's Congress, 'NPC', or its Standing Committee), which sit at the same level of hierarchy and occupy the same field as the CCC; (2) foreign civil codes that have exerted influence on the CCC, such as civil codes in Germany and Switzerland; and (3) the more detailed application or implementation rules and judicial decisions associated with the provisions of the CCC. This chapter will attempt to assess one particular aspect of the CCC by using the aforesaid benchmarks. The aspect to be investigated concerns the systematization of the CCC. Systematization is widely accepted as an essential character of a Code, particularly when it results from a process of codification rather than compilation. The assessment of the systematization of the CCC will go some length in revealing whether the process of revising and finalising the CCC from late 2019 to its date of enactment is better classified as a codification or compilation and, more importantly, what implications this might have for its future interpretation and application.

2 Codification and Systematization

Before we embark on the aforesaid assessment, some basic concepts relevant to the subject must be clarified. A code, or codification, has been defined as 'an instrument to bring about a transformation of the structure and content of the law' and a 'complete conceptual-institutional change-over of the legal field'.[2] This definition stresses that codification must have a strong element of legal reform and thus represents a narrow and strict sense of the term. A paradigm of this narrow sense of codification is the French Code Civil and the German BGB, which were both epoch-making instruments that brought about an entire upheaval of the law of the jurisdiction at the time. In modern days, however, the term 'codification' has been used in more diversified senses ranging from mere collection, compilation, consolidation to the above reform-centered codification. However, even when used in the broadest sense, codification is generally more than mere 'graphic expression of the [existing] written law' and involves 'the restructuring of the rules of law as a coherent whole'.[3]

Among the different senses of codification, a distinction is generally drawn between 'substantive' codification in the traditional European style and 'formal'

---

[2] Varga (Sándor Eszenyi et al. trans., 1991, p. 223), reviewed by Legrand (1994, p. 9) Tulane European & Civil Law Forum 1.

[3] Steiner (2018, pp. 26 and 27).

codification that dominates common law jurisdictions.[4] Systematization seems to be recognized as a watershed between the two:

> The distinguishing criterion, then, is whether the codification merely wants to order and structure existing laws, with or without some updates and the solving of inconsistencies, or whether it aims at systemizing rules within a domain of law on the basis of a specific set of fundamental principles or a specific angle.[5]

Clearly, here, 'systematization' comprises more than mere ordering, structuring or updating existing laws or removal of inconsistencies. However, it is conceivable that even reordering or restructuring of pre-existing legal rules might introduce changes in the substance of law, where the rules are set up under a new nexus that imposes legislative coherence on a legal field. Such systematization, characterized by the substantive changes it introduces, needs not to reach the height of the revolutionary French or German civil codes in the 18th or nineteenth centuries but should be distinguished from consolidation, which has commonly been employed in common law jurisdictions to restate existing laws (including cases and statutes).[6]

What, then, does 'systematization' of a code mean precisely? A code in the civil law tradition is said to have to be comprehensive (or exclusive), authoritative and systematic. Since authoritativeness is self-explanatory, the other two characters, namely, comprehensiveness and systematization, can be compared. The comprehensiveness of a code is essentially an outward-looking feature, since its key feature lies in the exclusory effect of the code on norms not included in it. However, comprehensiveness must be viewed with qualification. No code can be all-embracing, self-sufficient or exhaustive in a domain of law. The move to decodification, in fact, denotes both a preference for resorting to more specialized norms[7] and a greater role to be played by judges in interpreting and developing the law.[8] In light of this, comprehensiveness is better understood to refer to a complete framework or structure 'at the level of general principles or rules', which provides a platform for the further development of detailed propositions of law through an exercise of legislative or judicial power.[9] Accordingly, a modern civil code must cover four central topics: persons, property, obligations and liability.[10] In contrast, systematization is evidently a distinct feature of a code.[11] Systematization is generally understood as a way of presentation—'synthetically and methodically organizing a body of general and permanent rules' governing the relevant areas of law.[12] Simply put, the systematization of a code concerns the relationship between different parts or provisions

---

[4] Bergel (1987, p. 1073).

[5] Popelier (2017, pp. 253 and 257).

[6] Teasdale (2017, pp. 247 and 252).

[7] Popelier (2017, pp. 259–261).

[8] Baudenbacher (1999, pp. 333 and 336 et seq).

[9] Legrand, (1994, p. 31).

[10] See Rudden (10 July 1992, p. 27).

[11] Stoljar (1977, p. 16).

[12] Bergel at 1074.

of the code. Furthermore, the systematization of a code consists of an internal order that not only arranges interrelating principles and rules but also structures legal analysis or thinking. Such systematization promotes rationality and legal certainty by having 'a whole built on "n" articles, each essential to the whole', on the basis of 'a fixed rapport between all the elements of each institution', 'a precise correspondence between the headings and the provisions they encompass',[13] as well as 'the formulation of concepts and of general principles and the use of logical classifications'.[14] A primary characteristic of such systematization is the organization of the code via resort to 'generalized statements of principle' which 'help to organize legal thinking, to allow the formation of clusters of similar cases, to make the law manageable and findable, and to provide a language in which a meaningful discourse between lawyers can take place'.[15] Consequently, a solution is to be found often through logical connections between the general and the particular and sometimes in a composite of both, since 'each code article has a meaning only because of its relationship to a cluster of articles to which it is linked; each institution has a meaning only because of its relationship with the whole system to which it belongs'.[16]

Accordingly, the systematization of a code seems to encompass the following tasks: arranging the contents in a logical sequence; adopting appropriately differentiated levels of generalization/abstraction; removing any obsolete, irrelevant or inconsistent provisions; ensuring that related provisions are compatible and complementary and work coherently; introducing new groupings to order homogeneous sections; renumbering sections and subsections; adjusting internal references to sections or subsections; merging sections that regulate the same subject.[17] To assess the systematization of the CCC, it should therefore be investigated whether, and if so how well, these tasks have been performed during the law-making process.

3   The Chinese Civil Code and Its Systematization

Since the establishment of the PRC in 1949 and until the enactment of the CCC, there have been several attempts to codify civil law in China, but all these attempts have failed.[18] Shortly after the Fourth Plenary Session of the 18th Communist Party of China Central Committee in October 2014, a two-step strategy was adopted by the NPC, which involved the enactment of the General Provisions of the Civil Law in

---

[13] Levasseur (1969–1970 at pp. 693, 700, 701 and 703).

[14] Tallon (1979, p. 4).

[15] Kötz (1987, p. 6).

[16] Bergel, (1987, p. 1083).

[17] See Albanesi (2017 pp. 268 fn 12) (citing Xanthaki (2014, p. 276)*et seq*), 275 (citing Pagano (2004), p. 80 et seq).

[18] For a historical account, see He Q, Li X, Chen Y (2003), An overview of the drafts of Civil Code in new China. Additionally, see, Liu (2020) Several main issues regarding the Civil Code, p. 51 et seq.

2017 to be followed by a review by the NPC Standing Committee of each of the other parts of the draft Civil Code.[19] The other parts of the draft Code were to be derived from Laws that had been separately enacted previously, including the following:

- the 1985 Succession Law[20];
- the 1986 General Principles of Civil Law[21];
- the 1995 Security Law[22];
- the 1998 Adoption Law[23];
- the 1999 Contract Law[24];
- the 2001 Marriage Law[25];
- the 2007 Property Rights Law[26]; and
- the 2009 Tort Liability Law.[27]

Drafts were then prepared for individual Books primarily on the basis of the 2017 General Provisions and the above Laws, also incorporating other relevant laws such as Judicial Interpretations issued by the Supreme People's Court ('SPC'). These drafts were combined to form a draft Civil Code submitted on 23 December 2019 to the NPC for final deliberation and enactment. The CCC was adopted on 28 May 2020, containing seven Books with 1260 articles. All except one of the seven Books are primarily based on the above Laws (including the 2017 General Provisions). The only exception is Book IV 'Personality Rights', which is a new Book developed partly from the 1986 General Principles and the 2016 Cybersecurity Law.[28] Below is a list of the prior Laws to which the individual Books of the CCC correspond:

- Book I: General Provisions (the 2017 General Provisions)
- Book II: Property Rights (the 2007 Property Rights Law, the 1995 Security Law)
- Book III: Contracts (the 1999 Contract Law, the 1995 Security Law)
- Book IV: Personality Rights (the 1986 General Principles)
- Book V: Marriage, Family and Adoption (the 1998 Adoption Law, the 2001 Marriage Law)
- Book VI: Succession (the 1985 Succession Law)
- Book VII: Tort Liability (the 2009 Tort Liability Law)

---

[19] Chang T, Lu L (2017), The "Two steps" compilation of the Civil Code, issue 6.

[20] Succession Law (adopted at the Third Session of the Sixth NPC on 10 April 1985).

[21] General Principles of Civil Law (adopted at the Fourth Session of the Sixth NPC on 12 April 1986).

[22] Security Law (adopted at the Fourteenth Session of the Eighth NPC on 30 June 1995).

[23] Adoption Law (adopted at the Twenty Second Session of the Seventh NPC on 29 December 1991).

[24] Contract Law (adopted at the Second Session of the Ninth NPC on 15 March 1999).

[25] Marriage Law (adopted at the Third Session of the Fifth NPC on 10 September 1980).

[26] Property [Real Rights] Law (adopted at the Fifth Session of the Tenth NPC on 16 March 2007).

[27] Tort Law (adopted at the Fourth Session of the Sixth NPC on 26 December 2009).

[28] Cybersecurity Law (adopted at the Twenty fourth Session of the Twelfth NPC on 7 July 2016).

Overall, the CCC has been described by the legislature as a 'systematic legislative project' that 'deals properly with and coheres the relationships between all types of norms under the codified civil law system'.[29] It has further been stated that:

> drafting the Civil Code is not making entirely new civil law, nor is it a simple compila-
> tion of law, but consists of editing and revising the existing civil legal norms, altering and
> ameliorating provisions that are no longer suitable for actual circumstances, and making
> new provision addressing new circumstances and issues arising in the economic and social
> life.[30]

However, the codification process from December 2019 to May 2020 appears to fit what had been described as a mere 'compilation' of the Laws that preceded the Code.[31] Indeed, it has been pointed out that there are issues of incoherency in earlier versions of the draft CC.[32] Nevertheless, it would be inconceivable if such Laws, particularly the 2017 General Provisions, had been enacted in total disregard of each other, and it could be argued that the systematization had, at least partly, been conducted in drafting and revising such Laws. The remaining question is, therefore, whether, and if so to what extent, the codification process has achieved a systematic code. To answer this question, it is useful first to outline some of the main changes made to the text of the CCC during that period. According to the Weixin account of Faxin (法信), a specialist legal database, a total of 313 'substantial changes' have been made during the codification process, including 55 to Books I and II, 145 to Book III, 67 to Books IV–VI and 43 to Book VII, including all changes in expression that may affect the interpretation and application of the relevant provisions (such as 'danwei' [单位, unit] altered to 'zuzhi' [组织, organization], 'month' altered to 'thirty days'). Apart from these changes, there have been 197 new additions to the text of the CCC not to be found in any prior law. These changes and additions do not comprise, however, those made during the enactment of the 2017 General Provisions. A considerable number of changes and additions made to Title 1 (General Rules—通则) of Book III (Contracts) are in the form of provisions referring to 'obligations' in general rather than contracts, which is only one form of obligation. As will be seen in Sect. 6, these changes and additions adversely affect the systematization of the CCC. Apart from that, most of the other changes or additions do not relate to the systematization of the CCC. Some of the changes are fairly significant, including formality requirements for a floating charge (Article 396) or a pledge over right (Articles 441–445), electronic contracting (Articles 469, 482, 491), a third party's claim under the contract (Article 522 para. 2), contract assignment (Article 544 para. 2), new contract termination right or power (Articles 563 para. 2, 580 para. 2), contributory negligence in contract liability (Article 592 para. 2). However, generally speaking, none of such changes or additions could be said to relate to the systematization of

---

[29] See Chen, Vice Chairman of the NPC Standing Committee's delivery at the thirteenth NPC meeting, Third session on 22 May 2020, Explanations on the draft Chinese Civil Code.

[30] Ibid.

[31] Sun (2016), The issue of systematization and scientization of civil legislation in China, issue 6.

[32] Liu J (2018) The systematic dilemma and outlet of the codification of Civil Code, p. 153 et seq.

the CCC, hence making it a more organized whole. In the following passages, we will focus on a number of changes or additions that are clearly 'systematic' in that sense.

4 The Relation Between Book I (General Provisions) and Other Books

The systematization of the CCC could be assessed against the six interacting elements of the BGB, the high watermark of modern civil codes: (i) a high reliance on concepts, (ii) a high level of abstraction, (iii) the allocation of rules to the highest possible level using concentric circles and (iv) some overlapping circles of scope, (v) the use of models and cross-references and (vi) a top-down approach with frequent use of general clauses supplemented by specific provisions.[33] The CCC has been drafted in a style generally comprehensible to a layperson, primarily because of the efforts of people working in the legislative committee of the NPC who tend to avoid the overly technical terms used in previous academic drafts. Nevertheless, the CCC still makes wide use of concepts similar to the German concepts, which form concentric circles at different levels of generalization. If we take the example of a sales contract, the circle of the highest generality (circle 1) consists of rules applicable to a sales contract as well as the rest of private law, such as those concerning 'civil subjects' (民事主体) and 'civil capacity' (民事能力). At the next level (circle 2) is 'civil juristic act' (民事法律行为), which covers both unilateral and bilateral 'declarations of intention' (意思表示) during the negotiation of a sales contract. When the General Provisions of Civil Law was enacted in 2017, some rules previously confined to the ambit of the 1999 Contract Law were elevated to a more general level and made applicable to all types of 'civil juristic act', such as effective time (Articles 137–139), interpretation (Article 142), fraud (Articles 148–149), duress (Article 150), unconscionability (Article 151), expiry of right of rescission (Article 152), illegality (Article 153) and so forth. Moving on to the still lower level of generalization (circle 3), we will find general rules applicable to all contracts, including contract conclusion (Chapter 2), validity (Chapter 3), performance (Chapter 4), preservation (Chapter 5), variation and assignment (Chapter 6), cessation (Chapter 7) and liability (Chapter 8). It is obvious that compared to the German system, there is one level missing from the CCC, namely, rules applicable to the entire law of obligations. As we will see, the legislators decided not to have a separate Book to make general provisions for the law of obligations but instead to absorb such rules into Title 1 of Book III (that is, circle 3 above). Title 1 of Book III also contains rules applicable only to synallagmatic contracts, which allow one of the parties to suspend performance (Articles 525–527) and demand appropriate assurance (Article 528). The level of the lowest generality is, in our example, the specific part of Book III, which contains rules applicable to a 'typical contract', such as a sales contract (Chapter 9). Therefore, the CCC

---

[33] Dannemann and Schulze (2020, p. 8 at [28]).

does have a 'from general to specific' hierarchy of rules, but this is a somewhat simplified system that contains fewer concentric circles compared to the German system. Likewise, overlapping circles are less frequently used. One notable feature of the CCC is that it does not endorse the German principle of abstraction and hence does not recognize an 'act' or 'contract' to create, modify or extinguish a proprietary right. Therefore, at least in a conceptual sense, the law of obligations embraces, rather than overlaps with, the entire law of contract. However, such overlapping circles do exist; for example, the proprietary effect of a sales contract is to be found under the provisions for the delivery of moveable property (Book II Chapter 2 Sect. 2). Likewise, while the use of cross-referencing under the CCC is fairly restrictive, examples can be found that support the hierarchical and logical structure of the relevant rules, such as the reference made to general rules of contract law for some noncontractual scenarios (see below). Therefore, broadly speaking, one could say that the overall conceptual structure of the CCC is similar in kind, even though differing in degree, to that adopted by the BGB, which is indisputably systematic.

Having said that, the systematization of a code goes beyond the adoption of such a conceptual structure and imposes more concrete requirements regarding the relations between different parts of the code. In this and the following sections, we will reveal some of the problems jeopardising the systematization of the CCC through three sets of such relations. The current section focuses on the relation between Book I and other Books. A principal feature of the BGB is that it starts with a General Part (*Allgemeiner Teil*) overarching the rest of the Code by laying down rules applicable to the entire Code and indeed private law as a whole; the drafting method adopted is one in which rules contained in the General Part are 'factorised' (*vor die Klammer ziehen*) and placed before specific rules.[34] Often, such general clauses are placed at the beginning of a Book, Title or Chapter and set out broad principles to be applied by judges by exercising the discretion granted under those principles.[35] The CCC follows this top-down order of the BGB and starts with Book I (General Provisions, 总则). Unlike the BGB, the CCC designates its very first chapter, Chapter 1 (Basic Rules, 基本规定), to a number of general clauses overarching not only Book I but also the entire Code. Such general clauses comprise the principles of voluntariness (Article 5), fairness (Article 6), good faith (Article 7), public policy (Article 8) and efficiency and eco-friendliness (Article 9), all of which are given paramount importance and apply wherever 'civil subjects' engage in 'civil activities'. In the following passages, two distinct issues with respect to such general clauses in Book I will be explored. The first issue is consistency, particularly whether the same meaning is given to the same term that appears in both Book I and other Books of the CCC. The exploration will focus on the use of the term 'good faith' as an example. The second issue concerns whether certain provisions in Book I genuinely perform the role of general clauses, particularly by covering areas not covered by the corresponding provisions in an ensuing Book. In other words, questions may be asked about whether such provisions

---

[34] Dannemann and Schulze (2020) at 3 [11]: *vor die Klammer ziehen* is 'the German mathematical expression for finding a common denominator and placing this outside of brackets'.
[35] Baudenbacher at 347.

in Book I should rather belong to a subsequent specific Book. The chapters on 'Civil Rights', 'Civil Juristic Acts' and 'Civil Liabilities' will be briefly discussed to show where the problem lies.

Book I of the CCC retains much of the provisions of the 2017 General Provisions, whose broad structure is similar to that of the 1986 General Principles, comprising basic rules, civil subjects (natural, legal and other persons), civil rights, civil juristic acts, civil liabilities and temporal provisions (limitation period, etc.). The 1986 General Principles is clearly outdated, as it has been pointed out that all but 20 of its 156 articles have either been replaced or lost relevance in the enactment of the 2017 General Provisions.[36] The first issue, regarding the consistency between Book I and other Books, can be explored by looking at Article 7 of the CCC, which provides that 'civil subjects shall adhere to the principle of good faith, by keeping honesty and promises, when engaging in civil activities'. What is the scope of this principle of good faith? It appears that Article 7 applies to all types of 'civil activities', including all 'civil juristic acts' whether they relate to property, contract, family or inherence. With respect to acts not involving a declaration of intention, such as a tortious act, 'good faith' cannot be seen as a standard by which such an act is performed. However, in Chinese judicial practice, there are many cases in which the principle of good faith is applied to the allocation of losses flowing from a wrong, including a tort or breach of contract. Therefore, the term 'civil activities' seems to be broadly conceived of as comprising a civil subject's bearing legal liability as a result of an application of law. The placement of Article 7 as part of Chapter 1 Basic Rules seems to suggest that it applies both to Chapter 6 (Civil Juristic Acts) and Chapter 8 (Civil Liabilities). On this note, a problem of inconsistency appears to arise between Article 7 and specific provisions in which the term 'good faith' is used. As noted by the present author in an earlier work, one of the existing problems with the principle of good faith in Chinese law is that there lacks credible guidance on how 'good faith' could be applied in practice and where the limit on the court's discretion lies.[37] When the 2017 General Provisions were enacted, the lawmakers attempted to redress this problem by defining 'good faith' as 'keeping honesty and promises'. Unfortunately, this may be a step too far in the other direction: it is a definition that is so narrow that it tends to considerably diminish the value of such an important general clause as Article 7. In short, the very purpose of a general clause is to offer flexibility and adaptability to the courts when deciding concrete cases. If a line should be drawn as to what 'good faith' entails or not, this should arguably be done by the judiciary rather than the legislature. Moreover, the definition given under Article 7 is clearly too restrictive. 'Keeping honesty and promises' might be a commonly accepted meaning of 'good faith', but the latter is far from being confined to that single meaning. For example, when we turn to a specific provision such as Article 509, which provides for the observation of the principle of good faith in the performance of contract, it would make little sense to confine that provision to requiring a contracting party to perform the contract honestly and in conformity with its promises. At least in

---

[36] Xinhua (2020 p. 21).

[37] McKendrick and Liu (2017) in DiMatteo and Chen (eds) pp. 77 and 78.

some cases, good faith might be equated with reasonableness. There is thus patent inconsistency between the definition of the term under Article 7 and the application of specific provisions such as Article 509 to cases that do not involve dishonesty or breach of promise but merely instances of unreasonable conduct. Similarly, honesty or promise-keeping could hardly be applied to the abovementioned allocation of loss cases or as a criterion of interpretation under Article 142 (interpretation of a declaration of intention) or Article 466 (contract interpretation). These examples indicate that when the definition of 'good faith' was added to Article 6, proper consideration of the systematization of the entire Code has not been carefully made.

The second issue concerns a number of provisions in Book I that ought to be relocated to other Books. Chapter 5 (Civil Rights, 民事权利) serves as a fitting example. At the outset, the title is misleading since the chapter provides for both civil rights and civil interests (Article 126). 'Interests' are used in the context of, for example, a tort where what is infringed may be a right, an interest or both (Articles 120, 183 and Book VII Tortious Liabilities). Chapter 5 consists of 24 articles (Article 109– Article 132) that can be divided into two categories: provisions relating to specific types of civil right and provisions relating to all types of civil right. The latter category of provisions forms a minority under Chapter 5 and addresses matters such as acquisition (Article 129), noninterference (Article 130), lawful exercise (Article 131) and abuse (Article 132) of civil rights. These provisions naturally belong to Book I. By comparison, most of the Articles in Chapter 5 fall into the first category and state that civil subjects enjoy a certain civil right, which finds more detailed provisions in other Books of the CCC. This gives rise to concerns over where is the most appropriate home for such provisions. The concern lies first in the fact that such provisions are sometimes too specific, relating to a type of civil right (such as the right to personal information under Article 111 and the specific personality rights under Article 110) rather than a group of similar rights. More fundamentally, the concern lies in the fact that such provisions, by stating that civil subjects enjoy property rights, contractual rights and so forth, merely repeat or rehearse what is to follow in the corresponding specific provisions in other Books of the CCC. This thus amounts to a waste of space and introduces provisions that have no practical application value. Furthermore, such provisions sometimes even use terms inconsistent with the subsequent specific provisions. For example, prohibited acts dealing with a natural person's personal information are described differently under Article 111 (as a list of specific acts) in Chapter 5 of Book I and under Article 1035 of Book IV Personality Rights (as a generic concept of 'handling' [处理], which is then defined by a different nonexhaustive list of acts). Consequently, an act of 'acquiring' or 'buying or selling' is only to be found under Article 111, while an act of 'storing' is only to be found under Article 1035. Article 111 is therefore not only an unnecessary repetition of the subsequent specific provisions (including Article 1035) but also at variance with Article 1035. Similarly, Articles 121 and 122 provide exactly the same rules (about a claim based on unjust enrichment) as those under the first paragraph of Articles 979 and 985, respectively, but under both of them, different wording has been used. For example, Article 122 provides that 'a person who suffers a loss *by reason of* (因) another person's obtaining an unjust benefit without any legal ground *is entitled to* (有权) demand that person to return *the unjust benefit* (不当利益)'. By comparison, Article 985 para. 1 provides that 'where an *enrichee* (得利人) obtains an unjust benefit without any legal ground, a person who suffers a loss *may* (可以) demand the *enrichee* to return *the obtained benefit* (取得的利益)'. It remains to be seen whether such different wording might cause a difference in judicial application of the provisions. At any rate, it is wasteful and confusing to make repetitive provisions for the same rule, and furthermore, it is inviting trouble to adopt different expressions in those repetitive provisions.

Cross-reference is sometimes used in the CCC to link different parts of the Code and avoids unnecessary repetition. Thus, since some of the contract rules are now generalized into rules applicable to all civil juristic acts and provided for under Book I General Provisions, the relevant provisions of the 1999 Contract Law have to be abridged when incorporated into Book III. For instance, Article 466 contains a cross-reference to the general principles governing the interpretation of an expression of intention under Article 142(1) of the Code, which applies to contract interpretation, and adjusts the specific rules concerning the interpretation of a contract drawn up in two or more different languages to suit such general principles. Likewise, the effective time and withdrawal of an offer is stipulated under Article 474 or 477 by way of cross-referencing to the more general provision for an expression of intention under Article 137 or 141. By comparison, since there is no general rule governing the revocation of an expression of intention, Article 477 has to make specific provisions for the revocation of an offer.

5   The Relation Between Different Specific Books

The systematization of the CCC also requires that related provisions contained in different specific Books are consistent and free from contradiction and that they are not repetitive but deal with distinct aspects of a legal matter in a coherent way. For example, the provisions of the Security Law are allocated to Book II (Property Rights; Rights *in rem*) and Book III (Contracts), depending on whether they are of a proprietary or contractual nature. A 'guarantee' is a type of contractual relationship that does not create a property right and therefore forms the subject of Chapter 13 of Book III, whereas proprietary forms of security, including mortgage and pledge, are provided in Title IV of Book II. There remain some provisions that are not in strict compliance with the distinction between property law and contract law. Article 388 (definition of a 'security contract'), for example, addresses a contract matter but is included in Book II. This raises the question of why a 'security contract' is not stipulated as one of the 'Typical Contracts' in Title II of Book III and whether and to what extent the provisions of Chapter 13 (Guarantee Contract) might be applied to other forms of security contract. The answer to this question probably needs to be addressed by the SPC in the future. Presently, the ensuing passages focus on Book IV (Personality Rights) and its relationship with Book VII (Tort Liability).

Book IV is the only Book within the Code that does not have a corresponding Law enacted before the promulgation of the CCC. Of course, Book IV has not been created from scratch. Some of the provisions in that Book are adapted from previous Laws, such as the 1986 General Principles and the 2016 Cybersecurity Law, and the relevant Judicial Interpretations. During the codification process, it has been suggested that there is no need for a separate Book on personality rights given that most of the provisions can, and should, be placed within Chapter 2 (Natural Person) of Book I and Book VII (Tort Liability).[38] In particular, regarding the relationship between Book IV and Book VII, Professor Liang Huixing criticized the adoption of a separate Book on personality rights on the grounds that the coexistence of Book IV and Book VII would give rise to a problem of 'double application' (双重适用) in practice.[39] In short, it was argued by Professor Liang that many provisions in Book IV were 'incomplete provisions' (不完全条文) and therefore had to be applied in combination with the provisions of Book VII to determine the cause of action and legal liability in question. Consequently, this would cause overcomplication in the application of law and hence a waste of judicial resources and an increase in judicial risk (that is, the risk that judges might err in interpreting and applying legislative provisions). To counter, Professor Wang Liming argued that the presence of a large number of 'incomplete provisions', including provisions making cross-references to provisions in a different Book, was not confined to Book IV and that 'double application' was fairly common in judicial practice.[40] An example given by Professor Wang suffices to illuminate his point. Article 238 of the CCC provides that where a property right is infringed upon, thus causing damage to the right-holder, the right-holder may lawfully claim damages and may lawfully pursue other civil liabilities. The claim for damages under Article 238 links to provisions of Book VII, such as Article 1184 (measure of damages for infringement upon another's property). In this sense, Article 238, which belongs to Book II (Property Rights), has to be applied along with Article 1184 in resolving a concrete dispute. This 'double application' is, however, both common and normal and does not call for any surprise. Viewed from the conceptual and logical structure of the CCC, the point made by Professor Wang is not to be faulted. Book VII, like its predecessor the Tort Liability Law, does not cover the whole field of the law of tort(s) but is, as its title suggests, confined to tortious liabilities. The task of defining the scope of rights and/or interests whose infringement would constitute a tort is left to other Books. Accordingly, the relationship between Book IV and Book VII resembles the relationship between Book II and Book VII. The former Book (Book IV or Book II) provides for rights/interests and their infringement, while the latter Book (Book VII) provides for liabilities and remedial consequences. It is not an

---

[38] Liang Huixing (2018), Major debates in the drafting of the Civil Code, issue 3.

[39] Liang, ibid.

[40] Wang (2020), Several controversial issues in the compilation of the Civil Code—miscellaneous responses to professor Liang Hui Xing's various opinions, issue 4. See also, Wang (2020), The adoption and application of the dynamic system theory in the personality rights of the Civil Code, issue 4, p. 1 et seq. and Shi (2018), A commentary on the controversy of the independent editing of personality rights, issue 4, p. 179 et seq.

anomaly to find that a provision in Book IV must be applied in conjunction with a provision in Book VII.

On closer look, it appears that the attack on Book IV is more grounded on Book IV's difference from Book II than on its relationship with Book VII. In his article, Professor Liang stated that personality rights were 'defensive' rights in the sense that the purpose of the legislation is not to provide for the creation, exercise or transfer of such rights but to provide for ways of protecting such rights from unlawful infringement.[41] The argument is, therefore, that, unlike Book II, there is not much to provide for in a Book having its focus on personality rights, aside from protective provisions already contained in Book VII. Much of the criticism is directed at how some of the provisions in Book IV have been drafted. For example, Article 1002 (Book IV Chapter 2) provides:

> A natural person enjoys a right to life. A natural person's life safety and dignity are protected by law. No organization or individual shall infringe another's right to life.

The first sentence is a repetition of the general provision for personality rights (including a right to life) enjoyed by a natural person under both Article 110 (Book I Chapter 5) and Article 990 (Book IV Chapter 1). The second sentence seems to define a right to life as a right to either safety or dignity of one's life. However, the sentence is not so drafted as to confine a right to life as such. The third sentence seems to suggest that a right to life is effective toward the whole world and its legal protection is absolute. However, one might say that both are natural features of a right to life and that there is no need to spell them out. Similar provisions may be found in other articles in Book IV, such as Articles 1003 (a natural person's right to his/her body) and 1004 (a natural person's right to his/her health). Overall, it may be criticized that such a provision is drafted for a declaratory purpose and does not provide much guidance in clarifying what the protected right comprises in real-life disputes. The same cannot, however, be said of all the provisions in Book IV. We only need to look at some provisions to appreciate their importance. For example, Articles 999/1025/1026 seek to strike a delicate balance between promoting the public interest in access to the media and protecting personality rights such as one's right to reputation or honor. In practice, the line between fair news reporting and defamatory reporting is often blurred and difficult to draw. It is thus essential to set out rules clarifying the limits to one's personality right and what constitutes an infringement of such as right. Therefore, providing a 'duty of reasonable verification' (合理核实义务) to be borne by the media or one who publicises an opinion is both necessary and significant. Similarly, the question of whether there is an infringement of the relevant personality right is answered, to varying degrees, in a number of different contexts, such as sexual harassment (Articles 1026) and infringement upon one's right to portrait/image (Articles 1019–1020) or privacy (Article 1033). This is not to say that all of such provisions have been drafted in a satisfactory manner—to the contrary, future improvements by way of restructuring or rephrasing can be suggested for many of them. However, the point being made here is that

---

[41] Liang, fn 39 above.

there is a need for laying down rules governing special issues concerning personality rights, such as establishing an infringement, and that there seems to be a sufficient body of rules to justify concentrated treatment in a separate Book. Therefore, the real reason for having a separate Book on personality rights does not rest on the perceived importance of such rights in modern Chinese society, with civil law being described as 'a law of persons'.[42] Instead, it is suggested that Book IV must center upon a distinct body of rules delineating the scope of various types of personality rights and specifying what constitutes an infringement of such rights. By doing so, a systematic relationship could be maintained between Book IV and Book VII, which focus, respectively on the right (and its infringement) aspect and the liability (including remedy) aspect of the law of persons.

6 The Internal Relation of Different Provisions Within One Book

Different provisions contained in the same Book may have a general-specific relationship so that in principle the specific provision shall be applied prior to the general provision. For example, Book III Contracts contains rules applicable to all types of contracts in Title 1 (General Rules). Logically, these 'general rules' of contract law apply only where the matter under investigation is not provided for in the specific provisions contained in Title 2 (Typical Contracts) and Title 3 (Quasi Contracts). Where however, no such general-specific relationship exists between the provisions, it might be asked whether there is any inconsistency or repetition between them. For example, Articles 143(3) and Article 153, both of which reside under Sect. 3 (Validity of Civil Juristic Act) Chapter 6 (Civil Juristic Act) of Book I, are said to be repetitive.[43] Article 143 provides for three essential conditions precedent for a valid civil juristic act, one of which is stated in para. (3): '[the act] does not violate any mandatory provision of a Law or Administrative Regulation and is not at variance with public order and good moral'. In comparison, Article 153 stipulates that an act which violates such a mandatory provision is invalid unless the provision does not have the effect of invaliding the act and that an act at variance with public order and good moral is invalid. Professor Liang Huixing contended that there was no repetition since Article 143 was an abstract generic provision, while Article 153 was a specific provision that should be first applied by a court or arbitral tribunal.[44]

---

[42] Contrast: Wang (2020) The reasons for adopting the seven compilations of the Chinese Civil Code and its contributions to the world, issue 4. It has been suggested that since personality rights are more important than property rights, Book IV ought to have been placed before the Book on property rights as Book II, consistent with the order of these different types of civil rights under Article 3 of the CCC. See also, Shi (2018), The historical evolution and trends of personality rights legislation 66(4) p. 140 et seq.

[43] Chen (2018, 48: pp. 257 and 278).

[44] Liang (2017), Urgent Suggestions for Restoring Article 155 of the General Provisions of the Civil Law (third-draft review).

However, this argument appears difficult to sustain. To say that A is an essential condition for an act to be valid and that an act may be invalidated if A is not satisfied seem to be two sides of the same coin. There is nothing preventing a court or arbitral tribunal from applying Article 143 directly and holding that a juristic act is invalid for its failure to satisfy condition (3). In addition, as far as a mandatory provision is concerned, the relevant parts of the two Articles are not identical and give rise to inconsistency. Therefore, a juristic act may violate a mandatory provision without being invalidated under Article 153, where the particular mandatory provision does not invalidate the act (because the provision is, for instance, of an administrative nature). In such a case, is the act valid under Article 143? It does clearly violate a mandatory provision, and hence, one of the essential requirements for its validity, that is, condition (3), is missing. The act thus does not acquire validity under Article 143 notwithstanding that the mandatory provision which it violates does not have the effect of invalidating it. The patently opposite conclusions reached by applying these two different Articles show that a serious systematic problem has not been fixed and remains in the CCC.

A major problem with Title 1 of Book III is that contrary to what Title 1 suggests, it contains not only general provisions for contracts but also general provisions for the entire law of obligations. A 'zhai' (债) can be translated into an 'obligation', referring to 'the *vinculum juris*, or bond of legal necessity,' between two persons.[45] Under the CCC, a simple 'zhai' is not often used (Article 514 is a rare example), and two Chinese words are used to refer to the two correlative sides of an obligation, namely, a right *in personam* (债权) and the correlative duty (债务). Article 118 provides that a right *in personam* is a right arising from a contract, tort, *negotiorum gestio*, unjust enrichment or any other provision of law and is a right to demand a specific obligor to do or not do a certain act. The CCC thus recognizes that there is a general concept of obligation and that there are some rules applicable across the board. During the codification process, a debated issue was whether a new Book on the general law of obligations that overarches Book III (Contracts) and Book VII (Tort Liability) and provides for additional categories of obligations, including those arising from *negotiorum gestio* or unjust enrichment, should be added to the CCC. The legislature eventually decided not to add such a new Book on the grounds that Book III and Book VII are well settled, that there are few species of obligations apart from the four mentioned above, and that the new Book on the general law of obligations would have a narrow scope of application and very limited use.[46] Consequently, provisions that logically fall under the general law of obligations are absorbed into Title 1 of Book III. There are many such provisions, relating to the performance, preservation, variation, assignment or cessation of obligations in general, placed in various chapters within Title 1. However, although these provisions are usually expressed as dealing with obligations in general, they are placed under a chapter

---

[45] John Salmond, in Glanville L. Williams (ed), *Jurisprudence* (10th edn 1947) 460, quoted in Black's law dictionary (9th edn 2009) 1179.

[46] Wang (2003) Some issues in need of research concerning the making of the Civil Code. Issue 4, p. 9 at [10].

with a heading encompassing the word 'contracts' and are mingled with other provisions whose application is apparently confined to contracts. This thus brings about interpretative difficulties as to which of the provisions are confined to contracts or extendable to other types of obligations and whether provisions concerning obligations in general should be narrowly interpreted to avoid obvious contradiction with the heading of the chapter in which they are found. Potential issues of order of application or inconsistency may also arise between the two categories of provision under the same heading. Thus, for example, Article 509 provides that a party shall observe the principle of good faith in performing 'duties' (义务) and avoid waste of resources or pollution of the environment in performing 'contracts'. While Article 509 must be intended to apply to the performance of all obligations, a judge when interpreting it must wonder why the lawmaker uses 'duties' instead of 'obligations' and whether it is possible to extend the principle of waste avoidance to obligations other than contracts despite the clear words used by the legislature. Conversely, Article 580 provides exceptions to the remedy of specific or actual performance where a party fails to perform its 'nonmonetary obligations'. Although this is clearly worded to be generally applicable to all such obligations, whether they arise from a contract or otherwise, it remains to be seen whether the exceptions provided for apply with the same vigor to nonmonetary obligations not arising from a contract. Therefore, the absorption of provisions concerning the general law of obligations into Book III Contracts tends to create disorder between provisions in that Book.

In light of the absence of a general law of obligations, Article 468 provides that Title 1 of Book III, except for those provisions that are inapplicable by their nature, 'applies' to an obligation not arising from a contract where the law governing that obligation makes no provision. This 'extraterritorial' application of general provisions in the Book on Contracts has been criticized by commentators during the codification process. The principal criticism lies in the fact that for the legislature to leave it to the judiciary to decide whether, and if so which of, the provisions in Title 1 Book III are to be applied to a noncontractual obligation leads to unnecessary complexity and almost untrammelled judicial discretion.[47] It should be noted that Article 468 adopts a different wording from Article 464, which replaces 'natural persons, legal persons or other organizations' with the unitary concept of 'civil subjects' and allows the provisions of Book III to apply 'referentially' to agreements concerning 'civil status such as marriage, adoption and guardianship', where the law applicable to such status makes no provision. Similarly, Article 467 largely adopts (with only minor adjustments) Article 124 of the 1999 Contract Law and provides that Title 1 of Book III applies to 'innominate' contracts, and provisions on the most similar contracts under Book III or other laws shall apply 'referentially' to such contracts. Compared to the simple expression of 'apply', the phrase 'apply referentially' is generally understood to mean 'apply *mutatis mutandis* or by analogy' and confers on courts a wider

---

[47] Yu (2018), Problems and remedies for the legislative thinking of the general principles of contract law instead of the general principles of the obligation law—from the methodological nature of "reference application". Issue 2, p. 31, at [32] and [33]. See also, Liu (2007), Several issues concerning the establishment of the general principles of obligation law in our Civil Code. Issue 4, p. 3 et seq.

discretionary power, thus creating greater uncertainty. In view of this concern, the legislature has removed the word 'referentially' from the draft Article 468. However, such a move has merely reduced, rather than eliminated, the uncertainty arising from the discretionary nature of that provision. For example, by providing that the 'relevant' provisions of Title 1 'apply' rather than 'shall apply', Article 468 is ambivalent about whether the court may decide not to apply a provision of Title 1. Furthermore, there seems to arise some sort of dilemma for judges when deciding whether to apply a provision such as Article 509 discussed in the foregoing paragraph. On the one hand, both the principle of good faith and that of waste avoidance under Article 509 are by their nature applicable to the performance of noncontractual obligations, and Article 468 clearly authorizes courts to apply both. On the other hand, close attention to the words chosen by the legislature requires the principles (particularly the principle of waste avoidance) to be confined to the performance of contractual obligations. The legislature thus creates challenging tasks for the judiciary to choose whether to follow the clear words used or the commonly accepted legislative purpose or intent behind such words.

7   Conclusion

This chapter has applied the internationally articulated definition and benchmarks of the systematization of a code to assess the CCC in terms of its systematization. It can be seen that the CCC has generally followed a general-specific structure and a top-down approach akin to the BGB. At a macro level, the use of concepts, concentric circles and general clauses in the CCC is of a similar scale to a mature code such as the BGB. While being controverted, the legislature's decision to adopt a new Book IV Personality Rights seems to be logical and in line with other Books such as Book II Property Rights. The macro structure may be easy to imitate and transplant. At a micro level, that is, when the detailed content and expression of the provisions are scrutinised, however, the scene becomes more complicated. From the limited survey conducted in this chapter, it can be seen that inconsistency between different provisions, either under a general-specific relationship or another relationship, is a problem that arises rather too frequently. This problem arises, for example, between the definition of 'good faith' under Article 7 and other more specific provisions about 'good faith'. Repetition is another problem that has been observed a few times during our assessment. This problem arises, for example, between the general provisions for civil rights in Book I and the corresponding specific provisions in a relevant ensuing Book. This phenomenon reflects the fact that cross-referencing has been used perhaps inadequately or inefficiently in the CCC. More importantly, it reveals that some of the provisions have been drafted too broadly and hence lack distinct substance. This might constitute the real challenge faced by the new Book on Personality Rights. Without the benefit of a prior Personality Rights Law, at least some of the provisions in Book IV appear to be hard to apply in practice. An uneasy relationship also currently exists between provisions governing obligations in general and provisions governing contracts only within Title 1 of Book III Contracts. That they sit next to each other and that their borderline is not always clearly set out will create difficulties in judicial application and increase judicial costs. These shortcomings in turn reduce the compatibility and coherency between Book IV or Book III and Book VII Tort Liability.

The making of the CCC has been referred to as 'a process of systemic integration'.[48] In the meantime, it has also been, however, pointed out that 'the CCC is not a finished work, nor is it immune to changes; rather, it allows for future reforms and further development by leaving an interface for future laws'.[49] In many respects, the CCC remains a young code and it is imperative that it grows into a more systematic whole. The more important work ahead is for the SPC to synthesise, revise and update the rules contained in the relevant judicial interpretations. One would expect that at least some of the problems at the micro level indicated above may be fixed in this subsequent process of judicial law-making.

Acknowledgements I am grateful for Zhu Chen for her research assistance.

References

Adoption Law (adopted 29 December 1991) Seventh NPC, Twenty second session, Shouyangfa [收养法]

Albanesi E (2017) Codification in a civil law jurisdiction: an Italian perspective. Eur JL Reform 19:264–284

Baudenbacher C (1999) Some remarks on the method of civil law. Texas Int LJ 34:334–360

Bergel JL (1987) Principal features and methods of codification. Louisiana L Rev 48:1073–1097

Black's Law Dictionary. 9th ed. BA Garner, editor, West Group, St. Paul., Minn.

Chang T, Lu L (2017) Minfadian bianzuande 'Liangbuzou' [民法典编纂的'两步走'] (The "two steps" compilation of the civil code). People's political circles [中国司法观察], China's Justice Observer (updated 29 March 2020), 6. Retrieved from https://www.chinajusticeobserver.com/a/chinas-first-civil-code-on-the-way

Chen J (2018) Re-conceptualizing private law: the struggle for civil codification in China. Hong Kong LJ 48:257–282

Chen W (2020) Guanyu《Zhonghuarenmingongheguo Fadian (Caoan) de shuoming》[关于《中华人民共和国民法典 (草案) 》的说明] (Explanations on the draft Chinese code), delivered at thirteenth NPC meeting, Third Session, Retrieved http://www.npc.gov.cn/npc/c30834/202005/50c0b507ad32464aba87c2ea65bea00d.shtml

Contract Law (adopted 15 March 1999) Ninth NPC, Second session, Zhonghuarenmingongheguo Hetongfa [中華人民共和國合同法]

Cybersecurity Law (adopted on 7 July 2016) Twelfth NPC, twenty fourth session, Zhonghuarenmingongheguo Wangluoanquanfa [中华人民共和国网络安全法]

Dannemann G, Schulze R (2020) German civil code volume I: Books 1–3 article-by-article commentary. Beck, Munich, Nomos, Baden-Baden

---

[48] Liu Rui, 'Five key points to understand Civil Code', National People's Congress of China (NPC Magazine), 2020, Issue 2, at 24, available at http://www.npc.gov.cn/npc/c16175/202008/d3f85e213abc4d7abe500b8e4293b6f9/files/cbcc2d851148457ca463955232fbe6ad.pdf.

[49] Liu, NPC Magazine, ibid. at 25.

General Principles of Civil Law (adopted 12 April 1986) Sixth NPC, fourth session, Zhonghuaren-
    mingongheguo Minfatongze [中华人民共和国民法通则], as *amended* by the decision of the
    NPC Standing Committee on 27 August 2009 and passed on 15 March 2017

He Q, Li X, Chen Y (2003) Xin Zhongguo Minfadian Caoan Zong Lan [新中国民法典草案总览]
    (An overview of the drafts of civil code in new China). Law Press, Beijing

Kötz H (1987) Taking civil codes less seriously. Modern Law Rev 50(1):1–15

Levasseur A (1969–1970) On the structure of a civil code. Tulane Law Rev 44:693–703

Liang H (2017) Huifu Minfa Zongze (Sanshengao) Di yibaiwushiwutiao de jinji jianyi [恢复民法
    总则 (三审稿) 第一百五十五条的紧急建议] (Urgent suggestions for restoring Article 155 of
    the general provisions of the Civil law (third-draft review)). Chinese Law Network [中国法学
    网]. Retrieved http://www.iolaw.org.cn/showArticle.aspx?id=%205118

Liang H (2018) Minfadian bianzuan zhong de zhongda zhenglun [民法典编纂中的重大争论]
    (Major debates in the drafting of the civil code). In: Gansu Political Sci Law J [甘肃政法学院
    学报] 3

Liu J (2007) Woguo minfadian yingshe lizefa zongzi de jige wenti [我国民法典应设立债法总则
    的几个问题] (Several issues concerning the establishment of the general principles of obligation
    law in our civil code). China Law Sci [中国法学] 4:3 ff.

Liu J (2018) Minfadian bianzuan de tixi xingkunjing ji chulu [民法典编纂的体系性困境及出路]
    (The systematic dilemma and outlet of the codification of civil code). Gansu Soc Sci [甘肃社会
    科学] 2: 153 ff.

Liu J (2020a) Guanyu Mainfadian de jige zhuyao wenti. In Zhongguo Sifa [关于民法典的几个主
    要问题] (Several main issues regarding the civil code). Zhongguo Sifa [中国司法] 9(249): 51 ff.

Liu R (2020b) 'Five key points to understand civil code', National People's Congress of China
    (NPC Magazine) Issue 2, available at http://www.npc.gov.cn/npc/c16175/2020b08/d3f85e213
    abc4d7abe500b8e4293b6f9/files/cbcc2d851148457ca463955232fbe6ad.pdf

Marriage Law (adopted 10 September 1980) Fifth NPC, third session, Zhonghuarenmingongheguo
    Hunyinfa [中华人民共和国婚姻法]

McKendrick E, Liu Q (2017) Good faith in contract performance in the Chinese and common
    laws. In: Di Matteo L, Chen L (eds) Chinese contract law: civil and common law perspectives.
    Cambridge University Press, Cambridge

Pagano R (2004) Introduzione alla legistica. L'arte di preparare le leggi, Giuffrè, Milano

Popelier P (2017) Codification in a civil law jurisdiction: a Northern European perspective. Eur J
    Law Reform 19:253–263

Property [Real Rights] Law (adopted 16 March 2007) Tenth NPC, fifth session, Zhonghuarenmin-
    gongheguo Wuquanfa [中华人民共和国物权法]

Rudden B (1992) From customs to civil codes. Times literary supplement, July 10, 1992

Security Law (adopted 30 June 1995) Eighth NPC, fourteenth session, Zonghuarenmingongheguo
    Danbaofa [中华人民共和国担保法]

Shi G (2018a) Rengequan duli chengpian zhenglunpingshu [人格权独立成编争论评述] (A
    commentary on the controversy of the independent editing of personality rights). China Univ
    Political Sci Law J 4:179 ff

Shi J (2018b) Rengequanlifa de lishi yanjin jiqi qushi [人格权立法的历史演进及其趋势] (The
    historical evolution and trends of personality rights legislation). China Univ Political Sci Law J
    [中国政法大学学报] 66(4):140 ff.

Steiner E (2018) French law: a comparative approach, 2nd edn. Oxford University Press, Oxford

Stoljar SJ (1977) Problems of codification. Australian National University, Canberra

Succession Law (adopted 10 April 1985), Sixth NPC, third session, Zhonghuarenmingongheguo
    Jichengfa [中华人民共和国继承法]

Sun Xianzhong (2016) Woguo minfa lifa de tixihua yu kexuehua went [我国民法立法的体系化
    与科学化问题] (The issue of systematization and scientization of civil legislation in China).
    Qinghua Faxue [清华法学] 6

Tallon D (1979) Codification and consolidation of the law at present time. Isr Law Rev 14(1):1–12

Teasdale J (2017) Codification: a civil law solution to a common law conundrum? European J Law Reform 19:247–252

Tort Law (adopted on 26 December 2009) Sixth NPC, fourth session Zhonghuarenmingongheguo Qinquanzerenfa [中华人民共和国侵权责任法]

Varga C (Eszenyi S et al. trans., 1991) codification as a sociohistorical phenomenon. 14–15:31 and 223, reviewed by Legrand P (1994) Strange power of words: codification situated, 9 Tulane European & Civil Law Forum 1

Wang L (2020a) Minfadian bianzuan zhong de ruogan zhenglun wenti – dui Liang Hui Xing jiaoshou ruogan yijian de jidian huiying [民法典编纂中的若干争论问题 – 对梁慧星教授若干意见的几点回应] (Several controversial issues in the compilation of the civil code—miscellaneous responses to professor Liang Hui Xing's various opinions). Shanghai Univ Political Sci Law J [上海政法学院学报] 4

Wang L (2020b) Minfadian rengequanpian zhong dongtaixitonglun de cainai yu yunyong [民法典人格权编中动态系统论的采纳与运用] (The adoption and application of the dynamic system theory in the personality rights of the civil code). The Jurist [法学家] 4:1

Wang Liming (2020) Zhongguo minfadian caiqu qibianzhi de liyou jiqi shijiegongxian [中国民法典采取七编制的理由及其世界贡献] (The reasons for adopting the seven compilations of the chinese civil code and its contributions to the world). Comparative Law Res [比较法研究] 4

Wang S (2003) Zhiding minfadian xuyao yanjiu de bufen wenti [制订民法典需要研究的部分问题] (Some issues in need of research concerning the making of the civil code). Fa xue jia [法学家], (4), 9 at [10]

Xanthaki H (2014) Drafting Legislation. Art and Technology of Rules for Regulation. Oxford and Portland, Hart Publishing

Xi J (2020) Chongfen renshi banbu shishi minfa dian zhongda yiyi, Yifa geng hao baozhang renmin hefa quanyi [充分认识颁布实施民法典重大意义依法更好保障人民合法权益] (Fully understand the significance of the enactment of the civil code, better protect the rights and interests of the people lawfully). Qiushi [求是] 12. Retrieved from http://www.qstheory.cn/dukan/qs/2020-06/15/c_1126112148.htm

Xinhua (2020) Civil Code, better protecting people's legitimate rights and interests. National People's Congr J [《中国人大》对外版] 49(2):19 and 21

Yu F (2018) Hetongfa zongzi tidai zefa zongzi lifa silu de wenti ji mibu – cong "canzhao shiyong" de fangfa lunxingzhi qieru [合同法总则替代债法总则立法思路的问题及弥补 – 从 "参照适用" 的方法论性质切入] (Problems and remedies for the legislative thinking of the general principles of contract law instead of the general principles of the obligation law—from the methodological nature of "reference application". Suzhou University Press: Law Edition [苏州大学学报: 法学版] 2:31

Qiao Liu DPhil (oxon), is Professor and Deputy Director of the Centre for Chinese and Comparative Law, School of Law, City University of Hong Kong. He was Associate Professor at the TC Beirne School of Law, University of Queensland; Lee Ka Shing Visiting Professor at the Faculty of Law, McGill University; and specially appointed Tengfei Adjunct Professor at Xi'an Jiaotong University School of Law. Professor Liu is Honorary Professor at the TC Beirne School of Law and holds a Visiting Professorship at Xiamen University School of Law. He is the author of over fifty publications concerning contracts, commercial law, unjust enrichment, international commercial law and financial transactions. with a particular interest in the comparative study of Chinese and Anglo-Australian private law. He is the co-editor-in-Chief of *The Chinese Journal of Comparative Law.*

Reinforcing the French Legacy While Borrowing from the Common Law: The Civil Code of Quebec (1991)

Michel Morin

Abstract After recounting the history of the coexistence of civil law and common law rules in the private law of Quebec, this chapter reviews the various steps that led to the adoption of a new civil code in 1991, including the development of separate protective legislation and the discarding of proposals that aroused strong opposition. It then provides an overview of the Code. The preliminary provision emphasizes its fundamental importance in the legal system of Quebec. Indeed, this preeminent position is well accepted by judges. Codal innovations include the recognition of good faith, trust, and hypothecs on movable property. Most of the amendments made after 1991 pertain to persons or the family, notably to address issues for LGBTQ+ persons and for Aboriginal Peoples. However, de facto spouses are generally ignored. Overall, the new Code has assimilated some common law concepts and increased the protection of vulnerable persons, with some important exceptions, and its English version has been immensely improved.

1 Introduction

In 2014, the preliminary provision of the (fourth) Code of Civil Procedure gave the following direction to courts: "This Code must be interpreted and applied as a whole, in keeping with civil law tradition."[1] One may deduce from this statement that this approach had been eschewed in the past. In 2019, an enactment affirming the "laicity" of the (provincial) State included among the characteristics of the Quebec nation the "civil law tradition", alongside "distinct social values and a specific history".[2] Furthermore, since 2022, "it is incumbent on the Parliament of Quebec to confirm

---

[1] Code of civil procedure.

[2] An Act respecting the laicity of the State, preamble.

M. Morin (✉)
Université de Montréal, Montreal, QC, Canada
e-mail: michel.morin.3@umontreal.ca

the status of French as the official language and common language in the territory of Quebec and to enshrine the paramountcy of that status in Québec's legal order".[3]

In summary, this is what the recodification of 1991 is about. It confirms that the connection between civil law and Catholicism (or Christian morality) has been severed; it rejuvenates the French version of the Code while being oblivious to its English counterpart, and it strengthens the civil law tradition by drafting a French-style code that refashions or discards various common law rules introduced in Quebec by the courts or in legislation. It also emphasizes the foundational role of the Code in the legal system of Quebec.

Forty years earlier, substantial modifications to the Code were strongly resisted, for fear that they would be based on common law models. The era when the Supreme Court of Canada relied on common law principles in civil law cases was also vividly remembered. At the same time, the language and the substance of the Civil Code (CC) of Lower Canada was becoming anachronistic, and its traditional values were being challenged. Eventually, this criticism won the day, and the legislature decided to recodify the civil law.

To understand how this project came to fruition, this chapter will recount the history of the coexistence of civil law and common law rules in the private law of Quebec. It will review the various steps that led to the adoption of the Civil Code (CC) of Quebec (1991), including the development of separate protective legislation and the discarding of proposals that aroused strong opposition. It will provide an overview of the Code and of the more important amendments made after its adoption. It will suggest that in Quebec, the autonomy of the civil law tradition is now secure, for francophone and for anglophone civil lawyers.

The chapter is divided as follows. Section 2 explains the reasons for the adoption in 1866 of the CC of Lower Canada (this refers to the official name for Quebec at the time). Section 3 examines the evolution of civil law after Quebec became a Canadian province, notably some significant amendments, as well as the interpretation of the Code by a court of last resort dominated by common lawyers. Section 4 presents the different stages of the recodification project, which began in 1955. Section 5 discusses the status of the CC in the legal system of Quebec and the treatment afforded to it by the Supreme Court of Canada. Finally, Sect. 6 focuses on the ten books of the code and the more important changes that have occurred during the last thirty years. Section 7 offers some concluding observations.

2   Civil Law in a British Province, 1760–1866

Following the British Conquest (1760), the Royal Proclamation (1763) provided that English law would apply in the new Province of Quebec.[4] This led to many complaints. In 1774, the British Parliament adopted the *Quebec Act*, which restored

---

[3] Charter of the French language, preamble.

[4] Morin (2013a).

the law in force in New France, but only for "property and civil rights", i.e., private law. Criminal law was to remain English, as well as public law. The *Quebec Act* itself and subsequent legislation adopted specific rules and principles of English law, such as testamentary freedom, optional trial by jury in commercial matters or for cases of personal injury, rules of evidence for business transactions, adversarial trial, corporations, etc. Occasionally, British legislation was copied word for word. In the legislature or before the courts, many attempts were made to replace French law with English law, but they generally failed.

The civil law of Lower Canada was based on the law in force prior to the British Conquest. The Custom of Paris (1580) contained the law of property, successions, and matrimonial regimes. The case law and the legal literature of prerevolutionary France governed obligations and contracts. As a result, authors such as Robert-Joseph Pothier (died 1772) were widely admired in Lower Canada. In 1837, Thomas Erskine, speaking for the Judicial Committee of the Privy Council (the court of last resort in the British Empire), opined that there was no "more satisfactory authority" than the "clear and intelligible" principles of Pothier; these had been reproduced "in the [French] Code Civil [...] which, though not an authority binding in Canada, may be considered [...] in the nature of a commentary on the French law, as laid down by Pothier, respecting those matters in which there is no apparent intention to introduce alteration."[5]

References to the French Code by lawyers or judges soon became an everyday occurrence in Lower Canada; certainly, jurists harbored no hostility toward it. However, this Code did not always reflect local law. Furthermore, the antiquated rules of the Custom of Paris needed to be coordinated with Lower Canadian statutes, some of which were based on English Law. All this produced considerable confusion. Nonetheless, by the middle of the nineteenth century, anglophone and francophone judges generally refused to rely on English law to interpret the applicable rules of French law.

In 1857, the legislature thus explained the need for codification: there was no official translation for the parts of French or English law that applied in civil matters; the legal literature of prerevolutionary France was becoming inaccessible, since it was not being reprinted; France had derived great benefits from codification, as had Louisiana with its bilingual code of 1825.[6] A specific act provided for the appointment of three codifiers who were required to prepare a bilingual draft. After restating the existing law, they could propose amendments. This would be done in reports explaining their reasoning and the sources they examined.[7]

The legislature declared that the code must be "framed upon the same general plan" and contain, as far as possible, "the like amount of details upon each subject

---

[5] JCPC, *Bellingham v Free*r, Judgment of 1837, E.R. 12, pp. 845 and 847.

[6] An Act to provide for the Codification of the Laws of Lower Canada relative to Civil matters and Procedure; see, among many publications, Brierley (1968), Greenwood (1995), Brierley and Macdonald (1993, pp. 24–32), Young (1994), Cairns (2015), and Girard et al. (2018, pp. 425–439).

[7] An Act to provide for the Codification of the Laws of Lower Canada relative to Civil matters and Procedure, sec. 7.

as the French Codes", i.e., the CC, the Code of Civil Procedure and the Code of Commerce. This signaled a rejection of the convoluted drafting of statutes in the common law tradition. However, the Lower Canadian code would encompass rules pertaining to both "Civil Matters" and "Commercial Cases".[8] In other words, there would be no Code of Commerce. A Code of Civil Procedure would also be prepared. In this area of the law, the influence of the common law was much more pronounced.

The codifiers, one anglophone and two francophone judges, completed their task in 1864; most of their recommendations were accepted by the legislature the following year.[9] The *CC of Lower Canada* came into force in 1866. In general, it was similar to its French model, but with important differences.[10] For instance, religious officers (Catholics, Protestants, or Jewish) were authorized to create acts of civil status and to solemnize marriage; emphyteutic leases and "fiduciary substitutions" (*substitutions fidéicommissaires*) were recognized, but not adoption and divorce. Because of testamentary freedom, whose ambit was clarified by legislation in 1801, descendants had no reserved share in the succession of their parent. The fourth book pertained to commercial laws.

The codifiers espoused liberal value for the law of obligations: they abolished lesion (akin to unconscionability) between adults of sound mind, as well as the power of the courts to reduce the amount stipulated for liquidated damages or penalties.[11] This sense of innovation did not extend to family law, where the traditional authority of husbands was preserved or reinforced. As a general rule, in their reports, French legislation and French legal literature represented the main source for the Law of Lower Canada, except for public law issues that were addressed incidentally in the code and for commercial law.[12] On this last subject, for some issues, English law was expressly referenced as a suppletive source of law.[13]

3   Civil Law in a Canadian Province, 1867–1955

In 1867, the *British North America Act* (known since 1982 as the *Constitution Act, 1867*) divided the legislative and executive powers between the federal and provincial governments.[14] Federal jurisdiction extends to an idiosyncratic list of subjects, many of which pertain to Commercial law[15]: international and interprovincial trade and commerce; navigation and shipping; transportation and communication lines extending beyond the limits of a province; banking; bills of exchange and promissory

---

[8] Ibid., sec. 4.

[9] Canada (1866).

[10] Niort (2004).

[11] Canada (1866, secs 640, 751, 1012, 1076 and 1135).

[12] Morin (2015, pp. 619–627).

[13] Canada (1866, secs 1206, 2340 and 2388).

[14] Constitution Act, 1867, sec. 91–95.

[15] See ibid., sec. 91.

notes; companies with national objects; insolvency; intellectual property. Following this, the book on commercial matters contained in the CC of Lower Canada was replaced by federal legislation, with the notable exception of insurance law, which fell under provincial jurisdiction.

In 1867, it was feared that the remarriage of divorcees would not be allowed in provinces where Catholics represented a majority of the population. Therefore, the legal capacity for marriage and divorce became a subject matter of federal jurisdiction.[16] For provincial legislatures, their exclusive jurisdiction includes property and civil rights, a phrase that refers to private law in general, except for any subject matter already assigned to the Canadian Parliament.[17] Federalism has allowed Quebec to maintain its civil law heritage in matters of private law. In all other provinces, common law applies for private law matters.

Until 1949, the Judicial Committee of the Privy Council sitting in London was the court of last resort.[18] Since 1949, judgments of the Supreme Court of Canada are final; three of the nine Justices must be appointed from the Quebec Bar or from the Courts of the Province of Quebec.[19] These are "Quebec" Justices. Both the Privy Council and the Supreme Court of Canada hear cases in any area of the law, whether provincial or federal, including cases in which the CC must be interpreted. These decisions are written like any other common law judgment, even by Quebec judges. They provide a lengthy review of the facts, arguments, case law and legal literature. In this regard, the contrast with the extremely terse style of French judgments is striking.

Until 1918, Justices of the Supreme Court of Canada did not hesitate to draw on common law principles in civil law cases, despite the occasional protest from Quebec Justices. They recognized the relevance of common law cases if a provision was derived from English law (for instance, issues surrounding testamentary freedom and wills, or the special action given to dependents after the accidental death of a parent). More controversially, they referred to Common law for rules of public order, or when an issue was not addressed by the Code (for instance, offer and acceptance).[20] In the words of Taschereau J, "It strikes one as an astounding proposition, to say the least, that what is undoubtedly licit in England, under the British flag, which covers over two-thirds of the maritime carrying trade of the world, should be immoral and against public order in the Province of Quebec [...]".[21]

In 1918, after his appointment to the Court, Pierre-Basile Mignault denounced the practice of relying on common law cases to interpret the CC. The Court as whole agreed with him. It became settled law that the civil law system of Quebec is independent of the common law (except for comparative purposes, an approach

---

[16] Constitution Act, 1867, sec. 91 .26.

[17] Ibid., sec. 92 .13.

[18] An Act to amend the Supreme Court Act, sec. 3.

[19] Ibid., sec. 1.

[20] Brierley and Macdonald (1993, pp. 54–59) and Normand (2008, pp. 79–82).

[21] SCC, *Glengoil SS. Co. v. Pilkington*, Judgment of 1897, SCR 28, pp. 155–156; on Taschereau, see Young (2004).

that was not used in the first decades of the twentieth century). The Privy Council also acknowledged this point. In the twentieth century, it was criticized for being too innovative, but it is not clear that this was due to a reliance on common law principles, as was alleged at the time.

In the 1920s, many statutes were criticized for being based on British or North American models and for departing from traditional values enshrined in the code. By way of example, one may mention the power to grant injunctions given to the Superior Court of Quebec,[22] the introduction of trusts,[23] the statute on adoption,[24] or the power given to corporations to issue bonds or indentures secured by trust-deeds affecting their moveable and immoveable property.[25] By the 1950s, the CC of Lower Canada had achieved an iconic position in Quebec. Its substantial content was generally considered a legacy that must be preserved for later generations for nationalistic or religious purposes. Social innovation was frowned upon or rejected, for instance, social programs for workplace injuries or labor law generally. This is illustrated by the negative reaction of the Supreme Court of Canada to French cases that adopted new interpretations of the Code to protect weaker parties.[26] Indeed, from 1876 to 1963, among the four jurists most often cited by the judges of this Court, one finds Pothier and Belgian author François Laurent (died 1887), a herald of the exegetic school who criticized French jurists who, in his view, interpretated the code too freely.[27] However, the situation would soon change.

4   Recodifying Civil Law, 1955–1991

In the 1960s, during the Quiet Revolution, the Catholic religion waned.[28] College, universities and health institutions became public and were funded or largely subsidized by the Quebec government, which tightly controlled their activities. Like other Western countries, in a decade or so, Quebec would become very liberal on moral issues. During the same period, the rights of consumers, workers, women, victims of a car accident, and many others were considered far too limited. Many traditional values enshrined in the CC of Lower Canada were considered outdated in every area of the law. In time, this would lead to recodification.[29]

---

[22] An act to provide for the issue of the Writ of Injunction in certain cases, and to regulate the procedure in relation thereto. See nowadays Code of civil procedure, secs 509–515.

[23] An Act respecting Trusts; Canada (1866), secs 981a–981n (as amended).

[24] An Act respecting Adoption.

[25] An Act to amend the Revised Statutes, 1909, by inserting therein articles 6119a, 6119b, 6119c and 6119d.

[26] Morin (2000, pp. 359–371) and Jobin (2010, pp. 611–613); see also Devinat and Guilhermont (2012).

[27] Morin (2000, pp. 373–381).

[28] Durocher (2013).

[29] Normand (2008, pp. 42–43, 2021).

In 1955, it was decided to undertake "a general revision of the Civil Code" that "would permit the improving of its coordination and the making of such improvements as may be opportune".[30] Thibaudeau Rinfret, a former Chief Justice of the Supreme Court of Canada, was the "jurist" entrusted with this task. He produced modest reports.[31] By 1960, more ambitious goals were assigned to this project. Four "codifiers" were to "study the reports, observations, proposed amendments and recommendations of such jurist, as well as the suggestions and information which they may obtain from other sources, and to prepare a final draft of a new Civil Code."[32] André Nadeau, a lawyer, replaced Rinfret. He and his colleagues turned to the legal status of married women and matrimonial regimes. In 1964, married women were finally able to enter into contracts independently of their husbands.[33] That same year, limited protection was afforded to debtors of monetary loans.[34]

In 1965, Professor Paul-André Crépeau of McGill University replaced Nadeau. He was authorized by the government to create the Civil Code Revision Office (CCRO). Numerous committees, composed of judges, lawyers, notaries, civil servants, and academics, were then set up with the participation of many anglophone jurists. They worked on various parts of the future code, invited comments, made some consultations, and produced a draft chapter. These were later stitched together and harmonized. The result was a bilingual draft of the complete code, accompanied by explanatory comments. In 1977, it was delivered to the Quebec Minister of Justice and published.[35]

Meanwhile, new social values triggered a stream of reforms, some of which were inspired by the CCRO: the right to divorce was recognized for the first time in 1968 (by way of a federal statute)[36]; that same year, civil marriage became possible (before that, only religious officers could solemnize marriages, although some Protestant denominations did not inquire into the religious beliefs of the future spouses).[37] In 1969, a new matrimonial regime for married spouses replaced the community of property; this reform was inspired in part by the laws of Sweden, Denmark and West Germany after an examination of Ontario law.[38] A legal framework for condominiums was put in place.[39] During this period, there was a strong emphasis on the need to modernize civil law while remaining faithful to the traditional characteristics of codified law. The Supreme Court of Canada acknowledged that older precedents based on Common law rules should no longer be followed and that the code should

---

[30] An Act respecting the revision of the Civil Code, preamble.

[31] Normand (1994, 2008).

[32] An Act to amend the Act respecting the revision of the Civil Code.

[33] An Act respecting the legal capacity of married women.

[34] An Act to protect borrowers against certain abuses and lenders against certain privileges.

[35] Civil Code Revision Office (1977a, b), Brierley and Macdonald (1993, pp. 84–93), and Normand (2008, pp. 42–45).

[36] Divorce Act.

[37] An Act respecting civil marriage.

[38] An Act respecting matrimonial regimes; Brisson and Kasirer (1995, p. 426).

[39] An Act respecting the co-ownership of immoveables.

be interpreted as a coherent whole, even if a provision was historically derived from English law.[40]

In the 1970s and 1980s, more protective measures appeared for persons considered vulnerable when entering into a contract, such as consumers,[41] tenants,[42] and insureds.[43] Discrimination against natural children was gradually eliminated.[44] To a certain extent, these measures were more extensive than what the CCRO had proposed. On the other hand, some of its proposals were not accepted by the legislature, such as the recognition of de facto spouses or a general protection against lesion in contracts. In fact, the government began the drafting process anew; it did not use the CCRO report as a starting point.

In 1980, the Quebec government decided to proceed incrementally and to begin with Book II on family law, with a chapter on adoption that replaced preexisting legislation.[45] Some of its provisions came into force in 1981, while others came into force in 1982. As a result, the legal community had to work with two incomplete civil codes: Book II of the CC of Quebec and the CC of Lower Canada, except for the provisions on family law that had been repealed in 1980. In 1986, after a change in government, a steering committee was established. Its members were two public servants, lawyer Marie-Josée Longtin and notary André Cosette; judge Georges Chassé; and Professor Jean Pineau of the Université de Montréal.[46] In 1987, Books I, III and IV on persons, successions, and property, respectively, were enacted.[47] By that point, the idea of having two codes had become very unpopular, so this act never came into force. This did not prevent the legislature from making some last-minute changes to the CC of Lower Canada[48] or from adopting a statute creating securities borrowed from Common law jurisdictions.[49]

In 1989, Book II was amended to put in place a primary regime from which there would be no opting out for couples married after the coming in force of the act. Inspired by Ontario legislation, this "family patrimony" (a misleading name) obligates spouses to share the net value of certain family assets, regardless of which spouse had title to the property.[50] The avowed objective was to protect the spouse who had no employment or had a reduced income because of child-rearing obligations, most often women whose marriage contract imposed separation as to property.

---

[40] Baudouin (1985), Brierley and Macdonald (1993, pp. 57–59), Normand (2008, pp. 79–83).

[41] Consumer Protection Act.

[42] An Act to establish the Régie du logement and to amend the Civil Code and other legislation.

[43] An Act respecting insurance.

[44] This began with An Act to amend the Civil Code respecting natural children.

[45] An Act to establish a new Civil Code of Quebec and to reform family law.

[46] Marx (2009, p. 214) and Pineau (2009, p. 224).

[47] An Act to add the reformed law of persons, successions and property to the Civil Code of Quebec.

[48] An Act respecting the Public Curator and amending the Civil Code and other legislative provisions.

[49] Act respecting bills of lading, receipts and transfers of property in stock.

[50] An Act to Amend the Civil Code of Quebec and Other Legislation in Order to Favour Economic Equality Between Spouses; Brisson and Kasirer (1995, pp. 442–443).

Significantly, the bill was shepherded in the National Assembly by the Minister for the status of women, independently of the ongoing recodification process. Although often criticized, the regime remains in force today. The same legislation imposed important restrictions on testamentary freedom to protect needy dependents on the death of a family member.

From 1986 to 1988, the government published draft bills of the missing books and proceeded to important consultations.[51] Among other controversial proposals, the draft on obligations provided that a contract entered into by a physical person could be annulled for lesion, except if the person was acting in the interest of an undertaking.[52] Lesion would occur when the exploitation of one of the parties created a serious disproportion between the prestations of the parties. The draft also contained 171 articles reproducing some detailed provisions of the Consumer Protection Act. These articles departed substantially from the rules applicable to ordinary contracts of sale, loan or services. Professional organizations representing lawyers and notaries, as well as other business interests, reacted very negatively to the tenor of this draft, arguing that it would jeopardize the stability of contracts.[53]

In 1990, the recently appointed minister of Justice, Mr. Gil Rémillard (a former Professor of Constitutional Law of Laval University, like his predecessor, Mr. Herbert Marx, who taught at the Université de Montréal), established an advisory committee composed of Justice Jean-Louis Baudouin, a Université de Montréal professor of civil law that had recently been appointed to the Quebec Court of Appeal, Me Michel Jolin (Bâtonnier), Professor Raymond Landry (Dean, Civil Law Section, Faculty of Law, University of Ottawa) and Professor Robert Koury (Notary, Professor, Faculty of Law, University of Sherbrooke). Only the recommendations of the committee were made public at the time. In one on them, the authors argued that as a general rule, lesion should not be a ground of annulment for persons capable of entering into a contract.[54]

Following this, a new bill replaced (and renumbered) the first version of Book II, as well as the books that were adopted in 1987 but had not been proclaimed. It added the missing books. In 1991, the new Code was adopted. It came into force in 1994 and is often called the 1994 code for that reason (as opposed to the 1866 Code).[55] In general, parliamentary debates were not partisan, since the two political parties who took turns in governing in those years supported the project. Some contentious issues were ignored or postponed, such as the lack of protection for de facto spouses (almost entirely omitted from the code, even today)[56] or the possibility for physical persons

---

[51] These documents are available online: Bibliothèque de l'Assemblée nationale du Québec Le Code civil du Québec: du Bas-Canada à aujourd'hui.

[52] Assembly national of Quebec (1987), Avant-projet de loi portant réforme au Code civil du Québec du droit des obligations, sec. 1449.

[53] Rémillard (2005), Laflamme (2005), Parent (2005), Wilson (2010), and Paquin (2014).

[54] Baudouin (2005).

[55] Civil Code of Québec; Brierley (1992), Normand (2008), Baudouin (2009), Pineau (2009), and Morin (2019).

[56] *Quebec (Attorney General) v. A, 2013 SCC 5*, Judgment of 2013, S.C.R. 1, paras 105–110.

acting in their personal interest to grant a hypothec on movable property.[57] Finally, contemporary French law was no longer a predominant source of inspiration for the drafters of the new code. The law of many jurisdictions was examined, including those belonging to the common law tradition.[58]

Turning to the wording of the code, one should note that the English version was prepared hastily and disgraced the code.[59] In the early 2000s, with the support of the Department of Justice, a Committee of the Barreau du Québec and the Chambre des notaires was formed to address this issue.[60] With the help of various subcommittees, the English version was completely revised by Casper Bloom, Edmund Coates, Martin Boodman and Nicholas Kasirer (both from McGill University), and Jeffrey A. Talpis (from the Université de Montréal). Finally, in 2016, the problem was remedied.[61] The French version, although generally enjoyable to read, has not escaped censorship either.[62] Professor Pineau provides the following explanation for some of these problems: "going straight to the point and being concise are perhaps no longer such easy rules to follow as they used to be" in the days of Portalis because "the solutions are less straightforward and more subtle than before".[63] On the other hand, some provisions can be traced back to Portalis.[64]

5   Living with a New Code, 1991–2021

Following the adoption of the new code, lawyers and notaries were obligated to attend continuing education lectures.[65] The minister also published commentaries to provide in a few sentences the gist of each article and some of the sources consulted.[66] This document has been recognized as having some persuasive value.[67] A specific enactment also contained detailed transitory rules.[68] Ten years after the coming into

---

[57] Civil Code of Quebec, sec. 2683 (as orginally enacted); Rémillard (2005, pp. 304–308).

[58] Glenn (1993), Brisson and Kasirer (1995), Normand (2008, p. 47), and Jobin (2010, pp. 614–615).

[59] Brierley (1993) and Legrand (1995, 1996).

[60] Coates (2011, p. 54); information on this subject was provided to the author by Professor Jeffrey A. Talpis; Morin (2013b) and McClintock and Meredith (2015).

[61] An Act to ensure better consistency between the French and English texts of the CC.

[62] Brierley (1993) and Legrand (1995, 1996).

[63] Pineau (2009, p. 227).

[64] Kasirer (2004, p. 23).

[65] Regulation respecting compulsory training for advocates relative to the reform of the Civil Code of Québec; Regulation respecting the mandatory training of notaries concerning the reform of the Civil Code of Québec.

[66] Québec (1993).

[67] *Doré v. Verdun (City)*, Judgment of 1997, S.C.R. 2, paras 12–14.

[68] Act respecting the implementation of the reform of the Civil Code.

force of the new Code, interviews with practitioners revealed that they considered the reform very positively.[69] This opinion seems to be widely shared.[70]

The preeminence of the code was affirmed in its preliminary provision (an article in itself), which read as follows:

> The Civil Code of Québec, in harmony with the Charter of human rights and freedoms [...] and the general principles of law, governs persons, relations between persons, and property.
>
> The Civil Code comprises a body of rules which, in all matters within the letter, spirit or object of its provisions, lays down the jus commune, expressly or by implication. In these matters, the Code is the foundation of all other laws, although other laws may complement the Code or make exceptions to it.

The first paragraph affirms the fundamental importance of human rights in Quebec law, notably the principles of equality and dignity.[71] The reference to "general principles of the law" ensures that the code is not closed upon itself. It allows interpreters to draw on the values and concepts accepted in a large number of legal systems.[72] The second paragraph emphasizes the structural qualities of the code ("a body of rules") and its open-ended nature, which commands a generous interpretation that takes into account the "letter, spirit or object of its provisions" to discover its express or implied meaning. This is a clear rejection of the traditional common law approach to the interpretation of statutes.[73]

As for the *jus commune*, if truth be said, this translation of *droit commun* avoids a more literal rendering such as "the common law" of Quebec. It comprises the rules generally applicable to persons, relations between persons, and property. No self-respecting minister of Justice in Quebec would propose that a code lays down the common law for fear that it would be somehow connected (yet again) to the common law of England. The intention here is to ensure that issues unaddressed in legislation will be answered by the CC if they are relevant to the problem at hand.[74] Furthermore, the Book on obligations applies to the "to the State and its bodies, and to all other legal persons established in the public interest, subject to any other rules of law which may be applicable to them" (s. 1376). Thus, public organizations can be bound by the Code, except if a "rule of law" provides otherwise. In Quebec, this includes, for public law issues, Canadian common law (historically derived from England), as well as legislation or regulation.[75] "It may seem surprising that a public

---

[69] Cantin Cumyn (2005, p. 467).

[70] Niort (1994), Lortie et al. (2005), Arroyo I Amayuelas (2003), Masse (2003), Laidler (2005), Normand (2008, p. 95), Pineau (2009), Baudouin (2009, pp. 507–508), Morin (2014b, p. 172), and Samson and Langevin (2015, p. 745).

[71] Samson and Langevin (2015).

[72] Brierley (1992, pp. 499–501), Bisson (1999), Normand (2008, pp. 72–73), Jutras (2009), Andò (2015), Jukier (2018), and Morin (2019).

[73] Bisson (1999, p. 551) and Normand (2008, pp. 72–73).

[74] Brisson (1993) and Normand (2008, pp. 48–50).

[75] *Prud'homme v. Prud'homme, 2002 SCC* 85, Judgment of 2002, S.C.R. 4, paras 27–31 and 46.

law rule would be found in the *CC of Québec*", but this is because it provides the basic law (the *jus commune*) of Quebec.[76]

Federal legislation had to be revised after the new CC came into force.[77] The modern approach consists of using terminology drawn from civil law and common law in both English and French (in New Brunswick and Ontario, the common law officially exists in French, in law schools and before the courts). Furthermore, the Federal Interpretation Act provides that for private law issues, provincial law will be the suppletive law for a Canadian enactment. In Quebec, this refers to "civil law".[78] The respect afforded to the civil law tradition is illustrated by a federal statute on the capacity to marry that was adopted in 2001. It provides that the sections applicable in Quebec "are to be interpreted as though they formed part of the *Civil Code of Québec*".[79] In 2005, this legislation was amended to allow same-sex couples to marry.[80]

For the courts, although the style of judgments rendered in Quebec is indistinguishable from that of common law jurisdictions, the reasoning is more logical. It focuses on concepts and pays high attention to doctrinal opinions. Continuing a trend that started in the 1970s, the Supreme Court of Canada emphasizes that civil law cases and common law cases may produce different results.[81] Occasionally, it is criticized for striving to achieve similarity while using civil law concepts and methodology, but this is not a recurring concern, as it was in the past.[82] Furthermore, in civil law cases, justices trained in the common law write learned reasons for judgment that often attract the support of their colleagues.[83] Overall, twenty-first century jurists no longer view the common law as a threat to the integrity of Quebec's civil law system.[84]

---

[76] Ibid., paras 28–29.

[77] Canada, G of, Bijuralism and Harmonization (online).

[78] Interpretation Act, sec. 8.1; Normand (2008, pp. 83–84) and Allard (2009).

[79] Federal Law—Civil Law Harmonization Act, No. 1, sec. 4.

[80] Civil Marriage Act, sec. 9 (as originaly enacted).

[81] LeBel and Le Saunier (2006), Baudouin (2009, pp. 511–513), Jutras (2009), Jukier (2018) and Morin (2019).

[82] Juneau (2016) and Gardner (2017). *Mennillo v. Intramodal inc., 2016 SCC* 51, Judgment of 2016, S.C.R. 2 (Côté J., dissenting); *Jean Coutu Group (PJC) Inc. v. Canada (Attorney General), 2016 SCC* 55, Judgment of 2016, S.C.R. 2 (Côté J., dissenting).

[83] For instance: *Cinar Corporation v. Robinson, 2013 SCC* 73, Judgment of 2013, S.C.R. 3 (McLachlin C.J.C.); *Mennillo v. Intramodal inc., 2016 SCC* 51, Judgment of 2016, S.C.R. 2 (Cromwell J.); *Churchill Falls (Labrador) Corp. v. Hydro-Québec, 2018 SCC* 46, *[2018] 3 S.C.R.* 101, Judgment of 2018, S.C.R. 3 (Rowe J., dissenting); *Brunette v. Legault Joly Thiffault, s.e.n.c.r.l., 2018 SCC* 55, Judgment of 2018, S.C.R. 3 (Rowe J. for the majority); *Barer v. Knight Brothers LLC, 2019 SCC* 13, Judgment of 2019, S.C.R. 1 (Brown J., concurring); *L'Oratoire Saint-Joseph du Mont-Royal v. J.J., 2019 SCC* 35 (Brown J. for the majority); *Yared v. Karam, 2019 SCC* 62 (Rowe J. for the majority); *Newfoundland and Labrador (Attorney General) v. Uashaunnuat (Innu of Uashat and of Mani-Utenam), 2020 SCC* 4 (Brown and Rowe J., dissenting).

[84] Baudouin (2009, p. 509), Moore (2011, p. 211), Morin (2014b), Samson and Langevin (2015, pp. 724–725), and Morin (2019, pp. 156–157).

Ironically, the influence of civil law on the development of common law in Canada is now being criticized. In 2014, this trend culminated with a judgment of the Supreme Court of Canada in a case coming from Alberta. The Court recognized that good faith is an organizing principle of the common law. This marked a watershed because the civil law experience helped alleviate fears that this development would undermine legal stability.[85] In 2019, Justice Nicholas Kasirer was appointed to the Supreme Court of Canada. This noted comparative law scholar and former Dean of the Faculty of Law of McGill University sat for ten years on the Quebec Court of Appeal. Recently, with the support of four colleagues, he wrote[86]:

> In its modern jurisprudence, this Court has recognized the value of looking to legal sources from Quebec in common law appeals, and has often observed how these sources resolve similar legal issues to those faced by the common law [...]. Used in this way, authorities from Quebec do not, of course, bind this Court in its disposition of a private law appeal from a common law province, but rather serve as persuasive authority, in particular, by shedding light on how the jurisdictionally applicable rules work.

This attracted strong criticism from the four other members of the Court. They agreed that Quebec's civil law should be examined when the Court developed the common law. This could be done to fill a "gap" or to answer concerns about the consequences of a change. Otherwise, a comparative approach can render "the law obscure to those who must know and apply it", especially unilingual practitioners who have never studied civil law.[87] It must indeed be noted that the level of bilingualism outside Quebec is extremely low, so that most Anglo-Canadian jurists know neither the civil law nor the French language in which it is primarily expressed.

These Justices claimed for the Common law provinces the autonomy achieved by Quebec's civil law system[88]:

> The direction that civil law developments must be consistent with the overall civil law of Quebec applies with equal force when considering potential modifications to the common law. Maintaining the distinct character of each of Canada's legal traditions requires administering each system according to its own scheme of rules, and by reference to its own authorities [...]. It follows that any enrichment from another legal system must be incorporated only insofar as it conforms to the internal structure and organizing principles of the adopting legal system [...]. Ultimately, the golden rule in using concepts from one of Canada's legal systems to modify the other is that the proposed solution must be able to completely and coherently integrate into the adopting system's structure [...].

Finally, we should observe that anglophone legal practitioners from Quebec are generally proud of the CC. The civil law tradition has also taken root and prospered in the anglophone community, notably at McGill University.[89]

---

[85] *Bhasin v. Hrynew, 2014 SCC* 71, Judgment of 2014, S.C.R. 3, paras 82–85 (Cromwell J. for a unanimous Court).

[86] *C.M. Callow Inc. v. Zollinger, 2020 SCC* 45, para. 58.

[87] Ibid., paras 123 and 169 (Brown and Rowe JJ); Côté J., dissenting, agrees (par. 191).

[88] Ibid., para. 172.

[89] Pilarczyk (1999), Normand (2008, p. 38), and Morin (2014a, p. 120).

6   The Ten Books of the Quebec Civil Code After Thirty Years

The ten books of the Code pertain to the law of persons (I), family (II), successions (III), property (IV), obligations and contracts (V), securities for the performance of obligations (VI), evidence (VII), prescription (VIII), publication of rights (IX), and private international law (X). If the overall structure and contents of the Quebec CC have been relatively stable, numerous changes have occurred, some of them minor.[90] Only a general overview of the contents and evolution of the code can be provided here. One may note that, as in France, the CC of Quebec has been called a "civil constitution"; this entails a flexible application by the courts and adaptation over time.[91] In this view, although they are unavoidable, targeted amendments dealing with specific issues may create unforeseen problems because of their interaction with other codal provisions. On the other hand, the need for the legislature to update the code has been repeatedly emphasized to avoid a disconnect from the needs and values of Quebec society.[92] Indeed, a few days before the final vote on the Code, the opposition party in the National Assembly of Quebec demanded the establishment of a law reform agency.[93] This was done the following year, but the legislation was never implemented, although it was never repealed either.[94] Its absence is keenly felt.

The Code does not contain a general part. However, the first title of Book I is entitled "Enjoyment and exercise of civil rights". It defines personhood and patrimony. It guarantees the inviolability and integrity of the person.[95] It imposes an overarching duty of good faith and prohibits the abuse of one's right, thus codifying jurisprudential innovations (s. 6–7). Title II regulates consent to medical care or procedure, confinement in an institution and psychiatric assessment, children's rights, reputation and privacy, and respect of the body after death.

Title III provides rules on a person's name, domicile and residence, the property of missing persons, and registration of acts of public status. Finally, a unified system independent of legally recognized religious authorities was established. Since 2016, a person whose gender identity does not correspond to the designation of sex in his or her act of birth may have that designation, and if necessary, his other given names changed, with no requirement of prior medical treatment or of a surgical operation (s. 71).[96] In 2017, Aboriginal customary adoption was officially recognized

---

[90] On some issues that were overlooked when the Code was drafted, see Caron et al. (2015).

[91] Cabrillac (2005), Crépeau (2005, p. 25), Kong (2005), Rémillard (2005, p. 284), and MacDonald and Kong (2006, pp. 29–45).

[92] Pineau (2009, p. 228), Baudouin (2009, pp. 509–510) and Morin (2011).

[93] Rémillard (2005, pp. 310–311) and Pineau (2009, p. 228).

[94] Act respecting the Institut québécois de réforme du droit. Moore (2011).

[95] See Kasirer (2008), Ricard (2016), and Macdonald (1995).

[96] The amendments have been held discriminatory for trans persons: Centre for Gender Advocacy c. Attorney General of Quebec, 2021 QCCS 191; but see An Act respecting family law reform with regard to filiation and amending the Civil Code in relation to personality rights and civil status.

(s. 132.0.1). In such a case, a certificate is issued by the "authority that is competent for the Aboriginal community of nation of either the child or the adopter"; this will be legally effective, as long as the interest and rights of the child are respected, and the consent of the persons concerned has been obtained (s. 534.1).

Title IV pertains to the capacity of persons, including majority, tutorship and, for persons of full age whose incapacity is total and permanent, curatorship, as well as less intrusive measures. In 2017, suppletive tutorship was recognized to allow the sharing or delegation of the offices of a legal tutorship when it is impossible for a father or a mother to assume these duties (s. 199.1). This suppletive tutorship may be established according to the rule of an Aboriginal custom; in such a case, the authority mentioned above for Aboriginal customary adoption will grant a certificate (s. 199.10).

One should also mention the protection mandate introduced in 1989 in the CC of Lower Canada. It is given by a person of full age in anticipation of an incapacity to take care of himself or herself or to administer property and becomes effective "upon the occurrence of the incapacity and homologation by the court upon application by the mandatary" (s. 2166). If it "does not fully ensure care of the person or administration of his property, protective supervision may be instituted to complete it; in such a case, the mandatary must report, on request and at least once each year, to the tutor or curator" (s. 2167). A recent reform, not yet in force, abolishes curatorships and makes significant improvements to this title.[97] Finally, title V regulates "Legal persons" endowed with legal personality (i.e., moral persons or corporations). These can be established in the public interest or for a private interest (s. 298). This basic framework is supplemented by detailed rules contained in specific legislation (s. 300).

Book II, which replaced the version first adopted in 1980, pertains to marriage (including matrimonial regimes), filiation (including adoption), the obligation of support, and parental authority. Since 2002, marriage may be solemnized by clerks, notaries, mayors and other municipal officers, ministers of religion licensed by the Minister of Justice (this has existed since 1866) and "any other person designated by the Minister" (s. 366). That same year, same-sex couples and unmarried heterosexual couples were allowed to enter into a civil union (s. 521.1–521.19). This provided them with the rights enjoyed by married couples, but only for issues governed by provincial law. However, in 2005, a federal law granted the right to marry to same-sex couples.[98] Nonetheless, a de facto relationship is still considered preferable to marriage by many couples, regardless of their sexual orientation.

Matrimonial regimes consolidated the existing law. The family patrimony introduced in 1989 and discussed above, from which there is no opting out, is the primary regime; partnership of acquests is the default secondary regime, but instead of this, a couple can choose separation as to property or a personalized regime that does not offend the rules of public order. A de facto spouse cannot benefit from these regimes

---

[97] An Act to amend the Civil Code, the Code of Civil Procedure, the Public Curator Act and various provisions as regards the protection of persons.

[98] Civil Marriage Act.

upon a breakdown of the relationship unless a contract renders these rules applicable to them. Nor can they claim support for themselves from them their ex-partner (as opposed to support for the children under their care). A constitutional challenge alleging that this exclusion was discriminatory failed.[99] A special committee was set up to study the need for reforms, but its recommendations have not been followed up.[100]

Surrogate motherhood agreements are absolutely null (s. 541). On the other hand, assisted procreation is permissible with the use of the genetic material of a third party, through artificial means but also by way of sexual intercourse (s. 538.2). Regarding adoption, we have already mentioned the recognition of Aboriginal custom (s. 543.1). Since 2017, an adoptee has the right to obtain his or her original surname and given names, those of his parents of origin and information allowing him to contact them, unless they have issued a veto barring disclosure or contact, as the case may be (s. 583). Finally, one should mention the hasty abolition in 1996 of the obligation of support between grandparents and grandchildren (s. 585).

Book III pertains to the law of succession. Testamentary freedom is still the governing principle, although limited protection is granted to dependent family members. A spouse or a descendant may be entitled to a maximum of one-half of the share he could have claimed had the entire succession, including the value of the liberalities made during the previous three years, devolved according to law; of course, on must take into account what he or she actually receives from the succession (s. 687–688). The contribution granted to a former spouse is equal to the value of 12 months' support, and that granted to other creditors of support is equal to the value of six months' support, but in both cases, it cannot exceed 10% of the value of the succession, including liberalities (s. 688). Title V was an innovation in that an organized liquidation procedure replaced a heterogeneous system based on universal transmission. It applies to both intestate and testate successions. There have been few amendments to this book. However, since 2013, a new procedure has allowed deaf persons who cannot speak, read or write to make a will (ss. 722.1 and 730.1 C.C.Q.)

Book IV defines the various kinds of property, notably ownership and its modalities (i.e., co-ownership and superficies) and dismemberments (i.e., usufruct, use, servitudes, and emphyteusis). Title V also allows "restrictions on the free disposition of property" stemming from a "stipulation of inalienability" in a contract of gift, a will, or a substitution. Title VI establishes "patrimonies by appropriation", for public purpose foundations and for trusts (s. 1260–1298). This very original concept has recast common law trusts in a civil law mold. It is generally agreed that this new institution must be analyzed through the lens of civil law and that analogies with common law principles will often be problematic.[101] In part, this is due to Title VII, entitled "Administration of the property of others", which contains the powers and obligations of "any person who is charged with the administration of

---

[99] *Quebec (Attorney General) v. A, 2013 SCC 5*, Judgment of 2013, S.C.R. 1.

[100] Comité consultatif du droit de la famille (2015) Pour un droit de la famille adapté aux nouvelles réalités conjugales et familiales.

[101] See the 15 papers in McGill (2013), Kasirer (2008, pp. 466–467), and Smith (2008).

property or a patrimony that is not his own" (s. 1299). This would include tutors, trustees, and mandataries. Seventy-one provisions define their rights and obligations. There have been few amendments to this book. However, in recent years, the rules pertaining to the administration of immovables held in divided co-ownership have been revised (s. 1063–1109). Furthermore, since 2015, "Animals are not things. They are sentient beings and have biological needs. However, except for any special legislative provisions, the rules concerning property nonetheless apply to animals" (s. 898.1 C.C.Q.).

Book V, entitled "Of Obligations", includes nominate contracts and contains no less than 1,274 articles. Following the strong opposition of the Bar, the Chamber of Notaries, and business interests that was discussed above, lesion was not recognized as a generic ground of annulment for persons of full age capable of entering into a contract (s. 1405). Three exceptions introduced in the previous code were retained: renunciation by one of the spouses, by notarial act, of partition of the family patrimony (s. 424); renunciation of partition of the other spouse's acquests (s. 472); loan of money (s. 2332). Lesion "results from the exploitation of one of the parties by the other, which creates a serious disproportion between the prestations of the parties"; if such a disproportion is present, exploitation is proven (s. 1406 1st par.). This is called objective lesion. For minors and protected persons of full age, lesion "may also result from an obligation that is considered to be excessive in view of the patrimonial situation of the person, the advantages he gains from the contract and the circumstances as a whole" (s. 1406 2nd par.). This is subjective lesion.

The definition of objective lesion was based on the Consumer Protection Act adopted in 1978.[102] Section 8 of this legislation gave a court the power to annul a contract entered into by a consumer or to reduce his or her obligations, where the disproportion between the respective obligations of the parties was so great as to amount to exploitation, or where the obligation of the consumer was excessive, harsh or unconscionable. In French, "unconscionable" was rendered *exorbitant*; there was no mention of *lésion*, although scholars agreed that this was the relevant concept. Section 8 is still in force. This means that there is a general protection against lesion in consumer contracts.

The CC of Quebec did not oust the Consumer Protection Act (s. 1384). However, three provisions afford special protection to consumers and to adhering parties (i.e., those who enter into a contract in which the essentials stipulations were imposed or drawn up by one of the parties, or for his or her benefit, and were not negotiable) (s. 1379). For these persons, external clauses will not be binding if they were ignorant of its contents, and it was not brought to their attention (s. 1435). Secondly, a "clause which is illegible or incomprehensible to a reasonable person" is null if it occasions an injury to a consumer or an adhering party, unless he or she received a reasonable explanation of its nature and scope (s. 1436). Finally, an abusive clause may be annulled, or the obligation arising from it may be reduced (s. 1437 1st par.). The Code provides a convoluted definition that is hardly a model of civil law drafting. Such a clause "is excessively and unreasonably detrimental to the consumer or the adhering

---

[102] Consumer Protection Act, sec. 8.

party and is therefore contrary to the requirements of good faith"; furthermore, "a clause which so departs from the fundamental obligations arising from the rules normally governing the contract that it changes the nature of the contract is an abusive clause" (s. 1437 2nd par.). Nonetheless, these three sections provide a substantial level of protection for persons considered vulnerable.

Other rules apply to everyone. Two are worthy of mention. First, the Code prohibits exclusions or limitations of liability for a moral injury that results from an intentional or gross fault and for a bodily or material injury (s. 1474).[103] Second, the amount of a "stipulated penalty may be reduced if the creditor has benefited from partial performance of the obligation or if the clause is abusive" (s. 1623 1st par.).

Notwithstanding the absence of lesion, a person who is neither a consumer nor an adhering party still enjoys substantial levels of protection through the principle of good faith (repeated in s. 1375 for obligations), abuse of rights, restrictions on exclusions or limitations of liability, reduction of penal causes, and the importance of "free and enlightened consent" (s. 1399). These are not equivalent concepts, of course, but they do achieve a certain level of fairness. On the other hand, "unforeseeability" (*imprevision*, akin to hardship) is not recognized in Quebec.[104] For some, the new code errs in entrusting to the court a mandate to consider issues of distributive justice.[105] For others, their narrow power of intervention is a betrayal of the humanist vision of the CCRO.[106]

A few sections are inspired at least in part by common law rules. For instance, if a debtor is in default by "operation of law" (see s. 1597–1598), or because he or she has not performed the obligation in time, the creditor may consider that the contract is "resolved or resiliated without judicial action" (s. 1605). Punitive damages may also be awarded if a legal provision authorizes the court to do so, not as a general rule (s. 1621 1st par.). They are assessed according to specific criteria that differ from those employed in common law jurisdictions (s. 1621 2nd par.).[107] As mentioned, such sections are interpreted and applied using the lens of civil law.

Title II of Book V addresses nominate contracts, namely, sale, gifts, leasing (transfer of movable property to a lessor who is financing a sale for an enterprise, the buyer becoming the lessee), lease, affreightment (a contract by which all or part of a ship is placed at the disposal of the charterer, for navigation), carriage or transportation, employment, enterprise or services, mandate (akin to agency), partnerships and associations, deposit, loan, suretyship, annuities, insurance, gaming and wagering, transaction (i.e., out of court settlement), and arbitration agreements. The code carries over the strong protective measures introduced in 1979 for the lease of a dwelling

---

[103] For a recent discussion, see *6,362,222 Canada inc. c. Prelco inc., 2021 CSC* 39.

[104] *Churchill Falls (Labrador) Corp. v. Hydro-Québec, 2018 SCC 46, [2018] 3 S.C.R.* 101, Judgment of 2018, S.C.R. 3, paras 92–110.

[105] Valcke (1996).

[106] Normand and Jobin (2019, p. 58), Jobin (2020, pp. 831–832), and Tancelin (1994, p. 757).

[107] *Richard v. Time Inc., 2012 SCC 8, [2012] 1 S.C.R.* 265, Judgment of 2012, S.C.R. 1, paras 148–157.

(ss. 1892–2000). For the contract of employment (ss. 2085–2097), its bare-bones framework must be supplemented by detailed rules contained in specific legislation.

Book VI on prior claims and hypothecs revamps the latter. This real right can affect movable or immovable property (s. 2660), including corporeal or incorporeal property, whether individual or multiple, and property comprised in a universality (s. 2666), including personal claims (s. 2676). The pledge is a movable hypothec with delivery; however, a debtor may remain in possession of movable property that is hypothecated—this is called a "hypothec without dispossession", a straightforward if inelegant phrase (s. 2665). For an enterprise, this regime may include customer accounts, patents, trademarks, and, prior to their alienation in the ordinary course of business, things used in manufacturing or in processing or kept in inventory (ss. 2674 and 2684). Furthermore, the effects of a "floating" hypothec are suspended until the creditor brings about crystallization of the hypothec by serving a notice to the debtor following his or her default (s. 2715). Under this regime, businesses can grant security interests such as those found in common law jurisdictions, such as chattel mortgages or floating charges.[108]

Hypothecary creditors "may take possession of the charged property to administer it, take it in payment of their claim, cause it to be sold under judicial authority or sell it themselves" (s. 2748). In doing so, they must comply with numerous conditions imposed by the Code. Some protective measures for debtors have been put in place, such as prior notices. These rules apply to the taking back of property sold under an installment sale if the buyer is in default (s. 1749) or to a trustee acting in the interest of creditors who are the beneficiary of a trust securing the performance of obligations (s. 1262). Furthermore, before taking in payment the hypothecated property, the creditor must obtain the prior authorization of the court if the debtor has already discharged one-half or more of the obligation secured by the hypothec (s. 2778). Many amendments have been made to this book. One may mention the adoption in 2008 of a separate and derogatory regime, based on s. 8 of the U.S. Commercial Code, for the transfer of securities and "security entitlements" (ss. 2714.1–2714.7). The wording of these sections and their contents is completely divorced from traditional civil law concepts.[109] Specific legislation also supplements this book.

Book VII, on evidence, streamlines and simplifies a regime that combined civil law and common law influences for historical reasons, the latter being more evident in commercial law. In 2001, amendments recognized that electronic documents could be used in evidence, but the most important rules on this subject are found in separate legislation.[110] Book VIII, on prescription, also eliminated arcane distinctions due to the historical influence of the Common law. In 2020, special rules were added for actions in damages for bodily injury resulting from a criminal offence (s. 2926.1). It is prescribed by 10 years from the date the victim becomes aware that the injury suffered is attributable to that act. However, such an action cannot be prescribed if

---

[108] On the resulting tension with traditional Civil law concepts, see Macdonald (1995) and Brierley (1993).

[109] Macdonald (2014).

[110] Act to establish a legal framework for information technology.

the injury results from sexual aggression, violent behavior inflicted upon a child, a spouse, or a former spouse, or conversion therapy imposed during childhood. If more than three years have elapsed after the death of the victim or the alleged abuser, the action can no longer be instituted.

Book IX regulates the publicity of rights. Initially, the intention was to create a registration system for immovable rights that would make registered rights unassailable (as a general rule), such as the *Torrens system* of common law jurisdictions. The idea of creating a system with very few possibilities of challenging the validity of registered rights was discarded in 2000. Instead, the old system was retained: only rights contained in registered documents could be set up against third parties. On the other hand, registers have all been computerized and made accessible online. Numerous minor adjustments have been made to the registration system of personal and real rights.[111]

Book X deals with all the essential questions pertaining to Private International Law. Title one contains general provisions, while Title two focuses on Conflict of Laws. Title three is devoted to the international jurisdiction of "Quebec authorities". Title four provides for the recognition of foreign decisions or the jurisdiction of foreign authorities. This book drew on a report written by Professor Jeffrey Talpis that updated the 1977 draft of the CCRO and reflected recent international conventions, as well as a 1987 Swiss law and common law rules on the law applicable to movable securities.[112]

Four principles underlie these new rules, in ascending order or importance: proximity (favoring the law of the State most closely connected to the dispute), party autonomy (allowing choice of law and designation of a forum in a juridical act), protection of the weaker party (for instance, consumers or children), and respect for the mandatory interests of the forum.[113] This book is resolutely international in its outlook: for instance, there is no distinction between interprovincial and international disputes. Additionally, domicile and residence may determine the applicable law, not nationality. A Quebec Court may, exceptionally, decline to exercise its jurisdiction "if it considers that the authorities of another State are in a better position to decide the dispute" (s. 3145). This provision approximates the common law doctrine of *forum non conveniens*. However, it is not applied in the same way because it must be reconciled with the concepts and provisions of the Code.[114] Foreign judgments, in general, will be recognized if Quebec authorities assume jurisdiction over a similar case (s. 3164). When making this decision, the Court cannot consider the merits of the decision (s. 3158). Amendments to book X were linked to modifications to

---

[111] For a good introduction to these issues, see *Ostiguy v. Allie, 2017 SCC 22*, Judgment of 2017, S.C.R. 1.

[112] Goldstein (2008, p. 436).

[113] Talpis and Goldstein (2009, p. 343).

[114] *Spar Aerospace Ltd. v. American Mobile Satellite Corp., 2002 SCC 78*, Judgment of 2002, S.C.R. 4, paras 14–23.

other parts of the Code. These new rules of Private International Law have met with widespread approval.[115]

7 Conclusion

During the nineteenth century, in Quebec, attempts to eliminate or severely restrict the role of the civil law tradition were unsuccessful. In 1866, the strong determination of Francophone jurists, with the crucial support of Anglophone members of the legal community, made possible the adoption of the CC of Lower Canada. This bilingual document reflected the needs of a liberal economy and reflected patriarchal values. By the turn of the century, the Supreme Court of Canada looked to common law principles to interpret the Code, an approach that was discarded in 1918. Meanwhile, important modifications to the private law of Quebec were made outside of it. By 1955, the need for a revision was accepted by the legislature, but the decision to draft a new code was made only in 1960.

At that point, family law and the law of obligations were considered outdated because of their incompatibility with the principle of equality and because of a newly felt need to protect weaker parties in a contractual setting. In 1966, the CCRO was set up. Various committees composed of anglophone or francophone judges, lawyers, notaries, and academics were involved in the preparation of the draft code published in 1977. During this period, the law was thoroughly modernized, and important protective measures appeared in legislation pertaining to insurance, consumer protection, and the lease of dwellings.

Book II of the CC of Quebec, entitled "On Family Law", was first adopted in 1980 and then put in force. This step-by-step approach was not well received by the legal community. Other Books were adopted, but in 1989, significant changes were made to the CC of Lower Canada and to Book II, including the addition of a primary matrimonial regime recognizing the right of each spouse to share the net value of some assets, with no possibility of opting out for future spouses, and a restriction of testamentary freedom to provide limited support to dependents and ex-spouses. The draft bill on Obligation met with a strong opposition from the Bar and the Chamber and notaries, and it was scaled down for this reason.

In 1991, a completely new code replaced the books already enacted. It proclaimed its fundamental character and the need for the courts to interpret it according to the canons of the civil law tradition; the direction has been complied with. In general, the Code consolidates existing law, but some important innovations can be singled out. Good faith is an overriding principle. There is a government-run secular system of civil status. Liquidation rules apply to both intestate and testate successions. Patrimony by appropriation has become the conceptual foundation of trust. Specific provisions govern the management of property by a tutor, curator, trustee or mandatary. Consumers and weaker parties in a contract of adhesion enjoy special protection. In

---

[115] Goldstein (2008, p. 521).

every contract, an abusive penal clause may be reduced. Punitive damages can be awarded, but only if a specific legislative provision grants to courts the power to do so. Hypothecs apply to movable and immovable property (among many important innovations). A complex regime for the publicity of rights has developed. Rules of private international law are thoroughly codified and must be interpreted accordingly, including the provision replicating the doctrine of *forum non conveniens*.

Amendments have been numerous in the fields of the law of persons and family law. LGBTQ+ have generally benefitted from them. On the other hand, de facto spouses are generally overlooked by the Code, and contracts of surrogate motherhood are still null, as in 1991. Since 2017, Aboriginal customary adoption has been recognized, as well as Aboriginal customs providing for suppletive tutorship. Amendments to the law of obligation and contracts are far less numerous, comparatively speaking. The ones that have been made to other books are generally of a technical nature.

Of course, the CC of Quebec is not flawless, nor is it particularly coherent on a conceptual level. Practitioners have been able to work around these difficulties, and provisions that were initially based on common law principles or institutions are now considered an important feature of the civil law of Quebec. The contents and the language of the code are modern, and difficulties in its application do not reach an abnormal level. Thanks to the ceaseless labor of Anglophone jurists, the English version is now fluidly written. The underlying values of the code have evolved over time and are not divorced from Quebec society. If access to justice remains an urgent problem, the code does not exacerbate it. Overall, no one would dream of going back to the CC of Lower Canada, and that is undoubtedly a good measure of its success.

References

Allard F (2009) La disposition préliminaire du Code civil du Québec, l'idée de droit commun et le rôle du Code en droit Féderal. Can Bar Rev 88:275–312

Andò B (2015) The Feature of Droit Commun in the Disposition Preliminaire of the Civil Code of Quebec: A Clue to the Bijurality of the Legal System? In: Farran S, Hendry J, Rautenbach C (eds) The diffusion of law: The movement of laws and norms around the world. Ashgate, Farnham, pp 147–168

Arroyo I, Amayuelas E (2003) From the code civil du bas Canada (1866) to the code civil Quebecois (1991), or from the consolidation to the reform of the law: a reflection for Catalonia. In: MacQueen H, Vaquer A, Espiau Espiau S (eds) Regional private laws and codification in Europe. Cambridge University Press, Cambridge, pp 267–287

Baudouin J-L (1985) La Cour suprême et le droit civil québécois: Un bilan, un constat. une prospective. In: Beaudouin GA (ed) La Cour suprême du Canada, Actes de la Conférence d'octobre 1985. Yvon Blais, Cowansville, pp 125–134

Baudouin J-L (2005) Le Comité aviseur sur la politique législative du nouveau Code civil. In: Lortie S, Kasirer B, Belley J-G (eds) Du Code civil du Québec. Contribution à l'histoire immédiate d'une recodification réussie, Thémis. Montréal, pp 321–381

Baudouin J-L (2009) What does the future hold for the Civil Code of Quebec? Canadian Bar Rev 88:506–514

Bisson A-F (1999) La Disposition Préliminaire du Code Civil du Québec. McGill Law J 44:539–567

Brierley JEC (1968) Quebec's Civil law codification: viewed and reviewed. McGill Law J 14:521–589

Brierley JEC (1992) The renewal of Quebec's distinct legal culture: the new Civil Code of Quebec. Univ Toronto Law J 42:484–503

Brierley JEC (1993) Les langues du Code civil du Québec. In: Côté P-A (ed) Le nouveau code civil, interprétation et application - Journées Maximillien Caron 1992. Éditions Thémis, Montreal, pp 129–146

Brierley JEC, Macdonald R (eds) (1993) Quebec civil law—An introduction to Quebec private law. Emond Montgomery Publications, Toronto

Brisson J-M (1993) Le Code civil, droit commun? In: Côté P-A (ed) Le nouveau code civil, interprétation et application - Journées Maximillien Caron 1992. Éditions Thémis, Montreal, pp 293–315

Brisson J-M, Kasirer N (1995) The married woman in ascendance, the mother country in retreat: from legal colonialism to legal nationalism in Quebec matrimonial law reform 1866–1991. Manitoba LJ 23:406–449

Cabrillac R (2005) Le Code civil est-il la véritable constitution de la France ? Revue Juridique Thémis de l'Université de Montréal 39:245–259

Cairns JW (2015) Codification, transplants and history: law reform in Louisiana (1808) and Quebec (1866). Talbot Publishing, an imprint of The Lawbook Exchange, Ltd, Clark, NJ

Canada P of (1866) Civil Code civil of lower Canada from the amended roll deposited in the office of the clerk of the legislative council as directed by the act 29 vict. chap. 41, 1865. Cameron, Ottawa

Cantin Cumyn M (2005) Les innovations du Code civil du Québec, un premier bilan. Cahiers de Droit 46:463–479

Caron V, Berthold G-A, Torres-Ceyte J (2015) Les oubliés du Code civil du Québec. Thémis, Montréal

Civil Code Revision Office (1977a) Draft Civil Code. Éditeur officiel du Québec, Québec

Civil Code Revision Office (1977b) Commentaries. Éditeur officiel du Québec, Québec

Coates E (2011) The English voice of the Civil Code of Québec: an unfinished history. Revue du Barreau 71:45–61

Crépeau P-A (2005) Une certaine conception de la recodification. In: Lortie S, Kasirer B, Belley J-G (eds) Du Code civil du Québec. Contribution à l'histoire immédiate d'une recodification réussie, Thémis. Montréal, pp 23–162

Devinat M, Guilhermont É (2012) La réception des théories juridiques françaises en droit civil québécois. RDUS 42:459–504

Durocher R (2013) Quiet Revolution. The Canadian Encyclopedia

Gardner D (2017) L'harmonisation des solutions en droit privé canadien: un regard sur quelques arrêts de la Cour suprême. Les Éditions Thémis, Montréal

Girard P, Phillips J, Brown RB (2018) A history of law in Canada. Published for The Osgoode Society for Canadian Legal History by University of Toronto Press, Toronto

Glenn HP (1993) Le droit comparé et l'interprétation du Code civil du Québec. In: Côté P-A (ed) Le nouveau code civil, interprétation et application - Journées Maximillien Caron 1992. Éditions Thémis, Montreal, pp 175–222

Goldstein G (2008) Private international law. In: Grenon A, Bélanger-Hardy L (dir) Elements of Quebec Civil Law : a comparison with the common law of Canada, pp 433–522

Greenwood FM (1995) Lower Canada (Quebec): transformation of Civil Law, from higher morality to autonomous will, 1774–1866. Manitoba Law J 23:132–182

Jobin P-G (2010) La circulation de modèles juridiques français au Québec. Quand? Comment? Pourquoi. In: Mélanges Adrian Popovici, Les couleurs du droit. Thémis, Montreal, pp 599–629

Jobin P-G (2020) Paul-André Crépeau: un personnage. Cahiers de Droit 61:825–852

Jukier R (2018) Canada's legal traditions: sources of unification, diversification, or inspiration? J Civ Law Stud 11:75

Juneau M (2016) The mixite of Quebec's recodified Civil Law: a reflection of Quebec's legal culture. Loy L Rev 809–828

Jutras D (2009) Cartographie de la mixité: la common law et la complétude du droit civil au Québec. Can Bar Rev 88:247–273

Kasirer N (2004) Portalis now. In: Kasirer N (ed) Le droit civil, avant tout un style? Thémis, Montréal, pp 1–46

Kasirer N (2008) Translating part of France's legal heritage: Aubry and Rau on the patrimoine. RGD 38:453–493

Kong H (2005) Changing codes and changing constitutions. Cahiers de Droit 46:629–670

Laflamme L (2005) La Chambre des notaires du Québec et le Réforme du Code civil. In: Lortie S, Kasirer B, Belley J-G (eds) Du Code civil du Québec. Contribution à l'histoire immédiate d'une recodification réussie, Thémis. Montréal, pp 403–428

Laidler P (2005) The distinctive character of Quebec legal system. In: Place and memory in Canada: global perspectives. Polska Akademia Umiejętności, Kraków, pp 277–287

LeBel L, Le Saunier P-L (2006) L'interaction du droit civil et de la common law à la Cour suprême du Canada. Les Cahiers De Droit 47:179–238. https://doi.org/10.7202/043886ar

Legrand P (1995) Bureaucrats at play: the new Quebec Civil Code. Br J Can Stud 10:52–76

Legrand P (1996) De la profonde incivilité du Code civil du Québec. Revue Interdisciplinaire D'études Juridiques 36:1–13

Lortie S, Kasirer B, Belley J-G (eds) (2005) Du Code civil du Québec. Contribution à l'histoire immédiate d'une recodification réussie, Thémis. Montréal

Macdonald RA (1995) Reconceiving the symbols of property: universalities, interests and other heresies. McGill LJ 39:761–812

Macdonald RA (2014) Book VI of the Civil Code of Québec—Prior claims and hypothecs. Les livres du Code civil du Québec. Les Éditions Revue de Droit de l'Université de Sherbrooke, Sherbrooke, Québec, Canada, pp 189–228

Macdonald RA, Kong H (2006) Patchwork law reform: your idea is good in practice, but it won't work in theory. Osgoode HLJ 44:11–52

Marx H (2009) Introduction of Professor Jean Pineau by the honourable Herbert Marx. Can Bar Rev 88:213–214

Masse C (2003) The positive experience of the Civil Code of Quebec in the North American environment. In: MacQueen H, Vaquer A, Espiau Espiau S (eds) Regional private laws and codifciation in Europe. Cambridge University Press, Cambridge, pp 260–266

McClintock B, Meredith RC (2015) Twentieth anniversary of the Civil Code of Quebec: the English translation of the Civil Code of Quebec: a controversy. Journal of Specialised Translation

McGill LJ (2013) The civil law trust. McGill Law J 58:793–966

Moore B (2011) Rapport de synthèse. In: Dorato JA, Ménard J-F, Smith L (eds) Le droit civil et ses codes: parcours à travers les Amériques. Thémis, Montréal, pp 187–212

Morin M (2000) Des juristes sédentaires? L'influence du droit français et du droit anglais sur l'interprétation du Code civil du Bas Canada. La Revue Du Barreau 60:247–386

Morin S (2011) Pourquoi j'emmenerais le législateur au musée s'il voulait discuter de l'avenir du Code civil du Québec. In: Dorato JA, Ménard J-F, Smith L (eds) Le droit civil et ses codes: parcours à travers les Amériques. Thémis, Montréal, pp 87–116

Morin M (2013a) The discovery and assimilation of British constitutional law principles in Quebec, 1764–1774. Dalhousie Law J 36:581–616

Morin M (2013b) Réflexions sur la qualité de la loi au Québec et au Canada – ou ce qui est bon pour les francophones du Canada ne l'est pas pour les anglophones du Québec, pp 247–277

Morin M (2014a) Blackstone and the birth of Quebec's distinct legal culture 1765–1867. In: Prest W (ed) Re-interpreting Blackstone's commentaries a seminal text in national and international contexts. Hart, Oxford, pp 105–124

Morin S (2014b) Quebec: 'First impressions can be misleading.' In: Farran S, Örücü E, Donlan SP (eds) Study of mixed legal systems: endangered, entrenched or blended. Ashgate, Farnham, pp 165–212

Morin M (2015) Blackstone et le bijuridisme québécois de la Proclamation royale de 1763 au Code civil du Bas Canada. In: Rousseau S (ed) Un juriste sans frontières Mélanges Ejan Mackaay. Thémis, Montréal, pp 585–632

Morin M (2019) Dualism, mixedness and cross-breeding in legal systems: Quebec and Canadian law. In: Saucier Calderón JP (ed). Viajes y fronteras de la enseñanza del derecho comparado. Pontifica Universidad Católica del Perú, Departamento Académico de Derecho y Centro de Investigación, Capacitación y Asesoría Jurídica, Lima, pp 151–167

Niort J-F (1994) Le Code civil face aux défis de la société moderne: une perspective comparative entre la révision française de 1804 et le nouveau Code civil du Québec de 1994. McGill Law J 39:845–876

Niort J-F (2004) 'Notre droit civil…': Quelques remarques sur l'interprétation du Code Civil français et du Code civil du Bas-Canada au Québec. In: Le Code Napoléon, un ancêtre vénéré? Mélanges offerts à Jacques Vanderlinden. Bruylant, Bruxelles, pp 173–199

Normand S (1994) La première décennie des travaux consacrés à la révision du Code civil. Revue de Droit McGill 39:828–844

Normand S (2008) An introduction to Quebec Civil Law. In: Grenon A, Bélanger-Hardy L (dir) Elements of Quebec Civil Law: a comparison with the common law of Canada, pp 25–97

Normand S (2021) La célébration du centenaire du Code civil du Bas-Canada: moment propice à l'écriture d'un nouveau récit. Revue Juridique Thémis De L'université De Montréal 55:193–232

Normand S, Jobin P-G (2019) La pensée de Paul-André Crépeau à travers ses écrits doctrinaux. Cahiers de Droit 60:3–93

Paquin J (2014) La soif de certitude et la peur du chaos dans la réforme du droit des contrats: une analyse rhétorique du discours du Barreau et de la Chambre des notaires du Québec. Les Cahiers De Droit 55:385–416. https://doi.org/10.7202/1025754ar

Parent S (2005) Le Barreau du Québec et le Réforme du Code civil. In: Lortie S, Kasirer B, Belley J-G (eds) Du Code civil du Québec. Contribution à l'histoire immédiate d'une recodification réussie, Thémis. Montréal, pp 429–444

Pilarczyk IC (1999) A noble roster: one hundred and fifty years of law at McGill. Montreal

Pineau J (2009) A very brief history of a recodification and its problems. Can Bar Rev 88:223–229

Québec M de la justice du (1993) Commentaires du ministre de la Justice - le Code civil du Québec, un mouvement de société. Publications du Québec

Rémillard G (2005) Le nouveau Code civil: un véritable contrat social. In: Lortie S, Kasirer B, Belley J-G (eds) Du Code civil du Québec. Contribution à l'histoire immédiate d'une recodification réussie, Thémis. Montréal, pp 283–320

Ricard L (2016) La Philosophie Politique et le Code Civil du Québec: L'Exemple de la Notion de Patrimoine. McGill Law J 61:667–719

Samson M, Langevin L (2015) Revisiting Québec's Jus Commune in the era of the human rights charters. Am J Comp L 63:719–746

Smith L (2008) Trust and patrimony. Revue Générale De Droit 38:379–403. https://doi.org/10.7202/1027041ar

Talpis JA, Goldstein G (2009) The influence of Swiss law on Quebec's 1994 codification of private international Law. Yearbook of Private International Law 11:339–374

Tancelin M (1994) Les silences du Code civil du Québec. McGill Law J 39:747–760

Valcke C (1996) The unhappy marriage of corrective and distributive justice in the new Civil Code of Quebec. University of Toronto Law J 46:539–648

Wilson K (2010) Alive and kicking—the story of lesion and the Civil Code of Québec. Cahiers de Droit 51:445–465. https://doi.org/10.7202/045637ar

Young B (1994) The politics of codification, the Lower Canadian Civil Code of 1866. McGill-Queen's University Press, Montreal

Young B (2004) Overlapping identities: the Quebec Civil Code of 1866: its reception and interpretation. In: Le Code Napoléon, un ancêtre vénéré? Mélanges offerts à Jacques Vanderlinden. Bruylant, Bruxelles, pp 259–284

Michel Morin is Full Professor at the Faculty of Law of the Université de Montréal. His research focuses on Comparative Legal History of public or private law and the evolution of Aboriginal Peoples' rights. In 1998, the Humanities and Social Sciences Federation awarded him the Jean-Charles Falardeau prize for his book *L'Usurpation de la souveraineté autochtone* (The Usurpation of Aboriginal Sovereignty, 1997). He has published, in French, a Historical introduction to Roman, French and English Law (2004) and, with Arnaud Decroix and David Gilles, *Courts and Arbitration in New France and Quebec, 1740–1784*. This book was awarded the Rodolphe Fournier 2013 prize (ex aequo) by the Fédération des sociétés d'histoire du Québec (Federation of Historical Societies of Quebec) and the Chamber of Notaries. He is grateful to his colleagues Jean-François Gaudreault-Desbiens and Jeffrey Talpis for comments on an earlier version of this chapter.

The German BGB: What Needs to Be Changed and Why

Christoph G. Paulus

Abstract The German BGB, like all its continental sister codifications, is meant to be the central Code for private law. Due to modern technological developments, the law of property within that BGB, however, is increasingly losing its importance, shifting more and more toward what is generally called intellectual property (IP) law. The present contribution proposes a way by which the BGB could regain its former centrality in this field and adapt the time-honored codification to the needs of the present-day economy.

1 Codifications as Mirrors of Their Times

The history of codification reaches back deep into history. Suffice it to refer to examples such as the Codex Hamurapi, the town charter of Gortyn, or the compilation of the Corpus Iuris Civilis by the Emperor Iustinian approximately 530 AD. They all share with the much more modern emanations of the codification idea the legislative intent to provide a comprehensive collection of rules for a certain section of life. Insofar they serve for a simplification of the access to law and try to improve thereby knowledge of and compliance with the law. This becomes particularly evident with the praetorian edict[1] that the ancient Roman Praetor exposed outside his "office"—, i.e., literally on the street or on the square—on which all clauses were listed that the particular Praetor was ready to grant and which informed the citizens about the applicable law.

---

[1] Despite its purpose to support, complement, and correct the *ius civile* (*iuris civilis adiuvandi, supplendi, corrigendi gratia*), it transcended more and more from a mere gap filler into a codification—particularly when it, in the first half of the second century AD, became eternal, *edictum perpetuum*, by the eminent jurist Iulian.

C. G. Paulus (✉)
Humboldt-Universität zu Berlin, Berlin, Germany
e-mail: chrpaulus@t-online.de

© The Author(s), under exclusive license to Springer Nature Singapore Pte Ltd. 2023   249
M. Graziadei and L. Zhang (eds.), *The Making of the Civil Codes*,
Ius Gentium: Comparative Perspectives on Law and Justice 104,
https://doi.org/10.1007/978-981-19-4993-7_14

However, these historical remarks shall not be pursued further; they are supposed just to broaden the understanding that each and every codification—like any other human work—mirrors the social legal and economic situation of the time of its creation. Since the present author is a German[2] professor of private law, it is hopefully forgivable that the BGB (Bürgerliches Gesetzbuch = Civil Law Code) will be presented in this text. It entered into force on January 1, 1900, thereby ending an almost 90-year struggle within German scholarship for the need, timing, and contents of such codification.[3] The BGB, thus, represented more than other German codifications[4] a peak of the preceding efforts to unify the numerous German states into one political entity; in this context, it appears to be not just accidental that at about the time of the BGB's entering into force the later Chancellor von Bülow proclaimed in a parliamentarian speech (1897) the (in)famous claim of German politics to get its "place at the sun"—thereby alluding to colonial ambitions.

Wieacker[5] characterized the BGB to be "more the fruit of previous legal thinking than semen for a new one". Evidence for this statement is manifold; suffice it to mention but a few: The Common Part of the BGB, its first book (Allgemeiner Teil), is structured in parallel[6] to the famous textbook of the classical Roman jurist Gaius, the *Institutes* (approximately 160 a.d.): the law of persons (sec. 1 et seq.) is followed by the law of things (sec. 90 et seq.) and by procedural law (sec. 194 et seq.[7]); the acquisition of rights, i.e., contract law, is dealt with in sec. 104 et seq. and forms part of the law of things, namely, how to transfer them. It is thus fair to say that the Allgemeiner Teil climaxed the "Historische Rechtsschule", which dominated German legal scholarship in the nineteenth century and which is alternatively branded as "Pandektenwissenschaft", i.e., a revitalization of the classical digests.[8] I will return to this below.

Another example is the list of types of contracts that were explicated and shaped in the Special Part (Besonderer Teil) of the BGB's second book, the law of obligations (Schuldrecht). They mirror quite obviously Roman law, at least as it was presented in the leading textbooks on Roman law at that time. The most famous textbook was written by one of Savigny's former pupils, Prof. Bernhard Windscheid from

---

[2] Being, thus, also a European citizen, a European codification could (or should) have been made subject of the subsequent deliberations; however, this is left to others, more qualified scholars, as, for instance, Lehmann (2020).

[3] From the almost innumerable literature, just see, quite recently, Becker (2015) and Hattenhauer (1971, 69 ff).

[4] Most prominently the so-called four "Reichsjustizgesetze" (Empirial Judicial Acts) from 1877, comprising the Criminal Law Code, Civil Procedure Code, Bankruptcy Code, and the Judicature Code.

[5] Wieacker (1967, 478).

[6] Cf. ibid., 487 ff.

[7] These rules deal with the statute of limitations which was in previous times of the so called "aktionenrechtlichen Denken" an exclusively procedural remedy.

[8] On this connection cf. particularly Zimmermann (2007, 1 ff).

the University of Leipzig, who was not only a member of the BGB's first drafting committee but also a very influential one. It does not come as a surprise, therefore, that some commentators of the legislative process coined one of the last drafts of the BGB as being the 9th edition of Windscheid's textbook.[9]

The said retrospective approach also becomes visible in the omission of something[10] as seemingly modern as the protection of human dignity.[11] With the invention and increasing popularity of photography toward the end of the nineteenth century, this value had its chance to greater popularity—after all, a photo of the Chancellor *v. Bismarck* on his dead bed gave rise to an important and heavily discussed court decision[12] that based the prohibition of using this photo for journalistic purposes exactly on this value, a violation of human dignity. However, the class distinctions in that society were still just too large to justify a homologation of this value.[13]

Instead of adding further examples—for instance, from the 5th book, the law of succession, where the legislator obviously felt the need to establish with sec. 2102 BGB a norm that solves the issue of the *causa Curiana*, a famous case from the first century B.C. (sic!), of which Cicero reports in his writings several times[14]—the question shall be raised in what follows whether the BGB, this "fruit of the nineteenth century", has to (or should) undergo revision in order to adapt it to the needs of the present time—whereby coining this time as the twenty-first century would be somewhat over optimistic, given the increased celerity of grave social, political, economic and legal changes. An answer to this question shall be given (or better: tried) in the next section.

---

[9] Cf. Wolf (1944, 580).

[10] There are, at best, just indirect hints to the validity of a doctrine which is central for the functioning of modern economy, namely, *pacta sunt servanda*. The likely reason for that is that this rule is just the opposite of what constituted classical Roman law (where the rule was: *pacta non sunt servanda*); the modern version was formulated only on a Bishop synod in Africa in 348—for religious reasons; on this, Paulus (2016, 740 ff). On its possible connections with Muslim law cf. Boisard (1980, 429, 441 ff).

[11] This value is currently commonly seen as the fundament of Human Rights law, cf. Tomuschat (2014, 85 ff), Besson (2018, 22, 34 ff), and Clapham (2007).

[12] RGZ 45, 170 ff; on this decision Kohler (1900, 196 ff) and Brüggemeier (2005, 297 ff).

[13] On this, cf. Farhount (2020).

[14] Just cf. Manthe (1997, 74 ff). The case was all about whether a reversionary heir can also be, by means of interpretation, seen as a substitute heir; sec. 2102 BGB equates the two positions.

2 Modernization of the BGB

2.1 Past Proposals

2.1.1 General Overview

In German scholarly writings, one finds every now and again reasoning about improving the existing structure of the BGB.[15] Suffice it to mention *Fritz Schulz'* seminal article (actually book) "System der Rechte auf den Eingriffserwerb"[16] (system of the rights derived from an infringement) in which he tried to establish a separate class of actions directed at the recovery of the benefits gained from an infringement. Another example is *Klaus Hopt's* search for a new type of contract that he calls "Interessenwahrungsvertrag" (contract on the maintenance of someone else's interests),[17] which inspires one's own curiosity as to which types of contracts would be chosen for the Special Part of the law of obligations today by someone with little if any knowledge of ancient Roman law. That is, by someone who does not look back into what we have achieved thus far but who asks what we will need in the future? Even a brief glimpse through the existing part of the Schuldrecht (law of obligations) discloses the urgency of such a question: numerous new contract types have been included only recently, such as construction contracts, patient rights contracts, architect contracts, and travel contracts. In addition, many of those new codified contract types make the informed observer feel slightly uneasy as they seem to be rather the product of an actual urgency than of thorough and thoughtful reflections. Nothing proves this point better than that there is not yet any rule on the license contract even though it plays an essential and central role in the entire area of the law of immaterial goods.

The following deliberations (below at 2.2) are devoted to a similar exercise; they shall prove that there is (or at least: can be seen) a need for another restructuring of the BGB as it is today. What is advocated for is the introduction of a new General Part, this time in the BGB's third book on the law of property. The reason for this proposal is, first, to keep the BGB sufficiently prepared to cope with the most modern trends and developments and, second, to thereby strengthen this codification's central role for the private law as a whole.

---

[15] To be sure, proposals to improve the existing legal system have a long tradition: Apel (1540), was by far not the first representative in this line and even more certainly not the last one; on this book, Wieacker (1959, 44 ff); *idem* (as in fn 4), 80 ff.

[16] AcP 105, 1909, p. 1— 488; on this Ernst (2004, 105, 113 ff).

[17] Hopt (2004b, 1 ff), idem (2004a), 213 ff. Cf. Paulus (2005, 1948 ff).

2.1.2   Special Example: General Terms and Conditions

With regard to the latter point, a previous development turns out to be informative, that of the legislative treatment of general terms and conditions (Allgemeine Geschäftsbedingungen). The fundamental principle of freedom of contracts is probably something like a central pillar of the present-day economic system as such[18]; it is hard to think of any more basic, essential rule in this context. However, when and if a codification from the second half of the nineteenth century, such as the BGB, adheres to overly liberalistic ideas and assumes that all parties of any contract are approaching each other on a level playing field, thereby ignoring that for huge parts of the population, this assumption is wrong, the freedom of contract principle serves as an invitation to the more powerful party to (ab)use this freedom to its own benefit.[19]

That was indeed done so for decades. The German Supreme Court (then the Reichsgericht) tried to straighten things in the worst cases, and just a few authors made this inequality and injustice subject of their writings.[20] However, neither the court decisions nor academia had a visible impact; it was just US president Kennedy's appeal to consumer protection ("we all are consumers", 1962), which ignited respective legislation in Germany by, i.a., a special code on general terms and conditions.[21] The European Economic Community (as it was called then) picked up this trend and enacted a Directive on general terms and conditions in 1993.[22] Some 10 years later, in 2002, happened what is so informative about this development for the present context: the thus far separate statute was incorporated into the BGB; its subject was seen as too important to not be included in the main codification of private law.[23]

2.2   A New Proposal

2.2.1   The Confinement of the Law of Property

With this general terms and conditions example as background and model, we now turn to the proposal to create a General Part for the third book of the BGB, dealing with the law of property—literally translated: the book of things (Sachenrecht). The literal wording is key for understanding the setting of the agenda: a thing in the BGB is a term of art, defined in sec. 90 BGB. It runs as follows[24]:

---

[18] Informative in its contextualization Mazzoni and Malaguti (2019, 143 ff).

[19] On the fragility of the debtor-creditor-relationship cf. Paulus (2020, 39–52).

[20] Cf. Grossmann-Doerth (1933) and Raiser (1935).

[21] Gesetz zur Regelung des Rechts der Allgemeinen Geschäftsbedingungen from 9 December 1976, BGBl I, 3317.

[22] Cf. Council Directive 93/13/EEC on unfair terms in consumer contracts from 5 April 1993.

[23] On a more general level, instructive: Stürner (1996, 741, 742 ff).

[24] Translation of the BGB here and henceforth taken from: https://www.gesetze-im-internet.de/englisch_bgb/englisch_bgb.html#p0270.

Only corporeal objects are things as defined by law.

Needless to point out that the equation of a thing and a corporeal object is a translation from Latin, i.e., the term *res* is transplanted from ancient Roman law to modern German law.[25] This is no surprise at all, since Roman law was, until December 31, 1899, not only the dominant applicable law (Gemeines Recht = Common Law), which in case of legislative lacunas was still applied; moreover, German scholarship was branded as Pandektenwissenschaft, which was probably the most sophisticated scholarly treatment of Roman law ever. This was developed over approximately 100 years and was a blossom of Roman law and was as such deeply engraved in the minds of the BGB's drafters.

Unfortunately, however, these drafters have chosen the narrowest translation of *res*[26] and have, thus, by restricting things to corporeal objects such as a book or a real estate (but not a receivable, let alone an immaterial right), confined the applicability of the Sachenrecht (i.e., the German law of property), respectively, to regulating only such "things". Accordingly, the rules on property are reserved for corporeal things; in German law, property of receivables, for instance, is a misnomer.[27]

This is all the more surprising as up to that time, i.e., end of the nineteenth century, those who did what is today coined intellectual property law used to speak about "geistiges Eigentum" (intellectual property). It was then that the leading academic figure in that field, Prof. Dr. Josef Kohler from the Friedrich-Wilhelm University in Berlin (today Humboldt-Universität zu Berlin), declared this area's independence from the common private law of the BGB[28] by branding it from then on "Immaterialgüterrecht" (immaterial assets law) and understanding it from then on as a "Bruderrecht" (brother law) to private law. This marked the ever since accepted bifurcation of these two branches of law, at least within German jurisprudence. This means that at the time of the codification of private law—which was, as we have seen supra, the result of almost an entire century of heated debate—it was taken for granted that this brother law was not to be included in the civil law codification. In sec. 903 BGB, there is a definition of what it means when property is at stake;

> The owner of a thing may, to the extent that a statute or third-party rights do not conflict with this, deal with the thing at his discretion and exclude others from every influence....

Until the drafting of this rule, it was absolute standard to speak about intellectual ownership—and all what the drafters have to say about this parallelism is that there are certain analogies which might justify in some cases the analogous application of the BGB rules.[29] This is hard to understand and needs deeper investigation which,

---

[25] On the connection between Pandektistik and sec. 90 BGB cf. Von Savigny (1814, 99), idem (1840, 338), Puchta (1845, 47), Esmarch (1860, 9), and Windscheid (1862, 343). For the BGB: Johow (1880, 17–21).

[26] On this, cf. Rüfner (2003) and Becker (1999, 55 ff). On the philosophical origins of that particular meaning of *res* v. Sokolowski (1902, 28 ff).

[27] Cf. Mugdan (1899, 142).

[28] Cf. Busch (1887, 169 ff).

[29] Cf. fn. 27.

however, shall not presented here. Since the main focus of the following lines is the attempt to advocate for the bridging of the gulf between Sachenrecht and Immaterialgüterrecht (i.e., law of property and intellectual property law)—at least to a certain degree and based on the assumption that the dogmatic construct of property must not infringe on any of the achievements of modern immaterial asset law (IP law).

2.2.2   Structure of the BGB

Unlike the Swiss Code on Obligations (Obligationenrecht) or the Private Law Code (Zivilgesetzbuch), which are products of the more or less sole authorship of Prof. Eugen Huber who presented legislations made for the user—, i.e., in common language and in understandable German—the German BGB was a piece of art made by experts for other experts only. It is brilliant in its precision, it is conceived in a way that triggers admirations, and it is construed like a gothic cathedral—but it lacks any down-to-earth quality. The actual addressees are kept away and dependant on professional intermediation.

Part of this conceptualization is that the most general features of private law are put into the very first book of the BGB, which is called "General Part" (Allgemeiner Teil). It was already mentioned supra that this part's structure is derived from Gaius' *Institutiones* from approximately 160 AD! Thus, since contracts do play a role not just within the law of obligations but also in family law (book 4), the law of succession (book 5), and even in the law of property (book 3), the mechanism of concluding a contract is regulated in the Allgemeiner Teil. Offer and acceptance as the fundamental elements of any contract[30] are to be found in that first book, sec. 145 et seq. Similarly, representation is dealt with there, too, since not only contract parties but also children, for instance, are represented by their parents when they enter into a contract. Moreover, the above-cited sec. 90 BGB is part of the Allgemeiner Teil. Accordingly, as in Maths, when certain numbers precede brackets and therefore are to be multiplied (or whatever) with every number within those brackets—whenever the word "Sache" (thing) appears in the entire BGB, it is to be understood as defined in sec. 90 BGB.

---

[30] On the German scholarship's influence on the Common Law doctrine regarding the conception of offer and acceptance, cf. Riesenfeld (1985, 267, 269 ff).

To be sure, this mathematization, as it were, of the BGB's structure does not stop here. The second book, called Schuldrecht, is devoted to what might be translated as the law of obligations. It covers all sorts of contracts, quasi-contracts such as the ancient Roman *negotiorum gestio* (Geschäftsführung ohne Auftrag, agency without specific authorisation), unjust enrichment, and the law of torts. The commonality of all these disparate institutions is that they result in an obligation that one party (creditor) has against the other (debtor); in case of a lease agreement, for instance, the landlord, after the conclusion of the contract, has a claim against the tenant for payment of the rent, whereas the tenant has a counterclaim against the landlord for letting the apartment and keeping it this way; after a car accident, the one who got hurt has a claim for damages against the one who culpably caused the accident; etc.

In this book on the law of obligations, there is again a General Part in the beginning. Since all these obligations do have something in common—for instance, how, when, and where to perform; how to calculate damages in regard to a duty to pay for damages; under which circumstances is a debtor to be assumed to be in default, and under which a creditor, etc. The structure of the Schuldrecht, thus, is General Part of book 2, Special Part with subdivisions on contracts, *negotiorum gestio*, unjust enrichment, and torts.

2.2.3 Law of Property

2.2.3.1 The Value of Precision

With this information about the structure and contents of the BGB, we can now turn to the main subject of this presentation, the Sachenrecht. Its primary purpose (there are many additional rules and purposes, to be sure) is—in the words of the historic legislator "the regulation of the rights in rem;"[31] in other words: the determination of who is holder of a particular right and who is not.

It is this either-or contrast that makes this field of law both appealing and difficult. Unlike in the law of obligation where more or less all duties might become subject to some modifications—and be it due to the good faith clause in sec. 242 BGB[32]—the property law has to decide precisely whether person A is the owner of the house or

---

[31] Motive zu dem Entwurfe eines Bürgerlichen Gesetzbuches, vol. 3, Berlin 1888, p. 22 ff. From reading this passage, Seiler's impression is justified that the structure of this book was of little concern for the drafters, cf. Seiler (2007).

[32] In terms of the abovementioned mathematical precision of the BGB's structure, the positioning of this absolute central norm for the entire private law is a failure: it stands in the General Part of the 2nd book (law of obligations) and should, accordingly, be applicable just in the law of obligation. As a matter of fact, this norm has quickly been seen as essential for all books of the BGB (and even beyond); it should therefore be positioned in the 1st book (General Part of the BGB). The legislator had thought, however (and somewhat naïvely), that it would be enough when the general norm of "good behavior" under the law would be just to abstain from chicane. This rule is, in fact, in the

person X. It is hard if not impossible, for instance, to build a system of taxation on unclear ownership. Similarly, when a want-to-be borrower of a bank loan is asked to provide security, the bank is likely to be quite unhappy with an answer to the property question: it is possibly me who is the owner of this land. A similar situation is it in regard to the enforcement of a money judgment or to the debtor's insolvency. The creditors want satisfaction of their claims but are entitled to receive it just from the debtor's assets.[33] Whatever is owned by or encumbered with a right in rem for someone else, is either out of reach or subject to special restrictions.

Thus, a clear determination of rights is indispensable and key in any modern and functioning market economy.[34] When a strong economy such as the German economy is based on 70% external capital, it is evident that the collateral security law is quintessential for the system's stability. Accordingly, a precise attribution of rights in rem is of utmost importance. Under these circumstances, it is somewhat irritating that the scope of the Sachenrecht's regulations is limited to things, i.e., corporeal objects. This is true at least when one is inclined to see the private law codification of the BGB still as the focus point of all essential rules in daily life. As we have seen supra, some 20 years ago, in 2002, the German legislator saw the need to incorporate the law of general terms and conditions into this central code for private law since it was felt that this area is so important that those rules should not be separated into a special statute. Accordingly, we have to see now if the same holds true today with regard to the narrowness of the Sachenrecht and its restriction to corporeal things.

2.2.3.2 On Blurring Boundaries

The incremental digitalization of the modern economy and world in general carries with it the potential to correspondingly undermine the importance of things and, as a

---

General Part, sec. 226 BGB: "The exercise of a right is not permitted if its only possible purpose consists in causing damage to another."

[33] A modern appearance of the problem connected with this statement is when an insolvency debtor owns cryptocurrencies: are the creditors entitled to have them included into the estate? In 2018, an insolvency court of first instance in Moscow denied it on the ground that this kind of ownership is not regulated in the Russian Civil Law Code; this decision was repealed in the higher instance, cf. Paulus and Berg (2019, 2133, 2134); further decisions on this same issue: Ruscoe v Cryptopia Limited (in liquidation) [2020] NZHC 728 (High Court, Christchurch, Gendall J, 8 April 2020; B2C2 Ltd. v Quoine Pte Ltd. [2019] SGHC(I) 3, [2019] 4 SLR 17 [B2C2 (SGHC)]; Quoine Pte Ltd. v B2C2 Ltd. [2020] SGCA(I) 2 [B2C2 (SGCA)]; Vorotyntseva v Money-4 Ltd. [2018] EWHC 2596 (Ch); Shair.Com Global Digital Services Ltd. v Arnold (2018 BCSC 1512); AA v Persons Unknown [2019] EWHC 3556, [2020] 4 WLR 35. See, additionally the response of the German Federal Government to a so called brief enquiry at: https://dipbt.bundestag.de/doc/btd/19/211/192 1157.pdf.

[34] On this connection insightful Kozolchyk (2005) and idem (2007).

consequence, of the Sachenrecht.[35] This is not so much true with regard to real estate, which is likely to remain for quite some time into the future the prime collateral for any securitization purposes, but it is very likely true with regard to corporeal things. This is where automatization,[36] smart contracts, blockchain and the internet of things come into play.[37] For a better understanding, it might be helpful to begin with a rather simple clarification of some extralegal information:

Software comes along in two ways, as so-called firmware (or operating system or control software) and as application software. The former is in charge of making the device (computer, TV, car, robot, etc.) work at all; the latter, in contrast, is there to fulfil certain tasks or to solve them. For writing this text, for instance, I need an application software which transforms my klicks on given keys into sentences on the computer screen. Possible is this, however, only when and if prior to this writing the firmware has started my computer and keeps it running. The firmware, thus, is something like the brainstem—with the particularity, however, that it usually comes integrated with the device but that this is by no means necessary.

The "brainstem" and device are thus not dependent on working together in one and the same unit (computer, TV, cell phone, etc.)—they do their respective jobs also when their respective locations are different. While the device is in my office, the firmware might be saved on a tablet that I carry around—or it might be stored in a completely independent block chain. When now adding the so-called internet of things into our deliberations, it becomes visible that the firmware is the "master mind", which connects two (or more) things by transmitting messages between them—usually by what is (irritatingly[38]) called a "smart contract". It is thus possible for a landlord to give the tenant a chip card instead of a traditional key for the premise (not unlike what has become standard in hotels), which has the peculiarity that (a) the chip controls the regular inflow of the lease rent on the bank account and (b) the sanction mechanism that the chip card no longer opens the door when the rent has not been paid for a day (a month, or which time span ever).

Leaving aside that the use of this technical possibility might be illicit under the law, the example does nevertheless reveal the possibilities of the internet of things. Whenever in a contractual situation the nonowner has factual power over an asset of the other party—lease, rent, trust, etc.—the owner might obtain completely new control mechanisms. Two examples from real life prove this point: (a) Even though the landlord might act illegally when blocking the tenant from access to the apartment, it might be legal (at least under German law) to reduce the heating that can technically

---

[35] To be sure, this is all but a new discovery, cf. Hoeren (2002, 947 ff). who writes on p. 948: "Because the BGB corresponds in its concentration on things and rights with the needs of the commodity society, it is utterly out-of-date" (translation by me).

[36] On this, e.g., Zech (2016, 163 ff).

[37] On what follows, see already Paulus (2019, 119 ff).

[38] Irritating for lawyers insofar, as the transmission is neither smart—but just the execution of an order—nor that the result is necessarily (or just regularly) a contract; informative on this Paulus, D. and Matzke (2018, 431 ff) and Möslein (2019b, 81 ff).

be done by a cell phone from which place so ever on the globe. (b) A man who had rented a car in Berlin had not told that he was planning to drive to Poland; approximately 10 kilometers after having crossed the border, his car stopped and could not getten running again. His phone call in the rent office revealed that there was a respective automatism foreseen for the cars; he was allowed to turn around and to return to Germany in the direct way. It needed a switch in the rent office to get the car started again.[39]

For a lawyer, the lesson to be learned from these examples is that movable things such as heaters, cars, machines of what kind ever might increasingly become dependent in their functionality from a program that is located or stored somewhere else—or is portable and might, thus, be temporarily in the thing and at another time outside of it. Without going into the insolvable puzzle of what is more important (that is, a hen or egg question), so much is (or should be) clear that a traditional car with full functionality on board is more valuable (irrespective of its purchase price) than one which runs only as long as the controller of the firmware is willing and ready to have it run. When and if this controller is a third party, the owner of the car is likely to be confronted with some difficulties in convincing his bank that the car is a good collateral for security purposes. In other words, the digitalization of our world carries with it an enormous increase in the importance of the legalization of immaterial rights such as copyrights and patents. Which corresponds with a respective decrease of the importance of classical law of things (Sachenrecht).

This is similar to the principle of communicating vessels: the increase on one side corresponds with the decrease on the other. However, both sides are dependent on each other. They belong together to reveal their respective full capacities. Under such circumstances, it is to be assumed that it becomes increasingly questionable whether a particular legal issue is rather one of the thing as such (then one would have to look for a solution in the third book of the BGB) or one of intellectual property (then one has to search for which other statute is the appropriate one). In other words, it will become increasingly difficult to specify which face of the Janus head is the relevant one; the boundaries between the two areas are blurred. Technically speaking, the traditional centrality of the concept of property in the Sachenrecht as defined in sec. 903 BGB is bound to decrease if not to fade away. We will return to this particular observation below.

2.2.3.3 A General Part for the 3rd Book of the BGB

Building on what has been said supra with regard to a codification's role in general, and the BGB in particular, the preceding description of the Sachenrecht's loss of

---

[39] On this, see just Möslein (2019a, 313 ff) and Paulus and Matzke (2017, 769 ff).

significance should make all alarm bells ring.[40] The idea of comprehensive and all-encompassing coverage of the code is about to fade away to the degree that the described effects of digitalization extract more and more relevance from the 3rd Book of the BGB. In this area of law, the BGB is about to lose its aspiration for being the legislative center pillar.

It would be naïve to advocate for the total inclusion of the law of intellectual property in the BGB. Not only would the BGB swell from a voluminous code (of approximately 2400 sections) to a gigantic one; it would also need years and years of hard work to adapt and adjust the two thus far separate parts of the law and to align their respective logics. However, there is a much easier way to achieve a similar result—and that is the said General Part for the 3rd Book—possibly in addition to a few minor amendments in the (then) Special Part of this Book.

Regarding the latter, another codification technique could serve as guidance. It can be found, for instance, in the Civil Procedure Ordinance (ZPO), to be more precise: in its 8th Book, which regulates the law of enforcement. In the context of enforcing money judgments, sec. 869 ZPO addresses an enforcement against a plot of real estate—more precisely, by means of an enforced auction and/or receivership. It does so by just stating:

The enforced auction and receivership have been provided for in a separate statute.

That's all! The separate statute has 190 sections and is notorious for its complication, but it is taken as a given that the starting point for all deliberations is that this statute forms part of the Civil Procedure Ordinance. Accordingly, it would be that simple to bring the entire (or just parts of it) Immaterialgüterrecht under the roof of the BGB.

What is presently more important, however, is the interlocking of the Material- with the Immaterialgüterrecht by means of a General Part. This is far less revolutionary than it might appear on first sight, since the Civil Code of the Netherlands could serve as an example.[41] However, the primary question to be answered—even when one feels, in principle, sympathetic with the idea—is what should be regulated in this General Part? For this, it is necessary to reflect on the purpose of the 3rd Book of the BGB. As we have seen supra, today, the starting point is property as a legal tool to attribute rights over a thing (in rem) to a particular person. However, since the attribution of rights to the owner of a thing is likely to be something (entirely) different from the "owner" of data or a copyright, sec. 903 BGB cannot serve as a model any longer. Accordingly, for the attribution of rights, a sort of meta-level must be found. This would be the prime candidate for being addressed in the new General Part, at least as an elementary concept.

---

[40] It is telling that in a rather comprehensive collection of writings on the general theme: De Franceschi and Schulze (2019) not a single explicit contribution is devoted to the law of property. However, cf. at least Leyens (2019, 47 ff).

[41] Cf. Art. 3:1–3:31 of the Civil Code, available at: http://www.dutchcivillaw.com/civilcodeboo k033.htm. To be sure, although, this General Part does not undertake the task envisaged in this paper, namely, to establish commonalities of the law of material and immaterial goods.

Additionally, the BGB also addresses in its Sachenrecht the law of possession and transfer of rights and, even though just implicitly, the notorious principle of abstraction. These are the four candidates that will subsequently be presented as potential candidates for becoming included in such a General Part.

2.2.3.3.1 Possession

Seen from the present German law perspective, it seems to be misplaced to include possession in such General Part. Since under present private law, possession is confined to corporeal things as defined in the above cited sec. 90 BGB.[42] This is most likely a result of von Savigny's[43] early publication on the law of possession,[44] in which he tries to prove that possession is thinkable and reasonable just with regard to "physical", i.e., corporeal things. However, a closer look reveals that this is less mandatory than it sounds and feels in front of an authority such as von Savigny. A look alone to the Austrian legislative equivalent to the BGB, the Allgemeines Bürgerliches Gesetzbuch (ABGB = Common Civil Law Book) shows that it is very well thinkable to grant possession (and, thus, the respective possessory protection) to the holder of a right, cf. sec. 311 ABGB.[45]

What is of primary interest for most practical purposes is the possessory protection that is granted in the chapter on the law of possession, sec. 854 ff. BGB. Even though there might be a number of justifications why it might be reasonable to confine it to corporeal things, there are certainly cases in which the same protection would be desirable for the holder of a "mere" right. Therefore, rules should be included in the General Part.

To be sure and to reject all counterarguments that are too simple: What is proposed here is not meant as a plain statement of the kind: the possessor of any right has the following protection .... As a matter of fact, all sorts of modification can and shall be made when and if they are of a more general nature; and when and if such protection is not justified for a specific right, such exemption could also be included in the particular statute in which the right is specified. After all, this statute could be incorporated into the Specific Part of the Sachenrecht in the way as described before (cf. sec. 869 ZPO).

---

[42] See also Kuschel (2020, 98 ff). underpinning the need and possibility to expand the applicability of the present possession-rules.

[43] Before him, one finds explicit confinement to corporeal things also at Kant (1797, 27).

[44] Von Savigny (1803, 443, 448), idem (1814, 99 ff). This was contrasting to the previous width of the term in the preceding Naturrechtskodifikationen (codifications of natural law), cf. Rüfner (2003, T§ 90) mar. no. 5. On Savigny's critical attitude toward the natural law codifications just see Paulus, G. (1979, 16); on von Savigny's critique toward Kant, see Nörr (1994, 73 ff).

[45] On this, just see Kodek (2002, 105 ff). The idea of extending the possession rules on incorporeal rules is old, cf. Wacke (2002, 8) (fn. 19).

2.2.3.3.2 Principles of Abstraction and Separation

These two principles probably form the most specific characteristic of the German law of transactions, the details of which are highly complicated.[46] The fundamental idea behind them, however, is that it takes two steps to transfer title, right or empowerment and that both steps are to be seen, interpreted, and treated completely distinctly. The first step is the conclusion of a contract that gives rise to an obligation to perform. The second step is the fulfillment of that obligation. The primary consequence of this somewhat weird and complicated construct is that when and if it turns out after performance of a contract that the step one contract (the *causa*) was or is invalid, then the recipient of the performance is still justified to possess or own the title, right or empowerment—but is under the obligation to return it on the basis of unjust enrichment, sec. 812 ff. BGB. When and if, however, step one is valid but step two has a deficit, the obligation stemming from the step one contract has not yet been fulfilled so that a new attempt is to be made.

Again, the details of these principles are intricate and complex, but they are likely to be the single most important feature of German private law; however, they are nowhere explicitly addressed in the entire BGB. The usual reference to the rather isolated norm of sec. 137 BGB needs a lot of preacquired knowledge to understand that this is (supposedly) an expression of the two principles. It would thus be worthwhile to seriously consider whether a clearer determination of this fundamental pillar of the entire business and daily transactional law should be positioned in the 3rd Book's General Part.

This is all the more advisable as there is an intense debate going on in the field of the law of immaterial goods (Immaterialgüterrecht)—and here, in particular, in the copyright area—about whether or not the principle of abstraction is still to be applied there.[47] It is unfortunate that this debate is lead in isolation, as it were, without the somewhat parallel (and less dramatic) developments in the general delineation of the relationship between the 2nd and 3rd Book of the BGB (law of obligations and law of things).[48] For the inner coherence of the entire system—after all, that is what codifications are made for and what they are praised for—it would be appropriate to have these (and similar) discussions lead with feedback to the source and center pillar of private law, the BGB.

---

[46] Cf. just Stadler (1996), Flume (1965, § 12 III), and Felgentraeger (1927).

[47] Just see Wandtke (2019, 186 ff).

[48] On this, cf. Wiegand (1990, 112 ff).

2.2.3.3.3 Attribution of Rights

As we have seen supra, the primary purpose of the 3rd Book of the BGB is the determination of property and that is who is the owner and who is not. In other words, the core element of this book is the attribution of rights.[49] We have seen, furthermore, that such attribution is essential not only with regard to corporeal things but also to all other sorts of rights and empowerment. The question is who owns what, whose creditors are entitled to enforcement in which assets; it is here where we have to come back to the threat of the Sachenrecht losing its importance and centrality due to its outdated concentration on corporeal things.

To regain—or at least to increase—that importance, it might be a good idea to establish in the General Part also some basic guidelines on which requirements are needed to attribute an asset of which quality so ever (corporeal thing, idea, data, etc.) to a certain person.[50] To provide a level playing field for material as well as immaterial assets, it is inevitable to bid farewell to the abovementioned centrality of the traditional property concept as defined in sec. 903 BGB; as fitting as it might be for corporeal goods, it does not go with the immaterial goods.

Therefore, in the General Part, a higher level of abstraction is indispensable—as it is amply demonstrated today with regard to one of the most heated debates on a private law issue—namely, who owns data.[51] Nobody knows to whom they belong— and it is both an interesting and frightening intellectual game to consider what would happen with all those personal data when and if a company like Facebook would go bankrupt.[52]

As a first approach to the legislative attempt to provide some guidance for the concept of the attribution of rights, the following elements are submitted here as a kind of first approach: specificity, assignment, and marketability. They are distilled from experience—thereby following the usual method of how lawyers approach unknown territory: they survey a similar known territory and examine then whether at all and if so to what degree that survey can be carried forward to the unknown territory.[53] After all, the advantage of this approach is an embedding of the new results into the existing body of law and thereby guaranteeing continuity and prevention of dogmatic proliferation.[54]

---

[49] On the deeply rooted basis of this phenomenon cf. Kant (1797, 51 ff). in which the First Part of the Common Law Doctrine (Allgemeine Rechtslehre) is devoted to the discussion: On the Mode of Having Something External as His (Von der Art, etwas Äußeres als das Seine zu haben).

[50] Note that this approach is slightly different from earlier attempts to incorporate into the BGB a definition of legal objects (Rechtsobjekte); on this Rüfner (2003, 10 ff).

[51] The literature on this is endless on all levels: national, European, global. Just see, with many further references, Paulus and Berg (2019, 2133 ff), Adam (2020, 2063 ff), and Leyens (2019, 47 ff).

[52] This question is the background of the well-known battle of Mr. Schrems against Facebook; cf. CJEU, decision from 19 September 2016,—C-498/16; on this decision cf. Paulus (2016, 199 ff).

[53] On this method which can be found already with regard to the famous Twelve-Table legislation from 450 AD cf. Paulus (2002, 563, 567 ff).

[54] See also Akgun (2021).

2.2.3.3.3.1 Specificity A closer look at the law's mechanism for attributing rights reveals that it works very much with a kind of virtual reality. The example of a claim proves the point best: Nobody has ever seen a claim in the real world, and yet lawyers are—after thousands of years—working with it as if it were a thing in the real world.[55] The same is true with regard to the technical term of "ownership" (Eigentum), legal person, etc. When this car or real estate is owned by X or when Y is creditor of a claim against Z, the lawyer uses these labels as sufficient for attributing those rights.

However, let us go a step further and take a look at the evolution of the copyright. It was obviously always felt that a plagiarist breaches the rules of mores and decent behavior; the most prominent example is Martial's epigrams in which he accuses Fidentinus on having presented Martial's epigrams as if they were those of Fidentinus.[56] It was his (= Martial's) work, and this should have been made sufficiently clear. The failure to do so was sanctioned by those epigrams that were likely to lead to Fidentinus' social degradation but not to a legal consequence. The special relationship between the author and the work entered the legal sphere only many centuries later. It was not before the seventeenth and eighteenth centuries that this special relationship was flagged under the term "work", which then was a sufficient specification to grant legal protection.

The equivalent in patent law is the term "technical invention". It might be noted as an aside that a similar and somewhat parallel development can be observed in the work of the UNESCO: Its economically and politically enormous important, prestigious and lucrative badging as world cultural heritage has by now long gone beyond buildings and natural settings; today politicians (sic!) strive for getting such a badge for "the French cuisine" or "Pizza Napoletana". Here, too, it is all important to narrow down the respective phenomenon to an indicative term, which is indispensable for specificity.[57] This search can be observed presently with regard to data; which data shall be attributable? Shall data protection law with its term "personal data" be sufficient to transfer all data into my "property" that I create with my Facebook account, with my car, or which are made of me by the social screening mechanism? The time has not yet come to give a definite answer to these questions.

2.2.3.3.3.2 Assignment Once a position has achieved sufficient specificity for legal protection, the next question arises as to whom protected position is to be assigned. In the case of property, the BGB has a very explicit rule in the first sentence of sec. 903 BGB[58]:

> The owner of a thing may, to the extent that a statute or third-party rights do not conflict with this, deal with the thing at his discretion and exclude others from every influence.

---

[55] Interesting discussion on the specificity of claims in Wiegand (1979, 282, 288 ff). On what follows, cf. Paulus (2011, 151 ff).

[56] Cf. Martial; on this Schickert (2005, 69 ff).

[57] Cf. also Johansson (2009) and Vandevelde (1980, 325, 329, 333).

[58] Important on this: Zech (2019, 488 ff).

There is no equivalent regulation with regard to claims. In addition, yet it is recognized for literally millennia that it is an asset which, for instance, in case of the creditor's insolvency, forms part of the estate—which means that the creditors of the insolvent creditor are entitled to receiving satisfaction from this claim as they are with regard to corporeal goods of their debtor. Whereas legislative silence is thus harmless with regard to claims, enormous uncertainty does exist with regard to data and their assignment. Is it a correct legal interpretation when the CEO of a carmaker says with regard to the abovementioned data stemming from my driving with my car that they belong "us", i.e., the carmaker?

Additionally, an assignment can be made by contract. A teaching example is the expectancy right ("Anwartschaftsrecht"), which is usually[59] defined as the "coessential minus of property" ("wesensgleiches Minus gegenüber dem Eigentum"). What is meant with this slightly cryptic definition is primarily the result of the widespread use of retention of title on the German business life. The buyer who has received from the seller possession of the purchased good but not yet full title as owner shall be protected. Leaving aside that the division between the legal owner and the legal possessor ties nicely to a centuries-old discussion on the relationship between the *dominium directum* and *dominium utile*,[60] it was in the thirties of the last century that the purchaser was awarded a position which was then called "expectancy" (Anwartschaft) and which enjoyed a particular protection. In the course of the ongoing discussion on this legal institution, the mere "expectancy" grew increasingly into an "expectancy right" and is today irrefutably established—even far beyond the purchase under retention of title.

The example shows that an assignment can be done by means of a contract not unlike the assignment of rights under a license agreement when, for instance, the licensee is given an exclusive right of use.

2.2.3.3.3.3 Marketability Even though not all rights in rem would be affected, one could consider including a rule on marketability in the envisaged General Part. The ownership of completely invaluable goods is protected by the respective rules in a similar way as is an enormously valuable know-how of which the holder does not have the slightest intent to dispose of. Both cases share two commonalities. First, creditors have no access to those assets—be it that they are barred by the debtor protection rules in the law of enforcement, sec. 803 par. 2 ZPO, or be it that the common understanding is that a know-how becomes accessible for the creditors only when and if the holder has demonstrated in which way ever to make this asset part of a transaction.[61]

---

[59] Ever since BGH, decision from 24 June 1958—VIII ZR 205/57, BGHZ 28, 16, 21.

[60] Cf. Wiegand (1976, 118, 154) and see also Walter (2017, 863 ff).

[61] Cf. Uhlenbruck et al. (2019, § 35 mar. no. 253), Lwowski and Peters (2020, § 35 mar. no. 400). Cf. Additionally, Schmoll and Hölder (2004, 743 ff, 830 ff).

The second commonality is more interesting in the present context: The marketability of those goods depends on the will of the market participants. When a person wants to sell his old suit, he is likely not to find a buyer; when B does not want to sell her know-how, she cannot be forced to put it on the market. In contrast to this freedom to choose, sec. 400 BGB imposes the legislative prohibition to dispose of certain rights:

> A claim may not be assigned to the extent that it is not subject to an attachment.

In the context of the law of enforcement, in the aforementioned 8th Book of the Civil Procedure Code, there are rather impressive lists of assets that are exempted from attachment because of debtor protection. Accordingly, sec. 400 BGB parallels (like its procedural counterpart in sec. 851 par. 1 ZPO) transferability and enforce-ability. The sanction for ignoring the prohibition in sec. 400 BGB is the nullity of the respective contract.[62] This is true not only with the assignment of claims but also with the assignment of any other right (as opposed to the transfer of corporeal goods), sec. 413 BGB (on this, see below).

In other words, it is here the statute—rather than the market participants' will—that determines the marketability of assets. The justification for the legislative limita-tion in sec. 400 BGB is said to be the necessary protection of the creditor who wants to assign its claim.[63] If that is deemed to be a valid argument then it is hard to see why the same should not also be true with regard to corporeal things—and why in one case the private autonomous decision shall govern and on the other the statute.

2.2.3.3.3.4 Transfer of Rights The present regulation of transfers of rights in the BGB is somewhat miscarried. To be sure, this is not true for von Savigny's and his pupils' logic but for an approach that puts all assets into one category. For von Savigny, as we have seen supra, things could only be corporeal goods; accordingly, a claim was not a thing and had, therefore, no place in the Sachenrecht (law of things). As a consequence, transferring ownership over corporeal things is regulated in that 3rd Book of the BGB, sec. 873, 925, 929 ff., whereas transfer of a claim (assignment) is dealt with in the 2nd Book, the law of obligations.

The assignment is regulated in sec. 398 ff. BGB. Regarding the historical back-ground of this group of rules, it might be noted in passing that it was far from clear whether the BGB should have at all rules on assignment; after all, the ancient Romans never got fully to this instrument because they allowed transfer just as a novation[64]—arguing that the change of the creditor is essentially changing the rela-tionship.[65] What is particularly interesting with this group of rules is that the very last section, sec. 413 BGB, a rule is given about the transfer of "other rights":

---

[62] See Busche (2017, § 400 mar. no. 1).

[63] Cf. Busche (like previous footnote).

[64] On the evolution of this "novelty" cf. Wieacker (1974, 68 ff, 76 ff) and Wacke (2002, 15) (with the interesting observation of a contradiction between § 137 and § 399 BGB).

[65] This argumentation—long time almost ridiculed as being completely outdated and inappropriate for modern economic needs—was sort of reactivated in 2008 when private equity funds entered the German real estate sales market, i.a. through the secondary market, and protection was sought for

> The provisions relating to transfer of claims are applied with the necessary modifications to the transfer of other rights unless otherwise provided by law.

This means that the most fundamental and general rule on the transfer of "ownership" over an asset is placed in a context where pursuant to the German Civil Code system, nobody would even think of looking. Because of the abovementioned principle of abstraction (in combination with its twin, the principle of division), the transfer rules cannot be part of the law of obligations, as its subject is just the coming into existence of and further requirements for a causa. The fulfillment of an obligation is to be found in the law of things.

As we have seen that the restriction to corporeal things is castrating the eminent importance of property law, it would be a good idea to transplant at least sec. 413 BGB into the 3rd Book's General Part. It could run, for instance:

> A transfer of any right is done by a contract unless otherwise provided by law.

Thus, if there is no "otherwise" specification, a contract suffices for transferring the claim, the right to use a patent, or a website or what else. The specifications that exist thus far are—in the case of a movable corporeal good—a handover (as an act of publicity) or a registration in the land register in case of rights in a real estate. Any other register could do equally, at least theoretically.

3 Conclusion

What is submitted in this text is an attempt to give back to the Third Book of the German Civil Law Codification its central position. As such, it is also meant to form an opposite pole to a widely observable trend and tendency to contractualize private law relationships in general. Instead of clear-cut rules, preference is increasingly given to common understandings that are subject to interpretation and that are flexible. To be sure, there is not much to be said against this trend, but it must not be forgotten that there are situations in which there is an either-or indispensable rather than a maybe so-or maybe the other way. These situations are, for instance, secured transaction law, tax law, law of enforcement, insolvency law, etc. It would be inadequate for the BGB and its aspiration to have a more or less empty shell as its Third Book.

However, it needs to be emphasized that such a revaluation comes at a price for traditional understanding: given the social, economic and legal overall importance of the law of immaterial goods, it would be naïve to believe that an inclusion of that law into the existing Third Book could be done by preserving the model character that sec. 903 BGB thus far has as the paradigm of attribution of rights. It is more or less exactly this approach that served as a main reason for keeping the law of corporeal and that of immaterial things apart. It is for this reason that the present

---

the owner of houses burdened with a land charge (Grundschuld), cf. sec. 1192 par. 1a BGB; see, additionally, sec. 354a par. 2 HGB.

proposal submits the idea to get, as it were, a step higher in abstraction (meta-level) and to set up rules on attribution of rights that serve as guidance in both fields of law.

References

Adam S (2020) Daten als Rechtsobjekte. Neue Juristische Wochenschrift, 2063–2068

Akgun M (2021) A comparative analysis of the securities over moveable property and the analysis of the efficiency of the Cape Town convention on international interests in mobile equipment (Diss Berlin)

Apel J (1540) Isagoge per dialogum in IV libros Institutionum. Nurnberg

Becker C (1999) Die "res" bei Gaius – Vorstufe einer Systembildung in der Kodifikation? Heymann, Köln

Becker C (2015) Lehren aus dem Streit zwischen Savigny und Thibaut. In: Rosenau H, Hakeri H (eds) Kodifikation der Patientenrechte, Nomos, Baden-Baden

Besson S (2018) Justifications. In: Moeckli D, Shah S, Sivakumaran S (eds) International human rights law, 3rd edn. Oxford University Press, Oxford

Boisard MA (1980) On the probable influence of Islam on western public and international law. Int J Middle East Stud 11(4):429–450

Brüggemeier G (2005) Haftungsrecht: Struktur, Prinzipien, Schutzbereich. In: Enzyklopädie der Rechts- und Staatswissenschaft, Springer—Verlag, Heidelberg

Busch FB (1887) Archiv für Theorie und Praxis des Allgemeinen Deutschen Handels- und Wechselrechts. Berlin

Busche J (2017) § 400 mar. no. 1. In: Staudinger, Kommentar zum BGB, Otto Schmidt - De Gruyter, Berlin

Clapham A (2007) Human rights: a very short introduction. Oxford University Press, Oxford

De Franceschi A, Schulze R (eds) (2019) Digital revolution—new challenges for law. C. H. Beck, München

Ernst W (2004) Fritz Schulz (1879–1957). In Beatson J, Zimmermann R (eds) Jurists uprooted—German-speaking Emigré lawyers in twentieth-century Britain, Oxford University Press, Oxford

Esmarch K (1860) Grundsätze des Pandekten-Rechtes zum akademischen Gebrauche. Braumüller, Wien

Farhount I-A (2020) Gewinnherausgabe im Persönlichkeitsrecht: Persönlichkeitsschutz im Spannungsverhältnis zwischen geschriebenem und ungeschriebenem Recht. In: Berliner Juristische Universitätsschriften: Grundlagen des Rechts, Berliner Wissenschafts-Verlag, Berlin

Felgentraeger W (1927) Carl Friedrich v. Savignys Einfluß auf die Übereignungslehre. Göttingen

Flume W (1965) Das Rechtsgeschäft II. Springer, Berlin

Grossmann-Doerth H (1933) Selbstgeschaffenes Recht der Wirtschaft und staatliches Recht. Fr. Wagner, Freiburg

Hattenhauer H (1971) Zwischen Hierarchie und Demokratie – Eine Einführung in die geistesgeschichtlichen Grundlagen des geltenden deutschen Rechts. C.F. Müller, Karlsruhe

Hoeren T (2002) Zur Einführung: Informationsrecht. Juristische Schulung, 947–953

Hopt K (2004a) Prävention und Repression von Interessenkonflikten im Aktien-, Bank- und Berufsrecht. In: Festschrift für P. Doralt, Manz, Wien

Hopt K (2004b) Interessenwahrung und Interessenkonflikte im Aktien-, Bank und Berufsrecht – Zur Dogmatik des modernen Geschäftsbesorgungsrechts. Zeitschrift Für Unternehmens- Und Gesellschaftsrecht 33(1):1–52

Jatzow H (ed) (1888) Motive zu dem Entwurfe eines Bürgerlichen Gesetzbuches, vol 3. J. Guttentag, Berlin

Johansson E (2009) Property rights in investment securities and the doctrine of specificity. Springer, Heidelberg

Johow R (1880) Entwurf eines bürgerlichen Gesetzbuches für das Deutsche Reich. 3. Buch. Sachenrecht. Begründung. Erster Band, Reichsdurckerei, Berlin

Kant I (1797) Die Metaphysik der Sitten, Erster Teil, Metaphysische Anfangsgründe der Rechtslehre avaliable at: https://archive.org/details/in.ernet.dli.2015.358315/page/n81/mode/2up

Kodek G (2002) Die Besitzstörung. Manz, Wien

Kohler J (1900) Der Fall der Bismarckphotographie. Gewerblicher Rechtsschutz Und Urheberrecht 5:196–210

Kozolchyk B (2005) A roadmap to economic development through law: third parties and comparative legal structure. Arizona J Int Comp Law 23(1):1–35

Kozolchyk B (2007) Secured lending and its poverty reduction effect. Tex Int Law J 42:727–745

Kuschel L (2020) Digitale Eigenmacht. Archiv Für Die Civilistische Praxis 220:98–128

Lehmann M (2020) Lässt sich die Rechtsetzungsmethode der EU reformieren? Der Versuch eines europäischen Wirtschaftsgesetzbuchs. Referate im Rahmen der Vortragsreihe "Rechtsfragen der Europäischen Integration", Bonn

Leyens P (2019) Sachenrecht an Daten. In: Faust F, Schaefer H-B (eds) Zivilrechtliche und rechtsökonomische Probleme des Internet und der künstlichen Intelligenz, Mohr Siebeck, Tübingen

Lwowski J, Peters H-P (eds) (2020) Münchener Kommentar zur Insolvenzordnung. Beck, München

Manthe U (1997) Ein Sieg der Rhetorik über die Jurispriudenz. Der Erbschaftsstreit des Marius Curius – eine vertane Chance der Rechtspolitik. In Manthe U, Ungern-Sternberg JV (eds) Grosse Prozesse der Römischen Antike, Beck, München Martial Epigrams

Mazzoni A, Malaguti M (2019) Diritto del Commercio Internazionale – Fondamenti e prospettive. Giappichelli, Torino

Möslein F (2019a) Legal boundaries of blockchain technologies: smart contracts as self-help. In: De Franceschi A, Schulze R (eds), Digital revolution—new challenges for the law, Beck, München

Möslein F (2019b) Rechtsgeschäftslehre und smart contracts. In: Braegelmann T, Kaulartz M (eds) Rechtshandbuch smart contracts, Beck, München

Mugdan B (1899) Die gesammten Materialien zum Bürgerlichen Gesetzbuch für das Deutsche Reich, vol 3. Decker, Berlin

Nörr D (1994) Savignys philosophische Lehrjahre – ein Versuch. Klostermann, Frankfurt am Main

Paulus C (2002) Verbindungslinien zwischen Insolvenzrecht und Privatautonomie. In Prütting H, Vallender H (eds) Festschrift für Wilhelm Uhlenbruck, O. Schmidt, Köln

Paulus C (2005) Überlegungen zu einem modernen Konzerninsolvenzrecht. Zeitschrift Für Wirtschaftsrecht 44:1948–1956

Paulus C (2011) Die Handhabung von Wissen im Recht. In: Flick C (ed) Wem gehört das Wissen der Welt? Göttingen

Paulus C (2016) The erosion of a fundamental contract law principle—pacta sunt servanda vs. modern insolvency law. In: Unidroit (ed) Festschrift für Michael Joachim Bonell, vol I, Unidroit, Rome

Paulus C (2019) § 90 BGB, das Sachenrecht und die Digitalisierung der Welt. In Boele-Woelki K, Faust F, Jacobs M, Kuntz T, Röthel A, Thorn K, Weitemeyer B (eds) Festschrift für K. Schmidt zum 80. Geburtstag, vol II, Beck, München

Paulus C (2020) The everlasting power game between creditors and debtors in credit relationships. In: Vega Copo A, Martínez Munoz M (eds) El acreedor en el derecho concursal y preconcursal a la luz del Texto Refundido de la Ley Concursal, Thomson Reuters-Aranzadi, Madrid

Paulus C, Berg J (2019) Daten als insolvenzrechtlicher Vermögenswert des Schuldners. Zeitschrift Für Wirtschaftsrecht 45:2133–2143

Paulus C, Matzke R (2017) Digitalisierung Und Rechtsdurchsetzung. Computer Und Recht 33(12):769–778

Paulus D (2016) Die Grenzen zivilprozessualen Verbraucherschutzes. Zeitschrift Für Zivilprozess 21(2):199–234

Paulus D, Matzke R (2018) Smart contracts und das BGB. Zeitschrift Für Die Gesamte Privatrechtswissenschaft 4:431–467

Paulus G (1979) Die juristische Fragestellung des Naturrechts. Dunker & Humblot, Berlin

Puchta GF (1845) Pandekten, 3rd edn. Verlag von Johann Ambrosius Barth, Leipzig

Raiser L (1935) Allgemeine Geschäftsbedingungen. Hermann, Bad Homburg (reprinted 1961)

Riesenfeld S (1985) The impact of Roman law on the common law system. Lesotho Law J 1:267

Rüfner T (2003) § 90. In: Rückert J, Zimmermann R, Schmoeckel M (eds) Historisch-Kritischer Kommentar zum BGB. Mohr Siebeck, Tübingen

Schickert K (today: de la Durantaye K.) (2005) Der Schutz literarischer Urheberschaft im Rom der klassischen Antike. Mohr Siebeck, Tübingen

Schmoll A, Hölder N (2004) Patentlizenz- und Know-How-Verträge in der Insolvenz. GRUR, 9: 743–748, 10: 830–836

Seiler HH (2007) Einf zum Sachenrecht. In: Staudinger-Kommentar zum BGB, Neubearb, Berlin 2007

Sokolowski P (1902) Die Philosophie im Privatrecht. Max Niemeyer, Halle; available at: https:// archive.org/details/diephilosophiei00sokogoog/page/n6/mode/2up

Stadler A (1996) Gestaltungsschutz und Abstraktion. Tübingen

Stürner R (1996) Der hundertste Geburtstag des BGB – nationale Kodifikation im Greisenalter? JuristenZeitung 51(15/16):741–752

Tomuschat C (2014) Between idealism and realism, 3rd edn. Oxford University Press, Oxford

Uhlenbruck W, Hirte H (2019) Praß K (2019) Kommentar zur Insolvenzordnung. Vahlen, München

Vandevelde K (1980) The new property of the nineteenth century: the development of the modern concept of property. Buffalo Law Rev 29(2):325–367

Von Savigny F (1803) Das Recht des Besitzes: Eine civilistische Abhandlung. Heyer, Gießen

Von Savigny F (1814) Vom Beruf unserer Zeit für Gesetzgebung und Rechtswissenschaft. Mohr, Heidelberg

Von Savigny F (1840) System des heutigen Römischen Rechts. Vol 1; Veit, Berlin

Wacke A (2002) Das Studium des Rechtsobjekts: Ausbildung zum europäischen Juristen. In: Wacke A, Baldus C (eds) Juristische Vorlesungen und Prüfungen in Europa. Ein praktischer Versuch am Beispiel des Rechtsobjekts, Richard Boorberg Verlag, Stuttgart

Walter F (2017) Eigentumsökonomik – ein europäischen Rechtsvergleich: Eine Untersuchung des Eigentumsbegriffs des deutschen, englischen und sowjetischen Rechts. Zeitschrift Für Europäisches Privatrecht 4:863–889

Wandtke A (2019) Urheberrecht. De Gruyter, Berlin

Wieacker F (1959) Humanismus und Rezeption – Eine Studie zu Johannes Apels Dialogus oder Isagoge per dialogum in IV libros Institutionum. In: Id., Gründer und Bewahrer: Rechtslehrer der neueren deutschen Privatrechtsgeschichte, Vandenhoeck & Ruprecht, Göttingen

Wieacker F (1967) Privatrechtsgeschichte der Neuzeit, 2nd edn. Vandenhoeck & Ruprecht, Göttingen

Wieacker F (1974) Pandektenwissenschaft und Industrielle Revolution. In: Wieacker F (ed) Industriegesellschaft und Privatrechtsordnung, Klostermann, Frankfurt am Main

Wiegand W (1976) Zur theoretischen Begründung der Bodenmobilisierung in der Rechtswissenschaft: Der abstrakte Eigentumsbegriff. In: Coing H, Wilhelm W(eds), Wissenschaft und Kodifikation des Privatrechts im 19. Jahrhundert, vol III, Klostermann, Frankfurt am Main

Wiegand W (1979) Kreditischerung und Rechtsdogmatik. In: Berner Festgabe zum Schweizerischen Juristentag, Verlag Paul Haupt, Bern, Stuttgart

Wiegand W (1990) Die Entwicklung des Sachenrechts im Verhältnis zum Schuldrecht. Archiv Für Die Civilistische Praxis 190:112–138

Windscheid B (1862) Lehrbuch des Pandektenrechts, vol 1. Buddeus, Düsseldorf

Wolf E (1944) Große Rechtsdenker der deutschen Geistesgeschichte. 2nd edn. J. C. B. Mohr (Paul Siebeck), Tübingen

Zech H (2016) Zivilrechtliche Verantwortung für den Einsatz von Robotern. In: Gless S, Seelmann K (eds) Intelligente agenten und das Recht, Nomos, Baden-Baden

Zech H (2019) Die "Befugnisse des Eigentümers" nach § 903 Satz 1 BGB – Rivalität als Kriterium für eine Begrenzung der Eigentumswirkungen. Archiv Für Die Civilistische Praxis 219:488–592

Zimmermann R (2007) Römisches Recht und europäische Kultur. Juristen Zeitung 62(1):1–12

Christoph G. Paulus is Professor emeritus of Civil law at Humboldt-Universität, Berlin, Juristische Fakultät LL.M. (Berkeley); from 2009–2016: Director of the Institute for Interdisciplinary Restructuring e.V. (iir); 2008–2010: Dean of the Law Faculty of the Humboldt University Berlin; 2004–2008: Dean for international programs at the Faculty of Law of the Humboldt University, Berlin; 1994–2019: Full Professor of Civil Law, Civil Procedure and Insolvency Law and Roman Law at the Faculty of Law of the Humboldt University Berlin; 1992–1994: Associate Professor of Civil Law and Civil Procedure Law at the University of Augsburg.

Second Wave of the PostSocialist Civil Law Recodification in Russia

Andrej A. Pavlov, Natalia J. Rasskazova, and Anton D. Rudokvas

Abstract After the collapse of the USSR, the first recodification of Russian civil law occurred. The new Civil Code was adopted in parts up to 2006. However, soon after its adoption, the second recodification was launched, which considered the experience of the formation of a market economy in postSoviet Russia and the development of foreign and supranational law. Since 2012, large-scale changes have been made to the Civil Code of the Russian Federation to modernize it. Initially, an attempt was made to adopt the draft changes in their entirety, but it was met with fierce resistance from the legal community. As a result, the process of making changes to the Civil Code is still incomplete. In particular, the changes affected the law of obligations and contract law. However, important innovations took place in inheritance law and in a number of other sections of civil law. The proposed comprehensive reform of property law has thus far failed due to the obvious imperfection of the draft amendments, which, however, does not exclude that the legislator will return to this issue in the future. This article reviews those changes that have already happened and the reasons for their appearance in Russian law.

A. A. Pavlov · N. J. Rasskazova · A. D. Rudokvas (✉)
Law Faculty, St. Petersburg State University, St. Petersburg, Russia
e-mail: a.rudokvas@spbu.ru

A. A. Pavlov
e-mail: a.a.pavlov@spbu.ru

N. J. Rasskazova
e-mail: n.rasskazova@spbu.ru

© The Author(s), under exclusive license to Springer Nature Singapore Pte Ltd. 2023   273
M. Graziadei and L. Zhang (eds.), *The Making of the Civil Codes*,
Ius Gentium: Comparative Perspectives on Law and Justice 104,
https://doi.org/10.1007/978-981-19-4993-7_15

1 The Idea of the Second Civil Law Recodification[1]

The Russian Civil Code, which replaced the Soviet-era civil code of the RSFSR, was adopted shortly after the collapse of the USSR and the creation of the Russian Federation. At this time, a Research Center for Private Law was organized under the auspices of the President of Russia. In this Center, a large team of leading Russian civil law experts joined forces to develop a new Civil Code for the new Russia. Recodification was aimed at creating the necessary conditions for the development of a free market economy. The urgent and immediate need for a new civil law to regulate the relations of the market economy, which replaced the planned economy of the Soviet period, prompted the drafters of the new bill and the country's political leadership to adopt the Code in Parliament in parts, as each subsequent part of the draft is prepared. Therefore, the Civil Code of the Russian Federation (hereinafter CC RF) was adopted in separate parts from 1994 to 2006. This was the transition from Soviet civil law to the new civil law of the market economy.

However, almost simultaneously with the adoption of the final part of the CC RF, D. A. Medvedev, who at that time held the position of first Deputy Prime Minister of the Russian government, drew attention to the unsatisfactory quality of this Code, which was explained by its hasty development in a short time at the initial stage of the formation of a market economy in postSoviet Russia. For this reason, shortly after being elected President of the Russian Federation, Dmitry Medvedev initiated the second recodification of Russian civil law after the collapse of the USSR. This process was launched by Decree of the President of the Russian Federation No. 1108 of July 18, 2008. According to the Decree, the research Center for Private Law and the Council for the codification and development of civil law legislation under the President of the Russian Federation were assigned to develop a Concept for the development of civil law legislation. The mentioned concept was supposed to be the theoretical basis for developing the necessary CC RF changes.

The Council for the Codification and Development of Civil Law Legislation (here-after—Council for the Codification) was established by Presidential Decree No. 1338 of October 5, 1999. It is an advisory body that was created at the initiative of the heads of the higher federal courts to conduct legal expertise of draft laws that fall within its competence. At the time of its creation, the Council had 38 members. Approximately one-third of this number were judges and court presidents, the other third of the Council was formed from representatives of legal scholarship, and the rest of its members were government officials.

Decree No. 1267 of the President of the Russian Federation of 29 October 2003 prescribed that all draft federal laws aimed at regulating civil law relations developed by federal executive bodies must pass a preliminary examination by the Council for Codification before being considered by the federal government. To develop the mentioned Concept for the Development of Civil Law Legislation, the Council for

---

[1] This section of the chapter is based on the introductory part of a published article, with citation to the sources and further information: Rudokvas (2012, pp. 508ff.). See also: Rudokvas (2013, pp. 153–169).

Codification created 7 working groups to prepare separate concepts for the development of various subsectors of civil law. It was decided to prepare separate concepts for such sections of civil law as its General provisions; corporate law; property law; law of obligations; securities and financial markets law; private international law; and intellectual property. The working groups were attended not only by members of the codification Council but also by some other government officials, academics and practitioners. Preliminary versions of individual concepts have been subject to intense discussion in universities and professional associations of lawyers, having been published in legal journals in early 2009. As a result, the authors of the concepts received more than 500 critical comments. They consulted with experts from Germany and the Netherlands to resolve some of the complex issues.

As a result of the subsequent discussion of individual concepts, the Council for Codification formulated the text of the consolidated Concept for the Development of Civil Law Legislation. It was based on this document that the same Council for Codification prepared a draft of CC RF changes.

However, the draft CC RF changes proposed by the Council for Codification unexpectedly faced a wave of strong criticism. The General provisions of the draft and the provisions of the section on the law of obligations were most criticized. A strong skepticism about the draft was expressed by the Association of corporate lawyers, which existed under the umbrella of business associations and the Ministry of Economic Development of the Russian Federation and the Working Group on Creation of International Financial Centre in the Russian Federation, which was established in 2010 as attached to the Council on Financial Market Development under the President of the Russian Federation. They argued that Russia was losing out on the global competition of jurisdictions, both because of its inflexible and restrictive legislation and because of the imperfect judicial system. According to these critics, the draft law proposed for discussion was not able to change almost anything in this regard, being developed on the basis of traditional approaches to legal regulation in Russian legislation.

Data from a special sociological survey conducted among corporate lawyers of large Russian companies at the initiative of one of Russia's leading law firms, Egorov Puginsky Afanasiev & partners, showed that 62% of them prefer to hear their cases in foreign courts rather than in the Russian judicial system. In response to a question about existing obstacles to the application of Russian legislation, corporate lawyers listed the lack of adequate legal protection mechanisms for investors and large businesses in CC RF (10% of respondents), the legal inability to hide the beneficiary under Russian law (14% of respondents), the commitment of foreign counterparties to their own domestic legislation (14% of respondents), and unfriendly tax regulation in Russia (48% of respondents), confidence in the ability of foreign courts to ensure a fair trial and, conversely, lack of confidence in the Russian judicial system (62% of respondents), and inflexibility of Russian legislation that makes it inconvenient for doing business (67% of respondents). The skeptical attitude of corporate lawyers toward Russian law has led to the fact that, for example, of the total number of transactions, legal accompaniment to which was performed by another well-known Russian law firm, "Andrey Gorodissky and Partners", from 2004 to 2012 (for a total of 3.61 billion dollars) only 6% of transactions (in the amount of $240 million) were concluded under Russian law. As a rule, Russian corporate lawyers preferred to choose common law as the applicable law for transactions and British jurisdiction as the court competent to resolve disputes arising from these transactions.

In particular, critics of the bill insisted that it was flawed and ineffective from the point of view of economic analysis of law. Many of the new rules proposed in this draft were considered by corporate lawyers as additional useless obstacles to the functioning of the free market. On the other hand, they were active supporters of legal transplants from English and American common law, insisting on the possibility and desirability of such borrowings. For these reasons, the opponents of the bill under discussion have created several alternative drafts of their own to recodify certain sectors of civil law legislation.

In response to the Council's for Codification arguments about the impossibility of successful borrowing from common law to a system that belongs to the civil law tradition, their opponents turned to the experience of similar recent borrowings in Germany, the Netherlands, Italy and France. To justify this position, some leading European law firms, such as De Brauw Blackstone Westbroek N.V., Bredin Prat, Hengeler Müller & Bonelli Erede Pappalardo, commissioned by the Russian Non-Profit Organization for the Advancement of Corporate Law, prepared for March 16, 2012 a detailed comparative legal study entitled *Memorandum on Certain Aspects of Civil Law and Corporate Law using the Example of Dutch, French, German, and Italian Law.*

The appearance of such a strong and influential opposition to the bill proposed by the Council for Codification forced the Russian government to mediate between the conflicting parties. The Federal Ministry of Justice has engaged in reconciling competing groups and harmonizing their drafts. As a result, the parties to the conflict were encouraged to compromise by mutual concessions and the development of a compromise bill by the opponents, which was submitted to the Parliament in 2012 and successfully passed the first reading. Meanwhile, the other part of this bill, concerning the Law of Property, also caused a heated discussion, since it involved a radical reform of the existing system of real rights. In addition, this part contained many logical contradictions. Therefore, instead of the second reading of the bill as a whole, the State Duma—the lower house of the Russian Parliament - decided to adopt the bill in parts, as it was done 20 years ago with parts of the current Civil Code.

It is worth mentioning that at the very beginning of the legislative reform, its initiators also expected the bill to be adopted in parts. They hoped to see the country's Parliament approve the upgraded first part of the CC RF as early as 2010 and expected to see other parts of the updated Code made public later. The subsequent conflicts of the lobby groups had changed the deadlines, but probably no one could predict such a radical delay. At the final stage of the presidency of Dmitry Medvedev, 1 September 2012 was deemed the date of enactment of the updated Civil Code, and then—1 January 2013. Afterwards, the spring of 2013 became a new reference point, but the draft did not meet this deadline because in those times, some deputes of the Russian Parliament were foretelling the enactment of some parts of the draft only a year or two later. Therefore, in autumn 2012, the representatives of the Council for Codification were strongly resisting the enactment of the draft piecemeal because they were afraid that the opponents would benefit from such a structure of the legislative process by lobbying through their ideas. At the end of the day, it happened so that it had been decided to enact the draft piecemeal, and the process of the civil law recodification in Russia is not over until now, even if the major part of the proposed modifications are already implemented in the updated CC RF.

2 Features of the Second Recodification of Russian Civil Law

2.1 Principle of Good Faith

Until 2013, the CC RF had a rule prohibiting abuse of rights (art. 10 CC RF), but there was no reference to good faith as a general principle of civil law in the Code. The sanction established for abuse of the right (refusal to protect the right) did not allow the courts to confidently apply such a measure as compensation for damages caused by abuse. It often happened that to protect a party acting in good faith from abuse of rights by the other party, the Russian courts were forced to refer to article 1 CC RF "Basic principles of civil legislation"; however, in those times, the principle of good faith was not mentioned in it *expressis verbis*.

From 2013 article 1 CC RF includes two fundamental provisions: "When establishing, exercising and protecting civil rights and performing civil duties, participants in civil law relations must act in good faith. No one has the right to take advantage of their illegal or unfair behavior." Thus, unfair behavior is considered a violation of the law. In Russian practice, the requirement of good faith is understood in accordance with the classical approach as the requirement of *ut inter bonos agere oportet*.[2]

However, immediately after the appearance of the principle of good faith in the civil code, the jurisprudence of courts has tended to reduce the formulation of the *ratio decidendi* of its decisions to the reference to article 1 CC RF, instead of having to refer to specific rules to be applied to the disputed relations. Despite the fact that these rules provided a person acting in good faith with full protection from unfair behavior of the counterparty, the judges, relying on the fundamental nature of the general

---

[2] See: item 1 of the Ordinance of the Plenum of the Supreme Court of the Russian Federation dated 23 June 2015 No. 25 "On the Application by Courts of Certain Provisions of Section I of Part One of the Civil Code of the Russian Federation" (in Russian). The Ordinance of the Plenum of the Supreme Court is a peculiar source of law in Russia and other postSoviet countries. In the document, the Supreme Court provides rules formulated in the format of abstracts akin to statutory provisions. These rules, designed to fill gaps in the statutory law, are binding on the lower courts—Puder and Rudokvas (2019, p. 1098. n. 195).

prohibition, exempted themselves from a detailed analysis of the relationship. This unhealthy practice has gradually disappeared, and today references to violations of the principle of good faith are used only to fill the gap, that is, when it is impossible to protect the rights of a person on the basis of special rules.

2.2 Subject of Civil Law Regulation

In article 2 CC RF, an indication appeared that the subject of civil law regulation includes corporate relations, that is, relations related to participation in corporate organizations or their management. Strictly speaking, these relations were even previously considered civil law relations, and the legislator only brought the text of the statutory provisions in line with the realities of civil law turnover. There are a lot of amendments related to corporate relations and included in the CC RF during the last recodification, but even their general overview would require a separate voluminous text.

2.3 Decisions of Meetings

During the reform, a new Chapter 9.1 "Decisions of meetings" was added to the CC RF. It regulates relations regarding decision-making by groups of individuals in cases where the law links civil law consequences with such decisions, which are binding not only for those who participated in the meeting but also for those who had the right to participate in them. This group of persons is named in statutory provisions "civil law community" although it is not recognized as a legal entity (art. 181.1 CC RF). These include meetings of corporation members, creditors in bankruptcy, and so on.

The decision of the meeting, as well as the transaction, is an expression of will. However, unlike a deal, it binds not only those members of the civil law community who attended the meeting but also those who did not participate and might have voted against such a decision. The rights of those who did not participate in the meeting are protected by the rules on the avoidability and nullity of meetings (art. 181.3 CC RF). Like transactions, a decision that does not comply with the provisions of statutory law is generally avoidable unless such provision explicitly states that the decision is null and void. Thus, the decision of the meeting taken in the absence of a quorum is null and void.

2.4   Limitation of Actions

The recodification resulted inter alia in that now two variants for calculating the general limitation period which are distinguished but coexist emerged in the CC RF—a subjective variant of three years and an objective one of ten years (art. 196 CC RF). Pursuant to the subjective mode of calculation, the limitation period starts when a claimant learnt or should have learnt of the violation of its right and of the identity of the person against whom to file to have the violated right protected (item 1 art. 196 CC RF). The objective mode installs a cap in that, independent of circumstances, the limitation period expires ten years from the day when the violation of the right took place, unless otherwise is provided by statutory law (item 2 art. 196).

2.5   Real Rights

The attempt to radically reform the Property Law in the CC RF during the second wave of recodification failed primarily because of the imperfection of the proposed draft as it related to possession and possessory remedies[3] and because of the negative attitude of the majority of lawyers toward this idea.

2.6   Obligations and Contracts

The fundamental principle of regulating contractual relations is the principle of freedom of contract. The rules devoted to it (clause 1 of art. 1, art. 421 CC RF) themselves did not undergo significant changes during the 2012–2015 reform. However, a fundamental rethinking of the role and significance of this principle occurred at the level of judicial practice. It is the principle of freedom of contract that has allowed higher courts to change their attitude to the assessment of the imperativeness or dispositivity of the rules of contract law.

Previously, the opinion prevailed in judicial practice that contractual derogation from legislative provisions is possible only in cases explicitly specified in the law. The new approach is based on the need for a teleological interpretation of the law rather than a literal one. Changing the rules of contract law by agreement of the parties is now allowed as a general rule. Exceptions are cases where the imperative character of legislative provisions is due to the purpose of protecting public interests, protecting the interests of third parties or a weak party (for example, a consumer). Additionally, as a restriction on freedom of contract, there is a gross violation of the

---

[3] See about it, e.g., Rudokvas (2016, pp. 5–16; 2017, pp. 51ff.) .

balance of interests of the parties and a contradiction to the essence of legislative regulation.[4]

The reform of civil law legislation helped to codify the rules on framework contracts (art. 429.1 CC RF), the option for the conclusion of the contract (article 429.2 CC RF), subscriber contract (article 429.4 CC RF). Previously, these structures were used by participants in civil law relations but did not have a clear regulatory framework.

In the course of the reform, many institutions of contract law known to foreign national legal systems or international private law incorporations were reflected in the CC RF. Thus, article 434.1 of the CC RF regulates the issue of negotiations and the related issue of information duties of participants in the negotiation process. It also establishes rules aimed at combating dishonest or unfair behavior in negotiations and measures of responsibility for such behavior.

The new version of clauses 2 and 3 of article 428 of the CC RF protects the interests of a party that joins the standard conditions developed by the other party in a situation where a party with "low" negotiation capabilities (first of all, the consumer) acts as a party to the agreement. These rules have a significant similarity to the phenomenon of "unfair conditions" (articles II.-9:401–II.-9: 410 DCFR, §§ 307–309 of the BGB). Art. 431.2 of the CC RF introduces into the Russian legal order the institution of assurances about circumstances and responsibility for false assurances (a remote analog of these Russian norms are warranties and representations, well-known to common law). Art. 406.1 of the CC RF is devoted to the institute of compensation for losses, the prototype of which was such a common law institution as indemnity.

The norms on the interpretation of contracts (art. 431 of the CC RF) have not changed during the civil law reform, but they are actively developing. Thus, judicial practice introduces such methods of interpretation as *"contra proferentem"* (against the party who proposed the condition), "the principle of absurdity" (according to which the interpretation of the contract should not lead to such an understanding of the contract condition that the parties obviously could not have had in mind), and

---

[4] See: items 1–4 of the Ordinance of the Plenum of the Supreme Court of State Arbitration the Russian Federation from 14 March 2014 N 16 "On freedom of contract and its limits" (in Russian, hereinafter—Ordinance No. 16). The courts known in Russia as "arbitration courts" are in reality state courts, which deal with commercial litigation. The name is confusing a foreign reader as Russia also has nonstate courts of arbitration in the proper sense of the word "arbitration". However, the tradition of calling the state commercial courts "arbitration courts" is ascending to Soviet times and persists. Therefore, for avoiding confusions, these courts are referred to in this article as "state arbitration courts", which should be distinguished from the courts of general jurisdiction. From 1992 to 2014, the Supreme State Arbitration Court of the Russian Federation was the highest state arbitration court. The highest court of general jurisdiction was the Supreme Court of the Russian Federation. In 2014 the Supreme State Arbitration Court was abolished. After that the Supreme Court of the Russian Federation became the supreme court for both the courts of general jurisdiction and the state arbitration courts. See also on the new trends of the freedom of contract in Russian law: Karapetov and Shirvindt (2020, pp. 531–560).

"*favor contractus*" (priority of the interpretation option in which the contract remains in force).[5]

General provisions on obligations and their performance are concentrated in Chapters 21–22 of the CC RF. Most of these regulations are in line with current international trends in civil law regulation (sect. 1 of Chapter 6 of the UNIDROIT Principles of international commercial contracts 2016, Chapter 2 of book III of the DCFR). In this regard, these rules were only slightly adjusted during the 2012–2015 reform.

Thus, clause 3, article 307 of the civil code, established the requirement of a conscientious conduct of the parties obligations and mutual rendering by the parties of obligations necessary assistance to each other, as well as providing each other the necessary information. These requirements are an emanation of the General principle of good faith as one of the main provisions of Russian civil law legislation. In view of the universal nature of the principle of good faith, it was not necessary to duplicate it in the section on the law of obligations. However, a direct indication of the operation of this principle not only within the framework of the performance of the obligation but also in the process of its establishment, as well as after the termination of the obligation, obviously has a useful effect for regulating civil law turnover.

The new edition of the CC RF received a detailed regulation of the rules about alternative obligations (articles 308.1, 320 CC RF), i.e., obligations for which the debtor is obliged to perform one of several actions, and the choice between them belongs to the debtor, unless under the law or the agreement of the parties the right of choice is granted to the creditor or to a third party. This regulation is largely inspired by the provisions of article III.-2:105 DCFR. However, unlike these international standards that differentiate the procedure for granting the opposite party the right to choose depending on the nature of the delay of the authorized person (significant or insignificant), Russian legislation does not know such differentiation, assuming that the opposite party is given the right to choose, regardless of the nature of the delay.

Along with this, the rules on facultative obligations were also codified (articles 308.2, 320.1 CC RF). The latter are characterized by the fact that, providing for a single subject of the obligation, they establish the right of the debtor to replace it with another surrogate for the performance of the obligation, agreed upon in advance by the parties.

The idea of the provisions of art. 312 of the CC RF is to distribute the risk of performing an obligation to an improper person. Since, as a general rule, this risk is borne by the debtor, the rule of law should provide for means to minimize this risk for the latter. One of these means is the right of the debtor to suspend the performance and require a representative of the creditor to notarize his authority to accept it, as stipulated in clause 2 of article 312 CC RF. Taking into account the public register of notarial powers of attorney that exists in the Russian Federation, this rule largely removes the risk of providing a false power of attorney from the debtor.

---

[5] See: item 11 of the Ordinance No. 16, items 43–46 of the Plenum of the Supreme Court of the Russian Federation dated 25 December 2018 No. 49 "On Some Issues of Application of the General Provisions of the Civil Code of the Russian Federation on the Conclusion and Interpretation of a Contract" (in Russian).

Before the reform 2012–2015, provisions for the performance of an obligation by a third party without the consent of the debtor (item 2 of art. 313 CC RF) restricted the rights of a third party only when there was danger of loss of the right to his property by the debtor as a result of the creditor's foreclosure on the debtor's property. However, it is obvious that third parties may have other legitimate interests in the performance of obligations for the debtor. In this regard, the Concept of civil law reform proposed, following the example of art. III.-2: 107 (2b) DCFR, to allow a third party to perform the obligation for the debtor, in any case where such third party has a legitimate interest in the performance of the obligation, and the debtor is late in performing the obligation.

Unfortunately, this idea was not fully reflected in the text of the Code. The new version of clause 2 of article 312 of the CC RF establishes the right of a third party to perform any overdue monetary debt for the debtor, without indicating the need for such a third party to have a legitimate interest in such performance. A literal reading of the law can provoke unfair intervention by third parties. Therefore, the task of interpreting the text of the statutory provisions in accordance with the original goals of the legislator is assigned to the jurisprudence of courts.

The new version of clause 1 of art. 314 and art. 327.1 of the CC RF allows the parties of contracts to set the term of performance of obligations depending on the moment of counterparty's performance of obligations or the occurrence of other circumstances stipulated in the contract. This feature is widely used in contractual relations, primarily in the construction contract, being embodied in the contractual condition "I will pay when I get paid".

For example, the parties to a subcontract often postpone the payment period for work performed by the subcontractor until the general contractor receives payment from the main customer. Judicial practice sees this condition as a temporary imposition on the creditor (subcontractor) of the risks of nonreceipt of performance by the debtor from a third party (the main customer). If no such performance is received from a third party within a reasonable time, the creditor can effectively demand performance from the debtor. The question of the permissibility of the use of the terms "pay when I get paid" in the other contract designs (for example, the contract of the commission, which sets the time of payment of remuneration to the commissioner, depending on the receive performance from a third person with whom the commission agent on the instructions of the consignor has concluded the contract), as well as the use of contractual conditions "will pay for it if I get paid" in the Russian doctrine and practice is not completely clarified.[6]

The art. 319.1 CC RF, as a result of the recodification, imposes a general rule on how to determine whether the obligation is considered to be performed if the performance followed when the parties had several homogeneous unperformed obligations. The established sequence of criteria for attributing performance is as follows:

---

[6] See: item 3 of the Information letter of the Presidium of the Supreme Arbitration Court of the Russian Federation dated 17 November 2004 No. 85 "Review of the Commission's Contract Dispute Resolution Practice"; Ruling of the Supreme Court of the Russian Federation dated 27 October 2020 No. 305-ЭС20-10,019; Karapetov (2017, pp. 189–191).

an obligation defined by the parties; an obligation specified by the debtor during performance or without delay after performance; an obligation that has reached its due date; an obligation that does not have security; an obligation that is due earlier, or for obligations that do not have a term-an obligation that arose earlier; *pro rata*. Unfortunately, when establishing this sequence, the Russian legislator did not use as a model the requirements of paragraph 2 of article 6.1.12 of the UNIDROIT Principles 2016, article III.-2:110 DCFR, as a result of which the Russian rules on this issue look rather arbitrary and do not have internal logic.

If the above rules ration the allocation of the exercised performance (usually payment) to a particular obligation between the parties, the art. 319 CC RF provides special rules for allocating payments to the relevant part of the monetary obligation. Following the majority of modern codifications and international acts of unification of private law (clause 1 of article 6.1.12 of the UNIDROIT Principles 2016, article III.-2: 110 (5) DCFR), Russian legislation establishes the following order of repayment of claims: first of all, the lender's costs for obtaining performance, second—interest, and then—the amount of the principal debt. The peculiarity of Russian regulation is that the interest payable earlier than the principal amount is understood exclusively as regulatory interest (interest as a fee) and that judicial practice allows for the possibility of changing the order of repayment by agreement of the parties only for those claims that are explicitly named in article 319 CC Effort example, the agreement on repayment of the principal amount before the "regulatory" interest is not questioned. However, the courts are extremely negative about the agreements of the parties that establish the repayment of "protective" interest (as well as penalties), in priority in relation to the amount of the principal debt, recognizing such agreements as invalid.[7]

The rules of the CC RF on joint and several obligations have not changed in the course of the recodification. Therefore, the urgent problems of this institution are solved by the jurisprudence of courts. Thus, art. 324 CC RF on passive solidary plurality does not provide for the protection of the interests of solidary debtors in a situation where the debtor who performed the joint obligation did not use the available objections against the creditor. For these purposes, the Supreme Court of the Russian Federation, following the example of article 11.1.12 of the UNIDROIT Principles 2016, recognized that a debtor who is sued by another joint debtor who had performed a joint and several obligation has the right to use against such a claim all the objections that he had against the creditor.[8] Further development of this idea will allow maintaining the status quo of such a codebtor even in a situation where

---

[7] See: item 49 of the Ordinance of the Plenum of the Supreme Court of the Russian Federation dated 24 March 2016 No. 7 "On the Application by Courts of Certain Provisions of the Civil code of the Russian Federation on Liability for Breach of Obligations" (in Russian, hereinafter—Ordinance No. 7); item 37 of the Ordinance of the Plenum of the Supreme Court of the Russian Federation dated 22 November 2016 No. 54 "On Some Issues of Application of the General Provisions of the Civil Code of the Russian Federation on Obligations and Their Performance". See criticism of this approach: Karapetov (2017, pp. 149–150).

[8] See: Ruling of the Supreme Court of the Russian Federation dated 11 February 2020 No. 78-КГ19-6.

the corresponding personal objections of other codebtors were not available to the performing debtor.

Provisions on the creditor's remedies in case of default by the debtor are located in different chapters of sect. III of the CC RF.

An important place among these provisions is occupied by article 308.3 CC RF, which also appeared as a result of recodification. Clause 1 of this article establishes such a method of protecting the creditor as an award for specific performance. The availability of an opportunity for a creditor to file such a claim is recognized as a general rule. Otherwise, it may arise from the law, the contract or the substance of the obligation. For example, judicial practice recognizes that it is inadmissible to award a debtor for specific performance, if it is impossible to perform the obligation, or if there is a close connection between the performance and the debtor's personality.[9] This approach itself, as well as exceptions to it, generally corresponds to the civil law tradition of continental European countries and acts of international unification of private law (articles 7.2.1–7.2.2 of the UNIDROIT Principles 2016, articles III.-3: 301–III.-3: 302 DCFR).

An effective mechanism for forcing the debtor to specific performance is a "judicial penalty" (an analog of the *l'astreinte* known to some legal orders). Originally arose in Russia in the context of judicial law-making, due to the recodification the "judicial penalty" it was enshrined in sect. 1 of the art. 308.3 CC RF, according to which the court may award by the creditor's claim in his favor a sum of money (determined on the basis of principles of equity, proportionality and good faith) that the defendant should pay in case of default to comply with the underlying judgment of the court.

Clause 2 of the art. 328 CC RF provides for the possibility of suspension of performance in the event of a breach of the contract (including foreseeable), in many respects recalling the relevant provisions of article III. -3: 401, article III.-3: 504 DCFR, article 71–72 of the Vienna Convention of 1980.

According to sect. 3 of the art. 328 CC RF, none of the parties of the obligation, under which counter-performance is provided, is not entitled to claim in court for its performance, without giving to the counterparty what is due and payable under the obligation. As follows from the text of the Concept of civil law reform, these rules are intended to exclude the deformation of relations between the parties in a synallagmatic contract and are designed for the case when the sequence of actions of the parties to provide performance is not established by law or contract. However, since this last clarification is not directly included in the text of the law, judicial practice applies this rule without taking into account this restriction. As a result, the creditor cannot claim performance from the party that is obligated to perform first in turn (for example, to make an advance payment, transfer goods with deferred payment, etc.). This approach looks rather controversial, since it largely invalidates the parties' agreement on the order of performance.

A common and universal way to protect a creditor from non performance of an obligation is claim for damages (article 393 CC RF). Compensation for damages

---

[9] See: items 22–24 of the Ordinance No. 7.

is a traditional institution of Russian law. However, it was not actually used for a long time. The courts imposed extremely high requirements to prove the amount of damages, as well as the causal relationship between the damages and the debtor's breach of contract. The civil law reform was designed to remove these obstacles, making damages once again an affordable and effective way to protect the creditor. Thus, clause 5 of the art. 393 CC RF does not require an exact determination of the amount of damages, but only their determination "with a reasonable degree of reliability". At the same time, the court cannot refuse a claim for damages if the creditor is unable to prove their amount even with a reasonable degree of reliability. In this case, the court must determine at its discretion the amount of compensation that it considers fair and appropriate to the consequences of the breach of contract.

In the course of the reform, both the rules on specific (based on the price of the substitute transaction) and abstract (based on the current market price) methods for calculating damages upon termination of the contract in response to the debtor's breach were improved and made universal. Article 393.1 CC RF, which contains these rules, largely resembles the requirements of articles 75–76 of the Vienna Convention of 1980, articles 7.4.5–7.4.6 of the UNIDROIT Principles 2016, and article III.-3: 706-III.-3: 707 of the DCFR.

Provisions on the change of persons in the obligation are contained in Chapter 24 of the CC. In the course of the reform, point changes of these rules also took place.

Thus, the number of possible options for changing persons in the obligation was supplemented by the case of replacing a party in the contract, i.e., simultaneously transferring to a third party all the rights and obligations of the party. This model is known to many national legal systems, as well as international instruments for the unification of private law (see sect. 3 of Chapter 9 of the 2016 UNIDROIT Principles, sect. 3 of Chapter 5 of book III of the DCFR). Before the reform, this model was fixed in Russian law only for individual special cases (for example, in regard to transfer to the new lessee of the rights and obligations under the existing lease agreement to the same extent as they existed for the previous lessee), but now it has acquired a universal character.

With regard to the assignment of a claim, the regulation of the permissibility of assignment and the consequences of violation of contractual prohibitions and restrictions on assignment have been changed. Following the principles of UNIDROIT 2016 (article 9.1.9), Russian legislation has established a differentiated approach. If a contractual prohibition or restriction on an assignment is established in relation to a monetary claim, such prohibition or restriction is relative, and its violation does not invalidate the assignment. In this case, the assignor may be liable to the debtor for violation of the specified prohibition or restriction. If a contractual prohibition or restriction on the assignment of a nonmonetary claim is violated, such assignment may be declared invalid if the assignee knew or should have known about the corresponding prohibition or restriction (clause 4 art. 388 CC RF).

The rules on notifying the debtor of an assignment were significantly adjusted during the reform. If such a notification is sent to the debtor by the assignor, the debtor does not have the right to demand proof of the actual transfer of the right to the assignee. Protection of the debtor's interests is provided by the visibility of the right, which is created by the corresponding notification. In contrast, when the notification of the assignment is sent to the debtor by the assignee, the debtor is entitled not to perform the obligation to the assignee, requiring proof of the transition to the latest of the corresponding claim (clause 1 art. 385 CC RF). With the obvious justice of this decision, it turned out to be palliative. Since it is the debtor who bears the risk of performance to the improper person, he has the right to demand additional evidence of the transfer of the claim to the assignee. However, the assignee is fundamentally unable to provide the debtor with such evidence of the assignment that the debtor could believe unconditionally. In this regard, it seems to be reasonable the conclusion of the Supreme Court of the Russian Federation about the possibility of the debtor in a similar situation to suspend performance until receipt of proof of assignment from the assignor or the debtor's ability to get debt relief, by performing it to the assignor, despite notice.[10]

The rules on the assignor's liability to the assignee have also been adjusted. Keeping the general direction of regulation, known to many legal systems, - the assignor is liable for the validity of the assignment, but is not liable for the performance by the debtor, sect. 2 art. 390 CC RF establishes an indicative list of circumstances that fall within the scope of liability of the assignor (the existence of the requirements; the particular entitlement to the assignment; the absence of the previously executed assignment; the absence of objections of the debtor, etc.). Rules of article 9.1.15 of the UNIDROIT Principles 2016 and art. III. -5: A total of 112 DCFRs served as a prototype of this list. At the same time, following these international unifications, the CC RF also explicitly emphasizes the dispositive character of the relevant rules and the possibility of changing them by agreement of the parties.[11]

Above all, the reform resulted in the provisions of the CC RF about the transfer of debt being complemented by a model for such a transfer (adherence to duty) by agreement of the creditor with the new debtor, which is well known to many national legal systems and the acts of international harmonization (article 9.2.1(b) of the UNIDROIT Principles 2016, article III.-5:209 DCFR).

The termination of obligations (Chapter 26 CC RF) remained practically unaffected by civil law recodification. Its development is largely carried out by judicial practice.

Thus, the text of art. 410 CC RF does not directly reflect the moment of termination of the claims under the set-off. The Concept of civil law reform proposed consolidating the idea of the prospective effect of set-off, which is directly reflected in paragraph 3 of article 8.5 of the UNIDROIT Principles 2016, article III.-6: 107 DCFR. However, this proposal was never implemented. Russian judicial practice on this issue is quite chaotic. Higher courts assume that set-off has a retrospective effect, considering that the moment of termination of the set-off claims not the moment of

---

[10] See: item 20 of the Ordinance of the Plenum of the Supreme Court of the Russian Federation dated 21 December 2017 No. 54 "On Some Issues of Application of the Provisions of Chapter 24 of the Civil Code of the Russian Federation on the Change of Persons in an Obligation on the Basis of a Transaction" (in Russian).

[11] This dispositivity is directly established in clause 1 of art. 390 CC RF only for B2B relations. However, there is no serious reason not to extend it to other relations of equal subjects.

receipt of the application for set-off by the relevant party but the moment when the claims became capable of set-off.[12] However, this idea is difficult to take root in the practice of lower courts.[13]

With regard to such a method of termination of obligations as novation, the key principle "novation is not presumed", known to the vast majority of legislations worldwide, is not directly reflected in the text of the CC RF. However, this principle is certainly recognized by judicial practice.[14]

The last reform solved an important practical issue of debt forgiveness, taking into account the opinion of the forgivable debtor. Clause 2 art. 415 CC RF establishes that the obligation is considered terminated from the moment the debtor receives the creditor's notification of debt forgiveness if the debtor does not send the creditor objections to debt forgiveness within a reasonable time. However, these regulations leave open the question of the nature of debt forgiveness. Judicial practice believes that debt forgiveness is a contract with the implied consent of the debtor to its formation.[15]

The provisions of the CC RF on the amendment and termination of the contract did not change dramatically during the reform.

The general rule on judicial termination of the contract in the event of a material breach by the counterparty was retained (clause 2 art. 450 CC RF). This approach does not correspond to modern European national legal systems, which provide for the termination of the violated contract in such cases by means of a nonjurisdictional procedure (unilateral refusal). The decision of the Russian legislator unreasonably increases the burden on the judicial system and causes justified doctrinal criticism.[16] However, it should be noted that the general rule on judicial termination is dispositive; the parties have the right to establish an out-of-court procedure for terminating the violated contract (by notification) or even to agree on an "automatic" termination of the contract in the event of a significant breach of the counterparty.

To ensure the protection of a party whose counterparty enjoys the right to terminate the contract (by filing a claim in court or by unilateral refusal) and to introduce

---

[12] See: item 3 item 2 of the Information letter of the Presidium of the Supreme Arbitration Court of the Russian Federation dated 29 December 2001 No. 65 "Review of the Practice of Resolving Disputes Related to Termination of Obligations by Setting off Homogeneous Counterclaims"; Rulings of the Supreme Court of the Russian Federation dated 16 August 2018 No. 305-ЭС18-3914, dated 12 December 2019 No. 305-ЭС19-12,031; item 15 of the Ordinance of the Plenum of the Supreme Court of the Russian Federation dated 11 June 2020 No. 6 "On Certain Issues of Application of the Provisions of the Civil Code of the Russian Federation on Termination of Obligations" (in Russian, hereinafter—Ordinance No. 6).

[13] In almost 70% of cases, courts recognize that obligations that are subject to set-off are terminated at the moment when the counter-obligation creditor received a notice of set-off—Romanova (2019, no. 9).

[14] See: item 22 of the Ordinance No. 6; item 2 of the Information letter of the Presidium of the Supreme Arbitration Court of the Russian Federation dated 21 December 2005 No. 103 "Review of the Practice of Application by State Arbitration Courts of article 414 of the Civil Code of the Russian Federation" (in Russian).

[15] See: item 34 of the Ordinance No. 6.

[16] See Karapetov (2017, pp. 1072–1078).

certainty in the relations of the parties, Russian legislation uses the doctrine of "consistent behavior", which is well known to many national legal orders. Following the example of article 3.12, 3.13 of the UNIDROIT Principles 2016, clause 5 of article 450.1 CC RF provides that when a party authorized to terminate a contract confirms such a contract by its behavior, it loses its right to terminate on this basis.

The new version of art. 453 CC RF clarifies the consequences of the termination of the contract. In a situation when the contract is terminated because one of the parties did not perform it, failure to satisfy the claim of the other party, which in good faith performed its obligation, to return the assets transferred to the counterparty pursuant to the contract, seems clearly unfair. In this case, on the side of an unscrupulous counterparty, unjustified enrichment is formed, which is subject to elimination under the rules on obligations arising from unjust enrichment.

2.7 Securities

Chapter 23 CC RF is devoted to ways to secure the performance of obligations. It regulates in detail the relationship between the two classic types of accessory obligations—surety and pledge—and the independent guarantee.

The legislator recognizes other security instruments (retention of title for security purposes, provision of a security payment to secure the performance of a future monetary obligation, and others) and allows the creation of other security by agreement of the parties.

The general trend of Russian legislation on accessory security obligations is to weaken their accessory nature. Security may arise earlier than the obligation secured by it, or after its violation; under the contract, you can pledge property the mortgagor's property right to which will arise later (art. 336 CC RF), etc.

The idea that all the conditions of the secured obligation that collectively determine its risk are important to the security debtor is replaced by the idea that the debt itself is secured, individualized by its size and maturity. For example, if the parties to the secured obligation changed it, even significantly, without the consent of the guarantor, it continues to meet the same conditions, that is, to the extent and for the period that was originally agreed upon (art. 368 CC RF). This trend is consistent with the acceleration and complication of civil law turnover, which is particularly noticeable in the postsocialist economic space.

Regulation of relations of suretyship in the CC RF is fairly simple and since the advent of the civil code have not changed significantly. On the basis of the surety agreement, the surety undertakes to be liable for the debtor's failure to perform its duties under the secured obligation. As a general rule, the guarantor is liable jointly and severally with the main debtor and has the right to the same objections that the debtor can oppose to the creditor (art. 363, art. 364 CC RF). The guarantor who has performed his duties takes the place of the creditor in the main obligation (acquires a claim against the debtor by subrogation) (art. 387 CC RF).

The regulation of a pledge, understood in the CC RF as a limited real right to another person's property, which gives the pledgee a priority over the other creditors of the pledger, is generally in the traditional course of continental law.

However, in the course of the reform, the provisions of the CC RF on the pledge significantly approached the samples presented in the 9th book DCFR.[17] First, it is necessary to note the emergence of rules that guarantee the protection of a bona fide buyer of pledged property and a bona fide buyer of a pledge right. In these cases, we are talking about the so-called subjective good faith: a person is considered to be in good faith if he did not know and could not have known about the circumstances that prevent the satisfaction of his interests.

If the pledged movable property is acquired on a paid basis by a person who did not know and should not have known that this property is the subject of a pledge, the pledge is terminated (art. 352 CC RF). The inclusion of this provision in the Code had become possible due to the new rule that a pledge of any property can become public, thanks to the emergence of special public registers intended for the publication of the pledge of movable property (article 339.1 of the civil code). This means that any acquirer of property can check whether it is not encumbered with a pledge.

If the right to pledge is subject to mandatory registration in the state register, it arises only from the moment of registration. This relates to the security of real estate (registered in the state register of real property rights), pledge of share in the Charter capital of a limited liability company (registered in the unified state register of legal persons), the pledge of the exclusive rights for an invention, trademark, etc., of industrial property (registered in the state register of inventions, register trademarks, etc.).

When pledging undocumented security, information about the pledge is reflected in a special account that records the rights of its owner (article 358.16 CC RF). Although such registration is not a state registration, the right of pledge in this case also arises only from the moment of making an entry.

With a pledge of other movable property, a pledgee may apply to the notary a statement about the inclusion of the right of pledge in a special register maintained by the Federal chamber of notaries.

The recording of information about the pledge in the notary register is solely for accounting purposes and does not affect the time when the right to pledge arises. However, when foreclosing on the pledged property, the pledgee will be able to oppose his right to third parties only if there is an entry about it in the notary register (of course, except for the case when the third party knew about the pledge from other sources).

The CC RF does not contain a rule similar to that included in article IX.-3: 201: "Possession" DCFR: the right of pledge may be opposed to third parties only if the subject of pledge is transferred to the pledgee under direct physical control. However,

---

[17] Features of mortgage of real estate are regulated by the special Federal law of 16 July 1998 N 102-FZ "On mortgage (pledge of real estate)", which has not yet been radically changed.

experience has shown that if there is a public record of pledge to movable, the absence of this rule does not cause difficulties in practice.

The updated CC RF has a norm that protects a bona fide buyer of the right to pledge. If the property is pledged by a person who was not the owner or otherwise could not dispose of the property, which the pledgee did not know and should not have known (a bona fide pledgee), the owner of the pledged property has the rights and obligations of the pledger (art. 335 CC RF).

A significant part of the changes is aimed at maximum protection of the rights of the pledgee as a creditor. During the time of socialism, the legislator proceeded from the traditional idea of Russian law that support should be provided to the debtor as the weak side in the obligation. In the 20 years since the adoption of the CC RF, this approach has changed dramatically. Now, the legislator proceeds from the fact that for a fair balance of interests, it is necessary to protect the lender. After all, its willingness to lend determines the efficiency of the economy.

Now, the right to obtain satisfaction primarily before other creditors of the debtor applies to insurance compensation for loss or damage to the pledged property; income due to the pledger or the pledgee from the use of the pledged item by third parties and certain other amounts that replace the value of the pledged item (art. 334 CC RF).)

Under pressure from banks, the legislator allowed the pledge of the entire property of the pledger, the so-called "general pledge" (article 339 CC RF), in relations between persons engaged in business activities. However, such a pledge has not yet been applied in practice due to the lack of a mechanism for making it public.

Among the separate types of pledge specifically provided for in the CC RF (mainly defining the features of pledge for various types of civil rights objects), two new ones appeared during recodification.

First, it is a pledge of rights under the bank account agreement (art. 358.9 CC RF). Such a pledge only occurs if the pledger opens a special collateral account. If the secured obligation is not performed, the pledgee has the right to request the bank to write off funds from this account in its favor.

Second, a new type of pledge is the so-called "judicial pledge" (article 334 CC RF). If security claimed by the creditor claims the debtor has been restricted in the right to dispose of his property, since the entry into force of the court decision on the claim, the creditor acquires with respect of this property rights and obligations of the pledgee. The main practical question—how the rights of such a creditor relate to the rights of other pledgees—is resolved in the general procedure (art. 342.1 CC RF).

The complication of the practice of relations related to collateral has led to the specification of the norms of the CC RF on the multiplicity of participants in such relations. Now, the legislator has specifically regulated the relations between creditors who have independent claims. They received equal seniority of collateral rights to the same property (co-pledgees) (art. 335.1 CC RF). Their claims are satisfied from the value of the collateral item in proportion to the size of the claim of each of them, unless they have agreed otherwise.

If the previous and subsequent liens arise in relation to one object of pledge, the conflicts of interest of the pledgees is resolved on the basis of the classical principle of *prior tempore—potior jure.* In other words, the order of satisfaction of the claims of the pledgees (the seniority of pledges) is set depending on the moment of occurrence of each pledge (art. 342.1 CC RF). However, priority in any case is granted only to a bona fide pledgee who, when entering into the pledge relationship, did not know and could not have known about the pre-emptive rights of third parties to the subject of the pledge (art. 342.1 CC RF).

The law has a direct indication that pledgees have the right to agree on changing the seniority of pledges (art. 342 CC RF). Such agreements have never been prohibited. However, they were rejected by practice due to the tendency inherited from the Soviet times to allow dispositivity only where the legislator directly indicates it. Today, the situation has changed, and references to the principle of the freedom of contract are actively used in the jurisprudence of courts, which is due first of all to the OrdinanceNo. 16.

A significant feature of the regulation of collateral relations under Russian law is the procedure for the implementation of collateral rights. From the point of view of substantive law, the implementation of the right of the pledgee consists of two stages: foreclosure on the object of pledge and its sale to obtain the maximum possible compensation for the pledge by the creditor.

As a result of foreclosure, the pledgee confirms its right to pre-emptive satisfaction of claims at the expense of the value of the pledged property. The fact of foreclosure has material and legal consequences since it gives the creditor the right to sell the pledged property (art. 349 CC RF). As a general rule, the right of the pledgee to start selling the pledged property is confirmed by a court decision. However, by agreement of the parties, it can be confirmed by a notary's executive inscription or by any other method agreed upon by the parties.

In some cases, foreclosure is possible only by a court decision (if the object of the pledge is the only housing of the mortgagor, property of significant cultural value to society, etc.). The sale of the pledged item allows the mortgagee to satisfy his claim at the expense of the value of the pledged property. As a general rule, the pledged item is sold at auction, but in specially stipulated cases, the pledgee has the right to keep it at the market price (art. 350, art. 350.1 CC RF).

The Unified rules for on-demand guarantees issued by the International chamber of Commerce in 2010 (publication No. 758) are a model for regulating relations related to the provision of an independent guarantee for the Russian legislator.

The idea of independence of the guarantee from the obligation it secures hardly took root in the Russian legal consciousness. Guarantors often refused to pay on the grounds that the beneficiary had breached this obligation, and the courts, when considering claims against the guarantors for payments, investigated whether such a violation had occurred.

However, in recent years, there has been a correct practice formed by the Supreme Court of the Russian Federation. Its numerous decisions emphasize that the guarantor verifies the submitted claim and the documents attached to it solely on formal grounds. It is clear that the obvious abuse of the beneficiary is the basis for refusing the claim.

2.8 Financial Transactions

The rules on financial transactions were changed and supplemented to take into account the need for credit development and the complexity of settlements.

CC RF initially distinguished between a loan agreement and a loan. A loan agreement is a consensual agreement in which only the bank can act on the lender's side. The loan was always designed as a real contract and could be concluded by any person other than banks. Now the loan agreement can be concluded as a consensual agreement at the choice of the parties, however, provided that the borrower is not a natural person (art. 809 CC RF).

Chapter 45 "Bank account" CC RF is supplemented with new types of accounts: (1) a nominal account (the rights to funds held in such an account do not belong to the person in whose name the account is opened, but to the beneficiary—art. 860.1 CC RF); (2) a joint account (the account accounts for funds belonging to more than one person—art. 845 CC RF); a public Deposit account (it contains funds transferred under the control of a notary or a court—860.11 CC RF); a collateral account (the rights of claim against the Bank with respect to this account are subject to collateral—art. 358.9 CC RF); escrow account (art. 860.7 CC RF).

The escrow account is intended to serve the interests of the parties to the escrow agreement (article 926.1 CC RF). The regulation of relations under the escrow agreement, as well as under the escrow account agreement, copies the escrow construction in common law. In particular, under the escrow account agreement, the bank, as an escrow agent, opens an escrow account for depositing funds of the depositor to transfer funds to the beneficiary if the grounds provided for in the agreement arise. The difficulty in applying the escrow design is related to the inability to reconcile it with the understanding of a multilateral contract accepted in Russian law as a contract where all participants act to achieve a common goal.

2.9 Inheritance Law

In recent years, the section of the civil code on inheritance has been supplemented by three new institutions.

(1) Inheritance Foundation.[18] This kind of legal person emerged in the CC RF as a certain partial answer to the continuing debate on the necessity to implement the law of trusts in the good law of Russia. The decision to establish the Foundation, its property and the procedure for managing it is included in the will. With the opening of an inheritance, the foundation is established as a legal person and called for inheritance. The inheritance foundation uses the inherited property exclusively in accordance with the will of the testator, ensuring that the beneficiaries receive the income specified in the will. Beneficiaries of the

---

[18] See more on the inheritance foundations in Russia: Novikov and Rudokvas (2020, pp. 112ff.).

Foundation can be any person, with the exception of commercial organizations. The foundation can be created for general purposes.

(2) Inheritance agreement. It is concluded by the future testator with the future heir (or a third party) about who will inherit and what property. The contract may oblige its party to perform certain actions in favor of the future testator. Since the future testator is not deprived of the right to dispose of his property, as well as to make a subsequent will of any content, the design of the inheritance contract is not popular in practice.

(3) Joint will. It can only be performed by persons who are married. The rules on joint wills contain an exception to the seemingly unshakable rule that the inheritance includes property that belonged to the testator on the day the inheritance was opened.

Spouses have the right to bequeath their common property to any persons, as well as to determine the property included in the inheritance mass of each of the spouses, regardless of the moment of death of any of them. In other words, in the event of the death of one of the spouses, the estate that belongs to the surviving spouse may be included in the inheritance mass. However, as stated in the law, this is possible if it does not violate the rights of third parties. For example, the creditors of a surviving spouse. Such wills already exist, but there is no practice of executing them yet.

The will of the testator in all three cases is limited by the rules on the right of compulsory heirs (disabled dependents of the testator) to obtain a certain share of the inheritance regardless of the will (art. 1149 CC RF).

References

Karapetov AG (ed) (2017) Dogovornoe I Objazatel'stvennoe Pravo (Obshja Chast). M-Logos, Moscow

Karapetov AG, Shirvindt AM (2020) Freedom of contract in respect of price terms in Russian law: With a special focus on price terms in standard form contracts. In: Atamer YM, Pichonnaz P (eds) Control of price related terms in standard form contracts. Ius Comparatum—global studies in comparative law volume 36. Springer

Novikov AA, Rudokvas AD (2020) Il fondo ereditario. In: Crespi Reghizzi G, Popondopulo VF (eds) Diritto Commerciale Russo. Wolters Kluwer, Cedam, Milano

Puder M, Rudokvas AD (2019) How trust-like is Russia's fiduciary management? Answers from Louisiana. Louisiana Law Rev 79(4):1072–1102

Romanova OI (2019) Analiz sudebnoj praktiki po voprosu momenta prekrashenija objazatel'stva zachetom. Vestnik Ekonomicheskogo Pravosudiia Rossiiskoi Federatsii 9:172–188

Rudokvas AD (2012) Recodification of civil law in the Russian Federation under the aspect of the law of contracts. In: Global Legal Issues. Korea Legislation Research Institute

Rudokvas AD (2013) Contract formation and non-performance in Russian civil law. In: Schulze R, Zoll F (eds). The law of obligations in Europe: a new wave of codifications. Springer

Rudokvas AD (2016) Lanimo possidere e lanimus possidendi come elemento del possesso. In: Vacca L (ed) Dai giuristi ai codici. Dai codicii al giuristi. Convegno ARISTEC. Roma 20 febbraio 2012, Jovene, Napoli

Rudokvas AD (2017) Possession and possessory remedies in the draft of modifications to the civil code of Russian Federation in the mirror of Jhering's doctrine of possession. Transformacje Prawa Prywatnego 4:51–59

Andrej Anatolievich Pavlov PhD in Law, is an Associate Professor of the Civil Law Department of Saint Petersburg State University from 2001 to the present. Member of the Scholarly Advisory Board of the State Arbitration Court of the North-Western district of the Russian Federation. Member of the working groups for the preparation of draft model laws of the CIS: "On the law of obligations" (2018–2019), "On the law of contracts" (to date). Member of the working group on the draft Ordinance of the Plenum of the Supreme Court of the Russian Federation on the application of the provisions of Chapter 26 of the Civil Code of Russia. The author of approximately 100 publications on contract law and the law of obligations. Member of the editorial Board of the journal "Herald of Economic Justice of the Russian Federation".

Natalia Jurievna Rasskazova PhD in Law, Associate Professor 1981–1993—taught law in the N.A. Voznesenskij Financial-economic Institute; 1981–2000—taught at the Higher School of Economics of the University of Economics and Finance; and 1993-1999, head of legal department of "BNP-Drezdner Bank" (Saint Petersburg). Since 1999, she has taught at the Faculty of Law of Saint Petersburg State University. In 2006–2019, she was a chair holder of the Civil Law Department. Since 2019, she has been a chair holder of the Department of Notaries. She is member of the Scholarly Advisory Board of the State Arbitration Court of the North-Western district of the Russian Federation and of the Scholarly Advisory Board of the Federal Notary Chamber. In 2008–2019, she was a member of the Council for the Codification and Development of Civil Law Legislation attached to the Presidency of the Russian Federation.

Anton Dmitrievich Rudokvas Dr. Sci. in Law. Since 2006, he is Professor at the Faculty of Law of Saint Petersburg State University; since 2013, he is Full Professor of Roman law, Civil law and Comparative Private law at the Department of Civil Law. Since 2012, he has been a lecturer at the International Summer School "European Private Law" at the University of Salzburg. He is a Member of the Executive Committee of the International Association for Comparative Historical Legal Studies (ARISTEC) and Member of the Italian Society for the Comparative Law Studies (SIRD) as well a Member of the Advisory Council attached to the Standing Law Commission of the Inter-Parliamentary Assembly of the states—members of the Commonwealth of the Independent States. Since 2015, he has been a member of the board SAPIENTES of the Court for Trusts and Fiduciary Relations of the Republic of San Marino.

The Civil Codes of Switzerland from a Historical and Comparative Perspective: Some Reflections Based on the Swiss Experience

Pascal Pichonnaz

Abstract The fascinating process of codification involving an understanding of various cultures and legal backgrounds is examined using Switzerland as an example. In the nineteenth century, the French Civil Code influenced by natural law impacted many French-speaking cantons of Switzerland, whereas the Civil Code of Zurich and the cantons of the center of Switzerland were influenced by the Pandectistic ideas of the German historical school. When Switzerland decided to codify its contract law in the second half of the nineteenth century, it had to face the divide between these two different legal cultures. Through two examples, this contribution shows how the notion of contract was defined according to the Pandectistic approach and how the regulation of the transfer of risk in sales contracts was the result of a fortunate compromise between both traditions. It was then reinterpreted by the Swiss Federal Tribunal to conform with the underlying principles of Roman law. This emphasizes that codes may be the result of compromises between (legal) cultures; to remain a suitable medium of communication between society and itself, a code should have an open texture to adapt to the evolution of society through pragmatic interpretations.

1 Introduction

Law is culture. Codification in Switzerland is particularly interesting, as it provides one way to better understand the people of Switzerland in their diversity under a single legal regime.

Napoleon was very proud of his Civil Code. He stated that "*My code alone by its simplicity has done more good to France than the mass of all the statutes that*

P. Pichonnaz (✉)
Department of Law, University of Fribourg, Fribourg, Switzerland
e-mail: pascal.pichonnaz@unifr.ch

M. Graziadei and L. Zhang (eds.), *The Making of the Civil Codes*,
Ius Gentium: Comparative Perspectives on Law and Justice 104,
https://doi.org/10.1007/978-981-19-4993-7_16

preceded me".[1] A single code for the people of one territory: Is it a reality, or a myth to foster unification? The Swiss are usually proud of their codes (the Civil Code and the Code of Obligations), as they can be easily read and understood. One could therefore consider these codes to be typical expressions of Swiss culture. However, at the same time, Swiss law is quite often chosen as the applicable law for international commercial contracts. Is it because of the mixed influences from different philosophical and cultural backgrounds? If so, is it truly possible to consider Switzerland as constituted out of one territory, one people but two codes, to reiterate the words of Napoleon? At the heart of such a question, however, is already the quest for an answer to the issue of whether Switzerland is constituted by "one people", given that there are *four different national and official languages* and several *religions*, (most predominantly Protestantism, Catholicism and Judaism). Interestingly, however, the linguistic and religious borders do not coincide.

These are only a few of the questions to consider when taking a closer look at the issue of codification in Switzerland.[2] In its modern aspects, Switzerland is also the result of external events. First, Napoleon imposed upon Switzerland a Helvetic Republic between 1798 and 1803, but had to mediate a way out of this unsuccessful attempt in February 1803. Second, Switzerland's core features would be the result of the recognition by major States of Europe (the Austrian-Hungarian Empire, France, the United Kingdom, Prussia and Russia) of its perpetual neutrality at the Vienna Congress and through the Treaty of Paris of 1815. Currently, however, the people of Switzerland consider neutrality to be part of their DNA. One could therefore think that the creation of a Swiss identity was probably artificial at the very outset. However, it has become a shared identity that grew during the second half of the nineteenth century and became a reality during the twentieth century. The wave of codifications that occurred during that period was certainly a means to lead toward such a national identity. Given this background, it is not surprising that the codification of Swiss private law is a series of legal solutions developed through a process embodying compromise between different philosophical understandings of law and culture. Therefore, it is useful to look at how these first codifications emerged and what all were required to bring the different (legal) cultures forward together. Although this paper will not be able to review all the facets in detail, it shall cover some of the main features. This will lead to conclusion that a code or a statute might be considered a mirror held up to a society at a specific point in time. It is a medium for society to communicate with itself and reflect upon its very nature. However, it should be made clear from the very beginning that a code does not incorporate the law as such, but it is a mere expression of all possibilities which will then be fixed more concretely in light of specific cases.

---

[1] Palluel (1969, p. 244): "Mon seul code par sa simplicité a fait plus de bien en France que la masse de toutes les lois qui m'ont précédé".

[2] For fundamental analysis: Caroni (1988, 2015).

2 The Triggering Effect of Napoleon and His Helvetic Republic

Prior to 1798, thirteen Swiss cantons lived in a confederation of independent States with no real common statutes in matters concerning private law. The teaching of Roman law and of natural law in law schools (called academia), or at some universities, might have brought to life some common features in the application of law and of a specific methodology used by lawyers, despite the fact that they were mostly applying customary laws or specific statutes.[3]

In January 1798, French troops entered Switzerland. The *Directoire* in Paris then decided that Switzerland would be constituted into a single Republic: the Helvetic Republic (12 April 1798). This Republic survived for only five years, until 10 March 1803, the official date of the abolition of the Helvetic Republic. Napoleon Bonaparte helped to mediate a way out, although he was the one who imposed it. This way out was an act of negotiation under his auspices that resulted in the so-called *Act of Mediation*, dated 19 February 1803. This gave the people of Switzerland a new constitution and forced them to keep the six new cantons (new independent States) that were brought into existence during the Helvetic Republic.

Indeed, during these five years of the Helvetic Republic, Switzerland became a battlefield for Europe (1799), then suffered a civil war (1800–1802), but never managed to get to the "Code Unique" that its *Directoire* previously wanted, based on the model of the Napoleonic Code.

There is something very special about the people of Switzerland, as expressed by Bonaparte himself during the first meeting in Paris, which led to the signing of the *Act of Mediation*. He said the following: "*Switzerland does not look like any other State, neither by the events which happened throughout history, nor by the various languages, the various religions and this severe difference in mentalities between its different parts. Nature made your State federal, to try to change that would not be the aim of a wise man*".[4]

With the signing of the *Act of Mediation* of 1803, the endeavour to have a code for Switzerland was (temporarily) abandoned. The idea of a codification, however, remained alive. In the cantons that regained their legislative power, some politicians began to use the idea of codification as a tool to propose new ideas and legal developments, benefiting from more power within the political discourse.[5]

---

[3] Pichonnaz (2012, pp. 19–35).

[4] Monier (2002, p. 26): [Procès-verbal des Assemblées Générales des Députés helvétiques et des Opérations de la Commission nommée par le Premier Consul pour conférer avec eux] "La Suisse ne ressemble à aucun autre Etat, soit par les événements qui s'y sont succédés depuis plusieurs siècles, soit par la situation géographique et topographique, soit par les différentes langues, les différentes religions et cette extrême différence de moeurs qui existe entre ses différentes parties. La nature a fait votre Etat fédératif. Vouloir la vaincre ne peut être d'un homme sage."

[5] Pahud de Mortanges (2017, n. 324).

3   The Cantonal Codifications and the Difference in Understanding

3.1   Four Different Groups of Codifications

In the second part of the nineteenth century, cantonal codifications of private law began to flourish throughout Switzerland. One traditionally identifies four groups of codes[6]:

1. Codes influenced by the French Civil Code. The French-speaking cantons were of course culturally influenced by France. *Geneva* for instance formed part of France when the French Civil Code was enacted in the year 1804, since it joined the Swiss Confederation only in the year 1815. The canton kept this codification, which was influenced by natural law, while amending it in some areas of family law, inheritance law and of the law of immovables. *Bernese Jura* had also been part of France since 1799 and became part of Bern in 1815; this territory nevertheless kept the French Civil Code. Upon its recognition as a full canton in the year 1803, the government of *Vaud* decided to codify its civil law, drawing its inspiration largely from the French Civil Code. It was enacted in 1821 as the first modern civil code in Switzerland. *Neuchâtel* in 1854–1855 and *Valais* in 1855 enacted their respective civil codes, which were also largely inspired by the French Civil Code. The Civil Code of *Ticino*, enacted in 1838, was inspired by the French Civil Code and partly by the Austrian Civil Code (*Allgemeines Bürgerliches Gesetzbuch*) and the *Codice civile di Parma*. Finally, the Civil Code of *Fribourg* of 1850 was inspired by the Civil Code of Vaud, the Austrian and the Dutch Civil Codes; the latter of 1832 was almost a direct translation of the French Civil Code. I shall later address the specificities of the French Civil Code as a source of inspiration.

2. Codes influenced by the Austrian Civil Code. This second group of cantons was inspired by the Civil Code of Bern. Indeed, it was not possible for the restored patricians of Bern to take over the civil code from those who had defeated them in 1798. Therefore, a Bernese professor of law, who was former Supreme Judge during the Helvetic Republic, drafted a code inspired by the Austrian Civil Code, since he was an adept of the philosophy of Immanuel Kant, who significantly inspired Franz von Zeiller, one of the drafters of the Austrian Civil Code. Several cantons followed this example by adopting variations of the Bernese Civil Code between 1826 and 1831.

3. Codes influenced by the German historical school and Savigny. This third group has been inspired by a very different understanding of the law. Johann Caspar Bluntschli (1808–1881) and Friedrich Ludwig Keller (1799–1860) studied in Zurich; Bluntschli later went to Bonn and to Berlin, where he was fascinated by the teaching of Friedrich Carl von Savigny. Contrary to Savigny, he was convinced

---

[6] Pahud de Mortanges (2017, n. 332ff.); see also the diversity in languages of these cantons and codes, Pichonnaz (2017, pp. 124–141, 127).

that codification should be achieved as soon as possible and that it should be based on the understanding of the German historical school of thoughts. Keller had to step down as a drafter in 1839 for political reasons, which allowed Bluntschli to finish the work alone, although powerful people opposed his endeavour for roughly eight years. Bluntschli was not only well versed with the historical statutes of Zurich but was also an expert in Pandectistic and Roman law. The Zurich Civil Code ("Privatrechtliches Gesetzbuch für den Kanton Zürich" [PGB]), enacted in 1853–1855, was the first civil code of its kind, entirely based on the ideas of the German historical school. It has influenced not only seven to ten other cantons but also the Swiss Civil Code to a large extent.

4. Some cantons went without a code. Some remaining cantons had abstained from following the trend of codification, with the deep belief that the former city-statutes and other customary rules would be sufficient.

In the second half of the nineteenth century, the situation in Switzerland was therefore very peculiar and, in a way, even quite unique. One single state had seventeen different civil codes for many of its territorial and political subdivisions. At the same time, fundamental concepts would differ much between the natural law-oriented codes, inspired by the French and the Austrian civil codes, and the historical-school ("Pandectists") inspired civil codes. To point out some fundamental differences, I will mention two specific issues prevailing in these codes. The first one is related to the notion of contract,[7] the second deals with the transfer of ownership in a sales contract.

3.2 Two Significant Issues

3.2.1 The Notion of Contract

The French Civil Code had adopted the notion of contract advanced by Jean Domat (1625–1696) and Robert-Joseph Pothier (1669–1772). These two authors were inspired by Hugo Grotius and his treaty on the law of war and peace ("*De iure belli ac pacis*") of 1625. For Grotius, the contract was basically an exchange of promises.[8] To be enforceable, these promises had to essentially follow the idea that one promise was given in consideration of the other or, as the Roman lawyer Ulpian already expressed it in the third century AD, one promise (e.g., to give or to do something) had to be the cause of the other promise (to give or to do something).[9]

---

[7] See on this, Pichonnaz (2021, pp. 491–507).

[8] Grotius (1625/1993, p. 343); see also, Schmidlin (1999, pp. 187ff., 190ff.; 2010, pp. 61–86) and Pichonnaz (2021, p. 497ff.).

[9] Ulpian, D. 2,14,7,2; Pichonnaz (2021, p. 495ff.).

This appears very clearly in the following excerpt from the book, the civil laws in their natural order ("Les loix civiles dans leur ordre naturel") by Jean Domat[10]:

> In these first three kinds of agreement, there is a transaction in which nothing is gratuitous, and the commitment of one is the foundation of that of the other. In agreements where only one party appears to be obliged, as in the lending of money, the obligation of the borrower has been preceded by what he was obliged to give on the part of the other party to form the agreement. Thus, the obligation which is formed in these kinds of agreements for the benefit of one of the contracting parties always has its cause in the part of the other: and the obligation would be null if in truth it were without cause.

Similarly, Robert-Joseph Pothier stated the same notion eighty years later[11]:

> Every commitment must have an honest cause. In self-interested contracts, the cause of the commitment entered into by one of the parties is what the other party gives him, or undertakes to give him, or the risk he takes.[12]

It is therefore not surprising that Articles 1101 and 1108 of the French Civil Code of 1804 were influenced by the conception stated by both Pothier and Domat.

Article 1101 French Civil Code of 1804 reads as follows: "A contract is an agreement by which one or more persons bind themselves toward one or more others to give, to do or not to do something".[13] It is completed by Article 1108 French Civil Code of 1804, which states: "Four requirements are essential for the validity of an agreement: The consent of the party who obligates himself; That party's capacity to contract; A definite object that forms the subject matter of the engagement; A licit cause for the obligation". As I explain elsewhere, the new formulation of these provisions by the reform of the French law of obligations in 2016 (newly numbered Article 1101 and 1103), evolved and transformed the initial understanding of a contract as an exchange of promises into a contract as a result of the meeting of minds.[14] Other European civil codes are not alien to such evolution.

---

[10] Own English translation; Domat (1723, p. 20): "Dans ces trois premières sortes de conventions, il se fait un commerce où rien n'est gratuit, et l'engagement de l'un est le fondement de celui de l'autre. Et dans les conventions même où un seul paraît obligé, comme dans le prêt d'argent, l'obligation de celui qui emprunte, a été précédée de la part de l'autre de ce qu'il devait donner, pour former la convention. Ainsi, l'obligation qui se forme dans ces sortes de conventions au profit de l'un des contractants, a toujours sa cause de la partie de l'autre: et l'obligation serait nulle si dans la vérité elle était sans cause"; On the wrong generalization by Domat for unilateral contracts, see, Rampelberg (2005, p. 87ff.); see also Pichonnaz (2021, p. 498).

[11] Own English translation; Pothier (1821, p. 41): "Tout engagement doit avoir une cause honnête. Dans les contrats intéressés, la cause de l'engagement que contracte l'une des parties est ce que l'autre partie lui donne, ou s'engage de lui donner, ou le risque dont elle se charge".

[12] See also, Pothier (1821, p. 7) and Pichonnaz (2021, p. 498ff.).

[13] In the original French version: "Le contrat est une convention par laquelle une ou plusieurs personnes s'obligent, envers une ou plusieurs autres, à donner, à faire ou à ne pas faire quelque chose".

[14] Pichonnaz (2021, p. 502ff.).

Bluntschli's perspective concerning the Zurich Civil Code was quite different. For him, one had to rely only on the "will" of the parties to create a binding undertaking. He wrote[15]:

> The contract is founded on a declared meeting of the will of the parties, in consequence of which one party (the debtor) obligates himself toward the other one to a patrimonial performance.

There is no need for any specific "consideration" or "cause", contrary to the French Civil Code. For Bluntschli and the Zurich Civil Code, no specific formalities were needed for a contract, since what essentially mattered was that the "will" of both parties had been declared and would coincide, making it a binding agreement.[16] This is truly in line with Savigny's legacy, for whom the *"Rechtsgeschäft"* ("juridical act" as translated sometimes[17]) is fundamental. This means that the will is efficient and produces legal effects as soon as there is an agreement.[18] This flows directly from Immanuel Kant's explanation in his *Metaphysic*, where he deals with the notion of "joint will" (*"gemeinschaftliche Wille"*).[19]

This difference in perspective has several consequences.[20] One is certainly to influence the way a judge interprets and fills in potential gaps in the contract. If the will, and not the promise, is central, a more subjective perspective is appropriate, and gap filling is then done with reference to good faith, rather than through implied terms.[21] Of course, since the nineteenth century, a lot of these differences have been erased, or at least largely smoothed over by convergence. This is very well evidenced by both the French reform of the law of obligations in 2016, and the new Articles 1101 and 1103 of the French Civil Code,[22] and by other modern codifications, such as the new Dutch Civil Code of 1992 (NBW), which completely abandoned the approach followed by the old Dutch Civil Code, which was based on French law.

---

[15] Own English translation; Bluntschli (1855, p. 1 § 903): "Der Schuldvertrag beruht auf der erklärten Willensübereinkunft der Kontrahenten, in Folge welcher der eine Theil (der Schuldner) sich dem andern Theil (dem Gläubiger) gegenüber zu einer vermögensrechtlichen Leistung verpflichtet"; see also, Pichonnaz (2021, p. 501).

[16] Own English translation; Bluntschli (1855, p. 9 § 911): "In der Regel bedarf es zu der Gültigkeit und Klagbarkeit der Verträge keiner besonderen Form. Es genügt, dass derbeiderseitige Wille in verbindlicher Weise erklärt sei".

[17] See for such translation, the Draft Common Frame of Reference (DCFR), Outline edition, February 2009, Article II.-1:101 "Meaning of 'contract' and 'juridical act' (p. 183); Article II.-1:101 para. 2 DCFR reads as follows: "A juridical act is any statement or agreement, whether express or implied from conduct, which is intended to have legal effect as such. It may be unilateral, bilateral or multilateral".

[18] For more details, see Pichonnaz (2021, p. 501ff.).

[19] Schmidlin (1999, p. 199ff.).

[20] For details, see Pichonnaz (2021, p. 504ff.).

[21] Pichonnaz (2021, p. 505ff.).

[22] Pichonnaz (2021, p. 502ff.).

P. Pichonnaz

3.2.2 Transfer of Ownership by Sales Contract and Transfer of Risk

In French law, the way transfer of ownership is regulated reflects the natural law idea that the conclusion of a contract by itself is enough to transfer ownership (Article 711 of the French Civil Code linked to Article 1583 of the French Civil Code), even if the path leading to such a solution was disputed.[23] In the seventeenth century, Grotius set out a clear reason for this, since he stated that *"each perfect promise has an effect similar to a transfer of ownership"*.[24] The said solution was also the one chosen by the Swiss cantons, which were inspired by the solution provided in the French Civil Code.

The transfer of risk would then follow from the transfer of ownership, according to the principle recognised by the Roman law *"casum sentit dominus"*, where the risk is borne by the owner.

In contrast, the Zurich Civil Code followed the Pandectist model: a transfer of ownership was triggered by a transfer of possession and title[25]:

> The ownership of a movable object is transferred from the owner to his or her successor by the transfer of possession as a result of a legal transaction aimed at transferring, e.g., purchase, exchange, donation.

The cantons that followed the Zurich model adopted the same provision. Accordingly, the transfer of risk would be allocated to the buyer not upon conclusion of the contract, but at the moment of the transfer of possession, which was when ownership passed to the buyer.

4 The Unification Process Toward a First Federal Code

In Switzerland, the unification of private law was not self-evident for historical reasons, such as the aspiration to independence, which was very strong in the past. How could one merge the French oriented mentality with the German or Austrian kinship of the Central and Eastern parts of Switzerland?

To decide to what extent a codification could be possible, the Minister of Justice (Federal Councillor Jakob Dubs) in the 1850s sought several legal opinions analyzing the necessity and feasibility of a codification for Switzerland. A professor from Zurich, Heinrich Fick, explained the necessity of codifying commercial law, bills

---

[23] See about this discussion, Pichonnaz (2019, pp. 785–805, 796ff.; 2020, pp. 7–33, 21ff.).

[24] Own English translation; Grotius (1625/1993, p. 329): "… quae perfecta promissio est, similem habens effectum qualem alienatio domini"; see also, Schmidlin (1999, p. 62).

[25] Own English translation; Bluntschli (1855, p. 138 § 649): "Das Eigenthum an einer beweglichen Sache wird von dem Eigenthümer auf seinem Nachfolger übertragen durch die Übergabe des Besitzes in Folge eines auf Uebertragung gerichteten Rechtsgeschäftes, z.B. Kauf, Tausch, Schenkung.".

of exchange and transport by train[26]; thereafter, Walther Munzinger and Emanuel Burckhardt-Fürstenberger published a legal opinion that reached similar results.

They also had to determine whether it would be possible to reconcile the French (natural law-oriented) approach with the concepts laid down by the Pandectists[27] and what would be the extent of such a codification. Fick envisaged a Commercial Code in the French style, which was *more limited*, while the other two jurists wanted *a large codification.*[28]

Codification is always a compromise between tradition and innovation. This is also true for the first Swiss code, the so-called Federal Code of Obligations of 1881, which became possible because the Federal Constitution of 1874 provided for the exclusive power of the Federal level to legislate in the field of commercial law.

The codification process required a large work of integration.[29] First, the drafters wanted to *avoid particular laws for different categories of people* ("*keine Standesrechte*"[30]), since these would contradict key "Republican institutions", the principle of democracy and the principle of equal treatment.[31]

The process of codification also imposed the obligation to at times create new regimes as a result of political *compromise between the different orientations.*[32] The Drafting Commission wrote, for instance, in its Report on the Draft of a "Federal Statute on Obligations and Commercial law" of 1880, that this draft was "*a fortunate mix, which appears in numerous chapters, between elements of French law and of German law*".[33]

This will to find such compromises was very important, as underlined by Henri Carrard, a professor of law speaking before the Society of Swiss Lawyers in 1873: "[The Zurich Civil Code] has preserved with care peculiarities of Zurich Laws, which is useful for the canton of Zurich, and may be for the territories of the ancient Gau region of the Thur; it would be a fundamental mistake to impose it to the entire Switzerland".[34]

---

[26] Fasel (2003, p. 59).

[27] Fasel (2003, p. 59ff.).

[28] Message du Conseil fédéral concernant le projet d'une loi fédérale sur les obligations et le droit commercial, du 27 novembre 1879, FF 1880 I 126 (hereinafter: Message du Conseil fédéral, FF 1880 I 126); also Fasel (2000, p. 1213; 2003, p. 61).

[29] Bucher (1983, p. 262).

[30] Caroni (1988, p. 188ff.).

[31] Caroni (1984, p. 38) and his reference in note 103; Message of the Federal Council, (Federal Papers) FF 1880 I 174; see also, Fasel (2003, p. 64).

[32] For an analysis among others: Caroni (1988, p. 73ff.).

[33] Report of the Committee of the Council of States charged with examining the draft federal law on obligations and commercial law, of 31 May 1880, FF 1880 III 139, (Saturday 12 June 1880), p. 147: "... d'un heureux mélange, qui se rencontre dans bien des chapitres, des éléments de droit français et de ceux de droit allemand..."; see also, Meili (1901, p. 12).

[34] Own English translation; Carrard (1873–1874, p. 133ff.): "[Le code zurichois] a conservé avec soin les particularités du droit zurichois. Ce qui fait son mérite pour le canton de Zurich, et peut-être pour le territoire occupé par l'ancien Gau alémanique de la Thur serait un défaut capital dès qu'il s'agirait de l'imposer à la Suisse entière".

This approach is further illustrated by an example. Swiss law is known for a peculiarity, that is its specific rule on the passing of risk in sales contracts. Article 185 of the Code of Obligations now in force reads as follows:

Article 185 B. Benefits and risks

[1] The benefit and risk of the object pass to the buyer upon the conclusion of the contract, except where otherwise agreed upon or dictated by special circumstances.

[2] Where the object sold is defined only in generic terms, the seller must select the particular item to be delivered and, if it is to be shipped, must hand it over for dispatch.

[3] In a contract subject to a condition precedent, the benefit and risk of the object do not pass to the buyer until the condition has been fulfilled.

The peculiarity of the rule lies in the fact that the buyer bears the risk of the counter performance from the moment of the conclusion of the contract, although he is not yet the owner of the goods sold. Thus, according to this provision, the buyer has to pay the price, even if, after the conclusion of an unconditional sales contract, the goods are destroyed by an Act of God ("*vis maior*"). It comes down to the secular principle "*periculum emptoris*", "the risk lies on the buyer".

However, since the doctrine elaborated by Grotius in the seventeenth century, all legal regimes in Europe have brought together the transfer of ownership and the transfer of risk, merging the two Roman law principles of "*casum sentit dominus*"[35] and "*periculum emptoris*".[36] The Pandectist school of the nineteenth century adopted the same idea, leaving aside the "*periculum emptoris*" rule, to adopt the idea of a transfer of risk by the transfer of ownership (which for them took place at the time of the transfer of possession). Therefore, the idea of a "*periculum venditoris*" (risk to the seller) at the time of conclusion prevailed if there was no transfer of possession.[37]

In Article 204 of the Federal Code of Obligations of 1881 and in Article 185 of the (current) Code of Obligations of 1911, the Swiss retained the Roman principle of risk borne by the buyer, although the transfer of ownership of moveables is triggered by the transfer of possession (Article 199 Federal Code of Obligations of 1881 and Article 714 para. 1 of the current Swiss Civil Code).[38]

That was possible because in 1881 there was an intense discussion in the Swiss Parliament regarding the issue of transfer of ownership of moveable objects (Art. 199 Federal Code of Obligations of 1881). The question was whether one should follow the French model, based on transfer by consent, or the more modern solution of the Zurich Civil Code, based on the transfer of possession.

---

[35] Diocl. C. 4.24.9 [293 AD]; Pichonnaz (2019, pp. 785–805, 787; 2020, pp. 7–33, 10).

[36] Dig. 18,6,8*pr (Paul., lib. 33 ad ed.)*; Pichonnaz (2020), RDS/ZSR, p. 13ff.; Pichonnaz (2019, p. 789ff.).

[37] Pichonnaz (2020, pp. 7–33, 21ff.); see also, Pichonnaz (2019, p. 796ff.).

[38] See also for details, Pichonnaz (2019, p. 799ff.); for an overview, Pichonnaz (2008, pp. 183ff., 187ff.).

First, with regard to the conclusion of the contract, the Swiss Parliament followed the Zurich solution by stating that: *"there is a contract only if the parties have declared in a concurring manner their reciprocal will"*.[39]

Therefore, quite logically, the transfer of ownership should also follow the Zurich Civil Code by adopting the requirement of the transfer of possession as an essential requirement for the transfer of ownership. The Swiss-German cantons won this battle with Article 199 of the Federal Code of Obligations of 1881:

Article 199

For ownership of a moveable to be transferred following an agreement, the beneficiary has to be put into possession.[40]

One accepted, at the same time, the regimes of *"constitutum possessorium"* and *"brevi manu traditio"*. These enable the transfer of possession without a change of hands. French-speaking members of Parliament could therefore accept the new solution more easily.[41]

The discussion was, however, still lively, since the Pandectists' approach had won. This would have a very important impact on the everyday life of merchants in most Swiss French-speaking cantons, given that the seller would continue to be the owner even after the conclusion of the contract and would have to bear all the risks until the buyer took possession. For this reason, some members of the Swiss Parliament from these cantons were considering not voting on the final text.

To avoid a deadlock, the parliamentary commission on legal issues found a way out of this difficult situation. Just before the final vote on the whole text, the commission proposed introducing a new Article 204 in the Federal Code of Obligations, which would allocate the risk of loss to the buyer upon conclusion of the contract, even if ownership had not yet passed to the buyer[42]:

Article 204

Unless an exception flows from circumstances or a special convention, benefits and risks of the goods are borne by the buyer as of the conclusion of the alienation contract.[43]

The rule thus fit with the new trends aligning the dogmatic perspectives with the cultural and commercial needs of the French-speaking merchants. Therefore, it

---

[39] Federal Code of Obligations of 1881, art. 1: "Il n'y a contrat que si les parties ont manifesté d'une manière concordante leur volonté réciproque." And "Zum Abschluss eines Vertrages ist die übereinstimmende gegenseitige Willensäusserung der Parteien erforderlich."

[40] Own English translation; Federal Code of Obligations, art. 199: "Pour que la propriété mobilière soit transférée ensuite d'une convention, il faut que l'acquéreur ait été mis en possession."; "Soll in Folge eines Vertrages Eigenthum a beweglichen Sachen übertragen werden, so ist Besitzübergabe erforderlich"; Pichonnaz (2019, p. 801).

[41] Egli (1926, p. 67).

[42] On this in detail, Pichonnaz (2019, p. 801) and Egli (1926, pp. 65–70).

[43] Own English translation; "A moins qu'une exception ne découle de circonstances ou d'une convention spéciales, les profits et les risques de la chose sont pour l'acquéreur à partir de la conclusion du contrat d'aliénation"; see also, Egli (1926, pp. 65–70); and authors following his presentation: Cortesi (1996, p. 11ff.), Bucher (1970, p. 288ff.) and Cavin (1977, p. 29).

appears, the conclusion of the contract would still have the same effect as before, namely the immediate transfer of risk to the buyer, although the transfer of ownership would take place only upon the transfer of possession. *This fortunate compromise is one of the most evident impacts of the duality of cantonal codifications on federal codification proceedings.*[44] This solution of a *periculum emptoris* is, however, not completely unique, because a similar solution also exists in Chile (Article 1820 of the Chilean Civil Code) and in South Africa.[45]

The principle was discussed again in 1910, when the Swiss Parliament had to discuss again all the provisions of the old Federal Code of Obligation of 1881 to prepare the Civil Code, given that the Federal level had been granted the powers necessary to codify the whole private law in 1898. The above-mentioned provision was, however, not modified, fearing that this would trigger a battle between the people of Switzerland.[46] As a consequence, Article 185 of the Swiss Code of Obligations is largely similar to its predecessor.

This hybrid solution has, therefore, not been inspired directly by Roman law but largely reproduces it. Therefore, in 2002,[47] the Federal Tribunal (the Swiss Supreme Court) interpreted Article 185 of the Swiss Code of Obligations by taking into account the principle *"periculum emptoris"* enshrined in Roman law.[48] The Federal Tribunal highlighted that—as in Roman law—to allocate risk to the buyer makes sense when the conclusion of the contract and the transfer of possession has been agreed to in accordance with the buyer's interests to not occur at the same time, either because the latter could not immediately take the delivery of the goods purchased or because the buyer could not pay the full price at once.[49] In such cases, it seems justified that the buyer bears the risk of destruction of the goods, even if he is not yet their owner. As a result of a fortunate historical compromise, the Swiss rule on the passing of risks in sales contracts is currently interpreted in light of the principle established by Roman law. One can wonder whether this comes down to what the Pandectists had in mind when they reinterpreted the sources of Roman law (i.e., to interpret rules of Roman law in light of their contemporary needs). The path was, however, slightly different in Switzerland, since the result of the general rule of *periculum emptoris* under Swiss law was not aimed at reproducing the conclusions which met the needs of Romans; it rather aimed at taking into account two different legal cultures. Since both inspirational rules (natural law and Pandectists solutions) were embedded within the sources of Roman law, it is, however, hardly surprising that the interpreters of the solution adopted by the Swiss Parliament were finally eager to rebuild the link to Roman law by way of interpretation. This "romanisation" of the Swiss solution does

---

[44] Egli (1926, p. 68) and Pichonnaz (2008, p. 190; 2019, p. 802; 2020, p. 30).

[45] Bauer (1998, p. 182ff.) and Zimmermann (1996, p. 292).

[46] Pichonnaz (2011, p. 133).

[47] DFT 128/*2002* III 370 [12 March 2002, FT 4C.336/2000].

[48] DFT 128/*2002* III 370/373, reason 4b aa. [12 March 2002, FT 4C.336/2000].

[49] DFT 128/*2002* III 370/373, reason 4b aa. [12 March 2002, TF 4C.336/2000]; for an analysis: see also, Pichonnaz (2008, p. 183ff.; 2019, p. 802; 2020, p. 30) and Pfeiffer (2003, pp. 888–898).

not obliterate the origin of such a rule and the creative understanding of the different legal cultures that it represents.

5 Some Final Thoughts

I shall finally proceed to emphasize certain characteristics that emerged from what has just been discussed.

5.1 No Codes for Specific Groups of People

In this contribution, I have mentioned that the Swiss Parliament, but perhaps also the people of Switzerland, did not want to have different statutes for people of different status. Swiss law does not provide for a true consumer code, despite having statutes for specific consumer contracts. Swiss law does not provide for an independent commercial code, despite having provisions on commercial law both in the Code of Obligations and in some specific statutes, such as a statute on mergers. How did this result come about?

Commercial law in Switzerland was first codified with the codification of the law of contracts and the transfer of ownership over movables by the Federal Code of Obligations of 1881. When the powers to codify the rest of private law were given to the Federal State in 1898, the question arose whether there should be a civil code incorporating the law of contracts, as many other countries had a commercial code on commercial legal entities and negotiable instruments.[50] However, the fear of having laws for specific groups of people was still very much present, so it was decided to keep the Code of Obligations and the Civil Code separate and to integrate all (general) regulations on commercial law into the Code of Obligations.[51]

The Swiss Parliament, however, had not been able to redraft all the provisions of commercial law contained in the 1881 Federal Code of Obligations prior to the time established for the entry into force of the new Swiss Civil Code and the Code of Obligations on the 1st of January 1912. It was therefore agreed that the new provisions and modifications would be integrated at a later point in time. To make this possible, the Swiss Parliament kept open the possibility of creating a commercial code at a later time by considering the Code of Obligations as the last book of the Civil Code.[52] Thus, it had its own number in the systematic collection of statutes, along with its own name, but was formally designated Book 5 of the Civil Code.

However, in 1936, when the revised provisions of the commercial law were ready and could enter into force, no one dared to reopen the issue of legislating a commercial

---

[50] Pichonnaz (2011, p. 129ff.).

[51] Pichonnaz (2001, p. 130).

[52] Rossel (1929, p. XIII).

code.[53] Switzerland kept its Civil Code and Code of Obligations, which included commercial law, and abandoned the idea of having a commercial code or a consumer code of its own.

5.2 A Code Has an Open Texture

Another peculiarity of the Swiss Civil Code and Code of Obligations is the fact that it is written in three official languages,[54] all equally authentic and valid. Obviously, the text in all three linguistic versions is not always exactly the same, and by necessity, the words used refer to different preunderstandings depending upon the linguistic and cultural backgrounds of the readers (e.g., lawyers and judges).[55]

In this way, one could imagine that decisions may differ from one linguistic part of Switzerland to another. If a specific interpretation is not brought up to the Supreme Court, there is a significant risk that a given provision may be interpreted in different ways across the country, not in the least because of variations in the drafting of the respective linguistic versions, or variations in scholarly works, similarly written in those different languages.[56]

Moreover, it is probably difficult to explain any solution with a mere literal or grammatical approach, since words and grammar are different in German, French, and Italian. This leads one to wonder if such a situation has a disruptive effect on Swiss law.

Experience shows, however, that although it is not possible to exclude this completely, it is most likely not the case.

First, similarities arise through the lawyers' education system, which is not identical throughout the country but remains relatively consistent. This does not imply that the scholarly understandings across the linguistic borders do not differ, sometimes quite severely, especially given the different wordings of particular provisions.

Second, similarities also arise because judges tend to read decisions in many languages and may take into account a decision rendered in French, German, or Italian, even if this is not the language in which they themselves write their decision. One should not underestimate the central role of judges who aim to have a coherent law throughout Switzerland.[57]

Finally, and most importantly, the "father" of the Swiss Civil Code, Eugen Huber, drafted Article 1 of the Swiss Civil Code in such a way to conceive the Code as an

---

[53] Pichonnaz (2011, p. 130).

[54] Although a linguistic version in Romansh is available, that version can only be applied to people with this as there first language; see on this point, Pichonnaz (2017, pp. 124 ff., 125).

[55] On the difficulties of drafting statutes in all three languages but also on the opportunities, see on this point, Pichonnaz (2017, pp. 124–141).

[56] For a good example: Pichonnaz (2017, p. 133ff.).

[57] On the issue of multilingual aspect of judges, see Devinat and Pichonnaz (2017, pp. 271–287).

open text.[58] François Gény, with whom Eugen Huber was corresponding,[59] held that Article 1 of the Civil Code was the best summary of his methodology, referring in particular to Article 1 para. 2 of the Swiss Civil Code on gap-filling, which reads as follows[60]:

> [2] In the absence of a provision, the court shall decide in accordance with customary law and, in the absence of customary law, in accordance with the rule that it would make as legislator.

Already in the interpretation of the express provisions, the ideas of Eugen Huber, however, are central, as evidenced by Article 1 para. 1 of the Swiss Civil Code, which reads:

Article 1 [A. Application of the law]

> The law applies *according* to its wording or interpretation to all legal questions for which it contains a provision.

This English—unofficial—translation does not say "*wording and interpretation*" but states an alternative, "wording *or* interpretation". It is *not* a mistaken translation, since the alternative also exists in the three official languages (French, German, and Italian), as mentioned below:

> French: «La loi régit toutes les matières auxquelles se rapportent **la lettre ou l'esprit** de l'une de ses dispositions. »
>
> German: "Das Gesetz findet auf alle Rechtsfragen Anwendung, für die es **nach Wortlaut oder Auslegung** eine Bestimmung enthält."
>
> Italian: "La legge si applica a tutte le questioni giuridiche alle quali può riferirsi **la lettera od il senso** di una sua disposizione."

The French and Italian versions mention "*wording or spirit*", whereas the German version mentions "*wording or interpretation*". There is thus a further discrepancy between these versions, since "*spirit*" does not necessarily mean the same as "*interpretation*". The different wordings are probably the result of different perceptions; the French version with the word "spirit" constitutes at the same time an implied reference to Montesquieu.[61]

This Article 1 paragraph 1 of the Civil Code and the "alternative" also provides for some reasons (if needed) supporting the Swiss Federal Tribunal methodological approach, which is presented as a "pragmatic methodological pluralism".[62] For more than twenty-five years,[63] the Swiss Federal Tribunal (the Swiss Supreme Court) has considered that there is no predefined hierarchy among the various methods

---

[58] Amstutz (2007, p. 255 et set., p. 265).

[59] On contacts between François Gény and Eugen Huber, see among others, Gauye (1962, p. 91); see also Gauye (1973, p. 271); see also Gény (2016) and Werro (2010).

[60] Pichonnaz (2011, p. 205ff.; 2017, p. 130).

[61] On this, Pichonnaz (2017, p. 132).

[62] In German 'pragmatischer Methodenpluralismus' and in French 'pluralisme méthodologique pragmatique'; on this, Pichonnaz (2017, p. 136).

[63] For the first cases, see DTF 121/*1994* III 219 (25th April 1995); DFT 123/*1996* III 24 (2nd October 1996).

of interpretation (literal, systematic, historical, teleological, and comparative). In different cases (among others DFT 134/2008 III 16/18 reason 3), it is underlined that *the normative value of a legal provision lies not in the text but in the concretization of the provision in a given context, which gives to it the legal (normative) force.*[64] The Court seeks a substantive equitable solution within a normative structure to achieve a satisfactory result in light of the *ratio legis*.

Thus, it says in German:

> Die Gesetzesauslegung hat sich vom Gedanken leiten zu lassen, dass nicht schon der Wortlaut die Norm darstellt, sondern erst das an Sachverhalten verstandene und konkretisierte Gesetz. Gefordert ist die sachlich richtige Entscheidung im normativen Gefüge, ausgerichtet auf ein befriedigendes Ergebnis der *ratio legis*.[65]

In an unofficial English translation of the text, this is translated as follows:

> The interpretation of the law must be guided by the idea that it is not the wording alone that constitutes the norm, but only the law understood and concretised in the facts of the case. What is required is the factually correct decision in the normative structure, oriented toward a satisfactory result of the *ratio legis*.

In French, however, it reads, slightly differently:

> Le Tribunal fédéral ne privilégie aucune méthode d'interprétation, mais s'inspire d'un pluralisme pragmatique pour rechercher le sens véritable de la norme; en particulier, il ne se fonde sur la compréhension littérale du texte que s'il en découle sans ambiguïté une solution matériellement juste.[66]

In an unofficial English translation, it would read as follows:

> The Federal Supreme Court does not favor any particular method of interpretation, however it is guided by a pragmatic pluralism in its search for the true meaning of the norm; in particular, it relies on a literal understanding of the text only if it unambiguously leads to a materially correct solution.

Even in the cases decided by the Supreme Court, one can potentially find differences in understanding and identify variations in the expressions used to define the methodological tools: this is a given in the case of a plurilingual legal system.[67]

---

[64] DFT 134/*2008* III 16, reason 3: "[...] Das Gesetz muss in erster Linie aus sich selbst heraus, das heisst nach dem Wortlaut, Sinn und Zweck und den ihm zu Grunde liegenden Wertungen auf der Basis einer teleologischen Verständnismethode ausgelegt werden. Die Gesetzesauslegung hat sich vom Gedanken leiten zu lassen, dass nicht schon der Wortlaut die Norm darstellt, sondern erst das an Sachverhalten verstandene und konkretisierte Gesetz. Gefordert ist die sachlich richtige Entscheidung im normativen Gefüge, ausgerichtet auf ein befriedigendes Ergebnis der *ratio legis*. Dabei befolgt das Bundesgericht einen pragmatischen Methodenpluralismus und lehnt es namentlich ab, die einzelnen Auslegungselemente einer hierarchischen Prioritätsordnung zu unterstellen. Es können auch die Gesetzesmaterialien beigezogen werden, wenn sie auf die streitige Frage eine klare Antwort geben und dem Richter damit weiterhelfen."

[65] DFT 134/2008 III 16, reason 3.

[66] DFT 133/2007 III 555/562, reason 3.4.3.1.

[67] Devinat and Pichonnaz (2017, pp. 271–287).

Considering that law is in a steady evolution under the influence of changing needs and social contexts,[68] Eugen Huber, the drafter of the Swiss Civil Code, expressed a very interesting statement in a book published in 1920, which reveals his understanding of the role of statutes:

> Law is not created by legislation but is only reflected by statutes, while creation of law is left to forces on which legislation has no power.[69]

With this statement, Huber was anticipating the path, which the Swiss Supreme Court currently follows. This should make us humble toward codification!

This fascinating process of codification through understanding of various societal cultures and legal cultures is not privy to Switzerland but can be found in most harmonization or unification endeavours. May the Swiss experience enhance the understanding of those processes.

References

Amstutz M (2007) Der Text des Gesetzes: Genealogie und Evolution von Art. 1 ZGB. RDS/ZSR 126(II):255–286

Amstutz M (2008) *Ouroboros*, Nachbemerkungen zum pragmatischen Methodenpluralismus. In: Gauch P, Werro F, Pichonnaz P (eds) (2008) Mélanges en l'honneur de Pierre Tercier. Schulthess, Zurich, pp 19–31

Bauer M (1998) Eine dogmengeschichtliche Untersuchung zur Gefahrtragung beim Kauf. Dunker & Humblot, Berlin

Bluntschli JC (1855) Privatrechtliches Gesetzbuch für den Kanton Zurich: mit Erläuterungen, vol III . Forderungen und Schulden, Schulthess, Zurich

Bucher E (1970) Notizen zu Art. 185 OR (Gefahrtragung durch den Käufer). RDS/ZSR 89:288ff

Bucher E (1983) Hundert Jahre schweizerisches Obligationenrecht: wo stehen wir heute im Vertragsrecht? Bericht SJV RDS/ZSR 1983 II 251

Caroni P (1984) Der «demokratische» Code Unique von 1881, Eine Studie zur ideologischen Beziehung von Sonderrecht und Demokratie. In: Caroni P (ed) Das Obligationenrecht 1883– 1983, Berner Ringvorlesung zum Jubiläum des schweizerischen Obligationenrechts. Stämpfli, Bern

Caroni P (1988) «Privatrecht»: eine sozialhistorische Einführung. Helbing & Lichtenhahn, Basel/Francfort-Main

Caroni P (2015) Privatrecht im 19. Jahrhundert. In : Schweizerisches Privatrecht (SPR), vol. I, Helbing & Lichtenhahn, Basel

Carrard H (1873/1874) Etude comparative des législations civiles de la Suisse romande et celles de la Suisse allemande. RJB 9:133

Cavin C (1977) Kauf, Tausch, Schenkung. In: Vischer F (ed), Kauf, Tausch, Schenkung, in: F. Vischer (edit.), Schweizerisches Privatrecht (vol VII/1), Obligationerecht – Besondere Vertrangsverhältnisse, Helbing & Lichtenhahn, Basel-Stuttgart

---

[68] Huber (1893, p. 185; 1914, p. 16ff.) und/oder Huber (2007, p. 18ff.); also for an analysis: Amstutz (2008, p. 20).

[69] Huber (1921, p 255): "… Das Recht ist nicht durch die Gesetzgebung geschaffen, sondern wird durch die Gesetze nur widerspiegelt, während die Schaffung des Rechts Mächten überlassen wird, über die der Gesetzgebung keine Gewalt zusteht"; see also, Amstutz (2008, p. 20) and Pichonnaz (2011, p. 213).

Cortesi O (1996) Die Kaufpreisgefahr. Zürich

Devinat M, Pichonnaz P (2017), L'égalité des langues officielles devant les cours suprêmes: regards croisés sur le droit canadien et le droit suisse. RDS/ZSR 2017/3 I:271–287

Domat J (1723) Les lois civiles dans leur ordre naturel. Gosselin, Paris

Egli W (1926) Die Gefahrtragung beim Kaufvertrag, Weiss, Affoltern

Fasel U (2000) Handels- und obligationenrechtliche Materialien. In: Haup (ed), Bern

Fasel U (2003) Bahnbrecher Munzinger: Gesetzgeber und Führer der katholischen Reformbewegung (1830–1873). Stämpfli, Bern

Gauye O (1962) Lettres inédites d'Eugen Huber, RDS/ZSR 81:91ff.

Gauye O (1973) François Gény est-il le père de l'art.1 al. 2 CCS ?, RDS/ZSR 92:271ff.

Gény F (1919) Méthode d'interprétation des sources en droit privé positif. Vol III, L.G.D.J, Paris 2016 [reprint of the original of 1919]

Grotius H (1625) [1993] De iure belli ac pacis. (repr.) Scientia Verlag, Aalen

Huber E (1893) System und Geschichte des Schweizerischen Privatrechts. IV, Reich, C. Detloff's Buchhandlung, Basel

Huber E (1914) Erläuterungen zum Vorentwurf des Eidgenössischen Justiz- und Polizeidepartements, 1. Band: Einleitung, Personen-, Familien- und Erbrecht. 2nd ed., Büchler & Co. Verlag, Bern 1914, p. 1ff. (reprint: Reber/Hurni (ed.), Materialien zum Zivilgesetzbuch, vol II: Die Erläuterungen von Eugen Huber, Text des Vorentwurfs von 1900, Berner Kommentar, Stämpfli, Bern, 2007, p 1ff.)

Huber E (1921) Recht und Rechtsverwirklichung: Probleme der Gesetzgebung und der Rechtsphilosophie. Helbing & Lichtenhahn, Basel

Meili F (1901) Die Kodifikation des schweizerischen Privat- und Strafrechts. Orell Füssli, Zurich

Monier V (2002) Bonaparte et la Suisse, Travaux préparatoires de l'Acte de Médiation (1803). Helbing & Lichtenhahn, Genève

Pahud de Mortanges R (2017) Schweizerische Rechtsgeschichte, Ein Grundriss, 2nd edn. Dike, St-Gallen

Palluel A (1969) Dictionnaire de l'Empereur. LGDJ, Paris

Pfeiffer G (2003) «Periculum est emptoris» — Gefahrtragung bei Sukzessivlieferung von Aktien. ZEuP 4:884–894

Pfeiffer G (2013) «Periculum est emptoris» - Gefahrtragung bei Sukzessivlieferung von Aktien. Entscheidung 4C.336/2000 des Schweizerischen Bundesgerichts vom 12.3.2002 mit Anmerkung. ZEuP 11:888–898

Pichonnaz P (2001) La compensation. In: Schulthess (ed), Zurich

Pichonnaz P (2008) *Periculum emptoris und das schweizerische Recht: Ein Fall des Rückgriffs auf römisches Recht durch das Schweizerische Bundesgericht.* In: Ernst W, Jakab E (ed), Kaufen nach Römischem Recht, Antikes Erbe in den europäischen Kaufrechtsordnungen. Springer, Berlin/Heidelberg, p 183ff

Pichonnaz P (2011) Le centenaire du Code des obligations, Un code toujours plus hors du code. RDS/ZSR II:117–226

Pichonnaz P (2012) Harmonization of European private law: what can Roman law teach us; what can it not? In: Fogt M (ed), Unification and harmonization of international commercial law: Interaction or deharmonization? Kluwer Law International, Alphen aan den Rijn, pp 19–35

Pichonnaz P (2017) Legal interpretation in multilingual states: An opportunity. J Comp Law (JCL) 12(2):124–141

Pichonnaz P (2019) Le risque dans la vente: éléments diachroniques et méthodologiques. In: Chevreau E et al (ed) Liber amicorum, Mélanges en l'honneur de Jean-Pierre Coriat, Pantheon Assas, Paris, pp 785–805

Pichonnaz P (2020) Die Gefahrtragung beim Kaufvertrag: Methodologische und Diachronische Elemente. RDS/ZSR I:7–33

Pichonnaz P (2021), Les deux conceptions du contrat en droit continental et leur concrétisation en droit français. In: Deumier P, Gout O, Hiez, Maria I, Prüm A (eds) Mélanges en l'honneur de Pascal Ancel, Brussels, Larcier, pp 491–507

Pothier RJ (1821) Traité des obligations, vol I. Chez Thomine et Fortic, Paris

Rampelberg RM (2005) Repères romains pour le droit européen des contrats. Economica, Paris

Rossel V (1929) Code civil suisse y compris le code fédéral des obligations: édition annotée, 4th edn. Payot, Lausanne

Schmidlin B (1999) Die beiden Vertragsmodelle des europäischen Zivilrechts, Das naturrechtlicheModell der Versprechensubertragung und das pandektistische Modell der vereinigten Willenserklärungen. In: Zimmermann R, Knüter R, Meincke JP (eds) Rechtsgeschichte und Privatrechtsdogmatik. C.F. Müller, Heidelberg, 1999, p 187ff. (reprint in: B. Schmidlin, Le contrat en droit civil européen, Schulthess, Zurich 2010, pp 61–86)

Werro F (2010) Art. 1 CC. In: Pichonnaz P, Foëx B (ed) Commentaire romand du Code Civil, vol I. Helbing & Lichtenhahn, Basel

Zimmermann R (1996) Law of obligations. Oxford University Press, Oxford

Pascal Pichonnaz is Professor of Private Law and teaches Contract Law, European Consumer Law, Roman Law and European Private Law at the University of Fribourg. He is President of the European Law Institute (ELI), former Dean of the Fribourg Law Faculty and past president of the European Law Schools Association (ELFA). He has been a visiting professor at many universities, including Georgetown University Law Center (Washington, DC), Paris I, Paris II, Rome II, ECUPL (Shanghai), University Catholic of Santiago de Chile (Chile), Liège, Trento, Montpellier, Pisa, Glasgow, Clermont-Ferrand, as well as at the Center for Transnational Legal Studies (CTLS) in London. He is admitted to practice law and completed his LL.M. at the University of California (Berkeley). Professor Pichonnaz is coauthor of numerous books and publications at the national and international levels. He is also active as an international arbitrator in commercial and construction cases.

The 2002 Brazilian Civil Code

Ignacio Maria Poveda Velasco and Eduardo Tomasevicius Filho

Abstract The Brazilian Civil Code was enacted on January 10th, 2002, replacing the 1916 Civil Code. One can imagine that there was a request to change this law to respond to society's need for changes in the regulation of private relations at the end of the 20th century. In the Brazilian case, to understand the process that resulted in a new Civil Code, it is necessary to know much about the elaboration of the 1916 Civil Code, as well as when and why there were demands to replace it eighty years later. After considering these aspects, this contribution examines the debates on whether the 2002 Civil Code is actually a new code, or just an update of the 1916 Civil Code, and to what extent the 2002 Civil Code can be considered a law capable of regulating the Brazilian society in the twenty-first century. In fact, due to the passage of time, the 2002 Civil Code corresponds to the 1916 Civil Code as updated until the 1970s. The real impact of this new Civil Code on the regulation of private relations is then analyzed, explaining the reasons why some important articles of the Code were declared unconstitutional by the Supreme Court, and what should have been done for the Civil Code to be able to respond to the current expectations regarding its ability to regulate private relations.

1 Introduction

The enactment of a Civil Code is a fact of great relevance in most legal systems. This complex law is fundamental in people's lives because it structures basic legal relationships, such as marriage and contracts. It defines rules on the protection of one's integrity and assigns what belongs to each person, both in life and after death.

I. M. Poveda Velasco · E. Tomasevicius Filho (✉)
University of Sao Paulo, Sao Paulo, Brazil
e-mail: tomasevicius@usp.br

I. M. Poveda Velasco
e-mail: poveda@usp.br

© The Author(s), under exclusive license to Springer Nature Singapore Pte Ltd. 2023   315
M. Graziadei and L. Zhang (eds.), *The Making of the Civil Codes*,
Ius Gentium: Comparative Perspectives on Law and Justice 104,
https://doi.org/10.1007/978-981-19-4993-7_17

Because a new civil code defines relevant aspects—and unlike so many other laws—it engenders high expectations in terms of its effectiveness and capacity to respond to social needs.

In Brazil, the current Civil Code (Law 10,406, on January 10th, 2002) repealed the 1916 Civil Code. This new civil code was designed to provide solutions to important legal problems in Brazil; however, there was some skepticism in relation to the 2002 Civil Code. The cause of this malaise can be found in the long, stormy, peculiar process of civil codification in Brazil. Although the analysis may be concentrated on contemporary aspects, it is mandatory to know what happened in Brazilian Private Law throughout the 20th century.

Three questions are raised for the reader's assessment in the following paragraphs. The first is whether the desire for a new Civil Code drafted decades before its enactment corresponded to demands of a society that no longer existed at the end of the 20th century. The second is whether a new Civil Code was actually enacted in fact or there was just a small change in some articles of the 1916 Civil Code. The third is the extent to which the 2002 Civil Code has solved problems of 21st century Brazilian society.

2 Roots of the 2002 Brazilian Civil Code

Because Brazil had been a colony of Portugal for three centuries, Brazilian Private Law is affiliated to the Roman-Germanic-Canonical system. In the first centuries of its history, Portuguese Law was in force in Brazil, which corresponded to the Afonsine Ordinances (1446–1521), replaced by the Manueline Ordinances (1521–1603) and updated in the form of the Philippine Ordinances (1603). Portuguese Law inherited local customs, but it was drafted with a profound influence of Justinian Roman Law.[1]

At the beginning of the 19th century, to escape from the Napoleonic invasion in Portugal, the Portuguese Court, escorted by the English navy, moved from Lisbon to Rio de Janeiro. This fact implied the transfer of the entire Portuguese political-administrative-judicial organization from Europe to America.

Almost nothing changed from a legislative point of view because Portuguese Law remained in force in Brazil. With the end of Napoleonic rule in Portugal, King John VI returned to Europe. Due to the independence insurrections existing in America, Prince Peter I stayed in Brazil. Although there was an attempt to preserve Brazil as part of the Portuguese kingdom, Brazil's independence was inevitable because the Spanish rule in South America ended and new nations arose in the region, such as Argentina, Chile, Peru, Colombia, and Venezuela.

In 1822, Brazil finally became an independent nation, and Prince Peter I became the first emperor. This fact is of paramount importance because, in practice, Portuguese legal structures have been preserved here. In this way, the Portuguese

---

[1] Poveda Velasco (1994).

Philippine Ordinances remained in force in Brazil. To avoid any doubts, the Law of October 20th, 1823 was enacted, according to which all laws governing Brazil until April 25, 1821 [date of the departure of King John VI from Rio de Janeiro to Lisbon], as well as the laws enacted by Prince Peter I until independence, remained in force.

The beginning of the 19th century was a time when constitutions began to limit the power of monarchs. Thus, Brazil also had its own. The 1824 Constitution of the Empire of Brazil organized the powers and brought, in its final part, a declaration of fundamental rights in the form of guarantees of civil and political rights for Brazilian citizens. Article 179, XVIII, disposed that the elaboration of civil and criminal codes, based on solid bases of justice and equity, was urgent. A Criminal Code was enacted in Brazil in 1830, which became a reference in Spain and Latin America for its advanced features, representing a Brazilian contribution to the rights of peoples, instead of being a mere reproduction of European codes.[2] However the Civil Code codification process did not start immediately.

Thirty years after becoming an independent nation, Brazil did not have a civil code. In 1850, instead of enacting a Civil Code, a Commercial Code was made, which adopted the acts of commerce doctrine and brought contracts classified as commercial ones, among them the sale of goods, leasing, and deposit.

The first step in the attempt to advance civil codification occurred only in 1855, when Emperor Peter II hired the jurist Augusto Teixeira de Freitas to organize a civil code. He, who was an expert in Roman law, chose, at first, to systematize the Law in force in Brazil, with the argument that, in his opinion, it was necessary to know, first of all, what was in force, to only then proceed to code. In this sense, he carried out hard work to systematize Brazilian Civil Law in the form of a Consolidation of Civil Laws.[3] Once this work was done, Teixeira de Freitas took the second step: to write the Civil Code draft. As premises, he divided civil law, based on the nature of legal relationships, between personal rights and property rights. He also adopted the idea of a general part and a special part.

Surprisingly, he intended to unify civil and commercial obligations into a unique Code. However, his Civil Code draft was abandoned due to the existence of slavery in Brazil, which prevented declaring in the Civil Code that every human being was a person, as well as to the hard Teixeira de Freitas' genius, who had fallen out even with Emperor Peter II.[4] This work, however, served as a model for the Argentinian jurist Dalmacio Vélez Sarsfield to draft the 1869 Argentine Civil Code,[5] which has remained in force until 2015. Then, the Brazilian Government hired other lawmakers to draft a Civil Code, including Nabuco de Araújo, Joaquim Felício dos Santos and Antonio Coelho Rodrigues, but all of them failed.

In 1889, Brazil became a republic with the banning of the royal family to exile in Paris. Due to the vicissitudes of history, Brazil reached the 20th century with the Portuguese Philippine Ordinances as its civil law! It is worth noting that even in

---

[2] Poveda Velasco and Tomasevicius Filho (2018).

[3] Freitas (1876).

[4] Pousada (2006).

[5] Christofoletti Junior (2020).

Portugal, the Philippine Ordinances were no longer in force because the Portuguese Civil Code was enacted in 1867.

In 1900, the government decided to hire jurist Clovis Bevilaqua to prepare another Civil Code draft. He, who was a professor of comparative law and wrote civil law handbooks, accepted this task. Instead of innovating, Bevilaqua decided to use Teixeira de Freitas' draft and complement it with Felício dos Santos' and Coelho Rodrigues' drafts. Once the Civil Code draft was concluded, it was strongly criticized by Ruy Barbosa, an eminent Brazilian politician who alleged grammatical deficiencies in its wording. In any case, Clovis Bevilaqua's draft was being approved with several amendments and finally became the Brazilian Civil Code on January 1st, 1916.

Although it was promulgated in the 20th century, the 1916 Brazilian Civil Code had features of a 19th-century civil code.[6] The idea of a general part, advocated by Teixeira de Freitas, was adopted. The beginning of legal personality, the ability to act, the domicile, juridical acts, and limitation were ruled. In the special part, the books corresponded to Family Law (important due to the end of the Roman Catholic Church as the official religion in Brazil), Property Law, Law of Obligations—including contracts—and Law of Successions. To a large extent, this 1916 Civil Code was sufficient for the regulation of society at that time because Brazil was an eminently agricultural country. It was enough to regulate the main contracts—sale, donation, leasing, lease of services, mandate, deposit, and insurance—in addition to possession, property, and 'in rem' guarantees. Another feature of this Code—not by Clovis Bevilaqua's view—was the maintenance of a patriarchal society through inequality between couples, placing married women as incapable and dependent on their husbands, submissive to their legal powers. Divorce was prohibited in Brazil, and the distinction between legitimate and illegitimate children existed, including as such those who were children of parents who lived in concubinage.

Shortly after its enactment, the 1916 Civil Code became the object of criticism due to the new private law ideas in the first half of the 20th century, translated into the crisis of the autonomy of the will and the need for strict liability in tort law, which made the 1916 Civil Code a symbol of liberalism. In the 1930s, an intense legislative change occurred in Brazil in the form of public order laws. Interest rates were ruled by Decree 22,626 on April 7th, 1933, and anatocism was criminally punished. The sale of fixed-term properties, which resulted in the use of preliminary contracts with effects for third parties, was improved to protect purchasers through Decree Law 58 on December 10th, 1937. Finally, Italian corporatism was absorbed almost entirely in Brazil through the creation of Labor Courts with class representation. Therefore, in the 1940s, the government concluded that a new civil code was needed. Thus, three Brazilian Federal Supreme Court Justices Orozimbo Nonato, Hahnemann Guimaraes, and Philadelpho Azevedo were appointed to draft a new Civil Code. Nevertheless, this project failed.

In the second half of the 1950s and the beginning of the 1960s, important socioeconomic transformations occurred in Brazil, resulting from the international division

---

[6] Tomasevicius Filho (2016).

of labor after World War II and the postmodern moral and sexual revolutions. Such facts resulted in the industrialization of Brazil and the founding of the new capital, Brasília, as well as the definitive entry of women into the labor market. New social demands needed to be resolved and regulated by the 1916 Civil Code. In 1961, a new commission was appointed to develop two codes. The first one, a Civil Code, was drafted by the jurist Orlando Gomes,[7] from the Federal University of Bahia; the second one, a Code of Obligations, was drafted by the jurist Caio Mario da Silva Pereira,[8] from the Federal Universities of Minas Gerais and Rio de Janeiro. The idea was that a Civil Code no longer should have a Law of Obligations. A specific code to unify civil and commercial obligations should have been enacted, returning the advocated by Teixeira de Freitas in his Civil Code draft. However, in 1964, there was a Military coup d'état in Brazil, and these works were left aside, mainly because they were considered advanced in terms of family morality.

3   From Professor Miguel Reale's 1970 Civil Code Draft to the 2002 Civil Code

In 1970, when Brazil reached an important level of economic growth, the government appointed Professor Miguel Reale from the University of São Paulo to be the chairman of a committee of jurists to draft a new civil code. This commission included José Carlos Moreira Alves, who was a Supreme Court Justice and Professor at the University of São Paulo, along with Professors Agostinho Alvim, from the Catholic University of São Paulo; Silvio Marcondes Machado, from the University of Sao Paulo; Clóvis do Couto e Silva, from the Federal University of Rio Grande do Sul; Ebert Chamoun, from the State University of Guanabara (current State University of Rio de Janeiro) and Torquato Castro, from the Federal University of Pernambuco.

Professor Miguel Reale established as a starting point for this legislative work that a civil code could no longer be hermetic and quickly become outdated. Through general clauses, he hoped that case law could establish new meanings for the legal rules contained in the future Civil Code. To give concreteness to general clauses, he chose three fundamental values: sociality, ethics, and operability. This is explained by the fact that Professor Miguel Reale advocated in Brazil the three-dimensional-legal doctrine,[9] according to which Law is a cultural construction based on facts, values, and norms, unlike Hans Kelsen, who advocated the exclusion of extralegal elements in the conception of Law, reducing it only to legal norms.

Sociality was an attempt to escape from the liberal vision that characterized the 1916 Civil Code to impose the vision resulting from solidarity values. For this, the principle of the social function of the contract was chosen as a norm to limit the principle of the mandatory force of contracts, enunciated in Brazil as 'pacta sunt

---

[7] Gomes (1963).

[8] Pereira (2005).

[9] Reale (1968).

servanda'. Thus, whenever the application of the mandatory force of the contract resulted in an uncomfortable situation before society, courts have the power to modify the content of the contract in the benefit of the aggrieved party. In other words, the social function of the contract consists of fulfilling the purpose for which the lawmaker foresaw the contract as a legal institution. In addition to the social function of the contract, the social function of property was accepted in Brazilian Law, inserted as a counterpoint to the powers inherent to property rights. This was not a novelty in Brazilian law since the Statute of Land (Law 4,504, on November 30, 1964) and the 1967 Federal Constitution [repealed by the 1988 Federal Constitution] because both recognized the social function of property.

Ethics corresponds to the possibility of changing the text of the Civil Code through an interpretation consistent with morals through the principle of good faith, which was not established in the 1916 Civil Code as a general clause, as it exists in the German, Italian, Portuguese and Argentine Civil Codes. There was only good faith in specific rules regarding subjective good faith, like in the case of possession in good faith, marriage in good faith, agency in good faith, and inheritance in good faith. The absence of a general rule on good faith was due to the liberal view of contract that structured the 1916 Civil Code, which presupposed that the contractors were fully rational and capable of defending themselves against the disloyalty brought by the opposite party in the pursuit of self-interest. The principle of good faith in the German Civil Code allowed updating Private Law through its intense by courts, to the point of saying that good faith had become a "parallel German Civil Code". As Portugal adopted the principle of good faith in the 1966 Portuguese Civil Code, this was another stimulus for the adoption of good faith in Brazilian Law. In this case, the first rule was in the matter of interpretation, similar to § 157 of the German Civil Code. The second rule corresponds to the prohibition of abuse of the rights, with a rule very similar to article 337 of the 1966 Portuguese Civil Code. Third, in clear inspiration from § 242 of the German Civil Code, a general clause on good faith in contractual matters was inserted.

Operability consists of the possibility for courts to carry out their constructive work, just as judges should have more powers to arbitrate intersubjective corporation and family conflicts to overcome the abstraction of the legal rules. This opening to the role of the courts in this task was important during the 20th century in Brazil because it has suffered for decades with the problem of inflation, which altered the standards and reserves of value functions of the national currency. At this point, the 1916 Brazilian Civil Code was out of step with reality due to the nominalist principle of currency, which released the debtor by the mere delivery of the amount established in the contract. Brazilian courts did not usually intervene in the content of the contracts, allowing the revision of them based on the French unpredictability doctrine,[10] and needed to be legally allowed in the Civil Code to decree the breach of the contract in these situations. There were also other situations pointed out by Professor Miguel Reale, which would be useful the intervention of the judge to correct the effects of legal transactions, such as the possibility of authorizing the suspension of work due

---

[10] Rodrigues Junior (2002).

to geological difficulties during the performance of the contract and the break of inalienability of property clauses, which led people to a life in poverty due to the difficulty of preserving the state of conservation of immovable goods.

Once the three values were adopted as vectors of the future Civil Code, the Commission ended up preserving the text of the 1916 Civil Code, making only occasional changes, except for the inversion of the order of the Law of Obligations and Family Law Books. As expressly admitted by Professor Miguel Reale in the explanatory memorandum to the preliminary Civil Code draft, it was mandatory to 'preserve, whenever possible, the wording of the current Civil Law, as it is not justified to change its text, except as due to fundamental changes, or in case of semantic variations that have occurred over more than half a century of effectiveness'.[11]

In the General Part, the main change proposed was the insertion of a chapter on personality rights. The protection of physical integrity, privacy, and image was not foreseen in the 1916 Civil Code, except that the woman's name change was established as an effect of marriage. A general protection clause for the human person was adopted in Article 11 based on the teachings of the Italian jurist Adriano de Cupis,[12] whose famous work on personality rights was translated into Portuguese and started to circulate among Brazilian scholars in the 1960s. The possibility of safeguarding these rights was foreseen by resorting to courts, including the imposition of judicial censorship, and the legitimacy of the family was extended to protect the privacy and image of deceased persons. Rules were established on the right to physical integrity, disciplining the use of the body after death for clinical trials but prohibiting medical surgeries contrary to good customs. The right to a name was regulated, and rules on the prohibition of unauthorized use of the name and image were inserted, as well as the right to privacy.

The unification of civil and commercial obligations was insisted on, as advocated by Augusto Teixeira de Freitas. The 1850 Brazilian Commercial Code would be finally repealed, except for the book on Maritime Law. The division between civil and commercial contracts would be eliminated, and another book was inserted into the Civil Code: Business Law. The idea of Commercial Law as the right of the trader, characterized as the person who professionally performed acts of commerce, would be replaced by the adoption of the business doctrine, according to which the businessman is the one who arranges factors of production for the creation of goods and services. Doctrinal and case law understandings on business establishments were inserted; Company Law became part of the Civil Code, except for corporations and cooperative societies, and the insertion of the general theory of securities. Accounting rules were set up, which provide for the preparation of the balance sheets. However, unlike the Italian Civil Code, the legal discipline of labor remained in force through the 1943 Consolidation of Labor Laws.

---

[11] Reale (2002, p. 27).

[12] De Cupis (1961).

In tort law, a strict liability general clause was established based on the risk of the activity, in addition to the subjective civil liability general clause, based on the fault of the agent, which already existed in the 1916 Civil Code.[13]

In Family Law, the 1916 Civil Code instituted the patriarchal model, but it has indeed modified in Brazil over the years, starting with the so-called 1962 Statute of Married Women (Law 4,121, on August 27, 1962), ensuring greater freedom and equality of conditions between men and women within the family and the end of the partial capacity to act due to the fact of marriage. Divorce was allowed in Brazil through Law 6,515 on December 26th 1977. Article 226 of the 1988 Federal Constitution abolished the distinction between legitimate and illegitimate children and recognized stable unions as a family entity. Furthermore, the 1990 Statute of Child and Adolescent (Law 8,069, on July 13th 1990), the 1992 Law on the Recognition of Children out of Marriage (Law 8,560, on December 29th 1992), and the 1996 Stable Unions Law (Law 9,278, on May 10th 1996) were enacted. The Civil Code draft simply embodied the majority of these legal changes.

The Civil Code draft passed through the National Congress between 1975 and 1984, but for political reasons, there was no opportunity for further debates. However, when no one else believed in this idea, the Civil Code codification process was restored in 1997 and carried out to the end, resulting in the enactment of the Civil Code on January 10th, 2002. Nevertheless, on the eve of its promulgation, it was necessary to adjust it substantially so that it was not considered unconstitutional 'ab initio', for not bringing, for example, rules on stable unions that, however, were structured to recognize this family entity as less dignified than that arising from marriage. There was still an attempt to give a certain 'modern' aspect to the 2002 Civil Code in terms of presumption of paternity, ruling the assisted reproduction techniques developed since 1978, alongside the ancient Roman rules on the matter.

4 Does the 2002 Civil Code Respond to Contemporary Social Needs?

Since the 2002 Civil Code was the same 1916 Civil Code with the incorporation of the Teixeira de Freitas's idea of unification of the law of obligations and with the doctrinal and case law updates until the 1970s in the form of new articles, there was much criticism after its enactment. For this reason, the draft of law No. 6,960 of 2002 was submitted to correct the problems existing in the 2002 Civil Code, preferentially before the end of the 'vacatio legis', which would result in the alteration of practically ten percent of its rules. However, due to issues related to political scandals at that time, there was no political opportunity for discussing the 2002 Civil Code reform, and in the end, this draft was stopped. Therefore, the society has lived with a new Civil Code that did not considerably innovate Brazilian Law.

---

[13] Lima (1938).

For example, the rules on personality rights are insufficient in the 2002 Civil Code. In the case of the right to a name, the Law of Public Records (Law 6,015, on December 31st 1973) has still applied, instead of the two articles provided for in the 2002 Civil Code. Regarding the disposition of the body, the 2002 Civil Code prohibited sex reassignments. However, this rule becomes unconstitutional after the Supreme Federal Court's decision about the possibility of change of gender regardless of surgery.[14] The prediction that clinical trials can only be carried out after the person's death is completely surpassed due to all the existing regulations since the end of World War II on this matter. Concerning the right to image, Brazilian case law completed this discipline. The protection of the right to privacy through judicial censorship, as established in the 2002 Civil Code, was declared unconstitutional by the Supreme Federal Court, when invoked as an exception to the exercise of freedom of expression of thought,[15] not to mention the growing situation of cases in which people renounce their privacy frequently, as in the emblematic cases of participation in reality-show programs. These rules have been deficient for the regulation of privacy in the contemporary world, in which relations have been performed on the Internet. For this reason, two laws were enacted to regulate this subject instead of the 2002 Civil Code: the 2014 Internet Civil Framework (Law 12,965, on April 23rd 2014) and the 2018 General Data Protection Law (Law 13,709, on August 14th 2018).

Another controversial aspect concerns people with disabilities. In general terms, the original rules on the capacity to act in the 2002 Civil Code were the same as those in the 1916 Civil Code. The lawmaker only replaced the expression 'every mad people by' 'illness or mental disorder'. In this sense, the vision adopted until 2015 was protectionist, recognizing, 'ab initio', that the person with disabilities is absolutely incapable of taking care of his life. However, with the ratification of the New York Convention on People with Disabilities in 2009 by Brazil, it was necessary to adapt the 2002 Civil Code to this international treaty considered here as an amendment to the chapter on fundamental rights in the 1988 Federal Constitution. Thus, the 2015 Statute of People with Disabilities (Law 13,146, on July 6th 2015) was enacted, and adopted a biopsychosocial model, recognizing the autonomy of the person with disabilities in the exercise of his rights, including marriage and sexuality. Consequently, people with disabilities in Brazil have been considered capable of exercising their rights but, due to an interpretation of the new provision of the 2002 Civil Code, are considered partially incapable of exercising private patrimonial autonomy. This point has generated controversy in Brazil, not to say that 'tabula rasa' is made of these new rules in Brazilian courts.

In the Law of Obligations, the social function of the contract was the most used principle at the beginning of the 2002 Civil Code, indicating, perhaps, that there was a repressed demand for social justice in contractual matters. Courts now have the 'final word' in a contract because, although the parties have exercised their private autonomy, the mandatory force of contracts could be easily relieved through the

---

[14] Supreme Court, Declaration of Unconstitutionality 4275, on March 1st 2018; Extraordinary Appeal 670422, on August 15th 2018.

[15] Supreme Court, Declaration of Unconstitutionality 4815, on June 10th 2015.

recognition that the freedom to contract must take into account important values, including the person's life, physical integrity, and free development. In the current Brazilian case law, whenever the contract has as its object the protection of a fundamental right, the court may freely modify its terms. In terms of health insurance, it is admitted that a person must be treated even in case of lack of contractual provision. However, courts reject that debtors of products, such as automobiles, argue the social function of contract for not to pay the debt, nor allow manifestly abusive requests, such as choosing the best doctors and hospitals in Brazil using cheap policy insurance. In fact, this principle is an important improvement to Brazilian law.[16]

Regarding good faith,[17] there was an important debate about its applicability because this doctrine was associated with a supposed degree of complexity, based on the news about the German postWorld War II experience, in which good faith corresponded to a general rule capable of imposing duties of conduct, limiting the exercise of rights and serving as a criterion for the interpretation of juridical acts. It is true that, in the first decade of the 21st century, the social function of the contract was used more than good faith in Brazil. Nevertheless, in the last ten years, good faith has started to be used much more frequently by Brazilian courts. It is worth mentioning that due to the importance of the general clause of subjective civil liability existing in the 1916 Civil Code—and which was maintained and improved in the 2002 Civil Code—several problems related to damages, which were solved in Germany through the principle of good faith, were solved in Brazil through tort law instead, so that a possible uncritical import of German solutions did not occur in the Brazilian courts.

As for the possibility of contractual revision due to economic imbalance, the 2002 Civil Code adopted the Italian 'eccessiva onerosità sopravenuta' doctrine that allows courts to breach the contract by the request of the debtor, ensuring that the creditor can avoid the breach of the contract by encouraging him to provide a viable counteroffer to the debtor. Some years before the entry into force of the 2002 Civil Code, the Brazilian exchange rate was artificially paired with the United States dollar, and several automobile leasing contracts, whose financial resources were obtained by national banks in the international markets, were executed. In 1998, Brazilian monetary authorities suddenly ended this policy and finished maintaining this artificial parity, and those contracts immediately became excessively burdensome. In this case, part of the courts applied the French unpredictability theory (théorie de l'imprévision), and another part applied the right to revise the contract established in the 1990 Consumer Protection Code (Law 8,078, on September 11th 1990). During the force of the 2002 Civil Code, there were situations where attempts to resolve agricultural contracts due to the 'eccessiva onerosità', but these ones were not modified by courts under the grounds that climatic effects cannot be considered unpredictable events. The big test for this rule took place in 2020, with the COVID-19 pandemic, which forced local authorities to decree lockdown in commercial activity. As the 2002 Civil Code only provided for the termination of the contract—which was not convenient for tenants—it was seen that the 2002 Civil Code was obsolete. An attempt

---

[16] Tomasevicius Filho (2014).

[17] Tomasevicius Filho (2020).

was made to resolve the situation through the Emergency Private Law (14,010, on June 10th 2020) enacted in June 2020, in force until October 30th 2020.

Concerning contractual types, almost nothing has been changed from the 1916 Civil Code to the 2002 Civil Code. Those contractual provisions remained too simple for the dynamics of current private transactions. This is the case in terms of sale, structured for an agrarian society; loan, surpassed by banking law; works contract, surpassed by technological advancement; deposit and commission, insufficient to manage business activities. Urban real estate leases continue to be governed by Law No. 8,245 of 1991, which came into force before the 2002 Civil Code. Insurance contract rules remained practically unchanged and, therefore, are deficient for the regulation of the subject, which needs to be done through rules of the Private Insurances Authority—SUSEP. Transport contract rules, inserted in the 2002 Civil Code due to the absence of a legal provision in the 1916 Civil Code, were established based on Brazilian case law statements. As they are simple rules, they must be supplemented by the national agencies of land transport (ANTT), water transport (ANTAQ), and air transport (ANAC), generating the conflict between regulated law and private law. In addition, the 1990 Consumer Protection Code, which complements a good part of the contracts in Brazil, has been very often applied.

There were criticisms of the unification of civil and commercial obligations among business law scholars. Although the contractual types were the same, such as the sale of goods, their applications were different. For example, it would not be fair to use the social function of contract in a business contract as a hypothesis of its breach, as well as good faith should be applied with caution between businessmen, in comparison with situations in which laymen were negotiating. Therefore, the idea arose that a new Commercial Code should be enacted, repealing the Business Law Book in the 2002 Civil Code. In 2019, the so-called 'law of economic freedom' (Law 13,874 on September 20th, 2019) was enacted, which makes it difficult to apply the social function of the contract in business matters and reduces the power of the courts to modify contractual terms in the event of an economic imbalance. The specific rules about business contracts, such as commercial representation, agency, and distribution, have been practically inapplicable. Additionally, the legal discipline of accounting standards in the Civil Code is 'nonsense', whether the entire world follows international accounting standards. This fact requires companies to make two types of balance sheets simultaneously in Brazil.

In Family Law, the first reaction was the attempt to enact a 'Statute of Families' in 2007 to repeal the Family Law Book from the 2002 Civil Code. Criticisms that were made to the lawmaker, who had kept the model of the family based on marriage as the main family entity in the 2002 Civil Code, placed the stable union as an inferior family entity. No reference to the same-sex relationships exists in the code. Thus, the 2002 Civil Code remained out of date concerning the advances in the current assisted reproduction techniques, even when providing it as a hypothesis of presumption of paternity. As the lawmaker desired to establish fewer advantages for the partner in stable union in comparison with married people in matters of succession rights, the opposite effect produced: the partner was often privileged in relation to the married person. Therefore, the Supreme Court declared unconstitutional this part of the 2002

Civil Code[18] and affirmed the equality of rules between married and partners in stable union in succession matters. In 2011, the Supreme Court declared the prohibition of stable unions between same-sex people as incompatible with the 1988 Federal Constitution,[19] which resulted in the immediate permission of this type of family entity; months later, the Brazilian National Council of Justice allowed same-sex marriages to be celebrated.[20] Thus, in Brazil, heteroaffective marriages are regulated by the 2002 Civil Code, and marriages between same-sex people are regulated by an administrative provision. Finally, also by permission of the National Council of Justice,[21] socioaffective parenting is allowed so that a child can have three parents.

5 What Should Have Been Done?

As expressly assumed by Professor Miguel Reale, the 2002 Civil Code corresponds to the 1916 Civil Code updated with the doctrinal and case law statements of the second half of the 20th century, except for the insertion of the Business Law Book. In this sense, there was more effort to update the old Civil Code than to draft a new one.

Considering that a civil code is a fundamental text within the legal system, Brazil should have created a new type of civil code or adopt a new legislative technique. There were doctrinal debates on the continuity in the use of the codification model inherited from the 19th century. Professor Antonio Junqueira de Azevedo,[22] from the University of São Paulo, argued that the society of the beginning of the 21st century, characterized as a 'postmodern society', could no longer guarantee legal security only through laws. The multiplicity of values and interests led to normative hyperproduction, and it would no longer be possible to combine such diversity into a single code, just as the traditional forms of dispute settlement were insufficient to deal with the power relations among institutions. The different social groups demanded their own statutes, and different conflicts are decided outside the parliaments and courts. Thus, the paradigm of law, important in the 19th century, and the paradigm of courts, important in the 20th century, would be overcome. Professor Junqueira de Azevedo pointed out that 'The Civil Code draft, still underway in the National Congress, is an example of the outdated paradigm', as it was conceived from a strong State model, in which the judge would needlessly be called upon to participate in private life decisions. In his opinion, the way forward would be to enact several codes, including a Code of Obligations, a Code of Family, a Code of the Environment and the

---

[18] Supreme Court, Declarations of Unconstitutionality 646721 and 878694, on May 10th 2017.

[19] Supreme Court, Declaration of Unconstitutionality 4275 and Writ against Inobservance of Fundamental Rule (ADPF) 132, on May 5th 2011.

[20] The National Justice Council, Resolution 175, on May 14th 2013.

[21] The National Justice Council, Ordinances63, on November 17th 2017, and 83, on August 14th 2019.

[22] Junqueira de Azevedo (1999).

Goods, a Code of Personality Rights, and a Code of Successions. He was sympathetic to what had been done in Holland, in which fifty-two statements for a Civil Code were launched for debate. Only in this way would the different social groups be able to participate in the discussions for their elaboration, abandoning the idea of a single code.

On the other hand, contemporary private law has substantial new assumptions, or, in other words, its own epistemological status. Throughout the 20th century, Private Law underwent pendular publicity movements (from the 1930s to the 1980s), advancement by the State over areas such as Family and Inheritance Laws. In addition to this advance, especially after the 1988 Federal Constitution, a discourse of defense of a broad constitutionalization of Private Law arose. At the end of the 20th century and the beginning of the 21st century, due to the privatization of public services, which occurred in the 1990s, with the transformation of Family Law, which is moving strongly toward a space of less state intervention to expand private autonomy, there was reflux in the doctrine regarding the limits of constitutionalization and criticism of the model of direct effects of fundamental rights in private transactions. These movements place Brazilian Private law before a series of debates about its role in the legal system, considering that some of the excesses surrounding constitutionalization have been revised in light of general theory of private law and history of private law studies, according to which there was never a denial of the centrality of the constitution in the legal system or ignorance of the need to interpret ordinary rules of private law in accordance with the constitution. As a transversal element of this criticism, there is the need to expand controls at the level of judicial intervention in Private Law.[23]

6 Final Considerations

Except for the values of sociality, ethics, and operability, the 2002 Civil Code is actually the 1916 Civil Code with Teixeira de Freitas' idea, and with an updated text with the 1970s doctrine and case law. Nevertheless, also in 2002, Germany reformed the Law of Obligations Book in the 1896 Civil Code. In 2016, France reformed the Law of Obligations Book in the 1804 Civil Code. Brazil, for its part, instead of reforming the 1916 Civil Code, updating it as necessary, or adopting a new model of civil code, based on the criticisms already being made regarding the inconvenience of insisting on paradigms and values of a society that no longer existed, it chose not to do either. For a foreign observer, one may have the impression that Brazil has a new Civil Code, when, in fact, this is false. Unfortunately, with the 1916 Civil Code repeal through the enactment of the 2002 Civil Code, Brazil, unlike Germany and France, lost an important 'lieu de mémoire' of its legal culture.

---

[23] Rodrigues Junior (2019).

References

Christofoletti Junior V (2020) A projeção internacional de Augusto Teixeira de Freitas. Thesis (Ph.D. in Private Law). University of São Paulo Law School

Cupis A (1961) Os direitos da personalidade (trans: Caeiro AM, Jardim AV). Morais, Lisboa

Freitas AT (1876) Consolidação das Leis Civis. Garnier, Rio de Janeiro

Gomes O (1963) Memória Justificativa do Anteprojeto de Reforma do Código Civil. Brasília, Depto Imprensa Nacional

Junqueira de Azevedo A (1999) O direito pós-moderno e a codificação. USP Law School J 94:3–12

Lima A (1938) Da culpa ao risco. Revista dos Tribunais, São Paulo

Pereira CMS (2005) Instituições de Direito Civil. Forense, Rio de Janeiro

Pousada ELR (2006) Preservação da tradição jurídica luso-brasileira - Teixeira de Freitas e a Introdução à Consolidação das Leis Civis. Dissertation (Master in Private Law). University of São Paulo Law School

Poveda Velasco IM (1994) Ordenações do Reino de Portugal. USP Law School J 89:11–67

Poveda Velasco IM, Tomasevicius Filho E (2018) The 1830 criminal code of the Brazilian Empire and its originality. In: Masferrer A (ed) The Western codification of criminal law—a revision of the myth of its predominant French influence, pp 341–367

Reale M (2002) Exposição de motivos do Supervisor da Comissão Revisora e Elaboradora do Código Civil. In: Brasil, Novo Código Civil, p 27

Reale M (1968) Teoria tridimensional do direito. Saraiva, São Paulo

Rodrigues Junior OL (2002) Revisão judicial dos contratos. Atlas, São Paulo

Rodrigues Junior OL (2019) Direito Civil Contemporâneo - estatuto epistemológico, Constituição e direitos fundamentais. Forense, Rio de Janeiro

Tomasevicius Filho E (2014) Uma década de aplicação da função social do contrato - análise da doutrina e da jurisprudência brasileira. Revista dos Tribunais 940:49–85

Tomasevicius Filho E (2016) O legado do Código Civil de 1916. USP Law School J 111:85–100

Tomasevicius Filho E (2020) O princípio da boa-fé no direito civil. Almedina, São Paulo

Ignacio Maria Poveda Velasco is Professor of History of Law at the University of Sao Paulo Law School. Former Attorney General and Superintendent of Institutional Relations of the University of Sao Paulo (2018–2022), former General Secretary of the University of São Paulo, Dean of the University of Sao Paulo Ribeirão Preto Law School—(FDRP) (2007–2013), Chairman of the Graduate Commission of the University of Sao Paulo Law School (2003–2007), member of the University Council of the University of Sao Paulo (2007–2013), member of the Sao Paulo State Research Support Foundation (FAPESP) Superior Council, member of the State University of Campinas Council, and member of the Sao Paulo Virtual University Curatorship Council. Bachelor of Laws at the University of Sao Paulo Law School (1982), master's degree (1990) and a Ph.D. (1996) in Roman Law at the same Faculty. Postdoctoral internship at the Università degli Studi di Roma I—La Sapienza (1996–1997).

Eduardo Tomasevicius Filho is Associate Professor of Private Law and History of Law at the Department of Private Law of the University of Sao Paulo Law School. LL.B. from the University of Sao Paulo (2001); Master in History at the University of Sao Paulo (2012); Ph.D in Private Law at the University of Sao Paulo (2007) and Habilitation in Private Law at the University of Sao Paulo (2017). He is a lawyer in Sao Paulo, Brazil.

The Making of a Civil Code: The Hungarian Example

Lajos Vékás

Abstract Concerning the social influence of the private law codifications of the last two hundred years, one can differentiate between four generations of these codes: classical codes, second-generation codes, socialist and postsocialist codifications. Almost uniquely on the European continent, until 1959, private law in Hungary was mostly judge-made customary law. However, the first Code from 1959 was conceived and adopted in an era in which nationalization fully liquidated private property. Therefore, after 1990, a new codification was necessary. The new Hungarian CC, like the other codifications in Eastern Europe and the Baltic states from the last thirty years, belongs to the fourth generation of codification. These CCs were born in the course of the historically late reestablishment of the private property-based society. Although the privatization of the state property was implemented by separate statutes, the new codes, including the Hungarian CC from 2013, play an important social role, similar to the classical codes in the early nineteenth century.

1 Introduction: Late Codification of Private Law

Almost uniquely on the European continent, until the second half of the twentieth century, private law in Hungary was mostly judge-made customary law. Between 1900 and 1928, several high-quality draft codes were produced, but for mainly political reasons, none of them were enacted. The first private law code, Act IV of 1959 (hereinafter: the CC of 1959), which entered into force in 1960, was conceived and adopted in an era—between 1953 and 1959—in which the ruling dictatorial political power and nationalization almost fully liquidated the natural social conditions for property transactions (namely, private property) and for emerging personality rights. Among those economic, social, and political circumstances, we can appreciate the enactment of a high-quality code that was elaborated by professors who graduated before the Second World War and benefited from a high level of legal

L. Vékás (✉)
Eötvös Loránd University Budapest, Budapest, Hungary
e-mail: vekas@ajk.elte.hu

M. Graziadei and L. Zhang (eds.), *The Making of the Civil Codes*,
Ius Gentium: Comparative Perspectives on Law and Justice 104,
https://doi.org/10.1007/978-981-19-4993-7_18

education. We have to mention their names with respect: Endre *Nizsalovszky* (1894–1976), Miklós *Világhy* (1916–1980) and Gyula *Eörsi* (1922–1992). Thanks to its outstanding professional quality, the CC of 1959 could survive the radical economic and political developments leading to the changes after 1990 by more than two decades. Among the codes of that era, only the Polish CC of 1964 can boast as much success as the Hungarian Code of 1959. Nevertheless, it is understandable that the changes, as a result of which a market economy based on private property could evolve again in Hungary, had to be followed by frequent amendments. This progress resulted in such fundamental developments in the field of private law relationships that their governance rendered a comprehensive reform and the adoption of a new CC necessary. Recognizing this need, the government ordered the preparation of a new CC in April 1998. According to the Government Decree, 'the goal of the reform is the creation of a modern CC compatible with international practice and expectations, which shall become the fundamental statute of private law as the constitution of the economy'. Due to the government decree, the Drafting Committee on Private Law was created, along with working groups that started their substantive work in 1999. After preparatory work and thorough discussions between experts, taking more than a decade, a draft was prepared. The proposal of the Committee was submitted by the government to the Parliament without amendments on 11 July 2012. After accepting some amendments proposed by the members of Parliament, the Hungarian Parliament adopted Act V of 2013 on the CC (hereinafter: *CC* or *Code*) on 11 February 2013. It entered into force on March 15, 2014.

2   Social Model

After four decades of nondemocratic governments and misguided policies that resulted in economic and social deadlock, Hungary set out on the path of a social order based on private property and free enterprise in 1990. Social policy goals have followed since then, and the constitutional guarantees adopted to implement these consider the view of society as modeled in Europe (i.e., the pattern of the social market economy, prevailing in today's developed Europe and primarily in the Member States of the European Union). This political and social direction is intended to be served by the CC. The legislation departed from the premise that the new CC has to establish the conditions for a constitutionally protected market economy interwoven with social elements in private law. The CC primarily lays down the legal frameworks for property transactions. At the same time, it intends to provide protection for persons, including the personality rights of individuals and legal persons and personal relationships within the family.

The new social model required the far-reaching acceptance of the private autonomy of owners, in particular the full recognition and protection of private property. This principle (as the first pillar of private autonomy) pervades the entire CC as well as its detailed provisions. This is, of course, supplemented by public law and social constraints imposed on private property, for example, in the rules on the protection of public health, historic buildings, environment, etc., as well as in private law rules on protecting the interests of neighbors. The other fundamental consequence of private autonomy (the second pillar) is the acceptance of the principle of freedom of contract. Any limitation to this pillar of private law is justified only to the extent that this is rendered indispensable by the demand for social justice, and it is still possible under the conditions of free market competition. The law governing consumer contracts is the most important field that attempts to maintain this balance, which is difficult to achieve. The third pillar of private autonomy is the freedom of association, the demands of which are intended to be served by the CC through the institutions of associations, companies and cooperatives following the tested models of traditional private law regulations.

3 Tradition and Innovation

The drafters of the CC departed from the existing living law, and they intended to change it only if this was rendered necessary by the demands of the changed economic and social conditions. In accordance with this methodological point of departure of fundamental importance, the CC maintained the rules of the CC of 1959 wherever it was possible. They were also complemented by integrating the provisions of certain specific acts. In addition, the CC built in the results of the decades of Supreme Court jurisprudence on the CC of 1959, which had a lasting message, was ripe for codification and demanded positive law regulation. In case of doubt, the CC thus opted for the existing law and did not adopt new alternative solutions if they could have caused uncertainty in the legal system. On the other hand, the CC wanted to reform Hungarian private law: it intended to serve the needs of the changed economy and society by introducing new legal institutions, for example, in the field of collateral and contracts. The reduction of private law transactions under the conditions of socialism necessarily resulted in the impoverishment of private law, the disappearance of the shades of solutions based on legal dogmatics and the fading of contours. The edge of private law concepts known and applied for centuries was blunted and became a victim of the sometimes-undemanding court practice. The CC also wanted to compensate for these losses, e.g., with the separation of liability for breach of contract and extracontractual (delictual) liability or with new regulation of the assignment of claims. At the same time, the legislation by no means wanted to complicate regulation with superfluous innovations in legal dogmatics; it brought changes only in those questions to which more correct answers could be given based on a more nuanced approach of legal dogmatics. To mention only one example, the CC amended the rules on the transfer of property in accordance with this objective. Taking this into account, the rules on establishing a pledge and on the transfer of property, for example, were also changed.

The CC took into consideration that EU legislation directly influences the reform of Member State private law in several fields, and it intended to integrate the lasting core of EU private law directives organically (e.g., in consumer contract law and company law). However, the legislature did not endeavor to build the entire corpus of EU private law into the CC. The reason for this was that the rules in the EU private law directives are too fragmented, casuistic and often subject to changes and thus are not suitable in all their details for codification planned with a long-term perspective. The CC therefore opted for the lesser evil by leaving some rules based on directives in separate acts.

4   Foreign Examples

The CC did not choose a foreign model, but it drew abundantly on works of foreign codification. The drafts prepared during the first half of the twentieth century had already primarily taken the solutions of the Austrian (ABGB), the German (BGB) codes, and occasionally the French *Code Civil* into consideration; the Swiss ZGB also provided some examples for the draft of 1928. As such, the lessons of these large classical codifications had already been drawn on by Hungarian private law codification earlier. From the more recent national codes, the Dutch CC (Burgerlijk Wetboek of 1992) and the *code civil* of the Canadian province of Québec (1991) were considered the most modern CCs at the time. These codes served as a pattern in several respects for the Hungarian reforms (primarily in determining the scope of the situations to be regulated and the structure of the CC), but not even these were considered a regulatory model as far as the entire codification was concerned.

In addition to national codes, the CC also drew on international legislation that had achieved worldwide recognition among legal experts and had a broad impact on legislation and judicial practice. From these, the CISG, adopted in Vienna in 1980 (CISG), must be mentioned first. Model acts elaborated by academic groups also served as templates that could be considered and occasionally followed regarding the regulation of contract law, namely, the UNIDROIT Principles of International Commercial Contracts and the Principles of European Contract Law (PECL), as well as the Draft Common Frame of Reference (DCFR).

5   Comprehensive Character: Monistic Approach

Although the endeavors of the EU for legal unification have also reached the area of private law in recent decades and they have considerable influence on national legislations today, it seems that private law may still be codified comprehensively, even within the EU, at the level of the Member States only. This statement is justified by the fact that, in addition to the Netherlands (1992), a new CC entered into force in several countries in Europe, including Lithuania (2001), Romania (2011) and the Czech Republic (2014), and even the classical codes (the BGB, the ABGB and the Code civil) have been recently subject to substantial reform. This codification by the Member States is understandable because the EU Directives and regulations result in legal unification in narrow specific fields only and constitute small islands in the sea of private law rules.

The CC is a legal work that possesses the character of a code, and the advantages of this code are intended to be broadly profited. Of course, this method may not be an end in itself. The CC took into account that, even in addition to the most successful codification, some private law rules remain outside the Code. The CC must therefore provide for a subsidiary default legal framework regarding such norms. The substantive accord and the terminological unity of these separate private law acts with the CC must be ensured to the fullest extent; the concepts contained in the CC must be used with the same content in separate acts as well.

The CC took as a point of departure that it is appropriate to broaden the substantive borderlines of the CC as long as the positive effects of the codification, in particular terminological unity, the methodological homogeneity of the norms integrated and the possibility of compression and abridgment, facilitate legal practice. The integration of rules into the same CC is therefore desirable and expedient as long as the methodological unity of the norms to be integrated exists and as long as the systematization denotes the advantages of codification, including systemic rationality, coherent and consistent legal drafting, the certainty of terminology and clear and perspicuous solutions.

Taking all these into account, the legislature incorporated the material of family law into the CC. Partly for ideological reasons, this part of private law was regulated in a separate family law statute and not in the CC of 1959 during the decades of socialism. In the course of integrating it, the due expression of the peculiarities of family law relationships cannot be ignored. This is demonstrated by the fact that the legislator in Book 4 of the CC laid down certain principles, primarily for the protection of the interests of the child, applicable to such legal relationships only.

The legislator also decided in favor of integrating rules on commercial companies into the CC, and the relevant rules have been located among the provisions on legal persons in Book 3. This solution logically follows from the fact that the internal and external relations of legal persons take place in the framework of private law relationships, and thus, the object and the method of regulation is in accordance with the character of the CC. The integration of the rules on companies into the CC involves several advantages. The scope of the general rules on legal persons may be broadened, and the repetition of the norms may be avoided. Moreover, the mainly default character of the norms of the CC on contracts becomes self-evident. For this and some similar advantages in terms of codification, in the Swiss OR (1881), then the second Italian code (Codice civile of 1940/1942), and most recently the Dutch code (*Burgerlijk Wetboek* of 1992), other legislatures decided on accommodating company law in the private law code. The counterarguments commonly advanced, in particular on mixing of private and public law norms regarding the regulation of companies, the tradition of separating the regulations, etc., weigh less in comparison to the advantages of integration. The CC equally provides framework rules on cooperatives in Book 3 on legal persons, laying the foundations for a more specific regulation of the main types of cooperatives (carrying out production, service and credit providing, etc., activities).

Similar to the CC of 1959, the CC did not integrate the material of the separate acts on copyright and industrial property, although the subjective rights emerging in the legal relationships of intellectual property and the majority of the sanctions for their violation have an unequivocally private law character. The separate acts embrace mixed norms from different fields of law; it would be difficult to reconcile them as a result of their differences in character. The CC stresses at the same time the private law nature of the protection of intellectual property and other intellectual goods, and therefore the CC lays down its own background role regarding the separate acts.

Although the CC, and in particular the general rules on contracts, also constitute the legal background for the special regulation of employment relationships, the CC left the settlement of individual employment contracts to the Labor Code. The main reason for this solution is that the legal regulation of employment contracts today already has so many peculiarities, making it difficult to integrate this system of norms into a CC. The employee is conceptually a 'weaker party', and this characteristic is a distinguishing peculiarity in regulation. Moreover, the influence of EU law is more intensive here in comparison to other fields of private law. Regarding those contracts for carrying out work that do not fall under the scope of application of the Labor Code, the rules of the CC on mandates or contracts to produce work may be duly applied, depending on the characteristics of the service.

The CC encompasses the private law relationships of both businesses (i.e., the professional actors in property transactions) and individuals. This is visible in how it regulates contract law. By adopting the so-called monistic approach, the CC created such general rules on contracts that can be applied to relations on any legal subject. In regulating special types of contracts, the CC imposes the standards of professional business on contract types playing a role in both business transactions and relationships between individuals. The CC lays down exceptional rules only if the contract is concluded between a business undertaking (such as a corporation or partnership) and a consumer (business to consumer: B2C), i.e., it qualifies as a consumer contract. The CC contains provisions providing for special rights for consumers both among the general rules of contracts, notably in relation to the obligation to inform and concerning the norms on general contract terms and conditions, on warranty and the right to rescind, and among the rules on certain types of contracts (pledge agreement, guarantee, suretyship, etc.).

The so-called monistic approach and the mainly commercial law character of the CC are also indicated by the new contract types regulated by it. The CC intends to offer nonmandatory rules for those contracts that have been crystallized to the necessary extent in practice and that are not simply a combination of contract types, mixing the already existing contract types, but have content that is clearly distinguishable from other contracts. Following this approach, the CC regulates factoring and financial leasing among financing types of contracts and those contracts that mediate goods and services from producers and service providers to end users: agency contracts, distribution contracts and franchises. An important novelty is the regulation of fiduciary asset management contracts (a kind of trust). The comprehensive review of the rules on credit and account contracts and the extension of the number of types of contracts regulated here are in accordance with the selected codification approach.

The CC is not one among many statutes. The importance and complexity of the situations directly regulated by it demonstrates its paramount significance. The impact of the CC goes well beyond the relationships regulated directly by it and radiates through any relationship that is or may be settled by private law norms, irrespective of whether the given norm refers explicitly to the CC.

6 Structure

The CC divides its norms into books, parts, and then chapters. At the beginning of the CC, similar to the CC of 1959, introductory provisions summarize the purpose and principles of the whole CC. These principles include the principle of good faith and fair dealing, the requirement on acting as may be generally expected in the given situation, and the prohibition of abuse of law. After Books Two to Seven, containing detailed rules, the closing provisions may be found.

The books of the CC are as follows:

Book 1: Introductory Provisions
Book 2: The Individual as Subject of Law
Book 3: Legal Persons
Book 4: Family Law
Book 5: Right *in rem*
Book 6: Law of Obligations
Book 7: Law of Succession
Book 8: Final provisions.

Following the traditions of Hungarian codifications, the CC does not contain a general part, unlike some foreign private law codes such as the German BGB. Structuring norms in such a way may be justified by the fact that the rules on institutions, which play a role in several fields, are located in an independent structural unit highlighting them. This is the case with the 'legal transaction' in the BGB, when its norms, which can have a role in addition to the law of obligations, in terms of rights *in rem*, in family law, and succession law, are summarized in the general part. Proponents of this solution to codification used the legal literature to oppose Gusztáv *Szászy-Schwarz* (1858–1920), the outstanding Hungarian private lawyer of his era, in the course of the elaboration of the very first Hungarian draft code, published in 1900. Such proponents of this solution rightly pointed out that the concept of 'legal transaction' is an exaggerated and unhelpful abstraction in a code because the most important legal transaction is the contract, the rules of which should be determined in their own place in the law of contract instead of being outlined in some abstract manner. Furthermore, the last will, the most significant unilateral legal transaction, is regulated by separate provisions in Book 7. Having accepted this approach, all Hungarian draft codes and the CC of 1959 refrained from creating a general part putting the abstract 'legal transaction' at the center of their CC, as did the drafters of the CC.

The CC builds up the system of its norms in principle following the CC of 1959, but in a partly different structure. The most crucial change is that it gives place to the provisions on legal persons in an independent book (Book 3), separating them from the rules on natural persons (individuals) to accommodate the increased number of rules stemming from the integration of company law into the law of persons. In comparison to the previous CC, the other important change in the structure of the CC is that it separates from contract law the rules applicable to all legal obligations, including representation, the limitation period, multiparty obligations, and the norms determining the performance of obligations. These rules are placed in an independent part at the beginning of the Book on the law of obligations (Part 1 in Book 6). Moreover, the rules on legal declarations placed in this part may gain application not only to legal declarations in the law of obligations but also to those made in terms of rights *in rem*, family law, and succession law, unless otherwise provided. This structural solution is not unproblematic but unequivocally indicates that these highlighted norms are to be applied to any obligation. The situation is similar with regard to the common rules on legal persons in Book 3 of the CC. These were created mostly by generalization from the norms of company law and primarily play a role in regulating legal disputes involving companies, but they may be equally applied to any other legal person. In comparison to the CC of 1959, the last structural change worthy of mention concerns Book 5. This book bears the title 'Rights *in rem*' instead of 'Ownership Law' because in addition to private law norms on ownership, it regulates possession and limited rights *in rem* in a more detailed way than the CC of 1959. Among them are the rules on pledge, which, unlike in the CC of 1959, are not in the law of obligations. This latter change was justified primarily by the fact that the fundamentally new regulation of pledge retains its double nature (pertaining to rights *in rem* and the law of obligations) in relation to the most important types of collateral. In contrast, today, the rights *in rem* character must be emphasized much more than in 1959, when historically a debtor under the law of obligations and the debtor of rights *in rem* almost never differed, modern characterizations of such rights require distinctions to be drawn. The CC also accommodates the principles of the Land Registry in the Book on Rights *in rem*.

7 Codification Style and the Nature of Norms

The CC avoids casuistry; it does not want to make legal practice more difficult with speculatively created detailed norms. Instead, it creates more general rules that are capable of following social and economic changes and are thus more flexible. For example, the CC accordingly specifies a deadline expressed in days only where it is indispensable. Otherwise, it provides for acting 'without delay', which enables the circumstances of the case to be taken into account instead of a necessarily rigid deadline, and for the standard of conduct that may be generally expected to be applied in the given case. However, the CC does not intend to risk imposing legal uncertainty by an extensive application of open norms (general clauses). The intention of regulating in a general way where possible is also demonstrated by the fact that the CC provides for the obligations applicable to all contracts (e.g., obligation to cooperate with or to inform the other party) consistently among the general rules of contracts, and only the possible deviations appear concerning the particular types of contracts.

The CC applies referring norms only where this method makes it possible to avoid word-by-word repetitions and involves abridgment. This advantage is not compromised by the fuzziness or ambiguity of the provision. The CC avoids referring simply to the number of the appropriate sect. This is because such a solution renders the use of the code more difficult, as demonstrated in the German BGB.

The main guarantee of the freedom of contract is the nonmandatory character of the overwhelming majority of contract law norms, allowing the parties to agree freely on the terms of individual transactions. They are free to determine the content of their contract and can derogate from most of the rules of the CC. The Code created the nonmandatory norms in view of typical life situations and taking the interests of the parties into account in a mutual and balanced way.

As with the realm of contracts in the law of obligations, the CC recognizes the autonomy of the parties for the association of persons (of course, subject to the necessary deviations). Accordingly, the rules on legal persons in the CC also broadly have a nonmandatory character. The nonmandatory nature for a significant part of the law of companies and associations, similar to contract law, is traced back to the consideration that the legislature apparently cannot foresee the goals to be achieved by the parties for an enormous mass of clauses. As such, the CC cannot give room to the intention of the parties individually or according to company type. If there were a completely mandatory regulation, many contract clauses would inevitably be prohibited even if this was not justified for any reason. It is therefore more appropriate to follow an inverse regulatory method, instead of the method allowing exceptions to the general principle of mandatory regulation, and to open the door to the parties' freedom to determine the substance and limit this by mandatory provisions only where it is justified for overriding policy reasons. This method was adopted by the CC in regulating associations and commercial companies as well.

The function and significance of nonmandatory rules lies in the fact that the rules offered by the CC do not need to be 'invented' by the parties and they did not have to include them in their agreement as they apply by virtue of the law. They extend to the relationship concerned unless the parties agree otherwise. By this solution, transaction costs related to the formation of a contract or foundation of a company or association may be significantly decreased. As mentioned, the rules laid down in the Code for contracts and legal persons are generally of a nonmandatory character (i.e., the parties may in each individual case either simply exclude their application in whole or in part or modify their content to adapt them to the specific needs of the kind of transaction involved). We stress, however, that the CC makes it clear that the parties are entitled to deviate from nonmandatory norms only regarding the provisions establishing their rights and obligations. The parties cannot deviate from the norms determining the concept of legal institutions, not even by mutual agreement.

In the field of the regulation of contracts, companies, and associations, there are, of course, also mandatory norms from which parties cannot derogate. A contractual clause derogating from such rules is null and void. Mandatory rules are necessary primarily where the interests of third parties (e.g., the creditors), the minority members in the case of associations and companies or the protection of the moral value system of the society require mandatory norms to restrict the autonomy of the parties. Furthermore, the CC also contains mandatory norms where a significant lack of balance in economic power or expertise may be established behind the presumed equality and interdependence of the parties to a contract, and this asymmetry may result in the unilateral determination of the content of the contract. Such situations primarily include contracts concluded with consumers (B2C contracts). In regulating them, the CC provides for protective rules using mandatory norms to safeguard the interests of the weaker party effectively. The CC locates the rules protecting consumers thematically (i.e., it lays down special norms for the protection of consumers in answer to concrete questions). The CC makes the mandatory nature of these norms and the nullity of any deviation from them unambiguous.

In exceptional cases, where one of the parties' profits from the possibility offered by nonmandatory regulation in an inadmissible way and the flagrant failure of the desired position of balance between the parties may not be remedied in the absence of a concrete mandatory rule, the principles formulated in the form of a general clause by the CC give courts the power to intervene. Such an open norm may also be found among the general provisions on contracts, such as the rule declaring a contract obviously in breach of good morals as null and void. Moreover, the common principles of the CC among the introductory provisions serving to protect the legal order are also of application in the realm of contracts, companies and associations. The abuse of mandatory regulations may be impeded by relying on the standard of the principle of good faith and fair dealing or the prohibition of abuse of law, provided that this may not be achieved by a more appropriate legal instrument in the case concerned, such as the safeguards of the rules on general contract terms and conditions (e.g., by declaring an unfair contract term null and void) or by establishing a violation of good morals.

8 Conclusion

Concerning the social influence of the private law codifications of the last two hundred years, one can differentiate between four generations of these codices: classical codes, second-generation codes, socialist and postsocialist codifications. The Hungarian CC, like the other codifications in Eastern Europe and the Baltic states from the last thirty years, belongs to the fourth generation. These CCs were born in the course of the historically late reestablishment of the private property-based society. Although the privatization of the state property was implemented by separate statutes, the new codes play an important social role, similar to the classical codes in the early nineteenth century. So does the Hungarian CC from 2013, too.

References

Iudica G (2021) Lo Stato moderno e la codificazione – The Modern State and Codification (bilingual). Editoriale Scientifica, Napoli

Küpper H (2014, 2015) Ungarns neues BGB. Wirtschaft und Recht in Osteuropa (WiRO) 5/2014, 129; 6/2014, 174; 7/2014, 206; 8/2014, 234; 9/2014, 266; 11/2014, 327; 12/2014, 366; 1/2015, 12; 2/2015, 46

Menyhárd A, Veress E (eds) (2017) New CCs in Hungary and Romania. Springer International Publishing AG

Vékás L (2009) Über die Expertenvorlage eines neuen Zivilgesetzbuches für Ungarn. Zeitschrift für europäisches Privatrecht (ZEuP) 17:536–563

Vékás L (2010) The codification of private law in hungary in historical perspective. Annales Univ. Sci. Budapestinensis de Rolando Eötvös Nominatae, Sectio Iuridica, Tomus LI, pp 51–63

Vékás L (2014a) Rekodifikation des Privatrechts in Zentral- und Osteuropa zwischen Reformbedarf und Tradition. In: Welser R (ed) Die Rekodifikation des Privatrechts in Zentral- und Osteuropa zwischen Reformbedarf und Tradition. Manz, Wien, pp 115–124

Vékás L (2014b) Der Einfluss des UN Kaufrechts auf die Schadenshaftung im neuen ungarischen Leistungsstörungsrecht. In: Mankowski P, Wurmnest W (eds) Festschrift für Ulrich Magnus. Sellier, München, pp 115–126

Vékás L (2014c) Erfahrungen mit einer verspäteten Privatrechtskodifikation: das neue ungarische Zivilgesetzbuch. In: Okuda Y, Schauer M (eds) Geschichtliche Wurzeln und Reformen in mittel- und osteuropäischen Privatrechtsordnungen. Manz, Wien, pp 1–18

Vékás L (2015a) Zur Umsetzung der Verbraucherrechte-Richtlinie in ein kodifiziertes Rechtssystem. In: Welser R (Hrsg.) Die Umsetzung der Verbraucherrechte-Richtlinie in den Staaten Zentral- und Osteuropas. Manz, Wien, pp 245–257

Vékás L (2015b) Konzeptionelle Streitfragen in der jüngsten ungarischen Privatrechtskodifikation. Pázmány Law Review III, Budapest, pp 17–29

Vékás L (2016a) Über das ungarische Zivilgesetzbuch (ZGB) im Spiegel der neueren europäischen Privatrechtsentwicklung. Zeitschrift für europäisches Privatrecht (ZEuP) 24:37–52

Vékás L (2016b) Privatautonomie und ihre Grenzen im Gemeinschaftsprivatrecht und in den post-sozialistischen Kodifikationen. In: Stumpf C, Kainer F, Baldus C (eds) Privatrecht, Wirtschaftsrecht, Verfassungsrecht. Nomos, Baden-Baden, pp 98–103

Vékás L (2018) Private law codifications through the lens of cultural history. Hungarian Rev 3:64–73

Vékás L (2019) Das europäische Verbrauchervertragsrecht im ungarischen Privatrecht. In: Welser R (ed) Der Einfluss des EU-Rechts in den Jahren 2007–2017 auf die Privatrechtsordnungen der CEE-Staaten. Manz, Wien, pp 45–55

Vékás L (2020) Über das europäische Verbrauchervertragsrecht und die Herausforderungen bei der Umsetzung. In Benicke C, Huber S (eds) National, international, transnational: Harmonischer Dreiklang im Recht. Festschrift für Herbert Kronke zum 70. Geburtstag. Gieseking Verlag, Bielefeld, pp 1273–1282

Lajos Vékás is Professor emeritus of law and the author of nineteen books in Hungarian, English, and German on private law and private international law. He taught these subjects at Eötvös Loránd University Budapest (1963–2009), was Rector of this University (1990–1993) and founding Rector of the Collegium Budapest Institute for Advanced Study (1992–1997). He was a visiting professor at the University Heidelberg (1986/1987). Between 2014 and 2020, he was Vice-President of the Hungarian Academy of Sciences.

System Innovations: Characteristics and Contributions of the Chinese Civil Code

Liming Wang

Abstract Informed by insights from comparative law and situated in China's national conditions, the Chinese Civil Code (CCC) makes significant innovations in building a civil legal system. The CCC did not adopt the classic "three-book" or "five-book" paradigm of other civil law countries. Instead, it is divided into seven books, namely, General Provisions, Personality Rights, Contracts, Property Rights, Marriage and Family, Succession, and Tort Liability. Compared with the German Civil Code, the CCC added Books of Personality Rights and Tort Liability but did not include General Rules of the Law of Obligations. The system innovations of the CCC include a separate Book of Personality Rights, a unique contract-centered organization of creditors' rights, a separate Book of Tort Liability, and a Civil Code system with civil/private rights as its foundation and rights recognition plus remedy as its organizing structure. These are significant characteristics of the CCC, and they are also important contributions to civil law codifications worldwide.

1 Introduction

A civil code system is composed of systems and rules with internal logical connections and a system structure composed of internally consistent values. "The formulation of the civil code is based on the idea of codification, which is that private legal relationships involving people's lives should be fully regulated under certain principles".[1] Since the codification movement in the eighteenth century, codification has meant systematization, so a civil code is essentially characterized by systematization and the logic resulting from such systematization.[2] Hence, system is the lifeblood of

---

[1] Wang (2001, p. 22).

[2] Rivera (2013, pp. 37–38).

L. Wang (✉)
Renmin University of China, Beijing, China
e-mail: wang_liming@263.net

a civil code, and a "civil code" lacking system and logic can only be called a "compilation of civil laws" rather than a civil code. The continental law system is also called the civil code system, demonstrating that the civil code is an essential hallmark of the civil law system. As the basis for fundamental law and private law in the legal system, the CCC makes important innovations by drawing from comparative law and attending to the conditions of China and the development of the times.[3] It can be concluded that system innovations are significant characteristics of the CCC and extraordinary contributions to the codification of Civil Law in the world.

2 The System Innovation of a Seven-Book Structure in the Chinese Civil Code

A civil code system includes two aspects: a formal system (external system) and a value system (internal system).[4] The former refers to the books of a civil code as well as the organization and rules of these books, while the latter refers to the fundamental values that underlie a civil code, including the values and principles of civil law. The civil codes in the continental law countries have invariably adopted the value of autonomy of private law (understood as the autonomy of private ordering), namely, civil subjects are entitled to act within the scope of the law freely and may establish, change, or abolish civil legal relations of their own free will. The subjects of private law can exercise autonomy of the will in all areas not prohibited by public law. This freedom accords with one component of the rule of law, "the absence of legal prohibition means freedom." The recent decades have witnessed more robust recognition of humanistic and cultural values in civil law thanks to social development and high-tech advancement. Since the beginning of the twenty-first century, respect for and protection of human rights has become an international consensus. In particular, as society develops, personality rights and torts have become new growth points for civil law, precisely underlining the value of humanistic care. In summary, the CCC not only establishes the concept of autonomy of private law and safeguards personal liberty but also takes humanistic care as a paramount value of the code, protects the interests of the weak in society, advances social justice, and manifests the spirit of humanism. Therefore, the CCC's internal system aligns with the development spirit of the twenty-first century.

There are two typical civil code systems in civil law countries across the globe in terms of the formal system (external system).

The first is the Roman system, which was proposed by the Roman jurist Gaius in his book *Institutiones*. This system was adopted by the Roman Emperor Justinian I when he compiled all existing laws into one collection. Justinian I divided the Institutes into the Law of Persons, the law of Property, and the Law of Procedure.

---

[3] A fine English translation of the CCC completed by a group of talented civil law scholars from around the world has been recently published by Brill, see Chen et al. (2021).

[4] Bydlinski (1996, p. 48 ff.).

The French Civil Code adopted this three-book codification system. Nevertheless, the French Civil Code eliminated the Law of Procedure and further divided the Law of Property into various modifications of ownership and various methods of obtaining property. Hence, the French Civil Code was divided into three books: Book of Persons, Book of Property and the Various Modifications of Ownership, and Book of the Various Ways of Acquiring Ownership. This model was adopted by a number of continental European countries, such as Switzerland, Belgium, and Italy.[5] The French Civil Code was modeled on Roman law and aptly translated the economic rules of a new capitalist society into the language of law, thus "becoming the code used as the basis for the compilation of all new codes around the world."[6] In recent decades, however, France took the lead in breaking away from this three-book system. It added a separate Book of Guarantees to satisfy the needs of financial development.

The second is the German Civil Code system based on the *Digest (Digesta)* of the *Corpus Juris Civilis*. This system was built by the Pandectist School, which relied upon annotations of Roman law, particularly interpretations of the *Digest*. The German system organizes its Civil Code into five books: General Provisions, Law of Obligations, Law of Property, Law of Family, and Law of Succession.[7] It stipulates the General Provisions by "extracting common factors" and lays out the common regulations and rules of the civil code. Meanwhile, it distinguishes between real rights and creditor's rights and has a separate Book of Succession. Consequently, a fairly complete and unambiguous system is formed. The German Civil Code is the fruit of the Pandectist School and embodies the latter's high logical and scientific standards. This is why the German Civil Code is often referred to as "scientific law." With respect to logical organization, the German Civil Code is a complete modern civil legal system,[8] so it is considered the crowning achievement of codification of the nineteenth century. Many countries and regions that adopted the civil law system have accepted the German Civil Code system, including Japan, Thailand, South Korea, Portugal, Greece, Russia, Taiwan, and Macau. Japan, notably, also followed the "Anglo-Saxon" tradition and placed real rights before creditor's rights when accepting the German Civil Code system.[9]

The Swiss Civil Code of 1912 is also unique. It has an Introduction and combines civil and commercial law into one code. In addition, it places Law of Persons and Family Law before Property Law and protects personality rights in its first Book, Law of Persons.[10] Meanwhile, it does not have a General Provisions; and a Code of Obligations was promulgated separately as a stand-alone law applicable to other

---

[5] Zheng (2003, p. 40).

[6] Marx and Engels (2009, vol. 10, p. 598).

[7] Von Savigny (1840, p. 401 ff.).

[8] Zweigert and Kotz (2003, p. 220).

[9] Zheng (2003, p. 40).

[10] Xie (2004, pp. 66 and 74).

civil legal relations through the provisions of Article 7.[11] It should be noted that the CCs promulgated in recent decades, including the Dutch CC and the Québec Civil Code, adopt different structures from the German and French Civil Codes. Overall, although later civil codes mirror the development pattern of earlier Civil Codes, they should also deviate somewhat from the pattern to accord with the country's legal traditions and actual needs. For this reason, there is no set system. The Dutch Civil Code, for instance, has a separate Book of Transport to satisfy the actual needs of its maritime development. The Québec CC introduced a separate Book entitled "Prior Claims and Hypothecs" to protect creditors' rights.

Although the Roman and German Civil Code systems had significant influence on the civil codes of countries within the civil law system, the most prominent characteristic of the five-book model is that the General Provisions consists of the common factors extracted from the other Books, thus simplifying legal rules and preventing duplication.[12] Meanwhile, the five-book model distinguishes between real rights and creditor's rights and enhances the scientific nature of the code. Therefore, many countries and regions within the civil law system have adopted the German Civil Code system. Since the reform movements of the late Qing Dynasty, the legacy of German civil law has become the focus of civil legislation and theoretical research in China. The Kuomintang (Nationalist) government promulgated the Civil Code of the Republic of China, which systematically copied the five-book model of the German Civil Code. In fact, most of the Civil Code of the Republic of China was derived from the German Civil Code. Regarding the time of the promulgation, the General Provisions of this Civil Code was promulgated on May 30, 1929; the book on Law of Obligations was promulgated on November 22, 1929; the book on Property Law was promulgated on November 30, 1929; and the books on Family Law and Succession Law were promulgated on December 26, 1930. Today, this Civil Code remains still valid in Taiwan, China. "Six or seven out of ten current civil laws adopt the German Code, three or four out of ten adopt the Swiss Code, and one or two out of ten adopt the French, Japanese or Russian Code," according to Mr. Mei Zhongxie.[13]

After the founding of the People's Republic of China, the legislature abolished the "six-book Civil Code" enacted by the Nationalist government. However, the legal traditions established in old China have not entirely disappeared, and German law has always impacted China. It is acknowledged that German civil law is highly system-atic and logical, which helps us integrate China's fragmented and chaotic civil laws. Some of its advanced experience is worth learning from. For instance, a number of basic regulations set forth in the General Principles of the Civil Law enacted in 1986 were obviously influenced by German law on issues of legal acts, agency, and effects. The Civil Code system, however, is an open and developing system rather than a closed one. Throughout history, the rationality of humans has never been

---

[11] Article 7 of the Swiss Civil Code stipulates that: "The general provisions of the Code of Obliga-tions concerning the formation, performance and termination of contracts also apply to other civil law matters."

[12] Westermann (2013, p. 10).

[13] Mei (1998, Preface).

in a static state but has gone through a process of continuous development, transformation and sublimation.[14] As a Chinese saying goes, a wise person changes as time and circumstances change. The German Civil Code was drafted by the German Commentators more than a century ago and complied with the social and economic needs of Germany at that time but does not perfectly meet the China's present social and economic demands. For example, the German Civil does not set forth systematic provisions on personality rights and has been fiercely criticized for this. Soon after the German Civil Code was enacted, the German scholar Werner Sombart (1863–1941) pointed out that the Civil Code "placed more emphasis on property than on persons."[15] Some German scholars level criticism at the German Civil Code on this basis and hold that it was "designed and constructed to meet the needs of the bourgeoisie in commercial trade" and, as a result, places "more emphasis on property than on persons", a need specific to the bourgeoisie. Consequently, "it reduces the importance of the law on personal and familial relations and places it after property law".[16] Over the last century, immense changes have occurred in human society, with never-ending changes and improvements in science and technology. To comply with the development of the Internet, advanced technology, and big data, strengthening personality rights and interests, such as the rights to reputation, likeness, privacy, and personal information, has become a major issue and must be resolved in civil legislation. Explosive high-tech growth (i.e., infrared scanning, remote photography, satellite positioning, drone photography, biometric technology, artificial intelligence, and voice recognition) has delivered tremendous benefits to humankind. It, however, has a side effect: posing grave threats to personal privacy and information. Accordingly, one of the toughest challenges facing modern law is how to respect and protect personal privacy and personal information.[17] However, the German Civil Code does not protect personality rights due to the limitations of the times, which is an apparent system defect. If the actual needs were disregarded on the grounds that the German Civil Code does not have systematic provisions on personality rights and personality rights were scattered in a few clauses regarding civil subjects or tort law, such mechanical application of Western theory would not only ignore China's actual conditions, but throw away a great opportunity, and a sacred responsibility assigned by our times to contemporary Chinese legal scholars!

At the onset of the codification project, China established the goal of developing a scientific and rational Civil Code based on China's national conditions. In other words, China was to "promulgate a stylistically scientific, structurally rigorous, standardized and rational, and coordinated and consistent code that would satisfy the development needs of socialism with Chinese characteristics and conform to its national conditions."[18] This meant that the CCC could not be confined to the German or Roman model but had to be innovative. The promulgated CCC does

---

[14] Meng (2007, p. 12).

[15] Schwab (2006, p. 42).

[16] Medicus (2000, p. 24).

[17] Froomkin (1999–2000, 1461 ff.).

[18] Shen (2020), visited on June 5, 2020.

make remarkable system innovations. To put it differently, although the CCC draws on the successful experiences and practices of other civil codes, it gives more weight to responding to China's genuine social needs and reflecting the development characteristics of our times. Furthermore, it has made an array of innovations and contributions, with system innovations standing out as the most eye-catching.

The CCC comprises seven Books, including General Provisions, Real Rights, Contracts, Personality Rights, Marriage and Family, Succession and Tort Liability, and totals 1,260 articles. It has the following marked characteristics in its system of contents:

First, the system of CCC is constructed with civil (private) rights as its foundation. The General Provisions of the Civil Law includes fundamental rules on issues such as subjects, objects, and the exercise and protection of civil rights by extracting common factors from the other Books. The Specific Provisions concentrates on the protection of real rights, contractual creditor's rights, rights in marriage and family, succession rights, and various other rights. Civil rights have become the main theme that runs through the CCC, adding scientificity and internal logic to the CCC and thereby fully demonstrating the CCC's characteristic as a law of rights. The CCC prescribes and protects the basic civil rights of civil subjects, so it is a law of rights, a common characteristic of all civil codes. Compared to the five-book system, the seven-book system embraces a more complete system of rights, which not only encompasses property rights, creditor rights, rights in marriage and family (rights of relatives), and succession rights but also lays down systematic provisions on personality rights.

Second, the CCC adopts a structure that runs from confirmation/recognition of rights to remedy of rights. There is no right without remedies, and the confirmation of rights cannot be separated from the protection of rights. The CCC first enumerates rights and then sets out the five Books of Property Rights, Contracts, Personality Rights, Marriage and Family, and Succession, with a view to protecting every right of a civil subject. The Book of Tort Liability is placed last, which provides remedies for the infringement of rights. This conforms to the general structure that runs from confirmation of rights to remedy and further highlights the nature of civil law that it is not only a law of rights but also a law that protects private rights and provides remedies for victims. Compared with the five-book system, the seven-book system embraces a more complete system of rights. It encompasses property rights, creditor's rights, rights in marriage and family (rights of relatives) as well as succession rights. Moreover, it sets forth a special Book of Tort Liability for rights protection, which adequately embodies the remedy function of Tort Law. Therefore, the overall framework for the CCC is "rights confirmation plus remedies," proving that the CCC system is rights-centered. This model satisfies the needs of a risk society to strengthen remedies for (prospective) victims. Risks are ubiquitous as modern society has become a risk society. As a result,[19] the CCC should not only focus on risk prevention but also punish the infringement of civil rights and interests and provide sufficient remedies.

---

[19] Beck (2004, p. 3).

Third, every Book of the CCC is arranged in a general-to-specific structure and divided into General Provisions and Specific Provisions. This structure is adopted not only by the CCC but also by all the books. A general-to-specific structure enables the different Books to establish their own system with stricter logic, thus forming a tiered system of rules from general to specific. In the meantime, such a structure can simplify legislation. The common rules are abstracted by means of "extracting common factors" to avoid the duplication of legal provisions. While achieving legislative simplicity, it also strengthens the system of the various Books of the CCC.

Compared with the five-book German Civil Code, the codification style of the CCC possesses three innovations, namely, a separate Book of Personality Rights, a separate Book of Tort Liability, and the role of the General Provisions in the Book of Contracts as the General Provisions of the Law of Obligations. These innovations better reflect the characteristics of the CCC as a law of rights. On the one hand, the adoption of the seven-book system by the CCC better underscores the protection of people and fulfills the people-oriented value. The five-book system distinctively "places more emphasis on property than on people" and is, in fact, centered on property rights. By contrast, the seven-book system creates the separate Books of Personality Rights and Tort Liability. It stresses the dominant role of people and the humanistic care of the CCC, demonstrating *"hominum causa omne ius constitutum est*[All of law is enacted for the sake of humankind]"[20] and effectively preventing the objectification of people. Additionally, the "human written in capital letters" can be recognized in legislation, and "the rediscovery of person in civil law" can become a reality.[21] On the other hand, this system is more consistent with the times and responds to the questions of the times. "The law goes with and adapts to social change, but it also creates and guides such change and hence plays an important role in society".[22] In modern society, the rapid development of advanced technology such as the Internet and artificial intelligence has given rise to the separate Books of Personality Rights and Tort Liability, which fully demonstrates the CCC's contemporary character. Meanwhile, the CCC also answers the demand for legislation in the modern Internet and high-tech era.

In summary, the system of the CCC meets the needs of social development, displays Chinese characteristics and pragmatism, and meets the demands of the times. In addition, it improves the CCC system, systematically implements the protection of people, and realizes the people-oriented value judgment.

---

[20] Bonfante (1992, p. 29).

[21] Hoshino (2012, p. 437).

[22] Friedman and Hayden (2017, p. 263).

3   The CCC's System Innovations in the Separate Books

3.1   *A Separate Category of Personality Rights*

The emergence of a system of personality rights is the most crucial development trend of modern civil law. From a global perspective, countries have generally strengthened the protection of personality rights. However, thus far, the classic civil codes of the civil law system have not created a separate Book of Personality Rights, and there is no separate law concerning personality rights outside a civil code. The CCC creates a separate Book of Personality Rights (Book IV) to meet the needs of the Internet, sophisticated technology, and big data in modern society.[23] Book IV totals 51 articles and centers around the protection of personal dignity. Personal dignity is a primary value of the law concerning personality rights and means that a person should have the most basic social status of deserving respect from society and others.[24] Paragraph 2, Article 990 of the CCC safeguards personal liberty and human dignity in a general clause, thus declaring personal liberty and human dignity as the fundamental purpose and value of protecting personality rights. This clause also becomes the basis for recognizing miscellaneous other personality rights not enumerated in Book IV. Hence, all new types of personality benefits appearing in judicial practice are protected under the general clauses concerning personality rights, even if no provisions explicitly recognize these rights in the Book of Personality Rights. This is an open approach to the protection of personality rights.[25] Personal dignity is a fundamental value underlying each specific personality right. In establishing concrete personality rights, the value of personal dignity should be upheld to diversify its types and content. As a case in point, Article 1002 of the CCC not only recognizes the right to life but also stipulates that the connotation of such a right includes both life safety and dignity. The concept of life dignity can be extended to cover the protection of embryos, fetuses, and remains. Concerning the formal system (external system), the separate Book of Personality Rights has the following characteristics.

First, China's law of personality rights is a system with a general-to-specific structure. The General Provisions refines the common rules regarding personality rights by extracting common factors, uniformly stipulating the common rules, and achieving simplicity of legislation. The General Provisions in Chapter I of the Book of Personality Rights affirm the general and common legal rules concerning personality rights. These include the regulatory scope of the law of personality rights (Article 989), general and specific personality rights (Article 990), fundamental rules relating to the legal protection of personality rights of civil subjects (Article 991), rules permitting the use of personality benefits (Article 993), provisions on the protection of personality interests of the deceased (Article 994), provisions on the remedy for infringement of personality rights (Article 995), rules of concurrent damages for

---

[23] Wang and Xiong (2021, 703 ff.).

[24] Liang (2001, p. 119).

[25] Tang (Ed) (2001, p. 30).

breach of contract and for emotional distress caused by breach of contract (Article 996), rules authorizing injunction for infringement of personality rights (Article 997), rules the fair use of personality interests (Article 999), and on the holistic evaluation of damages for infringement of personality rights (Article 998). Chapter II to Chapter VI of the Book of Personality Rights stipulate the content of each specific personality right, how these rights are exercised, and rules on how these rights relate to other rights. The rights recognized in these chapters include the right to life, the right to body and the right to health (Chapter II), the right to name and the right to entity name (Chapter III), the right to likeness (Chapter IV), the right to reputation and the right to honor (Chapter V), and the right to privacy and personal information protection (Chapter VI). This system integrates the general rules and special rules. Through a general-to-specific arrangement, the Book of Personality Rights in the CCC has set up a complete system for regulating personality rights.

Second, the personality rights system in China is established based on the classification of general personality rights and specific personality rights. General personality rights are stipulated in the general regulations, while specific personality rights are provided in the specific provisions. General personality rights (*das allgemeine Persönlichkeitsrecht*), in contrast to specific personality rights, are highly generalized and collective rights safeguarding personal dignity, equality of personhood, and personal freedom. The Book of General Provisions of the CC stipulates the protection of general personality rights. Article 109 of the CCC provides that "The personal freedom and human dignity of a natural personis protected by law". Furthermore, the Book of Personality Rights stipulates that "In addition to the personality rights specified in the preceding paragraph, a natural person enjoys other personality rights and interests derived from personal freedom and human dignity." (Paragraph 2, Article 990). This clause further clarifies the protection of personality interests by general personality rights, by making clear that the protection scope of personality rights is open-ended. Apart from general personality rights, Paragraph 1, Article 990 of the CCC also stipulates specific personality rights, "Personality rights are rights enjoyed by a civil subject, including the right to life, the right to body, the right to health, the right to name, the right to entity name, the right to likeness, the right to reputation, the right to honor, the right to privacy, etc." This clause stipulates the specific personality rights in a typified way. In summary, the CCC lays out general personality rights and specific ones and sets up a complete system for the Book of Personality Rights. In this sense, the Law of Personality Rights centers on rights, which is different from the Law of Tort Liability, which centers on remedy.

Third, the system of personality rights focuses on enjoying, exercising, and protecting personality rights, treating these as the fundamental functions of the law of personality rights. These three functions are largely reflected in the content and system of the Book of Personality Rights. Article 989 of the CCC provides that "This Book regulates the civil legal relations arising from the enjoyment and protection of personality rights." To put it more precisely, the first is the enjoyment system of personality rights, which refers to civil subjects enjoying various personality rights owing to the confirmation by the law. The law of personality rights is mostly a law of rights. In other words, the main content of the Categories of Personality

Rights focuses on the positive confirmation of personality rights. Personality rights law confirms the types of personality rights, the scope of protection of personality interests, the content and capabilities of various personality rights, the exercise and effects of personality rights, and the conflict between personality rights and other rights. The second is the exercise system of personality rights, which delineates the scope and restrictions on personality rights during their exercise. As an illustration, the Article 993 of the CCC requires licensing to use another's personality bene-fits. Yet, the Article 999 authorizes reasonable use of another's personality benefits in news reporting, public commenting, and supervision. The third is the protection system of personality rights. A civil legal relationship generated by the protection system of personality rights primarily entails the rights and obligations arising from the infringement of a personality right. The Book of Personality Rights under the CC offers various means to protect personality rights. For example, the CCC grants victims whose personality rights are being or about to be harmed a right to sue for injunctive relief (Article 997).

Creating a separate Book of Personality Rights in the CCC is doubtlessly a front-page innovation in the civil code system and an epochal contribution to the world's civil legislation. First, this implements the principle of guaranteeing human dignity recognized in China's Constitution and strengthens the protection of personal dignity. In the new era, we need to ensure that people not only live a well-off life but also live with dignity. People's longing for a good and happy life includes not only having ready access to food, clothing, elderly care, housing, and medical services but also leading a decent life with dignity. For this reason, a separate Book of Personality Rights in the CCC is, in essence, to fully protect personality rights and to enable people to live with dignity. Since each personality right reflects the value of personal dignity, the elaborate provisions on the protection of the right to reputation, the right to likeness, and the right to privacy and personal information in the Book of Personality Rights effectively respond to the fresh challenges posed by modern technological development. The Book of Personality Rights stipulates the protection of the right to voice, prohibits serious forgery of another's likeness and stipulates bottom-line rules for research on gene editing, human embryo testing, etc., all of which are responses to new issues in the new era.

Second, a separate Book of Personality Rights underscores the essence of civil law as "human law" and helps to fix the system flaw in traditional civil laws of "more emphasis on property than on person". The classic civil code system, as represented by the model of the Institutiones and that of the Digest, is centered on property relations. The human component in the classic civil code system is exclusively about "subjects" and resolving issues such as a subject's legal or behavioral capacity to participate in legal relations. It does not recognize the independent role of personality rights and does not pay adequate attention to the status of a person in terms of value.[26] Although the traditional civil codes of the civil law system take on the responsibility of protecting personal rights and property rights, they only stipulate proprietary rights (real rights and creditor's rights) and rights in familial relations (provisions

---

[26] Chen (2003, p. 5).

on relatives and succession) in their specific provisions. These specific provisions do not stipulate the most important personal rights, i.e., personality rights, testifying to the system flaw in traditional civil laws of "more emphasis on property than on person."[27] A separate Book of Personality Rights in the CCC provides protection for such rights and corrects the said flaw.

As far as style and structure are concerned, certainly, the provisions on the Book of Personality Rights in the CCC are still to be improved. The main problem is that personality rights should be the second Book in the CC (followed by the Book of General Provisions) rather than the fourth Book. The main reasons are as follows: First, such an arrangement would be consistent with the provisions of Article 2 of the CCC. Article 2 clearly stipulates, "The Civil Code regulates personal and proprietary relationships between equal subjects, namely, natural persons, legal persons, and unincorporated organizations." Personal relationships are placed before proprietary relationships. Compared with Article 2 of the General Rules of the Civil Law of the PRC promulgated in 1986, this Article highlights the importance of personal relations. Likewise, the General Provisions of the Civil Law of the PRC enacted in 2017 mentions personality rights before proprietary rights.

Second, this practice could better uphold the idea of putting people first. Placing the Book of Personality Rights as the second Book of the CCC, followed by the Book of Real Rights and the Book of Contracts, could adequately embody a modern civil law's humanistic care for the individual. Third, such an arrangement would provide a model for civil laws in other countries that aspire to embody the value of humanistic care. In these other civil laws, rights such as the rights to life, body, and health, should be the most significant rights protected by the law. They should take precedence over proprietary interests and private ordering.

3.2 The Establishment of Unique Contract-Centrism

Traditional civil law theory believes that "[a] General Provisions of the Law of Obligations is necessary, irrespective of how a CCC is organized.[28] Historically, Roman jurists categorized the causes of debts into contracts, illegal acts, and other reasons stipulated by the law based on their observations about life.[29] The legal development of the traditional civil law system is heavily influenced by the distinction between "*ius in personam*" and "*ius in rem*" in Roman law. Although feudal law and canon law weakened the distinction between the two, the concept of debt in Roman law still profoundly impacted the codification of many CCs. The laws of the civil law system as represented by the German Civil Code and the Swiss Code of Obligations set forth general provisions for the codes of obligations. In the codification of the German Civil Code, people held different viewpoints on whether to establish a

---

[27] Sun (2001, p. 18).

[28] Fujii (2004, p. 178).

[29] Fei (2018, 28 ff.).

General Provisions of the Law of Obligations. The final promulgated code accepted the idea of a General Provisions.[30] During the reforms in the Law of Obligations under the French Civil Code, the general rules for obligations were abstracted, and a General Rules of Obligations was set forth.[31] Therefore, regardless of whether the three-book or the five-book legislative model is adopted, the majority of civil law countries have followed this distinction between *ius in rem* and *ius in personam*.[32] As a result, although the civil codes of various countries have adopted different organizational models, most of them have retained the idea of creating a general rules chapter for the law of obligations.

In contrast, the system design of specific provisions in the CCC does not adopt this idea and does not set forth a General Provisions of the Law of Obligations. Instead, it proceeds from China's actual situation that there is already a Contract Law with a complete system comprising general provisions and specific contracts, which plays the same role as that of a law of obligations. The CCC incorporates the Contract Law as its law of obligations. This is a crucial innovation in the civil law system.

First, the obligations arising from unilateral acts are included in the chapter on the establishment of contracts. Unilateral acts are entirely different from contracts, so the rules in the Book of Contracts, particularly regulations such as the right of defence in reciprocal contracts, are not applicable to such acts.[33] Nevertheless, obligations of unilateral acts are the same as those of contracts; (unilateral acts and contracts are simply causes of obligations). As a result, the consequences of performing or violating both types of obligations can be governed by the rules of contract law. Therefore, the Book of Contracts in the CCC places the obligations arising from unilateral acts in the establishment of contracts. Article 499 of the CCC stipulates that "Where a reward provider publicly declares to pay a reward to any person for completing a specific act, a person who has completed the specified act may request payment of the reward by the reward provider." The obligations arising from unilateral acts are specified in the chapter on the establishment of contracts, so such acts are not omitted due to the absence of a General Provisions of the Law of Obligations.

Second, the chapter regarding the performance of contracts (Chapter IV) sets forth the classification of obligations. The classification rules for the law of obligations are essential content of traditional law of obligations and are stipulated in the performance of contracts in the CCC. The classes of obligations include obligations of money payment (Article 514), obligations with a right of choice (Articles 515–516), several (divisible) creditors' rights and several (divisible) obligations (Articles 517), and joint and several creditors' rights and joint and several obligations (Articles 518–521). Although multiparty obligations appear in the Book of Contracts, the Book of Tort Liability, and the Book of Succession,[34] they are regulated in the chapter on the

---

[30] Xie (2018, p. 18).

[31] Li (2016, p. 4).

[32] Tang (2010, pp. 93–94).

[33] Wang (2019, p. 62).

[34] Looschelders (2014, p. 415).

performance of contracts because the Book of Contracts governs the performance of obligations. The chapter concerning the performance of contracts also regulates contracts under which a debtor performs an obligation to a third party (Article 522) or under which an obligation is performed by a third party (Article 524). These provisions typically are part of the General Provisions of the Law of Obligations. Additionally, Chapter VII "Termination of Contractual Rights and Obligations" stipulates imputation of payments (Articles 560–561).

Third, the Book of Contracts makes a rigorous distinction between creditor's rights and debtor's obligations on the one hand, and contractual rights and obligations on the other. For example, Chapter VI "Modification and Assignment of Contracts" regulates transfers of creditor's rights and debtor's obligations and use a special article for assignments of contracts where "the rights and obligations of the contract are transferred together" (Article 556). This suggests that transfers of creditor's rights and debts are noncontractual assignments, while the total assignment of a contract occurs in contractual relationships only. For another example, in Chapter VII "Termination of Contractual Rights and Obligations", Paragraph 1, Article 557 enumerates the circumstances where "a creditor's right and a debtor's obligation are extinguished": performance, setoff, escrow, release, merger, and other situations according to the law. Paragraph 2 of the same article separately stipulates, "Where a contract is terminated, the contractual rights and obligations are extinguished." The separate clauses indicate that extinguishment of the creditor's rights and debtor's obligations occurs not only in contractual relations but also in noncontractual debtor-creditor relationships, while extinguishment of contractual rights and obligations occurs only in contractual relationships. The separate clauses allow the Book of Contracts to play the role of an alternative to a General Provisions of the Law of Obligations while maintaining the integrity of the contract system.

Fourth, the rules regarding nominate contracts in the Book of Contracts also serve as general provisions of the law of obligations. The Book of Contracts has a chapter on suretyship contracts, which applies to suretyships not only of contractual obligations but also of various other obligations. The traditional view generally regards the guarantee as the guarantee method of the debt. China used to regulate the various types of security in the Security Law. Nonetheless, as security by real rights has been absorbed by the Property Law, it is beneficial to ensure that the whole security system is included in the CCC. In the CCC, suretyship is regulated as a nominate contract in Division 2 "Nominate Contract" of the Book of Contracts. As a result, the entire security system is incorporated into the CCC. A separate dedicated chapter can also effectively regulate suretyships. In addition, the Book of Contracts effectively unifies civil contracts and commercial contracts and includes some typical commercial contracts, such as independent contractor contracts, finance lease contracts, factoring contracts, contracts for construction projects, and warehousing contracts. The Book of Contacts in the CCC, therefore, integrates the elements of commercial law and imposes uniform provisions on civil and commercial contracts.

Fifth, the Book of Contracts creates a separate Division of "Quasi-contract" (Division 3), which regulates unjust enrichment (Chapter 28) and *negotiorum gestio* (Chapter 29). This practice is in line with the characteristics of various statutory obligations. The quasi-contract system is derived from Roman law and was initially referred to as "*quasi ex contractu*", indicating considerable similarity to contract. Later, it gradually evolved as "quasi-contract". Regulating unjust enrichment and *negotiorum gestio* by introducing the concept of quasi-contract helps to maintain the completeness of the system of the Book of Contracts. It should also be noted that the establishment of a quasi-contract Division in the Book of Contracts of the CCC no longer separates the causes of various obligations in the Law of Obligations. Instead, it links the unjust enrichment and *negotiorum gestio* system together with the contract system effectively. While this approach recognizes the existing legal differences between statutory and intended obligations (thus regulating them in separate divisions), it also highlights the legal similarities between these two types of obligations (thus integrating both under the law of obligations).

The application of the law is facilitated by allowing the Book of Contracts to serve the purpose of a General Provisions of the Law of Obligations. "The provisions of a good code should be duly abstract to regulate a considerable number of practical problems, but should not, for this reason, deviate from the real life it regulates and become pure declarations of theories."[35] Most rules that would appear in the General Provisions of the Law of Obligations of a civil code regulate transactional relationships. In the context of the CCC, these rules would overlap with the system of legal acts in the General Provisions of the Civil Law and the General Provisions of the Book of Contracts. On the one hand, creating a General Provisions of the Law of Obligations might indeed lead to needless duplication, posing difficulties to judges in identifying the appropriate laws. If such double abstraction were adopted, then judges would have to search for the right law in the General Provisions, the General Provisions of the Law of Obligations, and the General Provisions of Contracts to settle contract disputes, which would make the application of the law much more difficult. On the other hand, it would cause duplication of rules. However, allowing the General Provisions of the Book of Contracts to play the role of the General Provisions of the Law of Obligations can efficiently simplify legal rules. The norms governing common regulations on obligations in the Book of Contracts are mainly achieved through permitted clauses. Such clauses extend the scope of the rules of the Book of Contract to apply to contractual obligations. In addition, they remove the barriers between the rules on contractual and noncontractual obligations, minimizing the tedious procedures of application of law and avoiding excessive abstraction of legal rules.

Allowing the General Provisions of the Book of Contracts to serve the purpose of a General Provisions of the Law of Obligations helps to protect the integrity of the General Provisions of Contract Law. The General Provisions of Contract Law forms its own complete system that regulates the transaction process. To enter into a contract, the parties concerned need to conduct negotiations first and then enter into a contract. After that, the validity of the contract needs to be examined. For a legally established contract that has taken effect, both parties are obligated to perform the

---

[35] Berg (2006, p. 19).

contract. In the performance of the contract, the right of defense, such as in a recip-rocal contract with simultaneous performance, and the defense of uncertainty, may also arise. The contract may be breached, rescinded, or terminated if the performance or non-performance fails to abide by the agreed-upon provisions. A singular focus on the course of the transaction contributes to the prominent "homogeneity" of the rules of contract law. The CCs of traditional civil law countries set forth the General Provisions of the Law of Obligations, so they have to prescribe countless regulations regarding the General Provisions of Contract Law in the General Provisions of the Law of Obligations. This model leads to a lack of utility of the General Provisions of Contract Law and the inability of contract law to form its own system. Judges have to go back and forth between the contract regulations and the General Provisions of the Law of Obligations to find the right law. Nevertheless, if the provisions of Contract Law incorporate the General Provisions of the Law of Obligations, this model can tackle problems of dual application while maintaining the integrity of the General Provisions of Contract Law. Moreover, this model allows ordinary people to under-stand the General Provisions of Contract Law more clearly. In China, the Contract Law was enacted more than two decades ago, so people have been fairly familiar with its structural arrangement and have developed habitual thinking about it. In this case, creating a General Provisions of the Law of Obligations and breaking the original system of the Contract Law would bring huge operating costs to civil-commercial life and judicial practice.[36]

Accordingly, allowing the General Provisions of the Book of Contracts to serve as a General Provisions of the Law of Obligations is an uppermost innovation in the structure of the CCC. Such an arrangement has its strengths but also suffers the following weaknesses. First, it creates a gap between contractual obligations and tort obligations and disregards common rules regulating both types of obligations. This negatively impacts the integrity of the legal system of obligations. Second, with regard to the rules in the General Provisions of the Book of Contracts, it is often difficult to decide whether such rules are applicable only to contracts or also to noncontractual debtor-creditor relationships. The CCC has certain signals in the provisions (a provision will apply to all obligations if it uses the words "obliga-tion", "creditor's right" or "debt". By contrast, an article applies only to contractual obligations if it uses words such as "contract," "contractual right" or "contractual obligation"). In practice, however, it remains difficult for judges to find the law and accurately apply it. Third, the regulatory capacity of quasi-contracts is limited and cannot cover statutory obligations beyond unjust enrichment and negotiorum gestio. For example, compensation cannot be stipulated in the Division of Quasi-Contracts as an independent cause of obligation.[37] Likewise, reward advertisement as a unilat-eral act is stipulated in the chapter on the establishment of contracts (Article 499), which is also inconsistent with the organizational style. Even for the obligation of unjust enrichment, it mainly applies to restitution of unjust enrichment and cannot

---

[36] Liu (2020, p. 68 ff.).

[37] Wang (2014, p. 116 ff.).

cover the rules for non-payment of unjust enrichment. This will bring some difficulties to the application of the law. In the future, it is necessary to continue to overcome the above shortcomings through legal interpretation and other efforts.

3.3   A Separate Book of Tort Liability

In comparative law, traditional CCs of civil law countries tend to regard the tort liability law as part of the Law of Obligations and make provisions accordingly. "In the civil law system, particularly German law, which stresses systematization and abstraction, the fundamental concepts of private law were developed after long periods, and were extraordinary legal achievements", commented by Professor Wang Zejian on the legal system of obligations.[38] Nevertheless, in the twenty-first century, a risk society has emerged, so people are always bearing new risks associated with the continuous development and application of novel techniques and technologies. If tort law is still embedded in the Law of Obligations, it will be more difficult to establish a logical system for tort law, and it may lead to the oversimplification of regulations. For example, the French Civil Code has only nine articles stipulating tort liability, and the German Civil Code covers it in about twenty provisions. Obviously, this approach does not provide a sufficient remedy for or prevention of various harms as a risk society requires. In fact, comparative law informs us that tort law has become the most powerful growth engine for civil law. It has shown an unstoppable tendency to break away from the traditional Law of Obligations and become independent. Many scholars believe that a separate Tort Liability Law would better reflect the development of society and legal civilization.[39] Unfortunately, aside from the unified Restatement of the Law, Third, Torts: Apportionment of Liability formulated by the American Law Institute, in almost all civil law countries, the proposition of independent tort law is still at the stage of academic advocacy.[40]

After many studies and debates, China's legislature adopted the proposal of creating a separate Tort Liability Law. It began drafting a separate Tort Liability Law at the beginning of the twenty-first century and promulgated the Tort Liability Law in 2009. China's promulgation of a separate Tort Liability Law is a remarkable

---

[38] Wang (1998, p. 87).

[39] Wagner (2007, p. 1005).

[40] Since its inception, the European Union has been advocating the formulation of a unified European CC, and has put the unification of tort law on its agenda. Additionally, relevant drafts have been produced and are continuously being improved and revised. This trend is proved by the session of "Tort Law" in the Non-Contractual Liability Arising Out of Damage Caused to Another written by Professor Christian von Bar in the model law for European private law, the Unification of Tort Law: Wrongfulness (Principles of European Tort Law Set) written by Helmut Koziol, and the Proposals for Reform of the Law of Obligations and the Law of Prescription drafted by Professor Pierre Catala with Paris 2 Panthéon-Assas University as entrusted by the French Ministry of Justice in 2005. Large numbers of scholars predict that the unification of European tort laws would come true if a unified European contract law could be introduced.

innovation. The Chinese Tort Liability Law forms a complete system of tort liability. It contains 92 articles following a general-to-specific structure. It also features more substantive provisions and a more complete system than tort liability provisions in conventional civil codes. One can conclude that the civil law system has established novel modern tort law. The seventh Book of the CCC incorporates this legislative achievement. A separate Book of Tort Liability is created based on the legislative experience of the Tort Liability Law, essentially incorporating the content of the Law while making necessary modifications, additions, and improvements. Pursuant to the overall style of the CCC, the Book of Tort Liability establishes its own system with general provisions followed by specific provisions.

3.3.1 General Provisions

The General Provisions of the Book of Tort Liability establishes the common rules generally applicable to all tort liabilities. Although the Book of Tort Liability in the CCC does not have a division titled "General Provisions" (it has no divisions at all), its first chapter is "General Rules", and its second chapter is "Damages." Judging from its content, Chapter 1 stipulates the scope of application of the Book of Tort Liability and the general rules regarding fault liability, joint tortfeasors, situations where causation is unverifiable, forms of tort liability, the scope of damages, and exemptions. These are fundamentally common rules relating to tort liability.

In addition, it should be noted that the Book of Tort Liability combines general terms with categorization. As mentioned above, Paragraph 1, Article 1165 of the Book of Tort Liability in the CCC, creates a general provision regarding fault liability: "One who is at fault for infringing upon a civil right or interest of another person shall be subject to tort liability." This provision applies to all regular torts. The scope of application of this provision is incredibly broad, from damage to property to injury to person, and from infringement of rights to infringement of interests. The provision could apply to thousands of tort disputes that occur every day. The Book of Tort Liability in the CCC also stipulates special provisions such as the principles of presumption of fault and strict liability (Paragraph 2, Article 1165, and Article 1166). Regarding these thousands of torts, judges can apply the general provision on fault liability if they cannot find any special legal provisions when seeking a basis for judgment. The general provision, however, cannot replace specific provisions because special tort liabilities are governed by special imputation principles and, accordingly, must have special constitutive elements and defences. Consequently, there are huge differences in evidence adducing between special tort liabilities and general ones. The Book of Tort Liability in the CCC stipulates large numbers of special torts, thereby providing judges with precise bases for judgment.

3.3.2 Specific Provisions

The system for specific provisions in the Book of Tort Liability in the CCC is mainly built on two threads:

The first thread is the specificity of imputation principles. With respect to contents, the system for specific provisions in the Book of Tort Liability follows primarily special imputation principles. The Book of Tort Liability in the CCC clarifies that presumption of fault and strict liability only apply to circumstances "prescribed by the law," Hence, the system for specific provisions in the Book of Tort Liability lays down provisions under the circumstances where a presumption of fault and strict liability are applicable. For this reason, the first thread of building such a system is the specificity of imputation principles. In other words, torts to which special imputation principles apply are prescribed in the specific provisions of the Book of Tort Liability.

First, torts to which presumption of fault is applicable. Regarding the provisions in the Book of Tort Liability in the CCC, presumption of fault mainly covers the following circumstances: (1) Liability for traffic accidents caused by vehicles (Article 1208); (2) Liability for damage caused by medical maltreatment (Article 1222); (3) Liability for damage caused by zoo animals (Article 1248); (4) Liability for damage caused to others by the fall or drop of pieces of a building, structure or other facility or by the fall or drop of objects placed or displayed on a building, structure, or other facility (Article 1253); (5) Liability for damage caused to others by the collapse, fall or drop of piled-up objects (Article 1255); (6) Liability for damage caused to others by the piling, dumping or littering of objects that hampers passage on a public road (Article 1256); (7) Liability for damage caused by a breaking branch, a falling tree or falling fruit (Article 1257); (8) Liability for damage caused to others by the digging, repair or installation of underground facilities in a public place or on the side of a road (Paragraph 1, Article 1258); (9) Liability for damage caused to others by underground facilities including utility holes (Paragraph 2, Article 1258). Take the last category of circumstances for example, Paragraph 2 of the Article 1258 of the CCC stipulates that "if the damage is caused to others by underground facilities including utility holes, the manager shall bear tort liability if they cannot prove that they have adequately performed management duties."

Second, torts to which strict liability is applicable. These specific torts are as follows: (1) Liability of a guardian (Paragraph 1, Article 1188); (2) Liability of an employer for damage caused to a third party by its employee within the scope of employment (Paragraph 1, Article 1191); (3) In a labor service relationship between two individuals, liability of the party receiving labor service for damage caused by the party providing labor service (Article 1192); (4) Product liability (Article 1202); (5) Liability for medical products (Article 1223); (6) Liability for environmental pollution and ecological destruction (Article 1229); (7) Liability for ultrahazardous activities (Article 1236);(8) Liability for harm caused by raising animals (Article 1245 and Article 1246).

The second thread is the specificity of liable subjects. Given the diverse forms of tort liabilities and the complicated relationships between liable subjects, the Book of Tort Liability in the CCC builds the system of specific provisions by relying on a second thread in Chapter III "Special Provisions on Liable Parties." To be more precise, some torts are regulated together under "special liable subjects," In these cases, the party committing the injurious act is a separate party from the party bearing legal liability. In Chapter III of the Book of Tort Liability of the CCC, the specificity of liable subjects arises in injuries caused by the following persons: "person without capacity for civil conduct," "person with limited capacity for civil conduct," "employee hired by employer," "provider of labor service in a labor service relationship with another individual", "independent contractor", and "provider of Internet services." Among these types of torts, the party committing the injurious act is not the party bearing liability for the act. This type of liability is the so-called vicarious liability. Vicarious liability applies to those torts where a person assumes tort liability for another party due to their special relationship.[41] Many torts, as set forth in Chapter III of the Book of Tort Liability in the CCC, invite vicarious liability. Special relationships that can make a person liable for another's acts mainly include: employment relationship, guardianship, service relationship, and other types of supervision and management relationship between the tortfeasor and the liable subject. The rationale for vicarious liability is that a tortfeasor committed a tort because the legally liable person failed to fulfill their responsibility of guardianship, supervision, or management, thereby creating an opportunity for the supervisee to commit the harmful act. Consequently, vicarious liability arises. Although the imputation principle applicable to torts stated in Chapter III of the Book of Tort Liability varies, for example, some torts incur no-fault liability (e.g., liability of the guardian and that of the employer), and some incur fault liability (e.g., liability for breach of duty of safety protection and liability for accidents on campus), the torts set out in Chapter III share a common feature of special liable subjects. Thus a distinct system can be formed.

The CCC divides the Book of Obligations in the traditional civil law system and creates separate Books of Tort Liability and Contracts, thereby setting up an independent system for tort liability. This is a significant innovation of the CCC as well as a new attempt to comply with legal development. Its primary significance lies in the following. First, a complete system for the Book of Tort Liability has been constructed to meet the needs of a risky society. A separate Book of Tort Liability contributes to the establishment of an imputation system that makes detailed regulations on various special torts and corresponding liabilities. In addition, it enriches the rules for protecting civil rights, improves the "rights and remedy" structure, and meets the governance needs of a risky society. Second, the protection of people is underscored by creating a separate Book of Tort Liability, which best exhibits the characteristic of the CCC as a law of rights. The CCC prescribes and protects the basic civil rights of civil subjects, so it is a law of rights. This is a common characteristic of all civil codes. The overall framework for the CCC is therefore "rights confirmation and remedy." This structure builds a civil legal system centered on rights, which is markedly different from the five-book German Civil Code, which creates a civil legal system through legal acts. In this way, the characteristic of the CCC as a law

---

[41] Wagner (2011, p. 906).

of rights is better underlined. Conventional civil laws place tort liability in the law of obligations, resulting in straightforward rules in tort law, insufficient to protect the rights and interests of civil subjects or provide a remedy for victims. Evidently, a separate Book of Tort Liability fully highlights the value of the CCC in protecting private rights, proving that the CCC is the fundamental law for the comprehensive protection of private rights.

Third, the system of the CCC is improved, featuring rights as the main line and remedy at the end. The CCC centers on rights. It establishes the Book of Tort Liability following the Books of Real Rights, Contracts, Personality Rights, Rights in Marriage and Family, and Succession Rights, thus forming a system ending with remedy. After recognizing rights, the CCC provides a variety of remedy measures for rights and countermeasures against the infringement of interests. As a result, the system of the CCC is more exhaustive, consistent and complete than a conventional Civil Code. Placing the Book of Tort Liability as the last book of the CCC serves as a summary of China's legislative experiences. Since the General Principles of the Civil Law of the People's Republic of China, China's laws have adopted the legislative model of structuring civil liability at the end of the law. Putting the Book of Tort Liability last also represents the transition from rights to remedy, for tort liability is the mechanism for the protection of personality right, real rights, and rights in familial relations. In addition, the Book of Tort Liability offers all-encompassing remedy measures for rights and countermeasures against infringement of interests. Hence, the provisions in the Book of Tort Liability apply to the protection of various in rem rights. This model adequately reflects the logical order of rights followed by remedy, thereby distinct from the model of traditional laws of obligations in the civil law system where torts reside in obligations and where the system is constructed with a focus on creditors' rights. As a result, the Book of Tort Liability completes the CCC's structure of starting with rights and ending with remedy.

It is relatively rational for the CCC to structure the Book of Tort Liability at the end, as it reflects the idea of transitioning from rights to remedy. However, the problem lies in that the Book of Contracts adopts a unique contract-centric doctrine and exerts the function of the Law of Obligations to a certain extent. Therefore, some rules in the Book of Contracts will be applicable to the Book of Tort Liability. As a consequence, Article 468 of the CCC stipulates that "Noncontractual creditor-debtor relationships are regulated by legal provisions regarding this type of creditor-debtor relationships; absent such provisions, the relevant provisions in the General Provisions of this Book shall apply, unless the nature of the relationship precludes such application." This Article provides a legal basis for the general rules concerning the application of obligations for tort damages. In addition, the general rules for obligations may be applicable to obligations arising from torts under particular circumstances. For example, obligations arising from torts may face problems such as setoff, imputation of payments, preservation or even assignment under special circumstances. Nonetheless, the Book of Contracts is placed as the third Book away from the last Book of Tort Liability. This separates the tort liability rules from the contract law rules and complicates judges in finding the right law. For example, it may not be straightforward for a judge adjudicating a tort dispute that he should look in the

Book of Contracts for rules relating to joint and several obligations and apply them to the tort case. A more ideal way would be to place the Book of Contracts and the Book of Tort Liability closer together, for instance, placing the Book of Contracts right before the Book of Tort Liability.

4　Conclusion

"When laws change with the times, good order will be achieved" (Han Feizi, Surmising about the Thinking of the People). "Law goes with and adapts to social change, but it also creates and guides such change and hence plays an important part in society".[42] From the codification movement onward, constant development and improvements have been made in the system of codes in civil law countries.[43] The promulgation of the CCC, by no means, suggests that explorations of the civil legal system have been accomplished by legislation. Any civil law system is relative and developing. It should be continuously enhanced along with the development of social life. In particular, ongoing improvements in the legal system should be fueled through interpretation.[44] Facing twenty-first-century human society, in terms of building the civil code system, we should adapt to changes in social development and satisfy the needs of the times instead of adhering to a convention or applying others' experiences mechanically. The Civil Law mirrors social and economic life from a legal perspective, and a civil code summarizes and reflects the lifestyle of a country. The CCC has established a civil code system with Chinese characteristics by learning from the legislative experiences of the two major legal systems to serve China's actual conditions and the development needs of the era. It provides a Chinese approach for build-up civil code systems and, in this way, makes our due share of contributions. These structural innovations will enable the CCC to stand tall and firm in the world's civil codes and serve as a model for the foreseeable future!

References

Beck U (2004) Risk society (He BW, Trans) (风险社会). Yilin Press, Nanjin
Berg JL (2006) Major methods and characteristics of codification (Guo C, Trans) (法典编纂的主要方法和特征). Tsinghua Univ Law J 8:12–30
Bonfante P (1992) Textbook on Roman Law (Huang F, Trans) (罗马法教科书). China University of Political Science and Law Press, Beijing
Bydlinski F (1996) System und Prinzipien des Privatrechts. Springer Press, Wien and New York
Chen HB (2003) Several issues concerning drafting of Chinese Civil Code (中国制定民法典的若干问题). Leg Sci (法律科学) 5:39–51

---

[42] Friedman and Hayden (2017, p. 263).

[43] Rivera (2013, pp. 37–38).

[44] Kelsen (2008, p. 100).

Chen L, Ge JQ, He J, Liu Q, Wu ZC, Xiong BW (2021) The Civil Code of the People's Republic of China: English translation. Brill, Leiden

Fei AL (2018) Rationality of CC and general provisions of law of obligations (民法典的理性与债法总则). Bus Econ Law Rev 1:28–41

Friedman LM, Hayden GM (2017) American law: an introduction. Oxford University Press, Oxford

Froomkin M (1999–2000) The death of privacy? Stan L Rev 52:1461ff

Fujii Y (2004) Necessity of formulating general provisions of law of obligations and development of Tort Liability Law (Ding XS, Trans) (设立债法总则的必要性与侵权责任法的发展). In: Zhang XB (ed), Review on Tort Law 1. Law Press, Beijing

Hoshino E (2012) Basic issues of modern civil law (现代民法基本问题) (Duan K, Yang YZ, Trans). China University of Political Science and Law Press, Beijing

Kelsen H (2008) Pure theory of law (Zhang SY, Trans) (纯粹法理论). China Legal Press, Beijing

Li SG (2016) Coordination several primary relations in the construction of China's law of obligations (中国债编体系构建中若干基础关系的协调——从法国重构债法体系的经验观察》). Chin J Law (法学研究) 5:3–26

Liang HX (2001) The general theory of civil law (民法总论). Law Press, Beijing

Liu CW (2020) On the legislative orientation and system openness of the contract law part of the CCC (民法典合同编的立法取向与体系开放性). Glob Law Rev (环球法律评论) 2:68–82

Looschelders D (2014) Overview of German law of obligations (Shen XJ, Zhang JH, Trans) (德国债法总论). Renmin University of China Press, Beijing

Marx K, Engels F (2009) Marx/Engels Collected Works (马克思恩格斯文集), vol 10. People Press, Beijing

Medicus D (2000) Introduction to German Civil Code (德国民法总论) (Zhao JD, Trans). Law Press, Beijing

Mei ZX (1998) Essentials of civil law (民法要义). China University of Political Science and Law Press, Beijing

Meng GL (2007) A history of the renaissance (philosophy) (欧洲文艺复兴史). People Press, Beijing

Rivera JC (2013) The scope and structure of civil code. Springer

Shen CY (2020) Explanations on request for the deliberation on the draft of special parts of civil code (关于提请审议民法典各分编草案议案的说明). http://www.npc.gov.cn/npc/cwhhy/13jcwh/2018-08/27/content_2059319.htm. Visited on June 5, 2020

Schwab D (2006) Introduction to civil law (民法导论)) (Zheng C, Trans). Law Press, Beijing

Sun P (2001) Several issues concerning China's formulation of Civil Code (民法法典化探究). Mod Law Sci (现代法学) 2:17–25

Tang DH (ed) (2001) Understanding and application of interpretation of the Supreme People's Court on problems regarding the ascertainment of compensation liability for emotional damages in civil torts (《最高人民法院(关于确定民事侵权精神损害赔偿责任若干问题的解释)的理解与适用). People's Court Press, Beijing

Tang XQ (2010) Concept of real rights and distinction between Ius in Personam and Ius in Re in Latin Legal Family (拉丁法系视野下的物权概念及物权与对人权 (债权) 的区分). In Yi JM (ed) Private Law 8. Huazhong University of Science & Technology Press, Wuhan

Von Savigny F (1840) System des heutigen römischen Rechts. 1. Scientia Press, Berlin

Wagner G (2007) Comparative law. Oxford University Press, Oxford

Wagner G (2011) Vicarious liability. In: Hartkamp et al (eds) Towards a European Civil Code. Wolters Kluwer, Alphen aan den Rijn

Wang ZJ (2001) General principles of the civil law (民法总则). China University of Political Science and Law Press, Beijing

Wang Y (2014) Statutory obligation of compensation as an independent kind of obligation (作为债之独立类型的法定补偿义务). Chin J Law (法学研究) 2:116–130

Wang WJ (2019) Exploration of the right of concurrent performing under continuing contract (继续性合同之同时履行抗辩权探微). J Nanjing Univ (南京大学学报) 1:61–69

Wang LM (2021) Foreword. In: Chen L, Ge JQ, He J, Liu Q, Wu ZC, Xiong BW, The Civil Code of the People's Republic of China: English translation. Brill, p 1 ff

Wang LM, Xiong BW (2021) Personality rights in China's new civil code: a response to increasing awareness of rights in an era of evolving technology. Mod China 47(6):703–739

Wang Z (1998) Study on doctrine of civil law and precedents (民法学说与判例研究). China University of Political Science and Law Press, Beijing

Westermann H (2013) German civil law concepts (德国民法基本概念) (Zhang et al DJ, Trans). China Renmin University Press, Beijing

Xie HS (2004) Research on civil codes of continental legal system (大陆法国家民法典研究). China Legal Press, Beijing

Xie HF (2018) Origin of general provisions of German law of obligations in the 19th century (19世纪德国债法总则的缘起:理论内核与体系建构). Bus Econ Law Rev (经贸法律评论) 1:12–23

Zheng YB (2003) General principles of the civil law (民法总则). China University of Political Science and Law Press, Beijing

Zweigert K and Kotz H (2003) Introduction to Comparative Law (H.D. Pan, Trans) Law Press, Beijing

Liming Wang is a Professor and a Ph.D. in Law at Law School, Renmin University of China, Research Fellow at Research Center of Civil and Commercial Jurisprudence, Renmin University of China; Prof. Wang is the former executive vice president of the Renmin University of China, he has been the vice president of the China Law Society and the president of the China Civil Law Research Association. Prof. Wang has published widely on contract law, property law, civil law and civil codification and has had a leading role in drafting the Chinese Civil Code. His recent publications include *The modernization of Chinese civil law over four decades, Frontiers of Law in China*, 2019, 14(1), 39–72; *The Basic Issues concerning the Construction of the Rule of Law in China in the New Era, Social Sciences in China*, 2020, 41(1), 21–37. His book *Contract Law of China* was recently published with Hein.

A Brief Analysis of Cryptotypes in the Chinese Civil Code: Legalism and Confucianism

Lihong Zhang

Abstract The 2020 Chinese Civil Code (CCC) is strongly influenced by the Chinese traditional legal culture, dominated by Legalism and Confucianism as its main crypto-types. In today's China, this code cannot be understood, interpreted, and implemented correctly without taking into consideration the continued application of these two ancient Chinese legal philosophies. Various ethical norms and key socialist values are incorporated into this code. The protection of state and collective interests prevails overwhelmingly over that of individual interests, even though the equal protection between private, collective and state ownership is expressly recognized in law in book. Private autonomy is strongly restricted and limited by public authority. The traditional legalist way of governing the state, characterized by the combined application of law, political power and secret skill of ruling, is also adopted by the Chinese legislature in the drafting and implementation of this code. Due to the massive application of judicial interpretations of the Supreme Court, guiding opinions of high courts and the policies of the ruling party, in terms of law in action, today's Chinese civil law has already been decodified.

1 Introduction

The promulgation of the Civil Code of People's Republic China on May 28, 2020 (whereas its general part was enacted on March 15, 2017) is a tremendous event in human history, as it regulates the civil activities of 1.4 billion people, almost

L. Zhang (✉)
East China University of Political Science and Law, Shanghai, China
e-mail: lihongzhang111@qq.com; zhanglihong@ecupl.edu.cn

20% of the world population.[1] This code was drafted through the exercise of political authority,[2] the application of the technique of codification and the special legal reasoning based on the Chinese legal history and culture. Technically, this codification not only resulted from a large-scale legal transplanting of numerous Western legal terminologies, concepts, norms and institutions[3] but also carried out some Chinese creative skills of codification.[4] However, "[M]en are ruled by ideas, sentiments ad customs - matters which are of the essence of ourselves. Institutions and laws are outward manifestation of our character, the expression of its need. Being its outcome, institutions and laws cannot change this character".[5] Hence, the authentic Chinese characteristics of this code are the traditional Chinese culture and legal reasoning implied in the texts of this code,[6] the core of which is Confucianism and Legalism. On this point, Roscoe Pound (1870–1964), the leading American scholar serving as legal counsel to the Chinese government from 1946 to 1948, regarding the scientific interpretation of the 1929–1931 Civil Code of Republic of China, wisely affirmed that the discovery and correct understanding of received ideals, such as traditional morality, ethics and usages, accepted by the Chinese people as the fundamental guiding principles for the interpretation of law and crystallized in its millennium history, is indispensable and crucial for the modernization of Chinese Civil Law.[7]

Law is not a mathematical calculation of the rules or simple analysis of facts but rather the product of history, culture, logical reasoning, and language. The ethics, religion, or (and) ideologies behind the written text of a civil code are its cryptotypes, which denote all unconscious elements working "in a silent way," which produce

---

[1] For a general introduction of the history and development of codification of Chinese Civil Law, see Zhang (2009, pp. 1000–1040).

[2] This civil code was drafted to satisfy the political need of China, to build a sound socialist legal system with Chinese characteristics and to realize the socialist rule of law. Its political guiding ideology includes Marxism-Leninism, Mao Zedong Thoughts, Deng Xiaoping Theory, the important thought of "Three Represents", the Scientific Outlook on Development, and Xi Jinping's Thoughts on Socialism with Chinese Characteristics for a New Era. See Wang (2020, p. 252).

[3] For instance, this code adopts many traditional legal terms and institutions that are well known in continental legal systems, such as capacity for civil rights, capacity for civil conduct, juristic acts (*Rechtsgeschaeft*), limitation of action, creditors' rights, real rights, *gestio negotiorum*, unjust enrichment, right of habitation, the principle of abstraction of real rights (*Abstractionsprinzip*), tort liability without fault, the obligation of protection of safety (*Verkehrspflicht*), punitive damages and the chattel mortgage in the common law. Its structure is also modelled on the German Civil Code, featuring the general part and six special parts (Property Rights, Contract, Personality Rights, Marriage and Family, Inheritance, and Tort Liability).

[4] Like the Ukrainian Civil Code, it dedicates *ad hoc* an entire book to govern the protection of personality rights (the fourth book). It regulates the rules on *gestio negotiorum* and unjustified enrichment in the book of Contract (the third book), abandoning the traditional way of drafting a specific part on general provision of obligation in a civil code.

[5] Le Bon (1896, p. Vii) (preface).

[6] The different legal culture between China and the West makes also difficult to realize a correctly mutual understanding, perception, translation and interpretation between Chinese law and foreign law. For this point, see Seppänen (2020, 1 ff.) and Ruskola (2013, 31 ff.).

[7] Pound (1948, p. 749). For the importance of Pound's advices for the modernization of Chinese Law, see Ma (2012, p. 139).

normative effects on the legal reasoning of the legislature. The thoughts of judges and scholars involved in the drafting, interpretation and application of law of a country[8] constitute the basic orientation for the correct understanding of law.[9] The great ancient Chinese philosopher Mencius (371–289 B.C. 孟子) also caught this point when he said that "[L]aw cannot be applied only by itself (徒法不以自行)". Obviously, Pound's remarks on the importance of discovery of so-called "received ideals" are also appropriate for a correct interpretation of the 2020 CCC and even for the scientific build-up of the Chinese legal order. We will not be able to interpret the CCC and appreciate its true Chinese characteristic without understanding how Confucianism and Legalism are preserved in the code.

In the opening of his *Institutiones*, the Roman jurist Gaius (130–180 A.D.) points out that all people are governed both by law and by morality ("*[O]mnes populi, qui legibus et moribus reguntur...*)". In fact, the Chinese political rulers also governed the country by morality and by law. However, the understanding and functioning of law in China's history differ substantially from that in the West. In traditional Chinese law, the etymology of the word "*Fa*" (法) means justice,[10] similar to *ius ars boni et eaqui* ("law is the art of goodness and equity") in Roman law, but in the law in action, *Fa* means punishment in the conception of Chinese legislators and common people, and it only refers to punitive rules, predominantly criminal rules. It is adopted and applied by the rulers to govern the country in combination with the social and moral norms, i.e., *Li*, as one of the two basic means of governing the country. *Li* is the carrot through which the rulers persuade people to comply with social and moral norms and grant recognition for compliance, whereas *Fa* is the stick through which those who violate social and moral norms are sanctioned by kinship rules and, in serious cases, by the criminal law of the state.[11] Traditional Chinese law does not have a democratic system similar to that of the West, which is based on the separation of legislative, judicial, and executive powers. As a result, there is only **rule by law**, not

---

[8] That is the silent law called by Rodolfo Sacco. As he wisely observes in his chapter of this book (Sacco 2022), the norms of silent law are created by "unexpressed, implicit, implied, sometimes unconscious normative elements", together with the written word. "Thoughts not accompanied by action is law, namely law of silence". See Sacco (2015, p. 23). See also Sacco and Gambaro (2008, p. 46).

[9] In this sense, von Savigny also says that "[T]he general aim of all law is simply referable to the moral destination of human nature, as it exhibits itself in the Christian view of life; then Christianity is not to be regarded merely as a rule of life for us but it has also in fact changed the world so that all our thoughts, however strange and even hostile they may appear to it, are nevertheless governed and penetrated by it." See von Savigny (1867, p. 43). Following the same thought of von Savigny, Max Weber also attached great importance to the study of religion and ethics in his study on law, economy and sociology, with the publication of his books entitled "*The Protestant Ethic and the Spirit of Capitalism*" (1904) and "*Religions of China: Confucianism and Taoism*" (1915).

[10] The Chinese traditional character "Law" is written as "灋", which is composed of 氵 (Shui, Water), 廌 (Zhi, a legendary animal with the capacity of distinguishing goodness from evilness) and "去" (Qu, elimination of the bad men).

[11] For a general study on the interaction between law and morality and their important role in the legal history of China, see Ma (2012, 2 ff. and 27 ff.).

rule of law, in traditional Chinese society.[12] In Chinese history, there are two different understandings of whether legal rules or ethical norms should play a dominant role in how the state is governed. The ideology that places more emphasis on law than on morality is known as Legalism, while the ideology that places a higher value on morality than law is known as Confucianism. Both schools of thoughts originated in China during the Spring and Autumn Period (770–476 BC), and legalism slightly preceded Confucianism. Its prominent representatives are Guan Zhong (723–645 BC), Shang Yang (390–338 BC) and Han Feizi (280–233 BC), of whom Han Feizi epitomized the Legalist thought.

The main ideas of Legalism are as follows[13]: all people have a propensity for greed and are selfish so that they pursue only their own interest; The rulers need to fully realize that it is human nature to draw their own advantages and avoid disadvantages and govern the state by controlling society on all fronts and by ensuring the efficient functioning of the bureaucracy through considerable rewards and harsh punishment. "There are only two ways of governing a country, *Fa* or *Shu*. *Fa* (law), as a written rule of punishment codified by the ruler, shall be disclosed to the public; in contrast, *Shu*, as a skill of ruling over the bureaucratic officers, shall be concealed in the mind of rulers and exert a subtle influence on the officers. Therefore, *Fa* shall be known by all peoples, but *Shu* shall remain in secret" (Han Fei Zi, Three Miseries, 人主之大物, 非法即术也。法者, 编著之图籍, 设之于官府, 而布之于百姓者也。术者, 藏之于胸中, 以偶众端, 而潜御群臣者也。故法莫如显, 而术不欲见" <<韩非子·难三>>). Legalists advocate the codification of law and believe that *Shu* is the secret skill of ruling; essentially concerning political tricks, it is forbidden to teach *Shu* publicly. At any moment, a wise ruler shall govern his country by authority (or power), *Shi* (Han Fei Zi, Three Miseries, "凡明主之治国也, 任其势。" (《难三》)). "The reason for what the rulers with ten thousand war chariots and those with thousand war chariots can govern their countries well and dominate the vassal states is because they hold absolute authority. The authority is the muscles and bones (Han Fei Zi, Lords, "万乘之主, 千乘之君, 所以制天下而征诸侯者, 以其威势也; 威势者, 人主之筋力也。(<< 人主> >). It is universally known that Shang Yang helped the Qin dynasty unify six states by reforming its law, enriching the country and strengthening the army.

Confucianism, founded by Confucius (551–479 BC), differs from Legalism in that it holds that a state should be governed primarily by establishing and enforcing good moral and ethical norms rather than harsh legal sanctions. In the Confucian view, human beings are kind and good from the moment of their birth. Through the education of virtues, the rulers create a sense of shame that prevents bad conduct, including insulting (making others lose face). The Confucian approach emphasizes the importance of the observance of *Li*, which refers to all rules that uphold moral habit and serve to maintain social order and essentially consist of the ceremonies

---

[12] See Peerenboom (2002, p. 27).

[13] Fung (2007, 260 f.).

and civilized patterns of social behavior developed through the wisdom of the ances-tors[14] and pursued by everybody to reach perfect virtue (ren, 仁) by overcoming one's selfishness and restoring *Li* (Confucius, Analects, 克己复礼为仁,《论语》). The real-ization of a person's perfect virtue also means "Do not do to others what you would not want them to do to you" (Confucius, Analects, 己所不欲, 勿施于人,《论语》) and "do to others what you wish for yourself" (Confucius, Analects, 己欲达而达人,《论语》). To rule the country well, Confucius argues that moral education is primary and punishment comes as secondary (德主刑辅), and in terms of the effectiveness of ruling a country, thanks to its preventive function, *Li* shall prevail over *Fa* (law), which is punitive by nature. Upon the advice of the philosopher Dong Zhong Shu (179–104 BC), the Chinese rulers began carrying out Confucianism as the unique official ideology to govern the country. According to Dong's canonic interpreta-tion, the practice of Confucianism essentially means the observance of the so-called "Three *Gang* and Five *Chang* (三纲五常)". The *Three Gang* denote the fundamental ethical relationships in a society, namely, that between a ruler and his subjects, that between a husband and his wife and that between a father and his sons. The *Five Chang* refers to five enduring virtues: benevolence (*Ren*, 仁), righteousness (*Yi* 义), traditional rituals (*Li*, 礼), wisdom (*Zhi*, 智) and trustworthiness (*Xin*, 信). Through moral education, Confucianists argue that in a society, there must be less dispute and more peace and harmony, so they invite the people to settle disputes through arbitration and conciliation instead of through litigation before the court.

To a large extent, "In China, according to traditional notions, law is not different from morality. It is only the implementation of this morality. The latter suffices as a criterion of repression, the punishment being only a substitute for the rite, *Li*, which should normally have preeminence. If moral rules only intervene to complete the force of legal precepts elsewhere, in China, legal precepts only intervene to complete the force of moral rules. In civil obligation, the moral rule is everything. The ancient theories, therefore, remain valid today as they were yesterday. Legal dynamism is virtually unknown to the traditional Chinese mentality".[15]

Whereas Confucianism stresses the rule of virtue or the rule of man, Legalism emphasizes rule by law.[16] They differ vastly but have many common grounds.[17] Both attach importance to centralization of power, recognize the political authority of the monarch as the legitimate source of the binding effect of all legal rules, agree on the inequality of social status between people (although Legalism highlights the equality of all before the law), uphold and recognize the legitimacy and validity of family

---

[14] Fung (2007, 69 f.) "It is Li that males and females shall not allow their hands to touch in giving or receiving something." (Mencius, Men with Good Eyesight, 男女授受不亲, 礼也 (孟子·离娄子)).

[15] Escarra (1936, p. 70).

[16] For the detailed narrative on the ideological conflict and the rule of law in contemporary China, see Peerenboom (2002, 33 f.). It should be noted that the Confucian concept of the rule of man should not be understood in an absolute way, but should be recognized in the Confucian rule of law, which emphasizes the self-discipline of the ruler, the soundness of people's thinking, and the harmony with the rule of law. See Ma (2005, p. 91).

[17] For a detailed analysis on the common points and differences between Confucianism and Legalism, see T'ung (2011, 226 f. and 324 f.).

rules, and stress the precedence of national and collective interests over individual interests.

Influenced by legal thinking centered on Legalism and Confucianism, a unique Chinese cultural and psychological structure is therefore created, namely, the tripartite model of law-morality-power (法-情-权). Under this model, power is at the core of a legal order and is more important than law, while laws and ethical and moral norms are enforced to maintain and consolidate centralized political power. This set of ethical and moral norms is built upon the duty-based ethics that individuals should be subservient to the collective and the state.[18]

In conclusion, unlike other legal systems, the Chinese legal system is not directly influenced by religion and theology but by Legalism and Confucianism, which constitute the core theoretical basis of legal order.[19] In traditional Chinese society, the ethical precepts and rules of kinship are applied extensively to govern the country, together with the law of state and the totalitarian authority of rulers, which, as the core of the power of legislation and justice, enjoys the primary privilege of being protected and the political power is centralized in their hands. In terms of the protection of civil rights, people are not all equal. Bureaucrats and aristocracies enjoy statutory privileges, and common people and people from a low social class are punished differently for the same crime.[20] Due to the practice of Legalism and Confucianism, the ideal of power worship and the bureaucracy-oriented mentality is firmly established and incessantly practiced, and the protection of personal freedom is very limited in the history of China.[21]

After the founding of the communist regime in the People's Republic of China in 1949, the traditional legal culture, with Legalism and Confucianism at its core, was not eradicated by communism. Conversely, the emphasis and maintenance of highly centralized and unified political power, despite twists and turns, is still absorbed or tolerated by the socialist legal system with Chinese characteristics and is clearly laid out in Chinese law today.[22] The socialist system has been implemented, but regarding

---

[18] Yu (2018, p. 29).

[19] T'ung (2011, 226 f.).

[20] For a detailed analysis, see Zhang (1984, p. 683).

[21] Alford (1986, p. 945) "The state was neither the embodied product of free will nor an impersonal encroacher upon individual autonomy. Instead, at least in theory, the relationship with the state was far more one of trust, modeled after the family, in which the Emperor and his representatives were conceived of more as senior than public figures…As was the case the Chinese family, those in position of power owed an enormous, fiduciary-like obligation to those over whom they exercised power".

[22] Marx believes that law is the embodiment of the will of the ruling class (according to this thought, the law in China today is the embodiment of the will of the Chinese working class represented by the Communist Party of China), and both Confucianism and Legalism believe that law was the manifestation of the will of the rulers. Although the separation between the legislative, judicial and executive powers is recognized in the Chinese constitution, in fact, as the Communist Party of China highlighted, China does not implement the separation of the three powers like the West, and all legislative, judicial and administrative activities are under the leadership of the Communist Party of China. For this so-called Party-Led constitutional governance and its theoretical basis, see Ke (2018, 98 f.).

the law in action, the Chinese legal culture today is not essentially different from that in the Qing dynasty (1644–1912) owing to historical inertia. The Chinese traditional legal reasoning is incarnated in the following ways[23]: power makes law, law needs to conform to basic morals and ethics, and law is panmoralized; law is intended by the common people as both sanction and punishment; people are invited to choose mediation or arbitration instead of litigation to resolve the disputes; there is more emphasis on the fulfillment of family and social obligations and less protection of individual rights; moral education is emphasized to prevent the violation of the laws, as its primary function, over that of punishment to govern the country.

Now, we probe into how Legalism and Confucianism, as well as, in general, the abovementioned traditional Chinese legal culture and mentality, are reflected in the 2020 CCC.

2 Crystallization of Legalism and Confucianism in the 2020 Chinese Civil Code

2.1 Moral Justice and Legal Justice Are Conflated

First, article 1 of this code is a clear manifestation of the ideology of Confucianism, which conflates moral justice and legal justice. Article 1 affirms the following: "This law is formulated in accordance with the Constitution of the PRC for the purposes of protecting the lawful rights and interests of the persons of the civil law, regulating civil-law relations, maintaining social and economic order, meeting the needs for developing socialism with Chinese characteristics, and carrying forward the core socialist values."

The emphasis on the protection of civil rights as legislative purpose results from the modernization of Chinese civil law and the protection of human rights, a worldwide set of social values transplanted from the West. The words "meeting the needs for developing socialism with Chinese characteristics" in this article manifest China's adherence to the socialist system and reflect the guiding political ideology of this Code. However, the real Chinese characteristics affirmed by the article consist of the promotion of core socialist values as its guiding ideology of legislation. The core socialist values in China refer to Prosperity (富强), Democracy (民主), Civilization (文明), Harmonization (和谐), Equality (平等), Liberty (自由), Justice (公平), Rule of Law (法治), Patriotism (爱国), Highly Professional Dedication (敬业), Good Faith (诚信) and Kindness (友善). In judicial practice, Chinese judges directly cite these core socialist values to motivate their decisions.[24] On May 13, 2020, the Chinese

---

[23] Yu (2018, pp. 15–29) and Ma (2005, p. 199 f.).

[24] For example, in the case of Beijing Pu Rui Te State Grid High Voltage Transmission Technology Co., Ltd. v. Si Xinlu [(2021) Jing 0114 Min Chu No. 822, July 12, 2021, Beijing Changping District Court]. The plaintiff was a company in Beijing, the defendant had joined the plaintiff as its employee and had obtained the Beijing Residence permit (Hukuo), the release of which was strictly controlled

Supreme Court even issued ten guiding cases on the protection of core socialist values to strengthen their protection.

Any civil conduct is thus subject to the observance of good customs and the moral ideals received in the country. This is a common rule in civil codes across the world. The CCC has also absorbed this rule, stipulating that civil subjects shall engage in civil activities in compliance with the principles of voluntariness (article 5), fairness (article 6), and good faith (article 7) and shall not offend good customs (article 8). It also recognizes that when dealing with civil disputes, the judge may apply customs (article 10) where the law does not specify the applicable rule, provided that good customs may not be violated. These principles are also intended to promote the core socialist values. It is particularly noteworthy that the 2020 CCC provides for the equality of all civil subjects in legal status (article 4) as a fundamental principle of civil law, which is highly distinctive. This is not only a manifestation of the concept of equality as one of the core socialist values, but also a direct reflection of the Chinese Legalist thought that requires equality before the law.

The legalization of moral and ethical concepts is embodied in the following specific provisions of this code; these provisions in China may be considered in light of Confucianism, even if some of them are common to Western legal systems:

1. Any party that damages public interests by infringing the name, portrait, reputation or honor of a hero or a martyr shall bear civil liability, and special protection shall be given to them (article 185)[25]; the rescuer shall not bear civil liability for damage caused to the rescued in an emergency rescue voluntarily carried out by the rescuer (article 184).

2. The so-called "compensation without assumption of liability" (Bu Chang 补偿) is adopted by this code. It refers to the situation in which, to realize moral fairness, the wrongdoer shall pay money to the victim for relief even if he has no fault and shall not assume any tort liability. The code provides the following case of "compensation without assumption of liability" (Bu Chang): (i) in emergency avoidance of danger, where the danger arises from natural causes, the person acting to avoid such danger shall not bear civil liability but may be condemned to pay reasonable compensation (article 182); (ii) where a person acts in order to protect any other's civil rights and interests, thereby harming himself or herself, the infringer shall bear the civil liability, and the beneficiary may have to pay reasonable compensation. Where there is no infringer or the infringer has fled

---

by the city of Beijing, then he resigned from the company. Considering that the defendant wasted the plaintiff's share of Beijing Hukou, the court ordered the defendant to compensate the consequent damages suffered by the plaintiff, amounting to 250,000 RMB, because the defendant violated the core socialist values pursuant to the article 1 of the civil code.

[25] For example, in the famous case of "making fun of military heroes died in Korea War", Mr. Chang Ping Luo made fun of a company of Chinese military heroes in the North Korea War. These men were frozen by a catastrophic snow storm and died while holding the position of attack like some ice sculptures in 1950. On July 10, 2021, he was arrested and accused of the crime of insulting those heroes. He was were also charged for the assumption of the related tort liability. See Big V "Fool" Insults Publicly the Military Company frozen as "Ice Sculpture", https://xw.qq.com/cmsid/20211009a014fw00, visited on July 15, 2021.

or is unable to bear the civil liability, the beneficiary shall pay to the victim a reduced sum of money (article 183); (iii) where a fully competent person has caused harm due to the temporary loss of awareness or loss of control in his/her action, even without any subjective fault, he/she shall make appropriate compensation to the victim per his/her financial status (article 1190); (iv) where the party providing labor services has caused an injury or damage during the provision of labor services as a result of the action of a third party, the party providing labor services shall have the right to request that the third party bear tort liability and shall have the right to request that the party accepting labor services make compensation. The party receiving the services may, after making compensation, claim compensation from the third party (article 1192); (v) in the event of damages to others caused by objects thrown from buildings or objects falling from buildings, where it is difficult to determine the specific infringer upon investigation, the user of the building who might have caused harm shall make compensation unless he/she can prove that he/she is not the infringer. The building user who may cause damage shall have the right to recover the compensation from the infringer (article 1254).

3. The elimination of ill effects, the restoration of reputation and the extension of an apology are explicitly listed as ways of bearing civil liability (article 179). This provision manifests the Chinese style of this code strongly.

4. Unlike most of the civil codes in the world, the CCC considers the usual moral code of returning money found as a legal duty. Unless a loser has explicitly offered a reward for finding the property, the finder of a lost thing has no right to ask the loser to pay any reward (article 317).

5. The CCC does not recognize the donation contract as a real contract, as the principal other civil codes do; instead, the code provides for donations as consensual contracts. At the same time, it also stipulates that the donor may revoke the gift prior to the transfer of its proprietary rights to the granted property (Article 658). However, in the case of donation contracts to provide for public welfare or to fulfill moral obligations, such as donations for disaster relief, poverty alleviation, or disability assistance, the donor cannot revoke the gift, and if the donor fails to deliver the donated property, the donee may require delivery (article 660).

6. Chinese legislators clearly inherit the Confucian concept of the family as the most fundamental unit of society, actively maintaining and promoting family unity and harmony. The CCC stipulates a large number of traditional Chinese ethics and moral norms that focus on preserving loyalty between the spouse, filial piety, courtesy, righteousness, and the sense of shame between the members of the family: (i) families should cultivate good family customs, carry forward family virtues, and attach importance to the construction of family civilization. Husband and wife shall be loyal to each other, respect and care for each other; family members shall respect the old and cherish the young, help each other, and maintain the marriage and family relationship characterized by equality, harmony and civility (article 1043); (ii) in case of divorce, one party of a couple, who has performed more obligations for bringing up children, taking care of the elderly, or assisting the other party in work, has the right to obtain the compensation for

the above contribution that he or she has made (article 1088); (iii) where in case of divorce, one spouse has difficulty in supporting himself or herself, the other spouse, if he or she has a capacity of bearing the cost of life of the other spouse, shall render appropriate assistance (article 1090); (iv) the shattering of affection between the spouses is qualified as a unique but very general and ambiguous criterion for divorce. In case of divorce, conciliation shall be carried out by the judge, and the divorce may be granted only under the condition that the conciliation before the judge fails and mutual affection no longer exists (article 1079); (v) the mutual and mandatory duty of maintenance of the life or providing daily support between the close relatives is also provided in this code (articles 1074, 1075); (vi) children born out of wedlock shall enjoy the same rights as children born by a married couple. The natural father or mother who fails to directly bring up a child born out of wedlock shall bear the costs of maintenance for his or her minor children or adult children who are not capable of living on their own income (article 1071).

7. In the field of inheritance, it is clearly set out that all successors shall deal with property inheritance in the spirit of mutual understanding, mutual accommodation, amity and unity (article 1132). In statutory succession, due consideration shall be given to those successors who have special financial difficulties and do not have the capacity of working (article 1130). Widowed daughters-in-law or sons-in-law who have made the predominant contributions in supporting their parents-in-law shall, in relation to their parents-in-law, be regarded as successors in the first order (article 1129). A necessary portion of property shall be reserved in a testament for a statutory successor without the capacity of working or a sufficient source of income (article 1141).

8. Confucius says that "after the death of a friend of mine, I will take care of handling his funeral if no one shall. Gifts from friends, even valuables such as carriages and horses, as long as they are not sacrificial meat, I will receive them all without worship." ("朋友死, 无所归, 曰: 于我殡。朋友之馈, 虽车马, 非祭肉, 不拜", 论语, 乡党篇 The Analects of Confucius, Chapter of Folks). In other words, after the death of a close person who is not a relative, where there is no one to handle the funeral for various reasons, everyone should take care of it. For this reason, it is reasonable for the person handling the funeral to obtain some property of the deceased. Therefore, the CCC specifically sets forth a legacy support agreement, which is stipulated between a natural person and an organization or an individual without the status of the successor. Accordingly, the latter undertakes the obligation of providing maintenance and therefore supporting for life the legator and has the right to inherit the property of the former after his death (article 1158). Moreover, the right-holder under legacy support is entitled to inherit the property of the deceased in preference to any other statutory or testamentary successor (article 1123).

2.2 The Protection of Collective and State Interests Shall Prevail over That of Individual Interests

Under the strong influence of Western law, the CCC not only transplants a myriad of Western civil terms and legal systems but also emphasizes the importance of respecting and safeguarding individual rights. For this purpose, a chapter on civil rights is specifically set forth in the General Provisions, namely, Chapter 5 (articles 109–132), with a total of 22 articles, which set forth in detail the specific civil rights that may be enjoyed by civil subjects (personality rights, personal information rights, identity rights, real rights, credit rights, intellectual property rights, right of succession, equity and other investment rights). "Civil subjects shall, at their own will, exercise civil rights in accordance with the law without interference of any others" (article 130). It is worth noting that to highlight the respect for human rights, a specific book on the protection of personality rights (book 4, articles 989–1039) is dedicated to this code.

However, influenced by Confucianism and Legalism, the CCC has drawn a red line for the protection of individual civil rights, clearly stating that "[N]o civil subject may damage the national interests, public interests or the legitimate rights and interests of others by abuse of exercise of his own civil rights" (Article 132). In other words, the protection of individual interests is subject to that of collective and state interests. This idea of subordinating individual interests under state interests is clearly embodied in this code as follows:

1. Special protection is provided for state ownership and collective ownership. Land is the mother of all things on the earth. As far as the legal framework of the Chinese land system is concerned, the Confucian and Legalist idea of subordinating the individuals under the state is closely compatible with socialist public ownership. In China, land belongs only to the state and the collective unit, and no other legal subject is entitled to own the land. Nevertheless, other civil subjects may enjoy the right to use state or collectively owned land by putting it in mortgage, contributing it as registered capital of company, or alienating such right to others. Therefore, the right to use land for construction (mainly for state-owned land, article 344–361), the right to use land contract management (article 330–343) and the right to use collectively owned land for habitation (article 362–365) are set forth in this code as usufruct right. However, given that ownership is the most complete real right, the owners of land, namely, the state or collective unit, hold power for the final disposal of land, and the rights of land use are ultimately subject to state and collective land ownership. On the one hand, all such rights of use of state or collectively owned land have a time limit, upon expiration of which they are recoverable by the state or collective unit (although the land use right for residential construction will be automatically renewed upon the expiration of its time limit, this renewal is not free and unconditional, article 359). On the other hand, the state has the right to expropriate or requisition the right to use state-owned land at any time when necessary, and as a sovereign, the state can also deprive individuals of the ownership of their buildings and appendages

affixed on state-owned or collective land through expropriation and requisition (article 243–245). Although expropriation and requisition can only be used when it is necessary for the protection of the public interest and corresponding compensation should be given, the judgment on whether the operation conforms to the protection of the public interest and how to quantify the compensation for the relevant expropriation or requisition is entirely regulated by China's complex and diverse administrative regulations and the Chinese Communist Party's policies. The amount of compensation for expropriation and requisition is extremely uncertain and often varies according to the location, time or legal status of the expropriated person. This code does not provide that the state shall compensate the expropriation or requisition against payment of price, comprehensively, fairly and reasonably calculated at the market value of the object of expropriation or requisition (article 243).

2. Even if this code recognizes the socialist market economy and equally protects the legal status, development rights, and property rights of all market entities (article 206, 207), under the influence of Confucianism, Legalism and the socialist system, the state enjoys some unchallengeable privileges in terms of the protection of its property rights: (i) a large number of the most significant resources (such as mineral deposits, waters and sea areas, uninhabited seas, urban lands, radio frequency spectrum, defense assets, and all rural and urban-suburban areas, cultural relics, wildlife resources, etc.) can be owned exclusively by the state (articles 247–254); (ii) a lost-and-found thing belongs to the state, in the case of failure of claim of its property right by anybody within one year after the publication of the announcement on such claim (article 318). Although the same rule is also applied in many Western countries, for the Chinese understanding, it results from the continuation of Confucianism, according to which every citizen is born first for the state, then for his family; (iii) any property that is left by the deceased without a successor or a legatee shall be owned by the state (article 1160); (iv) generally speaking, the establishment, alienation or extinction of real property is subject to the completion of their registration before the relevant authority, However, in case of state-owned natural resources, such registration is not required (article 209); (v) to prevent the loss of state-owned property, usucapion is not provided in this code, which is extremely rare and probably unique in all civil codes; (vi) the code also highlights that "[P]roperty owned by the State shall be protected by law and shall not be occupied, looted, privately divided, withheld or damaged by any organization or individual" (article 258), underlining the special protection of state-owned property, emphasizing the obligation of private civil subjects to protect state-owned property. (vii) The managers, supervisory institutions and their personnel of state-owned assets should promote value preservation, increase the value of state-owned assets and prevent any loss of state-owned assets. Moreover, the private party shall assume civil, administrative, or criminal liability pursuant to the law for his abuse of official powers and dereliction of duties, which cause losses of state-owned assets (article 259).

3. Although the CCC clearly recognizes the principle of freedom of contract, when the state needs it, a contract must be concluded in accordance with the will

of the state. For the purpose of emergency rescue and disaster relief, epidemic prevention and control or other needs, the state may assign, direct or mandatorily order, and the relevant civil subjects shall conclude a contract with the state per the concrete rights and obligations provided by the relevant laws and administrative regulations. Any party obligated to make an offer in conformity to the provisions of laws and administrative regulations shall make a reasonable offer without delay. The parties with the duty to accept the offer in accordance with the laws or administrative regulations may not refuse the reasonable request of the other party for conclusion of the contract (article 494).

2.3 Civil Rights Are Protected with Limited Recognition of Private Autonomy and Restricted by the Control and Supervision Imposed by the Public Authorities

Private autonomy, as the core principle and spirit of civil law, denotes that, in the field of private law, every civil conduct is admissible except that which is forbidden by law. In contrast, in the field of public law, the holder of public power may not exercise its power except when authorized by law. In many Western civil codes, represented by the French Civil Code, the principle of private autonomy consists of the absolute protection of private ownership, freedom of contract and fault liability. The recognition of private autonomy stems from right-protection-oriented thought. Unlike the 1986 General Principles of Civil Law, the legislators of the 2020 CCC do not emphasize the right-protection-oriented idea in their legislative endeavor. This is so despite that, in the opinion of legislators of this code, its promulgation aims to "improve and enrich the types of civil rights, to form a more complete civil rights system, to strengthen the protection and remedy of civil rights, and to form a standardized and effective rights protection mechanism".[26]

Nevertheless, in view of Legalists, the people enjoy rights only within the limit imposed by the state power of the ruler. This idea is clearly incarnated in the CCC as follows:

1. Although equal protection for state, collective and private ownership is expressly recognized in this code (art. 207), as mentioned above, under the guidance of socialism, state ownership and collective ownership are protected with priority to private ownership in terms of the extent of objects of ownership and the means of their protection. Moreover, for the protection of the social interest, the public authorities hold power to expropriate private property even at a price lower than market value;

2. The principle of freedom of contract, set forth in Articles 4 and 12 of the 1999 Chinese Contract Law, is not reiterated in the 2020 CCC; however, it is repeatedly and strongly emphasized that civil juristic acts shall not violate mandatory regulations and/or public order and/or good morals (art. 143, art. 135);

---

[26] Wang (2020, p. 252).

3. Although, in principle, fault is considered an indispensable element for the assumption of tort liability and no-fault liability is recognized in an exceptional way only to protect some special interests or in the case of high-risk activities, in China, to a large extent, many civil tort liabilities are regulated by administrative law. For example, tort liabilities for traffic accidents, industrial accidents, medical malpractice, environmental pollution, infringement of consumers' rights, infringement of personal information, network liability, defective products liability, violation of adjacent rights in real estate, and condominium ownership are respectively and mainly regulated by administrative laws;

4. The criteria for verification of fault for the determination of tort liability are not expressly provided in this code; in China's legislative and judicial practice, how to verify the existence of illegality (*Rechtswidrigkeit*), which is a key element for the constitution of tort liability, is usually provided by administrative law;

5. In light of Xi Jinping's idea of ecological civilization, article 9 of the code provides that all civil subjects, while engaging in civil activities, shall help save resources and protect the ecological environment. This provision is unique in all civil codes in the world. This so-called green principle is defined as a fundamental principle of civil law, and obviously, as a result, it strongly restricts private autonomy.[27]

6. This code adopts very restrictive policies on the establishment of a legal person. All profit-making legal persons shall be established upon mandatory approval by the relevant public authorities on a case-by-case basis. They must be registered before the specific public body of registration according to the administrative law (article 77); in principle, the establishment of a non-profit legal person is also subject to such administrative approval by public authority, unless otherwise provided by law (article 90). The so-called special legal persons (namely, public bodies holding public power, rural collective economic organizations, urban cooperative economic organizations, and grassroots mass organizations) must be established in accordance with public law rather than under this civil code, sometimes even without any approval of the public authority (articles 97, 99, 100);

7. The urban residence committees and village committees are classified as special legal persons (article 101), but they hold the administrative power to participate directly, control, monitor, and supervise the civil activities of individuals (article 24, 31, 32, 36, 277).[28] In this way, the Legalist tradition emphasizing state control over the individual is clearly followed by this code.

8. The establishment of a legal entity without the status of the legal person is always subject to approval by the relevant authorities and registration before them (article

---

[27] Wang (2020, p. 257).

[28] In concrete, these two organs hold the power to apply to the court to restore the civil capacity of the natural person (article 24), to appoint a guardian, in the case of a dispute over the individuation of a guardian, to act as the interim guardian in case of lack of protection of the civil rights of the ward by other persons (article 31, 32), to apply to the court to disqualify the guardian (article 36), even supervise establishment and organization of condominium committee of building and its election and activities (article 277).

102). The sphere of legal entities without the status of legal persons is very large and includes mainly sole proprietorships, partnerships, and professional service organizations.

9. Under the strong influence of Confucianism and Legalism, according to which civil law essentially regulates the activities of the family, which is the basic unit of society, this code sometimes considers the family as an autonomous civil subject, as happens, for example, with individual businesses family and lease-holding farm households (article 54, 55).[29] Moreover, the right-holder of the leaseholding rights of rural land and homestead use rights in China are families rather than individuals (article 330, 362). According to this code, a joint property regime between the spouses shall be applied automatically upon the conclusion of the marriage, except otherwise agreed upon by the spouse (article 1065). Additionally, the code recognizes the reciprocal agency between spouses in the case of their carrying out any activities for their common interests (article 1060). All debts only incurred by one spouse during the period of cohabitation and resulting from their joint operation or acknowledged expressly by the other spouse shall have effect as jointly initiated debts of the couple (article 1064).

As far as the law in action is concerned, today, the Chinese civil norms consist not only of those norms that are included in this Civil Code but also of those norms established by countless judicial interpretations, administrative regulations, and even the policies of the Party, which fully demonstrates the Legalist idea of governing the country by the combined use of *Fa* (law), *Shi* (power or authority) and *Shu* (skill of ruling).

As mentioned above, Han Feizi, the prominent legalist, considers all three (*Fa, Shi, Shu*) indispensable for the ruling of state, he held that:

> "the intelligent ruler carries out his regulations as would heaven and handle men as if he were a divine being. Being like Heaven, he commits no wrong, and being like a divine being, he falls into no difficulties. His *Shi* (power) enforces his strict orders and nothing that he encounters resists him…Only when this is so can his *fa* (laws) be carried out and in concrete". (Han Fei, Chapter 8, "明主之行制也天,其用人也鬼。天则不非,鬼则不困。势行教严,逆而不违………然后一行其法。《韩非子,八经》)[30]

In other words, by means of the exercise of his power (*Shi*), the intelligent ruler acts in accordance with law fairly and impartially (which is a function of law—*Fa*) and handles his subjects without letting them know how they are handled (which is the function of his unpredictable skill of ruling—*Shu*). The Chinese ruler has also always been adopting this legalist way of government in the drafting, interpretation and implementation of Chinese civil law.

As far as the Chinese norms in action in civil matters are concerned, in addition to the civil code and special civil statutes, there is a huge number of judicial interpretations issued by the Chinese Supreme Court, which, being abstract interpretations on

---

[29] In principle, the debts of these two kinds of family subject shall be paid off from the family property, unless it can be proved that the activities generating the debts have been actually operated by a member of family (article 56).

[30] Fung (2007, p. 256).

written laws, produce the binding effect and work exactly as law or code, in the sense that they may be cited directly by the judges to make their decisions.[31] In China, these judicial interpretations aim to ensure the uniformity of the implementation of civil written norms and provide authoritative solutions and interpretation for concrete legal problems occurring in legal practice, so they are enacted frequently and massively, as well as in a fragmented way.[32] Usually, they take effect shortly after their issuance, sometimes even a few hours later, and their content may change unpredictably and suddenly due to the enactment of new law or judicial interpretation.

The number of judicial interpretations on civil matters is extremely large. For example, before the promulgation of the 2020 Civil Code on May 28, 2020, there were as many as 591 civil judicial interpretations. After the Code came into effect on January 1, 2021, by the end of 2021, 116 judicial interpretations inconsistent with the Code were abolished, but 76 new judicial interpretations concerning its interpretation and implementation, featuring 1,523 articles, were intensively promulgated, such as the *Judicial Interpretation on the Application of the Period of Limitation of Action in the Civil Code* (December 25, 2020), *Judicial Interpretation on the Application of Security Interests Institution in the Civil Code* (December 25, 2020), *Judicial Interpretation on the Implementation of Book on Real Rights in the Civil Code* (December 25, 2020), *Judicial Interpretation on the Implementation of Book on Marriage and Family in the Civil Code* (December 25, 2020), *Judicial Interpretation on the Implementation of Book on Inheritance in the Civil Code* (December 25, 2020).

In particular, some judicial interpretations of the Chinese Supreme Court concerning specific laws may also significantly influence the application of the CCC and may sometimes even modify it. For instance, pursuant to article 1179 of the Civil Code, the tortfeasor who caused the disability of others shall pay disability compensation and death compensation in case of the death of victim. However, according to article 192 of the Judicial Interpretation on the Criminal Procedure Law, issued on December 7, 2021,[33] those who are convicted of a crime causing disability or death of a person shall only pay compensation for property losses caused by their criminal acts. Since both disability compensation and death compensation also include

---

[31] For a brief analysis on the judicial interpretation as the source of Chinese Civil Law, see Bu (2013, p. 3).

[32] Some of these judicial interpretations concern civil laws enacted before the promulgation of the Civil Code, such as the Judicial Interpretation on Inheritance Law (promulgated on September 11, 1985), the Judicial Interpretation on General Principles of Civil Law (April 2, 1988), the Judicial Interpretation on Contract Law (1) (December 19, 1999), the Interpretation on Contract Law (2) (April 24, 2009), the Judicial Interpretation on Marriage Law 1 (December 25, 2001), the Judicial Interpretation on Marriage Law (2) (promulgated on December 25, 2003, amended on February 20, 2017), the Judicial Interpretation on Marriage Law 3 (August 9, 2011). Some are judicial interpretations on certain types of civil legal issues, such as Judicial Interpretation on Limitation of Actions (August 21, 2008), Judicial Interpretation on Property Service Disputes (May 15, 2009), Judicial Interpretation on Mental Damages (March 8, 2001), and Judicial Interpretation on Personal Injury Compensation (December 26, 2003), etc.

[33] Actually, article 138 of the 2012 Judicial Interpretation on the Criminal Procedure Law provides the same rule.

compensation of emotional damages suffered by the victim, which are not by definition property losses, according to this judicial interpretation on Criminal Procedure Law, the defendant shall not pay these two compensations. Undoubtedly, although this solution is unreasonable and contradicts the 2020 Civil Code, it is currently applied in practice.

In addition to its judicial interpretations, the Chinese Supreme Court also issues some directive documents to guide Court proceedings. They are not judicial interpretations, so they may not be cited directly by the judges for making their decisions. However, they may be taken as a reference for the motivation of judgments. For instance, the "Minute of National Meeting on the Civil and Commercial Trial" (so-called Meeting Minutes of Ninth Section of the Chinese Supreme Court) dated November 11, 2019, with its 130 articles, provides detailed solutions for many problems arising in the course of a civil case. Even if it is neither law nor judicial interpretation, it is one of the most important normative documents on civil matters in China. Moreover, the high court in each province produces thousands of guiding opinions to direct the way civil proceedings are conducted; they produce some judicial policies and unify the different solutions for the same legal problems in its jurisdiction. China has no constitutional court, so the problem of how to resolve the conflicts and contradictions between the CCC, special statutes, numerous judicial interpretations and guiding opinions, which happen frequently and massively, becomes urgent and serious.

Last but not least, some civil norms are provided neither by civil code nor public law, even nor by judicial interpretations, but are enacted in the form of the policies of the Chinese Communist Party. For instance, although regarding agricultural and forestry land the Civil Code recognizes the separation between ownership, landhold leasing rights, and land management rights (article 339, 340),the detailed rules on how to make use of three different real rights are mainly set forth in a document of the Chinese ruling party, the so-called *Opinions on the Pilot Work of Rural Land Expropriation, Commercialization of Collective Land for the Purpose of Commercial Construction and Homestead System Reform*, approved at the seventh meeting of the Leading Group for Comprehensively Deepening Reform of the Central Committee of the Communist Party of China on December 2, 2014.

In summary, in terms of the law in action, China's civil legal order has been clearly decodified now.[34] China's civil legal order is built up in a way similar to the solar system. In this system, the Civil Code is the sun, namely, the core of civil law; various special statutes (such as Insurance Law, Company Law, Labor Contract Law) are planets; various administrative laws and regulations regulating civil activities constitute minor planets; judicial interpretations of the Supreme Court and guiding opinions of different high courts are comets; civil customs and judicial policies of the state and the ruling party are sunspots. With respect to the Civil Code and the separate statutes, in terms of the stability of their effectiveness, all other civil norms are much fragile in the sense that they may be drafted, approved, promulgated, modified and

---

[34] For the idea of decodification of civil law, see Irti (1998, 27 ff.).

abolished quite unpredictably and by use of a very simple procedure.[35] In this way, China's legalist tradition of taking law (*fa*) as a derivative of political power and a tool for maintaining or strengthening political authority continues today, and it is also perfectly compatible with the Marxist's jurisprudence, according to which law is the manifestation of the will of the ruling class.

3 Conclusion

The 2020 CCC is deeply influenced by traditional Chinese legal culture, especially Legalism and Confucianism. Even if the main theoretical terminology and institutions in this code are transplanted from the West, the mindset and the social and cultural soil on which its drafting, interpretation, and implementation are based have many Chinese characteristics and are essentially different from those of the Western civil codes. On the one hand, it results from the integration of legal rules with ethical norms, as Confucianism advocates. On the other hand, under the strong influence of Legalism, its main objective consists of strengthening the authority of political rulers through the mixed application of *Fa* (law), *Shu* (power) and *Shi* (skill of ruling). Thus far, Western legal institutions or norms cannot be successfully transplanted into China unless compatible with Legalism and Confucianism. Private autonomy, as the fundamental principle of civil law, and civil rights-oriented ideals are still far from their realization under the 2020 CCC. Due to the massive application of judicial interpretations of the Supreme Court and the guiding opinions of high courts, Chinese civil law has already been decodified shortly after the promulgation of this civil code.

References

Alford W (1986) On the limits of grand theory in comparative law. Wash Law Rev 61:945–956
Big V "Fool" Insults Publicly the Military Company Frozen as "Ice Sculpture" ("沙雕"大V公然侮辱"冰雕连"). https://xw.qq.com/cmsid/20211009a014fw00. Visited on July 15, 2021
Bu YS (ed) (2013) Chinese civil law. C. H. Beck Press, Munich
Escarra J (1936) Le droit chinois. Librairie du Recueil Sirey, Paris
Fung YL (2007) A short history of Chinese philosophy. Tianjin Social Science Press, Tianjin
Irti N (1998) L'età della decodificazione venti anni dopo. Giuffrè, Milan
Ke HQ (2018) Part-led constitutionism and its rationality (党导宪政及其合理性). Governance Study (法治研究) 3:98–105
Le Bon G (1896) The crowd: a study of the popular mind. Macmillan Press, New York
Ma XH (2005) Li and law: historical connection of law (礼与法: 法的历史连接). Beijing University Press, Beijing
Ma HP (2012) Law and social change: the Chinese experience past and present (法律与中国社会之变迁). Airiti Press, Taipei
Peerenboom R (2002) China's long march toward rule of law. Cambridge University Press, Cambridge

---

[35] On the decodification of civil law in China, see Zhang (2017, pp. 16–17; Id. 2018, 217 ff.).

Pound R (1948) Comparative law and history as bases for Chinese law. Harvard Law Rev 61(5):748–762

Ruskola T (2013) Legal orientalism: China, the United States, and modern law. Harvard University Press, Boston, MA

Sacco R (2015) Il diritto muto. Neuroscienze, conoscenza tacita, valori condivisi. Il Mulino, Bologna

Sacco R, Gambaro A (2008) Sistemi giuridici comparati. Utet, Torino

Seppänen S (2016) Ideological conflict and the rule of law in contemporary China. Cambridge University Press

Seppänen S (2020) After difference: A meta-comparative study of Chinese encounters with foreign comparative law. Am J Comp Law 68(1):186–221

T'ung TC (2011) Law and society and traditional China. Commercial Press, Beijing

Von Savigny FC (1867) System of the modern Roman law (Vol. I and Holloway W, Trans). Hyperion Press

Wang C (2020) Statement on the draft of the Civil Code of the People's Republic of China (关于中华人民共和国民法典草案的说明). In: Civil Code of the People's Republic of China (中华人共和国民法典). Law Press, Beijing

Yu RG (2018) General theory of Confucian legal thought (《儒家法思想通论》). The Commercial Press, Beijing

Zhang JF (1984) Law. Encyclopedia of China (中国大百科全书·法学卷). Encyclopedia of China Press, Beijing

Zhang LH (2009) The latest developments in the codification of Chinese civil law. Tulane Law Rev 83:1000–1040

Zhang LH (2017) General part of civil code, solar legislative model and decodification of civil law (民法总则、"太阳系式"民事立法模式和民法典的分解). People's Rule Law (人民法治) 10:17–18

Zhang LH (2018) Legal normative base of economic institutions and study on function of the civil code—analysis on decodification of civil law and the rationality on the legislative model of Chinese civil law (经济制度的法律规范基础和民法典功能的考察---民法典分解现象和中国民事立法模式合理性之分析). Guang Dong Soc Sci (广东社会科学) 4:271–321

Lihong Zhang is a full professor of law at East China University of Political Science and Law (Shanghai, ECUPL), a holder of Ph.D. degree in law of the University of Rome "La Sapienza", Vice Secretary-General of China's National Society of Civil Law, Standing Director of China's National Society of European Law, Director of China's National Society of Comparative Law, and Director of the Roman Law and European Law Research Center of ECUPL. He has been a visiting professor at the University of Paris "Panthéon Assas", University of Turin, National University of Singapore, Münster University, Catholic University of Leuven, Jagiellonian University, University of San Francisco and University of Macerata, and he has given lectures at many world-renowned universities, such as Harvard University, University of California at Berkeley, Georgetown University, Hitotsubashi University, and the National University of Seoul.

New Civil Codes and the Environment: The Contributions of China and Argentina

Sabrina Lanni ⓘ

Abstract Critically reflecting on the current approach to uncontrolled economic development, which could lead not only to ecologic imbalance but also to an imminent crisis of civilization, this essay aims to demonstrate that markets are not necessarily enemies of the environment: they could, in fact, provide valuable support in protecting ecosystems, as illustrated by emerging legal thought. This poses new challenges for private law. The need to contrast an irresponsible model of a consumer society with the necessity to understand nature as a nonnegotiable asset are responses to environmental problems that involve the new civil codes, including in particular those of Argentina and China. Focusing on the concepts of *consumo sustentable* and *lüse yuanze* from a comparative perspective, the author emphasizes the so-called "greening" of civil codes, stressing how these principles will not be effective in ensuring the survival of the geo-human system if not coordinated with constitution-based and democratic decision-making. New Latin American constitutions have fostered the elaboration, by legal scholars, of a new critical approach to environmental problems, which appears to be a valid starting point for facilitating the response of private law to ecological issues: that is to say, first of all, to introduce contractual and civil liability systems that will give priority to environmental problems.

1 The Greening of Civil Law

It is undeniable that one of the most delicate aspects of postmodern and globalized times is the issue of ecology. Problems generated by environmental devastation and by the hyper exploitation of natural resources go beyond national boundaries.

This essay is published as part of the activities of the Jean Monnet Chair "ENFASIS" co-funded by the European Union. Its contents are the sole responsibility of the Chair Holder (Prof. Sabrina Lanni). The work presented here is part of a broader research, which is currently being published, on the environmental awareness of the new civil codes.

S. Lanni (✉)
University of Milan, Milan, Italy
e-mail: sabrina.lanni@unimi.it

M. Graziadei and L. Zhang (eds.), *The Making of the Civil Codes*,
Ius Gentium: Comparative Perspectives on Law and Justice 104,
https://doi.org/10.1007/978-981-19-4993-7_21

Global warming has a global impact: it is a central problem for the survival of humanity as a whole. From a legal point of view, preserving the environment and ecosystems is not limited to environmental law. The need for a new green deal is being discussed with increasing frequency in the most disparate legal fields—from international law to municipal law, from consumer law to the regulation of digital technologies, and from constitutional law to private law.[1]

The development of several green legal fields brings in many new and innovative ideas, concepts, and principles that stress the establishment of a complete system of ecological civilization. This invites an in-depth analysis of the new civil codes' response to environmental problems and problems involving natural resources.

This approach appears in the long-awaited Chinese Civil Code (the "CCC")—where the environment and natural resources have been severely tested in light of China's rapid economic development—so much so that some scholars, at the beginning of 2002, proposed identifying it with the concept of the "green civil code".[2]

The protection of public welfare and health from environmental damage appears to be the starting point for facilitating the response of private law to ecological issues; that is, contractual and civil liability systems have a certain weight that allows them to have precedence. However, there are many legal areas of the CCC that refer to the environment and that are not isolated from one another. It is possible to identify a common thread that serves as a general, uniting principle.

One remarkable innovation of the General Provisions of Private Law is the adoption of the so-called "Green Principle", embedded in article 9 of the CCC, which is considered to be the major Chinese breakthrough in solving environmental problems—an issue that will be explored in depth later in this paper. What is interesting here is the systematic positioning of the principle itself. It is placed at the beginning of the code as a sort of preamble, in line with the logic of the general principles of the BGB model,[3] and it balances the exercise of the right to property and the freedom of contract with public and private interests.

It is a first for China in that a private law had never before regulated legal relations between individuals, thus imposing a mandatory requirement for environmental and natural resource protection. This decision on the part of the Chinese is placed in what, from the point of view of comparative analysis, appears to be a marked trend of the new private law codifications.

In many countries, new civil codes and the updates of old ones have made various and distinct breakthroughs concerning environmental protections. They go beyond the scope of repairing environmental damage by questioning the sustainability of choices that fall within the private autonomy of individual actors. This perspective is

---

[1] To review the interdisciplinary frameworks of environmental legal problems, see Sands (1993), Hironaka (2014), and do Amaral Junior et al. (2019). For an approach to these problems based on comparative law under the influence of globalization see Pozzo (2017) in Graziadei and Serio (2017, p. 86).

[2] Cf. Zhai and Chang (2019, p. 2) where reference is made to Lv (2/2002, pp. 10–11).

[3] The CCC structure is believed to be patterned after the German Bürgerliches Gesetzbuch model via Japan: see Lei (2009).

evidenced by the relationship between language and law and the fact that new entries have indeed been introduced into the lexicon of the new civil codes.

There are lemmas such as environment, waste, pollution, animal welfare, and sustainability, which were unknown to the first wave of codifications of civil law, or, in any case, to those codes, such as the Napoleonic Code, that served in several cases as 'model codes'.[4]

In Europe, the Dutch Civil Code (1992) focuses on the recognition of environmental rights and states the consequences of the "pollution of air, water or soil" (art. 6:175), paying specific attention to the "operators of waste sites" (art. 6:176). In my reading of the code, the real innovation for ecological environment protection in the Netherlands are the tools recognized to protect environmental interests, particularly in art. 3:305 that allows anyone to establish a foundation to protect a public interest, such as the environment, against the government of the Netherlands.[5] Likewise, the reformed German Civil Code (2002) is also sensitive to ecological issues. Not only does it provide an immediate remedy, but it represents an innovation in the form of a new ecological way of rethinking the relationship between man and nature. An excellent example of this is the German Civil Code's recognition of the intrinsic value of animals, which states for the first time in a European civil code that "Animals are not things" (§ 90a).[6] Noteworthy is also the Ukrainian Civil Code (2003), which particularly in art. 13 stresses the application of the Civil Code in all the "spheres of use of natural resources and environmental protection", thus expanding its operations in this regard. The aforementioned civil codes innovate and supplement the codal provisions, which, according to a traditional approach, have been mainly aimed at remedying environmental damage. However, even exclusively with regard to this (more traditional) perspective, a new legal sensitivity emerges.

A notable example can be seen in the provision of art. 603 of the Romanian Civil Code (2009), which details the landowner's obligation to operate in an appropriate manner in regard to "environmental protection and to ensure good neighborly relations".[7] Of interest, as well, is art. 1248 of the revised French Civil Code (2016), which explains how the restoration of ecological damage is prioritized and that monetary damages will be required only in cases where it is impossible.

Among the Latin American civil codes, the new Argentinian Civil Code (2015) stands out because it refers to the environment, the sustainability of an individual's choices, and the renewed balance between individual and collective choices (arts. 14, 18, and 240). It is important to note that some deep-rooted scientific thoughts on this topic are also found in earlier civil codes. An example is that of the Cuban Civil Code (1987), where natural resources and the environment are set as a limit for

---

[4] On diffusion of the French Civil Code and its contents, see Graziadei, in Reimann (1993, p. 115 ff.; Id. 2019, p. 442 ff.).

[5] For the context of Netherlands' leading case on environmental issues, see Spijkers (2020).

[6] For similar reforms in Switzerland (2002) and France (2015) see arts. 641 and 528 of their civil codes, respectively.

[7] Duscă (2013, pp. 24–30), who points out that art. 603 of the Civil Code represents the literal transposition of art. 44 par. 7 of the Constitution, rather than an attempt to integrate in the code the contributions of European, international or comparative law.

property rights (arts. 86f and 131.1). Another illustrative example is provided by the Brazilian Civil Code (2002), which inspires innovation in the glossary of civil codes themselves through the articulation of new values, such as that of "environmental beauty" as well as that of "ecological balance" (art. 1228.1).

In Latin America, a real trend is emerging for the greening of civil codes, a trend that inevitably extends to all new civil code projects, with rare exceptions.[8] Of the aforementioned trend, I believe the model of reference can be found in the very recent draft of the new Colombian Civil Code (2020), where new objectives of civil law are invoked, including the preservation of the "ecological coexistence" (art. 276), the conservation of the environment and "social wellbeing" (art. 268) as values to be weighed against "economic activities and in relationships and development of markets" (art. 38).[9]

China fully emblemizes this trend of greening the civil code. The recent CCC (2020) marks the development of an ecological legal path, one which originated with the 1978 Constitution that contained the first formal rules in favor of the environment.[10] It was a very intense period, one in which the development of environmental issues was spurred on on multiple legal fronts, both nationally and internationally, in light of the growing Chinese desire for supremacy in the international community.

The different legal norms and the many lemmas, which can be found merely from reading the new CCC, suggest an awareness on the part of the Chinese legal system of the importance of the ongoing debate over ecological issues as well as the need to provide a concrete set of answers from a private law perspective through the development of a comprehensive model of a civil code.

A significant number of rules, approximately 20, refer to the many and varied problems that may affect the environment in a broad sense. After careful analysis, I conclude that it is possible to subdivide these into three groups. A first group of rules is connected to the "environment"; here, the intent of the code seems to be the regulation of the civil activities contributing to resource conservation and to environmental protection.[11] Another group of rules is that in which the fulcrum of the reasoning appears to be oriented using an "ecological" approach, in the sense that they seek to limit ecological damage that can be linked to the free activity of private

---

[8] The 2019 draft of the new Peruvian Civil Code (cf. *Anteproyecto de reforma del Código civil peruano* [ed.: *Grupo de trabajo de revisión y mejora del Código civil peruano de 1984*], Lima, 2019) appears to be silent on environmental issues, as it contains no innovative ideas in this respect. In all likelihood, this was probably a matter considered to fall within the scope of the General Environmental Law (l. 28611/2015); see Foy Valencia (2/2018, pp. 69–86).

[9] Reference is to *Proyecto de código civil de Colombia (Primera versión). Reforma del código civil y su unificación en obligaciones y contratos con el código de comercio* (the draft code is available online: http://derecho.bogota.unal.edu.co/proyecto-deactualizacion-del-codigo-civil/).

[10] Cf. Toti (2017, p. XII) highlights the development of Chinese measures for the environment and its regulation such as the Environmental Protection Law of the PRC of 2015 (*Zhonghua renmin gongheguo huanjing baohu fa*).

[11] See arts. 9 (as a basic green provision), 286 (concerning landowners' rights), 326 (for the usufructuary exercise of rights), 346 (for the right to use land), 509 (referring to the limits of contractual freedom), 619 (on sellers' duties).

individuals.[12] The last grouping of rules includes those that are directed toward the problems of "pollution" to limit environmental damage and establish the rights (and duties) of the injured parties.[13]

Overall, the aforementioned rules have in common the fact that they may serve to establish a connection between the CCC and other contemporary civil codes in regard to environmental issues. They give rise to the greening of the civil code in light of 'integral sustainability' and 'State coercion' and, as a result, bring in an overarching vision reflected in all fields of law.

2 Stopping the Consumer Machine or Listening to the Voice of Nature: Latouche V. Daly

State and international environmental protection policies must necessarily be related to State and international consumer protection policies to establish limits on the exercise of consumer rights in the market for the preservation of the environment as a common good. This perspective finds a certain anchoring in the Latin American arena: there is an interesting common denominator in the Model Laws of Parlatino for the Protection of the User and the Consumer (2006) and Mother Earth's Rights (2013)[14] as well as in the new Argentinian Consumer Law Project (2019) that notably deepens and expands the dialog between Consumer Law and Environmental Law.[15]

In the face of pressing multilevel protections of the environment and of the overlap between constitutional law and statutory law, the new Argentinian Consumer Law Project underlines the emergence of the need for a renewed balance, first between consumer law and environmental law (as well as their principles and values) and, second, between consumer law and civil law.

The environment appears to be an innovative point of contact between two academic fields—consumer law and constitutional law—which in recent decades have been distinguished, especially in Latin America, by a great dynamism of

---

[12] See arts. 1229–1235 (tort liability for ecological damage).

[13] See arts. 1233–1235, No. 4.

[14] The reference rules are essentially twofold: The first concerns the danger of environmental contamination (art. 10): "Tested by any suitable means, the danger, toxicity or capacity of contamination of the environment by [a] product… the authority will carry out the product for the immediate retirement of the market and the prohibition of circulation for the same… producer or supplier will be responsible for damages and losses caused by the action of same goods or products"; the second regards consumers' education rights (art. 71, 3 and art. 4): "… knowledge about the prevention of risks and damages that could be caused, both to people and the *medio ambiente*, by the consumption of products or the use of goods or services… education to sustainable consumption issues aimed at promoting changes in those production patterns that are harmful to the *medio ambiente*".

[15] For an overview, see Henrnández et al. (2020, pp. 1–5).

ideas.[16] This dynamism fits not into the development of that current of thought based on 'private law constitutionalization' but rather into the general acceptance of the protective principles rooted in the so-called 'source dialog' (art. 28).[17]

The need for limiting the uncontrolled development model has clearly emerged in legal thought. This limit is, first and foremost, reflected in the sustainability of economic choices, in the sustainability of production, and in the sustainability of consumption. Comparative scholars are being confronted with ideas that arise from the impact of constitutional law on civil law and that were largely mediated through consumer law, as well as international law debates. The use of 'sustainability' as a legal concept that has strongly entered the lexicon of civil law system is extremely meaningful in this regard.[18]

Sustainable consumption concerns the environmental impact of the patterns of consumption. It has come into force in the international debate and, consequently, in the soft law instruments of international environmental law, especially since 1992, when the relationship between consumption and the environment was consolidated through the very idea of sustainable consumption.[19]

Sustainable consumption as part of sustainable development is practically a prerequisite in the worldwide struggle against climate change and environmental pollution.[20] In current political and scientific debates on the strengthening of sustainable consumption, not only are the possibilities of fostering a green lifestyle for developed countries drawing attention but also those for the low- and middle-income classes of emerging countries.[21]

Approximately 800 million consumers of the BRICS countries (Brazil, Russia, India, China and South Africa) are expected to attain a level of consumption equivalent to that of more developed countries during the next 10 years.[22] It is believed that the environmental impacts of consumption are becoming all the more important, as 850 million long-established consumers in rich countries have recently been

---

[16] On environmental governance in Latin America: de Castro et al. (2016). Activism in the field of environmental law is sustained by movements vindicating indigenous people's rights as well; see Baldin (2017, p. 8) with reference to so-called 'Earth Jurisprudence'.

[17] This refers to the mandate to the courts to integrate the applicable rule of law with the different legal sources, ranging from the national constitution to the international treaties to which Argentina is a party, to consumer protection legislation, etc. Within this framework legal scholarship and jurisprudence are considered as secondary sources of law.

[18] Cf. Groppi (2016, p. 47 ff.), who examines the use of the adjective 'sustainable' in 54 constitutions.

[19] The definition of sustainable development may indeed help to determine the meaning of sustainable consumption within the framework of consumer law (cf. Besalú Parkinson, in Mackinson and Farinati 2001, p. 249). See Southerton and Ulph (2014) whose work highlights many pertinent multidisciplinary perspectives (psychological, historical, social, legal, etc.) on this issue.

[20] In the framework of the 2030 United Nations Agenda for Sustainable Development (2015), goal 12 for ensuring sustainable consumption and production patterns is directly relevant.

[21] Cf. Schaeffer et al. (2005, pp. 284–297). With reference the BRICS Countries, see Lange and Lars (2009) and Ali et al. (2018, pp. 2–14).

[22] Lorek and Vergragt, in Reisch and Thøgersen (2015, p. 19) underline the unsustainability of present consumption patterns in developed countries and their influence on the production of inequity.

joined by almost 1.1 billion new consumers in 17 developing and three transitioning countries.[23]

The adoption by an increasing number of people of the resource-intensive consumption styles of industrialized countries creates evident environmental difficulties,[24] just as the imitation of the same socioeconomic model represents a source of problems for the environment and for nature. This emerging awareness on the part of these developing and transitioning countries is leading to the adoption of European environmental policy, which is based on the principles of 'precaution', 'prevention', 'sustainability', 'rectifying pollution at source' and 'polluter pays'.[25]

The governments' strategy of addressing emergent consumer classes given the aforementioned issues is due to the expectation that emergent consumer classes could directly adopt a pattern of ecological consumption based on a kind of 'leapfrogging' over negative environmental behaviors and resource-intensive lifestyles of industrialized countries.[26] Evidence of a reduction in pollution and changes in social attitudes are supported by substantive economic theory, which leads to a reconsideration of the traditional view of the law-economy-society relationship.

The aim of market regulations that seek to better protect nature and the world's natural resources is characterized by a heated debate, the two 'opposing' ideological viewpoints of which are voiced by Latouche and Daly.[27] Confronted with a common interest in economic development, the impact of population growth on employment, resources, and environmental protection, the aforementioned scholars diverge on the role of growth. In the face of a steady-state economy (Daly), is opposed to the degrowth idea (Latouche).[28]

Latouche stresses the necessity of downscaling the economy (*décroissance*), stating that it is not an ideal but a necessity. Scholars must not confuse downscaling with negative growth, which is an oxymoron (i.e., a backward progression). We are faced with a line of thought that may be understood in the context of a nongrowth society. For one such example, we can look at consumer expectations for a product's life. One might ask: How many disposable products have any real reason to be disposable, other than just to feed the mass production machine?

In regards to what would seem to be an irreconcilable dispute, I think it is possible to recognize a common theme, which finds its theoretical foundation in the clear

---

[23] Myers and Kent (2003, pp. 4963–4968).

[24] The well-known examples of owning a private car, high household energy use, eating large amounts of meat, buying disposable products...etc., have been taken as general wealth standards for many decades in all industrialized countries.

[25] For a recent overview that takes theoretical foundations and governance solutions into account, see Orsini and Kavvata (2020).

[26] The expression is used by Schaeffer et al. (2005, pp. 284–297).

[27] See Latouche (1993, 2010) and Daly (1977).

[28] For a detailed analysis, see Latouche (2003). The French sociologist refers to how: "Hernan Daly has devised a measure, the genuine progress indicator, that adjusts a country's gross domestic product according to the losses from pollution and environmental degradation...growth under these conditions is a myth, even in well-to-do economies and advanced consumer societies...increase is more than compensated for by decrease".

conceptual distinction between 'development' and 'growth': the first is intended as a qualitative improvement of nonphysical characteristics, whereas the latter is a quantitative increase of physical dimension.[29] To illustrate this distinction, an effective starting point might be the Six Rs programme proposed by the Treaty on Consumption and Lifestyle drawn up by the NGO forum at the 1992 United Nations Earth summit in Rio de Janeiro, that is, re-evaluation, restructuring, redistribution, reduction, reuse, and recycling.

Given all of the above considerations, one concept becomes clear: the obligation to rethink the meaning of development and the consumer machine that characterizes the contemporary economy cannot be detached from private law. Private law is an important ally for defending our future, as we face the dark side of economic development as well as tremendous ecological challenges.[30]

In addition to what can only be characterized as a heated scientific debate, there is also a political resonance along the lines of a David versus Goliath battle in which the new civil codes are entrenched. Indeed, driven by global dynamics to protect ecological interests, the new civil codes rethink the nature of private autonomy for all those choices that affect the common good; they seek a balancing of interests between the need to protect the environment, on the one hand, and the imperatives of economic development and social progress, on the other.

In the search for what is a delicate balance, the structure of the new civil codes echo an ever-growing principle of legislation: The civil codes are a comprehensive statement of both specific rules and broad general principles not only in the fields of property law and contract law, not only in terms of the circulation of wealth but also in the matter of ethical values that relate to the environment and its preservation for future generations.

3 Where Civil Codes Intersect with the Constitution: From *Consumo Sustentable* to *Lüse Yuanze*

Environmental issues entail a renewed reading of civil codes, one that takes into account sustainable consumption as a new way of consuming, as opposed to consumerism and the uncontrolled exploitation of nature. Accountability for sustainable consumption is apparently shared by all the members and organizations of society: governments, businesses, unions, and environmental and consumer institutions all play important roles. However, this indicates the emergence of, above all, a new consumer and, more broadly, of a new citizen: one who is responsible and

---

[29] Cf. Daly (1977, pp. 17, 77, 270, 280).

[30] For a critical analysis of humanist knowledge historically linked to Western private law, see Mattei and Quarta (2018).

conscious of their actions as well as the possibility of influencing social, economic, and environmental habits.[31]

What are the objectives of the new civil codes of Argentina and China on the aforementioned environmental issues? Comparing the two civil codes, what differences and similarities can we see? In the framework of a 'greening civil law', do they symbolize a unique model code or, instead, two different model codes?

From a diachronic perspective, the Argentine legal experience deserves attention first and foremost. The new 2014 Argentinian Civil and Commercial Code marks a turning point in sustainable consumption. Given the widespread heightening of environmental awareness, a new rule on sustainable consumption entered into force: "the norms that govern consumer relations must be applied and interpreted according the principle of consumer protection and that of access to sustainable consumption" (art. 1094).[32] It stems from an interpretative criterion, dating back to scholars' contribution to the legal pursuit of knowledge and, more specifically, to a general rule of consumer contracts that was set in a prominent position among the sources of law.[33]

Beyond the significance of the presence of a specific provision on sustainable consumption in a civil code, there are two issues of great interest here: first, there is the possibility of qualifying a contractual clause that directly or indirectly harms an environmental legal right as abusive, as foreseen years ago by the Brazilian legislation[34]; second, there is the possibility of evaluating the negative-side effects of consumption by establishing consumers' duties and responsibilities for unsustainable consumption.

Faced with a global scarcity of natural resources, the well-known adage of 'doing more with less' has become the main challenge for producers and consumers worldwide. In EEUU, to address this challenge, a whole range of policies and initiatives aimed at sustainable consumption and production were introduced to improve the overall environmental performance of products throughout their life cycle, stimulate the demand for better products and production technologies, and help consumers make informed choices.[35]

---

[31] A critical consumer is a person who asks about the social and ecological conditions in which a good or a service has been developed and about the feedback that concerns that same good or service.

[32]) On the relationship between art. 1094 c.c. and Argentinean consumer law, see Stiglitz (2014, pp. 137–141) and Cafferatta (2014).

[33] The Argentinian Civil Code introduces meaningful change in the classification of contracts: the Drafting Commission (2012) split the unitary category of a contract into three contractual categories: (a) 'discretionary contracts' (arts. 957–983 and 988–1091); (b) 'general clauses and conditions contracts' (arts. 984–987); and (c) 'consumer contracts' (arts. 1092–1122). The specific reference to sustainability in the third category strengthens consumer rights in terms of environmental protection.

[34] For the purposes of comparison, the aforementioned transition finds multiple sources of support in other Latin American countries. Consider, e.g., the Brazilian Consumer Code, which deals with environmental issues in a multitude of ways, above all, in the contractual context. The code, for example, forbids unfair and deceptive advertising (art. 37, §2 and art. 51, XIV), including those practices that violate environmental values. See Costa de Azevedo (2002) and dos Santos (2015).

[35] Problems related to sustainable consumption and consumer behavior are the main topics of the reviewed 2012 Action Plan for Sustainable Industrial Policy (first published in 2008). See the

However, European national consumer laws appear to still lack an overarching structure to counteract unsustainable consumption. The answers provided in terms of products' legal guarantees—which differ depending on their origin in EEUU Countries—are not enough. The need to shift the focus of law from an anthropocentric perspective to an eco-centric or earth-centered one is paramount in regard to sustainable consumption. At least, this is the perspective of the new Latin American constitutionalism, to which scholars have not yet paid due attention in regard to consumer sustainability.

In the framework of the aforementioned outlook, the new Argentinian Civil Code marks a step forward in the protection of rights and interests that may undermine the expectations of future generations because it not only introduces—beyond the rule of consumer sustainability—the concepts of environment, sustainability, flora, fauna, water, biodiversity, and landscape but also because it includes in the collective environmental damages those linked to imprudent action, thus underlining the responsibility for dangerous or risky activities for the environment in the operative range of the civil code.[36] Of crucial importance is the connection offered in this regard by art. 14 in the matter of individual and collective rights, as it contains a specific mention of the environment as a limit to the exercise of individual rights.[37]

The Argentinian Civil Code marks a fundamental step in the greening of civil law in that it complies with the constitutional provisions on sustainability as a value to be protected in the community interest.[38] Of course, to understand the rule on sustainable consumption, it must be jointly read and coordinated with the general structure of the civil code and, in particular, with the principle of good faith and, above all, with that of the abuse of rights. The rule of '*neminem laedit qui suo iure utitur*' attributed to Ulpian (Digest of Justinian: 50,17,55) embodies the principle of the abuse of right regulated by art. 14.

What reads as a true reflection of the ecological principles of the greening of civil codes within the Argentine experience is implemented very differently in the recent CCC. In the preparatory work for the CCC, the dialog between the private law and constitutional law makers appears less active, and therefore, the green principle has been developed as an endogenous choice: The influence of the constitution on the CCC is more evident on constitutional legal thought than on the text of the constitution itself.[39]

Technical Report 061/2012 (Policies to encourage sustainable consumption) which identifies the main policy instruments currently in use and sets out new approaches and recommendations for change (available at: http://ec.europa.eu/environment/archives/eussd/pdf/report_22082012.pdf).

[36] Cf. Cafferatta (2014, p. 273).

[37] With reference to the "ecosystem's sustainability" see art. 240.

[38] From a regulatory point of view, the aforementioned approach is supported by a group of rules: arts. 14, 235, 1094, 2078.

[39] Some scholars questioned whether the CCC should be established on the basis of the current constitution, according to China's political ideology and its legal experience. Professor Long Weiqiu (Beijing Aviation University) argued that, according to its legal history, Chinese civil law was developed before the evolution of the constitution because "despite its higher status, the Constitution, in addition to political rights stipulations, should also respect the demands of civil law. This is

As a result of the economic boom, a growing perception of ecological issues and, plausibly, a reasonable awareness of being one of the leading countries in the world in regard to environmental pollution,[40] China has slowly moved toward the 'greening' of civil law. In the years preceding the entering into force of the new CCC, China had already made reference to the environment in the General Principles of Civil Law (1986), which regulated civil liability of those who pollute the environment and cause damage to others by violating environmental protections and rules regarding pollution prevention (art. 124) and, in even more detail, the Tort Liability Law (2009), which dedicated an entire chapter, chapter VIII, to 'Environmental Pollution Liability' (arts. 65–68), in which, among other provisions, the polluter-pays principle, tort liability without regard to fault, and the reversed burden of proof were introduced. These provisions highlight a useful legal and political precedent for concretely expressing environmental interests.

Comparative scholars readily note the foundation of European civil code models in these rules. However, China's reaction to environmental problems and their regulation through the civil code has not been passive but rather it has given rise to a deliberate policy, as both legal and academic communities have fully realized. An obligation to protect the environment was actually incorporated into Chinese civil law by art. 9 of the General Part of the Civil Code of the PRC: "when engaged in civil activities, all persons shall be aware of the need to save resources and protect the environment".

Strengthening the legal path launched by the General Principles of the Civil Law, the CCC shows a sensitivity toward green issues, as is shown above all, through its coordination with those that appear as real 'fundamental norms' (*zongze*). In other words, the comparison between the CCC and the Argentinian Civil Code is to be contextualized within the principles and framework of values of the civil law system in which they commonly enter into dialog, thus setting the stage for a discussion of individual rights/duties (Chinese code) along with collective rights/duties (Argentinian code) for environmental preservation.

The new CCC appears to be in line with the trend started by the Argentinian Civil Code; that is, a 'model code' emerges whereby the protection of the environment is closely linked to the principles of equality (*pingdeng yuanze*, arts. 2 and 4), free will (*ziyuan yuanze*, art. 5), fairness (*gongping*, art. 6), good faith (*chengxin yuanze*, art. 7), respect of the law, public order and good morals (*bu weifan falü, bu weibei gong*

---

evident from the development of Civil Codes in France, Germany and Switzerland, the leading civil law jurisdictions where the Constitution is not necessarily relied upon because political and civil rights should be treated relatively separately"; cf. Zhang (2016, p. 117). This remains a debated topic in Chinese legal scholarship (cf. Han in Wang 2014, p. 207). In any case, over time Chinese constitutions strengthened their approach to environmental issues (cf. Toti 2017, p. XII). The fourth and last Constitution of 1982, thus provides in art. 26, 1: "The state protects and improves the living environment and the ecological environment, and prevents and remedies pollution and other public hazards").

[40] There is plenty of literature on China's ecological civilization as well as on the new civil code; see Han (2014, pp. 201–212) and Zhang (2016, pp. 106–137). Concerning the range of world pollution, see https://waqi.info/#/c/34.777/103.24/5.1z.

xu liang su, art. 8), prohibition of abuse of the right (*bu dei lanyong minshi quanli*, art. 132) and, most of all, the so-called 'green principle' (*lüse yuanze*, art. 9) that receives specific attention in the CCC.

In light of art. 9, in which legal entities conduct legal transactions, they 'should' contribute to resource conservation and ecological environment protection.[41] This is not a rule confined to the general part because art. 9 limits the contractual freedom guaranteed in § 5 of the General Part of the Civil Code, in that the creation, modification and termination of civil relations depends not only on their free will but also on ecological standards.[42] This approach is clearer from the coordination of arts. 5 and 9 with art. 509, whereby it is established that "… the parties shall avoid wasting resources, polluting the environment, and destroying the ecology".[43]

Thanks to the '*consumo sustentable*' and the '*lüse yuanze*', a new mode of strategic planning regarding the problems associated with the hyper exploitation of natural resources and the violation of intergenerational obligations has been launched following the path set forth by the greening of the civil codes.

4 Nature's Rights: A New Paradigm for Humans' Private Ecological Approaches

Humans are damaging the environment faster than it can recover. What can be done in the face of such a seemingly unstoppable process? This question has been prompted by the reconceptualization of nature purely as a subject of law, which is sustained through legal research related to Latin American constitutionalism, not coincidentally defined as '*constitucionalismo de la biodiversidas*' or '*costitucionalismo de la naturaleza*'.[44]

New Latin American constitutions have sped up legal scholars' adaptation of a renewed, critical environmental way of thinking. The acceptance of nature being viewed in terms of individual and collective rights promotes a different perspective than that related to the precautionary principle, or even than that connected to

---

[41] The new CCC does not spell out the remedies for the violation of the green principle, hence its statement as a hypothetical duty; it is yet to be seen what interpretations the Courts shall develop, and how they shall establish what the 'conservation of resources' means and what it implies.

[42] These standards are taken into account in several cases, see, e.g., art. 619 on sustainable packaging: "… where there is no agreement on package manner in the contract or the agreement is not clear, nor can it be determined according to the provisions of Article 510 of this Code, the subject matter shall be packed […] favorable to conserving resources and protecting the ecology and environment […]". On freedom of contract according to environmental standards, see Lieder and Porzik (1/2019, pp. 58–66).

[43] Article 9 plays a gap filling-role in the absence of specific civil rules in the subsequent sections of the civil code, and, for this reason, scholars consider that it marks a great progress made by the Chinese legal system in this respect. See Zhai and Chang (2019, pp. 5 and 6).

[44] Biodiversity constitutionalism and 'ecological constitutionalism' mark a very interesting trend which gives 'nature' a legal frame of reference; cf. Baldin in Baldin and Zago (2014, p. 160 f.).

environmental protection as a fundamental right. Nor should it be confused with the promotion of 'sustainable consumption' or, more broadly, of 'environmental sustainability', although a more careful evaluation of raw materials, products, packaging, and consumption choices themselves inevitably have a positive impact on the protection of nature.[45]

The recognition of the rights of nature requires a multilevel and transdisciplinary re-evaluation of nature as a subject of law. An approach that goes beyond just the environmental dimension is gaining ground in civil law that conceives of nature as having a balanced order.

It should be noted that, in the face of an irresponsible approach that could lead not only to ecologic equilibrium but also to an imminent crisis of civilization, many relevant studies and scientific approaches show that the market is not only an enemy of the environment but can, indeed, provide valid support in protecting the environment. In response to the well-known position of Serge Latouche on the possible implications of a 'happy degrowth', it is possible to use the framework provided by Henan Daly and Vandana Shiva, who advocate for the construction of a condition of 'steady-state economy' to eliminate the inequalities produced by neoliberal capitalism.[46]

Following these same principles, the Andean constitutions (Ecuador and Bolivia) provide interesting proposals (the new constitutionalism for biodiversity) that deserve to be explored more deeply and taken into great consideration. These constitutions, including novel developmental paradigms of indigenous inspiration, propose the unity of humanity and nature through the founding principle of "good life/living well" known as *buen vivir/vivir bien* (in Spanish), *sumak kawsay* (in Kichwa) or *suma queña* (in Aymara).[47]

According to the so-called principle of nature, nature itself cannot be understood as a subject, as an "anthropic principle", and a sustainable environment cannot be understood to be at the service of the needs of human beings, or for their enjoyment and exploitation. The awareness of nature itself as a principle of necessary, balanced order—as an intergenerational obligation —is what has come to the surface.

---

[45] Therefore, they are supported by 'green public procurement' policies (174 of the EC Treaty). These have an impact not only on public entities but also on private rights and obligations and, especially, on consumers (for a general framework, see *Buying green!*, *A handbook on green public procurement* of the European Commission, p. 5, available at: http://ec.europa.eu/environment/gpp/pdf/handbook.pdf).

[46] My opinion is in line with the holistic thinking articulated by Shiva (2006) and Latouche (2010). Further key contributions are those of Motesharrei et al. (2014, p. 90 ss.), Carducci (2016, p. 154), Ferlito (2016, p. 201 f.), and Boyd (2017).

[47] From a regulatory standpoint the new Ecuadorian constitution (2008), arts. 72 and 73 are significant. They recognize the right to the restoration of nature as well as the environmental right to precaution and restriction against the alteration of the natural cycles and the destruction of ecosystems. This constitution represents a watershed in the history of Ecuador: it articulates new relationships with the general public, seen as an actor of social construction and with the protection accorded to health itself. Indigenous and other progressive organizations advanced innovative ideas that the new Constitution introduced as pioneering paradigms; they challenge some conventional Western understanding of concepts, such as development and health.

The understanding of nature as a '*Grundnorm*' strengthened its doctrinal authority. Colombian rulings have come to recognize the character of the 'subject of right' to the Atrato rivers (Judgment T-622 of the Constitutional Court of 10/11/2016), to Amazonia (Judgment STC4360 of the Supreme Court of Justice of 5/04/2018), and to the wasteland of Pisba (Judgment of the Administrative Court of the Department of Boyacá of 9/08/2018), thus guaranteeing the protection and conservation of the environment through a series of pronouncements.

The Andean movement proposes a different perspective from that of green consumption or sustainable consumption. It points to the presence of the two sides of the coin, so to speak. If it is true that the existing limits to the earth's resources and to its capacity to replenish itself indicate that green consumption is a fundamental concept underlying the idea of equity for both current and future generations, it is equally true that there is an apparent contradiction in the expression 'green consumption', since 'green' is a concept directly related to the conservation of environmental resources, while 'consumption' involves using, expending or depleting a resource.[48]

The answer can only be that of putting a limit on consumption and its model of life. Sergio Ferlito, in one of his recent works, has pointed out the problem unequivocally: It is like saying, stop the consumer machine and listen to the voice of Nature.[49] It might appear poetic; nevertheless, the same idea appears in the Latin American system, in which the protection and preservation of nature is suggested as a meaningful limit for the concept of well-being based on consumption, or at least for 'unsustainable' consumption. It could be said that it was not by chance that the aforementioned perspective inspired a peculiar Parlatino Model Law on the Rights of Mother Earth[50] in 2013. This model law, even before the various national laws proposed on the subject (case in point, l. 300/2012 Bolivia), provide the most interesting examples regarding the issues of Latin American environmental law.

From this perspective, that is to say one in which Nature is viewed as balanced order, which has been outlined until now by the new constitutional assets, the ecological choices proposed by the civil code's of China (arts. 9, 509, 619) and Argentina (arts. 14, 240),[51] where *inter alia*, a different form of ownership from a comparative standpoint is also taken into account[52] seems to have been fully integrated. These rules are innovative in terms of civil law codification. This is the first time that the contract rules of civil codes have mandated resource conservation and environmental protection tied to the performance of contracts. In addition, choices such as those

---

[48] Cf. Wagner Mainardes, et al. (2017, p. 661).

[49] See Ferlito (2016, p. 274 f.).

[50] In my view, it is one of the most interesting aspects of the Latin American System, as explained in Lanni (2017, p. 149).

[51] Art. 18 of the Argentinian Civil Code introduces the land rights of indigenous communities, referring to the "management of their natural resources as rights of collective perspective".

[52] It is well known that property law is rich in meaning and that also includes regimes governing communities living outside the official rules and States' law. For an in-depth overview of property law in comparative perspective, see Graziadei and Smith (2017).

of the Chinese and Argentinian Civil Codes provide, thanks to the innovation in the codification technique, for the holistic perspective from which they are derived.[53]

Nevertheless, the greening of civil codes may be ineffective if not coordinated with a constitutional and democratic perspective.[54] Michele Carducci has emphasized, for the purposes of comparison, that the concept of nature as 'non negotiable benefit' cannot be separated from democracy, since only democratic forms of State government and democratic decision-making by State authorities can jointly and effectively face the problem of survival of the geo-human system.[55]

The need for a renewed balance between 'individual interest' and 'collective interest' shifts from constitutions to new civil codes and then returns under a different form in the new constitutions. This perspective seems fully identifiable in the Argentine experience, where the joint evaluation of Articles 14, 18 and 240 of the Argentinian Civil Code constitutes the legal basis for the recognition of nature's rights category, such as 'collective rights' in the Civil Code.[56]

Moreover, there may be a correspondence between the idea of the public interest (such as that in art. 534 of the Chinese Civil Code[57]), which is placed in support of environmental ideas belonging to ecological legal thinking, such as the conception of the environment as a sphere of living beings and as a reference point for environmental subjectivity, both of which borrow from Chinese doctrine.[58] These subjects might be further explored in regard to arts. 9 and 1232 ss., that find, from an empirical point of view, a reference in the movements of 'ecosophy' and the 'Caring State'.[59]

The perspectives of 'nature's rights' and 'caring state' do not appear in the lexicon of the new CCC, although the legal issue is well identified in the discussions that

---

[53] With regards to holism, I want stress its ability to reverse the narrow approach which defines the law solely in terms of rules. The holistic approach of the civil code highlights a 'modern' function of the same; thus Chinese scholars underline how: "foreign law and indigenous law are originated from different sources [...] the proportion of each and their adoption and reformation must comply with the codifying principle and holistic function of the civil code" (see Sheng 2013, p. 128, note 2).

[54] In spite of that, in Europe more than in Latin America, scholars focus on green-consumption, probably following several European acts on 'green' and social policy; for an interesting discussion: Peattie (2010).

[55] Latin American and Chinese forms of government are obviously different, thus we must contextualize Carducci's analysis in reference to the Latin American system.

[56] This category has developed through the Courts: i.e., 'Halabi, Ernesto c. Poder Ejecutivo Nacional – l. 25.873 – dec. 1563/2004s/amparo ley 16.986', Supreme Court of Justice of the Nation 24/02/2009 (sentence, 332:221). The indigenous experience is also meaningful; it should not be forgotten that the Argentinian Civil Code is the first to recognize indigenous property.

[57] "Where a party uses a contract to endanger the national interest and public interest, market regulation and other relevant authorities shall be responsible for supervision and punishment in accordance with the laws and administrative regulations".

[58] A note is found in Toti (2017, p. XIX).

[59] On the idea of the Caring State, see Bagni in Bagni (2013, p. 19 ff.), who stressed how *buen vivir* is a crucial tool for identifying a new form of State, the so-called *Caring State*, in which the needs of humans are holistically considered, including those emotional and cultural aspects deriving from ancestral traditions. To learn about ecosophy, which views ecology through the lens of social sciences, see the fascinating work by Ferlito (2020).

preceded the final version of the Code.[60] Indeed, Draft 1 of the General Provisions of Civil Law fixed through § 7—corresponding to art. 9 of the final version of the same General Provisions of Civil Law—lends more relevant support, having established that the parties in civil legal relations "shall protect the environment and conserve resources, promoting the harmonious development of man and nature".[61]

From the vantage point of environmental law alone, the perspective of Draft 1 was different overall. First, emphasis was placed on the 'duty to protect the environment' rather than on the 'duty [to] contribut[e] to the protection of the environment', which is obviously a milder and less coercive prospect. Last, but not least, the parties were expected to have due consideration, so much so that they not only had to preserve but also promote the harmonious balance between human and nature.

Even in the absence of these clarifications, the CCC has implemented a significant development of civil law on environmental issues. This step forward, from a regulatory point of view, serves as a model for all new projects of codification and/or recodification of civil law, projects that must be effectively involved in governing the relationship between humans and nature through a legal yardstick that is capable of reversing the deafening silence of a world audience for the so-called 'big mouth-small ears route'.[62]

References

Ali S, Hussain T, Zhang G, Nurrunabi M, Li B (2018) The implementation of sustainable development goals in 'BRICS' countries. Sustainability, open access

Bagni S (2013) Dal welfare state to the caring state? In: Bagni S (ed) Dallo Stato del bienestar allo Stato del buen vivir. Filodiritto, Bologna, pp 19–59

Baldin S (2014) I diritti della Natura: i risvolti giuridici dell'ética ambiental exigente in America Latina. In: Baldin S, Zago M (eds) Le sfide della sostenibilità. Il buen vivir andino dalla prospettiva europea. Filodiritto, Bologna, pp 155–184

Baldin S (2017) Los derechos de la naturaleza: de las construcciones doctrinales al reconocimiento jurídico. Revista general de derecho público comparado: 2–28

Besalú Parkinson A (2001) Salud, Alimentos y Desarrollo. In: Mackinson G, Farinati A (eds) Salud, Derecho y Equidad. Ad-Hoc, Buenos Aires, pp 249–260

---

[60] An intense translation activity of the laws and civil codes of other legal systems into the Chinese language has forged a 'civilian' background for environmental issues. Beyond the European codes, several Latin-American codes were translated into Chinese; e.g., the Chilean Civil Code of 1855 (Beijing, 2002, ed. Xu Diyu); the first Argentine Civil Code (Beijing, 2007, ed. Xu Diyu); the 2002 Brazilian Civil Code (Beijing, 2009, ed. Qi Yun), and the 1984 Peruvian civil code (Bilu Beijing, 2017, ed. Xu Diyu). These translations helped shape the CCC model, see Zhang (2004, pp. 211–246; Id. 2009, pp. 999–1040), Lin in Oropesa García (2008, pp. 1–50), Zhang (2016, pp. 106–137), Schipani in Frustagli (2019, pp. 79–104), and Timoteo (2019, pp. 23–44).

[61] Th 'Green principle' underwent several changes before being established as basic principle in the General Provisions of Civil Law, for an in-depth analysis, see Zhai and Chang (2019, pp. 5 and 6).

[62] This is one the characteristic features of the Western legal tradition as understood by a non-Eurocentric approach: "It is said in Africa that western culture has 'a big mouth and small ears'"; see Glenn (2010, p. 90).

Boyd DR (2017) The rights of nature: a legal revolution that could save the world. ECW Press, Toronto

Cafferatta N (2014) El Derecho ambiental en el CC y Comercial sancionado. La Ley Suplemento Especial Nuevo CC y Comercial, La Ley, Buenos Aires

Carducci M (2016) Nature as "Grundnorm" of global constitutionalism: contributions from the global south. Revista Brasileira de Direito 12:154–165

Costa de Azevedo F (2002) O direito do consumidor e a questão ambiental. Livraria do Advogado, Porto Alegre

Daly H (1977) Steady-state economics: the economics of biophysical equilibrium and moral growth. W H Freeman & Co, San Francisco

De Castro F, Hogenboom B, Baud M (eds) (2016) Environmental governance in Latin America. Palgrave, New York

Do Amaral Junior A, De Ameida L, Kein Vieira L (eds) (2019) Sustainable consumption: the right to a healthy environment. Springer, Switzerland

Dos Santos LD (2015) Relação de consumo sustentável. A geração de resíduos sólidos sob a ótica daproteção jurídica do consumidor. Letra Jurídicas, São Paulo

Duscã IA (2013) The civil code and the environment. Agora. Int J Juridical Sci: 24–30

Ferlito S (2016) Il volto beffardo del diritto. Ragione economica e giustizia. Mimesis, Milano

Ferlito S (2020) L'ecologia come paradigma delle scienze sociali. Rivista catanese di filosofia: 37–59

Foy Valencia PC (2/2018) Aproximación ambiental al CC. Revista Kawsaypacha: 69–86

Glenn P (2010) Legal traditions of the world: sustainable diversity in law, 4th edn. Oxford University Press, Oxford

Graziadei M (1993) Changing images of the law in XIX century English legal thought (the continental impulse). In: Reimann M (ed) The reception of continental ideas in the common law world 1820–1920. Duncker & Humblot, Berlin

Graziadei M, Smith L (2017) Comparative property law: global perspective. Edward Elgar, Cheltenham

Groppi T (2016) Sostenibilità e costituzioni: lo Stato costituzionale alla prova del futuro. Diritto pubblico comparato ed europeo: 43–78

Han SY (2014) Civil law codification in China: its characteristics, social functions and future. In: Wang W (ed) Codification in East Asia. Selected Papers from the 2 IACL Thematic Conference. Springer International Publishing, Cham

Henrnández CA, Japaze MB, Ossola FA, Sozzo G, Stiglitz GA (2020) Antecedentes y estado actual del Proyecto de Código de Defensa del Consumidor. La Ley, p 39

Hironaka A (2014) Greening the globe. Cambridge University Press, New York

Lange H, Lars M (eds) (2009) The new middle classes: globalizing lifestyles, consumerism. Springer, Heidelberg

Lanni S (2017) Il diritto nell'America Latina. Edizioni Scientifiche Italiane, Napoli

Latouche S (2003) Would the west actually be happier with less? World downscaled. Le Monde diplomatique

Latouche S (1993) In the wake of the affluent society: an exploration of post-development. Zed Books, London

Latouche S (2010) Farewell to Growth (Eng. translation by Macey D). Polity Press, Cambridge

Lei C (2009) The historical development of the civil law tradition in China: a private law perspective. In: Centre for Chinese & Comparative Law Research Paper Series. https://ssrn.com/abstract=1479442

Lieder J, Porzik P (2019) Der Schutz der Umwelt als Grenze der Vertragsfreiheit. Ger J Chin Law 26:58–66

Lin L (2008) Historia del derecho chino y su Sistema jurídico contemporneo. In: Oropesa García A (ed) México-China. Culturas y Sistemas jurídicos comparados. UNAM, México

Lorek S, Vergragt PJ (2015) Sustainable consumption as a systemic challenge: inter-and transdisciplinary research and research questions. In: Reisch LA, Thøgersen J (eds) Handbook of research on sustainable consumption. Edward Elgar, Cheltenham

Lv ZM (2/2002) The enactment of a "green" civil code: a prospect of environmental and resource law in the 21th century. J Zhengzhou Univ: 10–11

Mattei U, Quarta A (2018) The turning point in private law: ecology, technology and the commons. Edward Elgar Publishing, Cheltenham

Motesharrei S, Rivas J, Kalnay E (2014) Human and nature dynamics (HANDY): modelling inequality and use of resources in the collapseor sustainability of societies. Ecol Econ 101:90–102

Myers N, Kent J (2003) New consumers: the influence of affluence on the environment. Proc Natl Acad Sci USA 100:4963–4968

Orsini A, Kavvata E (2020) EU environmental governance: current challenges. Routledge, London

Peattie K (2010) Green consumption: behavior and norms. Annu Rev Environ Resour 13:195–228

Pozzo B (2017) La responsabilità ambientale e l'apporto delle scienze sociali. In: Graziadei M, Serio M (eds) Regolare la complessità. Giornate di studio in onore di Antonio Gambaro. Giappichelli, Torino, pp 76–92

Sands P (ed) (1993) Greening international law. Earthscan, Abingdon

Schaeffer R, Szklo AS, Cima FM, Machado G (2005) Indicators for sustainable energy development: Brazil's case study. Nat Resour Forum. U N Sustain Dev J 29:284–297

Schipani S (2019) El nuevo CC chino desde el Sistema jurídico latinoamericano. In: Frustagli SA (ed) Derecho privado del siglo XXI. Librería del Jurista, Buenos Aires, pp 79–104

Sheng Z (2013) From an integration of Western and Chinese legal norms to comparative legislation: Codification of the civil law of the Republic of China. China Leg Sci 1:128–138

Shiva V (2006) Earth democracy: justice, sustainability and peace, South and Pr, London

Southerton D, Ulph A (eds) (2014) Sustainable consumption: perspectives in honour of Professor Sir Partha Dasgupta. University Oxford Press, Oxford

Spijkers O (2020) Urgenda and Dutch Dikastophobia: is this the end of public interest litigation for the environment. Available at https://gnhre.org/2020/02/17/urgenda-and-dutch-dikastophobia-is-this-the-end-of-public-interest-litigation-for-the-environment-and-the-end-of-article-3305a-dutch-civil-code/

Stiglitz G (2014) La defensa del consumidor en el CC y Comercial de la Nación, Suplemento Especial CC y Comercial de la Nación, Thomson Reuters - La Ley, Buenos Aires

Timoteo M (2019) China codifies. The first book of the civil code between western models to Chinese characteristics. Opinio Juris Comp 1:23–44

Toti E (2017) Il diritto all'ambiente della Repubblica popolare cinese. In: Leggi tradotte della Repubblica popolare cinese, VIII. Giappichelli, Torino

Wagner Mainardes E, Yeh T, Leal A (2017) Consumers' evaluations of the efficiency of actions to improve environmental quality: a comparative study between Brazil and China. Int J Consum Study 41:659–670

Zhai T, Chang Y-C (2019) The contribution of China's civil law to sustainable development: progress and prospects. Sustainability, open access

Zhang L (2004) The codification of civil law in China: history, current situation and prospective. Verba Juris (Brasil) 3:211–246

Zhang L (2009) The latest developments in the codification of Chinese civil law. Tulane Law Rev 83:1000–1040

Zhang XC (2016) The new round of civil law codification in China. Univ Bologna Law Rev 1:137–196

Sabrina Lanni is Jean Monnet Chair Holder—ENFASIS (European Novel Foods Agreement and Intercultural Sustainable Systems), 2020–2023; Associate Professor of Comparative Private Law at Milan University (Department of International, Legal, Historical and Political Studies), 2018–present; Recipient of the National Scientific Qualification (ASN) of Full Professor in Comparative Law, 2017; Associate Professor of Comparative Private Law at 'Magna Graecia' University of Catanzaro, 2015–2018; and Researcher of Latin-American Private Law at Italian National Research Council—University of Rome 'Tor Vergata', 2001–2015.

Codification and the Interpreter

Rodolfo Sacco

Abstract Civil codes have changed their nature and function since they were first put into force. The unifying ideas prevailing in the nineteenth century codifications are bygone. Legislation is often negotiated by a multitude of actors who pursue conflicting aims. Nonetheless, codification is still possible and useful. When a code enters into force, the problem of interpreting it is not yet solved. The text is open to multiple interpretations. The text shall eventually have the meaning attributed to it by its interpreters, who will inevitably rely on their culture to approach it.

1 The Changing Nature of Civil Codifications

I am pleased to be addressing legislators and codifiers.

At other times, I too have codified. In 1972, when Somalia became independent, I was part of a commission set up to prepare a draft civil code; the commission instructed me to draw up a preliminary draft, which I did. However, when I was preparing to present my preliminary draft to the commission, the political authorities dissolved the commission and decided to entrust the codification to jurists of the Islamic faith.

My record shows that I believe in the possibility and usefulness of the code.

This puts me at odds with some of my fellow Italians, in particular with Natalino Irti, author of a much-cited work, which appeared in 1979, entitled "L'età della

Rodolfo Sacco: Deceased.

This text is the English translation of the speech delivered by Prof. Rodolfo Sacco at the conference "The Making of the Civil Codes" (University of Torino, 15 February 2016). We are indebted to P.rof. Martin Solly for this translation [Michele Graziadei and Lihong Zhang].

R. Sacco (✉)
Emeritus of the University of Torino, Torino, Italy
e-mail: segreteria@sirdcomp.it

© The Author(s), under exclusive license to Springer Nature Singapore Pte Ltd. 2023   405
M. Graziadei and L. Zhang (eds.), *The Making of the Civil Codes*,
Ius Gentium: Comparative Perspectives on Law and Justice 104,
https://doi.org/10.1007/978-981-19-4993-7_22

decodificazione" (The age of decodification). He argued, and maintains, that codification—especially the codification of civil law—is no longer practicable and that, in any case, it is not fruitful for a number of reasons. Civil law, according to him, has lost its central position in the legal system of our societies because it has ceded its place to the constitution, to administrative law, to labor law, and so on. Moreover, what remains of civil law is regulated, rather than by the will of a legislator endowed with a higher authority, through negotiations and agreements concluded by bodies, categories, and interested parties (territorial, economic, political, confessional organizations). Let us add that when the law comes into play, it no longer has that characteristic trait of generality and abstractness that once distinguished it: every general rule is faced with ever-increasing quantities of derogations and exceptions. In short, a code has its raison d'être when it is inspired by unifying central ideas; these ideas were—in the nineteenth century—property and contractual freedom; and today these ideas have been corroded in the name of collective, social values, or with the aim of protecting citizens from their own lack of preparation, weaknesses, mistakes.

A few years later, in 1982, when the International Academy of Comparative Law gathered jurists from all over the world to discuss the theme: "Codification, an outdated form of legislating", I was entrusted with the task of preparing the Italian report on the topic.

To do this, I started from a point of fact. In the previous thirty years, forty-seven civil codes had come into force in the world (including the Osnovy of the Soviet Union, the Czechoslovak Opčansky Zákoník, and the Greek and Portuguese Codes), and at the time I mentioned, the Netherlands and Quebec were also codifying. The forty-seven codes even included the very same Somali Code that I myself should have drafted.

In that same period, thoughtful and authoritative scholars augured that the civil law of countries without a code (Scotland, for example) would be codified.

It seems to me that if institutions codify, it is difficult to deny the possibility, usefulness and functionality of the code. Analysis of Irti's argumentation has allowed me to confirm this opinion.

Of course, we can ask ourselves a further question: can any country codify? Can codification take place in any cultural, political, social, or economic situation?

I believe that it is possible to provide an answer to this question based on logic and confirmed by experience.

In the first place, to make a truly new code, one which breaks with the law and with the previous praxis, a great theorist is needed to enlighten a country, or a dedicated school to flourish, capable of setting out the rules of law in an orderly and intelligible way. Think of Domat and Pothier, who paved the way for the French Civil Code. Think of Savigny, Arndt, Dernburg, Jhering, Crome, Windscheid who paved the way for the German Bürgerliches Gesetzbuch. However, in most cases, a civil code is not created on the basis of national thought. A foreign code deemed to be good is taken and then translated. The Code Civil was imitated in Italy, Poland, Egypt and other Arabic-speaking countries and in Castilian or Portuguese-speaking countries. At other times, the code comes into being in a different way: that is, it reproduces the state of the jurisprudence as it is at the time of the drafting of the text.

In conclusion, nations and the legislators that they set to work refer with confidence to the codified law.

Those who draw up a code know that they are flanked by the theory of the sources of the law, of sociology, of recent history.

Those who set out to draft a code may look forward to a highly satisfying task.

2 The Code, the Interpreter, and Its Culture

And now let us talk about the code. The code of which I speak has been published; it has come into force, and its rules condition the judges who will apply it.

Let us look closely at what the judge does.

The judge has the text before them and interprets it. The point I am making holds good, in a more general way, for every interpreter; in particular, for the professor, who interprets the law, and then transmits their thought, their interpretation to the student, that is, to the judge of tomorrow.

During the moment of interpretation, the learned scholar is on their own, in the sense that they may not communicate with the legislator. The judge, in turn, may consult the learned scholar (who makes their thought known through their teaching or through their writings), but they may not consult the legislator.

The judge knows the rule of law through the written text. However, is the text able to univocally indicate the content of the norm to them? Does the text have one sole objective meaning? If a hundred judges read that law, will they all always agree when they establish the meaning of the law?

Alternatively, do different judges find different meanings in the law? Or may even a single judge, faced by the text, deem that there might be more than one interpretation? Or do factors and elements other than the text affect the interpretation?

The interpretation of the text and the practical and theoretical issues it raises have long attracted the attention of scholars, who may not be jurists. Very widely spread religions teach that the truth is inscribed in texts, whose content has been revealed by God. Obviously, the teachers of religious thought ponder the theoretical issues related to the interpretation of the text. The science that concerns the interpretation of messages containing doctrines or precepts is called "hermeneutics". More generally, the science concerning the relationship between word and meaning is called "semantics", or "semiology".

However, legal hermeneutics has never been able to teach the jurist a criterion for recognizing the true and correct meaning of the text and for distinguishing it from erroneous interpretations.

Semantics enables us to identify the meaning of the word only when the word corresponds in a recognizable way to the so-called "referent", that is, the real factuality indicated by the words. I say elephant, and the referent of the word is the elephant. However, legal terms do not have referents.

For seventy years—and especially since I have been speaking about a "diritto muto" (mute law)—I have been focusing my attention on the fact that unexpressed, implicit, implied, sometimes unconscious normative elements contribute with written words to creating the norm.

A century ago, many jurists believed that the text had one sole objective meaning and that an interpreter, provided they were able to avoid mistakes, might be able to discover this meaning. Today, this illusion has disappeared.

The sole meaning of the text is an illusion.

The objective meaning of the text is also an illusion.

The meaning of the text is what the person who is dealing with the text assigns to it. At the moment of the text's creation, the meaning is that conceived by the drafter (if the text is drafted by a group, its meanings may vary between one member and the next). At the moment of the norm's application, the meaning is that conceived (with absolute certainty, or in the midst of grave doubts) by the interpreter.

The thought and the will of the legislator are now distant, they are estranged.

The interpreter knows the text. In some cases they will also have information about the thought of the author of the text. However, it certainly cannot be said that they have before them the mind of the author. Moreover, the doctrine of sources teaches us that the norm is sound if it is promulgated and published, and only the text (and not the will of its drafter) has been promulgated and published.

What I say should not frighten us.

Formidable factors ensure a meaningful alignment between the thought of the legislator and that of the interpreter and the alignment in the thought of the thousand and one thousand interpreters.

They speak the same language, which means that in the normality of cases, they are accustomed to giving that word those given meanings and not others. There are also other shared bonds.

Hermeneutics shows the interpreter the routes to follow to find the correct meaning of the text. Even the doctrine that believed in the objective meaning of the declaration has developed a theory of "hermeneutical means", through which the interpreter identifies the will of the legislator, the history, the purpose or the function of the norm, the sociological data, and the relationship that binds each norm to the legal system to which it belongs.

However, this knowledge, addressed to the history, to the society, to the function of law, has as its object elements which are extraneous to the text, pre-existent to it. The interpreter is told that "one must" know them. Nothing is said about them being extratextual elements, which condition the meaning of the text, that are engraved in it. Nothing is said about the fact that, used to reveal the meaning of the text, they actually contribute to creating the meaning of the norm, working together with the text, cocreating the norm. If the text is the source of law par excellence, if it is the primary source, those other elements also have the effect of sources (some call them "secondary sources").

We need to ask ourselves whether the active presence of these factors in the interpreter's mind might create chaotic disparities in interpretation due to the number and variety of interpreters. Of course, we will answer that there is a certain degree of homogeneity in the culture of interpreters and that interpreters can also take care to avoid cultural differences that might trigger distressful conflicts.

It is good to keep in mind what experience teaches us. It provides us with two indisputable facts.

The first is that interpreters develop multiple and conflicting solutions. Indeed, two works of doctrine, by different authors, may contain significant contradictions. Likewise, a given supreme court sometimes changes jurisprudence. However, these interpreters are the upholders of one sole culture, or, in any case, of compatible cultures. In all the well-known historical cases, this has been enough to avoid an over muddled and chaotic management of the law.

Coming to the second fact. The historian could well teach us that the Justinian Pandects (taught in the universities for seven consecutive centuries) have undergone various interpretations. The progress of legal thought has produced a tireless evolution of the applied law, and there is no reason to regret that this has taken place. More recently, in the two centuries that have witnessed the application of the Code Napoléon, the interpretation of certain articles or the reconstruction of certain norms that are the basis of given solutions has changed with the advent of each new generation. The norm that the act of disposition of the heir apparent is effective against the bona fide third party has been reconstructed in six different ways by the six generations of jurists who have dealt with the issue.

Since it has become well known that the meaning of the text is not objective, the figure of the interpreter has become central in the general theory of the law.

We may speak of "an interpreter", in the singular, because for a moment we are playing down the differences that may exist—and in fact do exist—in the many interpretations made by individual jurists.

This "interpreter" carries out their work using their own culture. Society is responsible for the establishment of schools in which the interpreters of the law are trained. However, even before attending these schools, the future interpreter understands what the law says. In this regard, there has been talk of a 'Vorverständnis', that is, of a pre-understanding of the law, of a knowledge of the rules, ahead of the reading of the text. Well, this prior knowledge is to a very large extent common to all interpreters, even if they are poorly educated and not especially perspicacious. It is visible without the slightest effort, visible even to the least prepared person, not so much as regards "what, in that legal system, is norm", but rather as regards "what, in that system, is not—and will never be—norm". Even the man in the street knows, without ever having read the text, that the seller does not have to pay the buyer's price; he knows that he is not allowed to break the ground floor window of a house which is not his, to enter the house, search for money and then take it away; he knows that during a civil hearing he is not allowed to slap the judge.

The interpreter brings with them their own pre-understanding, they bring with them their own culture; the trained interpreter (judge or lawyer) brings with them the knowledge to which years of study and experience have given them access.

And how does this interpreter operate when faced by the text?

They will take a position on the issues posed by the language of the text.

They will ponder the extrajuridical rules, those parallel to the law (ethical rules, for example), or feelings that are nudging toward given solutions.

They will weigh up realities related to the law—the subjects' interests, the function of the norm, the values.

Language poses extremely interesting problems for the interpreter.

First, they know that there is a specialized legal language, different from the language we use for common needs. However, it may happen that the law is drafted in the language of common needs (historical examples: the Montenegrin Civil Code of 1888; the Civil Code for the so-called German Democratic Republic-D.D.R.-of 1975). It may happen that the legal language of a country contains two different matrices. This has happened in Italy because in the nineteenth century the Italians modeled their legal language inspired by that of France, but at the end of that century they introduced a network of words inspired by the German conceptual system, and so some words had two meanings ('nullo' sometimes means 'void' and sometimes 'voidable').

The interpreter knows the traditional rules, which suggest how to use the language. However, these rules are unreliable. There is the criterion according to which "where the law has willed, it has stated it; if it has not stated, it has not willed." However, there is also the opposing rule, according to which "if the reason for a decision is identical in two hypotheses, then the solution is also identical".

The most exciting page of the whole theory of interpretation concerns the weight of extrajudicial data.

We observe that sometimes it is the legal text itself, which refers back to deontic appraisals that have been affirmed in society. Here is the referring back to good faith, to good morals, and to public policy.

However, in the last hundred years, there has been an unexpected development in the use of elements to which the legislator has not made explicit references because in the past, the doctrine taught in schools did not formulate specific remarks.

Let us see what it is.

The interpreter is endowed with reason, they cannot believe that the legislator might depart from reason, they pre-understand that the law conforms with reason. They know that the invocation of reason was at the basis of the law affirmed with the French and American revolutions.

Justice is related to reason. It is clearly evident that the work and research of the interpreter will be guided and supported by their love of justice (by the love of their vision of justice, by the vision of justice that their culture has given them). This justice entails the application of a legal treatment, expressly provided for a hypothesis, for a broad, very broad class of hypotheses. This justice also makes it possible to restrict legal treatment to ceasing to apply it for those who deserve protection (e.g., the disabled, the sick).

The interpreter then finds, in the extratextual knowledge of (legal or nonlegal) teachings, criteria, which will make them more aware of the legal instrument that the text is intended to apply and of the social reality where the norm must be applied.

Here is the interpreter enlightened by history (especially by the history of the law). Here is the comparatist interpreter, trained by the law of countries similar to theirs.

Here is the interpreter who knows how to critically analyze social reality (political science and economics have provided them with the necessary elements).

I said a moment ago that the interpreter engages with realities related to the law. The law is not an end in itself. The legal norm imposes obligations and assigns rights to protect given interests and denies protection to undeserving interests. It protects health, the spread of culture, and the economy. It discourages risk creation, improvidence, oppression.

The norm is conceived in view of a purpose to which a function, a task, is entrusted. The rule that safeguards free competition—and, in general, the rule that protects private autonomy—is intended to prevent the bad producer from prevailing over the good producer. The rule that in some cases impugns the usurious contract is intended to defend the market from some disturbing cases (hypothesis of the ill-informed, coerced contracting party, and so on).

For some time, the interpreter has examined an element that is certainly significant: the values protected by the law. Now, the jurist reflects on the tasks of law, called to defend human dignity, the free use of one's own language, and the management of one's own life made in accordance with one's own culture (even if in a minority, even if linked to an underdeveloped society), especially in accordance with one's own religious faith.

I have mentioned interests, ends. It is well known that in the last century, a scientific movement, developed in Germany and christened Interessenjurisprudenz, argued that the law should be known, studied, and analyzed exclusively through the interests (sometimes opposing) that it protects.

It is also well known that a century earlier, also in Germany, a great jurist, Jhering, inserted references to the purpose of the norm into the very foundations of the general theory of law. In this regard, there is talk of a teleological vision of law.

Now, we observe that it should not be thought that the jurist willing to turn to the purpose of the norm, to the interests that deserve protection, to the values recognized by the legal system, will find precise and unambiguous indications readily available, easily consultable and practicable, capable of establishing the correct application of the norm. When we consider the purpose of law, we are faced with the purpose of that single rule, the purpose of the institution to which the rule belongs, and the purpose of the law in general. When we talk about the purpose of the norm, about the interests protected by the norm, and about the value that inspires the norm, we are talking about elements that are just as difficult to identify and reconstruct, as it is difficult to identify and reconstruct the meaning of the text.

I, interpreter, I, legislator manqué, I am addressing the jurists that I see in the guise of legislators, and I am telling them the little I believe I know about the legislator and the interpreter.

The legislator believes they are creating the law. In reality, they are creating a text to which others will give a meaning or more meanings.

The interpreter—hopefully at least—will be loyal; they will approach the text with the intention of uncovering its secrets, uncovering its meanings, and making the thought and the will of the legislator, in its entirety, their own.

However, to do this, the interpreter will resort to what they know about the meaning of the words. The interpreter is equipped with their own knowledge, their own morals, and their own experience; in other words, they are equipped with a culture. Even if they wanted to, they could not silence this culture of theirs. Armed with this culture, they will give the text meaning.

The interpreter sees in the drafter of the text an authority.

The legislator can see in the interpreter the operator who, with the breath of their knowledge, gives life to the text.

Let us add a last point. De facto, the legislator is always a teacher, the interpreter is a judge, a judge who yesterday was a student, a judge whose knowledge was given by their maestro.

Rodolfo Sacco was Emeritus of the University of Torino. He was Titular Member of the International Academy of Comparative Law; of the Institut de France, Accademia dei Lincei, Accademia delle Scienze, Academia Europea. Professor Sacco authored of more than 400 works in the fields of comparative law, civil law, legal theory, and legal anthropology. He received honorary doctorates from Genève, McGill, Paris II, and Toulon. His *Introduzione al diritto comparato*, 7th ed. (with P. Rossi), was published in 2019.